D1234528

turning tiny

the small-living paradigm that's reshaping
the way we think, live and dream

ɔters *by over 60 tiny house movement luminaries*
piled and presented by Darin Zaruba

Acknowledgements

This compilation book came about because of the amazing stories I have been following on social media for the past few years. Those stories literally came to life for me at the little event last summer that came to define the tiny house movement and its people: the Tiny House Jamboree of 2015. It was an unbelievable time; magical, and life changing for so many people. It was like the first family get-together of an entire movement. Most of us there knew that this was the start of something greater than a singular event or even a "movement". Out of the hundreds of stories that came out during the Jamboree at least some had to be shared and even memorialized. Some stories were old, some were being retold with more detail, and some were just starting. How to choose? *Turning Tiny* is just a small fraction of them. We knew even that August that we needed something to look back on; a way to relive the stories over and over. We also needed something to start from. Who knows where it will go from here. That's the fun part!

First and foremost, I would like to acknowledge the entire tiny house community who has both humbled me and inspired me with their vision, their passion, their mission, their lives, their dreams, and yes, their houses.

I would like to thank Andrew and Gabriella Morrison who inspired me and encouraged me to jump into this craziness, and Andrew Stewart who gave me an early vision of what a tiny house community could look like, and helping me to create that vision.

And I would especially like to thank the *Turning Tiny* section coordinators: B.A. Norrgard, Kim Kasl, Gabriella Morrison, Andrew Odom, and Frieda Bakker, for their dedication, time, and energy. Certainly though, much praise goes to Andrew Odom, without whose help organizing and coordinating this project, we would not have been able to pull off *Turning Tiny*. I truly bit off more than I could chew, and Andrew was my sanity.

Thank you all! Have fun turning tiny!

Darin Z

Preface

*Every successful organization has to make the transition from a world
defined primarily by repetition to one primarily defined by change.*
—Bill Drayton

Have you ever wondered what makes the tiny house movement an actual
movement? Have you longed to hear the stories behind some of your favorite
non-traditional homes? Do you wonder if the movement is more of a shift in
thought rather than a blip on the architectural screen?

Turning Tiny is your direct-access pass into the minds and lives of tiny
housers in various arenas including design, building, community planning,
and the emerging business around it all. It's a collection of stories from 60+
contributing authors of how and why they turned tiny.

It is no secret that tiny housers exist in all walks of life. Our interests are
in raising families in tiny houses, defining a tiny house, figuring out where
to park a tiny house, assimilating into a community, the future of the movement, and much more. In the following chapters are the answers to those
questions, written in the words of tiny housers themselves. Each chapter is
written by a different tiny house enthusiast from their personal perspective
and provides a microcosmic look into an issue directly impacting them.

Read on. By picking up this volume you recognize that the old real estate
American Dream has failed America. It is neither attractive nor sustainable
and that living on a smaller scale is becoming the new paradigm. So indulge.
Allow yourself to turn tiny with each page turn!

Contents

Part 6: Tiny House Business

Introduction

Angela Alcorn

Social Media Queen and a Tiny House Jamboree coordinator

At some point most of us have asked ourselves the deeper question, "*What is my purpose in life?*" Whatever your purpose may be, the one common goal we all seem to have is happiness. It seems cliché but it is true. Of course, today's society has led us to believe that bigger is better and the more we have the happier we will be. What I have learned in my lifetime thus far is that adage simply isn't true. Happiness comes from an emotional state of wellbeing; something that can only be found within us and not from material items. I can assure you that living in a tiny house won't magically give you a life purpose, or make you the happiest person alive. It will go a long way to opening up vast possibilities for a life otherwise non-existent.

Two years ago my family – Bobby, my husband, and our two daughters, Gillian and Callie – felt strongly that we had lost sight of what life was truly about. Routine had set in and obligation felt closer to us than each other. Bobby and I wanted to teach our girls how to live a purposeful life; one that would allow them the opportunity to forge a future based in experience and adventure rather than consumption and collection. God alone has blessed us in that journey and for two years now we have worked toward a life we never before knew existed. In just 140 sq.ft., we have rediscovered ourselves, each other, and the world around us. We are literally and emotionally closer than we ever have been before.

We certainly aren't alone in our pursuits though. It seems to be reality that there is a whole world full of people like us; people searching for purpose. This really came to light for us tangibly at the inaugural Tiny House Jamboree of 2015 where thousands of like-mined people convened into one spot! And we weren't "just" there. We were in the middle and the thick of it, in all of its glory, beauty, craziness and behind the scenes mayhem.

Our working relationship with the event began a few days after the announcement of the Jamboree. Hearing the vision that Darin Zaruba and his team saw for the event was an inspirational turning point in my understanding of the purpose behind the entire tiny house movement and philosophy. I wanted in! I wanted to help! I wanted to preach the word, and preach it we did. So I took on the social media campaign, and can now say I had no idea what I was really jumping into. The interest in it, and the movement seemed to come to a crescendo and overwhelmed us all. The passion and effort that the entire team had put into creating the Jamboree was herculean, and best of all it was something that seemed like it would make an actual difference in the tiny house community. I was brought on board the team alongside some very talented members like Marcus Alvarado, and Coles Whalen who helped pull this off in a matter of months.

Being a collaborative part of such a groundbreaking event has truly been an honor. It was a crazy and magical time leading up to the event, talking to hundreds of people about their stories. And the actual Jamboree exceeded all expectations for those involved. All said, it came together almost seamlessly, at least from the outsider's view thankfully! As I look back, it was obvious that the stories, the lives, and the passion of the community made this possible. We didn't want it to end. We just had to memorialize it. We had to try to capture lightning in a bottle. But how?

Most of America's attention has been drawn to tiny homes because of their charming and unique designs. The fascination surrounding tiny houses has also grown in popularity following the hype from popular tiny house television shows, news and Internet outlets. But the real tiny house movement isn't about the homes at all. It's the people. Living a more conscientious lifestyle allows you to focus on other things; perhaps, the *important* things. The tiny house movement is more than just our society's latest fad or an architectural bookmark. Rather, it's a lifestyle that's here to stay.

Thankfully there are people like the authors included in this book. Each one – with their individual story – has decided at some point to either reshape or reclaim the American Dream, or to avoid it altogether in an effort to reshape their value system. Thankfully they have chosen to memorialize those stories and share with America why they are *Turning Tiny*.

Enjoy your journey!

Part 1

The Tiny House

There seems to be no lack of attempts at defining the tiny house. There is the tiny house on wheels. There is the tiny house on a foundation. There is an argument that tiny houses by definition must be less than 400 sq.ft. There are groups of people that think tiny houses are only those built in the style of the original Tumbleweeds. A growing number of people recognize RVs, park models, live-aboard boats, converted cargo containers, sheds, treehouses, and a number of other unconventional domiciles, as tiny houses. The fact remains though – despite the conventional thoughts surrounding such – that a tiny house is nothing more than a moniker; a term relative to the person living within. It is as much a philosophy as a measurement. It denotes a shunning of traditional American home values, and seeks to empower the person within giving them equal parts freedom and grounding. But more than anything, a tiny house is a story. It is a collection of walls made up of laughter, love, anger, pain, smiles, and sadness. These are the stories of the tiny houses.

From Alienation, to Collaboration, to Community
A Tale of Finding Home in 140 Sq. Ft.

Vina Lustado

Vina Lustado is the founder/owner of Sol Haus Design, a design firm specializing in sustainable building in Ojai, California. In December 2012, Vina manifested her dream home in 140 sq. ft., a self-sufficient dwelling loaded with functionality, style and charm. Since then Vina's home has captured the imagination of the tiny house enthusiasts from all over the world and has appeared in countless media publications.

My love for simple living started at a very young age when I was growing up in the Philippines. My fondest memory was the big family gatherings at my aunt's nipa hut, located in a tropical jungle setting. Surrounded by palm trees, fruit trees and lush vegetation with a babbling stream nearby, this place was paradise to me. In our native language, we called this place the "linang."

I have a large extended family, which is typical of Filipino families. My parents had raised ten children. My siblings, cousins, aunts and uncles would pack the mules with straw baskets straddled on their backs. The baskets would be filled with food supplies for the journey. We would walk two miles on barefoot into the jungle. Sometimes it was seemed like the entire town was coming along because there were so many of us. Once arrived, we would go swimming in the stream and then prepare lunch and dinner. Since we didn't own bathing suits, we would jump into the water with just plain shorts and t-shirts. We would wash our clothes in the stream with a wooden paddle and beat them against a rock.

Food preparation was the center of activity. We picked fresh jackfruit and bananas from the trees. My aunt, Tia Estelita, would climb the coconut tree barefooted. In her 30's, she was a spinster and a beloved member of the family. Her long flowing grey hair was past her knees. And she never wore underwear. To go to the bathroom, we would dig a hole in the ground and use guava leaves for toilet paper.

The rest of the day was about being together, playing in nature and cooking. The meal was always cooked in a big pot over an open fire. We would eat with our hands. We made a dessert called minukmuk, made with a big wooden bowl, and mashed with boiled bananas and gabi (taro roots) and mixed with coconut milk to make it sweet. I remember cracking the coconut open and straddling a wooden bench with a grater to shred the coconut meat. Then I would put the shredded coconut in water and squeeze the liquid out to create the coconut milk. When the food was ready to eat, we all gathered together to eat by the stream.

In my memory, the excursions to the linang stand out as the most joyous occasion during my childhood in the Philippines. Even though I left the Philippines at a young age, the memory is still vivid and dear to me. I am grateful that I was exposed to this quality of life. It shaped my values and deeply influenced my later years.

My family and I immigrated to Los Angeles when I was seven years old. It was a big move for such a large family. We were five boys and five girls. My parents did not have a lot of money and had to work very hard to assimilate us into the American culture. They both worked long hours to support the family, so they didn't have much time to spend with the children. My eldest sister, Rosie (or Ate Salinda), took the role of caregiver. She finished nursing school and immediately started working to help the support the family. In many traditional cultures, such as the Philippines, it is typical that the eldest child takes responsibility for the rest of the family.

As the third youngest, I felt I didn't get the same attention as my older siblings. By the time I was born, my parents already had six children. My parents provided as much as they could given the demands of a new environment and a new culture. I think during the development stages of a child, growing up in a large family and then immigrating to another country at such a young age, I didn't have a deep sense of belonging.

As a "third culture kid" or TKC, I didn't fit in with a specific crowd in school. I lived in LA where it was a melting pot of different ethnic groups. I became good friends with kids from Korea and China and Mexico. I learned how to build relationships with other cultures easily, but lacked a cultural identity of my own. "Cultural homelessness" is typical of third culture kids, and I was one of them. This lack of identity and not feeling like an important part of my family left me feeling lost and alienated.

In many ways, I was a black sheep of the family. I wasn't like my brothers and sisters. While most of them established a stable job, got married, bought a house and had children, I wanted to go to a university, travel the world, and have life experiences.

While adjusting to the new American culture, I worked diligently in school, got accepted to UCLA, then to USC for an architecture degree. I saw architecture as a balance of creativity and function, and a way I could make a difference in the world.

After my architecture studies, I developed a desire to visit the buildings I studied in person from around the world. This led me to my first trip to Europe as a young single female traveler. Being on my own for three months, I was changed forever. Architecture was a lens into different cultures and different ways of thinking. I learned how to make connections and was inspired by different ways people live, work, and play. I also learned that people are inextricably shaped by design.

With all my worldly possessions in my backpack, simplicity, mobility and freedom became very important to me. Living simply became my mantra connecting me to my modest childhood in the Philippines. At this time, I also became addicted to the travel.

Throughout my career, I traveled abroad to re-assess my direction at pivotal points in my life. I traveled to Alaska for Habitat for Humanity, to Italy to help build an artist residence, and to South America to trek to Machu Picchu. Either for personal or professional reasons, I welcomed the opportunity to experience other cultures and other ways of seeing the world.

My architecture career also prompted me to live in different parts of the US: LA, Chicago and San Francisco. After more than a decade of climbing the corporate ladder, I became disillusioned with the architecture profession. I started to see that architects catered primarily to wealthy clients with big budgets, and even worse, contributing to projects that polluted the Earth.

I learned that the building industry is largely responsible for environmental degradation: greenhouse gas emissions, depletion of natural resources and major contributor to waste in the landfill. After years of working in that world, I yearned for something different that would fill my soul and make a positive impact in the world.

In 2002, I pursued an opportunity that would give me one of the most valuable experiences: an international fellowship to research ecological and affordable housing in Germany. For three months, I lived in Cologne to research residential projects, interview architects and residents, and compile information for research. The German way of life gave me invaluable perspective on a lifestyle that was inherently aligned with the environment. During that time, I learned that sustainability must be a mindset that pervades culture and way we live our lives.

Upon returning to the US and after completing the fellowship, I felt a renewed sense of purpose to pursue projects with environmental stewardship. I found employment in a small architecture firm in Ventura, California where I worked on small residential projects with an environmental focus.

At the height of the recession in 2008, after traveling to South America for three months, I forged my own path by starting my own business, Sol Haus Design. It was a huge risk, but I needed to take responsibility for my own financial stability in my profession.

I wanted my company to address social issues facing the world, such as affordable housing and environmental impact. Unlike most architecture firms, I wanted my target audience to include people of modest incomes. My solution to provide affordable housing for the masses was a guesthouse pro-

totype. It was a prefabricated structure using SIPs panels on less than 700sf of floor space. It employed passive heating and cooling strategies and could be built for less than $100,000. In short, this was a larger version of my "tiny house on wheels" built on a traditional foundation.

Looking back at my business plan in 2009, the title read: "We redefine people's lives by simplifying the way they live." I had clipped newspaper articles and gathered photos of compact efficient dwellings less than 300sf. Even many years before my tiny house was conceived, the mantra of living simply was clear in my mind.

After a few challenging years starting my own business, I was able to set a good foundation for Sol Haus Design. But what I really wanted was a personal project that would reflect my core values on sustainability and affordability. I wanted to design my own house or office space. I wanted to show others that it is possible to live well with minimal cost, and be kind to the environment at the same time. Perhaps more importantly, I wanted to prove to myself that it could be done.

With the high cost of real estate in California, and especially in Ojai, it was not possible to find anything within my price range. I waited for a few years until an opportunity presented itself.

My friend, and colleague, Arne Steffen, first introduced me to tiny houses. I worked with Arne in Germany during my international fellowship. He had known about Jay Shafer's tiny house, and he suggested I look it up as way to create my own design project. At first I was skeptical. The image I had in my head was of Jay standing in front of his Gingerbread-style miniature tiny house. It seemed unrealistic, and admittedly, hard for me to take seriously. How can he have a fully functional house in a doll-size dwelling?

As I researched more, however, I realized that Jay's tiny house was not really about the house, rather the philosophy behind it. The tiny house concept matched my values of living simply and efficiently. Even more appealing, I could design my house with my own aesthetics, like a modern reinterpretation of the traditional cabin. By building it myself, and without permitting fees, the cost would be greatly reduced and would fall within my budget. It was brilliant and I was thrilled!

There was just one (major) issue: I had no construction experience, and I didn't want to tackle the project on my own. Of course I welcomed the opportunity to learn how to build with my own hands. Lucky for me, my partner Cliff agreed to help me. He was all that I needed to start the project.

I met Cliff through a shared passion for the outdoors and a love of nature. I became intrigued by his little cabin that he built in Ojai, and by his simple lifestyle, living almost completely off the grid. His cabin was built with found materials from the property, and he uses only a headlamp for his source of light. Cliff also repurposed an old tub, which he placed outside of his cabin, underneath a large tree. At night, he would take a shower and gaze at the stars through the canopy of leaves.

Cliff's humble little home in the woods resonated deeply with me. It reminded me of my simple childhood in the Philippines, with fond memories of the "linang."

Upon meeting Cliff and eventually moving to Ojai, I felt I finally found "home" in the spiritual sense of the word. It was a sense of belonging that I hadn't experienced before. I later understood that finding "home" wasn't so much about the physical space that we occupy, as much as finding the emotional comfort of what we call "home." For someone who felt lost and alienated for most of my life, meeting Cliff and settling in Ojai finally helped me find my place in the world.

Building a tiny house requires a leap of faith and a willingness to take risks. While everyone thought I was crazy, Cliff was the one who supported me, and willing to help from the beginning. I didn't have all the details figured out – legalities, financing, and so many other considerations! But it didn't matter. I was compelled to take on the project for reasons I couldn't really explain at the time.

In September 2012, I ordered the trailer. At a cost of well over $3000, the purchase cemented my commitment to build the house. There was no going back. Cliff and I picked up the trailer one month later. I felt like a proud parent of a newborn baby. It was a very exciting, pivotal day.

Since then, Cliff and I worked on the trailer every night and every weekend, while working on full time jobs of our own. With his welding skills, Cliff customized the trailer for the tiny house for three months. It was the holiday season in November and December, and it often rained. We worked through Thanksgiving, Christmas, and New Years, completing the foundation with insulation and wall framing.

I remember distinctly when Cliff's birthday came, the day after Christmas on December 26th. I asked him what he wanted to do. To my surprise, he said he wanted to work on the house. The amount of work Cliff was willing to put into this project often surprised me. After all, he never planned on living in the house with me.

After four months of building intensely together, I couldn't keep asking Cliff to help me finish the house. I needed to get more help. Also, there was a deadline to finish the build in one year. My tiny house was going to be featured at Ojai's Annual Green Home Tour, which took place in October 2013. I was honored with the opportunity, but with that came a lot of pressure. In retrospect, the deadline kept me motivated to stay on track.

To expedite the schedule, I enlisted local artisans and craftsmen to help. More importantly, I wanted to involve the community and highlight the work of some very talented friends. I reached out to friends to design things like a custom frosted glass window, draperies, pillows and multi-purpose furniture. What came out of this collaboration is what makes my house truly unique and special. Many say they feel the positive energy and love when they walk into my house.

Kris McCourtney is a local finish carpenter who specializes in using reclaimed wood. He was largely responsible for the installation of the exterior cedar siding as well as all the interior millwork, cabinetry and custom furniture. I designed the pieces with multiple functions, like the sofa and the mobile coffee table, to fit the space precisely, and Kris built them to specifications. We used only formaldehyde-free FSC certified plywood with a natural finish.

We used a lot of reclaimed products throughout the build: two windows, French doors, pocket door, and all the materials on the exterior deck. My favorite part of repurposing materials is giving new life to something old, such as the case with my oak floors. Kris had salvaged the oak flooring from a client with an old house in LA. The oak floors had a dark stain which covered the natural grain of the wood. To give it new life, a lot of time was needed to plane it down to remove the stain, re-mill with tongue and groove, then re-finish with a natural stain.

Again, I reached out to my friends in the community to help with the task – Uta Ritke, Lisa Berman and Carmen Lo Maglio. Alongside Kris, we all spent hours at the woodshop re-milling all the planks and prepping it for the installation. Several days of hard work paid off. The oak floors are gorgeous. The original owner of the house where we got the floors from came to the Green Home Tour to see the final results. She gave it a big nod and was pleased with the new life the floor had been given.

For the interior, I kept the design of the house minimal and devoid of decoration. I wanted a peaceful space like a retreat, with nature as the backdrop. So I explored the idea of incorporating trees into my tiny house.

A very talented friend, Alicia Morris, shares my love of trees. A peek of her sketchbook inspired me to reach out to her to help with the interior. Alicia used the sketches of trees to create one-of-a kind embroideries on the pillows for my sofa. Each stitch was lovingly (and sometimes painstakingly) done by hand. The most intricate pillow took three months to complete (!), and it has become my favorite.

I also appreciate Alicia's desire to use found objects in favor of buying new. For the window covering at the large office window, she used repurposed branches and old leather laces for an elegant window treatment. To minimize costs, Alicia came up with the brilliant idea of using painter's drop cloth for all the textiles. Many people assume the fabric is Belgian linen, which is a far cry from the utilitarian drop cloth! After two years of lots of wear and tear, the pillows and drapery remain in excellent condition.

Another artist friend, Maria Trimbell, is an internationally accomplished muralist. I was thrilled she was able to contribute to my project. We explored ideas on continuing the theme with trees, and decided to use sycamore leaves to decorate my wardrobe closet. Maria took great care to place each leaf carefully on the door so they flowed naturally to the bottom. This treatment on the cabinetry is simple and subtle, but it gives a focal point as you first enter the great room and into the kitchen.

Lynn Hegney, a local glass artist, collaborated with Maria to develop the custom art glass on the pocket door. The pattern of sycamore leaves were embedded on silver leaf to create the stunning piece of art glass on the door. Lynn created several templates and experimented with the texture on the back. She literally used the trunk of a tree to create the rough texture behind the glass. The result is breathtaking: a warm glow of light streams into kitchen and the quality of light changes throughout the day.

In addition to her artistic talents, Lynn also contributed countless hours for construction. She installed the insulation, helped with the electrical wiring and refinished the French doors to its full glory. Lynn Hegney and her partner, Margaret Eliott, are the proprietors of the retreat center Casa De La Luna in Ojai. It was the construction site of my tiny house for one year. Margaret and Lynn graciously offered their property, to which I owe a debt of gratitude for their generosity.

Uta Ritke is a dear artist friend who helped tirelessly during the build, from installing hardwood floors to whitewashing my interior walls. She believed in my tiny house project from the very beginning, and I am so grateful to her! Her exquisite painting hangs above the sofa in the great room, titled "Life."

Carrie Bahu is another creative talent who designed the small pillows on the sofa. The pillows are uniquely designed and made with raw silk and down. Each pillow is individually handcrafted by women from India and curated by Lucky Uschi.

The collaboration with all the local artists gives special meaning to my house. Everyone who enters my little house say they feel the positive energy and love imbued in the artistic expressions throughout the house.

Living in a tiny space requires very carefully chosen art pieces. I prefer to keep the interior clean and uncluttered, so I've had to let go of many of my own previous artwork. The only piece of art that remains in my tiny space is a small painting that has a special meaning to me. It is a piece of art that was created by Alicia Morris (the textile artist) based on a dream by Kris McCourtney (the finish carpenter).

In the dream, Kris was inside the tiny house, looking outside, and saw large pine trees out of the windows. When he stepped closer to the window, he realized the house was floating high above the valley floor. The giant trees that he saw outside the window were actually floating as well, uprooted from its landscape. Kris could see the giant roots below the trees afloat as well. The tiny house on wheels had sprouted some wings and was flying high above with the clouds! It was like a scene from one of Salvador Dali's paintings. I was so intrigued with the image, I asked Alicia to paint it for me, and now the painting sits on top of my desk.

With a little bit of analysis, the dream can be a metaphor: a tiny house gives a sense of home and stability, but because it's on wheels, it allows freedom of mobility. It's a beautiful contradiction.

I also came to realize the painting is a representation of my life. I have lived as a nomad, as a traveler, as a person seeking "home" for most of my life. Coming from different cultures and growing up in a large family, I didn't have a strong sense of belonging.

After meeting Cliff, then settling into Ojai and finding my community, I finally found a place to call home. The journey of finding home is not so much defined by the physical space as it is by the emotional well being of what home means to us.

Building my tiny home is simply an extension of my ethereal concept of home. As many tiny housers would agree, the tiny house is not really about the house as the meaning behind it. I have never been as content in a dwelling (of any size) as I am of my little house. By enlisting my partner Cliff, artist friends and local craftsmen, my house embraces community spirit. Everyday I feel the presence of each person who has graced my home with his or her gifts.

I can still remember my father saying to me: "A rolling stone gathers no moss." I think he was concerned about me, and he never understood my propensity to travel to foreign countries, especially to Europe for the first time on my own. Now that my father has since past, I have come to realize that I am much like my father. Itay (aka "father" in my native language) had a passion to give back to his own community in the Philippines. He started a scholarship organization to benefit disadvantaged children with financial need. Now I see the same quality in me with a desire to give back, and I hope he is smiling from above, and seeing how I have inspired others to live simply with my own little tiny house.

I believe tiny houses can address critical issues in the world today: homelessness, affordable housing, global warming, and environmental impact, among others. Tiny houses can also incorporate concepts of the shared economy: shared vegetable gardens, shared work studios, shared libraries, and shared mode of transport like electric vehicles and bicycles. This can support local communities and invigorate local economy. We can also create self-suf-

ficiency by employing permaculture principles and energy efficient systems
with renewable energy.

My greatest hope is to create a tiny house community that allows for
connection in an otherwise disconnected world. Connection inspires
humanity, community, and a sense of belonging. This is the greatest gift my
tiny house has given me, and this is my wish for you too.

Searching For Home: Coast to Coast

Finding a place for a family to turn house to home

Baylie Carson

Wife, mother, tiny house dweller and writer. We cram our entire family, two adults, a toddler and a baby into a 204 sq.ft. tiny house on wheels and love every moment. I write tinyhousegrowingfamily.com to show how even though we live tiny, our lives are very full.

The nationwide search was on — we were looking for the perfect completed tiny house for our family. That makes it sound as though we were searching for a fugitive, but it wasn't that exciting, just my mother-in-law and I sitting across from one another in front of our computers pouring over Tiny House Listings. The first challenge was to find finished houses, so many half-completed dreams sitting there ready to become someone else's dream. When I would accidentally click into an ad that was only a half-built tiny for sale, I would think of the hours of the builder's life that had gone into those walls, the blood sweat and tears that had undoubtedly been poured into that home, and other things had been poured too. Like wine. And often I know because our first tiny house, in the same half-completed state, had been on the market days before. I knew their story well.

The search continued, the must haves: two lofts, large kitchen, stairs, washer/dryer, all of these were non-negotiable. It was like scratching off a lottery card, it might have the kitchen, stairs, and a washer, but missing the loft. Another had lofts, stairs, washer, but a toaster and a hot plate was not enough to constitute a kitchen for us. Link after link we would click expecting to be the next lotto winner, but instead we were always let down on the last scratch.

Tiny houses are unique; they are fully customizable and made for their inhabitants' needs. I demand a washer and dryer, you might be perfectly happy to hang at the Laundromat. (You are a freak, but I will only judge you in my head, and apparently here). We need a large kitchen because we are a family of four and I make all of our meals at home because of allergies, I wasn't going to settle for a toaster oven and a hot plate. How do tiny house dwellers with only a toaster oven do Thanksgiving anyways? I assume they must sacrifice the turkey tradition for a Cornish game hen? Anywho, I am high maintenance and if we were buying our forever tiny home it was going to be perfect. We would not be buying one with the need of remodeling because I was over it, so over it. Donate the hammer, saw, and drill because we are minimalists and I never want to build anything else ever again. Building the tiny house ourselves was never our intention. The reason we were buying a house was to get past the seemingly endless task of home building, or, because I'd had enough of that mess. Honestly, owning a tiny house was never our intention.

This one time, we bought something that looked like tiny house on Craigslist. "Food Truck for Sale." Sure, it was listed as a food truck, but it looked an awful lot like those tiny houses on Pinterest. That's how it happened. No joke. Complete impulse purchase, a house, a non-traditional one at that.

Could we live tiny? Expecting to be heartily laughed at by my husband, I slowly turned the laptop around and I showed him. His words: Maybe. Let's go look at it. This, to me, is basically a yes.

Jaw drop. I reach for phone quick before he changes his mind. At this point I am 100% in. That's just how I am.

I called the number on the ad knowing that I wanted to hold my cards close and not let him know that what he labeled as a "food truck" is what I wanted to live in. I know I am crazy, but I don't need strangers knowing that. Plus, I didn't want to be judged or for him to be unwilling to sell it to us if I used the terms 'Tiny House' and 'family' together. Of course he asks what my plan with it is and I returned his question with a question, "Have you ever heard of a tiny house?" The response I heard on the other end made my heart skip.

"Yes! I am a tiny house enthusiast," the fellow almost yelled overly excited. "I built this structure knowing that I could turn it into a tiny house later if I wanted to." At this point I am 150% in. It's fate.

We went and looked at the tiny house as soon as possible. I looked inside.

Positive: It was a lot more spacious than I had expected! It was a blank canvas, just a shell really. We could hire contractors and have it built just the way we wanted.

I felt my heart sinking because with the angel and the devil on my shoulders, the devil was starting to talk louder. The percentage was going down fast, and my level of confidence was quickly dropping.

Negative: Maybe this was not, in fact, a good idea. Too much work. Too much money. We had a toddler and a baby on the way. We just needed to rent another conventional home.

My other half peeked in the door of the "food truck" and did not see the same thing as I did. The skeptical one got far more enthusiastic once he saw that there were endless possibilities. The fact that the space was small meant that we could afford to make it just like we wanted. Ironic that we swapped positions. Even though my eagerness had faded, he talked me back up.

We bought it. We spent every last dime we had on that empty shell. We bought our first house. We were now officially "home owners."

Why would we even consider a tiny?

The beautiful glow of pregnancy and the cute round belly had passed. I was a whale and I had the full-on waddle. You once gazed upon a beautiful pregnant goddess, now your look is of pity on that poor haggard looking woman who is overdue. I might have been able to hold on to the glow longer, but the truth of the matter, yet again, just like the past 3 years, my husband had been given a pink slip.

When passion and work collide amazing things happen, unless you are a teacher and your job is underfunded. Due to budget cuts in education, the light at the end of the tunnel has been turned off and there we were, in the dark. My husband who is a passionate teacher had been laid off again. The situation is stressful for a small family!

We started brainstorming, could we possibly live in a motorhome? This way our house could move with us and we would have the opportunity to save more! My husband jokes about living a nomadic lifestyle as a teacher. We simply hitch up the house to the back of my mom car. For us the answer was no, the climate in Alaska is too harsh for sustainable motorhome living for a family with young ones.

Our plan was to hire contractors to finish out the inside of our tiny house shell. Here is where we found the unfortunate part of a tiny house. It's tiny. The smallness of the build makes the projects small. The smallness of the projects makes them cheap to complete. Low-cost means it is easy to blow off and go to the bigger job if you are a contractor.

We were left building the inside of a tiny that we hadn't intended to build, and let me tell you, that was stressful. We lived in our teeny tiny 115-square foot tiny house for a year that was never completed, and then we were given the opportunity to upgrade!

I have purchased all sorts of things on Craigslist: normal things, shoes, textbooks, tent, vacuum, and now, two tiny houses! Tiny House Listings wasn't turning up what we needed. In a moment of brilliance around 2 a.m. it came to me — search all of Craigslist. There she was waiting for is in Philly. Tiny House Climbing Gym that was built on Tiny House Nation.

My mother-in-law probably thought something bad had happened because I was texting her at 2 a.m., but it was out of excitement. My fingers were flying. I couldn't help myself. The text read: Look at this tiny house. It has everything! And I included a link to watch the episode of Tiny House Nation.

Apparently when I am super excited, I lack communication skills, that, or because I was texting at 2 A.M. What I neglected to tell my mother-in-law was that house had everything and it's for sale!

The next day she invited us over for a sit down, to talk about hiring a builder, having one custom made. I was so sad. She hadn't liked what I had found. I asked her if she had watched the show I had sent her. She said yes, that tiny house had everything. Perhaps we could hire a builder to replicate it. This is where I realized I had failed and I told her that I had found it for sale on Craigslist!

She jumped up in excitement! Hop on a plane! Go get it! Now! So we did.

Mothers-in-law have a bad reputation. You know Everybody Loves Raymond? Think the exact opposite. My mother-in-law is a saint. She is the most amazing soul to have ever walked the planet. We are besties.

If we had been in college together, we would have invented a drinking game together, but because she was in her 60s and I am in my 20s, we invented a game that simply made us giggle.

We didn't set out to make up a game, we set out to watch the Food Network. Cooking shows are my absolute favorite genre of television. The shows evoke more senses and emotions than a sitcom or a drama. Paula Dean and her love of butter makes me laugh y'all. Watching a fresh made loaf of French bread steam as it is broken open and then buttered by Jaques Pepén makes me long for the days before I was gluten free.

Bjorn's mother Perri would indulge my craving for food TV. The trouble was we enjoyed each other's company so much we would get to chatting during the commercials. Inevitably we would talk into the first five minutes of the show, which is when they are introducing what they will be cooking.

That's where the game begins. We had missed the intro. We now spend the rest of the episode guessing what the heck they are making with all ingredients lined up in tiny bowls.

Perri's crowning moment, when she won the day, the chef of the hour chopped onions. Not a few onions, a mountain of onions. The chef hardly visible from behind the mound, as spectators we watched on with mouths gaped open having no idea what recipe could possibly call for that many blooming onions. It wasn't onion rings, because they were the wrong shape. We stared on in awe of these onions figuring that this meal was going to feed 20. Then Perri shouted, "French Onion Soup!"

That was the day high fives were exchanged over a daytime cooking show.

You are probably wondering why she is such a big part of this story. It is because we were gifted a house by Bjorn's family; a completed tiny house on wheels.

We have an amazing, wonderful, incredibly giving family. Bjorn's mother and father have seen what we had sacrificed to live out our tiny dream. They have also seen everything that has gone wrong and wanted us to have something completely finished. One of their reasons: our living in a half-finished house stressed them out, so by gifting us a house, they would be less stressed.

It is hard to express gratitude for such a big gift, a huge gift, a house even! My initial thought was to decline.

We want to raise our children with generous spirits. It is part of the reason we choose to live tiny. We now have more resources and time to give. We have lived amazing lives, and want others to have that same opportunity. The flip side to giving is being able to receive. We need to teach them this too.

A thank you card doesn't seem enough but kissing their toes seems awkward. So here, again, I will take the opportunity to write a big, "Thank you!"

Our house is everything you could want in a tiny house and more. Our galley kitchen is more spacious than my uncle's, who lives in a conventional home. I have a full-sized fridge and freezer and ample counter space.

Our kids love our sofa, unusual right? Until you realize that their toy box is built into it! Soon we will have a dollhouse built into our bookshelves.

Ironically, the motto that brought us into this tiny house was 'go big or go home', meaning if you are going to get into something, go in, all in. Even though we have been tiny for years, my husband still adheres to this. When put in charge of buying our mattress and given the power of a measuring tape, he concluded that a California king mattress turned sideways would fit, and now we literally have a wall-to-wall mattress!

Our sleeping loft has too much space. Is there such thing as too much space in a tiny house? Since we moved from 115 sq. ft. up to 204 sq. ft. we had already pared down our belongings. We could easily fit 6 storage totes worth of stuff into our loft, but we don't. Our first tiny house was 115 sq. ft., with one loft, and our second house nearly doubled our square footage at 204 sq. ft., plus two large lofts! Someday we might fill it up, but not yet.

My toddler and I are at odds. She thinks the second loft is her office, and I think it is mine. We have come to an agreement and share. She will go up there when she wants to be alone. This is the most underutilized space in our house, and often becomes a catch-all for junk. Since I have become a writer, I use it as my sanctuary.

The Craigslist ad showed pictures of a den area under the office loft. My first thoughts were the uselessness of this space, and how closed in and cut-off and isolated it would feel because of the walls. But of course, since living in it, ironically it has since become my favorite. It is the kid space; they know that their toys need to stay within those walls. It is our parent place to relax alone after the kids have fallen asleep. It is our movie theater where we enjoy shows and popcorn. It is our library where our dozens of books are stored. It is the best.

One of the awesome parts about living tiny, especially with a family, is that it takes about 20 minutes to clean the house. The same thing that is a bonus is also a drawback, it takes about 20 minutes, every day. There is no skip day, there is no shove it in the back room and no one will see. To keep our house functional, it must be tidy. If I am to deep clean and scrub it takes me a solid hour, but I do that only once a week.

Our house does have drawbacks, it has a shower and no bath, though I really can't complain because it is the most luxurious shower you ever did see, even by conventional house standards. It hosts a bench so you are able to sit down and relax. In our first tiny house the tub was so important that we created the Sofub, which is a hybrid sofa and bathtub. It came with us to our new house and has become patio furniture. Tiny house dwellers are pioneers of multifunctional furniture.

Our first tiny had a Nest thermostat and radiant floor heat. This tiny is heated with a small Dickinson propane heater. I have to say, I wouldn't choose this heat source again. Without a thermostat, it can get too hot or too cold, sending you ambling down the stairs to it during the night!

When designing your tiny house 'forever home', take your hobbies and interests into consideration and make room for that; you can axe the other things that aren't important. One of the things that got the cut in our tiny house by the original owners was space for a dining room table, because they would eat on the couch. A tiny house built for a couple is now serving a family; I desperately miss having dinners around the dining room table.

Tiny house living is for us. We have sacrificed space for financial freedom and couldn't be happier. We spend most days in the great out of doors soaking in nature. If our lives change, and we decide to move cross country, which we have already done several times, our house just comes with us. Home is where you park it.

Build a Foundation, Pull Up Your Roots

Laura M. LaVoie

Laura M. LaVoie writes the blog Life in 120 Square Feet about her tiny home in Western North Carolina. Today, she frequently travels to speak about her experience of building and living in a tiny space.

The mists cascade over the rolling mountains known, and named, for the smoky haze. The trees sway in the morning breeze and I breathe in deep. I am at home in the mountains of Western North Carolina, finally. Sometimes I think I can feel the pulse of the quartz that bubbles to the surface of the soil all over our land. The home itself grew from the ground out of nothing. Or so it seems right now, while you're reading this.

It wasn't always here, this 120 square foot house that shelters us. This land, raw and wild, became ours in the summer of 2007. We broke ground two years later on the site where our tiny house now stands.

Let me start the story near the beginning.

Act 1: Concrete Evidence

I went to the woods because I wished to live deliberately, to front only the essential facts of life, and see if I could not learn what it had to teach, and not, when I came to die, discover that I had not lived.
—Henry David Thoreau

On a weekend in May 2009, I tapped into a hidden strength I didn't know that I had. Our site, inaccessible by car or truck, fought us at every turn. While many might consider us crazy, that was by design. To aid in our build, we bought a used ATV to get supplies from the road to our building site faster than on our shoulders, but the ATV was unreliable at best. On this late spring day, we set out to pour the eight concrete piers that would become our home's foundation.

We prepped the site weeks before and excavated the eight holes with a rented two-person auger. We hoped to begin pouring the concrete then, but the project had a mind of its own. We were just the pawns. Our task was to mix and pour the piers by ourselves in one two-day weekend. Oh, and did I mention that neither of us had ever poured concrete piers before?

First, we placed and leveled cardboard tubes, called Sonotubes, in the pox scars on the mountain. Matt, as a perfectionist, wouldn't rest until the margin of error was non-existent. I'm firmly in the "it looks good enough," camp. My lazy ways are overruled. Our biggest job involved transporting a small, borrowed cement mixer, thirty gallons of water, and twenty-four hundred pounds of unmixed cement to the building site. 300 vertical feet, up a mountain. The ATV threw a temper tantrum and declared that it would take no more than three bags at a time. If we pushed, it screeched its disapproval. We wasted half a day of our limited time driving back and forth, unloading bags of cement, one after another, and doing it all again. Then, we mixed and poured concrete for the rest of the day. By this time, it was already after noon on Sunday.

We were a well-oiled machine. One bag of concrete and one gallon of water filled the mixer each time. Bucket after bucket went into the tubes. As each pier set, we added the bolts to secure the posts that would eventually become the framing of our tiny home. With my hands and face caked in cement, I couldn't even visualize the house. Function in my joints seized from the concrete and exhaustion. The light faded as we scrambled to finish. Our panic manifested in different ways. Matt worried about perfecting every step and I fretted that we wouldn't have enough time to clean up and drive three hours back home for work the next morning. Anger flashed in flames with cruel reds and unforgiving oranges, punctuating our raised voices. I couldn't dam the flow of tears as frustration grew. As the last light of the sun dipped below the mountains in the same blaze of fire, we set the last anchor bolt in the wet concrete of pier number eight under the sickening yellow glow of a flashlight. Anger turned to apprehension as we hustled to clean up the worksite, pack the car, and leave the mountains.

The car's clock read 11:30 when we finally motored down the mountain, now shrouded in darkness. The ghosts of Appalachia haunted the silence of the gravel road. The only sound was the tires grating on tiny rocks that echoed loud enough that we were sure our rural neighbors would wake.

Though we both felt the pull of sleep, we kept ourselves awake to drive in shifts. Over three hours later, we were finally back in Atlanta. Our 2700 square foot home didn't feel alien yet, but it would over time. I knew a couple of hours of sleep wasn't enough, so I left a voice mail at my office letting them know I wouldn't be in first thing. It was the first time I let our project affect my work, but it wouldn't be the last. We dropped everything inside the door and zeroed in on our bed, crashing to oblivion.

In my mind, it was years before the gravity of what we had accomplished finally set in. Over time, the memory began to change.

From there, the puzzle pieces of the house snapped into place easily. At least, it seemed easy in comparison. With help from friends along the way, the structure grew in small increments. First the posts and the floor joists appeared in place. Then the walls rose. It was capped by a roof and one day we could stand inside the 120 square feet shell and see the possibilities.

Act 2: I Quit

Never look back, unless you're planning to go that way.
—Henry David Thoreau

It was three more years before fear gripped me again. As our home filled out with each trip to the mountain, we were closer and closer to leaving our comfortable lives in Atlanta behind to embrace this new experience. I longed for this freedom more than I had ever wanted anything in my life, but terror flooded every cell in my body.

The house, while very much a real thing, was a symbol of so much more. There are a variety of reasons for building a tiny home. Some want financial freedom and others crave environmental accountability. For most, it's a combination of reasons we're unable to articulate. And for me, the three years we spent traveling three hours away from where we lived to build a small home in the mountains was the embodiment of my next steps. With a tiny house, I had the freedom to quit but I wasn't entirely sure I had the fortitude. Maybe it was a crutch, but maybe not. The only way I would know was to let go.

These feelings pounded through my veins day I gave my notice.

An angst I hadn't known since writing bad poetry at age sixteen steamrollered me in bed at night. A racing heart and sleep don't peacefully coexist. Did you know unexplainable itching is a sign of anxiety? Now, I know. The anxiety shifted its weight on an early April day while the wind was still sharp and showers prophesized the coming flowers. I quaked in my ergonomic desk chair, afraid that my quick pulse and darting eyes would betray me. I could hear the blood in my veins. "I Quit!" had to be scrawled on my forehead in thick, black sharpie.

I shook uncontrollably as I padded into my boss's office, my body language timid. I held the envelope out to her and said, my voice faltering, "I need to give you my notice." She looked at me, wide-eyed, without a word. In the pause, I sat down hard on the chair that faced her desk. "The tiny house is almost done and we're moving to Asheville." I felt compelled to fill the silence.

A few moments passed before she added her voice. To my surprise, she was excited for me. It was real now. I would live in my own tiny home. I had said it out loud to the people who would be affected the most by our decision, besides Matt and myself. There was no turning back now.

"Maybe you can work remotely," she offered with exuberance.

"I would be open to that," I said. Though I was leaving to start a new life, a safety net sounded less terrifying.

Over the course of the weeks to follow, the idea of working remotely was shot down by my coworkers. To this day I have no idea why. I can only imagine the worst. They couldn't wrap their minds around why I would quit.

After I left it was apparent that completely pulling up these roots would be the better choice by far.

My last day finally arrived. I spent my final weeks tying up loose ends, leaving no knots untightened. My successor was successfully trained. Eight long years with the same people, and the curtain finally fell. "The End" scrolled across the screen. While I was good at what I did, and my coworkers were good people, I spent years suffocated by an invisible fog.

My coworkers gave me a gorgeous potted plant as a gift on my last day. New roots I could plant by the tiny house.

Within a year the plant had died.

Intermission

When God made me born a Yankee, she was teasing.
—Indigo Girls

The transition was smooth. Smoother than we thought. Our lives in this 120 square foot, off-grid home surpassed our expectations and our previous adventures in suburbia. This was how we were meant to live. Benefits bloomed like wildflowers from hidden cracks and crevices in the landscape.

Now, I rise each day with the sun as its warmth streams through the tiny house windows. My feet, in fuzzy socks, pad softly down the ladder and I put on a pot of water for tea. The touch of one button initiates the whir of my computer and I settle into my morning routine. Then I type. My job now? Writing. For a living. People pay me. This was what I had always wanted.

There are things I am responsible for in the tiny house. My day isn't all pajama-wearing and tea sipping. Eventually, I slip on my shoes, step outside, and fill jugs of water from the spring. Three gallons fill the water filter inside. In Atlanta, we wasted so much water each day but in the tiny house, use is down to just five gallons a day, complete with showers and overall cleanliness. Gray water collects in a bucket outside, hung under the shower drain. I dump the murky water into our small reclamation system over pumice and river pebbles that naturally filter the water, safe now for the yellow irises planted in the artificial wetland. Chores are a nice break from the daily routine. These are words I never thought I'd say after years of dishwasher convenience and lazy nights of nothing but marathons of mindless TV.

Six months in, the next chapters of our new adventure were scribbled on the scraps of paper cluttering the surface of the newly lived-in tiny home.

Act 3: The Tree

> *Even if I knew that tomorrow the world would go to pieces,*
> *I would still plant my apple tree.*
> —Martin Luther

The night before Halloween in 2012, as we prepared to spend two months with our families for the holidays, we packed up the tiny house. A winter storm of extinction-level proportions closed in over the Smoky Mountains. That afternoon, between packing sessions, Matt went outside just as the heaviest winds whipped through the canopy of brown and gold. "I need to move the chairs off the deck," he said as the door slammed behind him sending tremors through the house.

We built a deck, and called it the Folk-N-Ale, shortly after moving in. At twelve by twelve, it more than doubled our living space. On the deck stood a table and chairs so we could entertain or enjoy our dinner under the trees. With the storm rolling in, their stability was in question.

I've already established Matt as a perfectionist, right? I watched out the window as he moved the chairs against one tree. He stopped, contemplated, and moved them against another. Then, deciding that the first tree was superior, moved them back. After some time, he finally determined the chairs were, in fact, safe and ran back inside just as the winds picked up ferocity.

Minutes later, as he settled on the sofa with his back to the window, movement caught my eye. From my vantage point I watched as a massive, dead eastern hemlock caught the tempest. That hemlock had been a source of consternation for a while, and we knew it would come down one day. We just hoped it wasn't on the house. The cracking sound was amplified by the landscape. I pointed and stuttered, "The tree. That tree!"

Matt jerked his head around and we both watched the tree crash directly toward the deck where he stood only seconds before. What happened in the fraction of a second felt like an eternity in slow motion. A tall, but skinny, adolescent tulip poplar deflected the dead trunk, sacrificing itself for the Folk-N-Ale. Otherwise, the tree would have been a direct hit. Instead, it crashed directly on the chairs so lovingly placed beneath a tree for shelter in the storm. Brown, plastic shards exploded into the atmosphere. Obliterated.

We were paralyzed. There was nothing we could do but watch. We were just grateful that the direction of the destruction was woodswise, and not housewise. I knew that living in a tiny house would be hard and I knew there would be moments of frustration, but I never knew that I could watch a tree fall in the woods and be grateful it didn't crush my house.

The tree, like the foundation and like the plant skeleton still anchored next to the house, was another monument to the hard work, sheer luck, and unexpectedness of our new lives.

From the moment we nailed the first two by fours together, I knew this was a project unlike any other. We raised the walls. We designed the interior. We moved in. We lived comfortably in this tiny home as easily as if we had done it our whole lives. And we learned and grew from our experience.

Curtain Call

> *Before enlightenment; chop wood, carry water.*
> *After enlightenment; chop wood, carry water.*
> —Zen Proverb

Sitting on the Folk-N-Ale with a beer in my hand, I drink in the calm of Appalachia. In front of me is my tiny home, just a few years old now. To my left, I can peer through the trees and catch a glimpse of some of the old-est mountains in the world. I'm part of that history now, too.

My cat lounges in the window where I can see her, soaking up the dap-pled sunlight that filters through the forest. The same sunlight powers our house and our lives. I am content.

There is freedom all around me from the cackling of the crows harassing a hawk in the distance to the light rustling of the bright green tulip poplar leaves with each gust of warm wind. The wood from the fallen hemlock waits in neat piles for us to place them in the outdoor fire pit once the sun goes down, which it does earlier on our mountain than anywhere around us. We are above the horizon.

Before it gets too dark, I'll fire up the burner on the outdoor kitchen and whip up a meal. Our weekly trek to the farmer's market rewards us with a boon of fresh ingredients from nearby farms. In our lives we've built a foun-dation, torn up our roots, and planted them again, over and over.

It's never been about the house.

Epic Tiny House Journey

$400m, A Really Good Date and a Movie With Friends

Kai Rostcheck

Kai Rostcheck is the founder of Tiny House Lending, Tiny House Dating and I Love Tiny Houses as well as a co-Producer for the documentary Living Tiny…Legally! His articles about the tiny house movement have been published in Tiny House Magazine and on Boston.com, he appeared on WCVB-TV's "Chronicle" about the tiny house movement in Massachusetts and he has been interviewed for numerous Tiny House blogs. In everything he does, Kai evangelizes the belief that Turning Tiny represents a viable, conscious choice based on personal values and shifting socioeconomics.

I didn't set out to be a writer, speaker, documentary filmmaker, match-maker, community builder or financier in the Tiny House world. But somehow, in just a few years, I've become all of them.

More importantly, I've become true friends with many people who inspire me.

Builders, bloggers, do-it-yourselfers, trailer manufacturers and enthusiasts, this is my tiny house tribe. And these are some of the best relationships I've ever had. Heck, my girlfriend even calls herself a Tiny House Groupie and was thrilled to feel included as part of the team when my Tiny House Collaborative mates traveled from across the country to pow-wow in Orlando.

I do what I do for the Movement because I love the people. They, no, you resonate with me.

How did I get here? What have I learned? And what can I share with you that will educate and encourage you?

In The Beginning

My tiny house journey began like most, through tiny house porn: the pictures and then the videos of these adorable little houses that felt immediately like the "home" I've always wanted, always yearned for. A sanctuary. Some place that I could call my own because it feels like me, looks the way I want it to, understands me. I was literally dreaming of tiny houses and fantasizing about the life I could live, and what I could do, by going tiny.

Then I stumbled upon Kirsten Dirksen's documentary We The Tiny House People, which had already been viewed over a million times. Today, that number is hardly anything – commercials regularly score exponentially more views. But a few years ago, when my journey began, a million views was still a big deal...especially for a tiny little fringe movement.

What was going on here? Why all the interest? Where was it coming from?

My lightning-rod moment came during a segment in the film when Kirsten was interviewing Jay Shafer, the man who is commonly and belovedly known as "godfather" of the tiny house movement (and who also happens to be a hysterical Tiny House Dating contestant – more on that later). It was when Jay explained that he "Sold more books and plans than tiny houses" and said that sometimes he felt like he was "selling the dream" that I began to wonder why tiny house living is just a dream for so many people?

I couldn't get that question out of my head. Some people have mammalian and reptilian brains. I'm wired for creativity and business development – but certainly not for building – and I knew right away that my engagement in the Movement would come through owning a tiny house (someday), and by some other unique contribution.

So I started researching, and set out to understand three things:

- Who is following the tiny house movement?
- Why are they joining?
- Where is this heading?

I wanted numbers and facts, and set out (without preconceived notions or bias, I think) to determine "How real is this tiny house thing?"

It didn't take long for me to realize that the tiny house movement is very real.

How Big Is It, Really?

I started by quantifying social media data. How many tiny house related Facebook groups were out there? (Over 60 already, way back in the beginning of 2014). How many "hits" had tiny house videos received? What could I learn about Twitter influencers and followers?

After diving into the deep end of the tiny house pool for a couple of weeks, I came up with the following numbers. At that time, the Movement was already represented by:

- More than forty blogs
- Far more than one hundred articles including mainstream coverage via Boston.com, ABC News, CBS News, NBC News, Oprah Winfrey, Huffington Post, New York Times, Slate, The Washington Post, Los Angeles Times, Mother Earth News and many, many more outlets.
- Over thirty (U.S.) builders
- Six hundred seventy nine thousand people following tiny house Facebook pages in January, 2014. That number had already swollen to eight hundred twenty two thousand by the end of February, 2014 – a twenty one percent increase in less than six weeks – when I realized that tracking the growth was no longer feasible
- Six hundred eighty seven percent historical growth in "Tiny House" keyword searches from March 2004 thru December 2013

- Over fifty YouTube videos representing more than five hundred eighty videos, nearly two hundred thousand subscribers and close to thirty million hits

Wait. Thirty million hits? Lightning strike number 2!

Thirty million is a big number, especially for a cottage industry. Either a lot of people were consuming a little bit of tiny house media or a few people were consuming a massive amount of media. Either way, that number signaled a pretty voracious appetite for anything tiny house related.

I found a lot more data too, and subsequently published it in the article Is a Tiny House the Solution to Big Financial Problems? (Boston Globe, March 2014). But the "final" penny dropped when I turned to Twitter. That's where I was able to find aggregated profile data for followers of some of the tiny house movement's biggest influencers. Frankly, up until that time I had been thinking that this 'Do it Yourself' industry was made up mostly of lower income people. This theory could explain why so many people had "the dream" but weren't buying, right? Yet it turned out that the average tiny house "follower" was a single, professional woman, thirty-six years old, college educated and preferred shopping at Nordstrom and Starbucks.

Come again?

What's Going On Here?

Why were so many educated, seemingly successful (and hey, I admit it...I was thinking "eligible") women fantasizing about tiny houses? This seemed like a huge sociological shift to me so I started looking deeper for demographic trends that could help me understand the phenomenon. By studying U.S. Census data, and following threads in financial publications like Bloomberg and Forbes, I quickly began seeing the massive explosion in tiny house interest as a direct response to the great recession of 2007-2010.

If you lived through that time as a wage-earning adult, you know that some fundamental economic realities shifted. Tons of people were laid off and few of the jobs were replaced. Health care, education, energy, transportation and food costs all rose significantly meaning that workers were earning far less "real" income than they had in nearly a generation.

Soon enough I realized that while our 36-year-old female archetype (let's call her Naomi – she'll show up in this narrative again pretty soon) was the harbinger, she wasn't alone. The tiny house movement was drawing interest from an extremely diverse base of people whose ages ranged drastically (I remember first learning about Sicily Kolbeck – the 13 year old girl who built her own tiny house around the same time that I was reading posts from retirees who wanted – or needed – to downsize).

Still, I wanted concrete numbers – and I found them via statistics from the U.S. Department of Commerce[1]:

- Median middle class household income in 2012: $51,017 and in 1989: $51,681
- U.S. official poverty rate in 2012 = 15.0% (46.5 million people)
- Real household income declined by 8.3% from 2007 to 2013
- Young adults age 25-34, living with their parents, had an official poverty rate of 9.7%. But if their poverty status were determined using only their own income, 43.3% had an income below the poverty threshold.
- Average amount needed to send a child to an in-state college for the 2012-13 academic year: $22,261 and for a private college: $43,289
- 75% of Americans are nearing retirement with less than $30,000 in their retirement accounts. Forbes calls this "The Greatest Retirement Crisis in American History."
- Housing prices increased by 56% since 1990.
- 3/4 of us do not have enough money saved to pay our bills for six months.
- In 2012, healthcare costs for the typical American family of four exceeded $22,000, "Almost as much as the cost of attending an in-state public college ($22,261) for the current academic year."

Lightning strike #3 – I finally understood. We (Americans) have created an inherently unsustainable economic model. Something has to change. To some observers, the tiny house movement is about small houses. That's true, but in reality, it's a response to shifting economics and changing values. Not only are many people no longer able to "keep up with the Joneses" – more importantly, we don't want to. Who wants to commute two to three hours a day to a job where you are overworked, under-appreciated and under-paid only to return home sapped of energy and unable to appreciate the people and/or things that used to inspire you?

My friends in the tiny house movement are universally creative, inspired and resourceful. We want to live fully, and we care about connections and experiences more than stuff. I got it. I felt it! And back in research world, I began to see how this might play out for me in a couple of ways.

A Match Made In Heaven?

I like tiny houses. The world likes tiny houses too! This is working out pretty well so far.

Unfortunately, not everyone has that experience. While reading through countless forums a curious topic showed up several times.

Naomi, our quintessential tiny house enthusiast, had a problem. To hear her tell it in her own words, she would say, "I really love the idea of having a tiny house. It makes me feel alive, and opens up doors for me to travel or start my own business. The problem is, I want to find a partner, too. I connect with people who seem like a good match on the dating sites. But as soon as I mention tiny houses, 'poof' – they disappear. Am I going to have to live alone forever if I pursue my tiny house dream?"

It's an unfortunate problem, no? I thought so, too. And since I've had some success matchmaking friends in the past, I thought "Why not create a dating site for tiny house people? How hard could it be?"

About $300 and three weeks later, Tiny House Dating was born. We went live pretty quietly. I wanted to trickle the word out a little bit at a time so I could see how the site might grow organically. And really, I wasn't expecting much. Tiny House Dating was a free site. I figured maybe we'd approach a couple hundred members at any given time and I'd keep it alive as a hobby. For $4.99 in hosting costs it was worth giving up one coffee a month.

We enrolled six members during our first week. A couple dozen more enrolled during week two. All was good until Kent Griswold posted a blog about our site on Tiny House Blog and all hell broke loose. His readership showed up in droves and within a few days mainstream media outlets started posting articles about Tiny House Dating. Outdoor Magazine, Tree Hugger and others boosted our visibility and people started flooding in. We received several hundred new members in just a few hours. But that wasn't to be the peak. Yahoo! Finance linked to our site and the world, or more accurately, the site, blew up. Tiny House Dating received 1.3 million hits during six days while we struggled to keep the site online. But in the end there was just way too much traffic. The site architecture hadn't been built to handle the load or scale so I had to pull it offline.

Long story short, I crowdfunded enough money to duct-tape it back together and re-launch with a paid subscription model (in order to recover ongoing costs and prevent spammers from joining – another valuable lesson I learned from this experience). But the platform was just fundamentally unstable from the outset. So despite recurring interest from Reality TV producers and people who wanted to join, along with a live episode of Tiny House Dating – Bachelorette! at the 2015 Tiny House Jamboree (featuring co-host Andrew "Holy Shit He's Hysterical" Odom and the one and only Jay Shafer) I brought Tiny House Dating offline in late 2015. Currently the project is in "vacation mode." I do hope to re-launch a more structurally sound version in the future since it did provide a valuable community service.

FINAL NOTE: Yes, Tiny House Dating did bring together several couples. I'm aware of one who connected during the first week the site was live (they've been together for over two years now) and another who connected through the live episode at the Jamboree. Even though letting it go (for now) was a bit bittersweet I'm still inspired that the site made a difference for some people. I'm also still astonished by the massive amount of interest it generated. However, I've also been working on several other projects in the meantime.

What Are the Real Problems and What Can I Do About It?

Earlier, we explored the socio-economic shifts that are fueling the movement. But we haven't looked at the other side yet: factors that are inhibiting growth. In a nutshell, the tiny house movement won't hit mainstream until obtaining and living in a tiny is a regular commercial transaction like buying a car or a more traditional house. Those transactions are obvious. We know where to go to look at houses or shop for cars. We're clear about the buying process (including financing, if desired), how to insure them, how to protect ourselves (through consumer protection laws, etc.) and most importantly, where they belong.

The tiny house industry needs standards for building codes, zoning laws, titling and insurance. We've got a long way to go on those issues and each one of them is going to require champions working together – most likely for a long time without paid contribution – to create change. Still, the movement continues to grow quite rapidly. For example, I know of approximately 120 builders now, a quadrupling in less than two years. I estimate that do-it-yourselfers actually account for about 75% of the industry.

"With so much policy to change, what difference can I make?" That's what I was asking myself as I began exploring these complicated issues. I tend to avoid politics, and I don't have any kind of education in the building industry, but I understood clearly when I read post after post from people who were only dreaming about their tiny house rather than living in one, because they didn't have cash on hand to build or buy. Many of these people were stuck, and wanted to save money by making the financially responsible decision to go tiny, payoff a loan in a few years and avoid long-term debt via rent or mortgage. But nobody would loan to them.

Banks don't understand tiny houses. We've created a "gray area" that doesn't sit well for an industry that's heavily regulated and expects round pegs to fit in round holes.

We are more like triangles.

Tiny houses aren't "houses" in the traditional sense. Houses are usually collateralized by land and property. Those things stay in one place. Banks are essentially "invested" in your mortgage. And if you default, well, most people know how that goes (hint: repossession and eviction are a lot easier for creditors when they know where to find you).

Tiny houses aren't RVs either. Though sometimes categorized as such, the very definition of recreational carries with it a policy that often restricts people from living full-time in such a domicile. No good if you are looking to actually live in your tiny house.

With these complications, even non-traditional lenders don't want to touch tiny houses. I know that because I've spoken to hundreds of them, everything from micro-credit and/or peer-to-peer lenders to credit unions, CDFIs and more. Most of them have no idea what a tiny house is. The rest (even when chartered with 'alternative' financing such as low-income or minority housing) can't get their heads around how to loan for a tiny house.

Unfortunately, the lack of building standards, comparable pricing models and legal placement options are just too much for them to overcome.

Tiny House Lending is Born

I had another dream. We'd "crowdsource" micro-lending and build a system that offered peer-to-peer, social backed loans to people who want to go tiny. It would be democratic and innovative while returning us to the roots of sound financial policy. All I needed was a big bank with an existing loan management system.

Yeah right.

However, I did find one option that seemed nearly perfect: the personal loan. This financial product typically offers from $3-50k on terms of three to seven years with no collateral. Applications can usually be done online. If an applicant is approved the money is deposited into her/his account in full (within hours) and the can be used for anything: vacations, big purchases, loan consolidation or tiny houses! Whether you want to build your own or buy from a manufacturer this could be the ideal solution for you.

There's just one catch.

Since personal loans are not collateral-backed, they are riskier for the lender. Therefore, percentage rates are significantly higher than they would be on a car, boat or more traditional RV loan (or mortgage). Still, it seemed like this option could make sense for some people. I launched my financing "matchmaker" site (do you see the trend here?) Tiny House Lending in early-2015. The site has a filtering process that connects potential applicants to personal loan lenders based on credit score, residency and the amount to be borrowed. Tiny House Lending is doing well. We've helped dozens of people into tiny houses. But there's plenty of room for improvement and I am continuously looking for different lending partners and financial products that will solve this Achilles' heel once and for all.

In the meantime I can confidently say (through data gathered during Tiny House Lending's first year of operation) that tiny houses represent a market of at least $400 million dollars in annual spending. That's still small potatoes compared to most industries (like banking...another reason why it's hard to get lenders' attention) but we've got quantifiable numbers now. And the wheels on this tiny house movement keep turning faster every day, which reminds of a road trip. Yes. That is how my mind works!

Road Trip!

The first annual Tiny House Jamboree was epic in every sense of the word. First, I toured the country. I spent 11 days driving from New Orleans to Austin, out through Albuquerque, over to Sedona, up to the Grand Canyon and beyond into southern Utah then over to Northern Colorado before finally landing in Colorado Springs. I was in high spirits. Literally! And it only got better from there.

Within moments of arriving I was touring Garden of the Gods with "famous" tiny housers Alek Lifeski (The Tiny Project), BA Norrgard (A Bed Over My Head), Lina Menard (This is the Little Life), Vina Lustado (Sol Haus Design), James Taylor (Orlando Lakefront) and Lee Pera (Boneyard Studios). These people were like royalty to me at the time. It amazed me that within 24 hours of meeting each other we had planted the seeds that would become the Tiny House Collaborative: an organization dedicated to Empowered Individuals. Resilient Communities. Home Redefined. I knew then, and still feel every day that I've found my tribe. The Tiny House Collaborative website launched during January 2016 with several awesome tools including an interactive builder map. But we have much more planned.

There was more magic at the Jamboree too. I teamed up with Alexis DeHart Stephens and Christian Parsons (collectively known as Tiny House Expedition) – documentary filmmakers who are touring the country creating a film about Tiny House Communities. It was awesome. Even more awesome though is that we were all hearing the same feedback from Jam participants. Everyone was concerned about zoning. So the three of us cooked up the idea of turning little successes into a big story. We'd interview policy makers from tiny house friendly (and would-be-tiny-house-friendly) towns across the country and let them tell their stories in their own words.

How are some communities already successfully adjusting zoning to encourage tiny houses? Why are they doing it? What's the economic and/or social incentive? What obstacles have they had to overcome and how are they doing it? What lessons can they share with their peers in other towns and cities around the country?

Living Tiny...Legally! was crowdfunded in early 2016. Filming is occurring throughout the calendar year with an emphasis on communities in Florida, Texas, California and Colorado plus stories from states as diverse as North Carolina, Georgia and Nevada. Our plan is to premier the film at the 2016 Tiny House Jamboree, and then make it available for free on YouTube; for enthusiasts and community planners to reference as they create their own plans for legal Tiny Housing.

What's Next?

So what will I do from here? And will I ever have my own tiny house?

First things first. I am committed to building Tiny House Lending as a widely available, affordable financing platform for people who want to go tiny.

Next, I'll help finish up Living Tiny Legally! and connect Tiny House Expedition with the Tiny House Collaborative (match-making again). I think it will be a perfect pairing of teams who have complementary competencies and shared interests. We'll build out additional resources that help community planners and policy makers legalize tiny houses and we'll have a freaking good time hanging out with each other.

Then there's Tiny House Dating, which needs to come back from vacation some day. I am currently in discussion with a production studio about turning the concept into a non-scripted show. If that comes through I may actually get arrested for having too much fun during one lifetime. But heck, I'll risk it.

Also, there's insurance yet. And not to be overshadowed is my belief that high school students – the future of the Movement – and at the crossroads of that socio-economic/values shift I discussed earlier, have a huge role to play. There are some tremendous stories to be told in this space. A lot of influential learning can happen here.

Beyond that, I'll be eagerly looking forward to the next Jamboree. Then I'll be looking forward to the one after that, and then the one in 2018. Come find me. I'll be the guy grinning ridiculously from ear to ear.

Following Your Dreams and Designing a Life You Love
Life is short, design a life that you love and follow your dreams

Jewel Pearson

After downsizing her lifestyle over the course of 10 years, Jewel Pearson took her long-standing dream of a lighter, freer, mobile lifestyle and designed a life and a tiny house she loves. A project manager and consultant by day, she has taken her passion for living a lighter lifestyle and now offers that expertise to help others dreaming the tiny house dream while continuing to share her tiny living experience via her website, Ms. Gypsy Soul – all in hopes of encouraging others to follow their dreams, whatever they may be!

My dream started out many years ago when my daughter was very young and in elementary school and I got her to agree that she'd buy me a RV once she'd made it big. Of course at that age she really had no idea what she was signing up for. I just made it a point to remind her frequently that she had agreed so I expected her to make it big – if just for my RV alone! As she got older I'd talk to her about my plan to travel the country in my RV and not really have a permanent address and how I planned to just show up randomly wherever she was. I told her there'd be a Wal-Mart with a huge parking lot wherever she went and I'd just stay there for a few days while visiting. Needless to say she was never amused by any of my plans. While I was kidding about some of my plans, I absolutely was not kidding about the desire to live what I felt like would be a free-er, lighter lifestyle once my daughter was grown.

Well my daughter certainly made it big. She's a lawyer; a graduate of Harvard Law School and though she technically still owes me a RV, I obviously went in a different direction and built a tiny house. How'd I get to building a tiny house when my dream was a RV? Well in a nutshell, after going to RV shows and doing some research I soon realized that the RV models I was most interested in were in the $300k range and above, which didn't bode well for my plans of a free-er, lighter lifestyle. That meant I needed to figure out another route to get to my dream. And that, my friends, is one of the many beauties of a dream. It can morph into whatever it needs to become to satisfy your wishes. It's your dream.

While my daughter was growing up, we lived in a 3-bedroom/3-bath home. My thoughts at that time were more along the traditional lines of thinking regarding homes and raising children, though I'm so happy to now watch so many families embrace tiny living as a way of life for them and to be able to follow their journeys. When my daughter left home to attend college I also relocated from Georgia to North Carolina to be closer to her. I sold my home in Georgia and settled into leasing a 3-bedroom/3-bath condo in the suburbs of Charlotte. I knew my ultimate goal was my free-er and lighter lifestyle. I wanted the ability to move when the mood hit me so I went the route of renting after selling my home and from that point forward to make achieving my dream that much easier. Please know that I'm not against homeownership. I will always be for people doing what works for them. I just knew my plans and priorities to be different. Moving to a large condo meant I still had the space, but my commitment to that space was different. I could still change my mind to make another move versus being locked into a 30-year mortgage that required more planning and different decision-making. My dream was still there and I was still working toward it.

I had downsized some, but I still wanted much of the space that I was accustomed to from my home in Atlanta. I still kept a bedroom for my daughter for her visits throughout the year. I had a guest room for friends and family, guest bathrooms, a big kitchen (though I'm not fond of cooking) and lots and lots of space. When my daughter graduated from undergrad I no longer felt the need to keep a dedicated bedroom in my house for her because I knew she was well on her way. She was headed to law school so in addition to her taking her bedroom furnishings with her, I gifted her with some of my other furnishings to get her started, as well as allow me to continue my downsizing.

Life was changing and I wanted to get out of the 'burbs and get closer to the hustle of the city, as well as continue downsizing my space. My next move was to a 2-bedroom/2-bath apartment closer to uptown Charlotte. This was my first move to a mid-rise apartment, so not only was I closer to the pulse of the city I could also achieve my standing dream of following beautiful sunrises and sunsets – and through the course of my moves I have had some beautiful views. All in all, I'm still holding on to my dream, but I'm making moves and living life all at the same time. Which brings me to this: another beauty of following your dreams is in knowing that dreams don't have to be linear. My moves and downsizing actually took place over the course of ten years and a lot of other things happened and other dreams were realized in between. If a dream is important you'll keep it in your mind space as you live life.

Well guess what happened next? I decided to follow another dream of mine and I chased the sunshine, skipping winter altogether and moved to sunny Fort Lauderdale, Florida! How many dreams can one person have? As many as they wish! That's absolutely right. Remember that earlier point about dreams not having be linear? Well you can also dream in multiples and that's just what I do. So let me introduce you to this dream. It's about everything sunshine and my love thereof. Got sunshine? I'm there! I decided I didn't want to experience winter this particular year and I rode off into the sunset, literally. My apartment lease was up, I found an apartment in the Los Olas area of downtown Fort Lauderdale and I moved so I could enjoy sunning and funning in the sunshine and on the beach. The highlight of my stay there being the time I took outdoor swim lessons in December while my friends not too far away in Georgia and North Carolina were wearing winter clothes and dealing with cold weather. They made sure to tell me how much they didn't appreciate my pictures in my new city.

During my time in Fort Lauderdale I missed the southern hospitality I was use to in North Carolina and Georgia and I missed my friends so I returned to Atlanta and eventually back to Charlotte. Here's another thing about following your dreams. There's always the option to dream a new dream when the current dream no longer serves you. So I'm back in Charlotte, in a 2-bedroom/2-bath apartment and one night I stumbled on Macy Miller's story and her beautiful tiny home. Macy's story of independence and financial freedom with a tiny house really resonated with me and I decided, I'm building a tiny house! I told my circle of friends and family and

I poured myself into reading and researching everything tiny house related over the course of the next year and a half.

What I will say about my circle of friends is that while not everyone "understood" my desire to live in a tiny house and even tiny houses themselves they were all supportive and that's what's important. I don't believe that people have to agree with my dreams, my dream might not be for them, but I do believe that you should always surround yourself with people who will support your dreams and you should do the same for them. As my friends would see articles applicable to my journey they'd forward them, they'd ask questions about my progress and as I got further into the process they stood in support when I needed them the most. Surround yourself with great people.

In support of my new dream I started a separate account and aptly named it my 'Tiny House Fund'. I specifically began to set aside funds to support my plans and I added the account to my online banking profile so that it was visible and a constant reminder of what I was working on. During this time I downsized my apartment again to a 1-bedroom/1-bath that allowed me to save even more money and I was also working toward my goal of living in a smaller space. I researched everything I could about tiny houses; I bookmarked pages, printed out articles and started collecting the important information in a binder. I followed blogs and joined groups on social media. I bought books. I started networking and I decided I would attend a tiny house workshop. I'm a project manager and I wanted to become the subject matter expert for my project; even if I wasn't going to actually physically build my tiny house I wanted to know how to do so in theory. I wanted to understand everything I could about tiny houses and I wanted to be able to make the decisions regarding my tiny house that would be best for me. That all paid off so much in the end.

During the course of this time as I was researching I also started making a list of what my requirements would be for my tiny house and I adjusted them as necessary. I also paid attention to others who were already living in their tiny houses as they shared their lessons learned about their spaces. I watched all of the tiny house shows and made notes of things that appealed to me and the things that didn't. Building my tiny house was going to be an investment for me and I treated the project as such, versus making a haphazard effort or just following someone else's tiny house vision. I was willing to pay for the resources as needed to help me on my journey; consultations, books, tours, etc. I think it's important to understand everyone can't give away their resources and knowledge for free, nor should I expect them to. I don't believe you throw your money at every person who considers him or herself an expert; you obviously must use some discretion, but you should respect those who are perhaps charging for their time but can assist you in your process.

During this time I also got laid off. I didn't think of it as the end of the world. I've been laid off several times before and I know that everything happens for a reason. Each time I've been laid off I've landed in a much better place post that lay off and this time I decided I would trust the process. I thankfully was offered a severance package and I had the monies I'd been saving for my tiny house fund so I took some time off and away from corporate America. I slept late. I travelled. I volunteered more. I was able to support a friend and his business. I was able to spend some quality time with a family member who lost her Dad and I continued to research everything tiny house related I could. This time also helped reconfirm for me a big part of my "why" for my desire of tiny house living. I want to live and know freedom. I want to be able to make more decisions to live and enjoy life without having to always factor in finances and time off from work. I don't want those things to always be the drivers for my life. There are so many places to visit, so many sunrises and sunsets to enjoy in other places, so many new people to meet and so many loved ones to spend time with. Life is so very short and I want to do those things now.

I had started deciding on the specifications for my trailer purchase, but before I spent any money I wanted to ensure I was really, really committed to tiny house living and that it was going to be something I could really do. One Saturday afternoon I saw an invite for an Open House being held the following day by Music City Tiny House in Nashville, Tennessee. It was a 6-½ hour drive and I don't mind driving so I jumped online and RSVP'd for the event, made arrangements for a rental car and hotel and I set off on my way. The thing I forgot to factor in is that I hate driving through the mountains. That drive was definitely an experience I will never forget and I was very happy to make it to Nashville and back home safely. I spent most of the day that Sunday visiting Music City Tiny House, sitting in the space, trying to take it all in. I asked the hosts as many questions as I could and they were very gracious hosts. I looked around at the interior and exterior of the tiny house trying to get a visual understanding of some of the things I was already familiar with from the tons of research I had been doing. What I confirmed from my visit was that I could definitely live in a tiny home. I wasn't feeling claustrophobic or boxed in and I really enjoyed the space. Music City Tiny House is 24ft long and I decided that I wanted just a little bit more space in the bathroom and a 28ft tiny house was the direction I'd go in for my build. I always encourage anyone on the journey to a tiny house or considering it to try to spend some time in one to substantiate your decision making process. When I got back home I finalized my trailer specifications and placed my trailer order. In October 2014 I knew I was definitely going to build my tiny house!

Now I start to focus on my actual building plans. I go home and measure off 28ft x 8.6ft in my apartment and start paying a lot of attention to how I use my space. I've had a list of requirements for each of my apartments; things like lots of windows, bathroom counter space so my jewelry and perfumes can sit out, ample closet space and these are the type of things that I know will transfer to my tiny house must haves since they've served me well in making my apartments my home. My sister Dawn is an interior designer and also attended the tiny house workshop with me so we start collaborating on the build plans. It was very important to me that my tiny house not only was functional in the interior, but I was also concerned with ensuring it had symmetry on

the exterior with my window and door placement. Paying attention to how I used my space became so important as we worked to put my tiny house plans together. I had my list of must haves and some nice to haves and now it was just a matter of pulling it all together, which sounds easier than it actually was. In my opinion this was the most critical part of my tiny house planning; to get through to the end of your build and not have a home that's both functional and personal and that makes you happy is a fail. Every inch counts in a tiny house and each inch should make you happy. It took a lot of back and forth and numerous iterations to pull it all together, but we did it and it was done well.

The highlight of the planning for me was to the see the build come to life in Sketch-up, with the help of Jamie, also an interior designer, who'd worked previously with my sister and also joined my team. I'm a visual person and Sketch-up is an amazing tool for someone like me, I could look at those renderings and imagine myself in my finished space. The renderings were so amazing as we worked through all of the details and I knew I'd be disappointed if the actual final product wasn't as fabulous! We worked for a few months on the actual plans and the pre-work certainly paid off. I think I've said over and over that I decided I was going to live tiny, but I didn't want to feel as if I was giving anything up and I wanted to maintain the style and look from all of my previous homes. I wanted lots of windows for sunshine and to expand my space, I didn't want a cramped bathroom space, I knew I had to have a comfortable couch included in my space and then there was my closet. I had to have my closet.

My apartment lease was up in May and my plan was to not extend my lease and to be in my tiny house by that time so I started interviewing builders with that objective in mind. As my plans were coming together I felt like my tiny house was different from many of the others that I'd seen and that it had some components that most wouldn't expect from a tiny house. I felt that my tiny house build would be an opportunity for a builder who might be interested in a new niche market and I pitched it as such. I also started sharing my build on social media. Up to this point only a few people knew what I was working on outside of my immediate circle so I decided to share my project. I also didn't see many African-Americans involved in the tiny house movement and I wanted to share what I was doing to perhaps be an encouragement for other African-Americans interested in tiny houses.

Around the same time that I decided on the builder for my tiny house I also saw an application to appear on HGTV's show Tiny House, Big Living and of course I applied. Part of the application process was to tell them about your build, the features that set your tiny house apart from others and why you thought you should be selected. I applied on a Sunday and got the call for an interview on Monday and we made it on the show, I think they agreed with my answers! Some of the features that I felt would set my tiny house apart from others like my fold-up screened in porch and Juliette Balcony had only been on the "wish list" before applying to the show, but I had shared them with HGTV so now we also have to include those very cool things. We started filming in February and the build began in late March. Both were completed by the end of May.

Once the build began, it became apparent that my builder and I didn't work very well together, unfortunately. Fortunately, I did work well with his team of builders working on the tiny house and with the other sub-contractors I'd contracted with to work on my project and it all came together. I expected the project to be somewhat stressful. My build was over what I'd (under) estimated as my budget, which meant my finances got really tight as the build was progressing. Plus the whole tiny house build concept was new for all of us and I expected that to cause some challenges, however I hadn't anticipated not working well with my builder and it took a toll on me. During my build I really, really had to lean on my circle. I actually wanted to quit and I'm tough and so not a quitter. But my friends wouldn't let me quit. They stood me back upright, reminding me of my "why" for building a tiny house and they stood in for me when I couldn't stand on my own. Support from my circle is what got me through my build and I am forever grateful. Remember when I said surround yourself with great people? This is why, they help you remember your dream and help you follow your dreams when you get off track – and you should always do the same for them.

It was an amazing feeling to watch my tiny house come to life from all the conversations, my dreams and the conceptual images on paper and on screen. I sourced all of the material and the contractors for my build and I definitely learned a whole lot in the process. Jamie went into overtime helping me with the build details and she was onsite, whenever I needed her, putting in physical labor – we often worked through the night to be ready for filming. I was onsite every day, managing the project and the dream of my tiny house took over my life for a while. It wasn't how I imagined it, but I was committed to making sure my tiny house was something that I was going to love and thankfully it paid off and I do. Sometimes I'd sit in the shell of the house and look at the progress in amazement that it was all really happening since it was now a physical thing I could touch. The dream, though very, very hard work, became a reality. What's that saying about anything worth having? Checkmate.

I moved into my tiny house at the end of May as I'd hoped and planned. Though it was staged for filming my tiny house wasn't 100% finished when I moved in and I was completely at the end of my budget which meant I needed to recoup my funds to finish some of the things that were still outstanding. Living in my tiny house was tough since some of the things outstanding were key – like having AC in July – but all of the hard work of the pre-planning and the actual build had paid off and I could see the finish line. My tiny house, even with the work outstanding, was a space that I absolutely loved so I knew it would all be okay once everything was completely in place. It was okay for sure and it just keeps getting better.

My tiny house is still in Charlotte, now parked on a beautiful space that I'm renting from a wonderful property owner. While it is mobile, I haven't moved it very far other than within the city. My tiny house is a beast structurally, but I treat it like a baby because I just love it. If I move it out of this area, because of its size I'd most likely plan to stay at that new location at least 6 months to a year. But the bonus is that I know that I can move it should the mood hit me; there's a freedom attached to that. There's also a lightness and freedom attached to knowing I own my beautiful home and that my expenses associated with it are minimal. I definitely achieved my "why"! Living in my tiny house affords me a free-er and lighter lifestyle – I've achieved my dream!

Dreams don't happen through lack of effort, you're more than likely going to have to work hard at achieving them – follow your dreams. Achieving dreams isn't always easy, you may want to give up and you might forget the reason you began the pursuit in the first place – follow your dreams. Dreams often take time to achieve; the time is going to pass anyway. Follow your dreams. No one else may understand your dream. Know that it's ok that they don't. Surround yourself with great people and follow your dreams.

Finding Joy In My Empty Nest

Michelle Bradeson Boyle

In pursuit of a secure and loving place to call home, Michelle has experienced more than her fair share of setbacks that go back as far as she can remember. These events in her life, however, have left her more resilient, resourceful, dedicated, and stronger than ever. Michelle is a proud and outgoing single mom of two college aged children, a procurement professional, published author, accomplished speaker, patented inventor, creative blogger, craigslist stalker, and enthusiastic Glamper; as well a passionate tiny house enthusiast, designer, and builder.

Joy is not the absence of sorrow. Joy is a decision not to allow sorrow to rule my thoughts.

Joy is not a denial of life's challenges. Joy is refusing to let challenges get in the way of my personal growth.

Joy is not an escape. Joy is a space where I can go to think, and write, and rest and consider all that my future has in store for me. Joy is lovely, and warm, and welcoming, and it envelops my soul in a way that nothing else can.

And this is the story of how I found that kind of joy, by building a tiny house.

In many ways my story is very much like your own. We all grow, we all have challenges, and we all face them as best as we can. Life is full of loss and feelings of not being comfortable in one's own skin, and of wondering when we'll finally be worthy of love and acceptance. In these ways I am no different from you.

But where our similarities end, is where we find opportunity. And when we discover the things we do not have in common, we also discover the potential that lies in our ability to help and enrich each other's lives. It is my hope that by reading this, my story; your life is enriched and you will gain inspiration from my journey.

Two years ago I started the latest chapter of the life I now live. I discovered the tiny house "movement" and was almost instantly inspired by the concept of a simple life, a life that I could build for myself. I immediately started to plan, and scheme, and sketch. I made lists, I made decisions, I committed myself to a new project and I would not be deterred.

However, before I begin to tell about this latest chapter in my life, let's go back a bit farther.

At a very young age I was abandoned by my birth parents at the feet of my Grandparents. My Grandparents were angry, confused and overwhelmed with the decisions they were being forced to face. Their drug-addicted daughter had failed. Their son-in-law had moved far away and refused to accept responsibility for me, or my younger brother. Since he was an infant, they made the decision to care for him and passed me on to foster care.

Growing up I remember longing for a space to call my own. I built forts and made cupboards into dollhouses. I drew houses and day dreamed of having my own room. By age 15 I was working. On my way to work I rode my bike past this tiny abandoned farmhouse in the middle of a hay field and I remember thinking "I know how it feels." It seemed to be lonely, but determined to stand tall, just like me. There were no broken windows, the door hung where it always had, and the vines grew up the brick chimney from the ground to the rooftop. It had a story to tell but, sadly, a story I would never hear.

At the age of 18 I moved into the first "place" I could call my own; a 10' x 10' tack room in a large horse barn. I decorated it, and swept it every day. I hung curtains, made my cot every day, and padlocked myself in at night. I was blissfully happy. It was tiny, but it was mine.

After two marriages, two divorces, and the loss of two houses amidst the carnage of those divorces, I started my life over in Oregon. I arrived with two kids, two cats, two horses, a pregnant dog, and little more than the clothes on my back. Looking back, being a single mom has been the hardest thing I have ever done. But nothing that I have ever done has been as rewarding and filled me with a sense of pride and accomplishment as being my children's provider.

Twelve years have passed since the move and during that time I have discovered myself, embraced my talents, clarified my values and found love. It's amazing what love and support can do to transform one's self esteem. I have someone in my corner, someone to urge me on when life is kicking my ass (again). Love, however, has not deterred me from my new goal: to never again let the success or failure of a relationship dictate my domestic security.

And that brings me back to those lists, floor plans, and budgets; the vision that is the starting point of my tiny house journey.

Now you know that my desire to have my own space was created by loss and longing for home. But despite a lifelong journey towards the peace and love and joy that one's own home can bring, I have no illusions of grandeur. I have no expectations to live a big life. I now know that a tiny house is enough, just enough.

Knowing myself, defining my goals, and putting together my plan for the future was what drove almost every decision I made during the design phase of my tiny house. I drew the plans, with a pencil, a ruler and graph paper. I drew many, many, versions. I love to cook so I drew a big kitchen, with full sized appliances. I love to entertain and, although the idea of having a tiny house may not exactly seem conducive to cocktail parties, I drew a "great room" which connected the kitchen and the living room in one big open space. Aand, by the way, more people have visited my tiny home since it's completion than ever visited all the houses I ever lived in, combined. I want people to visit, to stay. I want my children to bring their children so I knew that a second loft would be needed. The more I drew, the closer I came to the real living version of my dream space.

Drawing a picture of a tiny house is one thing. Paying for one, however, is a whole other "thing". I had no savings, my wages paid (and still pay) my rent, and my children were college bound. I knew I would have to think outside the box. I would have to find a way to pay for my dream that didn't involve using my paycheck.

I do not know exactly why my first sponsor took a chance on me, why they agreed to help me build my tiny house by providing the windows. I do not know why the next sponsor agreed to provide the lumber, and the third one agreed to discount my tiny house trailer. Perhaps it was because I had demonstrating to them that I was worth their investment. Perhaps it was because I had something they wanted; a new and unique way to market their products in what was (and is) the growing tiny house market. But, they did help and in doing so they helped me to advance toward my goal. I didn't tell them a sob story about my birth parents. I didn't even tell them I was a single mom. I just advocated for myself and made a list of what I could do for them in exchange for their products.

So many people ask me how I did it. My success in this area (I collected almost $18,000 worth of sponsored products) was not, however, terribly different than anything else I have ever accomplished. I made lists. I stayed focused. I didn't let the 180+ doors slammed in my proverbial face deter me. I set timelines. I held myself accountable.

And I progressed.

The sponsors' enthusiasm about my project ended up also being the inspiration for me to stay on course on difficult days when the entire project seemed to be no more realizable than a pipe dream. I simply could not fail or let them down. They were on board, I was indeed progressing, but I knew I would have to augment what my sponsors had provided. So, I started to look for other sources of funding.

My neighbor had a vintage trailer and, when she moved, asked me to help her in exchange for it. I did, and she gave it to me. I gutted the trailer and replaced the wiring and bearings and tires and lights and interior walls.

When I sold it 8 weeks later, I immediately spent my profits on my tiny house trailer. I also cashed out my 401K. It truly wasn't much but was just enough to pay for the framer. I also sold my stuff on Craigslist, stuff I would be getting rid of, anyways. I sold vintage furniture after I had refinished it, and I bartered for supplies and small items at a local reclaimed material store. Funding wise, I was well on my way.

I attended my first tiny house Meetup event in January of 2014. It was hosted by none other than Dee Williams. I took my floor plans and was sure that all of my questions would be answered right then and there by Dee herself! It didn't exactly turn out that way because everyone else who attended had the same idea but the experience certainly set me on my way. I wasn't alone. There were so many others just like me. I thought that maybe, just maybe, I had found "my people."

To say that I am thankful for all the support of my sponsors and my boyfriend and all of my newfound tiny house friends would be a gross understatement. It was almost magical how it all finally started to come together. When the first truckload of lumber and roofing materials was delivered, and dumped on my front lawn I thought to myself "This is real!"

I decided to build my tiny house in the driveway of my rental home because it was easy. That's it. It was next to my garage, and adjacent to my front lawn with lots of space for storing bulky, long, and otherwise awkward materials. I didn't ask permission. I didn't even consider that anyone would complain. I just started to build and assumed that everyone would love it as much as I did.

My boyfriend, Mark, is a talented professional framer and photographer. And, he's been framing houses for over 20 years so it certainly made sense to hire him to build my tiny house. That decision, however, wasn't made without a fair amount of discussion. As the designer, project manager, owner, and control freak that I naturally am, I wanted I wanted final say on everything from what screws to use to how fast he was going to be expected to complete my project. He, however, finally convinced me that you can not rush, or micro manage, perfection.

Since there really was no reason to inject drama into the project, and no deadline that wasn't self-imposed, we agreed on a flat rate of pay for the whole build and I agreed that he could take as much time as he needed to complete it. I was so excited to come home from work every day to see the progress he had made! He worked during the day, and then after dinner I would clean up the job site, organize the tools, and sweep. We would then have a "production meeting." It was an excuse to drink wine and whiskey and sit in the not-yet-completed house, under the stars, every evening. We discussed what he had gotten done and what supplies he needed. He told me how thankful I should be for his talent and ability to work from my kindergarten level drawings. And we laughed.

It took him 15 days, working as much as the very hot and sticky summer weather would allow. He started by leveling the trailer and building the floor; and then he framed the house, sheathed it, wrapped it with vapor wrap, and installed the windows. It all happened so fast and it remains, to this day, my favorite part of the build. Because, after that, the build seemed to progress at a snail's pace. Bad weather, lack of time, lack of energy and tools and expertise and help wore on me as the Fall and then the Winter passed. I would recall, fondly, the collaboration Mark and I had enjoyed. It was now just me. He was working full time again and had little time for my tiny project.

I did, however, push forward. I spent the bad weather days staying organized, buying materials, coordinating deliveries, managing sponsors, updating my budget, writing blog articles, and collecting bids. However, when all the stars and supplies and free time aligned I would be out in my tiny house installing insulation and staining loft beams with a Pinterest inspired mixture of vinegar and steel wool. And I would measure, and measure again. I would put tape on the floors, and post-its on the walls and ceiling to use as location markers for electrical fixtures and outlets. And, I cleaned the windows. I think I washed them, inside and out, about a dozen times during construction. Silly. I know. But it was like therapy. I was nesting. It was cathartic.

Mark's influence over my project, however, was far from over. He had recently torn down an old building on what was his parents' property. It was originally built in the late 1800's and was a virtual gold mine of barn wood. He re-sided his boat house with it and then, after some affectionate cajoling, he allowed me to take what was left. Next thing you know, there I was, crawling in the un-lit attic of his shed throwing down barn wood that I hauled over 150 miles to my house. Next, I pulled out all the nails and sanded it, and cut out the bad sections. Then I set it on end to dry in the garage, with several heaters and a prayer that I wouldn't burn down the main house in the process.

And, just when my house project couldn't possibly get any more out-of-the-box, I hired my ex-husband as my electrician. He was more than happy to take money from me and use my tiny house as practice for his own eventual house on his recently inherited 150 acres. And I was more than happy to pay less than a third of what a licensed electrician would charge. (To be safe, however, I did hire a licensed electrician to inspect his work before I installed the drywall. He passed.) Even though he made a lot of mistakes that I later discovered while drywalling (can you say "outlet inset issues"?) and I ended up tearing out the fixtures he originally installed in the kitchen, I'm still pretty happy he was involved. The process also served as proof to my children that they would not have to look forward to awkward weddings and parties for eventual grandchildren. The post-divorce-angst was gone.

I decided pretty early on that my design aesthetic would be "Modern Nostalgia" and despite some late-in-the-build nervous energy about how it would all look together in the same space, I ended up with just that; a very unique and quirky mix of vintage, and modern, appliances and furnishings. I have neutral colored Marmoleum floors, which lead you through a lovely glass paneled door into the bathroom. I have barn wood wrapped lofts, a 100-year-old steamer truck from my Grandmother sitting alongside IKEA pillows and the cutest pair of tiny orange side tables you have ever seen in your entire life. I hung stainless steel pegrails as a modern replacement for upper cupboards in the kitchen and utilized club-style chairs in the adjacent living room, covered with shiny silver leather. I also used Mark's "time out" chair from his childhood home to stack books on, his father's old painter's ladder for my front loft, and the very drain-board-style sink he was bathed in, as an infant, now graces my kitchen.

When I watch TV shows about people buying houses, they often lament about the spaces they have or spaces they want for entertaining. In one of the houses I built with my ex-husband we even included a guest room but it was rarely used. I mention this because I think that so often we design, and buy, and move into houses not as a true reflection of who we are; but who we think we want to be or who others expect us to be. My tiny house, however, reflects my true and authentic sense of self and who I am now. And, I do not fear other's reprisal of my choices. It is small, and cozy, and eclectic, and has nothing more in it than I will ever need to live a fulfilling and simple life. And, since I have completed it, I have had more people visit me than have visited me in all of my previous houses, combined. People are drawn to authentic living. I believe people appreciate vulnerability and simple places. I believe there is no time better spent than that which is spent sharing a bottle of wine with friends, engaged in conversation.

You will often hear tiny house occupants and builders say that "it's not about the house." And it's not. Tiny houses are about finding yourself and pairing down and living in a manner, which reflects your values and your goals. Tiny houses are about being honest with yourself about who you are, what your future holds, and being bold enough to pursue those goals when people tell you that you're crazy for entertaining the notion of living in less than 250 square feet.

You will also often hear people say that "nothing worth doing comes easy" and, let me tell you, nowhere is that more true than when you embark on a tiny house journey. Whether you are downsizing from 2300 square feet to 1000 square feet, or find yourself staring at a huge empty nest that has lost its allure, deciding to go tiny will be very hard and expensive. It is truly mind numbingly difficult work. But. Oh. So. Worth. It.

When I started my build I wanted my project name to reflect not just what it is, but what it is to me. My project's name "My Empty Nest" ended up being both a painful and an inspiring moniker to hang my blog based hat on. As I look forward to my life without my kids under my roof, I want to smile, not cry.

Life as a single mom has been tiring and stressful. I always have a "what if" scenario running in the background of my thoughts. My career has been anything but stable so I'm always wondering "What if I lost my job again?" And, as I look forward to retirement, I think, "What if I need my children's help?" My tiny house, "My Empty Nest," has quieted those concerns and brought me peace. I am no longer as vulnerable as I have been, wandering and wondering where I will end up.

I have spent my entire life looking for a home, and a community, and longing for a family who accepts me and appreciates my eccentricities. And I have found them all, at long last. My children are the most amazing adults you will ever meet. They are responsible, and respectful, and supportive and loving. They are my family, and whether I am living in a tiny house or not, they will love me always. Yes, they were there all along. But the process of building my tiny house has drawn us closer together even as their growth into adulthood is pulled them away. My boyfriend has been loyal and helpful and an invaluable part of building my future. And, I have discovered so many new friends with whom I have so much in common and can share our journey and struggles.

I never thought that building a tiny house would do so much for me. That it would give me the opportunity to share my story, to inspire others, and to live a life that is in direct alignment with my values. I never thought, when I started this journey two years ago, that I would be accepted into this new, yet tiny, world. I never thought that I would find this much security, and happiness and joy. But I have. And, here I am. I have found it...

Joy in my life, joy in my future, and joy in My Empty Nest.

Bless This Tiny House

Living Faith and Values; the Kasl Family Tiny House

Kim Kasl

Kim Kasl and her family of four swapped their 2000 sq.ft. house for their lovely 267 square foot Tiny in September of 2014 with the intention of becoming a one-income family that homeschools, pursue's passions and adventure, and says Yes! to every opportunity. Through pictures and stories on her website BlessThisTinyHouse.com, Kim's pursuit is to normalize family-style minimalism in a culture where "stuff-gluttony" is the accepted norm and to affirm for families that on their journey to family-style minimalism they will remove the excess and be abundantly b*less*ed!

Together with my husband Ryan, our two kids Sully and Story, ages 7 and 6, and our curmudgeon of a dog, Brinkley, I have been living in a tiny house for nearly two years. In 2014 we gave away everything we own, sold our house (we lovingly call it "The Big House"), and completely embraced the tiny house lifestyle. Minimalism, or Family-Style Minimalism as I like to call it, is quite awesome. Before 2014 we were living the antithesis of family-style minimalism and after having walked the path of both, I can say that we very much prefer the kind of abundance afforded from having less stuff as opposed to the abundance that is the stuff itself.

Ryan and I did not just get together, decide to build a tiny house and shake on it. It was actually a story that took place ten years after we started our life together and it was a literal high-five that sealed the deal.

We started dating in high school, went to college together, got married after graduating, and moved into our first apartment. We both began full time jobs while Ryan also went to graduate school and I worked at developing my photography business.

Sully and Story were three and one when we finally ended the renting cycle and purchased our own 2000 sq. ft. home. By the time we finally felt settled, we had moved eight times together and accumulated massive amounts of stuff and stress.

We were raising toddlers, I was running a business, Ryan was still working full time while going to school full time and we felt like we were treading water. We were both looking for more time in the day than there was. Ryan's double full-time commitments made it challenging for him to ever take the kids so I could get work done during daylight hours. I longed to be less sleep deprived and distracted and to be more engaging and adventurous. I was struggling between wanting to achieve more in my work and wanting to be a better Mom. I constantly felt like I wasn't able to invest my best into anything.

Sully and Story were in preschool when we started having discussions about their education. The topic started in the realm of public school versus home school and then spread to broader questions.

With what values do we want our kids to grow? What are our family's goals really? What and whose goals are we achieving currently? What values are we modeling for our kids right now?

We knew we wanted to model great values for our kids: faith, family, giving, care, action, and pursuing passions and adventure.

Ultimately, we had to realize that our current life situation did not at all reflect our goals and values.

How can we create a best-life scenario for our kids and ourselves? How could we restructure our life so that our actions would reflect the values we want to model for and instill in our children? We had to do something drastic.

If we could somehow become a one-income family we would have the flexibility to homeschool and spend time adventuring, learning things the kids are interested in, volunteering, meeting new people, spending time with our family, and taking on new opportunities.

Obviously, if I stopped shooting weddings to homeschool our financial situation would be even more of a struggle. Plus, in two years Ryan would be finished with school, which would mean that we would have to start payments on student loans. We would be tackling two huge bills every month:

the mortgage and the student loan. With Ryan's future position we were confident that we could comfortably manage one of those. The mortgage was the
only bill we were not strapped to for life.

I stopped my business; walking away from something I loved was hard
but we really needed to step back, just stop and reevaluate, and pray.

"God we do not know. But you do. God, please bless us with a house
(ahem, preferably one that does not have a mortgage). Amen!"

Yes, I realize that prayer sounds ridiculous. It felt pretty ridiculous to
pray it. But God tells us to ask Him to fulfill our needs. He does have limit-
less resources, and He is radical. God started turning our hearts toward minimalism.

We were now more focused on our values and figuring out how we were
going to achieve them. We continued to pray with more fervor and discipline. The things that were in the way of us achieving our family goals started becoming more evident. They were physical and tangible things and they
were already in our house filling up closets, shelves, and even entire rooms of
our house. These things needed to be maintained, organized, and stored.
Clutter in our house was clutter in my mind and it needed to be removed to
make way for focus.

We could feel God preparing us for something big.

The urge to remove the unnecessary brought back memories of staying
in a cabin for a week when Sully was two and Story was only three-months
old. Our lives were very chaotic at the time and Ryan's parents gifted us a
bonus week of their timeshare to go up North and relax. We had no money
to spend and it was winter. I planned as many free activities as I could come
up with. Highlights were walks, bubble baths, going to the coffee shop in
town, and watching the fire. The cabin was so simple and quant: living area,
a big window, four bowls, four plates, one bedroom, and a fireplace. It was
the most restful, memorable, and healing time.

I sought out a YouTube video by Kirsten Dirksen that I had watched and
re-watched years earlier when I was pregnant with our first baby. It was about
a woman who made a home for her small family out of shipping containers.
At the time I was so impressed by her simple, outdoorsy, creation. Finding a
wealth of similar videos, also by Kirsten, I watched them all. I was especially
inspired by Austin Hay, a high school student who built his own tiny house

on a trailer in his parents' backyard, and then by Dirksen's documentary, "We the Tiny House People."

The prospect of living in a tiny house as a one-income family that also homeschools was one that we started to embrace. Ryan and I were fully inspired. I was doing a lot of research and I needed official confirmation that we were really going to move forward on this plan. I didn't want to fall completely in love with the idea, invest time into the planning, and then change those plans and lose hours spent on research for nothing. So we made the decision. Yes! We are going to build a tiny house, sell our big house, and be a one-income, homeschooling family. And so it happened. We were green lighted with a very official high-five! I was unleashed; I turned the dreaming into real research and planning.

I was soaking up all of the tiny house information I could find. I believe I was on the Tumbleweed website reading about their contest to win blueprints mere minutes after it had been posted. I have a love for contests and now had a newfound love for tiny houses. I put all mom duties on hold and went into contest mode. While I focused on obtaining blueprints, the kids pretty much ran wild; snacking on whatever they found, indulging in as much screen-time as they wanted, taking full advantage of my inattention. I called Ryan and told him about the contest, pre-apologizing for the eminent mayhem that he was going to come home to after work.

To win the tiny house blueprints I had to come up with the best bumper sticker slogan. I suddenly felt like a marketing genius. This was serious business, people! I subsequently came up with forty impeccable slogans any tiny houser would be happy to adhere to their tiny house trailer. The winning bumper sticker was, "If you can read this you're in my backyard." We were so psyched! "God just gave us a house!" Of course, they were just blueprints that I had won. With the plan to get the majority of our materials through the Craigslist free section, we were so glad to have already reduced costs by $800! Feeling affirmed we took this as a sign that this was exactly what God wanted for our family. We were ecstatic. The house was a disaster area but it was worth it.

Up until this point in our process we had kept our tiny house plans fairly quiet. We had really only shared our plans with our parents. Having never before heard of tiny houses they reacted with questions and doubt, waiting to see what actually would happen and assuming nothing really would. That's not completely unfounded, as we had no building experience, no tools, and really no time for an extra side project. Once we had the blueprints in our hands the dream started to morph into a reality. As we became educated, we shared more with our parents, and their doubt transformed into support, which Ryan and I were so very grateful for.

We really felt God's hand guiding the process. In January of 2014 I was scrolling through Kent Griswold's Tiny House Blog when I came across the very first casting call for Tiny House Nation. This opportunity was huge. Another contest that I could pour creative energy into. The casting process was an exciting rollercoaster!

The reality show route really jived with Ryan and me. With the responsibility of family, building on our own would have been a great challenge. Expert help and guidance brought relief. Our reason for turning tiny was to achieve goals and live out our life values; handing over design control to someone else was quite thrilling. What we would be given was a strong, beautiful, tiny house canvas that we would personalize as soon as we made it a part of our lives and were handed the keys. The dreamy part of our dream home wasn't inherent to its design. Although the tiny house is a major enabling element, we were working toward our dream life.

There were many months during which there was no communication and we didn't know whether or not we were being cast in the show. In July we were called and asked if we could increase our budget from $20,000 to $30,000. It was necessary in order to follow through with our episode. But it was that exact $10,000 that we already intended for another purpose. It was key in the sale of our big house.

We projected that when our big house sold, there would be $30,000 in equity. We were banking on it. That money was already allocated to two purposes: to pay off what would be the tiny house debt and to finance a new roof for the big house. The roof was in terrible shape. It was obviously very old, damaged, and frankly, pretty ugly. Getting a new roof was something that absolutely had to be done before we could sell the house. No rational person could justifiably slide that $10,000 into the tiny house budget knowing that there was no way the big house would sell without the roof repair. We would be stuck with a tiny house that was completely in debt and a big house that wouldn't sell.

We heard God say, "Say yes to every opportunity. Say yes to every opportunity." With no plan and nothing to fall back on we sent the full budget of $30,000 to the network, locking us into our episode, not knowing how we would get past this roofing situation in order to sell her big house. Three days later a little black car pulled up, a man stepped out, approached our front door and actually asked us if he could take a look at our roof.

Really? This was quite possibly the most bizarre thing that could have ever happened.

This guy said the he thought he could find wind damage on our roof and get us a new roof covered by our insurance. Anyone looking at the roof could see that that damage was from sun and time; a lot of sun and time. He wanted to see if he could make it work anyway. Of course we gave him the go-ahead to give it a shot. He called the meeting with the claims adjuster and together they climbed our roof. Ryan and I stood inside the house by an open window, straining to hear, praying fiercely, amazed at the conversation we were hearing. Affirmative. The claims adjuster approved a few roof!

We were floored.

God knew the budget. God knew the equity. God sent the roof guy. God had all the resources. We trusted Him and He provided! These scenarios continued to occur as we followed through our tiny house journey. We would see a closed door and God would open it. We would see a wall and God would cut a door out of it! Through our experience with the bizarre roof miracle, we learned that God wants us to say "Yes!" to every opportunity. Our family continues to say yes to every opportunity! It is now how we conduct ourselves. The tiny house itself feels like a giant opportunity. It goes without say that the majority of self-described tiny houses are on wheels. Isn't that completely awesome? When your home is on wheels, you can take on new opportunities, go on adventures, and literally follow God's plan for your life!

There is so much to love about our tiny house. We love that it's a Tumbleweed. We love that Zack Giffin and his crew were so dedicated to our build and to our family. We love that my uncle Pat Mattson, who was our contractor, and our family cared so much and played such critical roles in its design and craftsmanship. We love that are our aunts and cousins wrote Bible verses in the frame of the house. We loved our first parking spot at our Aunt Julie and Uncle Ron's place. We love the people we've met and the connections made through living in it.

Falling in love with our home helped us embrace the transition. So much good was happening and we celebrated every milestone. We had a lot to learn and together, we took on each new challenge with adventurous spirits. We made so many good memories with our children!

One of my favorite memories is towing the tiny house for the first time. We chose the time that we thought the 100 miles of highway would have the least amount of traffic. We scheduled our maiden voyage for 3 a.m. on a Sunday morning after bars closed and before Sunday church goers hit the road. The fridge was secured, the hanging light was secured, and things that had been on shelves were in boxes and put on the floor. The license plate was on and the trailer was hitched. Everything was in place. The anticipation had built up so much. It was like Christmas Eve to our kids. If they had missed out they would have been heartbroken. They went to bed early, excited to get up in the middle of the night to drive their tiny house to it's new home.

At 2 a.m. we readied ourselves, packed our snacks, and blankets and pillows were tossed to the backseat of the car with the kids. Ryan had a headset plugged into his cell phone so he could stay focused on driving the F250. As we pulled out, the kids and I cheered for Daddy from the open car windows.

We watched the brake lights and the blinkers. Everything was awesome. I called ahead to let Jack, Ryan's Dad, know that we were on track to meet at the next town. With one car ahead of the tiny house and one car behind, we felt that we had buffered our precious cargo the best we could.

We had a great drive. It was uneventful, except for hearing Ryan say, "Come on, baby" to the truck from the phone since we had both forgotten to hang up on our last phone call. The kids fell asleep right as we pulled into our new campground. It took about twenty minutes to navigate backing the tiny house into place. The sun was coming up, the kids roused awake, and we wrapped up in blankets on the playground to watch right as Ryan and Jack were getting the tiny house safely in its new parking spot. We celebrated with a sleepy breakfast and coffee at our favorite organic restaurant, caffeinating ourselves for a full day of skirting with my Dad and making curtains with my Mom.

Since that first trip on the road, we have fully experienced two campgrounds, two moves, and now our own lakeshore property.

SIDENOTE: whether or not a campground is your final destination; it is great to fall back on! And tiny housers need a backup. We enjoyed campground life at two very different campgrounds for six months each.

Full-time RV'ers are awesome. We've met so many kind, generous, hard working, goal-driven, full-time RV'ers! There are many shared values within a campground community (namely, minimal space and possessions, mobility, and a focus on life experiences), they work hard together (leveling, skirting, wintering, swapping child care, and watching out for each other), and enjoy the outdoors together (walks, campfires, swimming, and sunsets). We found great communities of people in our temporary neighborhoods and made lasting friendships. Tiny housers can learn a lot from living in a neighborhood of full-time RV'ers. Living on a campground, living with other people also living on a campground (that's folk song material), is truly a great experience.

Our first campground was where we transitioned into our tiny space. It was there that we moved all of our possessions in and completely left the big house behind. We had to follow the learning curve for water hookup, skirting, the composting toilet, and the wood stove, on top of getting accustomed to the small space. The playground right outside our front door was filled with new friends and made the transition easier.

The kids had no idea there was even a challenge to face! They were busy making friends, hosting parties in their loft, dropping parachutes and paper airplanes from the catwalk, riding bike, having campfires, helping Daddy build fires in the Kimberly Stove, and soaking in the view of the stars from their pillows.

Sully and Story rocked the transition into the tiny house. They were volunteering to do chores! They really took ownership of their new home. Taking out the garbage, stocking the wood pile, and churning the toilet was like playing house. Learning new tasks for our off-grid lifestyle was adventurous for Ryan and me, too. Being at the campground meant that we weren't completely off-grid so it wasn't an overwhelming beginning. Since then, we've come closer to reaching our off-grid goals. We are glad to have had the opportunity to pace ourselves.

Living in the tiny house has brought our kids much closer to nature as well. They go fishing, digging for worms, swimming, walking, finding paths in the woods, and collecting wood for campfires. They feed the hummingbirds, host neighborhood kid picnics, catch frogs, build kites, collect rocks, and climb trees! They once found a baby snapping turtle, created a large outdoor aquarium and kept him fed and cared for him for two weeks before releasing him. Then we found a huge Black and Yellow Garden Orb spider in our potted garden and we grew to love it! We caught wasps in cups, aimed their release at its beautiful web and watched as it would catch and spin up its dinner and eat it!

This is exactly what we had hoped for. Sully and Story seek their own adventures, get dirty, and learn a lot in the process. During the spring, summer, and fall the tiny house door is always open because everyone is in and out all day long. Every evening is family time. We aim dinnertime at sunset. We have a campfire that the kids built and light with supervision. We discuss our day, problem-solve some things with the kids, and sometimes play "Would You Rather?" Then it's flashlights until baths, reading, and bedtime.

Our Minnesota winters have a different vibe. We get out more. We sign up for activities like swimming lessons at the YMCA, go to the library once or twice a week, visit family often, and go to plays and museums. At home the kids still play outside but this winter the kids love to hang out in the loft, drawing and listening to audio books. Grandma comes for overnights; she brings a bag of books and the kids are eager to tell her everything they've been learning. On cold days at home we enjoy watching documentaries. We write in our journals daily, play piano, read together, drink tea, draw, bird watch, and play.

After one year of campground life we started searching for our own property. Of course there are a number of hurdles to jump for tiny housers in terms of putting a THOW on your own land but we just prayed for guidance as we looked at all our options. During one of my searches I came across a piece of lakeshore property that had two RVs on it and no house! We checked it out and it was perfect for us. We removed the RV that sat at the full-length porch overlooking the lake and put our tiny house into the space instead. We figured that if they could have an RV there, we could put our tiny house there!

We later learned that the property itself is too small to build on so they allow two recreation vehicles! Its not too small for us! There is a beautiful deck overlooking the lake, a dock, two campfire areas, hookup to electric, well water, great little garden plots, huge trees, cute steps everywhere (the whole property is on a hill), parking area at the top. And as an added bonus, the property has a '74 Silver Streak trailer with a deck! We plan to renovate this vintage gem and put it into service as a guesthouse and, of course, space to grow.

We feel like we found a true treasure trove!

Our new dreamscape is ideal. I'm so excited to watch the kids experience everything they can on the water. Ryan and I have a front row seat to watch our family grow gardens, build playhouses, and get to know the critters that surround us. We feel incredibly blessed to have an affordable home that literally feels like a vacation.

Our house is 267 sq. ft., has two lofts connected by a catwalk and one stairway to go up, a homey little porch with beautiful front door, a huge farmhouse sink, a Kimberly stove, composting toilet, wine barrel bathtub, and bookshelves galore. All of the wood in our house was left raw causing our home to smell rustic and earthy. We love that. The deck that runs the whole length of the tiny house is exactly what I had hoped for from the beginning of our tiny house planning stages. I've always enjoyed changing the arrangement of the furniture in the rooms in our homes. Surprisingly, I've been able to continue that in the tiny house. I change the layout of the downstairs often; I enjoy the fresh change it brings.

The place I spend the most time in the tiny house is at the kitchen sink. I love our kitchen sink. It's like my Mom Station. I'm centered in the house and watch over everything while doing dishes, making a meal, or enjoying my coffee. The view from the kitchen window is amazing. We get to watch the sunset over the lake! Sully's favorite place in the house is in his room. He's a thinker and he likes to read, build things, and organize his space. Story's favorite place in the house is at the steps leading up the loft. The kids treat it like a desk space. They sit on one step with their legs dangling down, and they use the next step up as a tabletop surface. They craft art projects and eat meals there. It's like our unintentional dining room table. Story hangs out there a lot. I think she likes that central space near me. She is a dreamer. She paints and dreams up stories with imaginary friends. Ryan's favorite place is the loft. Usually, he's there just to crash after work. And when he does he draws a crowd. The kids pile on top of him and then the dog has a fit and gets after them for being too rowdy; she really just wants to hog all of his attention. At night we all just love the loft. It's cozy, filled with books and pillows, and we all just want to gaze out at the water, even the dog. When the lake isn't frozen we get to fall asleep listening to the water lap at the shore and I feel like we live on the ocean!

We asked God for a house and He provided in a radical, huge way. This blessing is unconventional. We are grateful and joyfully content. Our home is a reflection of our values. It is a testament to the power of our friends and family. It is a culmination of goals made and dreams reached.

God, bless this tiny house.

Love is Large in a Tiny House

Our Journey to Tiny Living

Wesley Birch

After realizing that the typical American dream comes with house payments, other forms of debt, and many hours at a job, Wesley Birch decided to follow his own version of the American dream, which involves no debt, and many hours at home with his family. His family consists of his lovely wife, Breanne, and their beautiful daughter, Samantha; making the plunge into tiny living has allowed them to live with minimal stress, no debt, and many hours of family time.

Love grows best in a small house.
—Author unknown

I have been asked what led me to turn tiny. Well, the answer is quite simple: the American dream. Yes, my view of the American dream is a little bit abnormal, but I found that most "normal" American dreams had one big thing in common, and that one thing is debt. With the big house, big yard, and big car also comes a big mortgage, a big car payment, and more time at work. When I spend more time at work, it means I spend less time with my family, and I can't fathom following a dream that leads to less time with my family. My wife and I realized this one-year into our marriage and decided to change our idea of the American dream. We found that the more money a person makes, the more money a person spends, so we decided to figure out how to decrease our expenses instead of increasing our income. Instead of the "normal" American dream of making everything bigger we decided to make everything smaller, so that our time with each other was plentiful.

We stumbled upon the tiny house movement by searching the Internet for affordable living ideas. We fell in love with the idea quickly and decided it was something we were going to pursue. Once we got started planning our build, there was no looking back.

The first challenge we had to overcome was figure to out how to make our tiny American dream a financial reality. This was the tricky part, due to us having a very small amount of income. We did some research on how much it cost to build a tiny house: we were quite stunned when we found that the average price to build a tiny house was about $25,000. My wife and I both worked minimum wage jobs. Minimum wage in the Portland, Oregon area at that time was $9.15/hour. At the time, we had a $600/month rent bill, a $90/month phone bill, a $160/month utility bill, and a car insurance bill of $100/month. On top of all the monthly expenses, we also spent a lot of money on restaurants, gas, entertainment, and groceries. Needless to say, we didn't have extra money left over to build a tiny house. The first thing we did was to find a way to cut down as many expenses as possible. The restaurant bills were pretty easy to cut down, so they went first. The next thing I did was to trade my iPhone in for a basic phone to cut our bill down from $90/month down to $60/month. We were able to cut our car insurance payment down by selling our second car, which also gave us extra cash, so the only payments left to downsize were rent and utilities. We decided the best way to cut out rent was to build a tinier tiny house, for very cheap, to live in while building our dream tiny house. The plan worked out great. I bought a used travel trailer frame for cheap and got to work. This first tiny house took me two months to build, and was nothing fancy. It was twenty-four feet long, eight feet wide, and seven feet tall inside. It had a bucket with peat moss for a toilet, one small sink with no hot water, a mini fridge, a single burner electric cook top, and our bed. Even though our first house was nothing fancy, it provided a cozy, dry, rent-free place to live while we went to work on our more permanent tiny house. Our rent went from $600/month down to $0/month, and our utility bill went from $160/month, down to $40/month. The best part is that it only cost me three thousand dollars to build. For many people, that is less than three months of rent.

With all of our monthly expenses cut down, and one tiny house build under my belt, it was time to get to work on our dream tiny house and tackle our second challenge: the challenge of planning, which proved to be much harder than expected. When I Googled the phrase "tiny house designs," thousands of design plans and options popped up. My first thought was, "how could so many different things be done with only 200 square feet?" My wife and I had already decided to go with a 24' trailer, and since we wanted it road legal with no special permitting, we decided to make it 8'6" wide, and no greater than 13'6" tall. After talking to a good contractor friend of mine, he convinced me to use a flat roof style with a membrane covering and sloped roofing insulation to allow for water runoff. Even though I knew the flat roof would not be quite as aesthetically pleasing, I loved the idea of maximizing the headroom in the loft. The shape and size had been figured out, leaving us with a little over 2,000 cubic feet of space to make home.

Planning out the interior of our tiny house was the most overwhelming part of the entire building process. We spent countless hours looking through website after website, picture after picture, and design plan after design plan. I sketched out multiple interior drawings, which were quickly crumpled and thrown in the trash. We even made a full size scale of the inside of a tiny house using masking tape on the floor of the house we were renting prior to our first tiny house. I would make a plan in my head, fall in love with the plan, find some fault with the plan, and then start over at the beginning. I went through many plans that I thought were "the one" just to realize that they were not. We asked ourselves question after question. Should the bathroom and kitchen be on the same side of the house? Should we have stairs? Should we have two lofts? Should we have the door on the side or the rear of the house?

While we didn't know the answers to all of these questions, there were a few things that were on our must-haves list:

The kitchen and bathroom must be on opposite sides to separate cooking from... let's say the aftermath of cooking

- We needed stairs for the main loft
- We needed a large kitchen (we love to cook)
- We needed a small bathtub (for bathing a baby and a dog)
- My wife made it clear she needed a dishwasher (I'm very glad she convinced me to put one in)
- We needed lots of storage
- We needed a sitting area downstairs
- We needed large windows to keep us from getting claustrophobic.

I was finally feeling a bit more prepared to start designing our house in Google Sketch-up. Fortunately for me, I was able to find someone who had already done most of the planning and brainwork for me. It was as if they had looked at my list of must-haves, and designed a house around almost everything that I needed and wanted.

Gabriella and Andrew Morrison designed a tiny house that they call hOMe. After looking at the design of their tiny house, my wife and I fell in love with it. We decided that this was the house that we were going to build. Even though the Morrison's house was almost exactly what we were wanting, there were a few small changes that had to be made to make it perfect for us.

The original hOMe design was a 28' tiny house and since we still wanted to build a 24' house, we had to figure out how to modify the plans to cut out 4 feet of length. We could either cut out length in the bathroom, kitchen, living area/entry way, or a combination of those. We decided that having a full size kitchen was the most important aspect of our future tiny house, so we left the kitchen the same size.

We decided to shorten the bathroom and living area. It was still very important for us to have a full-size bathroom as well; so even though it was a bit smaller than I had originally hoped, I was still able to customize it to fit our small bathtub/shower combo, a composting toilet, a pocket door for privacy, and a decent sized bathroom sink and vanity. When planning the size of the bathroom, I made sure that the loft above would be large enough to

accommodate a twin size mattress comfortably. The only down side to shrinking our tiny house from a 28' plan to a 24' plan was the stairway.

In order to fit the stairs, we had to design them fairly steep, much steeper than a typical stairway. The stairs ended up being a bit harder to get up and down than we would have hoped, but it is still much easier and more convenient, to us, than using a ladder. So after using some creativity and Google Sketchup, we were able to customize the Morrison's design and make a tiny house design that we knew would be perfect for us.

With our first and second challenges out of the way, the only challenge left was to build our dream home. Before building our first basic tiny house, the only building construction experience I had was a remodeling job that I had helped a friend with. Even though I had very limited house building knowledge, I had grown up around tools and felt very comfortable using them thanks to my dad. Before building either one of our tiny houses, I decided it would be a good thing to expand my knowledge on building construction. I went to the library and checked out multiple books, and I did extensive research online. After learning a little bit more, I decided to jump in and begin building.

The first tiny house was quite simple to build. I was fortunate enough to have access to our landlord's airplane hangar and was able to build it undercover. This was a huge blessing since I had decided to build it during the winter months. The hangar was also equipped with electrical outlets and a bathroom, which made it the perfect place to build. I used the knowledge that I had gained from my extensive research and reading and also learned a lot as I went. I found YouTube to be an extremely helpful source. I would constantly come across something that I didn't know how to do. For instance, I didn't know how to flash a window. When something like this came up, I simply typed it into YouTube and watched video after video until I knew how to do it.

After a contractor friend of mine came over, checked my work, and told me I was doing everything right, I knew this method of learning was working. Another great tool that I used to help me learn how to build was a how-to DVD set purchased from the Morrisons that took me step-by-step through the process of building a tiny house. I am a visual learner, so this

DVD set and the YouTube videos that I watched were the main reason that I was able to build our two tiny homes.

The second tiny house was a bit more complicated to build. It was overwhelming to think of all the steps that I had to take to build our dream home, so I decided to break it down into very basic steps, and then tackle those very basic steps one at a time.

- Step 1 was the trailer.
- Step 2 was the framing and window installation.
- Step 3 was the siding and roof.
- Step 4 was the interior wall framing, staircase, and loft framing.
- Step 5 was the electrical.
- Step 6 was the plumbing.
- Step 7 was the flooring, siding, and ceiling paneling.
- Step 8 was the finished plumbing.
- Step 9 was the appliance installation and composting toilet installation.
- And step 10 was to turn the completed tiny house into a tiny home with our furnishings.

After breaking the building process into broad tasks, I was able to start working on each step without feeling overwhelmed with the whole journey ahead. To make it even easier on myself, I was able to recruit some help during the build: my brother-in-law helped with the framing, which made it possible to have the whole house framed up in two days; and my grandpa, an electrician for over 60 years, helped with the electrical work. I also had a lot of help from my pregnant wife Breanne during the build, though her help was necessarily limited.

Our dream home took about 5 months to build, the total cost was under $10,000 dollars, and we were able to include everything that we had originally planned with our must-have list. The bathroom has a luxurious composting toilet, a bathtub/shower combo, and a good-sized sink and vanity.

The living area has a couch/spare bed with lots of storage underneath, an electric fireplace, a washer, and stairs with plenty of storage underneath. The kitchen is our favorite feature in the house: it has a full propane oven with a four burner cook top, a full-sized dishwasher, a double basin sink, two cupboards, a large pantry with more than enough food storage, two storage drawers, plenty more storage in the cabinet under the sink, and a mid-sized refrigerator. The loft has enough room for a king-sized mattress, enough storage for both of our clothes, and enough height to sit straight up in bed and still have plenty of headroom.

Some other features that we enjoy are recessed speakers mounted in the ceiling, LED recessed lighting with dimmer switches in the loft, a ceiling fan, and a porch with enough room for my wife and I to sit, relax, and drink a beer together.

Living in our home has been one of the greatest experiences of my life. It allows for lots of family time, and really brought my wife, my daughter, and me together. In a small space, there is no room for anger, hatred, or jealousy. When we were angry with each other, we would have to work it out right away, instead of locking ourselves in our room, or ignoring each other. The only possible way for us to live in a tight living condition was to radiate love towards one another and work out our problems and differences right away. With enough love flowing from one person to another in a tiny house, the walls seem to expand, and it no longer feels like a small space, it feels like a mansion. And that is why love is large in a tiny house.

Our Tiny 401(k)

Sheila McChesney

Sheila McChesney and Jimmy Staton are building a rural homestead in the Eastern Panhandle of West Virginia. Their goals are to develop a self-sustaining life style that is both environmentally friendly and financially secure. Sheila, an educational interpreter with the public school system, Jimmy, a retired veteran and "jack-of-all-trades," and Zedediah, Sheila's 16-year-old son, have designed their homestead to incorporate a grid free, self-sustaining tiny home, permaculture practices, and small-scale farm. Follow their journey at Tiny Mountain Home.

You cannot achieve a new goal by applying the same level of thinking that got you where you are today.
—Albert Einstein

Life has a way of doing random reality checks at the most inconvenient times. It was during one of these reality checks that our tiny house became both a necessity to survival and a life's passion. The 2008 financial crash created the perfect storm here in West Virginia; employment insecurity and the loss of all savings through no fault of our own sent waves of fear through our community and our family. Playing by the rules and following the guidelines of how to secure a comfortable future did not work and it was at that point, Jimmy and I, decided to take our security into our own hands. Our vision was and still is to take a small farm in rural West Virginia and create a self-sustainable homestead to provide for our needs as we age without the constant stress and anxiety debt and instability can bring. Our tiny home is a major part of that plan, built to be independent through off-grid solar power and water catchment systems and definitely debt-free.

I have always had a fascination with small well-designed spaces and wanted to have a very small cabin in the middle of nowhere at some point in my life. Before we met and became the best of friends, Jimmy had an experience that was born out of an unfortunate break-up, and he relocated to a travel trailer to sort out a new direction in his life and begin again. Through his experience of what works and what does not in a small space, and my deep desire to live in a tiny space in the middle of nowhere- we put our paths together to create a dynamic partnership. I often think about the long conversations and endless questioning about what works well and what is just for vacationing in a camper situation. We would often joke and laugh about the learn-as-you-go portion of life and in these conversations. We would list the priorities and the luxuries of it all.

Having our home off-grid was a priority, not only for the cost savings, but also using alternative energy sources, as they were very important to our way of life. Walking our talk is a major theme and has kept our plan in check. Each step of the process has been a cash deal; if we wanted it, we planned and saved for it. Becoming more purposeful in our lives has brought with it a new perspective when it comes to our needs and wants in daily life. We have repurposed many things to work for us just because we already owned it here at the farm, and in many ways, it has always turned out to be an even better solution. An excellent example of this is an old ugly stove unit we tore out of the original camper, and when I say ugly, I mean hideously ugly with fake wood grain accents and rusted out chrome parts with plenty of mouse nesting material!

Jimmy took it apart and cleaned it with steel wool and lots of elbow grease, taking each part off and scrubbing it, he then bought automotive engine enamel paint in my favorite color, fire engine red, and gave it a few healthy coats and then clear coated the whole project and installed it in our home. It is a project I am very proud of, as it has character and it took a lot of time and commitment to make an old worn out stove into a beautiful working appliance, and the kicker is that it did not cost us anything except for 3 cans of paint. It is the experience of creating something out of nothing and having something for which you are very proud to display in your home.

We found an antique cast-iron sink and washboard buried in an old pigsty area we were cleaning out for chickens. At first we were going to take the heavy piece to the scrapyard but as we looked at it, the sink was such a unique piece that we took two days cleaning it up and the enamel was in great shape, installed it into the house, and this found treasure gives our homestead a real old-time farm feeling.

From the beginning, Jimmy and I both had a commitment to a simpler way of life that was not centered around consumerism and impressing the mainstream. We both had a deep sense of tradition and desire to return to old ways. We both had very basic skills, Jimmy is an all-around Jack-of-all-Trades, and I have always been very detailed and project-oriented with a passion for research and a major science geek. Zedediah, my 16-year-old son is homeschooled with an obsession for projects, big and small, with a can-do attitude. This new adventure provided an outstanding opportunity for him to use and learn skills that will serve him well in his life and hopefully spark a passion for a future career path.

Our first go round consisted of an old camper that we tore down to the bare bones of the chassis and measured 8' X 20', we recycled and saved all parts and pieces that could be later used in our tiny home. We drew countless plans on graph paper and built small models refining each along the way.

We prepped and started welding supports on the chassis getting ready for our build and then we came upon an old gooseneck tri-axle hay trailer that a local farmer was selling at an awesome price and that was it. We paid for the trailer and hauled her home and tore off all the old boards and reinforced the frame extending the width to 10'. Our new home would measure 10' X 23' with a 7' extension above the gooseneck hitch. The requirements were two sleeping areas, an ample kitchen, an area to lounge and study, and a bathroom. We wrote tons of lists of our basic needs and the things we wanted in a home; large windows with plenty of light were a requirement for both aesthetics and passive solar heating. We had chosen an area of land in the middle of a field where our home would be parked with a southern exposure to take full advantage of the solar panels and provide a stunning view of our mountains. We searched yard sales, thrift stores, craigslist, local Habitat for Humanity stores and many barter deals for the components we could use for the house. In many ways I think this was the most fun because with each component took on a whole new purpose in our home.

Old wooden wine boxes became kitchen shelving and drawers in the bathroom. They provide an interesting piece to mundane areas and much needed storage space. The lumber however, was bought new, and we commenced building May 2014.

I can't say we had a complete set of plans as we built, but more of a general idea of what we wanted to end up with. A life lesson that we have taken from the experience is, what looks good on paper does not always work in the real day-to-day living. We have tinkered with the one side of our kitchen multiple times to make it just perfect for how I cook and the flow of activity. What was once a recycled Hoosier cabinet and small cupboard has now transformed into a full counter with rolling cart storage underneath. This expands the space when needed and then tucks away when not in use. The cabinet sections have a ton of storage for kitchen and food supplies. Our life really does revolve around food prep, cooking, and spending time with friends. My grandmother always said, "The kitchen is for friends and those you love and a living room is for guests." Therefore, our living room space is rather small and more geared to quiet study and watching movies.

Moving into the house during construction was both beneficial and a bit frustrating. We laughed a lot and each step brought a pride I did not even know we were capable of. At first many people laughed at us and just rolled their eyes in that way that says, "You really are nuts." But as the project progressed, the trailer was placed and leveled, walls started going up, and the lay-

out of the space started taking shape. We saw a change in the way people reacted when they heard of our plan. A new, inquisitive look came to their eyes and requests for tours became a new reality. It was at this point, many of those people began realizing we were not so crazy after all and were quite impressed with the layout and what three people with basic skills and a vision could accomplish. One of the greatest benefits that came with the build was my son grew in confidence, self-esteem and in muscle tone. In his own words, he became one of the cool kids!

On a trip to Washington DC to attend a Boneyard Studios Open-house, Zedediah was so proud to tell everyone of our build. We moved into the house, still under construction, Labor Day of 2014 and have never regretted for one moment our decision to be tiny.

Our journey has taken us many places both virtually and physically, we have met some wonderful people within the tiny house movement and have built bonds that are greatly cherished. Our contacts have taken us all over the world virtually and we have had the pleasure of learning from others and also helping others to prepare their journey. When we were asked to participate in this book, the request was for us to explain what makes our Tiny House journey unique; I believe our most unique feature is that we want to homestead and build our lives around our home, land, and community; we have also used this opportunity as a learning and teaching opportunity for my son and our community. It has become a living, breathing classroom for us all, not only an outstanding opportunity for my son but a wonderful chance to learn and hone new and better skills for me and Jimmy. We have opened our home to anyone who is curious about our lifestyle. This is not only a home to live in, but a lifestyle that shifts values and priorities, and we have embraced those and have become much happier and meaningful in our lives and our pursuits.

Financial security is a great feature, but I believe the freedom we have found in living a downsized, simpler life has been the biggest perk. Starting all over at our age is a scary prospect, no matter who you might be, and being faced with a new beginning is also very exhilarating and liberating; an overwhelming feeling of boom-or-bust.

Having the knowledge today that if our world collapses we will be okay and the sun will come up in the morning. We have a passion to learn more and better ways of developing the farm in a sustainable way. It has freed up time, money to pursue developing our homestead, and strengthening our bonds with people we love. We now seek new opportunities to share our home with family and friends.

On one such occasion, we planned a full sit-down Thanksgiving dinner for 11 people, although my older children doubted the success, it went beautifully. We set up a banquet table down the center of the house and had plenty of space for everyone to sit down comfortably to enjoy a traditional holiday. It was so successful that we did another the following year, and now, we have the set up down to a science. We as a family have completely enjoyed the challenges our lifestyle has thrown at us. We take on each one with a sense of humor and a sense of gratitude for it. Something we are truly grateful for is the short amount of time it takes to clean and tidy up our home, about 20 minutes for a quick clean up and about an hour for a floor to ceiling cleaning; you can't beat that with a stick! We have a home for everything and that has taken a lot of the stress out of the day-to-day activities.

We still have our hobbies and have learned how to enjoy them and then clean up quickly and easily. I love sewing and have had many opportunities to sew for our local High School theater group and have had no problem incorporating it into our home. Many of our hobbies and activities are shared and living in such a small space has also provided plenty of opportunity to share these passions. If we need personal or alone time we all have our own areas and also quite a bit of acreage to be alone. Respect for one another is the key to tiny house family living.

A few of the unique features we have here is that our grey-water system is integrated into a hugelkultur, a no-dig raised bed with a difference. They hold moisture, build fertility, maximize surface volume and are great spaces for growing fruit, vegetables and herbs, ours is designed to grow perennial flowers in front of our home. The concept we have as a homestead is to create a permaculture environment, or as some call it, "an edible self-sustaining landscape." Being off-grid and energy independent not only saves money in the long run but also makes for an impromptu get-together when the local power goes out and everyone calls and asks, "Is your power out?" for us the answer is always, "No" and followed by an invite to come over and ride out the storm. It is very empowering to know that when the outside world is out of sync, our world continues to function properly.

Our system here has a deep-cycle battery bank and 12v pump system for our water. Propane provides our hot water and cooking, this is the only outside bought feature, but I can live with it!

We heat our home with an outdoor wood furnace that is installed underneath the gooseneck area and keeps that area warm throughout the winter preventing our water from freezing and is piped into the house through a single vent in the floor. We have never been cold here even though the temperatures have been sub-freezing. We also have plans in the near future to pipe the heat into a greenhouse so that we will be able to grow vegetables throughout the winter and experiment a little with year-round food production. Throughout the experience we have become far more aware of our impact on the environment around us and have developed better habits and practices along with a deeper understanding of the power we use daily and what it takes to generate it.

We are still at the very beginning of our life's adventure and it has been a wild ride so far! We have had so much positive support from our community and from those that have come to know us. We are at about 90% complete in the build of the house and hope to complete a deck during the summer of 2016. We are also beginning a new build, a shepherd's hut design, for my elderly mother so that she can have her own home close enough so that we can care for her as she ages, also providing her with her own space to enjoy that is also debt-free and close to those who love her dearly. Her home will make use of that original chassis and measure 10' X 20' and be designed to be on a single level to accommodate her physical limitations. The awesome part of this is that we can design the home to be completely custom to her needs, desires, and personality. Our own success has motivated us to promote our tiny lifestyle. Anyone that gets within earshot will hear about how great I believe our life is. There are so many questions that come up when others hear about our life style that I have to giggle because to my family and me this is the norm.

One of my favorites is, "What do you do in the house?" My response is always, "Everything you do in yours." I hope I have been able to give you a brief glimpse into our life and a sense of why we do what we do. The decision to go tiny has been one of the best decisions I have ever made and my only regret is that I did not do this sooner in my life. Hopefully my children or those young people around us will embrace the value of the tiny lifestyle.

Ch-Ch-Changes

*An omnivorous ranching consumer turns vegan,
minimalist and "tiny"*

Nina Zamudio

From a rancher in a pricey two-story farmhouse to a vegan minimalist in a 77 sq. ft. shack, California native Nina Zamudio let go of her possessions and searched the Internet for "small houses" and found a large supportive community in the city known for BIG. Nina is near completion on her own beautiful 160 sq. ft. tiny house, you can follow her community build fun at baninabegins.blogspot.com.

How is it possible to go from being a rancher in a 2-story farmhouse on 20 acres in my native state of California to a vegan in Texas building a tiny house? All kinds of degrees of love (good and bad) have made twists and turns in my journey: Love gone sour, a mother's love, false love, new love and the enduring love from great friendships. In that farmhouse I was an unhappy and disillusioned housewife that stayed in a dysfunctional marriage for far too long. I was at the height of my consumerism; I filled that huge house with "décor" and fancy things and we were the Jones' that neighbors wanted to keep up with. As I spent hours bucking hay and fixing fences I would talk to the dog, sheep, chickens or whatever animal was nearby...asking them what they thought was in store for me because I knew that that was not it. Not one of those dang animals warned me what I was in for.

After the divorce (big relief) I temporarily moved in with my mom. She asked me to stay and since I loved being with her, I stayed.

She had me late in life and was now in her 80's. She was still pretty spunky and independent and my moving into the house meant that I moved back into my old bedroom (which she'd never really changed) so I had the master bedroom and the small 3rd bedroom which I used as a gym and stored extra stuff. The rest of the house was already full.

I wouldn't characterize her as a hoarder but she liked her stuff and she had a lot of it. It was all very, very small. She liked keeping things from her life and treasured them just as much as she did the items she got at a yard sale last week. I thought I was helping her by buying organization tools and roll-away carts with drawers and cute bins and boxes. I was not. She would fill those places up and then have room for more stuff. Everyone has favorite things and my mom was no exception.

Among her top favorites (and in no particular order) were humming-birds, the American flag, JFK, Jesus, Princess Diana (and her sons), the American eagle and the color green. She was 88 when she passed away and when my friend Dawn offered to take vacation to attend the funeral, I asked her instead to come a month later, after all of the friends and relatives had gone back to their lives, when I would be left to my own emotionally wrought devices.

Dawn came from Ohio and we tackled the house. Jesus fit in 3 boxes and the church ladies picked him up. The hummingbirds fit into 2 boxes and went to the special display case at the local animal shelter thrift store that we had supported. We collected hundreds of vases from the entire house and they went to a program that puts flowers at the bedside of gravely ill children. You get the idea. It was ten solid days that we took to get the majority of the stuff categorized, packed up and taken to whatever organization or charity could use it the best. I had boxes of items labeled for family members and for her friends. Dawn was a champ and I will be forever grateful for that feat of friendship. And when Dawn was gone, it was the hard stuff, and I. I was left with the personal stuff.

We had put aside boxes of papers and things that I knew I would have to carefully go through. It was months before I had an evening without long emotional hours of sorting through my mom's life. I was eating simply, had been, following the course of ridding excess. Even from my diet I trimmed things away by adopting more plant-based foods. I was feeling healthier in that regard.

That's when I started noticing the empty space in the house. It wasn't depressing. It was a relief! I started to see space on the wall, on the floors, under beds, and in cupboards. I didn't feel the oppression of being surrounded by stuff that needed sorting. My mom's few remaining belongings were the crux of her life and I would keep and cherish them.

And then the other part of it hit me: the stuff that was left was my stuff. What was this stuff? I started questioning the items left in the house. Why did I own it? What did it mean to me? Did it make me happy on any level? Where did I get it? Do I use it? Do I care if it's gone? Can someone else use it? Does someone else need it and I just have it shoved in a drawer? Am I disrespecting this item? I had to be realistic here. I do not have any children and I don't know who would be tasked to deal with my stuff if I should die.

I decided to continue the process that I had just gone through with my mother's things and did it with my own. It felt so good to be able to make the decisions of where my things were going! The kid across the street was about to graduate high school and wanted to go to cooking school. I filled up the kitchen table with all excess kitchen tools and had him come over and take his pick. He took 90% of it. The joy on his face was payment and I tear up when I think about it. His parents came over afterwards with their eyebrows in a worried wrangle. "Are you sure?" Oh yes, I was very sure. I felt great! I felt so much freedom from all that extra stuff that I kept it up and as the 1200 sq. ft. house started echoing and looking as if I was moving out I thought, "I should move! This house needs a family and a dog to play out in the backyard."

I started looking online for available homes that were smaller but found that they were either too big or they were small but very old and needed a lot of work on plumbing and electrical systems. I'm not afraid of a little DIY but I didn't find it appealing, especially at the ridiculous prices they were asking. I put in the search terms "downsize" and "small house" and up came Jay Shafer's name with the most adorable pictures of miniscule homes on trailers and his new company was having its first seminar and building workshop in just a couple of months just a few hours away from me. I signed up.

I should mention that I wasn't getting a whole lot of support from friends and family. There were a few but for the most part I would get the side-eye look of concern. And I get it. It seemed like an extreme turn to take. Veganism? Tiny houses? They thought I'd gone off the deep end because of my mom's death. Nope, I was finally thinking more clearly than ever.

The workshop brought together about 25 people in the same room that were all thinking along the same lines as I was about downsizing. We each had our different reasons for it but the goal was the same; we wanted to live with less stuff and enjoy life more. I met some key people at this workshop.

Daniel Bell taught the construction end and Jay Shafer the philosophy and design. Fellow attendees B.A. Norrgard and Judy Reid and I made fast friends and had a great time building the shell of a tiny home for Jay's nanny. While there we toured several tiny houses and at a point when most people were busy, I pulled Jay aside and asked if I could go spend some time in his tiny house to see how it felt to me. He said yes and said he wouldn't let anyone bother me.

I spent about 30 minutes sitting in different chairs, pretending to make cook in the kitchen, pretending to shower, pretending to work at the desk, sat up in the loft and took it all in. I knew it was for me. I was on the right path. I called my real estate agent and said "yes, let's put my house on the market."

During lunch one of those build days Daniel was talking about how he needed to find a person who was ready to go, ready to build, ready to … B.A.'s hand shot up immediately. He looked over at her, knowing that she was from Texas, and said he wanted to make it a class project where he taught shop in Los Angeles. B.A. just kept nodding. As it turned out, the project morphed into one for his volunteer work called MAGIC Camp (Mentor A Girl in Construction) and they scheduled to start the build.

I packed my tools in my car and drove down to join in the fun when B.A. invited me to be a mentor. This camp would last a week and usually hosted smaller projects of wiring lamps or perhaps going as big as building a picnic table.

Over the course of the week, area high school girls who didn't know each other pulled together as a team and framed B.A.'s house. It was MAGIC. They thought B.A. and I had been lifelong friends. Little did they know we had only spent a few days together. In all honesty, it kind of boggled our minds as to how many parallels our lives had experienced up to that point. B.A. had her tiny house started and returned to Texas where she thought she would look for anyone who might also be interested in tiny houses and started a meetup group.

Upon my return from MAGIC Camp, I drove up to my house to see the "For Sale" sign had been put up that morning. By that evening, my house was sold. I had 45 days to find a place to live and found a place on Craigslist. I know, I know. People are wary of Craigslist but I was desperate. Luckily I found a great homeowner that had a tiny space for rent in the backyard, separated by a deck, with its own gate and entrance. It was 7' wide by 11' long and had a small sink, shower stall and toilet. There was one big picture window, no closets, and a heat/ac unit. It seemed perfect.

I went to work to make it my own and built it up to suit me perfectly. I rented a storage unit for all of my tools and started a year of shopping for tiny house components from local ReStores, Craigslist, and wherever I could. I was riding my bike to work, hiking on the weekends and feeling good about my simple little life. I lived there for a year and during that year I found that I had kept many things that I found that I didn't need or use. I owned very little and was still getting rid of things! Of course, there were a few things that I either gave away or lost that I did end up having to replace but that wasn't much.

I joined a local Time Bank and started helping others with their relationship to their stuff. I'm not the person who will tell you that you should only have one spatula as I still have three. But I'll go through the uses of them with you and wonder how many you might need. We are not all the same so there's no cookie cutter approach that will work on every last thing you own but I do have some general guidelines that I follow.

Word started spreading and I started getting more and more Time Bank appointments around town. I found that I liked it and was good at it, especially if it's to help with an estate of a person who has passed away and how that emotionally affects a person as the process goes on.

So how did I get to Texas? I was happy in California in my little shack, lowering my carbon footprint and going to the university that I worked at for 26 years. Why would anything change?

I got a call from B.A. She was moving to California and would only be a few hours from me! I flew to Texas to help her pack up her life and her tiny house for it first major trip. I met many of her friends at going away parties in the four days that I was there. The day before we were leaving, her friend bailed on the road trip and we had to find a stand in. One of her tiny house friends stepped in and on the long, long trip to California, he and I fell in love.

In a whirlwind of a few weeks, he visited, we road-tripped again, he proposed, I found a great job in Texas and I moved. I thought B.A. would kill me for switching states with her! I called in friends and used those Time Bank hours to help get me moved just in time to spend Thanksgiving with my new soon-to-be-in-laws and subsequently had a great time.

I started meeting his friends and co-workers and we settled in to a rented house with space to build our tiny house in the back yard. I started my job a couple of weeks later and on my fourth day on the job, I returned to our rental to find that he'd moved out. The culprit? "Cold feet." I prefer to call it cowardice. He was overwhelmed just 19 days after I moved to Texas. I was stymied. I called B.A. in California. She was murderous-mad and asked what I needed. I needed to get out. I would find a place but I needed help to get me moved because I had no vehicle and no friends. She put out an email about my plight and the next day I was getting texts from her friends (names I recognized from meeting them at her going away parties) that offered "I can help you Friday or Sunday," "I can help you all day Saturday and I have a truck," and so on. I didn't have much to pack but I needed help with my refrigerator and loveseat/bed. I secured a place quickly and Mitch and Craig showed up to help me at night (in the pouring rain) to move to a 2nd floor bedroom in an old Victorian house about a mile away and closer to my job. It was miserable move but they were so nice to me and I treated them to a pub nearby afterwards where we commiserated about relationships and they made me feel better.

I had to make some decisions. Stay or go? Where would my tiny house happen? How? Do I stay here where I don't know anyone? Do I go back to my old job in California? I like this new job but all of 'his' family is here. Can I handle that? Christmas was fast approaching and I was feeling a bit weird. B.A.'s friends were texting me to go out and have a beer or have dinner. I would say yes because, what else was there? Her friend Sara was away for the holiday and generously offered her condo so I could get away from room-mates and think. I had so much love and support pouring in from friends around the country but I had very few connections in Texas. Co-workers and my new friends were shuttling me around and being so kind.

Craig's family lives in Canada and since he wasn't going home, we hung out for weeks. Friends that I'd met through my ex-fiancé invited me to a movie on Christmas day. I was walking around in a bit of a fog when I was suddenly jolted awake one evening. I was walking to the local pub and my ex turned the corner. He didn't recognize me because I had all my winter gear on and was in the shadows. A million scenarios raced through my mind as he walked in. I looked into the window and saw that he was meeting a woman. Yep. I had to quit the awesome job and get out of town. I told B.A. my decision and she invited me to live with her in Los Angeles. Maybe we could build my tiny house in the backyard where Daniel rented? I said good-bye to the friends and co-workers who had been keeping me such great com-pany and I had grown to appreciate so much in just 30 days. I loaded up a U-haul and drove to Los Angeles.

L.A. meant living with B.A. in her tiny house and hers really is a tiny house. It's built on a 16' trailer but she built between the wheel-wells and used about 2' for porch. It is TINY. I had a clothing bag, my comforter, my gym bag and the "McGyver" messenger bag that I always carried with me.

Those days of living with her in Los Angeles can only be described as a Shenanigan-Fest. We were acting like we were back in college and I always chuckle at the revelry of those days. Just what my heart needed.

During this time B.A. and I traveled to a few workshops and meetups where she would exhibit her house and speak.

One workshop was a Four Lights workshop in San Diego and Jay Shafer asked me to speak on minimalism. I think it's really important for anyone considering a tiny house to address their relationship to their stuff first because if they don't, they'll end up thinking tiny houses are the dumbest idea ever. I've had that chat with people and some have realized that they need more square footage to be happy. It's a good thing to know before you embark on turning tiny.

Minimalism isn't about deprivation; it's about celebration of the few items you have to maximize the rest of your life. As a first foray into thinking about your stuff, forget stressing about what you'd get rid of but focus on the things you would absolutely want and need to keep. Imagine being surrounded by those things that have great stories in them, are functional for you and make you smile; the things you would absolutely miss. That's where you start to build the foundation of how you want your life to be; carefully curated and cherished. Build outward from the important things and pay attention to the wants and needs and reactions that you're having as you go.

Creative thinking is often necessary to incorporate interests that have accessories. You probably already have an idea as to what you would want to keep and make important in your life if you had to downsize, it's important to focus of those things and make allowances. For me? I love to cook and vegan food is a bit of an obsession.

My tiny house is all about the kitchen. Do you have sports gear or shoes or a collection or two? They don't necessarily have to go. But incorporation as to a functional display or artsy presentation is a must. There it is. That was a taste of how I start downsizing willing participants. It's a rather fun journey.

While living in Daniel's backyard, he and I talked about the design I had settled on: the Sol Haus. The open floor plan and roofline were my favorite parts of it. I was working with Daniel and Vina (the designer) on tweaking it to make it my own. Vina was kind enough to let us visit and tour her tiny.

I knew it was the best design on the planet for me. Daniel designed my trailer and we ordered it to be custom built. We were all having a great time and were formulating our future plans.

I had a place in Chico that I was welcome to build, but not much of an active support system around me. In Los Angeles it was just Daniel, B.A. and I and his landlady seemed to be cooling on the idea of us building there. We both knew that the biggest support system was back in Dallas, Texas, where she built hers. Back we went! I rented a big enough U-haul to pick up my trailer on the way out of L.A. and B.A. hitched up her house to her truck and we caravanned back to the state where everything is big, to build tiny.

This whole time in Los Angeles I had been keeping in touch with Craig and we admitted that we missed each other greatly. As it happens, during the holidays, we had been dating without realizing it so we started (knowingly) dating when I returned. He happily eats my vegan cooking and is a stellar minimalist. He built a 140 sq. ft. cob house that we've spent time in so we know that we'll fit nicely together in the 160 sq. ft. tiny house.

When we hit Texas I headed to the Career Design Associates property where Dr. Helen Harkness had hosted B.A.'s build. She was excited to host another build and was so generous with her property and resources. B.A. organized a workshop and we flew in Daniel with the proceeds. He taught attendees and my house was framed in 3 days. We met new tiny house enthusiasts and have had many subsequent workshops, volunteer workdays and open house tours where the community has strengthened and grown. The 2015 weather was a challenge (torrential rains, flooding, Hurricane Bill, more rain, tornadoes just 6 miles from the build site) and held up many a workday but the progress continued. I can't tell you how many times I wished I could click my heels and have Daniel stay for a month and finish it. I have wished for days off and clear weather so that Susan, Dale, Bryan, Cory, Rob, Robert, Scott, Shannon, Shmorton, Jared, Jet, Demere, Lewis, Tracy, Jay, Kim and Craig would join B.A. and I for about 10 solid days and "ta-da, finished!" Over the course of a year, we had less than two months of actual build days but for that amount of time, it's an impressive feat for a group of DIY tiny house enthusiasts.

People ask me how I could trust strangers to lay their (mostly) unskilled hands on my home. It's easy. I trust that they will soon become friends and

I trust that they are there to learn and will do their best. We have fun, we stress, we laugh, we scream, we cry, and we laugh more (and then we have beer). We have people in the tiny house Meetup group who came into the group just out of curiosity, people who are dreamers and planning for the future, and people who are ready to buy their trailer. They are all coming together and putting their stamp on my house. I will remember my friends with tools in their hands, who are not just my friends.

You've read my story. These people rescued me. When I participated in building for Jay's nanny and when I watched the girls frame B.A.'s house at MAGIC Camp, I knew that I wanted that same energy to go in, on and around my tiny house as it was being built. The way this whole journey has happened for me, the way I turned tiny was with the help of the tiny house community.

My house is built with love and care and belief. If you come looking for flaws you will definitely find them but all I see is the perfection of laughter and long days and sweat and funny stories and memories that will forever be my soft place to fall.

Part 2

Tiny Lifestyle

Every tiny house in America tells a unique story. If only their walls could talk. They would remember harder times when perhaps money was at a minimum or a recognized American Dream was little more than a daydream. They might tell of heartbreak and even reconciliation. But they might also talk about redemption and success; that moment when the tears dried up, the blood quit pouring out, and the sweat gave way to a cool breeze. Then the story would become about the tiny lifestyle; the reason behind the transition. Those stories are oftentimes lost in the shuffle of do-it-yourself vernacular. Fortunately this section brings those stories to light. Whether it be a tiny house where teenagers are treated as young adults, a tiny house serves as a vacation resort or second home, pets are given their own furnishings, or tiny houses act as little more than a stepping-stone to something else, the tiny lifestyle is a unique one with some very entertaining and enjoyable stories.

Tiny House as Teacher

Hari Berzins

Teacher, writer, and speaker, Hari Berzins not only designed and built a tiny house with her husband, but she lived there for 4.25 years (with a family of four) while saving for, designing and building the family's mortgage-free "big" house. She continues to teach and blog at Tiny House Family and will share with *Turning Tiny* readers the afterlife of living tiny, and how families can incorporate the lessons of living tiny into any size home.

My perspective on tiny house life likely differs from many presented here. That is, my tiny house story contains a marriage and two growing children in 168 sq. ft. The romanticism wears off quickly when there is mud in the foyer, coats on every surface, bored kids and tired grown ups, but somewhere in the steam cooker of tiny house family life, we learned to make it work for as long as it took to build our right-sized house without a mortgage.

Folks arrive at tiny life for many reasons; ours was to recover from the loss of our business and home, but more than that, we set out to prove to ourselves that we could build a homestead with zero debt.

My goal in this essay is to show that even if you don't live tiny forever, the gifts of extreme downsizing are numerous and long-lasting. If you are a family, couple or individual who dreams of simplifying may you find the encouragement to start right where you are.

> *The secret of happiness, you see, is not found in seeking more,*
> *but in developing the capacity to enjoy less.*
> —Socrates

The tiny house leaves no room for haphazard. It requires discipline and routine. This will whip the lazy housekeeper in you right into shape. Or you'll lose your mind. Your choice. Of course, I speak for myself, but the tiny house presents one with choices. Ultimatums, actually. This or that? Peace and harmony or insanity? There was seldom a middle ground, and so I learned, often reluctantly and screaming, to maintain a lovely 168 sq. ft. home with my growing children while (barely) keeping my marriage alive.

How did I do this? I looked at the tiny house as a teacher and opened myself to the lessons. The first lesson was the hardest: resign yourself once and for all to a daily routine. I know how helpful it is to create structure and routine for children, but being a creative type, I rebelled against daily routine for myself. Surely, novelty leads to more creativity. Turns out, it doesn't. Not in 168 sq. ft. In 168 sq. ft., you have to create a machine. I mean the functions of daily life need to be on autopilot, everyone doing their part at the right times. It really is the only way I found to choose peace and harmony over insanity on a daily basis. With daily routines on autopilot, we kept the tiny house tidy most of the time. A tidy house leaves room for creativity. Who woulda thought?

Clothes on the floor and stuff on every surface became the norm and caused a lot of friction in the beginning, but after a year of learning we found ourselves hitting a nice stride. Our daily routine looked something like this:

Alarm at 5:00 a.m. Climb down the ladder to make coffee, write and read.

Make breakfast. Take the dining chairs and tables off the wall and set them up.

Wake the kids. Eat breakfast. Put tables and chairs back on wall.

Make lunches. Get dressed. Wash dishes. Sweep. Kids catch school bus. Go to work in a little corner of the tiny house. Kids come home. Backpacks explode. Sort school papers and contain backpacks. Hang them on the hooks along with the chairs. Kids change into play clothes and have a snack. Put shoes away. Sweep. Sort the books and papers on the kitchen counter. Put it all away. Go through the house and gather all the things we don't need and either throw away or put in the donate bag (yes, we did this everyday). Make dinner. Take chairs and tables off the wall, but first move backpacks off the hooks that they share with the chairs. Set up the dining room. Eat dinner.

Clear table. Do dishes. Put dining room away. Sweep. Shower (one person each night, one person each morning). Read books, watch movie or play games until bedtime. Kids climb to bed. Climb up the ladder to tuck them in. Climb down the ladder for a few minutes of quiet before climbing up our loft ladder and going to bed. Lights out around 10:00 p.m. This routine had to be in place for my sanity. And, yes, we really swept three times a day. I never kept a very clean house. Now I do. Thanks, tiny house.

Every single possession takes up space in both the physical and mental realms. Because I needed to find every inch of space available to me, my attachment to stuff decreased exponentially with time. Clearing excess became a game rather than a chore. Everyday there was space to reclaim by simply asking myself. Does this thing matter? Things matter less and less when they take up valuable real estate. What mattered and what we kept are items that are both beautiful and functional. Some of our possessions are simply functional, but very few simply beautiful items claimed a permanent spot.

Looking at stuff with a critical eye is helpful in keeping it at bay. Just like the people allowed into my innermost circle, the stuff in my life has to pass a few tests. I learned this in the tiny house as a means of making it work. Keeping it going in the big house gives our home the simple intentionality we loved about the tiny house. If something is there, it is clearly functional in our lives. When you long for more space, get rid of everything you can,

and put everything away. If there isn't a place to put it away, let it go. Your home will instantly get bigger.

By getting rid of everything I could and keeping the house tidy, I created as much physical space as I possibly could, but I needed more, so I turned within. I didn't know I needed to turn within; I learned that one the hardest way. I felt like those caged leopards I saw at the Melbourne Zoo. Pacing back and forth and coming face to face with a wall every two steps, I couldn't muster the patience to respond peacefully to my young children's constant questioning, and I yelled at my kids more than I want to admit. Lucky for me, I wasn't a leopard helplessly captured in a cage, I had the capacity to create, and there were a few more ways I found to create the space I desperately longed for.

Solace was waiting for me between my breaths. The tiny house taught me to breathe like I meant it: deep and slow (and very quietly) with a pause between the in-breath and the out-breath. In this pause, I found infinite space—the space I longed for. Solace. Silence. Each pause gave me enough peace to move to the next chaotic moment. Soon I yelled less and laughed more. Soon, the tiny house was not a punishment, but an adventure.

Through my mindfulness practice and adjusted relationship with stuff, I found myself settling into contentment. Because I had no place for anything else, I wanted nothing. If there is space that could be filled, it's easy to fantasize about all of the nifty things with which one can fill a space; the tiny house allows for none of this fantasizing. The feeling of not wanting for anything is deep a contentment and freedom that is available to anyone any time one chooses to want nothing, or cultivate contentment.

Cultivating contentment requires practicing enough.

We want more land. *3 acres is enough.*

We want to buy a tractor. *Two digging forks are enough.*

We want a new car. *Your old cars are enough.*

Practicing "enough" naturally seeps into the way one sees oneself. Soon I was enough. The house, the stuff, the money no longer defined me. In my deep breathing, I included enough. *Breathing in I have all I need. Breathing out I am enough.*

It's a good thing to tell yourself this as often as possible, because you will be tested. Folks who've lived in close quarters with others will know exactly what I mean by the steam cooker effect. The process of finding space meant coming face to face with each other's desperation.

While we trained ourselves to put things away, we learned the nuances of breath. Breathing in and out can be peaceful and it can be angry. Consider the difference between a slow, quiet breath with a relaxed brow and a a gasping in-breath a forced sigh as out-breath. Both are breathing, but one communicates frustration and discontentment. It's the same with tone of voice. Words don't matter as much as tone. These factors existed long before we moved into our tiny house, but those four walls compressed us like a steam cooker, and the necessary learning happened quicker. We learned to be hyper-aware of our breath, tone, and body language because they were all so much louder in the tiny house.

In order to learn the skills for peaceful living with three other humans, we worked to improve our communication skills. The most helpful technique we found was non-violent communication (NVC), also known as compassionate communication. Here is the NVC process:

1. The concrete actions we are observing that are affecting our well-being.
   - "When I (see, hear). . ."
2. How we feel in relation to what we are observing.
   - "I feel. . ."
3. The needs, values, desires, etc. that are creating our feelings.
   - "Because I need/value. . ."
4. The concrete actions we request in order to enrich our lives.
   - "Would you be willing to. . . ?"

This simple process is a practice. We fall short quite often, so we return to the process and try again.

When desperation was especially intense, I turned to the outdoors. This necessity fostered a deep relationship with our land and a connection to the seasons. As I walked this three acre hillside in deep winter looking for signs of spring, I realized how connected I was to the seasons. Each season offers an opportunity to reflect on my own growth and change.

If the first year in a tiny house is a crash course in housekeeping, mindfulness, communication, contentment, and self reflection, then the years that follow offer the practice needed to make these new understandings part of your core.

This refining of life also brought my core values to the surface. Living with only the essential is an opportunity to notice what is missing. If I am to lead a life in line with the core of who I am and what I value, what needs to be added back in? What I missed more than anything was space to create and gather. For me, creation takes solitude, and I missed the space to be alone with my art. I missed the space to spread out and make an artist's mess. I missed the space to have friends over on the coldest and wettest days of the year. Luckily for me, we were designing and building a bigger house, and living tiny informed the design of our future home.

The last three years of living tiny were also years of building our mortgage-free "big house." Our focus was not only on making the most of our little house, but of designing and building a right-sized-for-us house that would work for our family for the long haul. This meant salvaging barns, searching for deals on materials, and spending every free minute on building. This was an emotionally and physically exhausting undertaking. You know, lugging two by fours up the hill in a foot of snow, climbing 30 ft. ladders to install giant windows, having no money left and wondering where to find the money to finish the house.

Making decision after decision about materials and placement is challenging no matter where you sleep at night, but these decisions added an extra challenge to our marriage because we were also living in such tight quarters. When Karl asked me to tell him where to put the windows, I pretty much freaked out.

Where do I want the windows!? There's so much to that decision, and so much of it is unknown. How will I want to live in this house? I don't know. Making decisions without all of the information is scary for me, and yet I kept making them with as much information as I could collect. *Someday* kept me going. *Someday we'll have a big party and celebrate being super awesome people who built their own home without a mortgage.*

Sitting down the hill looking up at the big house, I'd imagine the day we finally moved our measly belongings up the hill. That day stood out in front of me like Oz.

We skipped and trudged and crawled our way down the yellow brick road only to reach the finish line. What seemed to stand before us as the climax was rather anticlimactic. Turns out what I had been sharing with our followers on Tiny House Family was true: The joy is in the journey. We were journeying to a mortgage-free big house, and the journey was so full of learning and pressure and living on the edge, that we hardly realized how happy we already were. I remember a lady telling me from her own experience finishing building her own house very passionately, "You are going to be so happy."

And, yes, we are happy now in this big house. It's remarkable to sit in a home after hammering it together for three years, but the journey was more remarkable. We were doing something big. It was something to hold on to. We were left with *Okay, now what?*

The after the elation of passing our building inspection and sleeping in the big house, our son, Archer, expressed our feelings—

"I miss the tiny house."

"But it's right down the hill."

"It's different. Our stuff isn't in there. You guys aren't in there. Now we won't be on TV anymore. We're just a regular family."

I took him down the hill and we snuggled on the coach and cried.

Closing chapters is poignant. Some chapters are more clearly defined than others. Our tiny house chapter was punctuated clearly on each end. Move in. Move out. *Is that it?*

The little move up the hill was anything but simple because we tangled our identities with the tiny house. Could it be that the tiny house wasn't done with me yet? Those lessons keep coming.

When we moved into the tiny house, I started tinyhousefamily.com. I expected to share with our families and friends, and wasn't planning on being a REAL blogger. But a few months into my blogging, we got a message from a producer for a guy named Anderson Cooper. I read the message out loud, "Karl, who is Anderson Cooper?" "He has a news show, I think." I thought about ignoring the request for an interview for a day or so, but something kept telling me to say Yes.

Hari, you didn't start sharing with the world to hide. You have to say yes. So we flew to New York and appeared on Anderson's daytime talk show. What followed was pretty surreal. A fury of interview requests and a few more national television appearances later, and I was feeling pretty fabulous. Wow! People are really reading what I write. Maybe, I really am a writer now. The tiny house gave me something to say that people wanted to hear. This experience gave me validation I was apparently seeking because I loved it even though every time a big interview came out or we appeared on TV, I was terrified. There was recovery time in the beginning as I toughened up to the ridiculously judgmental commenters. Eventually, I stopped reading comments altogether. Don't read the comments.

With this newfound readership and fan base, I was on my laptop and phone more than I wanted to be. Like an addiction, I had to keep posting or maybe they'd go away, all those likes and validations. Every time I posted something on Facebook I'd stare at the likes as they grew. I felt a pop of adrenaline. My family was upset that I was staring into the screen. I had to learn balance and priority. Sure, I want to share with folks, sure I want to help people, but not at the expense of the time I have with my family. That balancing act is one I'm still learning. I venture to say you are, too.

The thing is, I got so many shots of dopamine from sharing about our tiny house, that when we moved out, I felt like I had nothing left to say. That's the risk of identifying too closely with the tiny house as status symbol. There is (or was) a badge of honor for living in the smallest tiny house. *Oh yeah, your house is smaller than mine, but we have more people and our square footage/per person is way lower than yours.* Admittedly, I spent some time in this thinking. And now my house is 1400 SQUARE FEET!! Yes, I yelled that. Status symbol gone.

I had to untangle myself from the "tiny houser" label, as we do with so many labels throughout life. You aren't this or that. You are a being having a human experience and you will grow and change. We outgrew the tiny house, and it's okay. We grew something from the experience and our new home is informed by what we learned. And it wasn't about the house, really.

It's true, no doubt. But I had to sit quietly and let this new home and time in life take hold in my heart. And while the time in the tiny house spotlight was fun, it was addicting and ultimately distracted me from what matters most. Without realizing it I added mental clutter with my tiny house sharing. The first months in the big house, I went silent online. Closing the curtains from the outside world, I took the time to assimilate the last four years into who I am now.

I'm changed by the experience of living tiny, and I'm born anew into more space. As I let go of the tiny house person label, I can more fully inhabit this new home and, ultimately, myself.

Letting go is slow-release joy. The more I release my hold on what was, the more room there is for what is. Simply profound. The joy appears in moments of deep gratitude for the last four years. Those years gifted us with freedom from stuff, debt, and the status quo. We own more humility now than before—there was some value in reading those awful troll comments.

Joy hits in between agony and delight. It's quick like a sunbeam through a prism. It arrives when there is space for it. I'm finding joy between the agony of closing a chapter of my life and the delight of a long bath in my deep bathtub. Oh how I missed soaking. There is joy in the mess of creativity. I want to keep my tidy tiny house ways, yet I revel in spreading out a sewing project and leaving it there for a whole two days. Friends recently remarked on how good it is to see my creative mess. I worked so hard to keep that messy side of myself in check. She's joyful to roll in her mess. Joy arrives with the laughter of dancing friends on a snowy night—more than two of them at a time. It's a miracle to witness thrashing arms in our right-sized living room. I delight in spending money on plane tickets rather than wood. It's a gift from our former selves, this freedom to roam. We sat still and learned hard lessons and worked our muscles sore to have a home that is all ours. Now we have two homes that are all ours and we get to see where this takes us.

So far it has taken us into adolescence with our growing children. All along, our plan was to move out of the tiny house before adolescence moved in. We made it in the nick of time. Our oldest, Ella, has grown a foot in the last six months. She turns 13 next month. Her bedroom door and desk are a blessing as she navigates these coming years. But her years as a 8, 9, 10, 11, and 12-year-old sharing a loft with her brother have left their imprint. She is a thoughtful, socially aware young woman who cares deeply for the well being of our planet and its humans and other animals. Living a radically different lifestyle has taught her that she doesn't have to be like everyone else to fit in. She belongs because she brings all of who she is. That girl makes mama proud.

Our boy had his 11th birthday in the big house. As he blew out the candles on his key-lime pie (his choice,) I remembered his 7th, 8th, 9th, and 10th birthdays. In the dark of January when tiny house living was hardest, we lit candles and celebrated in our little house. We had slumber parties and crowded kids into our 8' x 21' box, and the house fell away. We were left with the love and the candlelight. Archer loves the animals. He is a great gardener and enjoys helping on the homestead. Sitting here, now, I know that teaching our children about hard work and showing them the rewards will serve them very well when they leave us.

The More Things Change…

Now that routine is ingrained in how we live, we have big house routines, too. Turns out we still live tiny in our big house. By that I mean there is a system and structure to our daily lives. Everything in our big house is intentional and inspired from a tiny space.

We built to minimize possessions—closets are tiny and windows are large. All nooks and crannies function as storage. For example, the space under the stairwell contains a coat closet, both Karl's and my bedroom closets and a little compartment to store toilet paper and towels accessed from tiny barn doors in the bathroom. There isn't a linen closet because we only need the sheets on our beds, and towels fit nicely into custom shelves in each bathroom. The washing machine is under a counter in the kitchen and we skipped the dryer opting to hang clothes on the line or inside when the wood stove burns. Our dining nook is just big enough for a table and benches, so we can still get cozy with our guests. We liked the simplicity of knowing where things go, why we had them, and actually returning them to their place, so we spent time thinking through the flow of life in the big house. We built shelves and cabinets with specific functions. For example, right outside the front door is a big built-in shelf where we deposit our shoes before entering the house, and just inside the front door, we each have a cubby to stow our personal belongings until we sort and put them away for the day. This might sound rigid, but it doesn't feel rigid. It feels freeing. Because we know what needs to be done, we do it, and we aren't giving a whole day to house-cleaning, ever.

We built into our big house what we missed most in the tiny house: Space for solitude and artistic creation, TWO bathtubs, space to gather with friends, and we made sure to build nature in with giant windows allowing views from three directions in every room. Four directions in the living room. We continue to cultivate contentment by enjoying what we already have and finding new and surprising ways to make use of our stuff. And if it's not useful, we toss it.

Our relationships continue to evolve, and I know we are all better off for the time in the tiny house as we continue to experience a deeper understanding of and respect for each other's needs, improved communication, and more patience. And, yes, our sex life loves this new house with its locking bedroom door.

I am profoundly grateful to have what I missed, but even more grateful to know that I missed it in the first place. Stripping life down to the essential is a worthwhile endeavor and it has left me with clarity. I know what matters most, and I will live out my life with this knowledge.

Did I mention we own two houses free and clear? Thanks, tiny house.

Meaningful Homes and Lives of Purpose

Jay Shafer

Jay Shafer is not the first to have designed, built and lived in a little house; but there is probably nobody who has done more to popularize and politicize diminutive dwellings since Henry Thoreau. Jay founded his first, now defunct, company – Tumbleweed Tiny House – in 1999. Shortly thereafter, his pivotal Small House Book was released. Through his writing, international media appearances, and efficient home designs, Jay Shafer continues to bring little houses and the simple, sustainable lifestyle they can afford to the mainstream.

It'd be a mistake to think there's such thing as one tiny-house-lifestyle. There must be at least as many ways to live in small spaces as there are people living in them. Even the term, "tiny house" is hard to put a finger on. For me, it has always been, and still is, comprised of two words. One's an unquantifiable noun and the other's an ambiguous adjective. When asked, I just say a tiny house is any home in which every inch and everything's necessary and meaningful to its occupant(s). Whether it's a 100 square-foot cottage for two, or one man's 10,000 square-foot condo-castle, I'm not one to argue, so long as whoever's living there thinks they need every bit of it to feel safe and happy. That's not to say I don't sometimes wonder if they might be wrong. I just don't argue. It's their call.

There is, at least, one thing the varied lives of those living in well-edited homes seem to have, more or less, in common. Because we've generally spent a relatively large amount of time thinking about what we need to be happy (or, maybe, because we're prone to that sort of thing in the first place) and, because we've adjusted our homes accordingly, we tend have a relatively large amount of time to spend in a ways that are meaningful to us rather than in ways that might, otherwise, be expected of us if we were bound by a lease or a 30-year mortgage. In general, we tend to lead lives of purpose. When everything in your house means something to you, life itself can seem more meaningful; and there's a sense of freedom and clarity that comes with getting rid of everything else.

Beyond that, it's hard to know what goes on behind the closed doors of other tiny householders. I'm no more qualified to discuss those sordid details than I am to provide a more finite definition of what a tiny house is. I'll be sticking to my own story, here. That all seven of the homes I've occupied over the past two decades would, more or less, match what probably comes to mind for most people when they think "tiny house" is convenient. That so much of what I've experienced therein is bound to be a lot like that of others living in similar dwellings should help shed some light on what might be called a "tiny house lifestyle."

I'd start at the beginning, but, I don't remember much of my childhood, and what little I've been told about it should be discounted as heresy. Wolves raised me and wolves are prone to embellishment. Besides, the suburban house I was brought up in exceeds 4,000 square feet and doesn't come anywhere close to meeting my definition of tiny. Maybe that's why I felt more comfortable sleeping outside in the car. In any case, it seems that an aimless childhood spent in an oversized house in a particularly artificial section of 1970s suburban Orange County would prove to be the perfect blank slate from which to start my search for meaning.

It was my search for meaning that led to my love of tiny houses. To me, every well-edited, little house reads like both a portrait of its occupant(s) and of the socio-natural environment that created them/it. Each is a mandala depicting the seamless relationship between the individual and the indivisible world of which we're all part and parcel. This is definitely true of the little places I've designed, built and called home. If where I was living during one era or another isn't enough to provide a pretty clear picture of who I was, what I was listening to at the time probably would. I've had a theme song for every one of my seven tiny house builds. Each seems to say something about who I was, what I believed in and where I was headed when I made each structure.

I was 32 when I moved into my first tiny house. It was created from a 14'-long, totally derelict, 1964 Airstream trailer. I paid $2,200 for it, another $500 to rebuild the interior and another $600 for a solar voltaic system. I lived in it, off-grid, from 1997 until 1999, at the edge of a hayfield, 6 miles northeast of Iowa City. The soundtrack for my Airstream renovation was David Bowie's *Major Tom*. It's not like I listened to it non-stop for weeks on end or anything. I didn't have to. If I wasn't sleeping or listening to Teri Gross on NPR, chances are good that the words, "Here I am, floating in a tin can…" would be incessantly looping through my head. The lyrics pretty much sum up the special brand of domestic bliss I was after at the time. I'd be living in a metal Airstream way out in the country by myself.

In the 20 or so years that followed my time in my Airstream, I've lived in seven tiny houses with a myriad of other spaces mixed in among them depending on my life's needs. Initially I went even smaller with my house the XS, which measured 7' x 10'. The reduced size served the purpose of easy parking in northern California until I found some land on which to be a "groundskeeper" and lived surrounded by Redwoods. That first foray into living simply surrounded by nature is what shaped my future and my goals for my houses and designs.

There is of course that question that question that people love to ask, "Why not just buy an RV?" Having lived in an RV in Iowa, and spent a considerable portion of the winter with an ice scraper as my most frequent

indoor friend (accompanied by a sponge and a bucket for conversation, er, *condensation*) I can say for me, I am not interested in copying the (most common) RV standard of building fast and cheap and with glossy finishes in any way.

Tiny houses suit me: the flexibility they bring to my life, that they are an affront to authority – my first tiny house came about simply because I was told I couldn't – but most importantly, they are a true reflection of self and my needs. They contain nothing extra, and everything that I need. They are beautiful and functional. There is nothing about a larger, traditional house that is alluring to me in any way.

Aligning oneself with integrity is largely subtractive. Removing all of the extras – a systematic elimination of everything that does not enhance, allows one to reveal what's truly important and useful, and reflective of one's self. Getting down to just the items that serve a purpose is common sense, but we're often lead down the path that more is better, that bigger is better, and that gadgetry and button-pushing can "enhance" our living experience. Usually the case is that those things make life more expensive and more complicated – I don't have the time or the patience for that. I have made space that is adequate enough for beauty and truth, function and practicality.

Just as money, prestige or the law might play the ultimate authority for some, it is meaning that tends to govern the lives of those who've chosen to live so simply. All these other things may have had meaning ascribed to them, but, when all's said and done, they're just social constructs subject to the same meaning we're subject to.

For something to be deemed truly meaningful, it needs to serve as a good conduit between our world and us. Meaning is what makes us and our relationship to the world around us comprehensible. We find meaning in the universal symbols, beliefs and rituals that have been adhered to by people of all cultures throughout the world for ages. These archetypes have survived as meaningful because they, too, have shown themselves to be necessary. It is, in fact, as comprehensive as comprehensive gets. When we say something's of "integrity," we mean that it's i*ntegral* to that well-proven understanding that we all share. Unless you can, somehow, show me that 2+2=5 without asking me to disregard the comprehensive understanding that a few million other folks and I share with nature, it means nothing to me. It isn't of integrity.

A strong composition is one in which all the parts work to strengthen the whole. This is as true of music as it is of a painting or the design of a small house. There are seven principles of minimal design: simplicity, honesty, proportion, scale, alignment, hierarchy and procession.

It is ironic that *simplicity* is by far the most difficult of the principles to achieve. The more simplified a design becomes the more any imperfection is going to stand out. Everything in a plain design must make sense, because every little thing means so much.

In the most beautiful houses, no attempt is made to conceal structural elements or disguise materials. Wooden collar beams are understood as beautiful. Aspects that are purely ornamental are to a house what the comb-over is to a head of hair. The vast disparity between the intention and the result of these two contrivances is more than a little ironic. Both are intended to convince us that the homeowner (or the hair-owner) feels secure in his position, but as artifice, each other serves to reveal insecurity and dis*honesty*.

Honest structure and simple forms strike a chord with us because they are true to nature's law of necessity. Sound *proportions* strike a chord, too. Certain proportions (sacred geometry) seem to appear everywhere – in sea shells, trees, geodes, cell structure, and all of what is commonly called "the natural world." Proportion is one of the primary means by which a building can be made readable. Repeated architectural forms and the spaces between them are like music, the pattern (or rhythm) of which we understand because it is always with us. We intuitively understand good proportions because they are part of our most primal language. Once an increment has been chosen (plywood is milled to 4'x 8' pieces, lumber comes in 6', 8', 10' 12' and 16' lengths) we can begin to compose a home comprised of simple multiples and fractions of the unit. This process should be fairly intuitive.

The *scale* of our homes should be determined by the true needs of their occupants. In a restaurant, most of us prefer the comfort and security of the corner booth. Ideally, every room in our homes will offer the same sense of enclosure without confinement. The overall scale of our homes does not need to accommodate every possible activity under the sun. With little exception, home is the place we go to sit and lie around at the end of the day. There will also be some cooking, eating, hygiene, working and playing going on, but none of these activities need occupy a palace. Remember the

Japanese two-dimensional increment, the tatami mat: "half a mat to stand, one mat to sleep."

Gestalt psychologists have shown that compositions with long, continuous lines make more sense to us that those with a lot of little broken ones. Continuity allows us to read a composition as a whole. The principle of *alignment* is just one part of what some psychologist have termed the "simplicity" concept.

Good home design entails a lot of categorizing. The categories we use are determined by function. Arranging the rooms and objects in a house according to their relative importance is essential to making any space readable. Presenting such a *hierarchy* may require that some doorways be reduced to create a larger sense of space once you pass through it, or a ceiling may be lowered to downplay a room's significance. As always, necessity will determine these things inasmuch as it is allowed to.

While the principle of procession is still primarily about space, it also pertains to time. The best houses speak to us in a visual language with which we are all familiar. A gate in a picket fence that opens onto a narrow path that leads through a yard to an open porch that covers a door is a set of symbols we recognize as sign posts guiding us through increasingly private territory toward the threshold of someone's clandestine world. Such layering demarcates public space from semiprivate and private spaces. This serves to put us at ease, as it ensures that will we never be left to wonder if we have overstepped our boundaries as guests. Once inside a good dwelling, visual cues should leave us with no doubt that this is a home in the truest sense of the word. Some of the greatest residential designs employ the same formal geometry as that of sacred architecture. When we approach and enter a well-designed church or mosque, we immediately are aware of the proportions, symmetry and geometry. A well-designed little house will remind us just as effectively as any cathedral that we are not merely witnessing divine beauty, but that we are beauty.

A strong procession is created in the home by using some variation of the same three elements that are universally used to create it in sacred architecture: a gate, a path, and a focal point. A well-composed little house reflects the entire universe as no ordinary mansion can.

A structure offers shelter and security but a home is more than that. A sense of home comes from inside – your home reflects what you feel inside, and if you are at peace with yourself, you can be yourself and your home will reflect that. Strip away the pretentiousness and find your personal space that serves your needs. My homes have been my fortresses against chaos and the demands of others, a quiet space for drawing and designing free from the dilutions of the extraneous world. I am happy with less, and to be able to step outside of my home and into a community that surrounds me just makes it all the more sublime. Tiny houses are a reflection of everyone's truth – what's important, genuine and honest, and meaning manifests itself as truth, love and beauty.

Life in a Tiny House
Pretty Good, Some Problems²

Dee Williams

How much stuff does a person really need? This is a question Dee Williams has been mulling for years, and after a life threatening illness, her conclusion was: not much. Dee began limiting herself to about 300 things and commenced re-defining her understanding of the basics: community, gratitude, happiness and the compost toilet. Dee is a builder, teacher, author and occasional rabble-rouser. She's the founder of Portland Alternative Dwellings, a company founded on the principle that everyone can build the life they dream.

I grew up in the Midwest, where people are practical. I've used this bit of biographical information to explain myself to neighbors and friends who might question why I am comfortable cutting my bangs with the tiny scissors on my pocketknife, or why I often 'sew' my clothes with duct tape. I've used my Midwest roots to explain why I like cheap beer, cheese, and all the pitchforks, axes, and wood chippers on display at the hardware store.

For the most part, Midwesterners are a sincere, handsome people. We get along well with others, we don't ask for too much and find comfort in awesome creations such as Jell-O salad peppered with tiny fruits, and beer can holders that strap onto a ball cap.

We don't believe in over-sharing our feelings. In fact, we get a little nervous when someone admits that they're lonely, angry, afraid or head-over-heels in love. Big feelings are messy and as a practical people, we like to keep things focused on "real" issues: a broken lawnmower, laundry, or poor cable reception.

I'm telling you all this to explain how I've managed to live happily enough in an 84-square foot house without running water, and why I've only recently started to lean on my friends to deal with some of my more over-bearing uncomfortable feelings.

Dark raging fear isn't normally brought up when talking about tiny houses. In fact, most of the media makes living in a tiny house sound remarkably awesome. And of course it is: I love that I have more time and money to explore what life has to offer, but it's not perfect.

My house rests in my friends backyard, in an older neighborhood with small mill-town houses built in the 1940s and 50's; homes that often spend the winter wearing a stocking cap of blue tarps to prevent them from further collapsing into their soggy surroundings. My house doesn't sit in a park-like setting, alongside a brilliant alpine lake that reflects a canopy of 500-year old cedars. Instead, my house sits above a shallow, well-used yard that grows into a lake when it rains a lot.

Sometimes my house feels too small – a misplaced pair of pants could create an unavoidable obstacle, a traffic jam or a trip hazard. And sometimes, in winter my house smells dank because the "wet towel-raincoat area" is also the kitchen and the living room, and the bathroom and the "damp dog chewing her hinterland" area.

My sleeping loft is pinned to the gable roof, seven feet above the kitchen and bathroom. The headboard, a small triangle of wood with a sweet little window, juts out a few feet past the front door into the expanse of the yard. I love this elevated placement for spying on the world, except when I'm trying to take a nap in the middle of the day and the neighbor kids are below me, playing and shouting, and otherwise allowing their fun to crash into and over my bed like giant waves smashing into the bow of a boat.

My point is: this isn't a perfect set-up, but still pretty good. As an adaptable Midwesterner, I've not only made things work, I've come to love them.

Not long ago, I woke up at one in the morning and found my dog rolled over on her back with her feet hanging loosely above her body. Her nose was poking past the window sill into the backyard expanse, her head planted out the open window at an impossible angle. In the moonlight I could see her lips "pfffft" when she exhaled, and every once in a while her nose twisted and flared, following the smell of the raccoons in the alley. As I drifted back to sleep, I wondered what it would feel like to be so relaxed and vigilant at the same time.

A couple hours later I woke up again, and this time OluKai was on patrol peering down on the pre-dawn yard. Rolling over, I cranked open the loft window another couple inches, allowing her to lean further forward. "Hey Captain Ahab," I whispered to her. "What wild thing you hunting out there?" I've heard dogs can hear squirrels skittering down telephone lines a block away. They can smell the loose dirt excavated by a mole in the neighbor's lawn.

I rose up on one elbow to stare past OluKai into the shadows that dotted the lawn. It was the land of misfit toys: tricycles, wheeled carts, miniature lawn mowers, shovels, buckets, balls and bats. The view made me sigh and smile, remembering how emphatic the preschool neighbor boys had been earlier in the day, as they were explaining how this critical equipment, placed just so, would clearly prevent monsters from walking across the back lawn up to their house.

I could smell the grass and mud, and could feel my heart thumping slow and steady. I turned my head and tucked my hair behind my ear, but all I heard was someone further down the block dragging a rubbish bin out to the curb. I lay back down and closed my eyes, feeling my heartbeat lubbing away under my tee shirt. It was filling and emptying, working quietly to connect my brain to my lungs, to my feet in the loft. It had expanded and contracted eighty to one hundred thousand times during the day, banging about without much consultation from me until I rolled over to see my dog snoring with her head out the window. I couldn't imagine my heart could be any fuller or happier, because OluKai was running wild in the night from her perch in the loft.

Years ago, when I lived in my big house with three bedrooms and a basement, and cubby-holes around every corner, I had a different reaction to the occasional nighttime wake-up calls—especially when things would go bump in the night. This happened when I was home alone, when night sounds seemed most sinister and every thump or faint scratchy sound reminded me that I was soft and mortal. I'd lay paralyzed in bed for a time, cocking my head to hear more clearly what, or whom, might be slowly chipping away at the locks. I'd replay every horror movie I'd ever seen and eventually I'd wonder if I could lower my dog out from the upstairs window to fetch the neighbor. My more rational side would remind me how silly I was, and would suggest that it was probably just the wind. I would capitulate for an hour, and then my more practical upbringing would kick in and I'd creep down to the kitchen for a weapon.

Some people would respond to their fear by hiding under the blankets. Others would nail their windows shut or put electric alarms on the doors; they'd build panic rooms and security gates, and buy motion-sensitive lights, guns and ammo. Me, a gal from the Midwest: I'd go for the heavy kitchen knife, a spatula or frying pan. No need to bother other people or invest in an elaborate fix when a sturdy soup ladle could do the job.

I did call the cops a couple of times, when my big house felt too overwhelming, even for someone who can deftly weld a cookie tray. But some nights, there were too many doors, too many cabinets and closets, and a bathroom with a menacing shower curtain that could hide any number of boogies.

I'm lucky. Nothing bad ever happened to me in my big house. Always and without fail, my suspected burglars were imaginary. They were tree branches scraping up against the bathroom window, or the air ducts popping under the weight of a fresh supply of heat.

In my tiny house, over the past twelve years, I've never felt compelled to sneak down the ladder to grab a tiny fork to fend off intruders. Instead, I've spent a bit of time worrying that the roof or skylights would leak. I've been afraid that I'd light myself on fire, trying to ignite or repair my propane heater. I've worked through all sorts of temporal fears: electrocution while fiddling with the hundred-pound battery that powers my lights, skidding off the porch in an ice storm, decapitating myself with hedge clippers while trimming the neighbor's blackberry bushes, lightning strike, disease, pestilence, a collapsed car jack while crawling under the house to retrieve dog toys. These are what I'm calling transcendental HOLY SHIT experiences that come along in life, whether you live in a cute pillbox of a house or something larger.

Then there are the darker fears that can't be fixed or worked around, even for a stubborn Midwesterner.

The idea of my tiny house was born out of a troublesome time. I was living in my big house and had just been diagnosed with congestive heart failure (CHF). My internal alarms were going off. Who would walk my dog, how do you install grip bars in the bathroom, what if I can't drive a car and who's going make space in their living room for an oversized hospital bed?

The fear tied to losing my independence and dying at the age of 40 flooded into my bones and filled my lungs, and lodged itself alongside every other disappointing thing that had ever happened to me.

Here's the deal: we pin the human heart with so very much. We hope to cultivate a generous heart or a brave heart, and we give our hearts in love. We encourage each other to search our hearts for truth, for faith, or a path out of darkness; and we reach into its deepest caverns when we grieve. Collectively, we imbue the human heart with the full weight of our humanity, so what do you do when your heart threatens to fail?

Fortunately, through an article in a magazine, I came up with a no-nonsense course of action: I would sell my big house and get rid of my mortgage, to build a tiny house on wheels and see what would happen. In retrospect, this was problem solving with traditional practicality: the busier I stayed, the less I had to talk about my problems or experience my fear of heart failure.

I remember excitedly exchanging emails with my folks, trying to explain my rationale by quoting Walden:

> *Remember the creator in the days of thy youth. Rise free from care before the dawn and see adventures. Let the noon find thee by other lakes, and the night over take thee everywhere at home… grow wild according to thy nature, like these sedges and brakes, which will never become English hay.*
> —- Henry David Thoreau

My dad cheekily responded by telling me that he thought he: "saw some of those brakes (what ever those weeds might be) in his flower patch," and was now trying to get rid them with Roundup, an herbicide that is the backbone of many Midwest gardens.

In May 2004, I launched into the building project, spending three months and $10,000 on what I imaged would be 'enough' to be happy. As fate would have it, the year I built my house, my parents bought a hybrid sailboat called "Anuf" from a guy on the west coast. It was a beautiful boat built for the shallow sea shoals of the Pacific Northwest, small enough to tuck into isolated bays to watch Orcas or to slide out of our winter storms. Their idea was confusing to others because they live in the landlocked Midwest with a small lake that dries up in the summer and ices over in the winter. But all they wanted was Anuf and I understood that. Many decisions are made out of a desire for one last adventure, a last chance to dive deep or catch the sunset before it pulls the night down on our heads.

In September, I drove my tiny house onto the open highway, traveling from Portland Oregon to Olympia Washington. There, I landed in my friends' corner yard, pinched by an alley on one side and a view of the neighbor's 1972 VW beetle (and accompanying blue tarp) on the other. It wasn't necessarily ideal, but reasonable enough to explore my new simple life.

Everything felt like an adventure, from learning the best way to take a shower without a shower, to discovering that it works best to scoop up my fifty-pound dog like barnyard animal when carrying her up the ladder. This moment in time was spectacular for me because I suddenly became more than a heart patient. I became the keeper of the compost toilet, the fixer of the thingy-bob that makes the propane heater run, the backyard lounger and most impressively, Rita's friend.

I shared the backyard with Rita and her nephew's family (Hugh, Annie, Keeva and Kellen) and over the next nine years, I grew to love Rita. She was paralyzed on her left side from a stroke, but I never heard her kvetch. When

I'd help her get a sweater on, snagging her limp arm in the sleeve, she'd jok-ingly cluck in her thick Brooklyn accent: "Ah come on Lefty. Shape up."

In the last year of her life, after she had turned 89 years old, I sometimes helped Rita get dressed. I gave her sponge baths and dabbed ointments in the most private, horribly intimate spots. I laughed with her about the tights she wore as a young woman, trying out as a trapeze artist for a 1930s Circus troop. "My sister dared me to do it as a way to meet boys but I didn't get the job," she admitted cackling and holding her head in her hand, "I was too afraid of heights."

In those last several months, I became the person who would race out of bed, running across the lawn in my underwear if I thought she needed help. I became a caregiver, and my dark fear of dying slowly, of inconveniencing my friends, seemed to loosen. I didn't feel as compelled to race about, stay-ing busy, remaining distracted when I could just as easy be a home-body and recognize that moon has gently settled into my sleeping loft.

Rita died three years ago and I miss her. Sometimes I am racked with such intense sadness and desperation for things to go back to normal. I don't want to cry anymore, or feel empty, or wonder when all my sad-sadness will finally be used up. It's exhausting. My body is exhausted. But I must admit that more commonly when I think of Rita, I simply feel an intense sense of gratitude. She was such an amazing, kind, and funny lady who helped me find a home in her backyard.

Here's what I know is true: for most of us, the days whiz by with a brain full of clatter and before we know it, we make it to thirty years old, then fifty, then seventy. Before we know it, we've lived an entire lifetime with only a few moments of sincere clarity, depth and meaning; those are the moments we fall in love, lose someone dear, witness something beautiful, or scare the shit out of ourselves. In any case, time slows down in those moments and we begin to see things different.

Will I always live in my house? Maybe. I still love it, imperfect as it may be.

Will I always live in Rita's backyard? Maybe. I don't know. Most recent-ly, I've been wondering if I should move my house to a spot closer to my par-ents as they are growing older. I feel I am uniquely qualified for helping my parents at the end of their lives – at the point where they stare at me but can't articulate what they want, and they are on a routine of protein drinks; and they're crapping their pants and have finally been distilled into their most potent denominators: my mommy, my daddy, mine. At that point, since I've had years of living with dogs, I will be able to address their needs in a special way. I'll look them in the eye and say things like "are you hungry?" and I'll look for the slightest muscle flinch, and the tiniest nostril flare or small bit of panting, which will lead me to get another pudding from the refrigerator down the hall or not. I'll say things like: "Who's my favorite guy," and "who's the funniest girl?" I imagine the situation will be similar to the early years living in my tiny house: rife with new discoveries, some good. Some problems. I will massage their skin with baby lotion, and tuck small stuffed animals into their hands, and will cry my eyes out when they die.

The idea of shouldering that grief scares me witless – far more than anything else I can fathom including my own demise and eventual death. But I'm from hearty, clever Midwest stock. I know that some fear will never go away, but you can learn new ways of being with it, like learning to feed a tiger without losing an arm or combing honey by moving very slowly. I recognize it's not a perfect arrangement but perhaps good enough for the time being. In any case, we'll see what magical amazing thing happens next and how my sweet friends will continue to change my heart.

You Can Never Outgrow Tiny

Mario Soto

Mario has worked for Apple for over six years, teaching people and fixing their devices and computers. He combines his knowledge with heart by volunteering teaching blind people how to use Apple devices. He loves to snap photos as he travels in his tiny house that features wireless technology. To learn more about Mario and his house and travels visit TinHouMD.com.

Asked when I first imagined myself living in such a small space, I replied: Always!

In fact, my first tiny house lifestyle experience was living in a rectangle, Winnebego style travel trailer parked in the backyard of my Grandma's house in East L.A. Some of my earliest memories are of living in that trailer, so my personal story is as fresh and authentic as anyone's. My family was poor, but my brother Bobby and I lived a happy childhood with our parents in that narrow space. Perhaps it was there that necessity began training my curiosity for problem solving. Bobby and I were both really inquisitive boys, precocious and never ones to accept defeat. Only we didn't think of it that way back then. For us, a box of cereal, sans milk, meant rethinking everything. With the primary goal being to do nothing more than eat, we simply substituted water for the missing milk. We deconstructed the pairing first, reducing the meal to its essential truth. The milk was just a vehicle for delivering cereal to the belly. We ate it like that because we had to. We were thrilled though because it filled us up. We then congratulated one another's ingenuity.

As opportunities paid off for my family we ended up moving into our own 800 sq.ft., 2-bedroom house, in the suburbs. My brother and I wasted no time creating our two-story clubhouse out of recycled cardboard boxes. We crawled in the first floor and stood up for the second floor. The clubhouse mail floor was waist-high and only big enough for one and therefore reserved for the club leader. Politics being what they are, leaders didn't last long, so we all got to play king of the fort!

As I got older I never seemed to outgrow my affinity for small spaces. It was not uncommon for my parents to find me, after an exhaustive search, napping in some iteration of our clubhouse, with the seemingly endless litter of pit-bull puppies we raised. On any given hot, summer day, the plastic doghouse would get dismantled, flipped upside down and filled with water, allowing me to improvise a wading pool for the dogs and I. No matter the challenge, my childhood always benefited from a feeling of being just a step ahead of circumstances. Life was good.

In 2001, I joined the workforce as a mortgage loan officer, diving head-first into the American Dream. Most Americans remember those "boom" years fondly. I am no exception. "Million dollar club" awards marked my first milestones, several months in a row, very early in my career. Eventually, I would go on to work on teams closing 5 million dollars in loans every month. I was good at what I did. I was successful.

I felt fortunate to enjoy a career in an industry that seemed to have no limits. I was making more money than I knew what to do with and I mainly lived like a big kid. I had new skis, a $60,000 Jeep, season passes for the local ski resort and lots of technology gadgets, including iPods, cameras, phones, Apple laptops and things I can no longer remember. I do remember they were mostly disposable and frivolous because that was part of the fun of it. When something got old or was replaced by a newer version, I purchased that newer version. In with the new and out with the old! The other fun part was the research I did to learn about the latest gizmos.

For me, the most important thing is to know what you need from a particular piece of technology. Perhaps you want to simplify something – avoid or consolidate steps – like going into a bank branch to make a deposit. Technology has made that process so much easier. Now you can deposit a check with the Internet and your smart phone camera. Understanding what you need from a product or solution involves research and learning curves. I researched and learned before purchasing anything. Shoes, socks, underwear, watch, router, glasses; all were given the once, twice over, before being purchased. I Googled it and would go from there. I also searched for low prices. I don't like paying full price. It is always possible to minimize expenses and sometimes radically so.

By the way, I am a certified, self-declared, card-carrying, armchair expert in purchasing general goods. Just like I did in high school, I'll do the homework. I'll research and I'll compare. When I am passionate about something, I dive deep. I love the feeling I get from finding simple solutions to problems. It's a real rush.

So long story longer, I thought I was happy with what I had at that time in life. I had my toys, my ride, the Big Bear slopes, some good food and great people, and almost no want went unfulfilled! But the commission checks kept stacking up and I knew deep inside that they would one day allow me to buy a house. I helped mortgage residences for lots of people, for many years and I was good at it because I provided the best product I could possibly find. I treated all my work as if it were my own purchase. Home ownership for me was inevitable; another step up the ladder of success.

With South Orange County being what it is, I went big and all in on a 3-bedroom townhouse in a gated development for a price very near the one million mark. After moving in I realized that all I ever really had was a king size bed, a lawn chair in the living room, a cardboard box to hold my drinks and plate of food, fancy fridge, nice cookware, and a large format, big screen television. It was my first time on my own, in my own place, and I thought furnishing and decorating was for the birds. A bunch of stuff I would never use or need. My mother snuck in a couch toward the end.

I thought I was happy.

I guess I wanted more though. I felt lucky to meet a beautiful Egyptian princess and I wined and dined her until I had her convinced that we had fallen in love. Ah, the hubris!

I thought I was happy.

My pockets flush with cash and credit cards, I was head over heels for this girl. I felt grown and capable, eager to continue my march of success. So I decided I would propose marriage. And I did. We put on a great party at the historic Mission Inn in Riverside. I was at the top of my game and on top of the world!

Of course, this part of the story doesn't end well. By 2008 the writing was on the wall. The housing bubble burst spectacularly, leaving me blowing in the wind with over $250,000 in upside-down loans on my first home. By 2010 I had lost it all. My stake in the company, which was now bankrupt, was effectively worthless. My home was foreclosed on and charged-off. I was left dazed, insolvent, and unemployed. And to add insult to injury, I was divorced.

I am not sure if it was because of my youth or the power of the economic bubble that swept the mortgage industry like wildfire, but I had never imagined that anything could end the wild ride we were on so early in the Millenium. It didn't end there though. All my investments were in real estate. I lost everything. My whole life completely crashed around me.

My demise complete, I moved back in with my parents, who had also lost big in the real estate speculators market. We shared a 2-bedroom, 2-floor apartment unit and I mostly felt pretty bad about things for a while.

Eventually, my recovery began to take shape. Like a Phoenix rising from the ashes, I took to waking up early and running through the streets a la Rocky in the mean streets of Philly. Bill Conti's Gonna Fly Now billowing gushes of wind in my sails, I set myself on course to get back to where I once belonged: sort of.

It was at this time that I decided to pursue passion and not just money. I went after my first love and applied at a local Apple store. I wasn't making the wads of cash I had grown accustomed to, but it beat unemployment insurance benefit checks by a wide margin. Plus, I worked at Apple! And it was good. I wasn't happy-happy, but I was having fun at work, meeting tons of people and staying out of my head. And I learned so much about the Apple suite of devices and just how scalable the application solution market was becoming and how revolutionary it was for almost any imaginable practical application. Naturally, the Apple iPhone serves as a nexus device that allows me to run all of my wireless services, including TV, locks, lights, internet and security all from phone, via a local wireless network or the Internet.

So it really is a credit to Apple that I began thinking of a home again. Dreams of seamless ease of use and reliability left me imagining a different way to live in a house. At this stage in life, I still wasn't dreaming tiny, but rather smarter, wireless, accessible, scalable and more and more efficient.

Learning about these applications made me a better customer service representative at Apple, and nothing else. I still had no desire for a mortgage. I simply let a part of my brain enjoy the quest for a fully integrated wireless system solution that I can install myself.

I think I was happy.

Still, I took to cross country train rides and backpacking across Europe for weeks and months at a time. I went as often as it took me to raise the money.

Meanwhile, between international flights, I came to recognize that I had not been living my life's passion. It was as a customer service representative at Apple that I understood my passion for helping people. I hadn't really known this about myself prior to my current job. I was discovering that I really thrive helping people understand things, teaching and supporting people's desire to know more.

Travelling let me see just how much I appreciated learning from and understanding people from all walks of life, from all over the world. Sharing space on a train or hiking on a trail, or wine at the hostel after a night of intense sightseeing, sharing space with other travelers and hearing their stories left me profoundly altered. It opened up my worldview far beyond the life as a pastoral list of measures of success that I aimed to attack one at a time like making grades in elementary school. Instead, I was transported to a place filled with ease and conviviality in a way that I had never experienced before.

The trains, walks, hikes, campsites and late nights served as an example of just how easily I could dismantle the programming of life as a goal driven commercial strategy. Instead, I could just breathe and hang out in the common area and wait to see who might stop by. I was wandering about Europe re-evaluating what kind of life I really wanted for myself. It made me curious too about what kind of life I could have? I was already having a grand time of things. But what else was there?

Having failed miserably at the life I thought I was created to have, I felt like I had lost everything and would never do much better. But with Europe opening itself up to me, making itself vulnerable and available to me, I felt as if the world had been reborn and woken me up as well. A whole array of opportunity awaited me. I was, in essence, reborn on those European trails.

Looking back now, I can see that Europe really accelerated a process that had started long before. My values were changing and my true life was unfolding. All I wanted to do was travel, meet new people, visit old friends, catch the sites and come home with a bottle of wine!

I thought I was happy.

Then my parents announced they were moving from their apartment. It had only been a temporary stop for them too. They offered to let me take over the lease, but I figured that buying would be about the same cost as renting. There I was in 2013, just 3 years out of financial annihilation and I was seriously thinking of buying another home.

The numbers never squared well for me though. I did end up with a savings after the dust settled, enough for a modest down payment. But the prospect of pouring $30k into a loan, leaving me house poor and most likely stuck again with more space than I am comfortable dealing with. Plus, travel and freedom to go exploring as I pleased kept returning to the top of my priority lists. My hierarchy of needs required a cash-ready model to accommodate last minute adventures. Add to that the very nature of interest charges on these big loans, namely the cost for financing such a large sum. It just didn't make sense to me anymore.

So I began going back to that tiny house experience in East L.A., recalling how much I enjoyed feeling like I was camping when we first lived in a trailer. I visited RV parks and encountered container homes and really felt like I might build myself a container home, but metalworking seemed more complicated than I wanted.

Eventually my research led me to tiny homes. I saw "tiny," "house," "wood," "plans" and I thought, I can do this. I went into it with not too much information, which was good, because if I had more information I would have psyched myself out and wouldn't have done it. I had just the right amount of information to feel confident I could do it and enough awareness to understand that it would require immediate urgency to get started. So on June 13, 2014, I started construction on my tiny dream house.

The next two years of the build will remain as some of the greatest days of my life. Building this house has been an interesting journey, to put it mildly. And sure, I grew up with an inclination toward tiny living, but I had to lose it all and walk across Europe before I was ready to take on building my own home: one of the most technologically advanced tiny house in the United States.

Despite the house being tiny, it is packed with loads of cool and functional technology that not only makes it uniquely one of a kind, but also easy to maintain.

My first order of business was to buy a trailer and purchase plans. My house is built on a 20 x 8.5 foot Tumbleweed trailer sitting on two, 5,200 pound axels. The framing is hardwood from the big box lumber yard that has been treated with a natural borate salt product applied directly to all wood wall, beams and supports. The borate salt product is packaged with an additive that fights mold. The liquid is sprayed on and allowed to penetrate into the wood where the salts take root deep in the wood's fibers. This product came to my attention after a swarm of termites decided to feast on my house early on in the framing stage. Pest prevention companies quoted me $400 and $800 respectively for treatments, so I went online and researched my options. Wouldn't you know that one gallon of Borate was all I'd need to treat my entire house. After all it is a tiny house! I would need a $14 sprayer to apply the $60 gallon of syrupy salt care to the wood in my house. DIY, all day!

The framed structure is coated with 3.5 inches of closed-cell spray foam insulation from top to bottom for higher R-values, greater resistance, and better protection against moisture.

The siding I used is a beveled Cedar and I really wanted to preserve the naturally handsome features of the wood itself, so I tried to find a clear sealer that wouldn't fill my house with chemicals, but give the house that rich wood glow. I found a product called Verde Natural, which is actually a pure, all-natural Rosewood oil, and it really gives the house a luster.

By the way, some of my pieces of siding were 20 feet long, so I really had to be creative to figure out how to fasten them long pieces with falling off the ladder or losing the piece itself.

After laboring over roofing options, I settled on a weathered-copper look from Classic Metal Roofing Systems. It reflects 95% of U.V. rays and is made of light-weight aluminum panels that interlock with each other to make installation simple and keep a long-lasting tight fit. I made sure to get the foam insulation inserts that go between the panels to help with sound damp- ening, temperature regulation and condensation management. The foam also serves to make the roof more resistant, after all this is a road house, so lots of rocks are likely to hit the roof over time, so the foam increases the durabili- ty of the surface from hail and errant objects.

Grace Ice and Water Shield was my choice for the entire roof underlay- ment. It was pricey, but worth the extra expense in my opinion. I don't want any leaks and any money saved on a cheaper product may cost me in roof repairs down the line.

The roof has two skylights: one a Velux with solar panel built-on the out- side and equipped with a rain sensor, built-in battery and a wireless remote control so that I never have to reach up to open and close. I have my Velux Skylight programmed to open and close at various times throughout the day to release hot air that has built up along the loft ceiling. It serves as a natural air conditioning strategy that allows me to keep a cool house in the evening, even despite a hot day of green house heat accumulation. Oh, and if the rain detector senses moisture in the air, the computer closes the window automat- ically, whether I am home or not.

My other skylight is an Egress and also has many functions, however, being just above the loft area, its primary function is safety. In case of fire or some type of emergency that keeps me from using my front door as an exit,

I can open my Egress Skylight and hop onto the roof. And it also gives me the flexibility to control the slightness of the opening to control the amount of air that circulates in that loft sleeping area.

Another great thing about the durability of the roof is that I can actually pop on it anytime and lay up there on top of my loft without causing any harm to the shingle panels.

As you step inside the front door, you won't see a standard lockset. Instead I went with a Schlage Keypad locking system. This lock is compatible with my iPhone and Apple's HomeKit software applications, allowing me to open the lock from my iPhone interface before I even reach the door.

Hands loaded with groceries? I can ask Siri to open it for me! It also allows me to give people I want to have access to the house their own pass code or even open it remotely via web as they arrive. Anytime guests arrive, all i have to say is "Siri, unlock the front door into my iPhone or iWatch and the it's "Open Sesame!" Most importantly, for me the greatest benefit are Apple HomeKit's security features.

Step in the door and immediately to the left you will find two 2.6 Kwh salt water batteries, giving me the ability to discharge my batteries from 100% to 0% and not damage them in anyway. They are made of cotton, carbon, salt water, base oxide, and stainless steel. Not any other harmful material whatsoever, so I feel safe having these batteries inside thehouse. The batteries are capable of going 6,000 cycles and are listed as Zero-Maintenance batteries, which is a plus for me, the less I need to worry about the better!

To the right as you enter you find my kitchen, designed with cooking lots in mind. My sink is 30 inches wide and 9 inches deep stainless steel. The faucet suspends over the sink like you might find in a hotel dish room, which gives me greater counter space access and mobility when in the relatively small kitchen area. A custom cutting board fitted to sit over the sink when in use and inside the sink when stored, giving it a place to drain dry into the sink when cleaning or preparing food.

The cutting board is made up of the wood piece cut out of the counter block that was used to mount the sink. I used butcher block for my counter top, so there is a seamless design continuity that really looks great.

The stove is a four-burner range with one 55,000 BTU big burner that I use as my primary cooker. A stainless steel backsplash and stainless steel range hood powering a 66cfm fan inside completes the kitchen. The stove-top, backsplash and range hood are from Costco, as is my flooring.

Walk across the kitchen into my living area and you will find a large flat screen television mounted on the wall opposite my kitchen. As you look back at the kitchen you will see a small loft above the kitchen and front door. Up there you will find the Schneider Electronics Inverter/converter and solar charge controller. This is connected to the salt-water batteries and the solar panels. It is what keeps the whole house purring with electricity.

Inside lights are LED and can change into 16 million colors.

You also might notice that there are no light switches anywhere in the house. This is due to the fact that all my lights are wireless. They stick to the walls, never need batteries, and when you push a button to turn on the lights, you are charging them with the power necessary to activate the light switch. Best of all, I can twist-off the switch and remove it from the wall, taking it with me anywhere in the house. Of course, I can program the 16 million colors to show in any order or combination I want.

Outside, I have strips of LED lights wrapped along the roof overhang. These are Philips Hue Light systems giving me the option to dim the lights by percentage and program them on and off in any way I want, including color changes and other frivolous details, like flickering whenever my team scores!

Heating and air conditioning is the responsibility of the LG Art Cool Model split system, which comes with 27.5 SEER rating, also with a wireless feature that controls remotely via the iPhone. Oh, and it is very efficient. I can even check the temperature or air quality via my iPhone when I am not in the house itself. I can activate the air, heater or dehumidification mode while away. This way I can set my settings 30 minutes before arrive and be sure to find the house in an optimal state, every time.

Oh, speaking of climate control, my range hood also acts in this capacity. Capable of sucking smell, smoke or any undesirable airborne particulates right into the hood and clearing the entire house in a matter of four minutes.

Continue to the back and you will find the restroom and shower, lined with red cedar. Over the shower stands a roll-away cabinet designed to occupy the shower space when it is not in use. Most tiny houses will use the shower as a half-hearted storage area, as we all inevitably see the inefficiency of this space staying open and unused for the greater part of the day. This cabinet rolls out for shower time, and also houses my LG Washer/Dryer Ventless combo unit that drains water into the shower. I use the cabinet as a closet and houses all the electronics necessary to run the tiny house. I keep a cordless Dyson vacuum in there too!

For sleep, I have a queen size memory foam mattress and I employ a projector screen that rolls down to cover the opening of the loft. I have projector mounted to the back of the loft, so the screen becomes my own loft mini theatre!

The house is an airy, well-lighted space that feels expansive and welcoming. I get lots of high-fives and fist pounds for keeping the look natural, but for my money, the real benefit is that I am no longer tied to a payment. After 1.5 years of building, I am mostly finished. I've invested $35,000 in my home, sure, but I am looking at reaching a break-even point in two years as I subtract all the rental costs I am avoiding by living in my tiny house.

Perhaps the best thing though is that not only is my house affordable, but also mobile! To date I have logged over 15,000 miles pulling my tiny house across the country. I have visited Colorado, New Mexico, Arizona, Nevada and up and down California, and the journey has just begun!

My Sacred Space

B.A. Norrgard

In 2012, bucking societal expectations and following her inner guidance, B.A Norrgard shed her paralegal costume after 26 years in a downtown high rise and hand-built her tiny house. She is a passionate advocate for others following their dream of letting go of societal conditioning and being free to live a larger life in a smaller space. B.A. is a doer. She has traveled over 6,000 miles with her house and writes about her life on her website, A Bed Over My Head.

When I wrote these Intentions I had no idea how they would truly manifest.

My Intentions

I hope this house changes lives. Starting today. I hope it becomes a glowing orb of light showing everyone that even though it's small it holds an abundant life.

I hope this house inspires. Inspires people to find their true happiness. Inspires people to work together towards a common goal. Inspires people to give and to want to be a part of something different that is whole, and grounded and good. I hope it inspires people to think in new ways, about possibilities for lives they have not contemplated for themselves.

I hope this house is a teacher. To teach basic construction skills. To teach us that we can do more than we think we can, and with less. To teach us that every single one of us has something unique to share whether its time, a talent, an idea, or a dream. That each of us has value. That each of us can make a difference.

I hope this house challenges. Challenges us to reflect on the types of houses we are building. Challenges us to review how we are using our resources, glob-

*ally and personally. Challenges us to think outside the box about the structure of
our neighborhoods and the places we call home. Challenges us to try something
that we are afraid of and to change our experiences.*

I hope this house is a haven. *A dry place in the rain. A place that's safe
and happy in which to gather. A place where friends and family know they can
come to for support and love. A place where strangers come to make friends. A
place with food for strength, soul nourishing conversation, and quiet.*

B.A. Norrgard
MAGIC Camp, 2013

Whatever you do in life, it's important to be true to yourself. To listen to
your heart and your body, and what they are asking of you. When I decided to change my lifestyle back in 2012, it was all about *me*. What *I* wanted.
What *I* needed. I wasn't overhauling my life to prove a point. I wasn't doing
it to please someone else or to help others. The tiny house was for me. I literally built a house for one – really it can't be any more about me than that!
I put my heart and soul into it (because that's how I am – I'm either completely disinterested or I am in with both feet) and although I didn't plan for
it to be, it became a vehicle for personal challenges and personal growth. In
the end, the project became a roof over my head – or as it is, A Bed Over My
Head. I'll never be homeless.

The turning point of my life was in the summer of 2012. I was in my
mid 40's and I decided to take a leap and change everything in my life and
try something totally new – banking on outrageous happiness. And when I
say, "change everything," I mean *everything*. Sell my material
possessions. Sell the house that I had worked so hard to buy. End a 13-year
relationship that had fallen cold. Walk away from my 25-year career. Put it
"out there" that I was willing to relocate to another part of the country. I am
resourceful; I figured I'd either be a huge success or an epic failure – and
either way I would have a great story to tell.

I grew up in northern Minnesota, the youngest of five daughters. Up
until 2013 I was your typical girl from the Midwest. In my 20s and 30s I did
what was expected of me: I graduated high school, got a college degree and
got married. I landed the downtown 9-5 job and we bought a house. And
then, like so many others, I just kept going to work. It felt a bit…*circular,*

the earning and buying. But isn't that what society tells us success is? We are conditioned that more is better. Bigger is better. Those mantras are no longer in my success criteria. As adults, we have the freedom to say, "No. This isn't working for me anymore. This isn't how I want to spend my days."

I was blessed with enjoying the job for which I went to college, and having a successful career path. I worked for the same lawyer as a litigation paralegal for twenty years, preparing for and orchestrating complex commercial jury trials all over the country. My career path kept me on my feet during a divorce, brought me amazing learning experiences in and out of the court room, built spectacular friendships, got me involved in Dallas Area Habitat for Humanity, where I learned to do construction, and ultimately enabled me to buy a 1929 Tudor home in a coveted historical neighborhood near downtown. I was a princess in my own castle. It was a great feeling of accomplishment and I was insanely happy; until I wasn't. At the time my build began, I had been a paralegal for 26 years. I'd owned my house in Dallas for just 3.5 years.

I've been very vocal about my time with my career transition coach, Dr. Helen Harkness of Career Design Associates. I studied with her all day, every Saturday for nine months in 2012 to help me figure out what would make me happy in the second half of my life. I knew by August that I wanted to go tiny for both my lifestyle and my career.

It's funny how my perspective about my choice to change has itself changed over the years. Over the last 4 years I've acknowledged that I didn't like being financially tied down by a mortgage and also that I didn't like being materially ladened both with a house and possessions. The house wasn't just the house, either. There was the furnace in the crawl space, the air conditioner under the eaves, the sewer lines running to the street – all items that kept me up at night.

These days I tell people that the change that is forced upon us is often the best change – the change we need. We realize we need to make a change, but fear stops us. We ignore those subtle taps on the shoulder, those whispers about change in our ears, until we are whacked over the head with it – and forced to change. And then we are reacting to change, often from a place of fear, instead of being proactive and embracing change, looking for change. But at that time in life, I didn't know that.

I barreled through my build with such determination and drive that the days flowed into each other. In the beginning I was still working at the law firm and I would work on the house after work and on weekends. On weekends I would get up very early (the battle cry became, "Bibs and boots at dawn!"), pack a lunch, and drive the 25 miles to my build site. I'd work until it got dark, drive home, shower, eat, plan the next day, fall into bed and get up and do it all again the next day. I was sort of a maniac about it. I was just taking each piece as it came, without really realizing how much I was learning and doing that I had never done before. The last three months I worked on my house seven days a week. When I add up all my build days, I calculate that it took me about 150 days, or 5 months, to build my house.

My build grew into something else without me really realizing it; it took on a life of its own. It really changed when a reporter from the Dallas Morning News was in line behind me at a local specialty lumber company. She asked for my card, emailed me, and on December 15, 2013 I read my story on the front page of the Dallas Morning News, above the fold, next to coverage of Nelson's Mandela's death. In the coming months I was featured in various media forums. I had been quietly writing a blog to keep my out-of-state friends and family updated on my life. Strangers read it, and started contacting me, asking to come out and see the build, which became asking if they could pick up a tool to help and learn for their own builds, and we became friends. Soon I was being told that I was inspiring others. I was being told that I was *empowering* others – and I started standing up a little straighter. I realized for the first time that I enjoyed teaching. I enjoyed being a leader. I'd never in my life experienced that – I'd always been the loyal, reliable supporter in the background. It's where I'd always been comfortable.

Once I made the decision to radically alter every aspect of my life, my journey began to unfold in front of me. I'm not sure I even chose it – I think it may have chosen me. It's been a magical journey filled with synchronicities. The way events have unfolded, and the paths my path has crossed have been, and continues to be, surreal.

The personal growth aspect of my build is difficult to put my finger on but I have am definitely a different person now than I was back then. I had a lot of time for personal introspection while I was building and I think the realization of how much I had learned about myself sort of crept up on me. I became very grounded. My house grounded me. I was very in touch with my energy, the energy of my house, and the earth's energy. When I arrived at my build site each morning it was as though I had arrived at a place of meditation – as if a weight lifted off of me. And in fact, the very few times that I have been able to successfully meditate in my life were in the midst of construction of my house.[3] At the end of build days when it was time to leave my house it was like saying "good night" to a friend.

By 2012 I had been looking at tiny houses online for a year or two. I was reading stories about people like Jay Shafer and Dee Williams and countless others who were living their lives in tiny houses and their lifestyles seemed so unattainable. But once I started paying attention I realized I personally knew tons of people who were leading unconventional lives! Friends of friends were traveling the world, teaching English in foreign countries. They were living on houseboats. They were teaching AIDS prevention in Africa. They were buying one-way cruise tickets across the pond and following their dream of attending Oxford. I *knew* all those people. They were *living*. They were taking risks. How in the heck did they orchestrate their lives of simplicity? I felt like I was missing out on some big secret.

One afternoon during the months that I was driving back and forth to my build site, I looked at the cardboard box on my passenger seat. Inside was a measuring tape, a book on carpentry, my construction plans, a notebook of lists and telephone notes, a pair of gloves, the keys to my new house, and my water bottle. On the floorboard were two plumbing roof vents. On my feet? My work boots. And I realized: I was in the thick of it. I was making it happen. Right then. I was becoming one of those people.

In the words of Eleanor Roosevelt, "Making a big life change is scary. But you know what is even scarier? Regret." I voluntarily made big changes. I am comfortable telling you that even though the changes were voluntary, I had, and I still have, days that I worry. I'm doing things I've never done before. I'm living in a way that I have never lived before. Of course there is fear; but there is also challenge. And anticipation. And excitement. Some days I feel like I am climbing tall mountains with rocks under my feet. But I am *challenged*. I sort of like not knowing what's coming next – I am open. I am *happy*.

When you think in your mind of your happiest days, what memories bubble up for you? For me, one word sums it up – BANina. And at the very start, "BANina Begins."

I was living in my tiny house in southern California. My dear friend Nina had recently relocated to Dallas. I was feeling a bit beat up by California, and she was feeling a bit beat up by Texas, and we decided we'd share my tiny house for a while and help each other heal. In January 2015 she came back to California and moved in.

By this time we had a bit of a history, the two of us. We first met at Jay Shafer's workshop in northern California in February of 2013. I had flown in from Dallas, Texas, and she drove in from Chico, CA with her VitaMix in the trunk of her car, carrying her ubiquitous orange messenger bag. She blew into the classroom at the last moment and took a seat my table along with our soon-to-be friend Judy. The three of us became fast friends during those 5 days.

Then I didn't see Nina, or even talk with her, really, until April 2013 when my house was framed at MAGIC Camp[4] in southern California. A few weeks before Camp she emailed me that she had taken the week off work and she was driving south to help on my build. I couldn't believe it! I felt it was such a sacrifice, she said she couldn't imagine not being there.

MAGIC Camp cemented the bond of friendship that the workshop days had formed. People watched us in action together and suspected we had been childhood friends. "How long have you guys known each other, about 30 years?" We'd look at each other, shrug, and say, "What day is it? What is this now – our 7th day together, counting the workshop?" It was hilarious right from the start.

At night we had total shenanigans. Home Depot runs for supplies and Trader Joe's runs for avocados, followed by blogging and posting photos, and cooking and eating. And we'd fall into our beds at night, exhausted, and but always laughing, only to get up at 5 a.m. (her with perfect hair, me pulling on a ball cap) the next day to do it all again. On the last day of Camp, each of the girls stood up and said what they had learned, and what their favorite parts had been. There were many girls with teary testimonials who said that Nina and were such a huge example of friendship, and how they admired how we supported each other. Nina and I were encouraged by staff to be in the front of the room for "graduation" but we wisely chose a space on the floor, with a box of tissue between us. I don't know what exactly happened to us all that week, but it changed all of us girls to the core. I think Nina and I both knew our paths would cross again, although we never could have predicted how intertwined they would become.

During Camp, I started telling her about the business we'd start together Eric & Ernie's (we were both supposed to be boys, and those would have been our names) and how it would be something tiny house related. She scoffed at me. How could that possibly happen? We were both entrenched in 25+ year careers 1,800 miles away from each other. Nina was adamant that she'd never live in Texas, but I often said I could move to California. Every time I spoke about it, Nina would throw her head back and laugh. I'd hear her tell people, "She's always talking about us working together. I don't know. How could that happen?" And then she'd just laugh.

What I couldn't have predicted was how many U-Haul trucks we would rent between us or that eventually our tweeting friends at U-Haul would ask if they could use Nina's image on the side of one of their trucks, or how many times we would cross the country with or without a tiny house and/or a tiny house trailer. I couldn't have predicted how many times we would have encounters with curious and/or serious law enforcement while eating burritos...

I slept in my loft, and Nina slept on a twin futon in my living room. Each morning I'd awaken, and crawl to the end of my loft and peer over the loft's edge to see if she was awake. We'd take one look at each other and start laughing. Eventually I'd come downstairs, make us lattes, while she'd fold up her bed and get herself upright. Then we'd sit with coffee and my book of lists and review what we had accomplished the previous day, and list what we would do that day. It became our ritual. I'd kept a book of lists for some time, but now we began numbering the "BANina Days." I still keep a book of my daily lists; sometimes it's the only way I can remember what state I was in, and when.

As for "BANina," our friend Lewis coined that term, and we readily adopted it. We ordered magnetic car placards and business cards, never realizing that it was akin to romantically intertwined celebrity couples such as "BrAngelina." That realization dawned on us much later; while perusing social media one evening we found a discussion thread where people were speculating whether or not we were a couple! We replayed several conversations from across the country back in our heads, looked at each other in horror and started laughing. The result was that Nina immediately crafted a blog post entitled something like, "We Like Boys."

We spent about three months together in southern California. We largely behaved as though we were 20-somethings in college. We had shuffled off our responsible careers and cloaked ourselves in sheer glee. We'd go to the gym, we'd take our computers to the bookstore and "work," and we'd gorge on amazing vegan foods. We were planning her build, and plotting the coming months. Despite living such freewheeling lives, our calendars were dotted with commitments in various parts of the country, making our cross-country tiny house travel plans (*#tinyhousetrip*) quite complicated. We often had calendar months on the living room floor alongside a U.S. map. All we needed were pins and bits of colored string to complete the picture that we were preparing to bust a nationwide crime ring. We often said we should be worried about not having full time jobs with benefits, and a concrete plan of where our lives were going, but we never really were. Things always seemed to work out.

March came, and one day we over lunch we decided to pick up and haul ourselves back to Dallas and do Nina's tiny house build there. This decision launched a whole new frenzy of U-Haul truck rentals, and sorting of build materials and tools in storage units, and preparing my house and her trailer for travel. Another round of purging. Another round of strategically packing the truck for what things would need to come out first, or last, and in what city.

We finally got underway, leaving Los Angeles at 5 p.m. on a Friday (the most hellish rush hour I have ever witnessed in my life) headed back to Big "D." We had shenanigans the entire way back – and this time the combined length of our travelling caravan was about 80 feet. Finding adequate spaces to pull over involved the aerial view of Google Earth. Border patrol crossings were accompanied with frantic walkie-talkie communications that involved remarks such as, "Don't pull away until you see that I'm clear too – my passport is in your house!" and other hilarity. We frequently pulled over for pre-arranged tiny house tours, and we spent one night in Kansas City as guests in the very posh Garmin International compound.

Those three months are the most fun I have ever had in my life. We both did some healing through laughter and crying – often one simply morphed into another. We learned what basics were needed for a full life – shelter, showers and food – both the tangible grocery-type of foods, and the food that nourishes our souls – friendship, challenges, problem solving, soul searching. We knew each other's demons and dreams, and we pored over all of them within the walls of my house. The house was our safe zone, our sacred space – we preferred being inside over going out anywhere – which sounds really weird, but it was true! We could go in, and close the door, and have our happy little lives inside. With guacamole and hummus.

Eventually, of course, the party had to end. We returned to Dallas, and I parked in Garland, and Nina went to live in Coppell and some semblance of responsible adult lives resurfaced. We went about our lives and her build until it was time for my summer road trip to Minnesota. We took the BANina show on the road once again!

And then there was the August 2015 Tiny House Jamboree where I was the opening speaker. Nina told me she wasn't coming and Friday morning, just before my speech as I walked around the grounds, she was hiding behind tiny houses just yards away, texting me as though she was in back in Dallas… and then revealed herself to me in the front row during my presentation – words can't explain that morning!

And then in February 2016, Nina was moving her tiny house (still under construction) for the first time, and it was my turn to surprise her! I had to hide in the shrubs for an hour, drinking coffee (and of course, eating breakfast tacos) because I didn't know exactly what time she was arriving. It was a great reunion, and a successful house move.

We are always at each other's side for the big things. We always "show up." It's what we do.

My house has provided me with a slice of life that I never could have foreseen. It has nurtured me, pushed me, protected me, given me great friendships far and wide, inspired me and given me my footing. It's my sacred space, my proudest accomplishment, my safe haven and yes, my friend.

It used to be when I heard the phrase, "tiny house community," I thought of small houses on a piece of land. Over the last year that has changed – now when I hear that phrase I think of *people*. The tiny houses *are* amazing. They are cute, they are liberating – they teach you how much you can do – but the thing that stands out the most about them for me are the people that surround them.

I've been a tiny house advocate and luminary[5] for a few years now – first unintentionally, and now intentionally – living by example, being a spokesperson, and opening my house for strangers to see. I didn't plan on being a spokesperson – it just sort of happened. And then I discovered that inspiring others inspired ME. And along the way I learned even more about myself. And now, it's not just about me. It's about you. It's about us.

I've grown to love telling my story of transition, and then opening my house for the audience to come and stand inside and look around. I remember the first time that I stood in a tiny house. It was Jay's Gifford. Even though we were bursting with anticipation, each of us was exceedingly polite and patient as we took turns removing our shoes and stepping inside in wonder to take it all in. I recall it vividly – stepping onto the porch, and into the hallway between the kitchen and the bath – and just taking in all the details. Likewise I recall the first time that I opened my house for exhibit. It was at Earth Day Texas in Dallas, in April 2014. Friends and I had literally completed installation of the lights and mini-blinds at midnight the night before, inside the exhibit hall, and I had 1,000 people a day for the next two days walk through my house. It was mind-blowing. The joy of the tiny house tour experience is why I open my front door to strangers almost daily. I love being there for people's first time in a tiny house – to see the wonder on their faces, to see them light up as they have a concrete vision of what their life could be like. It's why I sit on my desk facing my front door during my open house events – so that I can see people's faces when they step inside for the first time – for me, it's magic.

But my crème de la crème is being with people in an immersive environment and talking with them about choice, and choosing to have less, and helping them think outside the traditional box and witnessing their realization that they have choices. Now it isn't just about me – it's about everyone else, too. "Why can't you change the way you live? You can. It's not easy, but you CAN. Let's talk about what is holding you back." What feeds my soul is that quiet moment when people realize they have choice, regardless of what society has taught them is expected of them. When the switch of realization flips it's like watching them awaken and wiggle their toes. Tiny houses are not for everyone – I know that. And even if with the power of choice they don't choose tiny, I love that I stretched their mind a bit in a new direction.

And now life has brought me more change. Along with my sisters I am care-taking our aging parents, and I also completely unexpectedly fell in love. As a result of those two things my year and a half of tiny house travel following good weather has come to a pause in Minnesota. I'm so grateful that my tiny house and my current lifestyle allow me the flexibility to adjust to life's circumstances. I'm also frustrated with the realization that my house is not big enough for two people. I don't exactly know what to do about that or what the future holds. But I know the adventure continues, and I'm excited to see what's around the next corner – for all of us.

Family-Style Minimalism

Kim Kasl

Kim Kasl and her family of four swapped their 2000 square foot house for their lovely 267 square foot Tiny in September of 2014 with the intention of becoming a one-income family that homeschools, pursues passions and adventure, and says Yes! to every opportunity. Through pictures and stories on her website BlessThisTinyHouse.com, Kim's pursuit is to normalize family-style minimalism in a culture where "stuff-gluttony" is the accepted norm and to affirm for families that on their journey to family-style minimalism they will remove the excess and be abundantly b*less*ed!

We are normal people, whatever normal is. There just is not one identifiable quality that makes someone a good candidate to live in a tiny house or even to live a minimalist lifestyle. Our family of four consists of myself, my husband Ryan, and our kids Sully, age seven, and Story, age six. We live in a 267 sq. ft. tiny house making our home a bit extreme in regards to the accepted or normal living situation in American culture. What I think is important to communicate before exploring *family-style minimalism* is that it is not for *other* people who have some intrinsic quality that *you* do not have. Minimalism is for anyone and everyone. It is not an exclusive lifestyle for only the most extreme people. I would argue that minimalism is quite normal. The problem is that as a culture we are so consumed with material possessions that our current reality is abnormal to our true nature. In the course of our family's downsizing process and resulting realizations, we came to term this unfortunate iniquity "stuff-gluttony."

Prior to our family's purge and transition into family-style minimalism we weren't particularly blind to our own stuff-gluttony but we were sidetracked by it. We didn't fully realize the problems our stuff was causing for us, nor the limits it was putting on our freedom.

Confession: we had a lot of stuff. To our defense, we were pretty wise about spending on limited budget. And while our stuff was not the direct cause of our debt, as we had both a mortgage and steadily increasing student loans, it did contribute at times. The only purchases we ever made were at thrift stores or items that were deeply discounted. The irony is that as a result of our frugality we kept everything. Because we couldn't afford anything of great value we place great, undue value on the things we did have. In addition to keeping everything we had, we accepted everything we were given. And because of our apparent state of need, paired with the love of their only grandchildren and inner drive to help, our parents gave us a ton of stuff!

We were blessed and thankful to never have to worry about clothing for the kids. Both Grandmas loved a good deal and bought any type of clothing or toy for the kids even if it was not yet the right size or age appropriate. There were bins of clothes stored for every age, size, weather condition and event for both genders for present, future, as well as past (just in case a third child came along). Because we never knew what may be given to us at any given time there were a number of instances where doubles and even triples would turn up. For example, I would find a pair of thrift store snow pants for next year and buy them. Unbeknownst to me the Grandmas would both have bought snow pants as well! Months would go buy, previous snow pant purchases would be forgotten and a fourth pair might be purchased! From the kids' Grandma's perspective, our state of needs seemed to never be met, so they continued to supply.

As the Mom, I was constantly organizing and taking inventory and the task was completely out of hand. Our house was a chaotic system of incoming items being stored for future use. I was responsible for making sure each item was used at the proper time, and then stored away neatly *just in case* it might be needed again.

Sometimes I handled this chaotic job with skill. Other times though it was the most ridiculous job for a stay-at-home-mother and small business-owner to maintain. Ryan and I did not dream of a luxury vacation with each other. Rather, we dreamed of a week in which someone would magically come along with nothing better to do but watch our kids and manage our day jobs, while we clean and organize our house! That was our fantasy!

Our stuff was literally taking over our lives. Stuff-gluttony! Its reach extended far beyond kids' clothes. It crept into Ryan and I's closets and drawers too. We were holding on to clothing of every size and style we had ever worn. And the kitchen! We had a so many dishes! We could easily prepare a meal for a party of fifty prepared using every kind of kitchen tool and served with a full set of dinnerware for each guest. And the toys! The toy debacle rivaled the clothing situation. After several attempts on my part to organize the toy room, that consequently followed, every time, with the devastating experience of watching the kids undo my fancy systems of toy filing with one swift blow, ignoring my cries, "Put everything back where you found it!" I gave up!

There were bins in the storage room, garage, barn, and closets, and the stuff kept coming. We were drowning in our own belongings, holding onto the security of *just in case.*

I want to emphasize that *we were so thankful for our needs being met.* These things were sent our way out of love and provision. Our needs were real. The problem was in the arrangement of our situation; our lifestyle was so upside down. Putting a stop to the incoming flow would not have been a solution by itself. We needed a complete reconstruction.

When Ryan and I started evaluating our lifestyle and values, made the decision to become a one-income, homeschooling family living in a tiny house and made the commitment to reach our goals, we didn't use the words *downsize* or *purge.* We didn't even discuss our stuff. "You know, we'll have to get rid of a lot of stuff." "Yeah." They were empty statements rather than real discussions. Getting rid of stuff was just a necessary part of the process.

We started very slowly. Initially, we had a garage sale. Weeks and weeks of work culminated into more work. We made $500, which we used on a car repair, and we were left just wishing that the garage sale had worked. We had expected it to be a solution in getting rid of everything. We still had a ton of stuff! A garage sale was not an efficient or successful way to get rid of all of our stuff.

The kids were three and four when we had the garage sale and they did not enjoy it. Sure, we used it as an opportunity to learn a little about money, sales, and trading but they had to give something up in order to get the payment. On top of that, it wasn't their choice to have a garage sale. The selling of their items was imposed on them, albeit gently, and in the context of a lesson. But I'm sure they could have thought of something more enjoyable to do than watch people walk away with their toys all weekend. It was a hard lesson for toddlers.

After the garage sale I pulled the book *The Treasure Principle* off of my shelf. I do not remember how I obtained it but am blessed to have read it at what seemed to be exactly the right time. It gave me a new perspective for my own possessions. It referenced Matthew 6:19-21, "Do not store up for yourselves treasures on earth, where moths and rust destroy, and where thieves break in and steal. But store up for yourselves treasures in heaven, where moth and rust cannot destroy, and thieves do not break in and steal. For where your treasure is, there your heart will be also." Through reading that book I realized that none of this stuff was really ours. We are just the *managers* of God's stuff. Each item was a blessing! (We happened to have a ton of blessings.) God was telling us that His plan for us was shifting. We needed to leave these things behind. It was time for us to pass these blessings on.

When I viewed our possessions as God's instead of ours I began making more rational decisions. Overcoming stuff-gluttony became much easier. "What do I want to do with this?" became, "What does God want me to do with this?" And God pretty much *always* says: "Give." God lit this fire in me and we started shedding everything.

It was not hard. I'd like to officially report that putting your stuff on the curb with a free sign is much easier that hosting a garage sale.

On occasion, we dropped off small loads at Goodwill. It wasn't my favorite route because the end owner did not get the item for free, which makes the item more of purchase instead of a gift. Someone in the middle profited. We preferred to take giant pickup-truck loads to the church. The church hosted "open-closet" hours in which everyone was invited to walk in and take whatever they needed for free.

Giving was something we celebrated with our kids. We cheered and exchanged high-fives at the church as we unloaded our truck. The kids carried heavy boxes of clothes they used to wear, reminisced over tiny shoes and costumes worn when they were babies, held doors open for each other, and chatted about the kids who might wear clothes Sully and Story had grown out of and play with the toys that they used to play with when they were younger.

Giving is an awesome experience for everyone. It was much more fun and beneficial than watching other kids come to their home, pick-up their toys, play with them, and purchase them at a garage sale. Teaching the lesson of gift giving and taking care of others is so much more valuable.

The kids' success in acclimating to their new tiny space was of utmost importance to Ryan and I. The purpose that drove our move to the tiny house was a better life for them. Throughout the process of purging we shared our excitement and positive attitude with Sully and Story, and were carefully sensitive to their transition.

Surely, if we had walked into the toy room with giant garbage bags, filled them, and walked out saying, "We gotta get rid of everything! Sorry kids. None of this is going to fit in your tiny room in the tiny house!" we would have been met by two, sobbing, blubbering, panicky, traumatized children! Think about it like this. You take your family on vacation to a new, adventurous destination. After several days away, do you think they miss their toys? Could they list off their top ten toys they miss most? Maybe they could; they might struggle after six or seven. What if you ask them to list *all* of their toys, what toys in their collection could they list? They would likely only be able to remember a small percentage. Once out of sight, they are out of mind. And while it would have been awesome to go away on a wonderful vacation and return to find that someone had sorted through our belongings and left only our top ten favorite items, it didn't happen that way. We had to process through every single possession.

Letting go of items became really easy and even a little addicting. Once the house started to really empty out I would dance around the house singing Red Hot Chili Peppers, "Give it away, give it away, give it away, give it away now!" Those were the only lyrics of the song that I knew, but it doesn't matter, for me it was the best part!

Each item had to pass a series of questions.
- Does this item serve an important purpose in our life or do we possess it *just in case?*

- Can I imagine its placement and easy fit in the tiny house?
- Will this item be more purposeful in someone else's possession?
- What is God's purpose for this item?

Once an item was destined to be given away I had to decide if it should be passed on to another family member (I have a large, close family that consistently shares and exchanges hand-me-down items), returned to someone who had given it to us, donated at church, or just be put on the curb for free. Sorting, piling, organizing, calling, offering, posting on the Craigslist free section, and delivering ensued. Our moving process was nothing like the average moving from one house to another. Usually you can say, "Well, I don't know if we want to keep that, but we'll decide when we get there." and then shove it in a box. In this case though there were no boxes, no packing tape, no storage garage, and no regular garage. A decision had to be made for every single item.

The kids' process was much easier, thank goodness!

We pulled out Sully and Story's favorite toy bins, which were really just colorful, glorified laundry baskets with wheels and handles designed for kids, and gave them a special purpose. I brought the kids into their room and said, "Okay! These are your very special toy bins. Look around your room and pick out your *favorite* toys and put them in your toy bin. You get to bring *everything* that you can fit in your toy bin to the tiny house!" At ages four and six this was a task that they could handle and even enjoy. They encountered

a few hard decisions. I watched as they considered the amount of space that a big stuffed animal took up. Keeping one large toy might mean leaving behind several small toys that they might value just as much. As they asked questions, I tried to always respond with a positive "yes" or "can do!" answer. "Can I put more in it?" "Yes, I bet you can fit a lot!" "Can I bring all of my toy cars? "You can bring your favorite ones!" "Can I bring my tutu?" "Yes! Fold it up really tiny so you can fit more toys!" We framed every aspect of the kids' downsizing in a positive, affirming way.

We kept the activity short and sweet. We cheered, celebrated, and encouraged. As toys were set aside, we emphasized that even though they weren't our favorite, they would probably become another child's favorite toy. That way we bypassed the feeling of loss or neglecting a toy and leaving it unwanted. I think it's important to emphasize that we didn't say, "You can *only* bring what fits in your bin." but instead "You get to bring *everything* that fits in your bin." Sacrifice vs. Celebration. We always used words that celebrated.

When the activity was over we moved onto something else quickly. I discreetly tucked the bins away and kept them out of sight (and out of mind!). This left Ryan and I to slowly pick away at the left over items when they weren't looking. They already knew and agreed to the decision that they would be donated and played with by other children and it was unnecessary at their ages to rehash that and draw it out.

They had only watched us put things out on the curb for free that they weren't attached to and we enjoyed watching from our big living room window as people took the free items. "What do you think they'll do with it?" "I bet they're excited that they found that for free!" and we waved to the people as they drove away. When the kids put toys to put on the curb, we did the same. We watched a young family load up a slide and we expressed excitement that the slide would be with new kids who would love playing with it in their backyard like we did. We noted that we were moving on to new adventures and looking forward to the playground we would have just a few steps from our front door.

Occasionally, Story would look outside and exclaim, "Oh no, we can't give that away!" One time it was Daddy's fifteen-pound hand weights. Even though Daddy didn't want them anymore, she decided that she did. So, we ran outside to get them. "*Yes*, we can keep them." If it was hard for her, in that moment, to part with them, we respected that. That doesn't mean that our kids were ruling the house. It means that our four-year-old was watching everything that she was accustomed to drift away and we needed to be careful in her processing of that. It was not too challenging for me to bring things back in the house at her request and then just run them back out when her awareness shifted. Being a parent to little ones is comical like that everyday anyway.

Shelves, drawers, closets, and entire rooms cleared and emptied. I loved the clean emptiness and realized that the clutter in our home had reflected itself as clutter in my mind. We were becoming liberated from the ties our stuff had on us and we felt a sense of freedom and joy. We had let go of everything that we had been holding onto *just in case*. Those *just in case* items are only important if something bad happens and they represented fear. Our homes should not be storage units for fear. I want our home to be a welcome retreat with the security and strength of family.

It's so normal in our culture to surround ourselves completely with stuff. We have been taught to believe that our stuff defines us, helps us express ourselves, and will make us happier. Couldn't we define ourselves in a better way by what we do with our time? Couldn't we better express ourselves through art, sports, words, or music? Couldn't we find more happiness in relationships with the people around us? Stuff distracts us from finding our true selves and purposes. It steals away our attention.

Life in the tiny house didn't help us exactly in the way s that we thought it would. We thought that having fewer expenses would make it possible for me to stay home and guide the kids' learning but *they don't need my guidance*. The kids are thriving and it's a result of the *minimalism*.

The toys and the screens and the clutter didn't allow their minds the freedom to drive their own creative process. Toys no longer entertain them, guide them, and occupy their thoughts. We removed the excess, the distractions, the useless *stuff*, and our kids have flourished because of it. They guide their own education! They ask questions and seek information according to their interests. They have an intrinsic motivation to achieve. They have tools, information packed books, craft supplies, and nature. Sully and Story seek out new ideas and creations. They are makers, doers, creators, leaders, explorers, musicians, builders, innovators, experimenters, and pretenders.

The abundance that stuff-gluttony provided couldn't improve our lives, situation, relationships, or health. Family-style minimalism doesn't leave us wanting because it didn't take away anything *good!* For us, it peeled away everything that hindered us from reaching goals and living a more valuable life. Underneath was an abundance of goodness and blessings.

We've easily settled into our tiny house and the life we looked forward to living in it. Ryan is finished with school and he loves his new position as a Special Education Administrator. I love the constant roll of activity as a homemaker in a homeschooling tiny house. I get to keep up with the tiny house movement, research opportunities for Sully and Story, and jump into new adventures and road trips whenever we feel the desire.

Family-style minimalism is not extreme. Looking back at the lifestyle we left behind, it is evident that *that* was the extreme situation. Now, we function at a pace that feels more like normal, enjoy peace that is more like normal, at a price that is much more normal. Family-style minimalism *is* normal...and awesome.

Dream Big, Live Small!

Living the Life You Were Designed to Live

Lora Higgins

Lora is a blogger, consultant and public speaker that has a passion for helping other people Dream BIG, live small and experience more in their everyday life! You can follow all her Tiny House adventures at tinyhouse-teacher.com. Moving into a tiny house changed her life and in *Turning Tiny* she is excited to tell you how and why it might just change yours too!

If you had asked me two years ago about tiny houses, I would have had no idea what you were talking about and I certainly would not have been in a position to talk about intentional living or lifestyle design. In fact, I was quite comfortable living in my 3- bedroom, 2-bath, 1,800 square foot townhouse. In my mind, I was living the American dream. A nice home, two cars (don't ask!) and a house full of stuff that I thought I wanted and needed. But life is funny, sometimes just when we think we have it all, we realize we are living the wrong dream.

Although my life looked like a version of the American dream I had always believed in, and thought I wanted, if I was honest with myself, it wasn't really going that well. I was stuck in a job that was toxic for me. I had a boss who I didn't see eye-to-eye with which created more stress than I had ever experienced before as a working adult.

I had recently gone through a divorce and was working on paying off some debt. I had just closed on my nice townhouse, but I was constantly feeling like I needed to fix it up. I was on a constant "earn to spend" treadmill and I had no idea how to get off. Most days I just felt trapped and worn out.

Over the course of a year, the worn-out turned into burn-out and ultimately depression.

The good news about the situation I was in is that it forced me to look a little deeper. I couldn't pretend that things were working well or that I was happy with my life. I realized I no longer wanted to trade my time at a job I didn't enjoy to pay for the stuff I never had time to use. I no longer wanted to spend my free time cleaning my space and trying to keep up with maintenance and repairs. And more importantly, I no longer wanted a life that left me feeling stressed and unhappy.

The good news about getting stuck in a position where everything just feels "off" is that we often start looking for other options. I realized if I wanted to change my life, the first step was to change my economic situation. At first, this included simply thinking about selling the extra car, or moving to a slightly smaller space. It meant looking at different job opportunities and deciding if I could pay the bills with a different form of employment. Eventually my plan included downsizing to a tiny house, moving across country and finding a new job.

I wish I could say that my first exposure to tiny houses was love at first sight. But I assure you it was not! In fact, when I first read about the idea in Tammy Strobel's book, *You Can Buy Happiness (and it's cheap!)*, I thought she was crazy. I couldn't imagine getting rid of enough stuff to move into a space so small. In fact, I had no idea who would ever decide to live like that. My adamant declaration of, "I could never do that!" should have been a warning.

I remember loving Tammy's ideas of aligning your time and money with the things that were really important to you, but I didn't initially embrace the idea of smaller living. I had to really look at what I wanted to accomplish in life. I had to spend time analyzing how I lived in my current space and what I would be giving up when I downsized. I also had to spend the time changing my fundamental definitions of what it meant to "live well." It took a few more months of soul searching and planning before I decided that tiny living was the right choice for me.

Over time, I realized that a tiny house was a perfect solution to some of the challenges I faced. My tiny house gave me the ability to move across country easily, which allowed me to apply for a new job. I realized it was the perfect solution because it gave me everything I was looking for, fewer expenses, more freedom and the ability to off-load the "stuff" that no longer added value to my life.

The best part about downsizing for me was that it taught me how to dream again. Dreams that I had forgotten I had. Dreams I had buried under piles of stuff and hours of meaningless work. Dreams that I was afraid to dream because I had no idea how I would accomplish what I wanted to do in life. Downsizing fundamentally changed how I viewed my life. It allowed me to spend my time and money in a way that was more consistent with what I want in my life on a daily basis. Living Tiny has made me a more intentional, grateful and happy person, and I want to share those insights with you.

Dream BIG!

I believe the first step in any journey worth living is giving yourself permission to Dream BIG! Most of us live complicated lives full of stuff, commitments and relationships that keep us from truly taking the time to dream. We spend hours trying to fit our lives into the little boxes we think we need to check to be happy. Most of us stop dreaming as we grow up, but if we want to live the lives we were designed to live, we have to be brave and take the time to start dreaming again. More importantly, we have to be willing to share those dreams with those around us.

As children, we all understand the power of imagination and dreaming. All it takes is spending a few minutes on the playground with children to hear all of the fantastic things they believe about life. They talk about being doctors, astronauts, teachers and ballerinas. Their imaginations are endless and their eyes are filled with wonder. They know without question they can do anything they want.

Unfortunately, most of us stop dreaming as we grow up. The world around us slowly conditions us to reach for the things that are "attainable" the things that are "practical" and the things that don't seem "too crazy." When someone asks us about our dreams as adults, they include more practical things, like finding a "good job," having a nice house or simply being able to retire someday.

What if we all reached for the crazy and ambitious dreams? What if we used our strengths, talents and experiences to make our lives better, the lives our families better and the community as a whole better?

The first step on my tiny house journey was giving myself permission to dream. My current dream includes helping other people live more intentional lives, it means making a positive impact on those around me. My dream life is full of work that feeds my soul and is continually moving towards a better version of me. My dream also includes practical things like retiring early from my current job, opening my own business and moving to the beach! What if you gave yourselves permission to dream again? What would your life look like? Who would it include? What would you be doing? How could you help others? Dreams are what give us the inspiration and enthusiasm for life, and if nurtured correctly, they are what can make life worth living.

Design Your Life

Once you start allowing yourself to dream big, you can begin to design a life that reflects your values and goals. Lifestyle design is popular because it allows you to make conscious choices about how you spend your time and money. It allows you to get out of the "rat race," and make better choices for you and your family. It allows you to build a home that truly reflects who you are and who you want to be.

For me, making conscious choices about how I wanted my life to look was the start of a fun and exciting journey.

When I started my downsizing journey, I knew I wanted no debt, fewer bills and more flexibility in terms of where I lived and how much I got to travel. I am still in the process of getting to this stage, but I am moving forward. I have realized that more stuff won't make me happier and smaller spaces encourage more intentional choices. To me, that has been the biggest benefit of living tiny.

It's easy for us to think our lives need to "look" a certain way to be successful. Sometimes cultural and family pressures make it challenging to do the things that make us feel alive. But here is what I have learned after my first couple of years in my tiny house. Creating your dream life is all about being true to who you are and what you want out of life. Your life doesn't have to look like anyone else's it just has to reflect who you are and who you want to be.

One of the things that I have found frustrating about this journey is the misconception that we are all going tiny for the same reasons and that we all have the same goals. Nothing could be further from the truth. Your life looks a lot different than mine and I am guessing we came to the decision to downsize for different reasons. I believe that is one of the best things about this lifestyle.

Tiny living allows many of us to reach our goals and live in-line with our values. For some the desire to downsize is driven by the goal of not having a mortgage, for others it is to focus on environmentally conscious living and others just want more mobility and flexibility. All of these reasons are great and your reason is great too. Don't get in the mindset that you need to downsize for a certain reason and don't feel the need to justify why you want to make this lifestyle decision.

One of the reasons tiny houses are gaining so much popularity is because they give us an alternative to the "American Dream," or rather they let us live our dream in a way that is meaningful to us. I know some people struggle with what others think about their dream when they start their downsizing journey. I will tell you, you will meet critics and skeptics who argue you can't live this way. I am here to tell you, you can.

As you think about designing your life, take the time to review your goals and values. Decide how you want to use your space each day. Make sure you know what activities add joy to your life and what material possessions make you feel connected to your space. For instance, when I downsized I kept some of my books. To me reading is not only a fun and relaxing activity and it also helps me grow as an individual. Although, some people think the space I devote to my books is wasted in my 234 square feet, to me the books add value. If you can articulate your why, you will find the critics and skeptics a lot less daunting!

I love my tiny house. For me, it is a huge part of my intentional living journey. It taught me the difference between needs and wants and made me much more conscious of how I spend my time and money. My tiny house gives me the freedom and flexibility that I want in this stage of my life. My lifestyle change has also encouraged me to share my new outlook on life with others, which has been incredibly exciting and rewarding. However, I know that I probably won't always live in my tiny house full-time, and that is okay too.

This lifestyle is a perfect fit for me right now, but here is my word of caution, a tiny house can't solve all your problems or fill all the voids and if not planned carefully, it might create more headaches for you than you currently have. For me, my tiny house is a great tool and fun lifestyle that fits in to the rest of my plan. It is imperative that you understand what motivates you and why. I challenge each of you to think through what makes you happy. Who are the people you want to spend time with and why? Understanding these things can help you decide if tiny living is right for you.

As you are creating your life plan, make sure you are honest with yourself about whether or not a tiny house is a good decision for you and your family. It is easy to get excited about this lifestyle. The national attention, the almost cult like following and the enthusiasm for tiny house can be exciting and intoxicating. A tiny house can be a powerful component in helping you achieve your dreams, but much like a large home, by itself a tiny house is just a structure to live in day-to-day. Take the time to evaluate if and how a tiny house fits into your larger life plan before you start building or sign a contract with a builder.

Take Action

Perhaps the biggest advice I can give you about this lifestyle is to remember to take action every day. It is easy to get overwhelmed with the whole process of lifestyle design and downsizing. One of the most important questions to ask yourself each day is, "are my actions today moving me in the direction I want to go?" If not, then stop what you are doing, make a choice, make a change and move in a new direction.

Again, I challenge each of you to slow down and take the time to really look at your goals, values, time, and money situation. Make sure tiny living is the right fit. Once you do decide it is, move forward! I see a lot of people who dream about going tiny. They have a Pinterest board of their favorite designs and they know what they want to keep, but they stay in the planning stage for months or years. Sometimes there are legitimate reasons to delay the decision to downsize, but for many it is just a result of a lack of intentional action.

I know it can be overwhelming to change your lifestyle, but know that there are tons that have gone before you and lots of great resources to make your journey more fun and less stressful. Deciding if you want to build or buy a tiny home, figuring out where to park, and downsizing are all big decisions, and choices that can be daunting. Know you aren't alone!

I encourage each of you to make a list of what you need to do to make your dream life a reality. Then break those things into smaller steps that seem less overwhelming. Once you've done that, take action each month, each week and each day. Make intentional choices about how you spend your time, and take action each day to move you in the direction you want to go.

Remember that sometimes bold action makes a big change less overwhelming. I actually decided to downsize, put a contract on my tiny house, moved across country, started a new job and got rid of almost eighty percent of what I owned in less than three months. Although, this was stressful in some ways, it also removed the indecision and barriers I had to taking action. I am certainly not advocating such radical changes for everyone, but sometimes bold action is required to make progress. I am encouraging you to not let excuses and doubts keep you from living the life you were designed to live.

Life is never a linear journey. Although I am huge advocate of dreaming, planning and taking action, I also realize that over time our goals can change. As you get ready to make this lifestyle choice, try to remember that if it ends up not being a good fit, you can always change again. Living an intentional life, one that truly allows you to be the best you and enjoy every minute, requires constant work and occasional adjustments. This may mean that a tiny house is just part of your journey.

As I have said, I love my tiny house, but I also know that this most likely will not be my lifestyle forever. I still have a full time job and I am still working my way out of debt, but I have a plan. I am confident this is the right choice for me at this moment. I also know that over time, this goal may change some, and that is okay. Don't let fear stop you from taking action.

When I started this journey, there were lots of aspects of my life that were out of balance and in some ways broken. My tiny house has helped me move forward. It has given me new enthusiasm for life, but I am not done growing as an individual. I am not done trying new things or reaching for new dreams. Remember you might not be able to get from your starting point to your dream destination in one stop. But you can move in the right direction.

Dream Big! Be bold, take action and live the life you've always wanted!

Tiny Ticket to Adventure

Christian Parsons

Alexis Stephens and Christian Parsons of Tiny House Expedition, are a filmmaker duo and ordinary couple taking an extraordinary road trip across the US & Canada with their DIY tiny house on wheels in tow. Through their documentary storytelling and direct community engagement, they seek to inspire people to think BIG and build small as means to provide more quality, affordable housing & more connected communities. Creative use of tiny housing is cultivating more connected community experiences and more meaningful relationships, for multi-millionaires to those transitioning out of homelessness; the tiny house itself is just the beginning of *Turning Tiny*!

Some people might think that this is a little out of the norm to but it wasn't that hard for me to go tiny. I have always been really good at adapting to my environment. I find a comfortable place in the space available and I am able to make the most out of it. I lived in a 400 sq. ft. apartment for years, traveled the country for a 40-day road trip and loved both. I even traveled around the world for two months with mostly just a suitcase. Those are the times I've been the happiest because I'm having a meaningful experience. That's what I see living in a tiny house on wheels as: a means to create more experiences.

I've been a homeowner before but it was much different. When I was newly married, I owned a 2,500 square foot, five bedroom, 100-year-old house. Buying such a big house was an adventure but became a burden very quickly. It was a lot of house to maintain, not to mention to heat. In winter we blocked off the upstairs because we couldn't afford to heat it all. After only owning the house for two years we divorced, and I knew there was no way I could afford my oversized home alone. I sold the house, most of what was in it, put all my remaining stuff in a 8 x 10 x 8 foot box and headed west. I knew it was time to go back to a simpler life.

Over the next couple of years I began to realize selling the house and having less gave me so much more. More time, more experiences, more interactions with the world outside my door. This was a revelation and part of what started my path to building, traveling and living in a tiny house on wheels.

It wasn't hard for me to just pick up and go. Traveling the United States has always been a part of my life whether it was when I was a kid car camping with my parents and my brother in Upstate NY, or as an adult, snowboarding with friends at Jackson Hole. I've always wanted to see new places and meet new people. Traveling across the country either, in a plane or a car made me think very thoughtfully about the things I absolutely need. Every time I would travel I would realize there was something else I should have brought, and something I should have left at home.

Jump ahead five or so years, after some time living in Park City, Utah and Brooklyn, NY and in North Carolina; I find this girl Alexis. After dating for just a short time we took a road trip to a place that wasn't too long of a drive, but somewhere completely new and different. We took five minutes, while looking at a map, to figure out our next ten days of vacation. It was Michigan, of course, one state I hadn't been to yet and neither had Alexis. It was about ten hours from Winston-Salem and knew we would find some interesting things on the way. So we went.

It didn't take long to realize that traveling together is a blast. The long time on the road didn't seem that long and space in the tent didn't seem that small. We found a rhythm in our days on the road. Sleeping in a tent and cooking on a camping stove; we found our strengths and weaknesses. We complemented each other very well. Alexis let me have my OCD moments, and she navigated us to all the great places. We saw many new things and realized how much we enjoyed doing this together. We ended up talking about the trip a lot in the coming months, and thought about other ways to travel together like renting a van or buying a teardrop trailer. Then it switched to building a teardrop, after finding out how much they cost. Not long after, I told Alexis about this thing called a tiny house on wheels (THOW). We started talking about THOWs a lot the next couple of weeks, but didn't really have anything set in stone. I just thought it was a cool thing.

Then Alexis hits me with a pitch! "Let's build a THOW, travel the country and shoot a documentary on tiny house communities." To me that sounded like a blast. I saw this as an opportunity to do so many things that I enjoyed, travel to different places, meet new people and hear great stories from people in the tiny house world, plus build my own tiny house! But most of all spend more time and share all those experiences with a woman I love. This project was right up my alley. The traveling is something I want to always be doing, and this meant I could do it and sleep in my own bed every night. How cool is that? Having my bed was one of the few conditions I had before starting this project. Having good A/C was another; I've lived in NC for a long time and humidity and summer are two things I don't like very much. One other was to spend a good amount of time in New Mexico, one of the most beautiful and weird states I've been to. I also wanted to hit a bunch of national parks on our days off. But the A/C and bed were the most important things.

The idea of actually building a house never seemed daunting to me; it was so much more exciting than daunting. The crazy thing is, I'm a photographer not a carpenter. I've never had any formal training in carpentry. I'd never framed anything, and I'd never done a complete project from start to finish using those skills. I tell people, when we are showing the house, "I know how to use tools and not hurt myself." And that is totally true. Growing up my father worked on every house we ever lived in. I learned from helping him and watching him work on everything that makes a house function. When he looks at some photos or sees a drawing of how something goes together, he can do it. I picked that up from him and that is what gave me the confidence that I could build our own tiny house on wheels. Thank you for that confidence, Dad. I was ready to build! I was ready to build a cute little house with all those cool little things that did like seven other things. A sofa that turns into a desk that is also a bed, and it makes coffee, sharpens knives and plays guitar. You know like in that tiny house on that show. All the multifunctional things in the tiny house excited me. Trying to think up clever ways to save space, like building shelves inside the studs of a wall, are the great things about a tiny house design.

After deciding to build a tiny house, we had to design it. I didn't want to build just a box with a bathroom and a kitchen; I wanted to build something extremely useful. Made for the way we spend our time at home and to enhance the experience of living, or sometimes just to make it easy. Alexis and I are both tall so we wanted some things that make life a little easier like 40" high countertops. Having the counters and stove higher up make cooking and even cleaning dishes in the sink much easier. Having as many big windows as possible was another thing we felt was a must. Always having that connection to the outside makes the house feel lighter. It also draws me out more to experience the world.

But to complete the design and to physically start the build, we needed a foundation. A THOW needs some wheels. So we started where everyone should start when building a tiny house on wheels, picking a trailer size. We knocked around going big, about 28 feet long and 8 feet wide, just so we could get a washer dryer unit in, and a nice long set of stair with adequate storage. Then we realized with as much traveling as we were planning to do – in the ballpark of 20,000 miles – we should make it just a bit smaller and more compact. We decided on a 20' trailer and to build inside the wheel wells, and have a full front porch to sip iced tea on. Building on top of the metal frame of the trailer instead of out to the edge of the wheel wells seemed stronger and more stable to pull behind a truck. So with that decision made we began to lay out our new life.

So what does a house require? And what parts are we sure we absolutely need, and how can we fit it all in our scale of an average house? Looking at how we lived our life in our 900 square foot house helped us figure out what was needed in our THOW. One of our new tiny house friends, James Taylor (no, the other one) had such a great idea to help figure out how often you use your things in your big home, to know what you really need in your tiny home. For a couple of months James would keep track of the items in his house he touched and used, by putting a colored dot sticker on that object he every time he used it. So if he woke up and made a cup of coffee with the coffee maker, it got a dot. Or open the fridge, dot, did laundry, dot; you get the idea. At the end of a few months, he realized how much he was using the things in his apartment and had his tiny house on wheels built accordingly. This is why he doesn't have a stove only a microwave, and why he has a washer/dryer where you might find a stove. Also why he has his 57" flat screen TV in his tiny house. Yes, 57 inches! Alexis and I watched it once; it's like being at a movie theater. It's how he relaxes, and it makes him happy. Well, I knew we didn't need space for a 57 inch TV. I could think of some things that I definitely wanted in our tiny house. These ideas came mostly from how were already living our lives. I know our tiny house would need to sleep three. Alexis has a 9-year-old son that will travel with us sometimes, so 2 lofts were needed for sure. We wanted to make G-man happy and feel included in the design process, so we asked him for input on what he wanted in his room. He came up with things I never thought of, like a desk. He needed a flat table to do his Legos on, so we planned desk that folds down from the wall. G-man also thought that carrying toys up a ladder was a bad idea. He was learning about simple machines in school and came up with the idea of using a pulley system, attached to a basket, to get his toys up and down from his loft. And we did end up putting those things in his room, and he absolutely loves it.

No matter what I wanted my Sealy mattress in this house. It's so comfortable, and sleep is important to me. Ok, what else? A kitchen. Alexis like to cook more than me and uses the oven a lot, so definitely a full stove. Also a nice big sink; not one of the silly little bar sinks that I've seen in some tiny houses. Other things in the kitchen area, a small fridge to fit under the countertop, a pantry for food storage, a coffee maker for sure, and a water storage tank. Then I started thinking about function of the kitchen. I'm pretty positive we will have bowls, plates, silverware, etc. Now where do I want to put them? I wanted to be able to wash dishes and just put them away like on a drying dish rack, but knew I couldn't use a real dish rack. After some leg-

work, I figured it out. I was walking through a Home Goods Store and found this thing for cooking sausages on a BBQ grill. The openings between the metal pieces looked like they could fit a total of 4 plates. So I bought it, and sure enough the plates fit in perfectly. I cut a hole just big enough for the sausage rack to fit on the shelving, and the plates slid right in and ride perfectly at 65 mph.

What about the bathroom? I don't need a bathroom sink when there is one 4 feet away from the bathroom, so nix that. Shower for sure, and let's make it comfortable 36 inches wide. I also didn't want to make it all fiberglass or plastic. So when we went to pick up our metal roof from a place called Triad Corrugated Metal in NC, we asked to go through their recycle dumpster. I pulled out enough powder coated metal sheets to do our entire shower surround.

Now for the poop conversation. It's something that every tiny houser has to deal with. So how do we want to do this; what makes the most sense for us on our planned expedition? We talked about RV and composting toilets. We kicked around the idea of a $900 Nature's Head composting toilet, but $900 for a toilet! That wasn't in our budget. So we decided on the simplest composting toilet there is: a 5-gallon bucket with a diverter to separate the solid and liquid. Alexis was cool with it too, so one $5 bucket and one $6 automotive funnel, and we have a toilet.

The living room has to be comfortable, have storage and also be used as our workspace. I wanted a sofa big enough so I could sleep on it. I came up with an Ikea hack for our table. I looked at a picture of their fold up table with storage drawers. I created my own version with only one side that folds up, and the deep drawers hold all my hard drives (we are making a movie after all). I also planned a power outlet inside, so the hard drives could always be plugged in and ready to go. Having shoe rack is a must, and a place to our hang coats. There were 10,000 other little things to design and plan that we didn't figure out until we actually started building. Coming to an agreement of what the house should contain is a great start, then it's about the layout. We chose a tiny house with an L shaped kitchen so the house feels more open and long. We laid out where things would feel right. The stove and sink in front of windows, and the front door at the end of the trailer but to one side to maximize our sofa size. We also wanted twelve windows and a door to let as much light in as possible, so it feels like outside.

Actual Building

I picked up our brand spanking new tiny house trailer from a place in PA, and after an hour or so of getting the guys to fix the trailer lights I was on my way back to NC. After getting back to NC, I spent the next couple of days checking out the trailer, all its metal parts and pieces because I've never owned a trailer before. I had been gathering materials for 6 months to use in our tiny house on wheels build, but nothing I could use to insulate or put in for subflooring. So I paused to put my plan together to insulate my brand new trailer floor, and spent a day going to Lowe's to pick out my materials. I was doing it. I was building a real tiny house on wheels! Well I was at least cutting board insulation to size to fit inside the cavities of the trailer, 2-¾ inches thick to be exact. I cut all the insulation in two days then took it all out, and did a time lapse of me putting it all back in and then starting to spray foam the gaps. TinyX tip: buy the $40 spray foam gun, and the $20 can of Great Stuff when you start your build. Trust me. At the end of each day when it's time to go home, I had to cover the trailer with tarps. I built in North Carolina, and had a very windy, rainy, snowy, cold, and hot nine months of a building. So until I had the house dried in, I had to tarp it every night and untarp it every morning. That was my most hated job the entire build.

The craziest day I had on the build was the first time Tom cut a piece of wood for the subfloor. Tom Elsner is a master carpenter and good friend. He and his family offered so much to help to make this build happen. We built the house on his land, a beautiful farm. I was able to use all of his tools, and some days, like the day we started sub floor, he was there to help. Well that day he was there to get me started. We talked, drank coffee for a while then he walked over to the trailer measured something, and then walked over to the saw and cut a piece of subfloor for the tiny house. I thought, "Oh, ok, I guess that's how you start, you just start." So we wrestled with the subfloor for a couple days, and broke I don't even know how many drill bits. In my eyes, that was really the day my build started.

Framing was really the hardest part for me. It was something I had never done before. I've just never had to. So being shown how to frame the first wall by Tom and friend, Toby, helped so much. When I completed the next wall, I had them check my work and was able to do the third wall correctly. To square the house, my buddy Pete came by to help, and man I'm so glad he did. My tiny house would have been so misshapen if he didn't come help those two days. You really need to know when to say, "I don't know how to do this," and get the help you need. After the framing and sheathing, Alexis helped me with putting in every window and with the vapor barrier. When it came to the 20' ridge beam, four of us got it up and rafters put in. That took four days. My buddy Neil and his roommate helped me sheath the roof because some steps are impossible by one's self. Even though I did about 80% of this build myself, I still needed so much help making parts of it happen. It takes a village. Thank you again everyone.

When we had the house finally dried in, I could finally stop tarping and untarping it every day. That was a glorious thing. And when we moved inside, that's where the fun stuff really happened, except maybe the plumbing and electrical. We had professionals come in and do that for us, just to be on the safe side. Some things would start going faster, when other things got slower, but I was busy every day of the build doing things, like putting up our tongue and groove walls we had pulled out of an old farm house. Or laying the newly planed 40-year-old oak boards that we found in a friend's old tobacco barn. Or building one of our favorite features of the house, the butcher block countertop. It was built from trees that fell in a tornado in Apex, NC. A tornado went over my parent's house and their neighbor's 50-acre farm. It knocked down a couple hundred trees. Alex – the neighbor – and his buddy decided to buy a mill and mill all of the wood to use for his farm, for out buildings and chicken coops. When he heard about our project from my parents, and he generously decided he to donate some wood, and boy, did he donate some beautiful wood. We used, what we call "tornado wood" for our countertops, our live edge ladder, live edge shelving, and the centerpiece of the house the butcher block countertop. What's more, wood that Alex donated literally got the house up off the ground; it includes every 2" x 4" in the entire house.

After putting the windows in, I realized we needed curtains. Here's something I love to do, repurpose what someone has thrown away. Every six months in North Carolina, there is the world's biggest Furniture Market, where people from all over come to buy the next great thing. Before every show, they get rid of last Market's discontinued items. Most of these things go directly to the landfill, unless I get my hands on them, like fabric swatches. I picked up so many 2' x 2' swatches that I filled the front of my pickup truck. I sold some of those swatches at a yard sale to make some money for our project, but we kept our favorite colored swatches. My mom sewed these into beautiful curtains for us. She did an amazing job of taking two small pieces of fabric to make one beautiful curtain. How nice was that? We didn't have much color in the house, dark floor with white walls, so curtains of red, orange, teal with chevron or organic patterns made the house into this warm and inviting space. These were some of the many things that we figured out along the way and truly made our house a home.

We always wanted to reclaim as much wood as possible to use in our tiny home, but never imagined that so many items that were meant for the landfill would become the heart of our tiny house on wheels. There are so many stories that go along with every aspect of build and in our house, because of the many different ways we acquired our materials, from so many amazing people.

Living Tiny

Having less stuff wasn't a problem for Alexis and I, we had pared everything down to make our THOW livable and comfortable. The new thing about living tiny was physically being in each other's space all the time. She sits 4' away from me, as I type these words. This was new to both of us and took some time to work out. Figuring out the rhythm of life in a tiny space took time and became second nature. Just the act of getting up 15 minutes before Alexis, to make coffee and get dressed, keeps me from getting in her way while she goes about her morning routine. Sharing chores is another aspect of our daily rhythms. Alexis likes taking on the cooking, and I actually like washing dishes. So we are in the kitchen at different times. Overall our small living space forces us to interact more. We definitely have our arguments. But having figured out that resolving them quickly by actually talking to each other about what is wrong has been the best thing for our relationship.

For us living tiny has been our key to a stronger, healthier relationship and our ticket to adventure.

The Transitional Tiny House

Without endings we can never experience new beginnings

Andrew M. Odom

Having built his first tiny house in 2009, blogger and speaker Andrew M. Odom has become a tiny house advocate on a number of levels in order to advance the idea of a more intentional life for all. He still maintains Tiny r(E)volution and looks forward to adding his voice to *Turning Tiny* by exploring the reasons why tiny houses simply are not an answer to social issues like homelessness and transitional housing.

I got married in February of 2009. I was 31 years old and had already lived what seemed like a lifetime. I had gone to and graduated from an undergrad program at Florida State University, a masters program at Regent University, and even started in on PhD hours. I had started a career after gaining experience in several fields of interests. I had had major medical surgery. I had traveled to over nine countries and 14 states. I had owned and sold a "starter house." I had bought and sold two vehicles. I was living the American Dream day after day. But even with all of that under my belt I truly had no idea what I wanted to be when I grew up, what I wanted from life, or even how to truly *live!* I was subsisting but having pretty good luck all the way. Yet as Superman with Kryptonite, so did I have my weakness. If I had a dollar, I was going to spend it. Savings accounts were for those who lacked present ambition and retirement was something for old people. Credit cards let you buy now and pay later because once you're in debt, you'll dies in debt. That was the secret to the American Dream. I had seen it displayed and played out by generations around me.

My new bride felt differently though. Having never really accumulated any personal debt and having no outstanding consumer debt, she truly lived day-to-day making wise decisions based on the money she presently had. For us – upon our wedding – meant the money we had came from her making just under $10/hour and me making just at $10/hour. Her work was seasonal though so it didn't bring in a large income over a year and mine was limited to 40 hours/week with no chance for overtime. After a few very tough love discussions I came to realize that we didn't fiscally have much and didn't stand to have much more without some major life changes. Every spare cent we had at that time was being budgeted toward paying off the $46,000 consumer debt I came to our marriage with. None of it straight out because all of it had interest firmly attached to it. Within months I was singing a different song though about this American Dream concept and I was realizing that credit cards weren't temporary loans and that savings accounts were for proverbial rainy days and that when left unchecked, it could all put you in a position of poverty.

As we approached a year of marriage it became clear that our time living with my folks, bouncing between seasonal jobs, and just trying to figure things out, was coming to a close. With her guidance and patience with me I was quickly gaining better understanding that my Kryptonite was what I now call the Wimpie Syndrome.

"I'll gladly pay you Tuesday, for a hamburger today!"

I made a proclamation to both my wife and, well, anyone that would listen, that I was aware of my weakness, I was aware of the responsibilities of owning a home and not just investing in a home, and that I refused to become house poor because of an inflated appetite for things I couldn't truly afford. We began looking for something affordable and that fit our lifestyle; whatever that had become.

Lucky for us it only took a few days of mincing ideas – a yurt, a cabin, a modular, a mobile, an RV, an apartment – before we both, almost simultaneously, discovered Jay Shafer and his little house on wheels.

I am getting ahead of myself though. Let's talk about that first house that had become my point of reference and was now proving to be an even stronger point of reference, but for different reasons.

Built in 1951, the first house I purchased was in the Cape Cod style (without any obvious additions) and more commonly referred to in the navy town of Norfolk, VA as a "cracker box." It was to accommodate the surging house market following the end of World War II. It originally listed for just under $3,000 and I closed on it in 2001 for just $52,500.

The house was just 720 sq.ft. and needed every inch to be gutted, reinforced, and then renovated. By the time I officially moved in the house had cost me in the neighborhood of $80,000 and countless hours of labor. At the time the monthly payment turned out to be $403/month (including personal property tax and homeowners insurance). After taxes my then salary was about $1,760/month. That meant that roughly 25% of my monthly income was going towards my house payment. That also meant I had just at $1,330/month left or $332/week for other expenses. Factor in utilities, water, telephone, basic Internet, food, entertainment, a small auto loan payment, gas for my car, and general upkeep, and it is easy to see that although I wasn't on the poverty line I was very much living paycheck-to-paycheck.

The house was also just a 1-bedroom / 1-bathroom which meant there was no room to take on a housemate. I also didn't have the equity yet to secure a loan to add an addition, which would afford me a roommate. It was kind of a dead-end situation in that regard. After being in the house for just over two years I made the decision to sell it in order to pursue other callings. I made a rather nice profit and honestly felt I had made good decisions during my time there. Looking back though I can't imagine that house being fit for a family.

In a 2014 interview with David Friedlander of TreeHugger[6] online Jay Shafer said, "I set out to build an efficient house. When I took out all of the unnecessary parts of the house, it turned out to be a very small house."

Was that what I had been living in? Was my little house a stripped down home? I didn't think so. In fact, weighed against Shafer's idea the house was completely superfluous save the 1-bedroom and 1-bathroom. The rest was poorly designed and unnecessary. It had small, choppy rooms, anchored by a dining room that could have possibly been a bedroom if it had had some sort of closet and didn't have a built in china cabinet piece.

Jay was also asked by Friedlander, in that piece why he thought – in 2014, mind you – tiny houses had become such a sensation. Jay's response was near perfect.

"There are so many reasons, but I think it comes back to nature. In every area of nature, efficiency is the law of the land. Efficiency just makes sense. The only thing I know of that doesn't abide by efficiency is the human ego."

The cracker box that had become my home was terribly inefficient. It lacked natural light, it had a poor layout with zero fluidity, the original insulation had long since turned to a crumbling nightmare of asbestos powder, it had an oil furnace, and the list goes on. Even my renovations didn't do much to improve on those elements. So just as Shafer before me turned to designing a tiny house in an effort to live in something more suitable than his Airstream trailer, I was more determined that ever to do a few things with this new opportunity:

- Make wise financial decisions
- Build a house that was efficient and served the needs of my wife and I
- Allow myself to think more freely and defy practicality

That last one though was going to be harder than I thought.

Growing up in the South has its own version of the American Dream ethos. That version never aligns with anything Turning Tiny. In fact, if I were to have to market it I would call it *The American Dream: Deep Fried Version.* Why, you ask? When you deep-fry something it does a few things. It pops and sizzles and spatters grease, making noise and calling attention to itself. It also puffs up as it absorbs the oil. And if you're not careful you will cook it too long and make it dry without any flavor at all. It will forevermore be just status quo. To my opinion the Deep Fried Version of life has you living out a "bigger is better" mentality. You get good grades in primary, secondary, and high schools, so you can attend a good college. Get good grades and make good connections in college and you can get a good job. Get a good job and you make a good salary. Make a good salary and you attract a good wife. Have a good wife and then you can embark on procreation; 2 kids ideally, but more is desirable. Have a good family and a good job and you get a good house. Said house allows for a bedroom for each child and one master suite for the parents. With the house comes a nice yard and a garage suitable for his truck and her SUV. The grass is green and growing greener all the time. It is nothing short of a Hallmark reality infused with Sundays at church, Christmas at the in-laws, and themed birthday parties to celebrate the passing of another year. But because we grew up very Southern I felt like it was my legacy. I had to go Deep Fried.

I initially struggled with letting go of the aforementioned Deep Fried life that I was bred to embrace. And for what? 200 sq.ft. of efficiency? Like I said, *I struggled*. Ultimately though I realized that the reason it has been called the American Dream for so long is because it was always meant to be a personal *dream* afforded to each person who sought refuge in America. It was okay if what I felt was euphoria wasn't shared by anyone else. The American Dream, as it were, allowed me to bypass the Deep Friend and instead take a look at a different menu. It was to be my dream and mine alone. Fortunately for me though, I had married a woman who found as much comfort and encouragement from this tiny house thing as I did. Within a week or so our minds had been made up and we were prepared to break down the white picket fence and instead roll our house on up to the top of our slice of the pie.

The next few weeks were spent looking at photos online, photos in older architectural journals, and even a couple of history books. At the time the tiny world as represented online was limited to about 3-4 websites including Tiny House Blog run by Kent Griswold and Tumbleweed Tiny Homes run by Jay Shafer. It became very clear to us though that what we desired had not yet been designed out, much less built. We called on the experience of a few family members and a few friends and combined it with our own knowledge, experience, and ideas, and decided we would build our own tiny house in our own style.

Several napkins later and a lot of graph paper we ended up with a basic rectangle which at 240 sq.ft. felt like a house divided into thirds. The first third was to be the full size, gourmet style kitchen. The second third was to be the living space, which would actually be risen 7" in platform style to allow for hidden ductwork. The third third was the bedroom suitable for a queen size Sleep Number bed. Perhaps though the coup d'état was that our tiny house was single level: no loft, no stairs, and no ladder. Why such a design? My thought always was, I don't want to climb up and down a ladder each time I access the bed and I certainly don't want to fall down a ladder in the middle of the night in an effort to use the bathroom. Besides, we wanted a feeling of lofted ceilings and that could only be achieved if we nixed the lofts.

The home cost us about $16,000 out-of-pocket to build and we documented each step of the process from securing materials to planning wood to building trusses to spackling walls. We also chose to build cash-on-the-barrel to make the build more affordable and to keep us out of debt and being "house poor" once we moved in. All in all it was a 19-month process that taught us a tremendous amount about budgeting, patience, building, relationships, and more! The tiny house was literally built with ample amounts of shed blood, salty tears, and southern heat-inspired sweat! Because we took our time we also made a lot of good decisions in regards to insulation, sustainable materials, non-toxic materials, and alternative energy. Being married, working decent hours for decent pay, and having no house payment, really turned the American Dream on its head and allowed us to maximize our living in a number of ways.

Happy ending. Yes? Not so fast. Our tiny house – the Tiny r(E)volution as it has become known – was designed for two adults with plenty of outdoor interests. The layout, the ample kitchen, the large bed in back; all of those elements were designed with just two adult in mind. Imagine then our surprise and brush with an "abandon ship" mentality when we found out just a few months into the build that we were to become parents. Needless to say we were beyond excited. But that was more about having a baby than it was about finishing the tiny house. Things changed quickly. We had to rethink the needs of a baby and what it meant for our house to now need to accommodate three humans. Could it even be done? How long could we thrive (not just survive) in 240 sq.ft? This is where the transitional home part comes in.

Ask Macy Miller of MiniMotives. Ask Hari Berzins of Tiny House Family. Ask Kim Kasl of Bless This Tiny House. And ask any number of other parents who are now raising families in tiny houses. It is all at once frustrating yet possible. It is challenging but rewarding. It is – in our experience – a time for a young family to bond like no other. Historically speaking the average size of the American house didn't even reach 1,000 sq.ft. until the decade post-WWII. During the Dust Bowl families of 6 or 7 would often times settle a claim in a house that barely exceeded 700 sq.ft. By those standards our 240 sq.ft. of living space was on part with the 100 sq.ft. per person equation. Our third person was only going to be a mini-human so she wouldn't need as much room as a full size adult.

We quickly decided to move forward with the build and just work in a place for a 3-in-1 pack 'n play for our newborn. We talked to several of our friends who had already raised babies and come to find out babies don't require their own nurseries with glider chairs, bouncy seats, door jamb swings, and even their own bathroom. Turns out most babies don't even want to be away from the heartbeat of their momma for months! Our decision worked perfectly. In fact, as our daughter approached infancy and started sleeping in her own bed we re-appropriated a space at the side of our central living area for her toddler bed. It was perfect for our needs! Our daughter was within arms reach of us almost all the time and she started on day one in a house where quality trumps quantity, need and want are not synonymous, and thriving in life is more important that just surviving. The outdoors was our living room and when we weren't sleeping or eating we were out adventuring and just enjoying life.

For 19-months we lived in our tiny house and enjoyed the spoils of a mortgage-free lifestyle. We were able to finish up paying off our mountainous debt that had held us captive for almost four years. We had been able to save up some money and towards the end, think about what might be next for us in life. Turns out we were itching to see America and complete the "great American road trip" with our inquisitive and fast-growing daughter.

Through a fortunate series of circumstances – personal and professional – we were able to turn this new dream into a reality and exchange our tiny house for a 28' travel trailer. It was time for Tiny r(E)volution v.2.0. Our home still had wheels. Our home still served more as a place to eat and sleep than anything else. And as an added bonus we got 60 more sq.ft. of living space! It was such a wonderful transition for our family.

For two years we traveled all over the Southeast region and worked our way out West seeing states that and sites that we had only read about until then. We were able to expose our daughter to national parks, state parks, ranger programs, cities, small towns, and all the sights and smells that accompany those. We never once regretted our decision and, in fact, often wondered why we hadn't chosen to travel more before then. Somewhere around the 20-month mark we started feeling a big fatigued though.

In September of 2015 our daughter turned 4-years old and started requiring more space. Not because she was accumulating more things but because her energy was exceeding what our space comfortably allowed. We began to dread rainy days and cold areas because it meant there was nowhere to run and play. My wife and I felt very strongly that it may be time for us to anchor down again and provide a bit more stability for our family. It didn't mean the adventures would end or that we would fall into the status quo we had worked so hard to avoid earlier in our life. Rather it meant that we were in a state of transition and wanted to see what else our family could explore. We wanted a more simple and sustainable life for ourselves. We wanted to return to our rural roots and go back to raising chickens, growing a garden, having room to run, and the like. We wanted to anchor down and were in a position to. Our debt remained low. Our needs were minimal. It seemed like a perfect time for another transition; a Tiny r(E)volution v.3.0, if you will.

I write this chapter from my small desk in our 'new to us' little farmette in rural eastern North Carolina. We have anchored down in a 900 sq.ft. house with 2-bedrooms and 2-bathrooms. It can effectively be called Tiny r(E)volution v.3.0. While it isn't tiny we still find ourselves employing the ideals of a tiny house lifestyle. We still make every effort to conserve, not abuse space, save and store only what is necessary. In fact, on any given day a quarter of our house is absent of life. What's truly funny is that while it is a more traditional small house it is essentially an open space with 2-bedrooms and 2-bathrooms jutting off the main area like octopus tentacles. To this day we still value our time together as a family and find that a small, open space facilitates more open communication, more connection, more patience with one another, and more grace towards each other. It is a tiny house lifestyle within a small house. But that is proof of how our initial tiny house shaped us; altered our mindset.

True. Our little home needed some work and some love (as well as vision) when we closed on it. We weren't able to afford alternative energy solutions. We are tied to the grid and we get city water. But our goal is to thrive in this next adventure, using the two acres we now own to return to our homesteading roots. We will again have a main food garden, an herb garden, a greenhouse, and probably a small hoop house. We will raise chickens. We will collect our water for use in the garden and other applications. We will plant and grow nut and fruit trees. We will care for the land as it has cared for us. It is another great adventure for us and one that was made completely possible by that fateful decision we made back in 2009 to go against the status quo, find what was right for us, set our goals (both short term and long term), and pursue them with diligence.

In these past seven years what we have come to realize is that tiny houses don't have to be the starting gate and the finish line both. They can even be any point along the racecourse. They are perfect stepping-stones to a more long-term goal. For us our tiny house on wheels allowed us to grow as a couple, as a family, as individuals, as homeowners, as eco-conscious people, and more! It allowed us to meet financial goals and learn fiscal responsibility. And in the long run it allowed us membership into one of the finest communities I know of: the tiny house community! Transition is part of life and I remember once being told that without endings we can never experience new beginnings.

Thriving in Tiny with Teenaged Children

Gabriella Morrison

Gabriella Morrison and Andrew, her husband, designed and built "hOMe," the modern tiny house on wheels. She is a mother of two teenagers and looks forward to sharing her perspective on living tiny with a family in *Turning Tiny*. Gabriella has found again and again that when people have the opportunity to live a mindful and simple life, amazing transformations can happen.

The way we talk to our children becomes their inner voice.
—Peggy O'Mara

Once upon a time, not so long ago, our family of four was taking a nose-dive into the pits of conflict, strife, and lack of connection. Our son, Paiute, was 14, our daughter Terra, 11 and they were both having what we could call a "typical" angst filled teenage experience. My husband, Andrew, and I were working full time to pay for a house that was much larger than needed and our collective stress levels were higher than any of us probably realized.

Stress has a knack for taking the fun out of life. Its effects can be cumulative and if not kept in check, it has the power of sabotaging even the best of circumstances. Here we were living in our "dream" home but our family dynamic was almost unrecognizable, a faint glimmer from the happier days while living a modest life in the country.

We were confused as to why we felt so atrocious despite finally being surrounded by the things we had always longed for (nice cars, big house, luxurious vacations, etc.). To compound the matter, we felt powerless to change any of it because at the end of the day, we were so tired that it was easier to let things slide than to put in the effort.

By divine intervention, a new friend, Kent Griswold, sent me an email with a link to www.TinyHouseBlog.com in the signature file. I visited the site and within a matter of minutes, was ¾ of the way down the rabbit hole. I purchased "The Small House Book" by Jay Shafer and was so excited when it appeared in our mailbox that I sat on the sidewalk and read the whole thing right then and there.

The more Andrew and I learned about tiny house living, the easier it became to understand the source of our disquietude. A veil had lifted and we could see the tall walls of the money trap we had fallen into. Before living in this house, we had always spent money within our means and found happiness and satisfaction in the small things in life. Our attempt to reach the next tier of wealth had taken a costly toll on our health and family dynamic.

There was no going back and a chain reaction was triggered. Our lives took a necessary and very fast turn. Within six months we had gotten rid of the house, 90% of our worldly belongings bought a pop up tent trailer and made a plan to head to the beaches of Baja, Mexico.

Our thinning out process was exhilarating. The sheer volume of possessions we had accumulated over the years was impressive. Not knowing where to begin the process we devised the 365 Day Rule and started pulling out every single item from each and every drawer and cabinet. If we hadn't used something within a year, it went into the garage. By the end of this exercise our non-vitals formed a small mountain 12' long x 8' wide x 4' tall.

The more possessions we got rid of, the lighter we felt and in this process we realized that there is an emotional burden to material things. It's subtle so we didn't realize it was there until our effects started going away. The kids got swept up in the excitement too and voluntarily purged the majority of what they owned. To this day I have zero regrets of giving away and selling everything that I did. There is nothing that comes to mind that I wish I had kept. Not a single thing.

In the midst of all this change and transformation, Paiute, a passionate ice hockey player, expressed his desire to attend a boarding school in Colorado that had scouted him. Initially we had discounted the suggestion, joking that boarding school is for naughty kids or those whose parents don't love them and neither of those profiles fit us even remotely. We also knew we couldn't afford the tuition but when they came to us with a sizeable grant package, we were forced to seriously consider the option. His desire to go and play for the team only increased and we finally had to admit that our valley couldn't provide the level of coaching and play he needed to reach his goal. Dropping him off in Colorado was one of the most painful experiences we've ever had.

To say that we were stepping into the unknown is a gross understatement. Though we were incredibly excited to set off on a new adventure, there were nights when I was filled with dread and anxiety. But there was no turning back. I knew without a shadow of doubt that regressing to our "normal" life was no longer an option. The only way was forward and that meant doing something totally new and different.

Getting rid of the house and the vast majority of our possessions allowed us to escape debt and to free up resources for about five months of travel. We had two primary goals in mind for this journey: 1) to reconnect with our distant and indignant daughter, and 2) to strip away cultural pressures so that we could learn what our personal definition of home was.

We purchased a used 22' pop up tent trailer with a mini kitchen and tiny fridge, toilet, table for four, sofa, and queen and king sized beds. Each of us brought a plate, bowl, cup, set of utensils, 3 pairs of shorts and pants, 1 jacket, 2 bathing suits, 2 pairs of socks, 1 sweatshirt, 7 pair of underwear, and 1 towel. Kitchen supplies were very basic and included only a few favorite spices, 1 cooking pot, 1 frying pan, 1 wooden spoon, 1 spatula, 1 can opener, and 1 lighter. A big part of our curiosity was to see how little we could live with and still have our needs met.

We did splurge though by bringing our SCUBA gear. Being that Terra is a budding marine biologist and had just gotten her open water certification, there was no way we were going to pass up the opportunity to regularly dive in the fabled Sea of Cortez. Along the lines of entertainment, we also brought our favorite board games, cards, crossword puzzles, and a couple of books. Terra and Andrew each brought their guitars too.

Truth be told, our first month in Baja was hell. Three weeks into what was supposed to be a unifying family trip, Andrew and I seriously considered packing up and returning home, tails tucked between our legs. We were all suffering from electronics withdrawal, being bored, and struggling with our communication. Terra was furious with us because we had "stolen" her away from her life at home. When we reminded her that she had been just as involved in the decision making process to come down, she screamed "I DIDN'T THINK YOU WERE SERIOUS!!!"

Sometimes just when you think you can't tolerate something for another second, a transformation can happen. Just a couple days after talking about an emergency extraction from Baja, Andrew suddenly "landed" into the paradise that none of us had been able to notice for nearly four weeks. His withdrawal symptoms had lifted and his busy mind had finally slowed enough so that he could be present to where he was and what he was doing. The next day I stumbled into the same happy place and the day after that, Terra was with us as well. Just like that, the world became beautiful and sparkly.

For the next 4 months we found a joy and sense of calm that none of us had experienced since our early childhoods. We played, laughed, explored, went to sleep with the sun's rhythm, SCUBA dove, hiked, swam, learned Spanish, made our own tortilla chips, talked for hours on end, adopted a street dog, played board games, met people from around the world, and had the opportunity to really get to know each other. Distractions were minimal and our lives took on a richness and aliveness that all of us had been starving for.

We were able to see Paiute nearly every month during that time. It became evident that he was having his own positive transformation in boarding school. Living in a small dorm room and learning how to co-exist with his dorm brothers and the larger school community was having a profound effect on his confidence and maturity level. One side benefit of this was that he suddenly wanted to connect with us making our reunions particularly amazing. We especially noticed how much closer the kids were to each other. All of the fighting they had done was now gone.

During our time in Baja, Terra transformed into another person. Given the opportunity to rediscover herself without the stresses of a fast paced electronic rich world, she blossomed into a radiant young lady. Once combative and distant, she now opened up and shared her authentic self. Her sense of humor emerged and we would often spend hours sitting on the beach telling jokes, swapping stories or just enjoying the peace and quiet in each other's company.

Our original goals for our trip had been achieved: reconnect with Terra and gain an intrinsic understanding of what home means to us. In going down with the least, we had discovered the most and in living simply, we had found our greatest joy. Wanting to hang on to this sense of peace, we created a mission to set up a life in Oregon that supported this lifestyle. Our desire to live in a tiny house only intensified.

Eventually we found a piece of land outside Ashland to support our vision. Fortunately it was the least expensive acreage in our entire valley, which allowed for a cash purchase. It is a five-acre parcel nestled in the mountains and offers a ton of privacy, a forested landscape, and more wildlife than anywhere we've ever lived. A seasonal creek creates a magical sound during the winter and spring months. All of this and we are only 20 minutes from town.

When planning out our property with the kids, we decided on a main tiny house as well as cabins for each of them. This scenario made the most sense for several reasons: 1) create privacy for Andrew and I in our home at night 2) create privacy for the kids when they want to have down time, hang out with friends, listen to loud music, sleep, etc. 3) have the ability to shut down their cabins when they leave for college (sparing us from having a larger than needed house once we become empty nesters).

The main tiny house on our land was designed with all of our previous life experiences inspiring the way. We were clear on what we needed but perhaps even more importantly, what we didn't. Our tiny house is now known as "hOMe" and boasts a full sized kitchen, comfortable stairs into our master loft, tons of storage, secondary loft for guests (or when the kids aren't feeling well and want to sleep in the house), home office, relatively large bathroom, and a light and bright modern aesthetic. It sits on wheels and is 207 sq. ft. with an additional 110 sq. ft. in lofts.

hOMe is very well suited for our day to day lives, even with both of the kids living with us full time. Because Paiute was missing living with us after four years at boarding school, he decided to stay at home this year and to play on the local Tier II Junior ice hockey team, despite having opportunities to play on better ones in other states. Terra is a junior in high school and I'm delighted to share that the changes she experienced in Baja have stayed with her all these years.

Typically during our workday, I sit downstairs and work at our desk, Andrew sits up on our bed working on his laptop, and Paiute, when not practicing with the team or away at a tournament, hangs out in the lounge loft. When we are quiet and working on each of our projects, it's easy to forget that there is anyone else in the house. Terra is at school 5 days per week and comes home around 5-6 p.m. She is very chatty and likes to be a part of conversations so homework and cooking time are often lively while we all catch up on the day's events.

Terra's "Lookout" is a 10' x 12' single room cabin that sits just steps from hOMe. In it you'll find a raised queen sized bed, a small closet for hanging clothes and a large storage unit that fits underneath the length of her bed, providing space for the majority of her clothes. Above the bed hang her acoustic and electric guitars, a map of the world with dots marking the places she's visited, and a shelf with her favorite books. Between her bed and the tiny closet are a desk and a chair. This space, though simple, easily accommodates all of our daughter's personal items. We named it the "Lookout" because it's built up on piers and the large picture window overlooking the conifer dotted hills below, creates the illusion that one is a bird in a nest.

Paiute's request was for us to build him a tree house. It perches over our seasonal creek and in the wet months, he can hear the water flowing below. It is 10' x 16' and has a 16' x 6' deck on the entrance side. The floor framing begins 7' above the ground and a solid set of stairs with guardrails creates access to the deck. The interior is paneled with untreated plywood yielding a very contemporary look. He has a comfortable seating chair, a full sized bed, a large desk, and even a walk in closet. This is a very special tree house and frankly, it is my favorite structure on our land.

When I describe our lives with our teenaged kids to others, I sometimes have to pause and marvel at how well things are going. There was a time just 5 years ago that I was quite concerned about our family dynamic and who our kids would grow up to be. Despair and helplessness were things I remember feeling a lot.

It turns out that what was needed was a priority change. Once we shifted our focus from just surviving/working to creating a healthy family dynamic, we could easily see what changes needed to be made. Implementing them was not always easy and sometimes I couldn't even tell if we were making progress but we kept at it and over the months we all started to get the hang of it. Many mistakes were made along the way but as parents we did our best to stay humble, to apologize when needed, to learn from our mistakes, and to try again.

Communication is now key in our family. Living in close quarters has taught us that everything is so much easier when we are honest as soon as something is bothering us, rather than when it's already been festering. We treat our kids with respect and listen to what they have to say, even when it's an uncomfortable topic or our feelings are hurt. The temptation to sharply react during those times is still there but we have learned to pause before we respond and to ask ourselves if our reaction is going to invite deeper conversation or to cause them to become defensive and retreat. We are certainly not perfect at this but it is a priority so we do our very best.

If someone could have shown me a short movie back in 2011 what our lives would be like as a family in 2016, I would have dismissed it as Hollywood magic. I am grateful beyond belief for Kent Griswold's initial email and Jay Shafer's book. They were the motivation we needed to extract ourselves from a life that was fortunately not destined for us. Dismissing the status quo and forging our own way has been the very best thing that could have happened. We took a risk and looking back, I wouldn't change a speck of a thing that has happened along the way.

At The Heart of It All

Trevor Gay

Trevor Gay and Mary Benasutti live in Dayton, Ohio with 4 furry felines. They built their "Heart Of It All" tiny house together with the help of family and friends in 2015 and are living happier ever since. The charming couple are animal experts and enjoy spending time outdoors as much as possible. You can follow their story and adventures at Heart of it All House.

It was a sunny afternoon in Xenia, Ohio. There was a feeling of warmth on your skin, the smell of freshly cut grass, and the sounds of people outside enjoying the longer and warmer summer days. I was 13 at the time. My mom had just picked me up from middle-school. She would often bring my little brother, Barney, with her most places that she went. She even came to my school to do talks and presentations with him. When Barney originally came to us as an eight year old, we didn't get along very well. We had very typical sibling rivalry issues. Until Barney acclimated to his new family dynamics he would blame me for every situation gone wrong. When Mom would tell him "no," he would immediately blame me for his error which would result in various household items being hurled at me. For a little guy he had an accurate pitch! When things were going smoothly we got along great.

On this particular beautiful warm and sunny day in Ohio, Barney was in his Sherpa carrier on the front seat of the car when mom picked me up from school (oh yeah, I should mention that Barney, is a Capuchin monkey!) I climbed into my parents early 90's Saab and head for home in the country-side – windows down and sunroof open just taking in the fresh air. As we drive through town, Barney locked in his carrier now on my lap, is also enjoying the summer air.

I'm telling mom about how awesome my science teacher is and that it's definitely my favorite new class. I was mid sentence in my story when I saw his long skinny E.T. like finger poke out of the side of the cage. It was definitely one of those moments... like those milliseconds before a catastrophic car crash where everything slows down and gets super quiet. I watched that little finger manipulate the lock like a master and slide the zipper open within a second as I just sat frozen in panic!

Almost like a monkey being shot out of a cannon, Barney jumps straight up and out of the sunroof! My only reaction was to grab the short leash coming off of his waistband and hang on for dear life. I grabbed him pulling him back into the car after which he immediately jumped out of the side window and, like a rock climber missing a grab, he swung down and jumped back in the car onto my lap all while I'm skeptically hanging onto his leash. Within one fast motion he attaches himself to my face clinging onto anything he can possibly grab! Barney is screaming at the top of his lungs sounding like a 2-year-old child being burned at the stake. I'm screaming at Barney to let go of my face, and my poor mom is trying to pull the car over shouting over our screams trying to save the situation! This, in a nutshell, is how I grew up, with all sorts of animals (pretty much everything except for lions and tigers). They would come later in life.

I grew up as an only child with the mindset that all animals were my brothers and sisters (like Barney.) We lived in a rural town about 30 minutes outside of Dayton, Ohio. It was a nice place to grow up. Farmland. Go karts and bicycle jumps, horseback riding, modest people, and relaxed school environments. I was always outside, and always on my bicycle. Things haven't changed much over the past 30 years. I just take my bicycle to new places to meet new people. I've been lucky enough and worked hard enough to have some pretty cool jobs over the years that take me to new places and meet tons of new people, which has always been important to me. My mom, Barb, was a nurse for 23 years and then changed careers to horse training, lessons, and animal rescue. She later went on to open a photography studio with my dad. My dad, Gary, has been in environmental science for 26 years and supported my mom's missions to save animals and basically have a zoo for a home.

To say that animals play a large role in our family's lives is a serious understatement.

In December of 2012, I met this crazy girl named Mary Benasutti at some friends' Christmas party. In the months prior, I had just recently ended a serious 5-year relationship. I wasn't looking for another relationship and that's exactly when your dream girl strikes. Mary was in the Air Force at the time, with two cats, and had recently become vegetarian. She hit too many of my "must-have" traits and qualities. She's funny, caring, athletic, loves animals, wants to travel, introvert at home, extrovert with friends, into similar music, just crazy enough, and is just plain beautiful. Her plans to leave the Air Force and go back to school to become a veterinarian sealed the deal.

Within a month we made our relationship official. I bought a house in Dayton and we moved in together. The house, built in 1916, is a 1,110 sq. ft. bungalow style. It has a 2-car detached garage, finished basement, 2 bedrooms, and huge living rooms. It was perfect for Mary and I, and our four cats… or so we thought.

At the time, I had two cats of my own, Cleo and Merry. Cleo, who I raised from birth, resembles an evil feather duster or even a creature from "Where the Wild Things Are." She has kept some of my tougher friends from entering certain parts of my house. She creepily stares at people and chirps at them from dark corners. Merry, adopted during Christmas time, is thick long hair mostly white, brown, and grey, is the lioness of the house. She's the oldest, most loving, and most needy. She also hates to be picked up and awkwardly tries to attach herself to anything in site anytime humans take her precious gravity away.

Mary had two cats at the time as well: Jinx and Kiki. Two girls, both short haired Siamese. Jinx most certainly has the attitude of a nerdy doomsday prepper who was always given a hard time in school. She's tiny and faster than lightning, also scared of lightning, and stronger than she looks. Kiki, quite the opposite, carries a near human like personality. Chubby and shaped like a dairy cow, her mocha colored markings resemble a big brown cardigan buttoned on her chubby chest. Kiki is the boss and lets everyone know it vocally.

After nearly a year of living in our new house, thankfully we didn't have to call Jackson Galaxy of the tv show "My Cat From Hell." The four fur balls weren't getting along fantasticly, but going into the relationship, we knew with all of the unique personalities of the cats that it would be a challenge. Around this time, my curiosity and thirst for simpler, tiny living was rekindled when Andrew & Gabriella Morrison released photos and a video of their tiny house in Oregon. I had originally fallen in love with tiny houses and the whole movement a few years prior to meeting Mary, but life circumstances at the time kept me from moving forward. Like anything new and exciting, I became obsessed with building one of the Morrison "hOMe" houses. Fortunately Mary was on board and didn't require much convincing. Our biggest challenge would be none other than – you guessed it – these freaking cats!

We started our build in the winter of 2014 in hopes of completing the build in less than 5-6 months. After a couple months of building, somehow we ended up being cast for the HGTV show, *Tiny House, Big Living*. Thankfully, being on the show expedited our build process and really pushed our limits, personally. My mom and dad, Mary's dad and grandpa, my aunt and uncle, and a few friends and I managed to finish our house working nights and weekends after work and in between animal feedings at the farm in less than 5 months. During our last "reveal" shoot with the production crew, being the clever gentleman I am, I figured this was also the perfect time to propose to Mary and ask her to marry me. Thankfully, she said yes!

It was finally time to move into our tiny house: 28' long by 8'6 wide (224 sq. ft.), complete with a full sized kitchen, shower, waterless composting toilet, 2 lofts, plenty of storage, and of course, special features for our special cats. Knowing that our cats already had social issues, we wanted to do as much as we could to ensure their health and happiness in the tiny house. Between Mary, Mom, and myself, we came up with a game plan and layout of features to incorporate into the house and how to introduce them into the new space. We incorporated a scratching post into one of the staircase legs, 2 dedicated litter pan locations, extended window sills, and, we even made a kitty cat rope bridge to give the cats access to the top of our cabinets from the stairs (yea, crazy cat people, I know).

So the big question is: how are the cats getting along in the tiny house?

The answer: So much better than we had ever anticipated. When I say our cats hated each other…. I mean they really, really didn't want anything to do with each other. When we moved into the tiny house, all of them quickly changed their attitudes. They most definitely still respect each other's spaces, but we rarely see or hear catfights, their moods have improved, and they're actually healthier. Why? Our hypothesis is that there is just so much more to do, see, and experience where our tiny house is located. They all have their own "spots" where we regularly find them. Kiki loves to hog the rope bridge, Merry claims the bed under the loft stairs, Jinx sits on top of the dresser in the bedroom, and Cleo sits in the bed along the top of the storage cabinets. They have 14 windows to look out of, dinosaurs (horses) to watch, and we've been letting them outside to explore (usually under supervision.) We believe they have much more independence and security inside of the tiny house versus our "big house" with too many corner, rooms, and their least favorite, the long hallways.

So the question is, does your pet fit the tiny house lifestyle? There are too many instances of people not taking their pets into consideration before moving into a new home (let alone a tiny house.) Is there truly adequate space for them? Will they have an area to play or exercise (inside and outside)? Are you planning on creating a special and dedicated area for their food (litter pans for cats and puppy pads for small dogs). These questions and more should be answered and planned out when in the design or build process of your tiny house.

Planning their space is equally as important to you as it is to your animals. For some reason or another, the last four places I've lived, my cat's litter box has always been in the kitchen. Space-wise, that's just where it seemed to "fit."I didn't want this for the tiny house (even though it's still only 8' away in a tiny house!) so we incorporated one litter box underneath the main stairs into one of the cubby storage areas. I designed our second set of stairs into the lounge loft, to start on a wooden platform leaving roughly a 20" high space for the second litter pan underneath. To support the stair platform I used a wooden dow-rod that seemed to be the "purfect" place for a scratching post. We wrapped the post with a Sisal style rope and now have a built in scratching post for less than $20 dollars. Our wooden jungle rope style bridge was made for less than $30 dollars and was fun to make. Special features like these make our cats more comfortable and make our house unique from others. It can be a fun challenge designing and conceiving creative ways to incorporate your cut into your tiny house.

Being conscious of sanitation and air quality in your tiny house is important to both you and your animals, especially if you have children living with you. The living space is much more dense than that of a large home, so it's a good idea to have some form of air filtration system to keep dust and dander out of the air. Some ductless mini-split air conditioner/heater combos have built in air filters and purifiers. The built in versions will help save floor space in your house.

Not only is cleanliness and health important, but mood and happiness should be observed as well. If you start to see signs of depression or mood changes in your pet's new tiny space, it's time to introduce forms of enrichment into their lives such as: time outdoors, new places, toys, play time, bedding, or even a secure place to hide or sleep. Some animals will adapt to tiny house living better than others, and some will not. Be observant of your pet's health and needs to ensure their life is the best it can be in your tiny house.

Aside from all the special features or considerations you can take, the actual process of introducing your pets to a new and different space can be just as important as the features in your tiny house. Introducing pets into new spaces should always be taken with serious consideration and patience. The slow approach is always better because you can't undo what's already been done when the process is rushed. In the case of our four cats, we introduced them to the new house one by one – without the stress of any of the other cats. We brought each cat over to explore and stay in the house for a couple days at a time with just us there to reassure and reward them. They were able to explore every nook, cranny, bridge and window to discover their own comfort zone. By move-in day, they were already completely comfortable in the new house.

Out of everything you can possibly do for you non-human family members, regular vet visits and checkups top the list. Always be sure to schedule regular vet appointments to make sure there are no lingering health issues with your pet. Establishing a good relationship with your local and favorite veterinarian can be life saving down the road.

I can't even imagine life without my furry brothers and sisters. Growing up with animals all around teaches us a great deal of care and responsibility. For many, this is practice for taking care of children later in life. For some, it's a priceless form of love and friendship. What better way to top off your personalized tiny house than to bring your best friend into your new space with you. Many people gawk when we tell them that we live with 4 cats in only 224 sq. ft., but we can't imagine it any other way. Our animals and pets add so much to our lives and we always want it to be mutual.

In the end, we're so thankful to have taken the time to make special accommodations to our tiny house for the cats. Somehow, they get along better than ever, and it most certainly makes our home life much more enjoyable without catfights. Making the decision to downsize has brought so much to our lives, including the animals. Until our next "home" adventure, we're all living happily ever after in the "Heart of it all House."

Part 3

Tiny Alternatives

Everyone seems to understand the current given definition of a tiny house. It is a quaint, Craftsman-style bungalow, situated on a trailer able to be pulled with a large-ish truck. It doesn't exceed 300 ft. and it accommodates 1-2 people in a sleeping loft. The kitchen is minimal and seating is limited. But what happens if the house is 305 sq. ft. for example? Of what if it is 500 sq. ft. yet fits a family of eight? And if that isn't extreme enough, what if the house is not on a trailer at all? What if it is floating down the Mississippi River? Just what does make a tiny house tiny, then? Truth is, nothing does, or does not. The term "tiny house" is completely subjective and relevant to the family inside. It may roll. It may sit still. It may be powered by the wind or even fly 30,000 feet in the sky. There are a number of tiny houses and people living in all sorts of them. There is a paradigm shift happening right now and these are just a few of those dynamic stories.

Four in a Boat Afloat

Living on the ocean is not all it is believed to be

Genevieve Stolz

Genevieve Stolz and her husband Eben turned tiny and moved into their first floating home – S/V Necesse – nearly six years ago because they concluded that this would be the best way for them to continue traveling the world while expanding their family with the addition of their two daughters. Genevieve hopes that by sharing their adventures of raising two little salty sailors gives people a glimpse into the lifestyle and lets them see that dreams don't have to end with the arrival of kids; kids thrive and benefit from having happy parents.

To move, to breathe, to fly, to float, to roam the roads of lands remote,
to travel is to live.
—Hans Christian Anderson

It's always interesting seeing people's wheels spin when we tell them we live on a sailboat with our two young daughters. There are so many preconceptions and misunderstandings about the lifestyle that it is fun getting to answer the many questions that pop up in conversation. Once we explain how it is our family really lives, it doesn't seem quite as daunting anymore. Let me tell you the biggest secret of it: living on a boat with kids, well its just as crazy as living on land with kids, the only major difference is that we are simply surrounded by water. Our children are adventurous little beings that are extremely portable so being able to live in a floating tiny home with them while traveling the Caribbean is a great fit for all us.

My husband, Eben, and I had done a fair bit of travelling and was something that we had hoped to continue doing for a while, even once we had children. But as a family, hopping from one backpackers' hostel to the next with our lives on our backs didn't seem feasible for us, both monetarily and for reasons of comfort and ease. The thought of being able to travel with our kids while bringing our home along with us sounded like the perfect alternative. We could keep our creature comforts, our daily activities, our structure, our stuff, our home, and be able to regularly change our backyard scenery. Our sailing "style" could be compared to RVing but again, just add water.

Neither my husband nor I consider ourselves to be "avid sailors," even now after nearly 6 years of living on a sailboat we struggle with the term. We didn't come from sailing backgrounds and we are both completely self-taught. In his twenties my husband had bought a small sailboat and took off on an adventure with his buddy, Jordan. They both learned how to sail from reading encyclopedias and many helpful and knowledgeable friends. When their time on the boat met an early financially induced end, they stored her in the Bahamas and returned back to Canada, thinking they would go back to her after a few moneymaking months. Several years later Eben and I married and then a year after had our first daughter. At that point we knew we should either sell the sailboat, since we were paying monthly to have it in storage, or use it. We opted for the more exciting adventure. I, in turn, learned all of my sailing from him. We thought this trip would last us about a year of Caribbean exploration while heading towards Panama or Guatemala and then we would move on to something new. But then the years flew by and we are still calling our sailboat Necesse, our home.

We see ourselves as travellers that live on a boat, rather than sailors that are out travelling. With the exception of the Virgin islands, you won't see us going out for fun day sails just for the sake of it. We prefer to live in our floating home for an extended amount of time in various locales, and when we are ready for a change we raise the sails and move on to the next island. Cheap and effective. We do stints of a few weeks up to a year in any given area, all-dependent on how much we love it. And since the Caribbean has been our sailing stomping ground, all of the islands are in relatively close proximity of each other. We have never had to go more than 3 consecutive days "at sea" to reach a new destination. Sure there are families that circum-navigate, cross oceans and cover larger distances, but that just isn't our style.

To translate our cruising world into "land" English. Our boat is our home, the ocean and beach are our backyard, we anchor in a rural community, our dinghy is our car, and the island is the closest town. We are not disconnected and out drifting the great big blue alone, we are living within a community of fellow sailors of all ages and types, and are usually within a 10-minute dinghy ride to town. We have access to most "regular" commodities (depending on the size of the island), such as a grocery store, clinic or hospital, shopping, schools, and different island activities. Because we stay and live for such long periods of time in each location we often rent, buy or borrow a car (which we then sell when we leave, so be careful if you lend us a car.) This brings ease to our land commutes, allows for spontaneous escapades, and makes hanging out with island friends much easier.

Adding our children to the mix of sailing, adventure, and travel wasn't that challenging for us and I attribute much of that to the fact that we started sailing with one baby in tow. We didn't go from learning to sail as a couple and then try adding a kid. The learning curve of "sailing with kids" was achieved at the same time that we were learning how to sail in general. The two melded together and we learned to make it work with a child on board because that was just the way it was always going to be. In short, we had very few sailing habits that needed to be curbed.

We started off sailing in the sailboat that my husband had purchased and used as a traveling bachelor pad on water those many years prior. Although it did "work" for us we quickly realized that maybe 33 ft. of length and a 9.5 ft. beam (width in the middle) might be a touch too small for our needs, especially since we were hoping to grow our family and add another kid to our exploits. Reality set in when our daughter was trying to learn to walk and she only had 3 ft. in each direction that she could wander to. We even removed our table from the boat to give her more space. But even still with that modification things felt tight, and she learnt to topple from support to support instead of moving her feet in an organized fashion. Adding a second child to that scenario would have been hard on both, space, and my sanity. We spent almost a year on the smaller boat when a larger one, 41 ft. long and 13.5 ft. beam, came up for sale. It was a real fixer upper, but it was the only way we would be able to afford the extra space. We made the purchase knowing that the extra volume would make a huge difference for our comfort levels.

Although there are several concessions that need to be made to go from living a "normal" land life to the life of a live aboard, we see just as many benefits. These benefits are why we chose to continue living this lifestyle and sharing it with our kids. We have been accused of being selfish in pursuing an unconventional lifestyle and "forcing" it on to our kids, but we see it quite differently. We see our choice of living in a tiny floating home and traveling with our daughters as a way to teach them about the bigger picture; about responsible living and travel. When talking to people about our lives and raising the girls on the boat there are three major recurring topics of conversation; safety, socialization/education, and space.

Raising children on a sailboat may seem like a dangerous choice, but we see just as many dangers in raising a child on land, they are just "different" dangers. Our girls have never fallen overboard. They have very strict boundaries when it comes to the boat and we do everything in our means to control potentially risky outcomes. i.e. Our girls are not allowed to play on deck without an adult present. If they are alone outside they must stay in the enclosed cockpit. No playing alone outside after dark. No touching things that are not toys. And when we are sailing there is not standing up on the cockpit cushions and no walking around unassisted by an adult. Since this is the way they were raised they understand the rules and don't push them. It's just like teaching your child that he/she is not allowed to leave the backyard or cross the street without an adult. Kids understand that stuff. At least ours do. We also taught our daughters to swim at a young age. Being that our home is surrounded by water it seemed only smart. Both our girls are now mermaids, so if they were to fall in the water (and not bang their head or freak out from the event) they are quite able to at least swim around and call for help. To a lot of parents this may seem like a risky way to raise children but we see it as no more dangerous as getting in a car or a child playing near a pool. Risk is everywhere. We are extremely cautious sailors! Our family's safety is our first priority. We do not take unnecessary risks with the weather and we will patiently wait for weeks, at times, for ideal weather windows. If things unexpectedly go bad, which they have once or twice in our several years of sailing, we are not talking "perfect storm white squall bad" but we have plans that we set in place and it is amazing to see how quickly our daughters rise to the occasions. In those moments no ones life is abnormally in danger, we are just getting rained on a lot more than expected, blown around, and often a little queasy. In reality, they often tend to handle it better than the two of us.

Socialization and education for our kids is a topic of concern for many. No one wants to see a child with cabin fever who is socially inept. It was also a slight concern for us before we had the girls. We knew we wanted our babies to have plenty of friends their age, as it is an important part of growing up. We just had to figure out how we could make that work with our nomadic lifestyle. Both of our daughters are home-schooled now, which was not initially the plan nor was it even a necessity at their starting ages of 2 and 4, but it fits nicely with our travels. I used to teach at the elementary level and we purchased the books needed to keep the girls on par with the curriculum for their age groups. But how does that affect their social lives? It doesn't change much, it just means that instead of sitting in a classroom with a bunch of other kids each day, they learn their school subjects from me, in what has proven to be a much shorter period of time daily, and then get to learn all the social aspects of being a kid in other activities, such as play dates on the beach, extracurricular activities we enroll them in, and other boat kids and local children. All of the islands we live nearby are inhabited, and so there is no lack of children for our girls to play with. Most of these islands are also "vacation destinations" meaning the girls get to make plenty of foreign friends as well. Also, when two sailing families cross paths, they often try to spend as much time as possible together, prioritizing play dates, since it's always fun to hang out with other people that understand and are living in a similar and obscure manner. Sailing with our girls has given them the opportunity to make friends from many different cultural and geographic backgrounds. It has taught them to be fluent in the "language of play" since sometimes there is no common language amongst them and they still manage to communicate just fine.

One aspect that we are currently trying to work into our family's life a bit more is our extended families. Living in a moving home has meant that relatives are not close at hand. We don't get as many large family dinners and hangouts, the girls aren't growing up near their cousins, and there are no quick relief babysitters. But the flip side is that it has given our families some wonderful vacation spots to come visit us in. They get to come spend a couple of weeks each year in a new tropical destination where they don't have to worry about paying for lodging or food because they have us there to host them. Being that our home is considered tiny doesn't stop them, we shuffle everyone around for different sleeping arrangements and no one minds getting overly cozy since we only get a brief amount of time together. Our distance and nomadic lifestyle means that our moments with family are extremely special, and we are so proud to be able to share this adventure with them. This season we even sardined 10 of us on board for 2 full weeks!

Space is a big one. Just like in any tiny home, the amount of space that you live in is cut down to a quarter. This affects both your personal life as well as your stuff. Your personal bubble gets much less private. Even if send your kids to timeout in their room, they are still within earshot. Actually everything is within earshot, you become extremely well acquainted with every sound that comes from your spouse, kids, and vessel. Quiet time usually only happens at naptime and bedtime, and forget having private space as pretty much all space is shared (even the bathroom).

The benefit to the close quarters is that no matter where the kids are playing, I always know what they are up to. I can either see or hear them and know if they are getting into trouble or danger. Living in a smaller space has also created an amazing bond in our family. Our daughters always have one

of their parents close by, to talk to, play with, or bombard with questions. Family time is all the time. It has created a great sense of security for both of our girls and given them the confidence to grow and try out new experiences knowing that someone they trust is nearby.

It's not like our daughters are cooped up either. They have their own room, which consists of a queen size bed (V shaped however), shelves for all of their toys and books, as well as a whole other storage area, which we have dedicated to their playthings. To get down on your knees and see our boat from the standpoint of a three year old who show you how it is a huge jungle gym with plenty of space to have fun in. As for our stuff, yes we have less storage space than a lot of people, but we have become masters at Tetris. Everything has its spot and this helps keep our boat clean. Because of the size of our home, our daughters were raised with the simple rule concerning their things, only one game at a time. If you are done with one toy or game, you clean it up before you pull another one out. This helps keep our home happy and clutter free. The size of our home has taught us how little we actually need to live a happy life, and how not to go overboard with material objects. Our daughters may not have rooms full of toys, but they don't need it. They have plenty of fun with the toys they have and both have developed a great sense of imagination.

Even if our living space is smaller, this doesn't mean that we are cooped up. Lots of people worry that our girls don't have the space that kids should have, to run around and be crazy. This is partially true, inside our boat they can only run a 40 ft. distance at a time, but if you step into our cockpit you will see that our girls have endless space. They have a 360-degree backyard of endless possibilities. They have the ocean to swim in, the have beaches to run on, they have islands to discover. The world is literally their playground and they have much more free space than many suburban kids because of it.

Living on a boat, or even in a tiny home, may not be our "forever" plan, but we have loved the experience and will always be happy to have been able to share that with our daughters. Both our girls are confident, independent, and adventurous. Much of that came from being raised the way that they have been. As a family we made some concessions and chose to live this lifestyle and although it was different in the beginning everything got easier and more familiar with time. Even if sailing didn't feel natural at first, the more we sailed, the more we anchored, the more we slept in rolly anchorages, the more we got used to it, and it became a huge part of who we are today. We are happy to have traded land risks for the ocean ones because it means there is a beautiful island to call home at the end of every sail. We are happy to have traded traditional school for travel because it has given us a deeper knowledge of the world. We are happy to have traded some living space for an extremely close-knit family. Since overcoming the initial learning curve we have seen more benefits than anything else in living as a family in a tiny unconventional way.

The Cob Tiny House

How to fall in love with the walls

Conrad Rogue

Conrad Rogue is a teacher of natural building, founder and director of House Alive, and author of "House of Earth." For over 15 years House Alive has taught more than 1000 students how earthen building materials can enhance and uplift our built environment in a simple and elegant way. You can find out more at HouseAlive.org

What is Cob?

Cob is an earthen building technique, as old as human civilization. Clay-soil, sand and straw are mixed together into a wet "dough" and then put on the wall (with the material still wet.) The building process sometimes feels like playing with modeling clay for giants. The end result is a super strong, sculpted, thick walled house, with the bulk of the materials coming from right below your feet.

Earthen building is still actively practiced by   of the world population, anywhere from South America to Northern India, and in a great variety of climates. Besides cob, other earthen building methods that are used prolifically are "adobe" and "wattle and daub." With adobe, bricks are shaped with the help of a simple wooden form and then dried. Thereafter they are stacked using the same material as a wet mortar. With wattle and daub, a woven structure (reeds, bamboo, willow, saplings) is used, to then slap wet clay-soil up against. Think mud huts in Africa, or Hogans in the American southwest.

In all earthen construction forms, people benefit from the qualities of clay-soil: it becomes soft and sticky when wet, and hard and strong once it dries out. Not only does it have these great qualities, there is a lot of it: if you would wrap all the clay there is on earth around the world, like peanut butter around an apple, it would be a mile thick!

In North America, the revival of cob as a building method started to become serious in the early nineties, and was strongly promoted as a way to build "tiny." The basic thought was: why build poorly designed large structures if you can do just as well, or maybe even better, with carefully designed small structures. Because of the nature of the material, it's malleability, cob lends itself so perfectly for tiny design features in the form of customized detail work, built-in furniture and book shelves built directly into the wall. The ease with which you can build round walls using cob has made living in tiny cob houses so much more pleasant: suddenly the oppressiveness of rectilinear shapes and corners are gone. This always becomes crystal clear to those who first enter a cob cottage: people feel a breath of relieve in the absence of hard angles.

The immediate and obvious benefits of tiny cob cottages were very simple: less to build, less to maintain, less to furnish, less to clean and less to pay for. Also, less of the world's natural resources would be required for housing purposes. These benefits appealed in particular to people who had a strong interest in spending less time working for money and more time with their friends and family, arts and crafts, gardening and spending time in nature. The phrase: "why work for money to pay for a house that you can't spend much time in, because you're working all the time" made then, and still makes now, a lot of sense to a lot of people.

However, there are some other, more obscure reasons why so many cob dwellings end up being tiny. As par for the course, many cob builders take pride in going slowly and not using machines for mixing and transporting the material. Building sites are often peaceful, child friendly places, with the only sound the squishing of bare feet through wet mud and the wind in the trees. Going slowly has the potential for a higher quality built structure, but also means that if you want to move in at the end of the building season, you have to keep it small.

Having said that, I don't think cob building is slow per definition, or in comparison with other building techniques. The more you approximate the methods of perceived faster building techniques, such as stick frame building, by introducing more young and strong people, more machines and power tools, more purchased building materials, the faster you will go. The myth that cob is slow continues to live on merely because a lot of cob builders *choose* to build slowly.

A not unimportant reason why cob buildings often end up being tiny is related to the legal aspects of building. In part because cob building have always been difficult to get code approved, builders have often looked for out of the way places, where a tiny structure made out of mud could easily be obscured by trees and hill sides. Also, many municipalities allow you to build auxiliary structures without a permit, as long as they are smaller than 200 square feet. You still are not allowed to live in them, but at least the smaller structures tend to cause less suspicion.

Life in the Jelly Bean

My Cob cabin, called "the Jelly Bean," is located in the mountains of Southern Oregon. It is part of a larger intentional community; just a stone's throw away from the cabin is a larger common house with bathroom facilities and a sizable kitchen. The Jelly Bean has both an earthen floor, as well as a ceiling made out of earth. All the structural poles/rafters for the roof were harvested from the surrounding forest. It has 2 large windows purchased second hand, providing it with a gorgeous view of the mountains across the valley. The entire building is almost completely devoid of any glues, paints, varnishes, or other petro-chemical products. A comfortable chair in the corner, a homemade barrel stove, a built-in desk, a little kitchen counter and a sheepskin rug are its main features.

I have now lived in it for well over 2 years and I feel very good about my experience. Sure it is small, but has provided me with some unexpected surprises and discoveries that I believe are worth sharing.

First of all, it has held up very well. All the earthen materials, both inside and outside have proven to be maintenance free so far. The interior earthen finish plasters are durable and beautiful and on the outside, the sideways rain that we get from time to time has not caused any damage. It's important to mention this, as earthen buildings sometimes evoke an image of just sort of "melting away in the rain."

Secondly, a tiny cob cabin makes for the best dance parties. A small speaker can fill the space easily and we have danced freely with about 8 people at a time, having enough space to express ourselves, while at the same time feeling the "heat" of dancing close to others. The earthen floor makes for a fantastic dance floor and feels great on your bare feet.

At the other end of the social spectrum, when I have had people over for a cup of tea or glass of wine, I could not help but noticing how quickly the conversation took on a depth and quality, more difficult to achieve in other spaces. Maybe it's because you are sitting so close to each other. It makes me think of how much I like to go on long car rides with people I like, because the conversation often becomes so interesting. Because the light bounces so beautifully past the thick walls and because the acoustics are so rich, nuances in facial expression and intonation are clearer and therefore more intimate.

Perhaps related to the previous point, the smallness and beauty of the space has consistently given me a feeling of deep safely. The larger the space, the more our psyche can imagine the possibilities for people to hide, for unexplained sounds and smells, for unwanted air flow and dark corners and rooms. In other words, larger houses "host ghosts."

Because of this feeling of safely, as well as the "audible silence" of the small earthen space, the Jelly Bean has given me my best place to play music, as well as record. I play the didgeridoo, guitar and harmonica, and have found that the earthen walls bring an aliveness to the sound unlike any other space I have played in. A good microphone and a cell phone or tablet is now enough to create high quality recordings, making it possible to lay down tracks without having a tower of equipment and a spaghetti pile of cables on the ground. Generally speaking I have found that the digital age has really facilitated the possibility of living small. I grew up with alarm clocks, typewriters and stereo towers, so needless to say that a lot of appliances have disappeared out of my life.

I also thought a lot about the relation of the size of a house and how we interact with the world around us, whether it be nature, city or community. I mentioned earlier that I live close to a community house. Here is my premise: the larger the house, the less we tend to connect with the things outside the house; and equally true, the smaller the house, the more we will want to explore connections with people, things, nature, outside of it. Another way to put it would be: larger houses limit our lives. Even not having a bathroom inside has given me some of the most amazing peeing experiences late at night under the stars. In the end, small private places nurture us, but wilderness, the commons, great cafes and movie theatres, parks and street art, musical performance is what feeds us, brings us to life!

Loving The Walls

Whenever people come and see my cabin, almost instantaneously they put one of their hands on the wall. They want to feel it, in part because their brain doesn't recognize it as something they have seen before, but their soul instantly realizes the familiarity of it. Similarly, during my recent cob building project in Northeastern India (on the border with Bhutan), villagers would come by, stare at the building and they would just start to smile. What were they smiling about??

The familiarity that our soul experiences the moment we step into a cob building comes from a couple of different sources. First and foremost, I believe that our relation to clay is very significant. Not only have we as the human race lived in clay houses for millennium, we also have used it for pottery, ovens, fireplaces, healing purposes, practically all of human civilization has had an intimate relationship with clay. It is edged in our DNA. Scientists even suggest that the moment of "first life on earth," the becoming of the first microorganisms, was facilitated by clay. It's interesting to note in this

context that the word "Adam" means "clay" and that many other religious traditions have strong connections between clay and creation stories.

With the absence of hard corners and petrochemicals, cob buildings give us the opportunity to be in the presence of nature, earth, in the form of a building. Although cob is not "nature," it does express an absence of the manufactured world. That is a very unique experience and almost unheard of in modern times. This then comes with the inevitable feeling of "homecoming." Probably one of the worst things of modern civilization is that it has significantly severed the ties we have with the natural world. Our feet don't touch the earth; our eyes don't stare into darkness much, we don't eat much from the garden anymore and mostly, we have started to consider "nature" as a commodity, rather than our mother, the one that sustains us. In cob buildings we suddenly feel somewhat connected again, the world around us has echoes of nature in the shapes and materials of the walls.

The almost universal love I notice for cob buildings has strong roots in the previous 2 points. A third reason I have identified is the fact that cob buildings have a very low embodied violence (my term). By this I mean the collective violence done in the form of sound, machinery, labor abuses, physical abuses of humans or animals, mining, cutting, shaping, sanding, transportation, poisoning, waste, and more. Not only does it have a low level of embodied violence, it has a high level of embodied love: each little bit of cob may have been mixed and applied in wonder, with care and curiosity, while making friends, while helping out friends, out of love for family, etc.

Because of the clay material, the natural design and feel of the building as well as the embodied love, the walls of a cob building lend themselves fantastically for tiny houses. The walls don't become a limitation of space, an ending of a room, but rather a celebration, something you want to be close to. The walls surround you in the form of a "living art" that embodies everything that we wish for: safety, health, comfort, beauty, connection, and in the end, belonging. By having the walls practically hug you, you can feel these things, which may get lost, at least in part, if a cob house was designed more like a average American home. In this context we may come to understand choosing a tiny house not as expression of care for the environment, or a wish for financial freedom, but simply a deep, deep desire of wanting to be close to your walls!

The Regenerative Lifestyle

Finally, I would like to talk briefly about the hope that is encapsulated in a cob building. I am sure that if you are reading this book, you are at least minimally concerned about the well being of the earth, the natural world and the human race. (Things are not going that well!) By many of us, the word "sustainable" has been thrown around a lot in the last 50 years as a way to measure a style of living by which the earth could take the blows that we deal and recover endlessly. The problem with this outlook on the world is that one person's house is only sustainable to the degree that not everybody else wants the same house. For example, if everyone in India would want an 8000 watt solar panel array, that would be hard to achieve, even though a house in the United States with such an array is often referred to as a "sustainable house." Even our 1000 square foot community space may be highly questionable if we were to take the whole world into consideration. In other words, sustainability can never be an absolute thing, because it always depends on what everybody else is doing!

Then how do we create criteria for living that would give us solid guidance and hope for the future? The answer lies in replacing the word "sustainable" with "regenerative." The word "regenerative" suggests that my actions not only give me what I need, but also improve the world as it is for future generations. The simplest way to understand this concept is by looking at how people can grow healthy vegetables while at the same time improve the soil.

In cob building it's more complicated, but nevertheless possible. Because we take clay-soil from the earth, we can do it in a way that facilitates the formation of ecosystem enrichment, for example by digging a pond. Because of cob's malleability, its relatively easy to use small diameter, round wood, instead of dimensional lumber. It happens to be so that the American west is very overgrown with small trees and needs a never-ending thinning job. Harvesting small poles will help you build your roof while improving the forest health. And a last example, growing grains in compacted soils can give you straw for the cob, flour for your bread and help bring health back to the soil.

People are not always conscious of it, but they do feel that there is something so right about a tiny cob house. It gives us the notion that it is possible to shelter ourselves in a regenerative way. Nothing is ever perfect, but knowing that it's possible can sure put a smile on your face!

The Stigma of Living as a Home-Free Urban Professional

Terri K.

Terry K.'s writing on the subject of intentional, small-space living has appeared in Salon, Yahoo! Finance, Business Insider, LA Weekly, MSN, and The Good Men Project, and on his blog, theofficehobo.com. Terry, who has lived in many odd spaces–his office, his truck, a converted barn–has given interviews on the topic for Fusion TV, CBS News, WGN Radio, La W Radio, The Penny Hoarder, and Business Punk Magazine, as well as performing as a keynote speaker at the 2016 Tiny House Jamboree. His chapter in *Turning Tiny* examines the taboo of odd-space living for urban professionals and the trials and tribulations of striving to lead an ordinary life despite living in an extraordinary space.

It's the end of the workday and you're packing up to head home. The week's been a hectic one, full of deadlines and conference calls and talks of a possible merger between your startup and a larger company. Your boss is riding you. Most of your coworkers are on edge. You wonder if it's all worth it—the modest pay, the long commutes, the stress. But all you can think about is kicking off your shoes and escaping with a glass of cabernet.

You think you're the last to leave for the day, until you look up and see your coworker at his desk. You consider approaching him to vent about the excessive workload, but think better of it. He's friendly but he keeps to himself, and lately it seems like everything just rolls off him. He's so *calm*. What's his secret? Maybe he's not carrying his weight? Maybe he's so sly and aloof, he's found a way around working so hard like the rest of you.

Then why's he still here?

You shake it off, thinking back to the cabernet. You wave goodbye and leave the office. The door closes behind you and your thoughts drift away.

Yet as you drive off, your stress levels somehow rise, battling the traffic on your hour-long commute home.

Back in the office, your coworker's weekend has already begun. It started as soon as you left, when he jumped up to lock the door behind you while dialing up the Indian joint around the corner for some chicken masala takeout. In the ensuing hours, his secret is revealed. He'll grab a change of clothes from the duffel bags stored under his desk, bike down the street to the 24-hour gym, and practice his guitar in the back room. He might field a call from the agent no one knew he had or update that anonymous blog for his thousands of followers. Or maybe he'll bed down early tonight, unrolling the box-store air mattress behind his desk, inflating his way to sweet workplace/sleep space sub consciousness.

I know this routine because I've lived it. For 500 days. I lived out of my office, sleeping beneath my desk until I built a tiny living space in the back of my truck. Then I started sleeping there, in the back parking lot, continuing to my perpetual office routine, keeping it all secret from my coworkers the whole way through.

An entire movement of folks just like me, living in odd spaces and working regular jobs, is spreading all over the world. We live ordinary lives on the surface, but with an extraordinary lifestyle secret. It is the financial incentive, the specter of expanded leisure time and reduced stress, the horizon line of a yet-unrealized ambition, which courts us into the lifestyle, and the often stigmatized, sometimes criminalized, societal confusion about how we live that persuades us to keep it a secret.

You may know more of us than you realize. We are your coworkers, your bosses, the people serving your meals and driving your Ubers. We're the ones running your nonprofits or organizing your media campaigns, processing your bank deposits or writing the next novel you'll read before bed. Some of us have graduated from the most prestigious schools in the world and written letters of recommendations for your employees. We might be your child's teacher. Maybe even your mentor.

Call us the *working homeless* if you want, but understand that our brand of lifestyle choice is distinct from those involuntarily living on the street. Unlike the involuntary homeless, we need neither sympathy nor services. Our life is one of *intention*.

Better yet, we are the urban, professional *home-free*. We work hard and live unusually, eschewing rent or mortgage in favor of a more flexible way of life, putting our money and time towards that which our renting counterparts may find ethereal—attainable goals of early retirement, lofty ambitions in arts and entertainment, boundless horizons of travel and exploration.

We are the supply and demand dropouts, recognizing ever-ballooning populations and the diminished availability of reasonably priced housing within practical proximity to our jobs, choosing a *voluntary* return to simplicity rather than scrapping to maintain a lifestyle we feel is both outdated and unsustainable.

We are the new generation of economically conscious adults, young and aged, eager to redirect the effort needed to keep a traditional house or apartment elsewhere, unwilling to cede our hard-earned money over to wealthy land moguls in exchange for two pairs of walls separating us from where we really want to be in the first place.

So why on Earth are we so secretive?

Ours is a practical imperative. Society is not *yet* fully prepared to accept our way of life. They began by writing us off and have continued by insulting us and fighting our advancements. They make laws against us parking on our own public streets and building accessory dwelling units in our friends' backyards. They tell us we can't sleep beneath our desks or install ecologically friendly dwellings on their rooftops. They preach on their television shows how we've "given up" and claim on radio appearances how we "threaten" their community.

As more and more people question the vulnerabilities of the modern middle class existence, this will change.[7] Ours is a reactive culture, prone to hanging on to traditions well past their sell-by dates. Little by little, our lifestyle will shift from a movement to a model.

Mine is just one of a growing number of examples of average citizens making the change.

That change came in the summer of 2012. The status quo was shaky, my life ruled by rent. I was working multiple jobs to salvage a prison-cell-sized pad with a Porsche Panamera pricetag. I was stretched thin by insurmountable student loans from a sexy grad school, by medical bills and car payments, by frozen raises and bonuses and an untimely identity theft, by rising cost of living and absurd gas prices. A head-spinning spending spree on stuff I didn't need, leaving my once optimistic and passionate personality consumed with worry.

What the hell am I doing with my life?

I used to have savings. I used to travel. I used to think of fantastical things like *my future* and *being able to afford retirement.* I had ambitions to become a writer but no time to sit in front of the computer, lest I fall asleep face down at the keyboard after so many hours of unrequited hard work. And for what? Just to have a home such as the one my neighbor had?

This is the path many of those like myself took to housing freedom, to *financial freedom.* We recognized an inordinately large portion of our monthly budget being thrown away on a place we barely had time to enjoy, a place far too cumbersome to do so anyway. Spend enough time dusting every shelf and countertop in the house or shopping for replacement hand towels and you may come to the same conclusion—once you start adding up the opportunity cost of it all, you may realize all the great things you could've been doing instead of organizing your second walk-in closet.

Stroll around your city's public spaces and you'll run into prime examples of folks the new urban professional home-free. Like Lizandro, a 43-year-old bachelor living in his Volkswagen in West Los Angeles. I met Lizandro after playing soccer at the park near where he beds down every night. He's perfectly content working his way up the Whole Foods career chain while he

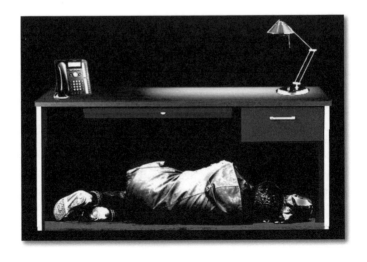

lives sans home. He's been doing it for years now, having made the decision after a divorce. Lizandro had a choice: Live farther from his place of employment or move into his van and live wherever the day's desires guided him.

"I can live somewhere else and pay more," he reasoned, "but then I waste more on commute. I love playing soccer, I love being at the beach. Everything kind of for me is right here."

Unlike most Angelinos, Lizandro is *saving* money. He sends cash home to his family in Guadalajara, Mexico, and enjoys eating healthy and attending concerts. His lifestyle is harmless. But it was, until recently, against the law. California's 9th Circuit Court changed that in the summer of 2014, striking down Los Angeles Municipal Code 85.02 banning vehicular dwelling. The law amounted to criminalized homelessness, and cities around the country have similar legislation on the books. Despite the ruling, Lizandro remains a model home-free citizen, taking steps to keep quiet around housed residents and dispose of his waste responsibly. He's a good neighbor. Just like he was when he had an apartment.

"I go to the gym, I have insurance, and I work. I pay taxes," Lizandro affirms. "I don't go to the neighbors with my music blasting, or talking loud. I'm not causing any harm."

He doesn't tell his coworkers, either. At least not unprompted. Lizandro's work ethic is his proof of upright citizenry. He fights silently against the tendency of others to misunderstand his lifestyle—and the misguided consequential legislation. Lizandro remains resilient, maintaining his positivity as well as he maintains his finances, persisting with his choice in the face of criticism.

"Society don't pay my bills," he says. "I can go back and prove to you that I'm not homeless. I can go rent me a place and be accepted into society. Oh, now I'm okay, you pat me on the back. I'm not homeless anymore. I don't care."

But some of us *do* care.

We are sensitive to the stigmatized status of our way of life. We're aware of the consequences and choose against boil our daily lives down to contrarian statements. Our main objective is to live in accordance with social norms in a great many ways—just not housing. Whether we do so temporarily or longer term.

I knew I'd be looked down upon—or worse—by my coworkers if I was found out sleeping in the office or in my truck. So I paid special attention to their needs, accommodating their routines to ensure that I wasn't. I tended to the trash on a regular basis and kept every file, every paper clip exactly how they left it. I devised a gym routine, alternating morning and end-of-work-day showers to ensure I was never both the first and last person at work.[8] I cut down my on-hand belongings to an absolute visible minimum. The company was a small one, so the task was manageable. Over time I grew to feel at home in the place. Living there was second nature.

Talking about it freely, however, never was.

Those who malign us in the media and elsewhere perpetuate myths about our lifestyle that keep us on the defensive.[9] The small-space, odd-space living movement, as of 2016, has yet to gain popular acceptance. But the tipping point is upon us.

There are places already setting the new standard for accepting the class of home-free urban professionals. Long known as a bastion for progressive thinking, Austin, Texas, is one place well ahead of the curve. The state's capital is well known for blending a Lone Star sense of independence with a college-town counterculture to concoct a vibrant subculture of odd-space dwellers.

My friend, John, is a reigning example. John is an account supervisor at an environmental marketing firm, spending his days arranging advertising campaigns and collaborating with fellow white-collar coworkers to devise strategic campaigns for partner companies. He's an expert in the field, someone his colleagues look to for advice.

Yet when John heads home, he walks along the side of the house to his backyard tool shed—his home. John discovered he could live in his tool shed while renting out his house during the South by Southwest music festival. He grew to like it so much, he decided to retrofit the shed for full-time living, and has been improving it little-by-little ever since. John likes that it nudged him to get out and interact more with the community he's grown to love.

"The idea that you would live in a big city and literally sit in a box of walls, "John said, momentarily incredulous. "There's so much to do! Get outside! Why imprison yourself?"

John's reward has been the renewed perspective on a return to essentials. He is the owner of the yard's main house, renting it out for discounted rates to budding artists in the community, saving much of his bi-weekly paychecks to support his goal of owning a second piece of land elsewhere. He is calmer, more relaxed than many of those in his field. He talks about walking to work—many miles, mind you—to get a better sense of the communities that lie between the two places, stopping by his girlfriend's place on the way.

Wait, someone who lives in a tool shed can have a girlfriend?

Yes. He can live in an office or a vehicle, too...*or* any number of places.

I doubted this when I began living home-free. I assumed the decision would render me a romantic leper; that voluntary homelessness would equate to involuntary celibacy. After all, how can a man be a viable mate if he appears unable to support himself?

It didn't take long for me to disprove the theory.

I've dated my fair share as a home-free urban professional. What I found was that the stigma of odd-space living was real, but not an inherent *obstacle* to dating. Even in a place like Los Angeles, known as a bastion for conspicuous consumption and keeping up appearances, there are eligible bachelorettes (and bachelors) accepting of unique lifestyles. But the creeping feeling that the next person you meet will be one of the faultfinders remains foremost on our minds.

Case-in-point: Samantha.[10] When I went out with Samantha, I knew the compatibility of my lifestyle with the popular culture would be tested. Samantha was a Vegas showgirl whom I'd met up with a couple weeks earlier, passing through the strip. She was in town for the night and asked me to meet her in Hollywood. I didn't think much of it. A simple hello, a couple drinks. So when I paid our tab and turned to find myself standing face-to-face with her, I was caught off guard.

"Let's go back to your place," she said, placing her arms around me.

For most men, a suggestion like this is a wild fantasy; for me, it was a logistical nightmare.

What was I supposed to do, ask her back to my desk?

Telling Samantha what was up now seemed impossible, in a swirl of dusty bar air and pulsing tunes. So I balked, deferring to all the naysaying voices in my head, deriding me for my living situation.

"How about I go back to yours?"

I took her hand and we left the bar. Before we reached my truck, I saw a van parked nearby. A van that was obviously lived-in. Being true to my playful personality, I grabbed for my keys and approached the van, pretending it was mine. Samantha pulled away.

"This is me," I said, deadpan.

"Oh, no no no!" said Samantha.

She stood in the middle of the street, horrified. I backed away and snapped my keys back onto my belt.

"Just kidding," I said. "My truck's this way. But *what if* I lived in my car?"

"Then I'd have to say goodnight now," she said.

Ouch.

Unfortunately, Samantha's remains the prevailing sentiment for much of the country. Folks like me are failures to be avoided. Hard stop.

Progressive places like Austin give both hope and a template for positive change.

No one exemplifies this more than Tab, the Executive Director of a non-profit called Project Schoolhouse, building schools and improving access to clean water in rural Nicaragua. In his free time, Tab is a salsa musician, playing his saxophone at gigs and festivals in his free time. And Tab has a lot of it, namely because he lives in a teepee in his backyard, having eliminated much of the overhead in his life. You can see the results in his face. He's at ease. The life of intention has done Tab well.

Tab moved into his first backyard teepee for 7 months while he renovated his new home. Years later, when he was running short on money in early 2014, he decided to rent out his place and move back into his teepee—this time a bigger, better one. Now he has time to visit his wide network of friends and family, visiting the often—regardless where they live. The last time I saw Tab, we sat around a fire in his teepee, cooking oysters from his recent trip to Northern California. It is the ascetic lifestyle which Tab cites as the main source of his happiness, allowing him to travel, play music, and serve the needs of those less fortunate than he.

"I like it out here," he says. "I don't know if I'll move back into the house."

What about Tab's love life?

"If she's the right person, she'll accept it."

Samantha, for me, was clearly *not* the right person. We did go back to her place that night, but I haven't returned her calls since.

I've grown confident in the future for odd-space dwellers like myself. The diaspora of home-free urban professionals living in secret is strong. But the tipping point is near. As more of us join the moment and share those experiences with others, the value of the lifestyle will become clearer and the stigma will subside, making it more common for those living unusual lifestyles to share their experiences more openly, more often.

Maybe then it'll make sense why that coworker sleeping under the desk next to yours is so relaxed—he's just got bigger and better things on his mind than worrying about making next month's rent.

Home Truths

Our journey to find (and redefine) our version of home

Julie Puckett

Julie Puckett and her husband Andrew moved into their beloved 1990 Bluebird school bus in May of 2015. Their creative natures allow them to thrive on the many challenges presented by tiny living, and the opportunity to problem-solve in beautifully unconventional ways.

You're already home where you feel loved.
—The Head and the Heart

My very first tiny house was one my father built for me in my family's backyard: it was a child-size, cotton- candy-pink cabin with a wood-paneled interior and orange shag carpet, and it was *beautiful.* Our family of five lived well below the poverty line for much of my childhood, so this amazing gift meant the world to me. It planted a tiny seed in my mind that a shack, if built with love, could rival a palace. It wasn't exactly a dream of mine to grow up and live in a school bus. I didn't watch The Partridge Family, or The Magic School Bus, but I did have a fascination with all things tiny. I still do.

Flash forward twenty years: the housing market had just crashed. Andrew and I were living in downtown Atlanta in a one thousand square foot apartment in a pre-war building. It was full of charm (*ancient*), had all of the original floors and windows (*it was freezing in winter and unbearable in summer*) and hadn't had many of the repairs it needed over the last seventy-five years. But it was in a great location, so naturally, it was priced accordingly... until our building was sold. The new owners adjusted the price upward or thirty percent without any accompanying improvements. We were already working insane hours to pay rent, bills and put a meager sum into savings each month. We told ourselves this was the last straw.

I then did what I had always been taught to do in a time of crisis: make a cup a tea. I made a list of our resources. In this case, we had about ten thousand dollars in savings, a strong desire to change our housing situation, and our personal fairy godmother of the digital age: the Internet. We keenly wanted to avoid the crushing weight of the thirty-year mortgages we watched our parents live in the shadow of the entirety of their adult lives. We knew too well how far-reaching the effects of debt on a family were, so a traditional home was never an option we really considered. Secondly, we needed to break free of the rent cycle that took so much of our income without giving us anything permanent in return. What choice, then, was left to us?

A lightbulb went on: tiny houses. *They were affordable. They were cute-as-all-get-out. They could be moved wherever and whenever we wanted.* We congratulated ourselves on being geniuses and I began the laughably easy task of finding our perfect tiny house.

Sounds too good to be true, right? Yep. It was.

The average cost of a tiny home varies widely, but typically begins around twenty thousand dollars for quality construction. That was already double our budget, and wouldn't get us the kind of finishes I really wanted. Secondly, most tiny house builders had a wait list of at least six months before they could even begin construction, and we only had four months left on our lease. Lastly, we would need a heavy-duty truck to tow a tiny house with, and didn't have any more money budgeted for a down payment for one. While many people would probably have moved on at this point, I'm famously stubborn. In this instance, it ended up saving the day.

The Bus

By sheer luck, I stumbled onto a site that specialized in something I had never heard of: school bus conversions.

I scratched my head curiously as I browsed through photos. *There was no way this was an actual thing people did.* A closer look told me that not only was it a viable way to live; it could be an aesthetically pleasing way to live!

Even more appealing was the fact that some of them were well within our budget and already partially or fully converted. The downside: the idea of buying a potentially ancient vehicle and then living in it was more than a little scary. I didn't feel it was possible for us to prepare ourselves adequately for this mammoth project in the short time we had, but every day spent fretting was one day less for problem solving.

For those of you who are considering converting a bus, or buying a converted bus, these are just a few of the things I advise you consider:

- How handy am I? Much like a stick-built home, things break in a bus. Sometimes the repairs are simple, sometimes not.
- How brave am I? Bus life isn't always a mirror of the luxury lifestyle you may have imagined.
- Do I have money set aside for potentially expensive repairs, or the know-how to fix them myself? Bus repairs can cost a small fortune for a mechanic to do.
- Do I have ample money/time for renovations, and a place to do them? Renovations can take years. Years. Allot more time for them than you think you need.
- Where will I park it once it's completed? I advise you have a solid answer to this before you even begin your renovation. I've heard too many nightmares about people finishing their buses, only to find themselves in a limbo with no permanent parking solution.
- Who will insure it? This was easily one of the toughest roadblocks we encountered. Our first insurer cancelled our policy within two months because they claimed they don't insure school bus renovations. Make sure to properly vet any company that claims to insure them. If you aren't sure about a particular company, use the resources at your disposal like the skoolie groups on Facebook or skoolie.net. They've both been incredibly helpful to us!

Granted, this list isn't comprehensive in the least, but these things are important to think about early on. This list is in no way meant to discourage anyone considering this lifestyle, rather it's meant to properly prepare you for some of the issues unique to bus life. It's a dream come true for us, yes. But it's also a hard and challenging way of life. I imagine the first American pioneers felt much the same as we do.

After a lot of consideration, research, and soul-searching, we had tentatively decided to go for it, when the discovery of a bus that was very close, almost finished, and in our budget sealed the deal. About a week later, we were driving up to Tennessee with our entire life savings in a cashier's check, praying the entire drive that we weren't going to get murdered. Spoiler: we did not get murdered. Even better, the bus (though not the fairest to behold) was going to make a great home once we were done.

We had a measly four months until our lease expired to finish the bus, pare down all our belongings, and move in. It was a tight timeline, and even though the difficult renovations were done, there was still a lot to do. A skilled carpenter among other things, my father agreed to help Andrew design and build the furniture for our bus. In a space with limited width, we decided everything should have multiple facets of functionality. A couch must also contain storage, a table must also transform into a dog crate, a bed should also be a closet, etc. My mother and I worked together to make insulated curtains, pillows and cushions for the bus. The four of us made a great team, and were able to discover a lot of clever, unexpected ways to make our bus as beautiful and functional as possible.

Tiny Design

Intentional design in any tiny space is absolutely imperative. When, from any angle, you can see the entirety of your home, it's paramount to choose colors and materials that won't overload your senses. I suggest keeping things fresh and light, with selective elements of contrast. For example, our bus palette is almost completely white and oceanic blues, but we contrast that with the dark floor and metallic finishes so it doesn't feel like a nursery. I also suggest putting quality furnishings and finishes in your home (though obviously, be smart about what you pay for things. Sales at high-end design stores are a great thing, my friends).

If you're having a difficult time choosing where to save and where to splurge, try to keep in mind that certain elements will drastically elevate the overall tone of your space. We opted for inexpensive fabrics, but balanced them with custom beadboard cabinets and furniture. Light fixtures are also a smart area to sink a bit of money into, since they have a ton of design impact as well as an important practical function. I can't stress enough how pivotal good lighting in a tiny home is- without it, your home could feel dark, cramped and depressing.

Tiny design isn't just about making your space look great, it's also about making it a place that you love spending time in. Investing in it is an extension of investing in yourself! If you absolutely love all of the aspects of your home, there's a much better chance you'll be able to sustain this lifestyle. Take the time, if you can, to make good choices and suss out the practical must-haves that are necessary to make your home the best home it can be for you. Our real-life example: when we were still in the building and planning stages, we were at a loss for what to do about our rescue dog, Starbuck's, crate. He had been trained to stay in his crate when we weren't home, and having his own private space had helped loads with his anxiety, so it was important for us to consider this in our future home. It would have been easy to just move his awkward, bulky, collapsible crate into the bus and say we would just make do, but I knew that we would get tired of that quickly. Instead, I had the idea to deconstruct his existing crate into something that could adapt to the space, and to everyone's surprise, it worked. His crate now snaps into the wall under our table, and can easily be folded up and stored behind the driver's seat when not in use. Starbuck has adjusted well, and loves his new home as much as we do.

One Year Later

It's been just over a year since that fateful voyage to Tennessee: a year jam-packed full of exciting, frustrating, growing experiences. Since this is the first home we've ever owned, we experienced a steep learning curve in home repairs arena. It's scientifically proven* that the second you buy property, eighty five percent of the previously functioning appliances in it immediately, inexplicably break (*data not based on any actual science or factual information). So it was with us, and our beloved House Bus. The water heater broke (thrice), the thermostat in our fridge went kaput, and the heater for the engine block decided it had lived long enough, thank you. Luckily we live in the age of YouTube, where merely Googling a problem will almost invariably yield some helpful tutorials on how to fix it yourself. A year ago, we would have just made a phone call to our landlord and let him take care of it, but now we've become much more independent and resourceful. Andrew fixed all three of the aforementioned issues, and I'm happy to report that they're all in working order.

Has tiny living changed us drastically? I don't think so. It seems to always disappoint people when I say that it isn't terribly different from living in a small apartment (living in downtown Chicago and Atlanta prepared us well for making this transition). We haven't missed the things we had to let go of to make this change- in fact, it's helped us be much more mindful of the things we spend money on, and prompted us to be ultra-conscious of what we bring into our home. In terms of our relationship, it's forced us to learn how to communicate clearly, quickly, and kindly. There's no room for anger and tension when you're in such close proximity to your spouse. It's important for us to work through problems instead of just suppressing them and hoping it'll go away, because it's imperative for the dynamic between us to be at its best. If at any point in your consideration of tiny living you think "My spouse and I could never do that," then maybe you're right. It's not easy, and it's not for the faint of heart. It takes a strength and commitment to your relationship that many might balk at. But believe me when I tell you, it is also brimming with rewards, both personal and shared, if you're willing to put the work in.

What's been the biggest adjustment? Andrew and I are both messy (don't worry, we're not slobs. Our bus just looks very "lived in" most of the time).

Keeping our home clean and tidy is an everyday challenge but one that's worth keeping up with. I can't describe how rewarding it is to look at this place after a good scrub-down, and smell that lemony-fresh scent that says, "That's clean!"

What do we love the most? It's everything we need, and nothing we don't. Living in a tiny space has dramatically shifted the focus of my life from making money towards pursuing fulfilling creative endeavors. Andrew now has the flexibility in his schedule to flourish artistically, and you can't put a price on that. I've begun to suspect that until you remove the need to constantly hustle, you're unable to be fully present in your own life.

What would we do differently? At the point we purchased the bus, the flooring and walls had already been done, for the most part, so we had little say in those matters. However, if it was ours to do from the start, I'd have made sure the floors had a more effective moisture barrier and were properly sealed. As it is, we get far too much moisture through the floors. As far as flooring material, I personally would have chosen wood versus laminate, or a wood-look vinyl, so that moisture wouldn't cause bowing and separation. I'd also have made sure the walls had spray foam insulation instead of just rigid insulate. It's not terribly effective, so we've had to rely quite a bit on our wood-burning stove and space heater to see us through the winter.

What's next for our bus and us? We've been invited to speak at a tiny house conference in Colorado this summer, so we're thrilled at the chance to travel with our home. We're also in the process of finishing our first full-length album, so after we record it, we'll be taking our bus on tour with our music. It's an exciting time for us, and we're very grateful for each and every opportunity that comes our way.

I hope that those of you with a tiny seedling of a dream will nurture it, cherish it, and give it the encouragement it needs to become something great. Don't ever let someone tell you your dreams are not worth doing! If we had listened to the scoffers and naysayers, we would have never had this marvelous adventure. Believe in yourself. Believe in the power of doing.

Little House in the Big Woods

Tara Alan

Tara Alan lives with her husband Tyler on their fledgling Vermont homestead, in the 12' x 16' timber frame and straw bale cottage they built by hand. They blog about their homesteading and travel adventures on their blog Going Slowly. In her chapter of *Turning Tiny*, Tara talks about the joys and logistics of hosting friends in such a small space.

Friends are my estate.
—Emily Dickinson

When we decided to build a house the size of a shed in the mountains of New England, we never imagined that entertaining friends would become an important part of our lives. After all, we were leaving suburbia in large part to divorce ourselves from a society we felt was deeply flawed. We had lofty goals of self-sufficiency, and looked forward to a solitary, Thoreau-esque existence.

In the winter of 2013, we bade a teary farewell to our beloved friends and family, leaving the Midwest to follow our hearts and homesteading dreams to Vermont. In our 8'x16' camper, we took up residence on a 10-acre woodlot in the Green Mountain National Forest. With the help of a rattling propane heater and the passion of long sought after dreams burning in our hearts, we settled into our new homesteading lives. We were two pioneers, with only blue mountain views and creaking skeleton trees to keep us company.

Or so we thought.

After a week, we decided it was time to meet the neighbors. We resolved to begin with the only house in the vicinity, a log cabin about a third of a mile away. Wanting to make a good impression, we baked a loaf of banana bread in our camper oven to bring as a goodwill offering. Then, we set off with the warm bundle in hand, wondering aloud who we'd find.

Would they be a kind elderly couple? Aggressive gun-toting yokels? Out-of-towners staying in their second home? Would they leave us in peace to start our homestead? Or, would they complain to the town hall about our unconventional goings on? If nothing else, we hoped they'd be neighborly enough to keep an eye on our place when we went out of town.

By the time we arrived at the cabin, we'd run through every possible neighbor-meeting scenario... except for the one we were about to experience. In response to our knock, a cheerful Argentine woman in her thirties opened the front door. A questioning look turned to a wide smile when we told her we were new in town. She introduced herself as Hercilia and invited us in.

Inside her home, we sat by a roaring fireplace, in a living room decorated with black and white photographs of Patagonia. With cups of tea in hand, we delved into a deep and meaningful conversation about life. While we chatted, her elderly German Shorthaired Pointer, Roscoe, vied for our attention. An hour passed in the blink of an eye. When we finally proffered the banana bread and said our goodbyes, Hercilia promised she'd bring her husband to meet us as soon as he got off work.

We practically skipped home. We'd hit the neighbor jackpot.

Hercilia was true to her word; she and her husband Jeremy came up to visit not long after. Jeremy, clad in colorful plaid, greeted us with a firm handshake and an easy-going smile. Just as we had with Hercilia, we hit it off right away. As dusk fell over our woods, we gave the couple a tour of our fledgling homestead. Roscoe sniffed around for squirrels, while we shared our hopes and dreams for the raw piece of land.

When it became too dark to see, our new friends left us with giant hugs and the promise that they'd come over the following weekend to help us install a hand-pump in our well. They seemed to be as excited as we were about the event.

As soon as they were out of sight, we whooped and hollered and pumped our fists with joy. From that day on, we were a budding community.

By the end of our first year on the land, we were anything but isolated homesteaders. Along with Jeremy and Hercilia, we'd befriended a second couple a little further down the road: Charlie and Becky. These fun-loving retirees rounded out a six-person neighborhood crew we semi-jokingly began referring to as "the 'Hood."

Together, we never let an opportunity to hang out slip by—anything was a good excuse to have a party. There were lazy summertime cookouts, impromptu afternoon visits, movie nights, weekend brunches, and holiday celebrations galore. No matter what the occasion, our friends were with us to soothe a homesteading meltdown, or raise a toast to a hard-won triumph.

Our camaraderie extended well beyond the social. We took advantage of our diverse collection of skills and many pairs of hands to make light work of any and every project. From shed-building to firewood stacking, we worked side by side to make the tasks more efficient and enjoyable.

This growing interconnectedness gave rise to a dramatic shift in our thinking. The notion of being entirely self-sufficient was discarded as a naïve and lonely relic. As integral members of a thriving rural community, we were now convinced that interdependence was far more far more desirable than independence.

As our thinking changed, we began to question our plans of building a tiny woodland cottage. The idea started to seem bizarre and selfish. Would we be excluding our friends by constructing a house so small? Would it even be logistically possible to invite four people to dinner? After a year of being welcomed into our friends' homes with open arms, we longed to be able to reciprocate.

Still, there wasn't much to be done about our concerns. We'd already poured a foundation and cut the 12' x 16' timber frame that would become the bones of our house. Since we couldn't easily enlarge it, we'd simply have to make it work.

When the spring of our second year in Vermont made its muddy entrance, the time had come to get started on our house. We kicked off the building season by hosting an old-fashioned "barn raising" party. On the morning of the event, our neighbors and friends from the community arrived one by one, hiking to our ridge-top house site. Some came with tools and work gloves, others with pitchers of coffee and baskets of baked goods. All came dressed for the drizzly, chilly day.

Despite the grey weather, there was something magical about the frame-raising. Between bites of scone and sips of java, we fitted tenons into mortises. While laughing and chatting, we drilled holes into each joint. With a massive hand-hewn wooden mallet, we hammered in each peg. When we worked together to lift each section of the frame and secure it in its new, vertical position, we all erupted into cheers. By the end of the day, most of the frame was raised.

As we toiled on our project throughout the following seasons, we celebrated each milestone informally with our friends. Together, we'd marvel at how our newly-installed roof made the space seem more house-like. As we stacked straw bales around our timber frame, our friends encouraged our progress and pitched in to help. When at last we plastered the walls, the transformation from straw to house felt miraculous. Our friends were nearly as excited about it as we were.

On a frigid November night, the rattling propane heater in our camper wheezed its final puff of warm air, and died. A few miserably cold days later, we finished installing the chimney and woodstove in our little straw bale cottage. It was the last piece of the puzzle, the final task that needed to be accomplished before the place would be livable. Though the "it" resembled a disaster area and represented a seemingly endless amount of work ahead of us, we moved in.

We've now been living in our cottage for a year. It's not completely finished—we still need to add slate to the roof and pour an earthen floor over our concrete one—but by this point, all the plaster splatters have been cleaned away, our kitchen is fully functional, and most of the interior finish

work has been completed. Mercifully, we no longer inhabit a construction zone.

It is with relief and joy that we're able to report our successes on the entertaining front: after years of yearning to reciprocate our neighbors' hospitality, we're finally able to. And it's glorious. Despite the cottage's diminutive size, it lends itself wonderfully to hosting friends. We've had Jeremy and Hercilia over for long, lingering brunches, and Charlie and Becky for fabulous dinner-and-a-movie nights. We've had other friends over for scones and tea, and cozy dinners by the woodstove. We've even hosted board game nights, holiday parties, and a full-on Christmas dinner!

When our friends visit us these days, they come by way of a curving woodland path that winds its way uphill to our cottage. As soon as they get close, we open our green front door wide and beckon them in, greeting them with hugs. Boots are removed; coats and hats are hung on hooks; tea is offered.

Though most of our friends have seen our house by now, occasionally we still get first-time guests. Their eyes grow wide with wonder as they scan our small but expansive, light-filled space. They run their hands along the off-white, gently undulating plastered walls, and our smooth, dark-stained wooden beams, murmuring about how beautiful the place is, how it feels larger than it is.

When our friends are finished with first impressions, we give them the tour, showing them as many details of our house as they wish to see. We begin in the kitchen, which takes up half of the one-room space. First, we show them our favorite window of the house, where we can admire views of our woodland and the mountains beyond while washing dishes in our 36" farmhouse sink.

There's something special about the wide sills and window reveals that straw bale walls afford. On the kitchen windowsill, we keep heaps of fruits and vegetables, and sometimes pots of herbs. The curving plaster reveals on either side of the window are so achingly beautiful, and somehow timeless, it makes us feel as though we've stepped into a Vermeer painting.

Continuing the tour, we point out the diminutive fridge, and our regular-sized propane-powered range. We show off the cabinets, which we designed and built ourselves, of which we are inordinately proud. There's a narrow, pullout pantry drawer for oils and vinegars. There's also a wider drawer for garbage and recycling, and a trio of drawers that house our cookware. Our favorite cabinets are the uppers, which we purposefully built with two rows of open shelves. On one, our flours, nuts, beans, and sugar are displayed in glass jars with pretty labels. Below that, two-dozen spices are easily accessible in smaller glass containers.

When the tour of the kitchen is finished, we turn to the other side of the house. There, we show our friends the nooks we carved in the bale walls for our speakers, and the stereo system that's housed in the trimmed-out, insulated knee-wall of our house. To maximize the storage space in the knee-wall, we also built rolling containers for shoes, out-of-season clothes and outerwear, and firewood.

In the living area is our wood stove, the adorable Morso squirrel, which sits in the corner on a hearthstone approximately the shape of a baseball diamond. Against the wall between the living room and kitchen is our gate leg dining table, which includes six ample drawers. When the sides of the table are down, the piece is only 10" wide! We usually use it with one of the sides raised, which creates a nice 3' x 3' working space. When both sides are raised, however, it seats six people!

Towards the end of the tour, we're proud to show off our two most recent and most fabulous additions to our little house. First off, there's the wooden ladder we built to reach our half-loft bedroom. It's simple but beautiful, stained dark to match our beams, and held together with wrought iron nails. The marvelous thing about it is the mounting plate we had custom-built by a friend of ours. The mount allows the ladder to swivel side to side, as well as tilt upwards. This allows us to rotate the ladder up and completely out of the way when we aren't using it.

The other most recent features of our house? A projector mounted on the kitchen ceiling, and a nine-foot screen, mounted to one of our tie-beams. When the screen is pulled down and the projector turned on, our little house transforms into private movie theater!

Everyone has their own priorities when it comes to tiny house design. We would never have guessed that entertaining would become so important to us! Here are some things we've learned from the experience of hosting friends in our little home:

Having a one-room open space is wonderful. Ours morphs from living room to kitchen to dining room to movie theater with very few adjustments. Divided into multiple spaces, this house would most likely feel cramped and crowded.

Before our current loft ladder setup, we were using a temporary metal ladder that took up nearly all of our house's open area. We'd fold it up when friends came over, but it still took up far too much space. Our custom-fabricated mount for our current ladder allows it to be swung up and out of the way completely, leaving more room to hang out!

We don't have an indoor bathroom, which affords us more space than we'd have otherwise. Instead, we have an outhouse, just steps from our front entrance. It has a Dutch door and a slate roof, and is the cutest privy we've ever seen. So far, no one has complained about our sawdust toilet, and folks seem to enjoy carrying an old-fashioned lantern outside and being able to look at the moon while they do their business.

Our multi-purpose dining table from IKEA is an entertaining godsend. It was ingeniously created to expand from just 10" wide to a full six feet. We love being able to adjust the size of the table to suit our entertaining needs. Bonus: the six drawers provide prime storage space!

Having a spacious kitchen, a large sink, and hot running water (via an outdoor cistern) makes it easy to cook for large groups and clean up after them as well. We even helped cater a 20-person weeklong event from our kitchen!

Having a house that takes care of itself makes entertaining easy. Our super insulated straw bale walls make it ridiculously comfortable and easy to heat even in the most brutal of Vermont winters. It stays nice and cool in the summertime without any effort whatsoever. Less fuss about our home means more time to hang out!

Just because we live off-grid in an off-grid cottage in the woods doesn't mean we can't enjoy modern luxuries. Our stereo and home theater system make our place a blast to host movie nights!

Wooden folding chairs are great. If too many people come over, however, we have to ask them to bring their own!

Just a few weeks ago, we crossed a new threshold with our entertaining when we hosted our first overnight guests. Our friends Ian and Melissa from

New York City were eager to see our house, and crash here to enjoy a week-end of skiing in Vermont. Despite our overwhelmingly positive entertaining experiences, we wondered how the weekend would go. What would our big city friends think of our little house? How would they deal with our out-house? Would they be comfortable? When they said they'd be fine sleeping on the floor, did they realize just how small our home was?

When at last they arrived, I was touched to see that after greeting us with hugs, they entered our house with the same rapt, delighted looks we often get. They were amazed and tickled, running hands along beams and plaster, stunned by the beauty of our place. And then, putting our small home to the test, they brought in all of their camping and skiing gear, which they stowed easily on our window seats.

They brought wine, and we lingered over garlicky pasta and Italian meats, chatting and reconnecting for hours, as the wood stove warmed us all. When the meal was finished, we put the table away, and we turned our little house into a movie theater. On the big screen, we watched funny clips and shows, until we were all spent and tired. Then out went the movie theater, and a large, open space was created once more, this time for Ian and Melissa's cozy nest of sleeping mats and sleeping bags.

We climbed our ladder to retreat to our own bedroom, and then we pro\ceeded to joke and laugh like kids because it almost felt like we were sleeping in a giant bunk bed, with us on the upper bunk, and them on the lower. We talked and teased and laughed until eventually, as if at a sleepover, we all dropped off to sleep, cozy and comfortable in this little woodland home.

Dude Making a Difference

Rob Greenfield

Rob Greenfield is an adventurer and activist on a mission to affect positive social and environmental change. He lives off the grid, in a 50 sq.ft. tiny house in San Diego, California where he harvests rain water for all of his water needs, uses only solar power, and of course composts his own poo! 50 sq.ft. is truly tiny but he does it as an extreme example to get people thinking about the benefits of living more simply.

I say I live in a tiny house. Truth is the 50 sq.ft. I call home is even less than tiny. It's truly the smallest house that I've seen in person or even on the Internet. One might refer to it as Micro. Because of the dimensions I can't even stand up inside and I'm only 5'10". Simply stated my home is a little wooden box, on a trailer, with a few windows and a door. It doesn't get much more basic than this. I love simple living. Don't get me wrong. Even I had something a little bigger in mind though when I imagined my *dream* tiny house.

During the entire dreaming and planning stage I knew I wanted to build my own tiny house to custom fit my needs. I was ready to get out of my apartment immediately so I knew I might have to scale back some to meet a reasonable timeline. I knew it would take a few months to build the house so I started on Craigslist with the idea of finding a camper to live in while I built. My eyes stopped scrolling the ad listings when I came upon a little wooden house sitting atop a trailer. My heart started racing when I read that it was only $950. I thought it must have been a typo because it looked too incredible to be just under a thousand dollars. I remember well. It was New Year's Eve and I called up the number on the listing, met on the other end by an old man named Chris Scott. The next day I was riding my bike up to his place five miles away with $1,000 cash in my pocket. It was going to be a new year and a new beginning for me. I bought the house on the spot not even stopping long enough to consider if it was a good idea or not!

Once the excitement of my purchase waned I had to find a place to put it. Whereas some people might spend endless hours looking up the legality of tiny houses, I'm a bit more of a rule breaker. My heart follows 'Earth Code' rather than city code, which means that if what I am doing is good for the Earth and its inhabitants, as well as causes no harm to others, than it is within code. I followed this notion and wrote a blog post titled *Looking for a Home for my Tiny Home* and explained the mutually beneficial relationship that I envisioned. I outlined that in exchange for an unused backyard I would set up a sustainable homestead with raised bed gardens, rainwater harvesting, and a compost bin, as well as do general labor to improve the land. I also explained in the post that I was looking for someone who is excited about being a part of these same efforts so that my presence would be of some benefit to them. A number of people told me that backyards don't truly exist in San Diego and that I'd have no chance, but the dozen or so offers that I received proved otherwise.

I came to an agreement with a gentleman by the name of Jim Bachman, who owns an alternative energy company and was excited about many of the same things as me. His backyard had gone unused for the last eight years and he was more than happy to have me living back there.

As stated before my goal went beyond just living in a tiny house. I also wanted to live in a very Earth friendly manner focusing on self-sufficiency. At the same time I wanted to live without traditional overhead costs or debt associated with an American home. I wanted to be largely independent of the systems that I choose not to support.

I see tiny house living as a way to accomplish much of what I'm most passionate about: reducing my personal destruction to the Earth and its inhabitants, decrease my dependence on money, to live a life of human equality with my neighbors, and to fill my time with purpose and passion. On a deeper level my goal remains to be a positive example for others and to serve as a source of inspiration and information to aid others in transforming their lives as well.

The most powerful way to do such is to literally lead by example. I did so by moving into what is now known as "The Teeny Greeny," my initial boxy, home purchase.

When I look at my life and the world around me I constantly think about overall global sustainability. Is what we are doing something we can continue doing? Rather than thinking of what I want first, I tend to think instead about what is best for the human race now moving past seven billion people worldwide, the countless species of animals we share the Earth with, and the Earth itself. It is the thought pattern that ultimately led me to living off-grid in a tiny house in the first place.

I find it important to note that off-grid living isn't synonymous with living in a cave or even removing oneself from all technology and facets of modern life. A better-suited definition for off-grid living is "for one to not be dependent upon public utilities, especially the supply of electricity." Being water independent is also standard for living off the grid.

In order to meet my electric needs I setup a solar array of just two small panels. My goal overall was to reduce the number of items I owned that were dependent on electricity anyway. I scaled back to my laptop, a headlamp, a couple of bike lights, a camera, an electric razor, and the three-watt LED bulb in my tiny house. By going on this electronic diet changed my needs in such a way that I didn't need a large solar panel and batteries. I was also much happier because I wasn't spending as much time on electronics and their usage.

Perhaps though the most challenging aspect of self-sufficient living that I encountered in San Diego is water. 85% of San Diego's water comes from either the Colorado River or the mountains in Northern California, both of which are hundreds of miles away. San Diego is considered a Mediterranean climate and is almost a natural desert. That said it rains about ten inches per year yielding a personal rainwater harvest potential of 10,000 gallons of water yearly for an average sized house. I managed to use just two to five gallons of water per day. The average San Diegan uses 80-100 gallons per day. 20 gallons of that water count is spent. I spent zero. Rather than setting up an off-grid solar heated shower, which would have been simple and spectacular, I just continued my routine of swimming in the Pacific Ocean. It was easy for me to meet my needs just from rainwater, even in a mega drought. Fortunately for me rainwater harvesting is legal in San Diego (unlike some other areas). The city actually encourages it and gives rebates to those building a rainwater-harvesting unit. Outlawing harvesting water from the sky is an unjust law that I'd happily break anyway.

Prior to moving into the tiny house I was coming up on almost two years without a traditional shower. I of course bathed, but did so in natural bodies of water like oceans, lakes, and rivers, or by using just a gallon or so of water from the sink. Living in "The Teeny Greeny," my "shower" time in the ocean was a time to connect with Earths elements. I find this exposure to be what keeps me feeling truly alive. As far as the rest of my personal hygiene I use very few products; just a toothbrush, toothpaste, floss, coconut oil, Dr. Bronner's soap, and essential oils. In the past this list would have filled up an entire paragraph but over the last five years I have taken back my body from the corporations and the chemicals they sell.

I have never been in another tiny house but I assume that a large percentage of them now have either a flush toilet or a septic tank of sorts. For me it was absolutely essential to set up a compost toilet. I could have made this quite complicated but instead I just threw together a simple system that revolved around two five-gallon buckets, a toilet seat, and a box that I made out of scrap wood. Instead of flushing my toilet after use, I covered what I left behind with natural elements like leaves, and when the bucket was full I added it to a compost pile. It was a perfect example of a humanure system.

Humanure is nothing more than composting human waste. It is a combination of the words "human" and "manure." The first question I am typically asked is, "Doesn't it stink?" The second question is "Is this safe?" It is not stinky and it is indeed safe. An entire book called *The Humanure Handbook* exists on this very topic. In the past I would have thought it absurd to poop this way but now I find it absurd that one flush (1.6 gallons) is just slightly less water than the average person living in mainland Africa gets in a day.

I did not stop there though. I live a near zero waste life in most areas of my personal life. In an average month I would create just a one-gallon Ziploc bag worth of trash. The average American creates that each day before dinnertime. I'm able to achieve this primarily by composting, buying secondhand items, avoiding disposable products, shopping for unpackaged food at the co-op and farmers markets, and buying quality stuff that I can repair if/when it breaks. A major plus is that I didn't need a garbage can or recycling bin, so there was also no need for trash pick up services.

Just outside my little abode I had a few raised bed gardens were I grew some of my own food. Contrary to some of the Internet stories I read about my place, I do not live a completely self-sufficient life (although I would like to) and do not produce all of my own food. In fact I produced less than 5% of the food I ate while at my house. This was one area where the mega drought largely defeated me. Not because it was impossible to grow food but because I prioritized other things in life. To keep money spending to a minimum I still do a fair amount of dumpster diving. Now I don't dive for half eaten sandwiches out of garbage cans. I'm talking about grocery store dumpsters filled to the brim with perfectly good food. You truly have to see it to believe it and Googling "Food Waste Fiasco" will more than likely amaze and disgust you both. I also bought a fair portion of my food at the co-op down the street. This activity accounted for the largest expenditure of money for me.

This leads me to the topic of money. The most common thing preventing my peers from living out their dream, whether it be living in a tiny house or a mansion, is money. The decentralization of money from my life is truly the largest factor in allowing me to live in alignment with my beliefs, while living out my dream. By moving into my tiny house I was able to achieve my aspiration of living without a single bill or debt to my name. Instead of paying rent I did a work exchange. Instead of paying utility bills I worked with nature. Rather than have my own Internet at home I used community resources such as shared office space, the library, or cafes. I was able to cancel my last bill – my cell phone plan – when I abolished my need for constant connection. I am still deeply connected to the world around me via the Internet but now I can more consciously choose when or when not to be connected. This is one of the toughest balances in my life, as I have some sort of dependency (or maybe addiction) to constant connection, as I imagine hundreds of millions of other people do as well.

The entire set up of my off-grid tiny house life cost right at $2,500 and I was able to do this by savings I had worked hard for in previous years. For many people that I know $2,500 is the equivalent of 2-4 months' rent.

Some would assume that by removing money from my life I find myself having to "mooch" off others. This simple couldn't be further from the truth. Removing money from the center of my life was the key factor in the equation of how I could dedicate my life to the service of others and the Earth. By doing this I have freed up the time to follow my heart, and my heart leads in the direction of helping those who have a hard time helping themselves. Since moving into my tiny house I've vowed to donate 90% of everything I earn from media (blogging, writing, speaking, etc) to grassroots efforts that improve the world. That has amounted to around $30,000 in a year of living in my tiny house.

Make no mistake. I am unapologetically and intentionally extreme. My message isn't to do just as I do or to take things to the outer limits as I have. Rather it is to take what you'd like to from my extreme message and adapt it to your life in whatever way that you see fit. We can't all do exactly what I am doing. Many of us don't even want to. But we can all live a more examined life and make sure that our beliefs line up with our actions. I lead by

example but simply can't be the example totality. For instance, San Diego has a very temperate climate, which makes living in my tiny house much easier than many other places. I'm not an example of exactly what to do in frigid cold winters of Canada or Wisconsin. However much of what I am doing personally can be adapted to life in Wisconsin with little to no effort. Other things do have to be adapted though in order to meet the cold winter. For example I believe 50 sq. ft. is too small for comfort in the frigid winter but I think a simple 250 sq. ft. log cabin, heated with wood, is an adequate tool for the elements there.

Another example is that I have chosen not to have children. Because of that personal choice I can't be a forthright example to families or parents. The good news though is that those examples do exist and are living by example in their own right. And in case anyone is wondering there are incredible partners out there who are also seeking the simple life. My girlfriend lived in an apartment while I lived at "The Teeny Greeny" but loved spending time at my house with me.

AUTHOR'S NOTE: You may have noticed that part of my story is written in past tense. When I started this chapter I did so sitting in my tiny house. After one year I decided to move onto other adventures. In my quest to simplify my life to an even greater extent I got rid of nearly all of my possessions. I have substantially less than 150 items, all of which fit on my back comfortably. I am finishing this story from an Internet café in southern Mexico. I am traveling for the time with my girlfriend largely in service to others. The goodness of "The Teeny Greeny" does live on though.

I turned my tiny house into ten tiny houses for people who do not have homes. I did this by partnering with an incredible woman who is starting a tiny house community in San Diego and using my house as a tool to cover the costs of the ten tiny houses that she wanted to build. I auctioned my house by fundraiser and successfully turned my $950 house into $10,000 for Homeless to Housed. I am very excited to see people benefit from these tiny homes far more than even I did.

In closing I deeply encourage you to seize the life you have and do what you feel that you are called to do. Again that may or may not involve a tiny house or a tiny life. You may be scared and you may not understand how it will all work out. But know that if you put your full passion and effort into living a truly purposeful life that you will come out where you want to. And even if you don't you'll likely feel so alive that you can just try all over again. It starts with little changes, one day at time. I've found with each little success the momentum picks up and it becomes easier and more enjoyable. It probably won't happen overnight though and it will take hard work. Start today though! There is no time like the present.

Finding Joy in Adversity

*How living in a historic 80 sq. ft. log cabin in the
Colorado Mountains changed my life*

Andrew Morrison

Andrew Morrison, a professional builder of 20 years, designed and built hOMe in 2013 along with his wife Gabriella. He shares his knowledge by teaching workshops and offering consulting at their website TinyHouseBuild.com. His tiny journey started 20 years ago when he and Gabriella lived in an 80 sq. ft., 100 year old log cabin in the mountains of Colorado while pregnant with their first child. He writes about finding joy in diversity.

I went to the woods because I wished to live deliberately.
—Henry David Thoreau

Tiny houses are not new nor are they a purely American concept by any means. In fact, people the world over live in tiny houses and have for generations. Here in the United States, there are examples of tiny houses all over the country from old beachfront homes in Florida to historic miners' cabins in the mountains of Colorado; and it is here, in one such cabin, that my tiny life story begins.

It's 1995 and my wife Gabriella and I had just graduated from college and moved from Massachusetts to Colorado. I was working full time on a geotechnical drill rig and Gabriella had part time work at Pizza Hut as a delivery driver. We were young and optimistic, and life was full of opportunity. We rented a two-bedroom home in the mountains outside of Boulder with Gabriella's brother and soon to be sister-in-law. We missed our autonomy and privacy, yet were painfully aware that the cost of living was really high in Boulder, and we simply could not afford to rent a 2-bedroom home on our own. That didn't stop us from looking though.

One day, upon my return from a long day at work, Gabriella asked if I wanted to go check out a nearby cabin she had found for rent. Keep in mind that this was 1995, and online property searches were not exactly "a thing" yet. The fact that she even found something nearby and in our price range was an amazing feat in and of itself. We got in the car and drove over Sugarloaf Mountain to what would ultimately be our home for the next eight months. It was late fall and the temperatures had started to drop; however, a particularly delicious Indian summer had stretched out over the days when we first visited the cabin, making our first impressions shine that much brighter.

The moment we got there, we both knew that it was the perfect home for us. It was everything we had wanted: remote, simple, affordable (by Boulder standards anyway), in a beautiful setting, and close enough to work for a reasonable commute. There were details that intrigued and excited us about the cabin that we had not previously considered when looking for a place to rent. For example, there was no running water or indoor plumbing, no power, and the cabin was a significant walk from the road (which I discovered matters more and more as the snow piles up). We had no idea what living in this historic cabin would be like, but we loved the romantic images our minds had created so we signed the lease and moved in.

Let me jump back a few weeks in time to set the stage for this move. Gabriella and I had enjoyed living with her brother and sister-in-law; however, we were ready to start our own "adult lives." It had somehow gotten into both of our minds that in order to truly start creating our own life, we needed to live in a house where we didn't have roommates. I guess the idea of roommates was too connected to college life, even though Gabriella and I lived alone my senior year at college in a one bedroom studio space off the back of an old farm house. I guess that was actually our first tiny house experience, but that's another story for another time.

A major reason for our sudden decision to officially become adults was the fact that Gabriella was pregnant with our first child. We quickly took stock of our lifestyle and made choices about what we wanted to create for our family moving forward. It was clear to us that starting a family in a shared house was not what we wanted, yet finding a place we could afford with our incomes was difficult. We searched for a while before Gabriella stumbled upon a flier at the local market, which read something like: "80 sq.ft. cabin. No water. No power. Remote. $400/month." To say were we interested would be an understatement.

Fast-forward a month from move in. Our lives and our experience with the romance of living in a tiny cabin were very different than they were just one short month ago. Much of that had to do with a change in the weather. The Indian summer had gone, temperatures had plummeted, and snowstorms continued to bury us in our simple mountain cabin. The reality of our choice to live in this space had landed squarely on our shoulders. Much of what we didn't know about the cabin in advance of moving in, (let's call them "quirks and fine details,") were rapidly revealing themselves to us.

As the challenges of living in this old, tiny cabin started to pile up along with the snow, we had a choice to make. We could choose to fight the reality of our situation, or we could choose to embrace it. Although there may actually have been several choices in front of us, they all ultimately boiled down to one of these two. Perhaps it was our youth. Perhaps it was our excitement for life and experiences. Perhaps it was less sexy than that and it was simply that this cabin was what we could afford. Whatever the reason or reasons that influenced our decision, we chose to embrace the experience of living in the cabin, with all of its challenges. I am so grateful for having made that choice.

The first challenge that was impossible to ignore was that we now lived on an unmaintained, two-mile long dirt road. This meant that no matter how much it snowed, there would be no plow coming to help us out. But hey, I had a 4WD car with studs on all four tires, plus two sets of chains, so I figured "how hard could it be?" That mindset proved to be part of the romantic vision I referred to earlier. The reality was that even with that great car and snow chains, when three feet of snow falls over night and high winds create six-foot tall snowdrifts, making any headway is really hard. I soon learned that a shovel in the back of the car was a must and that pushing through bumper-high snow at 6am, before my few and far between neighbors had left their homes, was always an adventure. Being 22 years old, I was all for adventure, so I chalked it up to another chance to really experience life. After all, how many people get to experience digging a car out of a remote, snow-covered road at 6am as they blaze a fresh trail through the mountains of Colorado?

Speaking of adventure, have you ever had to use the bathroom in the middle of the night? Not too adventuresome, I know; however, add to this mundane task the fact that your bathroom is an outhouse some one hundred yards away from your front door and the adventure starts to formulate. Add yet another detail to the growing image: that on multiple occasions, bear, elk, bobcats, coyotes, and mountain lions have been either seen or heard in the meadow between the front door and the outhouse. This was our life. It was just part of our every day experience. I should mention that trips to the bathroom are much more frequent when pregnant. Let's just say that Gabriella was a pro at making the two hundred yard round trip voyage, no matter what time of day or night.

Then there was the wood stove, which was a challenge completely unto itself. It was huge and took up an entire corner of the cabin with its five-foot tall stature and nearly three-foot diameter. This behemoth was good for two things: blasting us out of the cabin with sauna-like temperatures and filling the space with smoke. Unfortunately, it was our only source of heat so learning to use it, as best we could, was imperative. No matter how many times I tried, I could not find the recipe for creating the perfect sized fire. If I made the fire too small, it would smolder, smoke up the room, and go out. If I made it large enough to provide sufficient heat to draft the smoke up and out of the chimney, then we had to open up windows in order to survive the excessive heat the stove generated. During the day, although not terribly efficient, this was not a big deal; however, managing this stove and its impact on our lives during the night was an entirely different story.

Because the unit itself was so full of holes and leaks, the fires would always burn on high, with full draft to support the flames. This meant that I had the wonderful job of, not just stoking, but rebuilding the fire at least three times during the night. I'm talking about starting from scratch each and every time. Gabriella got used to the sound of crumpling newspaper and snapping sticks in her sleep and accepted the second major challenge of living in our cabin: all night fire duty.

Of course, if I had been able to manage the fire better, we wouldn't have had to live within the two extremes: major heat, due to the large and furious fire, and extreme cold, due to the fact that we had to leave windows open through the winter months. Not that leaving the windows open made a huge difference to our conditioned space. After all, we are talking about a one hundred year old log cabin with no insulation and single pane windows. In fact, I remember lying in bed often and looking through the walls into the meadow. And yes, I mean looking through the walls, not windows in the walls. The chinking in between the logs had deteriorated so much that in some places it was completely missing. There was nothing new and improved about this cabin, that's for sure.

In truth, the only "modern" conveniences we had in the cabin were a radio, one light bulb, and a gas cook stove. I should speak more to the power situation. The cabin was advertised as having no power and that is how I have shared it with you until now. The truth is that there was a single, very small solar panel on the roof and one small car battery under the bed. This gave us just enough power to either listen to the radio for an hour or two or use the light bulb for about an hour. To be clear, this was an either/or decision. If we mixed and matched, we might get 20 minutes of music and light together.

With all of these challenges, and there were others that could be added to the scorecard, the overall experience is something that neither of us would change. There were so many gifts in those short months that have positively impacted our lives. From our experience of actually living there, in the moment, to the life-long lessons that we took from that experience, our

months in the little mountain cabin influenced who we are today in ways that we may never fully understand or attribute to that time.

One of the great gifts that living in this space gave us was the ability for Gabriella to stop working. She was able to spend her timing focused on being pregnant and experience everything that journey had to offer her. Gabriella and I believe that there was no better way for her to bring a child into the world than to be totally present to the entire experience. Especially since that experience took place in a location surrounded by remote and beautiful wild country, connecting her back to nature every day.

Gabriella sometimes recalls her days in that cabin as peaceful, inspiring, slow, and nurturing. She would lie on the bed, looking out the long window at the meadow and watch deer, elk, rabbits, coyotes, and other wildlife pass by. She would journal about her experience and the future she and I were creating together. Her biggest job of the day was to gather snow and melt it on the camp stove so we would have water for cooking and cleaning. Those days were precious and were made possible by the nature of our living environment.

I was working long, labor filled days on a geotechnical drill rig in all kinds of weather from the scorching sun of the Colorado summer to the frigid colds of Eisenhower pass in February. No matter what my daily experience, coming home to our little cabin in the mountains was always a treat. There was a sense of calm and simplicity there that I so deeply cherished. Even though I would come home from work tired, I always found time to enjoy the land around our cabin. Gabriella and I would go for walks with our dogs (oh, I forgot to mention that we had two 80 pounds dogs during this time in our lives; a small and easily overlooked detail when living in 80 sq.ft.), sometimes in the snow, sometimes in the crisp mountain air while the soon to be falling snow considered its options, and well into spring and summer. We would drop down into Dream Canyon and walk along the river and marvel at the waterfalls. Nature surrounded us and embraced us, every day.

Other times, I would find solace in cutting and splitting firewood, or packing snow and ice into our ice box to keep our food fresh (we didn't have a refrigerator). The old adage of "chop wood, carry water" was actually a reflection of our lives. We lived a minimal and quiet existence and found joy in the simple experience of life itself. I think the biggest basis for our ability to experience our daily lives was the wealth we were living in. I use the word wealth intentionally here to perhaps surprise you. The wealth that we had was in the most valuable currency: time. We were not wasting our lives away with trivial tasks. Everything we did served us in some way. It was either a task required for survival or for relaxation and connection.

It's interesting that I remember having "time wealth" being that I worked longer hours than ever before, or since, for that matter. I think this is because when I look back at my time running the geotechnical drill rig, I see only positive experiences. I worked harder than I have ever worked and I absolutely loved it. It was yet another life experience. I worked with great people who inspired me to learn new things and to think outside of the box. In fact, it was my boss Lou who taught me about carpentry and gave me my first taste of building. In truth, without my experience at that job, I don't know if I would have ended up in construction and ultimately teaching. Perhaps it all would have come to fruition in its own way, but I find it interesting to consider that question while looking back.

What I do know is that I was absorbing everything I could get my hands and mind on. I would always step up to work extra hours when asked, partly because it was good to have some money to set aside for the future; but perhaps more importantly, because I was learning new skills. Being that life is simply a series of experiences, I was soaking up every one I could find and storing away any new information I came across.

What's intriguing about our time in that tiny little cabin in the Colorado Mountains is that it was perhaps the "hardest" time in our lives. We were preparing to welcome our first child into the world, which would ultimately change everything. Looking back, we wouldn't have it any other way; however, from our perspective at the time, we had no idea what to expect. We were stepping completely into the unknown, and that can be scary. So we had this potential fear of the unknown, coupled with long and tiring work hours for me, and a cabin that would challenge anyone who tried to live in it during a Colorado winter.

If we examine just one piece of that puzzle there would be ample reasons why we should have had a terrible experience during those eight months. But that's not what happened. We loved our time there. It is one of the best memories of my life, and I have a lot of great memories. I look back fondly, always with a smile, when I think about resetting and lighting those fires every night. I love the image of my beautiful wife sitting on the bed, gazing out the window as I walked the long, steep, cold path from the car to the cabin. I love that we had so little stuff to worry about. Everything we owned fit into that tiny space and it was perfect. I loved being so close to nature, even when a huge black bear was only an inch from my face, separated by a flimsy, single pane window. It was all a part of the experience.

I notice as I write this that I have used the word "experience" a lot. I don't think that is an accident. As I have already mentioned, "experience" is my way of defining life and that is what I gained in our mountain cabin. My wish for all of us is that we continue to experience life fully. I don't want to waste my time, a finite resource, on meaningless tasks. If I have to choose between cleaning a house and enjoying my family, the choice is obvious. If I have to consider if I'd rather spend my time working to pay for my mortgage or use that time to travel and learn about different cultures, the choice is obvious. I choose life and all of its experiences.

The other word that continues to resonate with me today is "simplicity." I believe that we, as a society, have fallen off of the wise path of simplicity and have instead begun to blindly follow the sirens of consumerism. We are sold on "making our lives easier" by buying things when, in fact, the truth is exactly the opposite. Stuff will never make our lives easier in the end. Sure, my smart phone helps me stay in touch while I travel and I can access emails, social media, and the Internet from just about anywhere, but does this really make my life easier? I suggest that it does not.

Can you remember a time when we were not as important as we think we are today? When airplanes used to land and people would simply gather their belongings and walk off of the plane, maybe sharing a few words with their temporary neighbor on the way out? That doesn't happen anymore. Now when the plane lands, the majority of people quickly turn on their phones to find out what they've missed during the flight. I find it hard to believe that we are all so important that the short time away from our phones has had that big of an impact on the world. My guess is that life has gone on without us, and that will always be true. No matter how inspiring or impactful I may be, or think I might be, in the end I am ultimately pretty insignificant to the global perspective. This may not be what you want to hear, but

I find it to be true and actually quite comforting. It helps me stay focused on the present and that is something that seems to be slipping away from our society.

This trend truly saddens me. I see people missing out on life because they are literally addicted to the information and images on their phones, which from my perspective, is just more stuff, and nothing of much value. I believe that the addiction comes from a desire to "not miss out" on anything that is happening. Unfortunately, everything that we see on our phones has already happened. We already missed it and now by watching the past, we are missing what is actually happening in the present moment. If we continue this trend, we will all miss out on life and its experiences. That is a risk I am not willing to take. I choose to stand in the present moment and experience life. As Henry David Thoreau once said "What lies behind us and what lies ahead of us are tiny matters compared to what lives within us." If we want to truly experience life, then we must look within and share ourselves with those around us, in our most immediate circles.

One thing I love about life, and am reminded of daily, is our complete connection with one and other. Life is a series of full circle moments that continue to roll forward, yet connect us to our pasts as well. From the present moment, we can experience it all. Our cabin in the woods is a great example of this. As I mentioned earlier, we lived there for about 8 months. The woman who owned the cabin lived in it for the remaining four months of the year and then moved to Mexico when the weather turned cold. Now here we are some 20 years later living in our tiny hOMe in the mountains of Southern Oregon. Each winter, we trek down to Baja, Mexico to enjoy the culture and weather that it offers us. I don't think it is coincidental. I think it is the magic of life that has looped our lives back to a pattern that existed only in our periphery 20 years ago. That is just one example of the many, often subtle, connections to something larger I find in my life.

I have also discovered that the simpler my life is and the quieter I get in my day-to-day practice of life, the more I am able to recognize these connections. I just found another one, literally right now. As I write this, I am sitting on my bed, looking out of a long window onto the meadow outside of our hOMe. I've watched coyotes, deer, turkeys, and other wildlife pass by this pane. Sure, our 207 sq.ft. house is almost three times as big as that cabin in

Colorado was, but our lives have once again shifted to a more simple time, where life, and all of the experiences that come with it, is what matters most.

To round out the balance of life within this chapter of my own story, I will leave you with a third a final quote from Thoreau. If there is a mantra that you can take from my story, I hope this will be it and that it will carry you forward to great things.

> *Our life is frittered away by detail. Simplify, simplify.*
> —Henry David Thoreau

Perspective, Priorities and Passion

Learning to live simply has helped me understand what's truly important

Jody Pountain

Jody Pountain lives compactly aboard a 42 sailboat with her boyfriend Peter and their dog, Betsy. She traded in the corporate conundrum for a life less ordinary and has been island-hopping around the Caribbean ever since. Between a quirky obsession with organizing, capturing pretty pictures, diving with turtles and burying her toes in the sand, she feeds a passion for writing by blogging about their adventures in search of surf, sun, sand and serenity Where The Coconuts Grow.

Collect memories, not things.
—Unknown author

The Spring of 2011 is when I met Peter. His devilishly charming personality and striking good looks were no doubt what caught my attention, but it was the underlying laid-back surfer essence beaming from within him that really intrigued me.

I had just moved to San Diego and within the blink of an eye had fallen in love with the warm sun and gorgeous beaches. Growing up in the suburbs of Seattle taught me to appreciate the outdoors but I had also grown tired of fleece zip-ups, puddle-soaked jeans from the knees down, and portable heaters under my desk. That year I was introduced to a culture of people that wore tank tops and flip-flops all year round, and I began to question my entire life up until that moment.

It was clear that Peter knew what his priorities were. He loved adventure, he loved to surf and he loved to fish. In June, we packed a few supplies into his 4-Runner and drove up to the Eastern Sierras with our two dogs. We found a trail in the middle of nowhere next to a peaceful little stream, hundreds of miles away from any other human beings. That weekend the stars looked brighter than I had ever noticed before. While sharing our dreams for the future, Peter told me he wanted to someday buy a boat and sail away, knowing it was the most cost-effective solution to reach all the epic surf spots and offshore fishing locations he wanted to visit. I listened intently, and although I had only known him for a short time, I knew in that very instant that *I was going with him.*

Two years came and went. There were a handful of conversations about setting off on some grand adventure. The most serious of them consisted of selling everything and moving down to Central America to open a surf camp where we could live inexpensively and Peter could take people out surfing and fishing every day. We were both more than ready to make a major lifestyle change, leaving us with really only two options: 1. *Do something adventurous,* or 2. *Buy a house and settle into a safe routine – because that's what everyone else does.* Clearly leaning toward option number one, we had a plan halfway in motion and a recon trip to Panama in the works. I knew the first obstacle would be figuring out what to do with all the *stuff* we had each accumulated.

Perspective

For years, I worked so hard to graduate college and pay off all my debt. I moved away from home when I was 18 and had always been proud of my accomplishments and all the high quality belongings I was able to purchase for myself. As the Susie-Homemaker type, I owned enough stuff to furnish a 4,000 square-foot home. Having already downsized to a quarter of those belongings when I moved from Washington State to California in 2008 helped a little, but there was still an overwhelming amount of *stuff* that was going to hold me back from any upcoming adventures.

My perspective began to shift. I began to see that for as long as I could remember, I had been seeking joy in my possessions. Sentimental value that had been attributed to childhood toys and gifts from the past suddenly started to crumble away. Countless plastic storage bins of *stuff* began to look like junk. It had all been moved from house to house throughout my life without ever reevaluating the joy those items still bring me. For so long, I had assumed that because I had saved those things before, I should still save them now. I was amazed at how my perspective had changed over the years. I could finally see that it's experiences and memories that matter, not material belongings. The first things to go were big ticket items like furniture, sold with the help of Craigslist. With the exception of an old rocking chair and a really cool wooden chopping block table, everything else was replaceable. I could always buy more furniture if I wanted to. A large pile was donated to a local charity organization and some of it was just too ridiculous to even give away, therefore ending up in the trash. The clutter dwindled away piece by piece and I found a new appreciation for the things important enough to keep.

Sooner or later, the conversation turned toward boats. Peter and I had both been around boats all of our lives, but each of us had been on a sailboat only *one time*. "*How hard could it be!? We'll just throw up the sails and see what happens,*" we both shrugged. My obsession at the time was getting lost in dreamy ideas on Pinterest, which proved to be the perfect place to get hooked on sailing blogs. For hours on end at lunchtime and after work I would read stories from other young cruisers around my age that had left everything from their previous lives behind and sailed away with their small children. I quickly became familiar with the well-known blogs like *Sailing Totem, The Rebel Heart, It's A Necessity* and *Windtraveler*. The photos they shared and the words they wrote tugged at my heartstrings, and I began to believe that if they were doing it... *so could I.*

It took an unusually short two months of searching to find the perfect boat. Not too big, not too small, and within our price range. Anything less than 40' felt too small, and anything bigger than 45' was very daunting and exponentially more expensive. Circumstances aligned in the most perfect of ways and we purchased a 1980 42' ketch-rigged sailboat on the West Coast of Florida in the Fall of 2013. Peter and I flew back to San Diego and spent what ended up being two more months whittling down our remaining belongings while we tried to decide what we would need to live on a boat.

That short period of time before we actually moved into our tiny floating home was the most intimidating part of the whole process. Downsizing from a 1200 sq.ft. house to a comparable 300 sq.ft. of usable space... *IN A BOAT...* seemed crazy. And with two large dogs? Everyone thought we were nuts! It was essential to take an honest look at each and every item we still owned. Every kitchen utensil, every shirt. *Just how important is it?* Where most people might feel as though their familiar luxuries were being ripped out from underneath them, I started realizing how many single-use items I still owned, taking up valuable space.

Did I really need 10 matching plates, bowls, and cups? No. Would I honestly use all of my casserole dishes and mixing bowls? Not a chance. Would any of it even fit into the cupboard space I was going to have? Maybe. For example, the oven on my boat is only 15" by 15" so I could only bring my smallest cookie sheet. The stove is only a three-burner design so one big pot, one little pot, one big pan and one little pan would be more than enough. Some things just didn't make sense to bring like my upright Dyson vacuum. The combined floor space inside our boat is smaller than a regular size kitchen. While I hated to part with it, I left the Dyson in an enclosed trailer along with a few other items Peter and I just couldn't let go of, parked in a family member's backyard in California. If we ever go back to 'land' those things will be there waiting for our return.

Everyone wanted to know if I decided to bring my glassware and real dishes from home or if I changed to plastic. You would think that having plastic dishes would be more conducive to being on the go and on a rocking boat but instead of buying *more* stuff, and remembering that my perspective had already began to shift, I recognized a feeling of 'letting go' as I made the decision to bring my breakables and enjoy them for as long as I can, until I can't enjoy them anymore. If they break, they break. Until then, there's no sense in getting rid of something I still love. I brought only the amount I thought I would need – 6 of each – enough for daily use and for light entertaining. I knew the space would allow for just that many. *Functional becomes a priority.*

From the second I stepped foot aboard our new home, my eyes lit up and my passion for organization raced through my veins. I immediately started making plans in my mind where everything would live. *A place for everything and everything in its place.* It took a couple days to do a deep-clean on the new-to-us boat but the previous owners had taken such good care of everything on board that there wasn't much else to do but make ourselves at home. I was intimately aware of every single item we had brought with us from

California and was beaming with excitement as I carefully put everything away. When you're working with small, low-visibility spaces, it's imperative that organization is the next priority. Finally... the perfect application for my weird obsession!

A boat is not just a tiny floating home. It's an incredibly awkward space with curved ceilings, removable floorboards, unusual shaped cabinets, and a million places to stub your pinky toe or slice open your knee. Because the interior and exterior shape of a boat is curved, most cabinets are miniature in size and never uniform. To be fair, boat designers must be incredibly gifted to plan out every nook and cranny. At first glance, most storage compartments appear to be an afterthought but a closer look reveals the shear genius of the designer spread across every inch of the boat. As each cubby is packed full, it's as if you're assembling the contents like a puzzle, like the kind you used to play as a kid where you have an odd shaped board with half a dozen odd shaped pieces that fit into the board only one way. On a boat, you've got to manage the storage space available by carefully fitting things together at strange angles to make sure not one inch of space is wasted. It's a given in the cruising life that you never know when you'll be able to replenish your supply of boat parts and food so in a way, we become organized hoarders. Extra jugs of engine oil are carefully wedged against the wide but shallow triangle-shaped compartment under the left side of our bed. The pantry shelves are strategically stacked with heavier items at the bottom and more important items in the front. If I ever need something from the back of any compartment, everything – and I mean *EVERYTHING* – in front of it has to come out first.

An important lesson I learned right away is that one project is really never one project. One project requires a whole compartment of items to be emptied onto the couch, which then seems more like a table, but then you need a tool that's in the back of another compartment under the bed. Then, everything *under* the bed ends up *on* the bed, and now I have nowhere to sit until Peter is done with this *one* project. But in the middle of a varnishing project, something breaks, like a hose clamp or electrical connection on the watermaker. Making water is more important than varnishing, so the drawer that contains all the electrical supplies has to be emptied onto the floor to find the right size heat-shrink tube from the container of parts at the very bottom of the drawer. Suddenly, 9:00am has become 4:30pm and my tiny 300 sq.ft. of usable living space looks like it was just ransacked by pirates. Good thing I love to reorganize and put things away!

Living on a boat has changed the way I think during every minute of the day. I subconsciously ask myself, "What is that for again?" like I'm testing myself to remember the value of every item on board. Every tool has at least one specific purpose. My wardrobe has been whittled down to items of necessity, with one or two pieces for each type of occasion. Even the fabric on my cushions is functional. Yes, maybe they look nice too, but I chose the fabric itself based on durability in a marine environment and the ability to be easily cleaned. Because I do live in such a compact space, I'm reminded daily that I only have enough room for the important things. Where my thinking has shifted is in my definition of 'important'. This lifestyle is a true confirmation that my experiences, adventures and happiness are far more important than the things I own.

Priorities

The idea of living on a boat is often glorified in books and movies by an image of a sailor that naps in a hammock all day, sipping from coconuts in the warm Caribbean sun, living a simple life, without a care in the world. After a few weeks living aboard, Peter and I were keenly aware of how hard boat life can really be. In a hurry to get off the dock and sail off into the sunset, we

were working long hours to get the boat ready every day for four months. Knowing that the luxuries of marina life would soon come to an end, our biggest priorities for outfitting the boat were power, water and safety.

With almost 900 watts of solar panels installed our power consumption is fully satisfied on sunny days. In fact, some days we have so much solar power coming into the boat that we have to run multiple systems to burn off the excess voltage. For this reason, we also have charge controllers hooked up to regulate the voltage going to our four 12volt batteries. Two rigid solar panels are mounted with stainless steel brackets on both sides of the boat, and two pairs of semi-flexible panels are affixed to the canvas cockpit enclosure and the forward deck. In the Caribbean, solar power is a sufficient source of energy though there are clouds and squalls that seasonally yet frequently pass through making it just as nice to have a wind generator. *Windy*, as we call her, sits high up on our mizzen mast pumping in a nice amount of amps from the steady Caribbean breeze. In the event that there is no sun or wind, we have a backup 5kw inboard generator and a portable Honda 1000 generator. If all fails we could always run our main engine to supply power as well.

Water is a precious commodity. Ironic, almost, that there is seawater all around us but we can't survive without fresh water. The previous owners of our boat understood the struggle well during their 16 years of cruising. They bit the bullet and installed a 12volt watermaker that can run off our house bank of batteries alone. No need to run a generator. It draws about 12 amps – hardly a drain on sunny days. To make room inside the boat, they removed one of the three water tanks but it was a very smart trade. 80% of the time the solar panels and wind generator are enough to power the watermaker, replenishing our fresh water supply and making us almost totally self sufficient.

Having the basics covered (power and water) is important, but when you live on the ocean there is a very intense level of self sufficiency required. If your engine fails, or if a hose bursts, you can't just walk out the front door, hop in your car and go down to the local hardware store. It takes a tremendous amount of energy, patience, logic and a drive to 'figure things out' when you live on a boat. Sometimes being able to figure out a solution is a life or death matter. Things can go from bad to worse very fast while floating on a deep ocean and being self sufficient is what boat life is all about. In most parts of the world accessible by boat, there is usually someone in the closest town or anchorage that can help fix or jury-rig whatever might break, but you're on your own to get your vessel and your crew to your destination safely.

I've always considered myself to be fairly competent in most situations, having enough common sense to figure out what I don't already know. Maybe it's the way I was raised. Maybe it's the education I received. Maybe a little of both. In any event, I have a certain mental drive to understand and conquer. Peter is really good at taking useful bits of knowledge from a vast range of experiences to complete any task at hand, where I'm the type that does better learning the big picture first. Between the two of us, we've survived a lot of 'firsts' and gotten out of some scary situations during our first couple years on the boat.

We work hard to play hard. Life on the water doesn't give you a choice about what your priorities are. Life on the water chooses them for you. Water and power are the biggest priorities but safety is equally as important. We've got fancy electronic systems with lots of redundancies like a GPS chartplotter, Radar, VHF radio, SSB radio, EPIRBs and a Satellite Phone to help us navigate but also to ensure we can call for help if needed. All of that may sound complicated or intimidating to land-lubbers but it's not hard to learn. Just like a new sport, or a new job, or a new tool – someone teaches us, or we teach ourselves. Some methods of communications are more dynamic an others but it's all designed to keep us, and others, safe. There is special safety gear to learn about and safety procedures for all kinds of situations that may happen while out on the water. Even though the learning curve can be a bit steep, the rewards for this lifestyle are even steeper.

Another skill to help me keep my priorities in order is one that slowly develops all on its own. The best way to describe this new skill is like the scene in the movie *Twister* where they hear the faint jingle of a wind chime from inside the diner. It draws them outside like a sixth sense, and they know a certain kind of storm is approaching. Just a hint of a change in the weather can indicate so much more to those with trained senses, and the rest of the world would never notice a thing. Peter and I have learned to hear raindrops from a dead sleep, jolting us out of bed to close the hatches before the approaching Caribbean squall dumps crazy amounts of rain on us just seconds later. One time I woke up to our wind generator preparing for lift off like a small helicopter – a sound it wasn't supposed to make – just minutes before an approaching squall caused a ferry to drag anchor in front of us, almost crashing into us before it ran aground. While sailing, we can *see* the wind change by reading the surface of the water and the clouds on the horizon. A slight drop in temperature usually means a storm system is moving in. We use our senses of smell and sound all the time to diagnose something 'not quite right' in the boat, usually before it turns into a disaster. If we hear the bilge go off, it could mean we have a serious leak inside the boat. If there is a new sound coming from the engine room, it needs to be investigated. Like I mentioned before, things can go from bad to worse in a matter of seconds and I think this lifestyle teaches us to be in tune with our surroundings at a level I never would have otherwise known.

Passion

What I find most amazing about living in a tiny floating home is that I have so much more opportunity for adventure. Every day is a new experience. Peter and I are constantly exploring new places and meeting new people. We dive with turtles, rays, octopi, reef fish and sharks. We catch and prepare fresh lobster, Mahi Mahi, tuna, grouper and snapper. Even on hard days, I never get tired of sailing on the crystal clear blue Caribbean waters with the sun on my face and a nice cool breeze through my hair. As we travel from island to island, we are able to bring our home with us and we have the freedom to enjoy each new adventure as long as we like with no ties holding us back to any one place. Every day we feel gratitude for the way everything has fallen into place, allowing us to live the way we do.

We had two dogs before this adventure started and it was never a question in our minds on whether they would come with us. Gunner was a Weimaraner. He was an old boy and it was a little challenging for us to get him in and out of the boat but the space was never an issue. He just wanted to be wherever we were. The majority of his life on land was spent at home – alone – while I was at school or at work so when we first bought the boat it was such a nice change to be with him 24/7. He got plenty of exercise swimming and running on white sandy beaches. I like to believe we gave him a really nice retirement on a yacht in the Caribbean. Eventually, old age took its hold on him and his body began to shut down. We lost him at almost 15 years old. It would have happened anywhere, but I'm grateful I got to spend so much quality time with him during his last few years. Our other dog, Betsy, is a Boxer/Pitbull mix and though she misses her brother she couldn't be happier. She goes wherever we go and continues to live a life that most people only know on their vacations.

After two years of carefree cruising with the weather as our only schedule, Peter and I decided it's time to work again. Neither of us could even imagine going back to land so we found a way to stay out on the water, doing what we love and sharing it with others. We are currently running a daysail catamaran taking vacationers sailing and snorkeling in the Virgin Islands. The best part is that Betsy gets to come to work with us every day! We'll work for a few more seasons to save up a bit of money before sailing off into the sunset once again. Someday we might end up in the South Pacific, but they say "plans are drawn in the sand" so we can't really be sure.

Of all the things I've experienced so far, I am most surprised by the incredible sense of community we have found in the cruisers we've met along the way. With a 'renewing faith in humanity' kind of way, I have been pleasantly surprised at how overwhelmingly kind and generous and like-minded everyone is on the water. We've met so many wonderful people and we've learned so much from them. We've also had more opportunities than ever before to pay it forward and help others in all kinds of situations – something that rarely happened back in the rat-race we lived in on land.

What I love the most is that is that we are *creating our story as we go along*. We aren't conforming to what society thinks we should be doing. We've transformed our lives into a simplistic rhythm as we follow our dreams and do what makes us happy each and every day. Life is too short – you never know what tomorrow might hold.

The world is such a big place with so much to see, do and learn. By telling my story I hope to inspire others to take a leap of faith as I have done, to set your fears aside, follow your dreams, make a change, and keep spreading inspiration to others.

UnBoxed Living

Sean David Burke

By day, Sean David Burke is a digital practice leader for a global architecture firm, believing strongly in the power of design to change the world. He is committed to resilient design and a minimalist lifestyle. Sean's observations on the tiny house phenomenon and documentation of BentoBox, a shipping container tiny house project.

Smile, breathe and go slowly.
—Thích Nhat Hanh

How I Started

When I first learned of the concept of the tiny house, I was early in my architecture career and had not figured out what I wanted to do when I 'grew up'. It was 1999, and having graduated from architecture school just five years earlier, I was still full of idealism and a change-the-world attitude. That feeling is returning to me, now for very different reasons.

The idea of what "home" was had been a work in progress for me. I knew I didn't want a new house built in a subdivision as I had experienced growing up. It would be the urban loft, the repurposed mill building, the clean lines of mid-century modern architecture, and more influences blended together into something that was an outward expression of my own personality.

I knew then that article on tiny houses I was reading was important. I knew I wanted a tiny house, someday. I also knew I did not want my some-day home to be like this gabled house with a gothic window, as this interesting man Jay Shafer (whoever he was) had done with his 'tiny house'. I knew

I wanted this dream of a minimalist lifestyle, however I had no idea how to achieve it or how it could be my own.

Why the Box?

The concept of the BentoBox house grew slowly from various tiny house influences. What likely was most significant was seeing the Seattle container port in operation. Up close. I spent a couple of years working in a office building with great views out to Harbor Island, home to thousands of containers. The rows and rows of stacked boxes created their own colorful pixelated landscape. I grew more fascinated with the giant ships being uploaded in the port, various transport systems and cranes that moved these boxes around.

Adaptive reuse was already an interest of mine and one day, fifteen years after seeing that first tiny house article, when I was really serious about making this a reality, something clicked. I had been sketching the traditional tiny house for several months, and now discovered the remaining piece. Later, I learned how many of these containers would sit discarded and empty, awaiting some new life that would have them no longer performing their intended task. Throughout the US, there are millions of containers that will remain in storage lots, because it's simply more expensive to send them back empty than it is to make more in places like China. I spent the remainder of that year researching all about containers and container architecture.

Choosing a container to build your tiny home and then putting it on a trailer is not something you can just run right out and find a DIY book about at the library. The audience so far has been very limited. Even now, after all the research and sharing online, I've only seen or heard of two others. Had I made a mistake? While happy to be a trailblazer, I didn't want to waste time and money, both of which I have in limited supply. It turns out, there are a lot of myths surrounding containers.

Soon after the research and a dozen or so designs in my sketchbook, I had the need to experience containers first hand. Sure, I'd seen them, but didn't pay as much attention as I would now. That's when you really start noticing them everywhere.

So, now the driveway had this big metal box. No one noticed. I was a bit disappointed, in a way. Then I looked around a bit more at the neighborhood. It seemed normal for there to be storage boxes, RVs, classic cars in various states of disassembly, boats waiting for their next adventure on the area lakes and Puget Sound. I was just part of the fabric. This became advantageous while plans became ready for making changes. I was intimidated by the reactions I expected of the neighbors. It turned out, they have continued to be supportive from day one in the best possible ways.

Myths

Although, not all below are myths, bear in mind there's always someone eager to tell you why you can't do something. Listen to all advice – however I recommend you do your own independent research. There are few obstacles you can't overcome with the right attitude and knowledge.

Unfortunately, many think the weight of an empty container is too high to build into a tiny house. In fact, a standard 20-foot long shipping container is only 4850 pounds (lbs). You will likely want to remove some of the material for things like windows and doors. I even cut out a large chunk of roof, so I could go a little taller. In all, about 800 lbs. of steel was removed from the original container. 4000 lbs. doesn't seem so unreasonable. It's just under the average weight of an American automobile. In my design, I'm using a 14,000 lb. capacity equipment trailer, which itself weighs about 3000 lbs. when the decking and ramps are removed. So, I've a remaining budget of 7,000 pounds to complete my house, including personal belongings.

Rust is usually a topic that comes up. I find it beautiful. In fact, my design incorporates some rust as a feature. There's a special type of steel used in the walls and roof construction of the shipping container. The generic name for it is weathering steel, often referred to as the trademarked Cor-Ten. Weathering steel is a special formula that when it rusts, causes the rust itself to seal the surface to prevent further oxidation. It doesn't need paint under normal environmental conditions. This coating on containers is primarily applied in response to the harsh conditions of salty sea air and spray. Hopefully, you won't be parking your tiny house on a barge in the ocean. Sanding and sealing any exposed areas just like you would your trailer, is a good idea, but not urgent. A container home should easily last 50 to 100 years. And the bonus is, at the end of its life is recyclable.

There's a concern that often comes up about the toxicity of shipping container materials. If anything, by becoming more aware of the effects on indoor air quality caused by various construction materials, you'll make smarter choices when selecting what goes into your tiny house, as well as how you mitigate risk. When applied, the coatings, sealants and paints used on the metal do have significant off gassing, and will do so for a time after installed. By the time the container gets to you, the materials are very stable. The plywood decking will have urea formaldehyde glue in it, like 95% of all plywood used in construction today, so allowing it to off gas for up to six months is recommended. The labels on the container will tell you when it was manufactured and exactly what materials were used.

While these pesticides have been used in transporting of our goods all over the world and we have already been exposed to them, they are now significantly safer than the older materials used prior to 1990. This is why I chose a newer container. You can also seal the floor panels with with a VOC blocking product, before placing rigid insulation and a new floor on it. Repainting exposed metal walls or ceiling is an effective way to encapsulate the container from the living environment.

Lessons Learned

Some people are excellent at estimating the time to accomplish a task. Admittedly, I'm terrible at this. Even after doubling my initial estimate, I'm often way too optimistic. Other times, I've not expected to encounter an issue that creates a setback. Like any tiny house build, you'll find yourself thinking you have all the items needed from the home improvement store, only to determine there's one tiny thing that you are missing. Worse, running out of fasteners can mean another trip and lowered productivity. It's OK. Progress, is still progress.

A container will definitely take you longer, and likely not save you money over a wood-framed house. This is despite starting with a nice weather resistant box—I inevitably needed to cut holes in it. In some cases, big ones. You may not. Despite the strength and security of a metal box to keep our goods safe during transport, I had no intention of trying to hide from some impending zombie apocalypse. I set out to create a home that feels light and welcoming.

Containers, being made primarily of steel, require different skills and tools than wood. Or for those tools that could serve as general purpose implements, take the common drill for instance, going for the extra-mondo heavy-duty variety might, just might, be enough to to do the job. I burned through the motor of one, and had to jump to the next larger size. Brushless, it turns out is best.

I had a fair bit of anchoring of the roof and wall framing to do, and once I had the right combination of tools, drill bits and fasteners, this part of the job went really fast. Sometimes, slow is better. Don't get over-confident. Always wear safety goggles and ensure your drill has a side handle. If (or most likely, when) the drill bit sticks, two things can happen – simultaneously, the bit can shatter in several places and the drill can suddenly turn in your hand – potentially spraining your wrist, or worse.

Cutting the openings in the steel required some very specialized tools. While an angle grinder is good for very small cuts, or cleaning up edges, a cutting torch, at the least, or a plasma torch will go through the corrugated metal steel walls like butter. For this work, I utilized the services of a capable neighbor who had the tools and skills. I learned a little while he was on the job site, however, I didn't want to become an expert and probably couldn't on one project. Don't be afraid to ask for or hire out help – especially when explosive gas and extreme high temperatures are involved.

It cannot be stressed enough: take all safety precautions, as well as read and understand how to use your tools. Take a hands-on class if you need to build confidence. Some things you can only learn through doing.

Planning is definitely one of the most important aspects of undertaking a big project like this. If you're on a limited budget and have limited space for storing materials and tools, like me, you learn to stage the project in the sequence of construction. One sequence I got wrong was deciding to buy a trailer later, after construction started and I had saved up enough (this is likely the single most expensive part of the project). I originally wanted to have a custom trailer made that was very light and strong, specifically for anchoring at the container's corner blocks. This turned out to be far more expensive and logistically challenging than I expected. So, a standard 8x20 deck-over equipment trailer was the ultimate selection.

A little over a year after I had the container delivered, it turned out lifting and setting down on the trailer was more physically and mentally demanding than I expected. Simply driving with a trailer to the container yard, they could have set the thing down in seconds. Instead, it took two people several stacks of timber and some serious muscle to operate the jacks over several days. The end result was the same. Everything happens for a reason. Going the more logical path, of course would have been free of the scary reality TV moments, like when the load shifted and a jack bent while trying to stabilize the container and square things up on the trailer bed. (Heart palpitations now nearly as strong as that day, just describing it to you). But hey, it makes for a fun scary campfire story.

About the BentoBox

My concept was simple: create a home that could expand when parked to create space that would soar, have a connection to nature and be flexible enough to accommodate different ways of living. I didn't want walls and fixtures that couldn't easily be moved or adjusted later. I was looking to create a truly open plan concept tiny house.

On the interior, only the bathroom is fixed. The kitchen, bay window, tansu stairs and even the bedroom loft are designed like furniture and can be

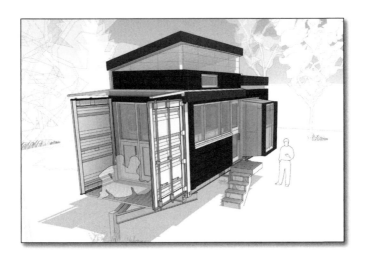

reconfigured at a future date. One day, the house may become something else. Since I cannot predict exactly how I'll use it over time, the modular nature of the components mean I can repurpose or even swap things out when needed.

The first thing that needed to go from the traditional tiny house on wheels was the loft. Having stayed in several tiny houses, I always felt that while the loft created a nice and cozy place to sleep, many of these spaces were not designed for much else, and even sitting up in bed is rarely possible without hunching. In its place, I designed a raised multi-function platform over storage and mechanical spaces that enabled a shed roof with full standing headroom. Once that decision was made, everything else came into place. The biggest trick for me in the design process was much like the downsizing process, decide what could be left out, not what absolutely needed to be put in.

None of these decisions came all at once, or even in the first five months after I purchased the container. Yes, I had the container delivered before committing to a final design. It was a known parameter that wasn't going away, so making that happen – getting it dropped into the driveway for everyone to see – added a bit of urgency to my planning. By October of 2014, after an exciting delivery where my new prize rolled off the back of a flatbed truck onto the driveway, I leveled it and by that afternoon set up a hammock inside my almost new container and daydreamed for a while. It's highly possible that daydream evolved into a nap. At that point, I was sure this had been the right decision; my new home.

The house unboxes when parked. This process is manually done, rather than opting for motorized RV style mechanisms, to keep costs down and to make the house easier to replicate if anyone chooses. The roof over the loft is higher than the top of the container, and while on the road the shed roof folds flat to be under the fourteen feet height limit of western states. At night, when parked this shed roof will seemingly float about a glowing lantern of translucent glass panels.

All 175 sq. ft. of living area is maximized with multiple purposes. The pop out bay window serves the function of a dinette, work area, storage, reading nook and pull out guest bed – all in a 3x5 foot area. To extend living space to the outdoors, there is a fold down porch that rests on the trailer yoke, suspended between the cargo doors. A lightweight polycarbonate roof allows protection from rain and minimally blocks daylight. As a coffee addict, I really needed a place I could swing open a window and sit on the edge of the bed, dangling my feet outside while enjoying a mug. For those sunny Seattle summers, an eight foot square roof deck over the kitchen and bathroom is accessed from ladder rungs on the back of the house.

Finding More Resources

When I started my research, I found a few great websites. The Intermodal Steel Building Units and Container Homes organization (ISBU-info.org) contains (couldn't resist the chance for a pun) plenty of materials for you. If, like me, you are looking for CAD drawings or 3D models, you may become a member for a modest fee and have access to download these for your own planning.

Some of the sites are certainly more eye candy than anything else. Lot-Ek, a design firm in New York City, http://www.lot-ek.com/, has sliced and diced containers in ways that will make you wonder how they could have possibly accomplished that. I've listed a few resources for makers of backyard container studios, which have similar principles to a tiny house that you may also find inspiring. I recommend you make contact with one before undertaking a project. Some, like Cargotecture (cargotecture.com) and ShelterKraft (ShelterKraft.com) have been active in my own community to promote further experiments in small living. Rhino Cubed (rhinocubed.com), originally based out of New Orleans, combines artistry and containers to create really unique tiny houses. I met the owners at the inaugural Tiny House Jamboree in Colorado Springs and was really impressed with their work.

Some criticism regarding the trend of using containers for habitation has been growing, so it's worth also pointing out an article written in September 2015 by Mark Hogan, "What's wrong with shipping container housing? Everything!", now widely talked about in the design world on Arch Daily, Treehugger and other popular websites, the original can be found on his blog: http://markasaurus.com. This was written not about the tiny house movement, but about the way some architects tend to paint the container as a panacea to the growing housing needs in cities with fantasy images of impractically cantilevering and twisting towers. He also published an alternative view, which touts the benefits of them. Hearing these pluses and minuses from someone who has actively been involved in multi-box container architecture is great food for thought.

Finally, for some fun reading, here's an enjoyably nerdy book recently translated to English, "The Container Principle: How a Box Changes the Way We Think," by Alexander Klose. While more of a collection of essays, this book will help you see containers in a new way, and I found it fascinating how they have completely transformed our world over the last 60 years. I'm looking forward to BentoBox and whatever is to come next to transform my life as well.

Part 4

Tiny Philosophy

The word philosophy is defined as the study of the fundamental nature of knowledge, reality, and existence, especially when considered as an academic discipline. In the setting of tiny houses, philosophy really seems to mean the innate understanding of what it takes to live purposefully and on a smaller scale. But can it be learned? Can the tiny philosophy only be something you are born with or can you adopt it as you experience life? One would argue that no, it can't be a learned reality. There is indeed a paradigm shift going on that involves moving to smaller, simpler homes and less consumption in order to enjoy more grand adventures. The following writers prove that the tiny philosophy is more often than not learned and gained through experience and adventure.

A Small Investment with Overwhelming Returns

*How our decision to go tiny lead us
far beyond financial freedom*

Jess Sullivan

After designing, building, and living with her husband in their tiny house since 2013, Jessica Sullivan has become a dweller, blogger, and inspirational speaker best known throughout New England. She continues to write their blog – Living In A Tiny House – and participate regularly in workshops, presentations, and conferences related to tiny living. Jess is excited to share the story of their adventure, in *Turning Tiny*, by examining how focused they were on giving certain things up, yet never anticipating the sheer scope of what they would soon gain.

When Dan and I began our tiny house journey, we thought it was about improving our financial situation and living a life more deliberate and in tune with our passion for the environment. I thought, surely, after all I had already been through, that these two things would be the course correction I needed to lead me home to happiness, inner peace, and my rightful place in the world. Based on past experience, I also figured this challenge would serve as the fast track to finding out what our bond would withstand. I never could have anticipated all that blossomed, grew, and branched out of this single decision. My life now is a vividly colorful, inspiring vision compared to the dull picture it once was. In order to paint so deeply contrasting a tale, I must start somewhere before it's beginning, somewhere near the sad end of a paler story.

It was 2010. I watched spots of sun dance across the carpet of my temporary room until my thoughts finally settled on the larger view of the last dozen years. I had just recently ended a serious relationship, and as a result, gave up my home, my budding business, and life as I knew it. So much felt out of focus. What I realized was that I had fallen into a default picture or path of life. One that I had not chosen, but rather, filled the void, because I had not stopped to really examine *my own* definitions of a life with success and happiness. I had never bothered to paint my own picture, nor truly question the one I followed. I did well in school so I could go to college, get that degree that promised a good job, and start building a life. I met a young man. We married, and decided to buy a house. Why? Well, because *that's what you're supposed to do next.* You find a partner. You marry. You buy a home. You fill it with nice things to show others how well you are doing. You have kids. You teach them to do the same. There was a hitch in our story however; one that served as a painful slap of reality.

The home we bought, which was barely within our means initially, turned into a serious undertaking in every aspect: financially, physically, mentally, and emotionally. We noticed the kitchen floor was squeaky and saggy, so we knew some floor joists would need to be installed. We had a contractor come give an estimate. He told us he would not do the work and that floor joists were not enough. The house was unsound. He had found that there was considerable water and insect damage to the structural components of the house. The contractor told us that we would need to rebuild the sub-floors. So our house, the one we had imagined would just need some hard wood flooring and a paint job, became the most epic project I had ever faced, and one that I had not volunteered for.

At one point, only the four outside walls were standing on our two-story house. We could see from the basement floor clear up to the rooftop. Still, we remained hopeful and ambitious... *for a while.* We could not afford to pay someone to do all the work so we had to do as much as possible ourselves. I learned how to frame, insulate, repair roofing, run electrical wiring, install light fixtures, basic plumbing, dry walling, mudding, installing wood floors, tile floors, tile counters, building and installing a stair case, interior doors and trim, and staining and sealing unfinished wood floors. As time went on, the romantic thoughts of the house faded and we were left with the truth. This was a lot of work, a lot of stress, and a lot of money.

We lived like hobos the first winter. We had a plastic utility sink, a hot plate, and two old cabinets that sat on the dirty sub-floors with a plank board across the top that served as our counter and pantry. Most of the house still had exposed two by fours and insulation, there were only a few lights even wired up. It was very drafty, cold, dark, and miserable. Every moment not spent sleeping, working, or running daily errands was spent laboring on the house. Our lives were absolutely consumed by it. As days went on, we saw progress, but could not fully enjoy it together. There was just too much fighting about how to do something, pointing fingers when a task wasn't accomplished on time or done correctly, and stressing endlessly about the debt we were sinking into. As the house neared completion, we became resentful strangers, utterly disenchanted with love, partnership, trust, and the idea of sweat equity.

This house that we had poured so much into was no longer our dream but our prison. We had just enough money to pay the necessities and stave off credit card fees each month. I was painstakingly aware of every last square foot of that house because we had to re-create it all with our own hands. It was too big, and too much for us to handle. I began to look at things differently. My ideas of a dream life, a dream home, and what it truly takes to achieve happiness changed forever. It was a painful lesson learned. The house that had been that "next step" toward the American Dream ultimately destroyed us. Our marriage lasted only two years.

So there I sat, in a spare bedroom at my Aunt and Uncle's house, feeling completely bare and raw. All I could really think about at the time is what I did *not* want in my future. I did not want a traditional house, ever. I did not want another long-term failed relationship. Most of all, I did not want to be in debt. I blamed so much of my despair on my debt. I was foolish to think this loose set of proclamations was enough to be my new path to happiness.

Two years later my life had improved considerably. I had a job that paid well enough, a modest apartment and a newer car. I had bills to pay, but I could manage them and still chip a little off my debt each month. I had met the man that I felt was my true match (only time would tell). But something was still wrong. This picture wasn't working for me. I felt stuck and my soul felt stale. My debt wasn't shrinking fast enough and I hated the idea of paying rent with no return on investment down the road. Meanwhile, I had been so focused on simply having more money and saving more money that I lost sight of the things that brought true value and fulfillment to my life. I thought about how passionate I used to be about the great outdoors, gardening, food, writing, living deliberately and with less environmental impact;

each of those passions fed my soul. I was proud to be the tree hugging black sheep of my family, but these days, I looked more like a corporate wolf. My hobbies collected dust while all my energy went into working a demanding job, or commuting to and from that job. It was time to define a clear path that truly fit my goals, my passions, and restored balance in my life.

I asked myself, "*If you could have any kind of life, what would it be like?*" I was surprised at how easily the answer flowed from me. I want to live quietly, deliberately, and with utmost respect for the environment as she is our only home and our only source of life. I want to live sustainably and depend on the outside world for as little as possible. I want my power to come from the sun and the wind, my water from a well or rain off my roof. I want as much of my food to come from my own land and animals as possible. I want a small, sensible home that is "green" in as many ways as possible- whatever form that may be. I want to be debt free. I want money to play such a small role that I could work less and switch jobs with ease if something wasn't a good fit.

I wrote it all down, so nervous to share this new vision with Dan. To my relief and delight he responded well to the idea, and we began brainstorming just how exactly we could get started. We researched all manner of alternative and earth-friendly housing, but the same roadblocks came up again and again. Every idea called for a sizable upfront investment and sinking majorly back into debt. Any of these dwellings first needed land to sit on. The idea of another mortgage made my stomach turn, so we kept searching. I was beginning to think my picture was out of reach. Then, one day, as I was combing through YouTube videos, I came across the video of a 16-year old who was building a tiny house for himself in his parents' backyard. The righteous spark within me burst into flame that afternoon. Here was this young kid, building a tiny house on a flat bed trailer. He was taking his time too. He built as he had the money, and used as many second hand materials as possible. He stood on his small porch talking about living a mortgage free life, and how a small home equaled a small cost of living. I was envious, but more over inspired.

I brought the idea to Dan. This was how we could begin our new journey. We saw the tiny house as a stepping-stone towards our final dream home, but at the same time it still rang true to my passions for living a life of less impact. For a comparatively small investment, we could ditch apartment living, save more aggressively, and eventually purchase land. Then, we could move the tiny house there, and live in that while we slowly built on the ground as we had money to do so. A project of this scale was also much more financially palatable. We could manage the start up cost of a trailer and initial building materials. We could work with the money we had coming in each month, and take our time collecting reclaimed materials at a fraction of the cost. We spoke with my dad about having a safe place to build, and Dan's dad about borrowing the necessary tools. It was October of 2012 when we made the single decision that changed our entire world.

We didn't have much support when we began our adventure. My family knew I would follow through, but did not really relate at all. Some decided to lecture and call us foolish. Some decided it would be the comedic topic of choice for the better part of a year. We've heard every tiny house, small space, closed quarters joke out there. We smiled our way through it, our bond already tightening, as we faced adversity from every source but one another. Dan's family mostly kept quiet and seemed a little thrown and confused. This was something radically different for the guy they knew. His father called it a "cute idea" with no shortage of sneer, and was very skeptical about it ever coming to fruition. Dan started holding his ground more often, and as we smoothly achieved one phase after another, his resolve and self-confidence grew, as did his family's respect.

So many people viewed our decision as a major sacrifice. Each time, I wanted to ask, "what exactly are we sacrificing?" I thought back to a tiny house video interview in which the man cited an interesting statistic. Since the 50s, the average square footage of the American home has doubled, yet our happiness rating has not changed. It's actually starting to fall. The most obvious fact this identifies is that your amount of space and stuff does not correlate with happiness. If more and more is not the way, why not try less and less? I read a quote decades ago that has stayed with me to this day, "Be careful that the things you own, don't one day own you."

Dan and I look around and see it happening everywhere. There are too many people out there giving their lives to their jobs, just barely making enough to cover all the payments that they have incurred for various pieces of stuff that they think they need. Payments on the big tv, the nice couch set, the dishwasher, the laundry appliances, the slick car, the clothes, accessories and gadgets that are "in" right now, and the big house to hold all that crap. I remember what it was like when I realized this for myself. I was struggling to make enough money just to sit in my home, keep the lights on, the temperature comfortable, and food in the fridge. I had barely enough money for gas to get to and from work. I couldn't even afford to take a weekend road trip. Maybe there are people who are okay with living life in a big, swanky cage, but not us. The way we see it is this: a small space is easy to heat, to cool, to clean, maintain, and repair. A small space can be designed with utmost efficiency, and one area or piece of furniture can have multiple purposes and functions. A small space is cozy and inviting. Perhaps most obvious, due to all the reasons above, a small space costs significantly less. In addition, a small space requires you to decide what is really important and worth keeping. This in turn is cleansing, liberating, and comforting. The weeding out and paring down forces you to focus on what truly matters, and in turn, poses less barriers to collecting what does make life grand: experience, perspective, and connection.

I'll admit, it wasn't easy to get rid of my unnecessary belongings, at first. I went through several rounds of evaluating the stuff I felt the need to keep. With each pass it got easier; as I unloaded junk, I gained clarity. It's funny the things we quietly lead ourselves to believe are a part of us. As if those things being gone would somehow detract from the person you are. The reality is, there are no objects that will truly contribute to your character. Remove as many distractions from your life as possible, and focus on exploring, developing, and understanding yourself. As the build progressed the simple task of ridding myself of life's excess transformed into a much greater notion.

As our home took on the shape we envisioned, so did many other areas of our lives. We were following a path that we defined. We were taking the route of our choice, building how and with what we wanted, while holding fast to one another and true to our convictions. Owning a home is a true point of pride in any person's life, but it withers in comparison to the pride and admiration I feel for Dan and the little place we built for ourselves. I wake up every morning surrounded by incredible memories. Some were intensely glorious and pivotal, like the day we raised the walls. It was the first, and one of very few times, that we asked anyone else for help. A group of friends and family helped us to lift and secure our walls into place. In just 40 minutes time, the planning and work of the last 6 months was suddenly a little building on wheels, and the attitudes and opinions of our family and friends changed starkly. Respect and admiration overtook the old jokes and skepticism. Suddenly, our goals became logical, perhaps even desirable. The sense of what we were doing was no longer lost in its oddity. I still remember the electrifying waves of triumph, reassurance, and tenacity that coursed through me as we stood inside that shell for the first time. I could not stop exclaiming to Dan, "Look at what we did together!" And from that moment on, not one doubt about this choice ever crossed my mind again.

Then there was the night of the yearly neighborhood block party. It was September and we were closing in on interior work. We had just finished putting up the pine shiplap on our walls. The inside was looking more inviting by the day. We were excited and wary for so many people to be around. The reactions we got were always varied. What we experienced was wonderful. I think we gave about 50 different mini tours of the house. We found we both really enjoyed telling the stories of each little piece, what plans we still had to come, and what it would be like living "outside" our home more. At the end of the night, after a few drinks, we even had a little commentary by ourselves in the dark. We sat on the back steps of my Dad's porch and stared at our tiny home, it's little windows lit with a warm glow. We admired every last detail and told our favorite stories of the best days and the worst days so far. We talked about our favorite details, the adventures we had while collecting supplies, and how much we have learned and grown from this experience. We took time to admire ourselves for the crazy things we had accomplished, and physical hell we endured while building. We praised one another and admitted that neither of us could have done it alone. It will go down in the books as one of my favorite conversations of all time.

There are memories of more difficult times too, like the day we learned we had installed half our windows wrong. Our time line was already sliding away from us, the weather was oppressive, and the work was tedious and slow going. To hear that we had to disassemble the last 4 days of labor and begin again was too much at that moment. Rather than explode into anger and begin firing blame in all directions like I used to, I thought back to my first home, and what resulted. I wanted to be better than that person, for myself and for Dan. So I changed my approach. I asked myself the same set of questions each time I was faced with a problem. Can it be fixed? Can it be saved? Can we adapt? Yes. Yes. Yes. Are you professionals? Was this common sense? Does there need to be blame? No. No. No. Who else has worked just as hard as you this entire time? Who else has trusted in you and agreed to take on this risky journey together? Who else would you want to face this challenge with? No one. No one. No one. Whose opinion matters most to you? Who's able to truly share in your joys and fears? Whose absence would hurt you the most? Dan. Dan. Dan. The answers were the same every time. Each fleeting moment of anger melted away into another opportunity to practice self-forgiveness, admire one another's best qualities, revel in the strength and depth of our bond, and process the sheer awesomeness of what we were accomplishing.

Our entire adventure served as an enormous and fruitful therapy session, for Dan, for me, and for us as a couple. From the outside, it doesn't look like we have changed, but I promise you that we are both wildly different people. Dan now walks with his head held high, no longer second-guessing himself at every turn. He has an entire arsenal of useful life skills and inspiring stories to share with others. He feels knowledgeable, helpful, and valuable as a person. He's become an overflowing fountain of positivity and encourage-

ment, not only for me but for the tiny house community. There's a special brightness to his smile when he tells people he built his house with "his own hands." He's a man's man now; the type of guy he had always admired, but never thought he could be.

As for me, one word covers it all: redemption. After the first house debacle and complete life reset, I didn't feel so self-assured in my character or capabilities. I questioned the existence of a true connection and deeply abiding love. I had almost started to believe the ridiculous claims of my ex, that I was too intense of a person, too far off the beaten path, and difficult to be around. Today, I laugh in the face of those words. I live a life I had only dreamed of just a few years ago, and now hundreds of folks look up to me, admire my intensity, respect that I chose my own path, and want to be around me if only to pick my brain or absorb some enthusiasm. With this newfound confidence and a lot more leeway financially, I also had the courage to walk away from the desk job and start to pursue a second dream, my own specialty food business. I've never felt more powerful or in control of my future.

Finally, as a couple, Dan and I are beyond rock solid. We didn't end up resenting one another but instead got married in the midst of our build! We learned just how much we could accomplish with our own hands and a healthy dose of perseverance. We learned to stand our ground in the face of adversity, and how wonderful and deeply gratifying it is to feel we belong in a special community. We learned to have just as much faith and pride in ourselves as we did each other. This tiny house did not take us down, but built us up into something so much greater, stronger, and more beautiful than I have ever experienced. I look around at my day-to-day life, and I feel overwhelming pride and love for how we choose to live. I no longer feel detached and adrift from my convictions. We are striving to inspire and lead by example. We are being the difference we wish to see. And to think that all we expected was to save big by living small.

Defining "Tiny" and the Importance of Social Stigma

Zach Giffin

Zack Giffin grew up in the small mountain town of Gold Hill, Colorado and was the middle child of three brothers in a tool manufacturing family. In the fall of 2011 he built his first tiny house with Outdoor Research, living and traveling to various mountain areas in the western US for three years before being hired to be the host of a television show called Tiny House Nation. Now in the end of the third season and with over 40 tiny homes built, Zack has become a prominent figure in the tiny house movement and is passionate about sharing the joys and lessons of living tiny to the greater world populace.

Fresno, California is not the first city in the United States to write into law regulations specifically intended to allow tiny houses on wheels. However, it is the first city to allow tiny houses to be used as permanent secondary dwelling units on existing properties. In effect, the law enables homeowners to use a house on a trailer as a rental property. This is a radical shift from most previous rezoning efforts by municipalities that, for the most part, focus on carving out specific areas of town in which people are allowed to live in trailers. Tiny house people call these places "Tiny House Villages" and "Eco-communities," but to the outside eye they can be hard to distinguish from something called a "Trailer Park." This brings into question two things, "What is the difference between a tiny house and a mobile home?" and "Why are tiny homes at this moment being accepted when tiny, mobile spaces like van's, RV's, and other options never have before?"

By the time I built my first tiny house, I had rented rooms in a number of crappy houses, lived in an RV, a van and on couches. I had experienced a large variety of living options and had certainly felt the social stigma that comes along with low-income housing. When I first started traveling and living in a tiny house my experience instantly shifted from being ostracized to the least visible public areas with my van, to being an invited and celebrated attraction at the center of many public events. The typical reception I got when parking my RV at a friend's house was being asked by the neighbor how long I'd be staying. With the tiny house, a typical reception is being asked for a house tour. Once the tour is over and the quality of my home is recognized, it becomes much easier to be welcomed. Basically, the way I'm treated by strangers and people of authority is completely dependent on their prejudices. How I am judged dictates the reception I receive and when I made the move from a van to a tiny house. Everything changed.

I have spent nearly five years trying to articulate an answer to "what defines a tiny house?" When I first was exposed to them, it was my belief that the definition of a "tiny house" was a cute, fully functional cabin, built on a trailer, basically a Tumbleweed Home. When explaining the differences, it is fairly simple to compare tiny house construction techniques vs. camper trailers and point to the difference in layout and insulation and materials and say things like "It's similar, only built for more permanent living." The main issue with that explanation (as many people like to point out), is that we already have the mobile home, which in essence is a trailer built for permanent living. Again it is fairly easy to contrast the building process and compare quality and longevity. "Like a park model?" is a typical question at this point that poses a very legitimate dilemma: If a "park model" mobile home is essentially a higher quality mobile home built with a different more custom aesthetic, isn't that exactly what a tiny house is?

In truth, "tiny house" is only a label. It is a title that is desirable because tiny houses have the ability to side step much of the stigma attached to almost all other low-income living options. There is no definition of "tiny house" that is universally accepted throughout the mainstream and still many people who would never live in a trailer park are moving into tiny houses. Cities around the country that would never allow trailers on lots are opening up to tiny houses. Girls that would never consider dating a guy living in a "van down by the river" are more than ok with a tiny house guy. A large portion of the value of my house is the reception I get from the community that

I desire to be a part of and without that acceptance the function of my house is actually compromised.

In my mind, many tiny home builders, especially ones who have not lived in their own tiny house, fail to recognize the significance of the aesthetic elements that form that distinction. If all we do is value pure function and maximization of every square inch, then every house has a flat roof. When we build tiny houses that look indistinguishable from mobile homes, we risk losing the good will that currently makes tiny houses so appealing. If we choose to dismiss the reality of prejudice, then we dismiss the very thing that has made the tiny house movement so successful. If Jay Shaffer's first tiny houses didn't have steep pitched roofs and an adorable Victorian aesthetic, my belief is we wouldn't have a tiny house movement at all. It was the aesthetics that formed that obvious distinction and it's that visual separation from common trailer homes that has allowed broad acceptance to be possible. Our future ability to integrate tiny houses into American cities depends, in large part on homes achieving the aesthetic requirements of the neighborhoods they intend to join.

The beauty of what Fresno has done is to include the entire community in a process of enjoying the financial and societal benefits of tiny houses. The truth is that a person's home is usually their biggest investment. By allowing property owners to rent spaces to tiny house owners, the effect of the new law is to give the greater community a way to also see value in tiny houses. At the root, it is about increasing population density in a way that doesn't infringe negatively on the existing real-estate market. Fresno has a number of common sense safe guards included in the new law to protect real estate values. There are requirements on the size of property (6000 sq. ft.), limitations to one tiny house per property, parking considerations and an inspection process to make sure the tiny house fits into the neighborhood. While many cities are looking to apartments as the only solution for increased density and affordable housing, Fresno is asking "can tiny houses used in tandem with permanent structures, both achieve this goal and offer sufficient separation for harmony to be possible?"

Perhaps the most important implication of the new law is that struggling, indebted homeowners can use their property to generate extra income. We have millions of homeowners in this country who for a variety of reasons, own properties they can barely afford. The situation is best described as "treading water." All over our country, people who once thought of themselves as well off, are now looking at their main asset – their home – as the liability that may be their downfall. The stress that can come from this type of insecurity is heavy, and the manifestations of living with perpetual fear can hugely affect mental health. Is it in our best interest as a country to have large portions of our population living with perpetual financial stress? Would it be better if all the people who are in over their heads sell their property and move?

Unfortunately, more and more of our country's total wealth is accounted by the ever growing value of our homes and these fluctuating assets are what has driven the banks' ability to loan money. If every property owner, who was living on the margin, were to sell his or her home, the result would be a massive and unacceptable loss of property values countrywide. Therefore, all of the interested parties have incentive to search for possible solutions that don't require major sales, and that is what I see Fresno, CA exploring. By allowing property owners the ability to rent a space to a tiny house, you give people struggling to pay their mortgage a way to instantly relieve some of the burden with zero upfront expense.

A second implication is that the rent bill can be lighter because the renter foots the construction costs of the house and the yearly maintenance. By contrast, many cities encourage homeowners to construct secondary dwelling units, basically mother in-law apartments, on their property. Property owners who are struggling to pay the bills are in no position to take on additional construction expenses. Owners who can afford the cost, have little incentive for property sharing. With new development, the need to pay off large construction loans drives up the rents and potential renters who most need affordable housing are excluded. If we increase population density without addressing the factors that drive increased rent prices, we do little to help our nation's housing problems or address the segregation of lower economic groups.

A third potential implication is that communities become economically diverse. When we speak about tiny houses by and large we are speaking of a low income demographic. I am all for tiny house communities, but the danger of consolidating any type of low-income housing option into one physical location is segregation of the communities and the concentration of poverty. Regardless of the title, concentrated poverty creates environments where families live, surrounded only by people in similarly destitute situations. The lack of contact with opportunities to move forward leaves people feeling helpless and desperate and the typical issues associated to poverty like crime and drug-use are manifested. Stigma associated with homes on trailers stems less from the perception of low quality construction and more from a general prejudice against trailer parks because of issues associated with concentrated poverty. It has very little to do with the concerns about portability or quality and everything to do with historic zoning policies forcing owners into "trailer parks." By allowing policies to be written that group tiny houses on wheels together, we make it easier to stigmatize them and this works to deflate the value of our homes. By working instead, to push for policies like Fresno's, that lend incentive to property owners who team up with tiny houses, we open the door for families of lower income to find real affordable housing and we give the millions of struggling home owners an attainable way to relieve financial stress.

The question really comes down to how we want our societies to function. I believe that communities that purposely involve a spectrum of people increase the quality of life for all. It is near consensus among tiny house enthusiasts, that if we include low-income families we also facilitate a more vibrant culture. Children that go to school together learn how to relate to each other regardless of social background and that process creates pathways for advancement over generations. Creating interactive, economically diverse populations with room for artists and musicians and teachers and police officers to actually live in the community is the goal of many city planners in the world today. Many people much smarter than me, are looking at all sorts of ways of achieving it, such as Nano-living concepts (Vancouver) and micro apartments (Seattle and New York).

Fresno is choosing to explore a much cheaper option of tiny houses on wheels. If Fresno is to succeed, it will be because housing prices do not fall and crime does not increase. It will be because we avoid the situation that the critics of tiny houses all fear: the neighborhood looking junky, property values depleting, crime increasing, and families losing their sense of safety. If what they see instead is traffic clearing up on the highways, families staying close, neighbors working together, and people less stressed because cute little houses are bringing solutions to struggling homeowners, then Fresno's experiment will spread.

Forming an actual legal definition of a tiny house will at some point be very useful. Until that happens, it will remain in my mind a relative term that is defined by the pride and perspective of the owners. The difference is that we enjoy living small and that pride of our choice is what has deflected the stigma and made tiny houses such an appealing option. Stigma has led to restrictions of many other forms of affordable housing in our cities but because tiny houses seem mostly exempt, they are in a unique position of being considered acceptable. I believe tiny houses could work to expedite relief to our housing crisis while bringing balance back to our communities, but in order for this to happen, it is important we work together to open up the legal restrictions in a positive way. By keeping our construction standards high and paying attention to the importance of aesthetics, we win acceptance in the urban neighborhoods. By allowing us permission to feel pride in the conviction of our choice to live small, we take stigma and classism and flip it on its head. By resisting efforts to consolidate tiny houses, we open the opportunity for people to live affordably in more desirable places and, in effect, work to secure a future with more accessible housing. If we choose to ignore the reality of prejudice, if we pretend that the size is the only thing that defines a tiny house, and if we allow the negative elements to place tiny

houses into segregated communities, we squander a really unique opportunity in time, and jeopardize our ability to be a force of positive change to the world.

As the co-host of *Tiny House Nation*, I understand that my actions reflect on our movement. I aim to be the best ambassador I can, so the message of "less is more" does not get lost on the messenger. I will do my part as best I can, but if we are to turn tiny houses into a more viable option for housing it requires all of us to be ambassadors. We all share incentive to be good neighbors: to work with our communities and maintain our building standards. All tiny house owners are representatives of this movement and if we can earn the good will of the country then Fresno's experiment with turning tiny, will become a template for change and progress.

Here's to the Misfits

Learning to find the way around the spider web

Frieda Bakker

Writer and speaker Frieda Bakker from the Netherlands believes that these times need misfits of all kinds in order for us to continue to grow as a civilization. Trying to fit into society for years herself, she has flipped the script organizing her basic needs in a way so she feels at home too, by building her own My Tiny House NL. Here's to the crazy ones. The misfits. The rebels! Here's to *Turning Tiny.*

Here's to the crazy ones. The misfits. The rebels. The troublemakers. The round pegs in the square holes. The ones who see things differently. They're not fond of rules. And they have no respect for the status quo. You can quote them, disagree with them, glorify or vilify them. About the only thing you can't do is ignore them. Because they change things. They push the human race forward. And while some may see them as the crazy ones, we see genius. Because the people who are crazy enough to think they can change the world, are the ones who do.
—Rob Siltanen

This quote touches me deeply and I believe it to be true. I know I'm not Ghandi, Nelson Mandela or Amelia Earhart. I'm probably more like you than we both think. Still, I feel I'm one of the misfits this quote is talking about. You are probably too. Why else would you read this chapter and this book about tiny houses?

I had my struggles with the current status quo: working more than I wanted at places where I did not feel comfortable, in order to pay for the home I felt was too big for me. Not being able to do the things I love or dreamed about because of that. Feeling trapped in this situation and feeling an enormous big bubble inside myself wanting to come out, being pushy and often not to be ignored. Nagging. All. The. Time! That bubble was me.

I felt it was time to take back control over my life and make way so I could come out; being the misfit that I am. Fully. And at the same time making sure I do not have to worry about these primal needs we all have: food and shelter. Because worrying about them makes it hard to thrive. An in my opinion often forgotten and overlooked aspect in our society, hence the project to build my own tiny home. Itself a misfit too. We like each other very much! This is my story about making a way for myself to fit in, and why I think we, as a society, should take better care of those who do things differently. It is likely because we need them, more than ever. Let's open up the housing market for more variety so we, as human beings, can thrive again.

Wow. Just wow! I'm in my car driving North to Colorado Springs area for the first Tiny House Jamboree after visiting friends in Alpine, Texas. I take the nicer roads, the empty ones, where I'm able to see this country – The United States – and take it all in without crashing into others. And I'm in awe! Miles and miles lay out in front of me. The sun is out; strong. After every corner lies a new scene even better and prettier than the last one. My camera is on the seat right next to me, trigger finger ready. I'm not used to this, this enormous amount of space. I'm used to crowded small lanes with agitated drivers, sound barriers alongside of it. This is a whole different story. The landscape is there, welcoming me. Opening up to me. Like an old friend waiting for me to come along: "Hi dear Frieda, enjoying the ride?" My response? Well, what the heck, I'm in my rental car; alone. The road is empty. Who care? I'm screaming; crying, laughing. My cup is clearly running over.

It's the road trip that was on my bucket list for quite some time, now grouped together with a tiny house hunt and my visit to the first Tiny House Jamboree, August 2015. And I'm doing it! I am doing it!! Wow! What took me so long?

To be honest, my entire lifestyle took me so long. I wasn't able to pull it off before. After graduating from college I jumped onto the career train. I got a bachelors degree. I learned stuff so this is what I should do, right? I hopped from job to job. I've been a harbourmaster, a job consultant, an agricultural advisor at a veterinary practice, a manager of an eco-visitors centre with a small farm, café, park, gardens and an exhibition, a team leader in a distribution centre, a sales woman at an import and export company of vegetables, and even more. I clearly searched for, well, me?

Some things just came my way, others I figured were jobs I felt I had to do because that's what I was taught to do and what was expected of me, by "them," the well known and invisible "they." In the meantime a nagging and unsatisfying feeling kept me busy for quite a while, reminding me of the fact that there is more to life than this. What I was doing did not move me at all, hence the hopping.

One day, in 2013, I came home from my job as a receptionist, social media geek, and ambassador for a project about sustainability at two big hostels in Amsterdam. It was a grey day in December, one of the darker months in the Netherlands. My cold fingers reached for my home key. I stepped inside, and I just stood there. [Sigh] Is this it? I took a good look around my home, nicely decorated but big. Sadness came over me. I suddenly felt that all that I am, a creative being with wishes, dreams, hopes for the future was basically numbed. Stuck in a clamp of work and bills. It made me cry inside. I'm not living my life! At that moment, standing in my doorway, it hit me hard. I needed to change things, drastically. And not by changing from job just yet again. No, I had to turn things around and go to the essence of it all: how my basic needs were organized. That was – what I felt in that very moment – what the problem was.

The change I needed was one I did not look at before. I came to realize that whatever it was I was doing, or trying to do work-wise, it was always based on one thing: I need a certain amount of money and work a certain amount of hours to pay for a home. Would it be an apartment, a regular sized rental home or a home with a mortgage? There is, in this current system, a standard amount you basically need – as a minimum – to pay for a roof over your head, for the utility bills, the insurances, and all simply because of the lack of variety in housing and the rules that cause that.

Why was this insight so important to me? Being in a situation where you worry about if you're able to keep that job that pays for your home, you maybe know that that is not a very stimulating environment to thrive and be creative. I stumbled upon that myself. When the idea of building my own tiny home hit me, my contract was not renewed just less than two months after. I had to find another job and thankfully got one. I also moved to the other side of the country into a smaller place six months after that. At that point, I was being busy with my basic needs, getting used to new situations and I found myself not being able get my project My Tiny House NL up and running. My focus was clearly on other things.

The home I moved into (and currently live in) is a co-house where I rent a small private room and share the kitchen and bathroom. It is my first step into transitioning into tiny. I downsized big time and because living like this is quite cheap, I no longer need to work that much and therefore already have more time for my project and other wishes. There are however not many co-houses out there, at all. Living like this is also not for everyone and also not for me in the long run. It's compromising and it can be exhausting! You're basically packed together in one home, living with people you don't know in the beginning. You have to make it work, adjusting without losing track of yourself. A challenge that is! It's also probably the best speed course on communication and on "how am I in groups?" It's providing me with a lot of knowledge about myself, about humans in general, and we have a lot of fun together too.

For those who do not wish to live like this but do have the urge to create, contributing to society in a different manner, and do the things they love, life can be a challenge. Some will never get to do what they love due to taking care of bills. Some simply cannot continue doing so. It's too much. It's like having two jobs, one to survive and one to thrive. What happens is that a lot find themselves with a dead end in those things they love to do. It is a slow death to themselves. That was what happened to me at least. Not because it's stupid or unworthy what they wish to do, no, simply because we, as human beings need to take care, that's how we are biological programmed, of our basic needs first. It's our survival mode. With the limited choices on housing and it being the standard that you work in order to pay for your home, not fitting the human scale, creativity that we need in order to grow as a human race is killed. And it's exactly this why I feel society is, or better phrased the rules and regulations are, not taking care of those who do and see things differently.

To be honest, I actually do not see myself as a misfit, even though I said so before. *I fit me.* You fit you. So we're all good. Then what is it with the concept of being a misfit? This comes into play as soon as society meets me, and you: education, family, work, housing and all that. Again, it's designed in a certain way. And that might not be my or your way, hence the word misfit. Let me tell you a bit about my own misfit experiences.

Besides looking for the "right" job, I somehow always ended up doing the exact opposite thing of what people normally would do. Not by intent. It just happens to be that way, all the time. For example, at college I needed to arrange my internship for six months. I wanted to be involved in this new development in agriculture I accidently heard about. It was a more holistic approach on the management of farms and as a result, healthier products. We were trying to capture that by setting new standards in measurements, scientifically. I mean, I'm here, in college, and I better take advantage of that. I want to learn, I want to grow and I'm eager. So I started talking to some folks and ended up having created my own unique internship. That happens when things are new. You have to arrange that yourself. We actually had to find a company to make it an official one as well, otherwise, school would not accept it. I found myself being the first student in the Netherlands to be participating in these developments. I found myself explaining this to the teachers. Shouldn't that be the other way around? It was kind of confusing to be honest, but fun and very educational too. Teachers picked up on them, getting other students enthusiastic about it too. I was pioneering without knowing it. It just happened because I asked questions and wanted to know. I soon became the quirky one with other ideas, looked at from a distance with some questioning heads or asked to be part of other new, funky, crazy stuff. Cool!

Work? Yep, I do not see myself as a misfit here too, but I simply think that most organisations out there have a very old fashioned, fear based approach on management. Not wanting you to thrive so you are the best possible you, but instead trying to control you and put you in this set-up box. I don't get the concept of hierarchy either. Energetically it feels unnatural to me. Why is my boss more or higher than me? Or why is anyone lower than me for that matter? Yes, your job description in the closet of human resources is different. So what? I also often found myself asking way too many questions to my managers or presidents. A lot of those questions were actually, I found out later on, directly related to the things that were not in order or simply wrong. Managers, therefore most of the time, liked me in the beginning. I was laughing, happy, fast learning, and eager Frieda. But later on despised me and wanted me to shut up. Too many eyes in my head I guess, unconsciously scratching on those things people wanted to stay hidden.

And now my own tiny home is in the making. I am bumping into rules, codes, and regulations here too. All I want is a home that fits me, and my so-called quirkiness. Is that too much to ask?

So I am fitting myself, but I find myself having trouble sometimes trying to find my way in this, to me, old fashioned, crampy, fear based world packed with "systems." Whether it be school, work or housing. It is one huge spider web. It's what makes me a society misfit. And I'm not the only one.

You feel where I'm going? Misfits. Crazy ones. Rebels. Those magnificent people make us see things differently and open up our minds. They raise the standard! Pave new ways with their new take on things. They are the ones who push things forward. It's exactly what we need, more than ever. I mean, look at the world. And again, I'm not saying I'm Ghandi or Amelia Earhart. I do have a voice though, so do you. Hoping to be contributing to society in my own unique way. Misfits should not be left out. No one should be left out! We need everyone in order to grow as a human race. So let us choose our own home! Okay, repeat after me: tiny houses! Tiny houses! Yes! And more. It's not *just* about tiny houses but hey, they are darn cute! We need to open up this housing market with all the rules, codes and regulations that keep it

just as it is: not fitting the human scale. Why should we adjust and try to fit into homes? Homes should be made to fit us, and our lifestyles. Right?

So I get it now. Simple basic needs are an often forgotten and overlooked part of our lives and can be the source of why we cannot go on and do the things we truly love. On that grey December day back in 2013 it hit me. Out of love for myself the plan to build my own tiny home was born, right there and then. I don't care if it's illegal or not. I want a home that fits me so I can live my life the way I see fit. I stopped looking for that perfect job and started my own business, doing… whatever, milking cows, writing, speaking. I stopped trying to fit in. And I started taking back control over my life. I am here and have the right to be here, in my own unique way. Bam! So do you. It's called freedom.

So be the misfit that you are. Without the pressure and responsibility of having to change the world. How weird that may even sounds. Just be you and that in itself will change everything, out of love for yourself. You are perfectly imperfect. We all belong here otherwise you wouldn't be walking the surface of the earth. Or? Be you: in a big home, in a small home. Just be you. Working 60 hours a week because you love it, or spending time writing a book that maybe only you will read? And I feel we should make way for that. We have all the means to do it. We are just, and nothing more, caught up in the insanity of having way too many rules based on mainly fear. Luckily they are man-made. So they can be unmade too. That's all there is to it.

It's Friday the 7th of August 2015. I'm in Colorado Springs. I just left the Tiny House Jamboree campground, off grid, with lots of cactuses right next to my tent. Waiting in line to get in. You can't see the site just yet. It's right behind the small hill that I'm on right now. After checking in, I walk up the hill and immediately stumble upon a man with a tag: Darin Zaruba, organizer. Cool! Beforehand they asked me to stop by during the event because I came all the way from the Netherlands just to see some tiny houses. He gives me a hug, welcomes me, and the rest is history. A staggering 40.000 people showed up. An amazing, ground breaking event that was. The Jamboree turned out to be the biggest in the world so far on living small. I met lots of people, all getting it. I had a blast and found out that I wasn't just the only Dutch person out there who had traveled the furthest, but also was one of the few, maybe even the only one, from Europe. They loved it and tagged me #FamousFrieda. What? Um, okay.

I made a friendship for a lifetime. After coming home to the Netherlands again, I tried to get back on the saddle with my project, talking to Dutch magazines and organisations. But we somehow just could not get things in line. Not a matter of lack of enthusiasm. The flow was just gone. It didn't matter what I was doing. Life has funny ways to show you where to go. At the same time, Tiny House Magazine showed interest in articles so I became a regular and proud contributor for them. The Tiny House Jamboree showed interest: "Want to be a speaker in 2016?" "Yes!" And now there is this chapter, and a possible build of my home right here, in the USA. This is what I wanted and set myself out to do! The flow crossed an ocean. And the story continues…

I'm sitting here, as we speak, in a café packed with cool bikes in Colorado Springs while writing this. It's February 2016. Looking out of the window where the sun plays with the peaks of the Rocky Mountains. I'm again visiting the States. Six and a half weeks this time. I had to borrow some money to do it but I just couldn't resist. I had to go. It is an investment in my own life. Going over these kind of hurdles of doing what I wish and following my heart, even if it seems too big and costs me some money, gets easier every time. Good! I'm here to finish the design of my tiny house, and maybe even find a place to build it. Things are looking great so far. It may end up being a project with a YouTube channel on the build and a blog alongside it. Hopefully having a factory interested in my home for a product line. Why not? I'm already brainstorming about it with a company. Who knew? I did and I didn't. I did because I did not change my basic needs to sit back and not thrive. I also didn't know this because it's too cool to imagine sometimes. I think I can honestly say that I found my way now, following my bliss. And it seems to fit me perfectly.

Our Journey to Simplicity
From Tiny to Not so Tiny

Ryan and Hannah Corson

Ryan and Hannah Corson currently live in rural Colorado on their homestead with goats, chickens, ducks, and cats – pigs, sheep, and a human baby to come soon. They love herbal teas, learning ways to simplify their lives, all things wooden, and cozy spaces. You can keep up with them at Restoring Simple or on Instagram.

Make it your ambition to lead a quiet life, to mind your own business, and to work with your hands. —1 Corinthians 4:11

The greatest fine art of the future will be the making of a comfortable living from a small piece of land. —Abraham Lincoln

Less is more. —Ludwig Mies van der Rohe

What fuels a movement for simplicity, like the current tiny house trend? As a culture, we are taught to value things; possessions. We are pushed to get the best education we can, then the best jobs so we can buy the best clothes, cars, and homes we can (or *can't*) afford. We are encouraged to push the limits of what we can obtain. But you don't have to look around very hard to see that people are still unsatisfied. We are still seeking more.

Millennials, who get degrees and work for a year in their field only to end up working in a coffee shop, are still seeking more. Retired empty nesters, who have spent their entire careers looking forward to the day they can collect their pensions, are realizing that the grass isn't necessarily greener.

Professionals who have been in their careers for years are finding themselves dissatisfied and aware of an absence in their lives. They are all seeking more.

Maybe what they are seeking is actually less. Now, I'm not saying that the tiny house movement is the answer to all of our problems. Living in a smaller space doesn't solve most of the issues facing our culture today. But perhaps there *is* something to living a simple, undiluted life that many of us struggle to find in our day-to-day routines and interactions. And maybe for some, living in 150 square feet is a means to a less distracted and more intentional life. But is the tiny house approach the only answer?

Our story intersects with tiny living in some unique, and honestly, slightly messy and complicated ways. We have a passion for living a simple, productive life together. Rather than focusing on an accumulation of material possessions, our faith and desire for an authentic life are the motivation behind our goals. We strive to: be productive in what God would have us do, be active and intentional in our community, and enjoy simple moments together.

We met in a coffee shop in 2012 and had a lot in common. We're both oldest children, both fairly stubborn, both enjoy learning, and both want more out of life than our current culture is offering as "normal." Ryan already had some exposure to simplistic living (in the tiny house sense) by transforming a garage in an affluent area of the country, into a livable space; complete with gravity fed water system, composting toilet, and functional kitchen. Rent in that area was prohibitively high, so it was the most attainable solution for a low cost living situation. This experience also stimulated him to start thinking about more attainable and sustainable ways of life. Hannah's experience with simple living came from growing up with five younger siblings and being taught to be content and resourceful with what was available.

When we met, Ryan had already designed several small homes that could be built for under $20,000. He had a desire to create alternative living options for individuals and families who could not afford traditional, stick-built homes. He found enjoyment focusing on basic needs and efficiency rather than excessive square footage. In addition to tiny houses, many of his designs were cob, earth bag, or other forms of alternative architecture.

Not too long after we met, we began making plans for our wedding and the beginning stages of our own tiny house. We were attracted to building a tiny house because, as a young couple just starting out together, this was actually an attainable goal for us. We liked the idea of a housing option that allowed us to be debt-free and allowed us flexibility with where we could live. Our hope was to, in time, buy a piece of land to park the tiny house on, while we developed a larger alternative architecture-based home for an eventually expanding family.

At our wedding, instead of registering for gifts, we asked our guests to contribute to a tiny house fund. We started building the house a few months later, and actually lived in it for a short time during construction. But as construction projects often go, our home took more time and resources than we had planned for, and with a Colorado winter approaching, the house was put on hold for a while.

It was discouraging to feel like we were taking a step backwards. But that didn't deter us. We were extremely focused and committed to our goal of living a sustainable, attainable life together. We weren't willing to settle for less than what we felt called to – even though the path often seemed completely overwhelming.

During the next few years, we moved more than a dozen times, within three different Colorado cities. We lived in friends' basements and spare bedrooms, hotels, and multiple rented houses, cabins, and rooms. We moved from one city, to another, and back to the first again, all to pursue different opportunities to get ahead. Ryan worked up to 121 hours a week for a period of nearly a year. This was not an easy phase to go through – especially being newlyweds – but we had a vision for what our life would look like, what we felt like God had put on our hearts to pursue, and we weren't willing to settle for less, even though that required much sacrifice.

We ultimately settled in a small town named Westcliffe, in the southern mountains of Colorado, and purchased a log cabin on 6.5 acres, complete with a barn, several pastures, and chicken coops. The square footage of the house is "normal" measuring 2,300 sq. ft. The kitchen is an average size. We have a large living area with couches and a wood burning stove.

The size of our home, and the more traditional construction, were both significant deviations from our original plans, but not from our goals. On our journey to find a simpler life, we learned a lot about each other, and about life; that plans change. Sometimes when things don't go as you initially envision, adjustments are needed.

We say all that to emphasize the point that the size of your home may or may not play a role in your desire and actions towards living a simple life.

There are many reasons why we chose to move to Westcliffe. One being that there aren't many building codes here – which allows for more freedom and creativity in creating sustainable architecture. But we also fell in love with the community. Being an hour away from the nearest Walmart, everyone who lives out here is determined in the same ways we are: to live a simple, sustainable life in peace. We have developed such great relationships with the folks in this little town, and cannot imagine calling anywhere else home.

We are now finally settled, for the first time in our marriage. We are able to pursue more sustainable methods of living than we ever have, and while there are parts of our lives that have that rhythm and cadence of simplistic living, we aren't living in a tiny house.

Our tiny house is currently being stored a few lots down from our property on a neighbor's land. It has been there for almost two years, and it is still sometimes a struggle for us to see it. It's difficult to see it's almost-finished state and remember the thousands of hours and dollars that have been put into it already; not to mention energy designing it, and time spent researching deals on craigslist for building materials. Moving it from its original

building location to it's current one was stressful; not knowing if it would actually hold together while traveling down the road! There were many places that it barely passed height requirements on the highway and going under bridges.

It was the place that Hannah first struggled with learning how to use power tools, and while living in the barely-dried-in shell, realized that living in a construction zone was *not* ideal. It was the place where we had some of our first big arguments of marriage, and where we learned a lot about each other; the good and the ugly. It was one of the first structures that Ryan actually built and designed. We had so many friends and family help with the building process in various ways; whether it was through the GoFundMe page, or the actual construction; this was a group effort from the beginning.

But at the end of the day, it's just a house, right? In its most basic form, it is some boards that we nailed together so that we would have a place to sleep at night. We have memories associated with it, because it was our home for a time. But those memories and experiences have been much more valuable to us than the building itself.

We do plan to make the tiny house a part of our future. We hope to purchase the lot behind us and place it on a permanent foundation. We would love to rent it out either long or short-term, providing tenants with goat milk, soap, and lotions, farm fresh eggs, and other locally made goodies.

Our days now are extremely full, as we both currently work full time and take care of 40-50 animals. Our day starts around 5 am with milking the goats and processing the milk, collecting chicken and duck eggs, and feeding and watering the menagerie: our 8 goats, 20+ chickens, 11 ducks, and 2 barn cats.

We also keep busy learning to make cheeses, caramels, soaps, and lotions with the goat milk. We've been learning different methods of preserving, like canning and dehydrating. We plan to develop a large garden, from which we can eat, preserve, and sell some produce. Bread making is another skill we're attempting to master. Our summers now consist of foraging for herbs, berries and flowers. Autumn consists of preserving the goods collected and grown during the summer. Winters are all about keeping everyone warm, knitting and reading inside by the fire, and finally spring has been about baby goats and the birds finally laying eggs.

Living simply can, in some cases, be enhanced by the small size of the place that you live, but we've determined that it's not the only viable approach. Living simply can be valuable because you're living an undiluted life. What we mean by this is that you have an intentional approach to life where you are more connected to the things, and more importantly, people around you.

There are many ways that this can be done, regardless of where you live. In our case, our community is not only something than enhances our day-to-day living, but it is a necessary part of our life here. We rely on one another for support, encouragement, and guidance as we've jumped into this homesteading lifestyle. For example, when we first bought our farm, we ordered some chicks but had no idea what we were supposed to feed them, how much, or how often. Oh, they needed a heating lamp? Good to know. We bought our goats within a week of owning the place, but neither of us had ever owned small livestock before and had to immediately adjust to milking them twice a day! Without the support of the folks around us that had been doing these things for years, we would have been completely lost. This has made us extremely connected to our community because of necessity. It definitely helps that they are now also some of our best friends.

Another way that we are attempting to live intentionally is by trying not to be blind consumers of our food, but being aware of where it comes from, and striving to make choices that are sustainable long term. This is also something that can be done in phases and is easy to get overwhelmed with very quickly because we are used to going to the grocery store and finding everything that we need, quick and easy, no questions asked. But we are slowly attempting to have a more sustainable approach to what we eat. We currently have chickens for both meat and eggs, and goats for meat and milk that we drink and make cheese with. We have hopes of growing lots of our own food, and would love to process more of our own meats as well. We aren't there yet, but the attempt to become more aware of the sustainability of our foods is something we'd like to grow in.

Whether you are living in the country, the city, a big house, or a tiny house; the choice of how to live is yours. Are there ways that you can simplify your life to focus on things that are really important to you? We understand that these answers may not come overnight. Remember, we moved 15 different times to get to where we are currently. The past few years for us have been an adventure to say the least; a challenging, exciting, exhausting-at-times adventure, mind you. We've had to constantly evaluate and re-evaluate a lot about life and the type of life we desire to live. And so we've found ourselves at multiple points across the tiny house/simple living spectrum. Our perspective is slightly unique because we started off super focused on building a tiny house in order to live simply and our plans have changed and now we're attempting to live simply in different circumstances than we had planned on.

So what have we learned from it all? Life is messy. But it is so worth it. It's worth taking the risks to pursue a dream of the life you see when you close your eyes and breathe in deep. And when what you've envisioned doesn't work out (because it won't always work out), and you have to revise your dream, well, you tend to learn a lot. That's where we are now. We're learning to cherish those learning moments. It's what keeps life interesting and full of fun challenges. We plan to continue learning. We plan to continue the pursuit of our goals of simple sustainability and meaningful community no matter what sort of house we live in. So as long as we're together, we're going to strive to live in a way that finds joy in the people around us and encourages others in their journey to discover themselves capable of creating a simple, fulfilling, self-sustaining lifestyle.

So stay posted. We'll be sure to let you know what we learn.

Skoolies In Session

The tiny life won't ruin your children, I promise...

Nina Nelson

Nina Nelson, creator of Shalom Mama, is a natural living writer and wellness advocate for women who want to live a more intentional lifestyle. After convincing her husband she wasn't crazy, they rebuilt a 'skoolie' and moved their family of 6 into it for one year. (Spoiler Alert: *no one died.*) She is feverishly writing in *Turning Tiny* about her experience and why living tiny won't ruin your kids.

A few years ago, I got this crazy idea after binge reading someone's blog all night. What if we sold or got rid of most of our stuff and moved into an RV just like they had done? I excitedly told my husband about my thoughts and awaited his reaction. It was pretty immediate. He thought I'd lost my mind. He just couldn't fathom why I'd want to live in such a tiny place. What about privacy? What about space? What would we do with all our stuff? There was also a more obvious reason why the idea was nuts. We had children. Not just one or two, but four. Surely moving into an RV would be a terrible experience for everyone. So my crazy idea remained just that – an idea.

Over the course of the next few years, though, we explored the idea a bit more. Or rather, I subtly steered us in that direction (my husband says I have an evil cat mind). I culled more possessions and looked for ways we could experience living tiny, if even for just a weekend.

During those years we camped more and stayed in little yurts and the kids just loved it. Not only were they excited about exploring the outdoors but they really liked that we had more family time together when there wasn't space for each of us to spread out to. And then five years after that blog sparked my crazy idea, we did it. After watching a documentary that featured a family with 5 kids living in a converted school bus (a 'Skoolie'), my husband turned to me and said, "Ok, fine. Let's try it. I'll give it a year."

Not long after I found our bus on Craigslist (before he could change his mind) and he drove from our home in Central Oregon to Idaho with my brother to pick it up. When he arrived back home in a 36-foot school bus with a patchwork exterior, I couldn't believe it. We were actually doing it!

Over the next few months my husband spent all of his spare time at my dad's farm turning our new-to-us bus into a home. Though it had been previously converted everything was saturated with cigarette smoke and done in a style most unattractive. There was shag carpet and everything was dark brown. We ended up tearing it all out and just starting over.

A few months into the project we moved out of our house into my parents' 22-foot trailer. The trailer was right next to the bus, which gave us more time to work on the behemoth of a project. It also gave us the chance to experience what tiny living was actually going to be like with our kids. The trailer was much smaller than the bus but we made it work. The kids spent tons of time outside or hanging out with Grandma and Grandpa, which they loved. It was cramped but it was a perfect step for the situation. After that experience the bus forevermore felt huge!

We moved into the bus as soon as the beds were ready and lived there for a little more than a year while my husband finished it (mostly) around us. It was quite the experience. During that time I had plenty of opportunity to observe my kids and how they were reacting and adapting to a tiny lifestyle. Face it. It's really easy to focus on why going tiny with kids is a terrible idea. Come to think of it, it's really easy to do that sans kids too. But for every con there seems to be at least two pros. These benefits can have a lasting positive impact on your children and your family as a whole and though the benefits were many, there were four that stood out to me the most based on our personal experience:

More Time Outside

There is only so much time that can be tolerated inside roughly 250 sq.ft. of space, no matter how well-designed it is. It's great though because there's so much to explore outside, especially here in Central Oregon. One of my main goals of moving into our Skoolie was to spend more time outside; both me and the kids! During our time in the bus our kids spent more time outside than they ever had (and have since). They dug holes, played in the garden, helped Grandma with the chickens and rode bikes around the farm I grew up on. It was comforting to this mama's soul. My oldest and I even did school on the bus roof when the weather was nice!

Less Stuff

Have you ever tried to clean up a giant mess only to get overwhelmed by the magnitude of it? It's hard. And that's what I used to ask my children to do every day. Finally I realized that they just had too much stuff, which I was mostly responsible for. As we got rid of more and more stuff the fights over cleaning became fewer and fewer. Our kids also explored their creativity more, finding new ways to use the few possessions they had.

Simply put, decluttering brought more peace to our lives.

Before moving into the bus each of our children was given a shoebox-size bin and asked to pick their favorite toys to bring with us. Though we had done a lot of purging this was still a significant move. They did it though and without a fuss. Most remarkably though is that during the time in the bus they were happy with the toys they had chosen. (I only wish the oldest hadn't chosen to fill his box with Legos. Ouch!)

More Creativity

Children are such creative beings by nature. They can turn a simple corrugated cardboard box into a spaceship or gourmet kitchen or any number of things! But the more stuff and distractions they have, the less creative they become. Thankfully, we were able to witness firsthand the creativity that can be sparked when the distractions are taken away. Our kids came up with countless imaginative games to play during our time aboard the bus. One night the four of them put together a puppet show together. They secured a blanket to our broom handle to make a curtain and set everything up behind it. They even invited Grandma and Grandpa to come watch. It was a blast and remains in my mind as one of my favorite memories of our tiny life.

Closer Family

The puppet show was only one of many fun nights spent together as a family onboard. When people ask what my favorite part of living in such a small space was I tell them it was all the time we got to spend together as a family. (Ok, first I tell them how much I loved being able to clean my whole house in just ten minutes. But still.)

Our children loved it, too. In no particular order, their favorite things were:

- Bedtime stories
- Family movie nights in the "living room"
- Snuggling (oh, so much snuggling)
- Listening to audiobooks together
- Talking to each other at night after bedtime since our beds were so close together
- Being so close to Grandma and Grandpa
- Playing games on the wobbly table

Each day gave us the opportunity to connect more as a family thanks almost entirely to our limited space.

Sounds like sunshine and roses, no? Please don't get that impression. It wasn't. There were days I climbed out of bed and stepped right onto a pile of Legos because the kids didn't clean up the night before like I'd asked. Some days they would argue and argue (and argue) with each other or I would hit my introvert people-limit and kick everyone outside and claim the bus as my own personal refuge.

But you know what? I still deal with all that stuff. Almost two years, in a house, out of the bus, and I still deal with all of that stuff. Truth is no matter where you live, if you're living with children, there's bound to be conflict. However, if you're going to be living tiny with them, there are some special things to consider ahead of time:

Personal Time/Space

As an introvert this was a huge consideration before we moved into our tiny house. It was very important that each person had their own personal space to retreat to if need be. For my husband and I, that meant curtains that we could put up with magnets to create a door to our "room" if we needed some space. The kids each got their own bunk with a light, shelf and curtain. We wanted them to have a space that was just theirs, where they could retreat to day or night.

Sex and Intimacy

We actually didn't put much thought into this at all before moving into the bus. But this must be a serious consideration for lots of people because I get asked about it all the time. "How did you um, you know, have sex on the bus with kids around?" Um, quietly? Seems simple enough, right? This question always makes me laugh because I wonder how "normal" couples have sex with kids living in a "normal" house. Sex and intimacy has always been and always will be an important part of our relationship. It was no different on the bus. So when we wanted to have sex we'd wait until the kids were asleep; really deep, REM-like sleep. It was then that I was so glad I had been intentional about making household noise at night when they were babies because now they can sleep through anything! When it was appropriate we even had the option to send them to Grandma and Grandpa's house to watch a movie. Where there is a will there is most certainly away!

Belongings

I'm not a sentimental person. Getting rid of my personal stuff was fairly easy. I can't say the same about my husband or children though. It was extremely important that they had a say in what they kept and what went out the door and when they disagreed with me on getting rid of something, we talked about it, openly and honestly. We ended up putting some of their stuff in storage when we moved into the bus, but we also got rid of a lot, too. We had an idea ahead of time how much space we'd have and what we'd be storing their stuff in, so we went through their belongings with that in mind. Thankfully my husband did such a great job with the design that they were able to keep much more than we thought we'd have space for. I can't say this with enough emphasis. So many stuffed animals on that bus!

The key to not ruining your children in a tiny living situation is communication. It all boils down to communication! Come to think of it, what is any relationship without communication? If you're even so much as thinking about going tiny with kids it is hugely important to discuss it with them from the start. Find out what they think about it and consider their concerns. Or course, this is assuming they're old enough. Even toddlers are capable of giving input, though. Different age groups will obviously have different concerns, but regardless of their age, their concerns are valid. Before moving forward talk about it as a family and make sure you discuss these points:

1. What are the overall concerns?

This is the time to hear all their fears and concerns even if you think they're silly. Remember when you were a kid? Little things felt really huge. If we were to move into our Skoolie again we'd go back through this process and spend more time addressing all of our kids' questions and concerns in their entirety.

As an example, we know after living in our current house that living near friends is really important to some of our kids, mainly our explosive extrovert. When asked if he would move into the bus again he said no which sort of surprised me. When we asked more questions we found out that he would, so long as we're still close to his friends.

The great thing about really hearing them out during this step is that it gives you a chance to discuss their feelings – their concerns – and mitigate them just by having them heard.

2. What's the plan for when they need more space?

This is important when designing your space when kids, especially those in the 'tween stage, are involved. In our case my husband built two sets of bunk beds, one on either side of the hallway with the intention of living in the bus for a year or so. At that point our oldest was 9-years-old and, unbeknownst to us, about to hit a massive growth spurt. He still fits in his bunk these days, but barely. If the plan was to live on board any longer we would have altered the floor layout a bit. Word to the wise. Before going into your tiny space, be sure to think about what you'll do if they're still growing.

You may also want to consider what your children's future space needs might be beyond the obvious height changes. Maybe they'll want more privacy? If so, making a curtain option in their bunk would be good. Or perhaps more cubbies or space for their special collections would work well. It only takes a little time to think out but you'll be so happy you did.

3. How can it work for everyone?

This is a great question to ask because it gives you a chance to hear what's ideal for each person. And it might surprise you. My ideal layout involved personal space to retreat to, enough space to have friends over and a bathtub. I'm pretty easy to please. My husband needed to be able to have a quiet space if it got too loud in the bus. Outdoors? Check. The kids wanted to make sure they had their favorite belongings and that they'd still get to play with their friends. Done.

Funny, but looking back on it, nobody ever said anything about needing a minimum amount of space.

When you approach tiny living with a list of what's most important to everyone involved it's so much easier to make things work smoothly. But be prepared. There's a chance it might not work out.

We moved into the bus with the intention of living in it at least a year but knowing that we could decide to leave in a month. If we did, we knew we'd have to find a place to live, replace some furniture and possibly sell the bus. But that was okay. Moving into the bus wasn't about proving anything to anyone, but rather seeing what the experience was like for my family.

We also didn't have a bunch of expectations about what the experience would be like, which I think was really helpful because there was no ideal we were trying to strive for and thus be disappointed by if we didn't meet it. Just know that there's a chance it won't work out and that's okay. Make the best of it wherever you are on your journey and know that it will be a memorable experience for your family either way.

It's been almost two years since we moved out of the bus and it turns out our turning tiny didn't ruin our children at all. In fact, I'd say it was one of their most impressionable experiences because through it, they were able to experience so much including:

- Conflict resolution
- Contentment with less
- Exploring the great outdoors
- Growing food and taking care of chickens
- Dealing with people who teased them for doing things differently (and doing it well)
- Deepening relationships with their grandparents
- Adapting to new situations
- Entertaining lots of people in a really small space

And a lot more I am sure. Kids are so resilient and can grow through any situation if given the chance. Don't be afraid to give your kids the chance to experience something new. Don't let them be your excuse. Let them be your reason!

The Pursuit of Adventure

Tabatha Mehl

As a Cincinnati native, graphic designer and dog mom, Tabatha Mehl documents her experience living and building a tiny home semi-trailer with her husband on their blog, Mehl Family. In her *Turning Tiny* chapter, she investigates how the pursuit of adventure turned her into a tiny dweller.

Noah signed his name and put the pen down. He looked at me for a long minute and said, "Are you sure? We have to be absolutely sure because there is no going back."

I smiled at that. My husband's caution warmed my heart. For me, there was no question; I knew in that moment that I was ready. It would be almost two years later that I would begin to understand why.

As a daughter of a single, hard working mother in a middle class family, I moved often. We had many apartments through the years – some with large rooms with natural light, and some with small square windows and walk-in closets. Ultimately, every experience was similar: we packed up all of the rooms and everything in storage and moved to a new apartment across town. My childhood was spent ping-ponging all over the west side of Cincinnati. A new school and a new bedroom awaited at each address. Growing up, I felt different from my family and my peers. I never felt like I was interested, or had the capacity to be interested, in normal social expectations and conventional thinking. I was by no means extraordinary; I just lived comfortably within my introverted self. I thrived on creativity and imagination.

I was one of the last generations to spend my formative years without devices and technology – things I now feel clog the imagination. I was free to explore the woods behind our various apartments, swimming through the creeks and climbing trees. At an early age, I enjoyed the peace and quiet offered to me when I was alone in the woods. There was a great sense of calm that permeated my core and one that would slowly begin to deplete as I grew into an adult. I also escaped what ever was happening in my family or school life by turning closets and basement nooks into private spaces for my mind to recharge and my imagination to grow.

Secretly, I craved structure and order but lacked the aptitude to follow the herd. I would later grow up part of a generation accustomed to social and professional networks like Facebook, Instagram, Twitter and so on, but unlike my peers, I felt so disconnected. In virtual world full of people I felt alone. I lacked whatever it was in that early culture that became fixated on gadgets and digital connectedness. While my friends were texting on their first cell phones, I still craved a world of freedom, imagination and nature. To this day, I am still one of the last of my peers to join the new network or buy into the new device.

The shift into teen years and early adulthood had me feeling very lost, as I'm sure most people do during that time. Somehow it was different for me though. I dealt with it all by holding onto lots of things; old relationships, clothes that didn't fit, pieces of art or even left over hobbies that no longer held any special meaning for me. In the span of my four years in college I moved five or six times. The load though remained the same during that time because I carried everything with me. I wasn't a hoarder and I didn't walk around like a pack mule but I did carry everything I owned from one place to the next. Maybe that was the result of growing up with a modest amount of material items, which gave me a sense of urgency to hold on to things? Ultimately, that kind of thinking held me back because it became more about putting those things in order and having enough closet space just to store things I never used. It turned into more things that I had to dust or take care of and for a long time I didn't think about it – these things just simply exist-ed. The reality is that I've always been someone who struggled with order. As much as I crave it and want that structure, I find it difficult to consistently keep things organized and clean, which just results in more time spent cleaning or looking for things.

I met Noah in the summer of 2011. Our personalities differ in some major ways: Noah is a dreamer, schemer and doer. He came to the relationship with a wide knowledge of many things, including technology and construction. He quickly became my rock and constant source of encouragement. By 2014, we were married.

Before our wedding, Noah and I had been renting an apartment in Over The Rhine in Cincinnati, Ohio for four years. The location was amazing but renting began to wear on us both: the noise, the people, and the general quality of materials and building management of the loft. For me, my frustrations with our living situation slowly manifested itself in mental and emotional ways. After living in the 1,200 sq. ft. concrete loft for four years, I started to crave trees and fresh air so badly it hurt. Eventually, it didn't matter that we only lived a few blocks from a park because I missed the ease of walking barefoot outside, hearing the wind blow and seeing stars at night. With little natural light in our loft (just two small windows) I felt like I was slowly dying; it was as if all the concrete and noise were sucking the life from me. I felt weighed down by our furniture and everything within.

"The things you own start to own you."

Eventually, I wasn't the only one who was suffocating in our loft. Noah and I both felt that a change needed to be made. We first explored options in our neighborhood, quickly realizing that the perfect place (at the right price) didn't really exist in Over The Rhine. When we looked into renovating one of the historical homes in the area we realized finances would be problematic (with both of us being young, relatively new into our careers, and strapped with student loans). We also knew the capital required for a renovation would be beyond our means. With a historic neighborhood there could also be hidden costs because old buildings are known to have possible water and foundation damage, among other things.

Many of my peers would (and have!) chosen a home in the suburbs. Conventional wisdom tells us that we should stop renting and buy a house or condo in a nice neighborhood. For Noah and I, that wasn't really our style. To find a solution that better suit us, we asked ourselves a lot of questions.

Do we want to be in the same place for 15 years? Do we want to live in a suburb? Are we having kids in the next few years? Do the houses available meet our needs with regards to design and infrastructure? Do we want to spend $100,000 or more to take on a mortgage? The answer to most of these questions turned out to be a resounding "No!" Since that was so obviously the case, what were our options? We knew that we were heading down a path that wasn't conventional. While we were mulling over these questions, we started researching what people were doing unconventionally. Through the Internet, talking with friends and attending housing seminars, we realized the options greatly varied. People all over the world have discovered alternative ways to live and build homes, such as container homes, RVs, various trailers, boats and even tree houses.

Through the research process, we realized a big problem for us would be being tied down to a single location, for a very long time. As a Cincinnati native, I had spent my entire life living within the tri-state area. I had long since dreamed of exploring different parts of the country, and so for me, moving away from a foundation home was an easy decision, and in deciding to do so, eliminated a weight that I had carried for a long time.

Because we wanted freedom to travel, we immediately had our first parameter, which was that our solution should be mobile. In our particular situation, with just a good Internet connection, both Noah and I have the ability to work from home (or on the road). In addition, I knew going mobile would afford us the opportunity to connect with the world and see friends and family.

Noah first approached the subject of tiny homes with me years before we found our tiny home. It was a surprise to even myself when I realized that I had little concern about getting rid of our possessions or how we would handle living in such a small space. I did, however, question if it was the right time. Was this a change a 20-something person should make?

The early discussions that went on between Noah and I were slow and deliberate. I recall my heart beating fast and my mind moving slowly as I processed what my life would be like as a tiny home dweller. What would it mean to leave behind convention and move into what can most be described as a full time adventure? I began to think back to the little girl exploring the great woods and creek behind her home: her heart would swell each morning that she awoke in a home she built, a home that yearned for nothing. And so, my anxious and scared heart slowed to an even and calm pace. I began to open and stretch my mind to tiny dwelling. It became a question of, "Why Not?"

Even so, the fear remained. It didn't even occur to me to tell anyone about our plans until it had already happened.

After years of research and after exploring the logistics of customizing a tiny home, we remained invested in a solution with wheels, giving us the ability to easily move it and all of our belongings for future travel and land ownership. It represented a freedom from a mortgage and a freedom from material items. And for me personally, it represented a goal in mind for my mental well-being; somewhere within I knew this could be the answer to alleviating some of my anxiety.

We explored many tiny home options, like shipping container renovations and prefab RVs, but we eventually arrived at a 53' dry van semi trailer. A semi trailer would give us maximum allowed size for a home on wheels (53' length, 8.5' width, and 13.5' height), and unlike building a custom trailer from the ground up, the semi came with walls and a roof, sealed and ready for all road and weather conditions. It would only take a few days of searching before we found a trailer that would fit our needs (a used 2005 steel Trailmobile). By the following week, I stood in what would later become my home. As we prepared the check, Noah asked me the question that would be the turning point for the biggest change in my life: "Are you sure?" – and just like that we put down the money and had the title in our hands.

By mid-fall 2016 it will be just at two years since we received the title for our tiny home. Since the beginning my mind has opened and flowered with the possibilities of what lies ahead. A major lesson the tiny home has brought to the forefront of my thoughts is this: In life, when something new or different scares you, it probably means you should take the leap and find out what you're really made of. We've spent countless hours over-engineering our tiny house so that we won't be limited by any location, weather or road conditions. We essentially build a wood box within a steel box within the trailer so that we have maximum structural support. Our trailer has been transformed into a home with real windows, sliding glass doors, a toilet, bedroom, AC, furnace and so on. It is more than my wildest dreams could have imagined and not one day has gone by where I've questioned our decision to go tiny.

Going tiny has changed my philosophy on life. By the nature of the times we live in now — the need for technology and need for excess — I likely would have ended up like may of my peers in a traditional home with a mortgage. I may very well have that eventually but for now, going tiny has allowed me to go back to the basics of who I am and what I need to be happy. For me the decision to go tiny was effortless. Although going tiny was scary and intimidating, it was an adventure that found me at a time where I was ready.

Even though there have been struggles and challenges with going *(and building)* tiny, I find that going tiny has changed me for the better. For the rest of my life I'll be able to have this as part of who I am. I'll be able to tell my children about this and to share this time and these memories with my husband. And no matter what happens to me in the next 80 years I know I've lived and gone after something that so many people feel is out of their reach.

What a Terrible Word – *Things*

*Starting your marriage with a trip around the country,
one road after another...*

Heath and Alyssa Padgett

Heath and Alyssa Padgett moved into their first RV just four days after their wedding in 2014. In their first year of marriage the couple traveled to all 50 states and have since upgraded RVs to continue a mobile lifestyle. In their *Turning Tiny* chapter, the Padgetts talk about why experiences are the most valuable thing they own and how to turn tiny living into opportunities.

"You still have to register for gifts," my mom reiterated to me for the tenth time.

"But we're going to be in an RV. We won't have space for them. We won't need anything else!" I argued.

"But you will want it and people want to buy you things, not just give you money."

Telling my family that my soon-to-be husband, Heath, and I planned on quitting our jobs, buying an RV, and traveling to all fifty states for our honeymoon wasn't exactly easy. My mom kept pestering me about registering for fancy towels, dishes, and kitchen gadgets. It was all things I knew we didn't need and wouldn't need for at least a year.

But she insisted.

Her words kept echoing in my head while I pondered if anyone would support our honeymoon fund over buying us a toaster oven. *People want to buy you things.*

What a terrible word. *Things.*

As Heath and I planned our 50 state road trip—an adventure that we estimated would take the better part of a year—we set up a crowd funding account so people could donate to our "honeymoon fund." Our friends and family could help contribute to getting us to the next state on the map in lieu of gifts.

Our unorthodox idea to travel to all fifty states wasn't a plan for a lavish, leisurely honeymoon. Heath and I both worked monotonous office jobs. You know, the typical recent college grad jobs that felt like we were wasting most of our days doing meaningless work for someone else instead of pursuing the work we really wanted to do.

We wanted something more out of life. Something we wouldn't find if we stayed in our jobs, found a nice apartment together, and just enjoyed life in Austin, Texas like all of our friends.

That's when Heath approached me with an idea. We were already flirting with the allure of a 50 state honeymoon, but struggled to figure out how to sustain a year of traveling.

"What if I work a job in all 50 states?" Heath suggested. "I don't like my job. I have a ton of ideas of businesses I want to start or books that I want to write, but I don't know where to start. What if I work a different job in each state we visit to try figuring it all out?"

To be honest, my immediate reaction was to rebuke him for even considering working during our honeymoon, but I eventually came around. The more we thought about it, the more the idea grew into the ideal project for us to pursue together. We even partnered with an online job board called Snagajob who agreed to help Heath find the jobs and even sent us film equipment to turn the adventure into a documentary.

Heath would work a job in each state and I would film our journey, all fifty states, all fifty jobs. It was the most bizarre, but somehow perfect, plan to propel us out of our boring lives and into an adventure.

We bought a 29-foot, 20-year-old motorhome off of Craigslist for our first home together. It was old and musty and roughly 50 different shades of brown. There was blue shag carpet that we quickly removed and replaced with laminate wood floors. More than one person commented on our home's likeness to the mobile meth lab in *Breaking Bad*.

More difficult than moving into our RV and deciding to film a documentary was the hurdle of explaining these decisions to everyone around us. They instantly prattled off questions.

An RV? Why not a tiny house? What will you do with all your stuff? All your furniture and clothes? How are you going to stay married in such a tiny space? What if you get in a fight? You won't even have a car to take a break from each other if you wanted to. What are you going to do about Internet? TV? How are you going to watch the Bachelor every Monday?

I didn't know the answers to any of their questions. But we knew staying home out of fear of jumping to something unknown would be far worse than anything we would face on the road. Well, we hoped anyway.

After a few cosmetic updates, Heath moved into the RV a month before our wedding and instantly filled every cabinet with clothes, books, and mostly junk. Before I moved in with any of my things, we went through the entire RV—twice—to purge all the things we decided we didn't need, like books we'd already read, winter clothes, tote bags, hats, DVDs. More than half of what we owned (plus every gift from our wedding registry, except a travel-size grill) was packed and sent to our parents' homes. Our siblings claimed pieces of furniture and I gave my smart TV to my sister on loan, wondering when I would watch Netflix again.

We hit the road four days after the wedding, setting aside everyone's worries and determined to see the country.

Ten days into our adventure, RV life had turned us upside down.

We had broken down twice and had mechanic bills and an insurance claim to deal with. We had gotten lost countless times—Did you know

there's actually no limit on the number of times a couple can argue over the GPS? We maxed out our data plan on our phones, and quickly learned that Internet at RV parks rarely works, if they have it at all. Money was tight, and we wondered if we hadn't made the wrong decision.

We had to learn how to be married, how to travel full-time, how to work together on a documentary, and where to put our shoes so the other person didn't trip over them.

It took time.

During our first month on the road, we made it all the way west to drive the Pacific Coast Highway. I was driving one afternoon, giving Heath a break after an already long day of sightseeing. We were talking excitedly about our adventure, the way newlyweds gush about their honeymoon, when I took a turn a little too fast and Heath's coffee mug—which he left unattended on the dash, by the way—tipped over, spilling the dark liquid onto the floor.

"Ah!" Heath yelled. "That coffee mug has been sitting there all day while I drove and it never tipped over once!" His condescending I'm-better-at-driving-the-RV tone did not go unnoticed.

"You leave your coffee on the dash and it's my fault?!" I retorted. My blood boiled beneath my skin.

"Yes it's your fault! You drive like a maniac!" He screamed.

I silently slammed on the brakes, parked the RV on the side of the road, and stormed away from the driver's seat toward our bedroom. I opened the door to our shower, which opens and locks into place to create a makeshift wall blocking off our bedroom from the living area, and threw it open in anger trying to separate myself from my husband.

Instead of locking into place, the door bounced back and closed itself politely, making me even angrier.

So I threw it open again, with more force, and it once again bounced back and closed.

I gave up on the dramatic door slam and opted to throw myself onto the bed crying hysterically instead. What had we gotten ourselves into?

Later that night after we had made up from our fight, Heath continued driving us up the highway while we tried to find a place to park for the night. We had no cell service and every park we passed had giant signs outside saying "campground full." The sun was 15 minutes away from setting and we started discussing sleeping on the side of the windy road.

"I'm just going to pull over and ask this campground if they really are full," Heath said as we drove past another park.

"We've stopped at campgrounds all evening and they all say full! There's no way."

"Look at this place! It's right on the ocean, I can hear the waves, it's beautiful. I just want to ask."

Heath parked the RV on the shoulder and hopped out, crossing the highway and jogging out of view toward the host's campsite. I sat and waited making contingency plans. I wondered if all those no parking overnight signs we'd seen at scenic overlooks meant we might be woken up by the cops in the middle of the night. We didn't really have another option.

What felt like ten minutes later Heath opened his door and hopped back in the RV.

"So…?" I asked.

"So, the park host said these campgrounds book out like six months in advance."

I groaned internally. Of course they do.

"But a guy booked three nights this week and never came. The park ranger was holding the spot in case he showed up, but it's the last night on his reservation and he said we could have it."

In record time, Heath parked and set up the RV while I reheated the fixings for tacos just in time for us to sit outside and catch the sunset over the Pacific Ocean. Our RV sat on the bluff and waves crashed rhythmically on the rocks below. The air was cool and refreshing after a long, frustrating day of travel.

When I think about why we still live full-time in an RV, I think about this day. It wasn't an easy day. We fought *at length* about a spilled cup of coffee (which turned into a fight about doing the dishes, which turned into a fight about the small space, which turned into a fight about respecting each other—if you're married you understand) and drove for over an hour not knowing if we would have a place to safely sleep that night.

But the next morning we woke up to the sound of waves and hiked down a small trail to the rocky coast. Sitting on the rocks getting splashed by the salty mist of the waves made it easy to wonder why we let ourselves get so caught up in the stress of traveling instead of enjoying the moment. If we wanted to keep going, to make it to all fifty states and actually enjoy our honeymoon, we needed to stop thinking about RV life as just a road trip and start thinking about our RV life as a mindset.

No matter where we lived, the fighting was inevitable. In a big house or modest apartment, we would argue about driving and messes and whose turn it was to clean the dishes. We chose to move into a motorhome and chase an epic adventure: to visit all 50 states in our first year of marriage. In order to do that we needed to stop focusing on all the *things* we didn't have and focus more on what traveling in our motorhome could make possible.

It didn't happen all at once, but after that particularly rough, yet exponentially rewarding day, we started to get the hang of our tiny lives in the RV. The more we traveled, the more we learned how to appreciate the small sacrifices we were making for ourselves. This meant no 9-5 job. No meaningless work. Definitely no monotony. We spent *literally* all our time together, but we created memories at national parks and rinky dink RV parks. We spent more time outside and watched less TV—and only partially because we couldn't stream Netflix over the 1990s dial-up speed of RV park wifi. Every day was new and exciting in its own way. We traveled along the coast, across the Rocky Mountains, and into the heart of America.

By the time we made it to the midwest, we were broke, tired, and suffocating in the August heat. We crossed the state line into South Dakota and found ourselves quickly surrounded by bikers. Hundreds, no thousands, of hard core bikers. We had stumbled into Sturgis Motorcyclist Rally, the largest biker rally in the world with attendance soaring over half a million.

We found a decent RV park in what we thought was the middle of nowhere in South Dakota, nearly an hour from Sturgis, and still nearly every campsite was still taken by people attending the event. Despite the constantly rumble of Harleys, Heath and I decided to stay at this campground for a few extra nights because it offered two huge amenities: a swimming pool and excellent Wifi.

We spent our days writing blogs and catching up on everything we'd missed in our first few months on the road. We settled onto the couch one night to stream Gladiator on Netflix. Neither of us had watched the movie in its entirety, so we made popcorn and enjoyed a simple movie night.

Rain came down outside, echoing the intensity of the film. Somewhere in the middle of Russell Crowe conquering everything, the lightning started getting a little too close for comfort. It poured rain outside and the nearest building was a solid 100-yard dash.

Heath pulled out his iPhone and opened his lightning app, which told us real time where lightning was striking in relation to our location. Little red lightning bolts struck a mile to our west and the rain roared on our thin, now leaking roof. We tossed a towel on the floor, paused Gladiator and made a decision. Coming from Texas, we were no stranger to thunderstorms, but thunder boomed every ten seconds with growing force. We could ride out the storm or sprint through heavy rain to the bathroom building on the other side of the park.

We slipped on water shoes and decided to sprint through the puddles to safety. An open field of a hundred metal motorhomes and trailers seemed like a landmine for lightning and staying inside seemed too risky.

After a half an hour of waiting indoors, the dark red of the radar passed over us and the lightning subsided. We ran back to the RV in the pouring rain and found everything slightly different than we left it. Half the lights were off, our microwave blinked 00:00, our leveling jacks and generator wouldn't work, and the towel we left on our floor was soaked.

We were only 12 states into our trip. We had a *long* way to go. We couldn't film a documentary about working in a dozen states. We had to keep going.

So we stayed broke, bought new batteries for the RV, and head north to find respite in a northern fall. Several weeks and three mechanics later, we found out lightning struck close enough to our RV to melt our house battery. Scientifically speaking, I'm not sure how that happens, but I'm glad I wasn't in the RV to find out that night.

We blew up our fridge, shattered our brake pads, froze our holding tanks, battled snow, and backed into a parked car. Heath struggled to find jobs for our project and I had more than one person yell at me that they in fact did *not* want to be on camera.

The more struggles we ran into, the closer we grew to each other.

It's kind of like being married in dog years. We crammed a lifetime of adventure and travel (and stress) into our first year of marriage and decided to stick with it no matter what. When our fuel pump gave out in the desert of Arizona or when we lived without a refrigerator for a month because we couldn't afford to replace it, we didn't have any else to turn to or any place to hide from our problems. Our 29-foot RV forced us together.

Everyone talks about how living tiny teaches you to not value things. We learned that early on in our adventure. We didn't need real plates or a flat screen TV (Which, by the way, halfway through our trip, our parents bought us one. They were astounded that we had made it four months without it.)

What living tiny really taught us was how to be better people. When we first got started, we let things like the GPS and constantly bumping into each other in the RV drive us a little crazy. We would often yell at our computers for loading email at a positively glacial pace and talk about how much we missed owning a dishwasher. We were so focused on comforts, on making our lives easier.

But living tiny isn't popular because it's easy. We all want to move into trendy tiny homes and downsize our lives because we know these life changes force us to grow into the people we want to become.

We became better people when we started doing work that mattered to us. As I dove into film, I found myself less worried about getting from point A to point B and more focused on creating a work of art. As Heath worked different jobs in each state, he learned the value of connecting with others instead of staying in our own small worlds. Working together brought us closer, strengthening our marriage and teaching us how to partners in everything we do.

The more we leaned into our adventure, a new world of opportunities opened for us, ones we didn't expect.

Word of the newlyweds traveling in a 20-year-old RV trying to find work in all fifty states started getting around. By the time we made it to New York City, we were asked to appear on Fox & Friends, then Huffington Post Live, then CNN, and then news crews from England and Australia were reaching out.

The tale of our RV honeymoon went straight to the front page of Yahoo and helped us land a few amazing gigs for our documentary, like being zombies at Six Flags during Fright Fest and stand up paddleboarding with whales when we flew to Hawaii.

After a year living and traveling in our RV, it came time to drive to Alaska for our fiftieth state. Through a friend of a friend, the Chief of Climbing at Denali National Park asked Heath to work his final job at basecamp for (then) Mount McKinley. We choppered up to base camp at 7,200 feet, worked with the park rangers, and stayed the night on the glacier.

We woke up the next morning—hold on, let me rephrase that. We woke up multiple times that morning because I have *never* been that cold in my life considering our mattress was roughly 1,000 feet of pure ice. Plus, the sun really never goes down during an Alaska summer making it impossible to sleep or know the time. Halfway through the night Heath and I both squeezed into the same single person sleeping bag to keep warm, which was nothing like a romantic honeymoon moment and everything like the most uncomfortable night of sleep in our lives.

When we woke up the next morning and opened the tent to find ourselves surrounded by mountain peaks breathing in the fresh air, we had to stop and wonder how on earth we got here. How did we go from being two unhappy kids wanting more out of life to waking up next to each on a glacier next to the tallest mountain on the continent?

People are constantly dreaming about throwing caution to the wind and traveling the world. But we let fear win. We let fear tell us we will waste all our money and look like a fool. Trust me when I say our adventure is filled with moments where we ran out of money and looked like fools. I have hours of documentary footage to prove it.

Looking back on our footage of Denali, I know these opportunities only came our way because we took the leap to live a different life.

This move was risky. Everyone doubted us or warned us against it. No one understood. After returning from Alaska multiple of our close friends admitted they never thought we would actually make it across the entire country without our RV dying or just giving up.

Now, a year after returning from our fiftieth state, we are still pursuing tiny life in an RV. We leveraged our publicity into a sponsorship with

Winnebago and upgraded to a beautiful new rig with more table space for us to sustain our work on the road. We filmed a TV show and were cast as extras in an upcoming feature film. We paid off over $14,000 in student debt in less than a year. Our story went on to People magazine and CBS primetime news, which landed us offers for speaking gigs talking about work in America to multiple Fortune 500 companies. We recently completed our documentary and are eager to release it to the world.

I'm inclined to say this is all happened because Heath was working these jobs during a time when minimum wage was a hot button topic, or maybe it was because we had the support of a company like Snagajob to help us attain press, or maybe it's just because I married an amazing man who never gave up.

The people we were before moving into the RV couldn't accomplish all these things. Moving into a less than 200 sq. ft. home forced us to grow. Every breakdown and freak lightning storm, violently pushed us out of our comfort zone and refined us.

We started on this adventure with a clear, simple goal: visit all fifty states. But long before we hit the last frontier, we knew we wouldn't leave the RV lifestyle for years to come.

Living tiny makes our lives bigger. It hasn't just led to opportunities. It gives us the freedom and courage to pursue them; to dream bigger, to do bigger. That's our tiny philosophy.

What is the Tiny House Philosophy?

...and why it should not matter what size of house you live in

Kent Griswold

Being the very first blogger to write about the modern day tiny house movement with his site Tiny House Blog and later publishing the Tiny House Magazine most everyone would think author Kent Griswold lives in a tiny house. He does not though. However he lives what he considers the Tiny House Philosophy, a topic he explains further in *Turning Tiny*.

For the last nine years I have enjoyed my role in the tiny house movement. My name isn't a household one and most people don't recognize me when we first meet and I am ok with that.

I stumbled upon tiny houses while researching basic small cabins as I had a dream of building one in the mountains one day. I had been bookmarking all these different construction techniques and construction companies that built these cabins when I stumbled across Jay Shafer and Tumbleweed houses.

At this same time I had been learning about blogging and decided to put all this information I had gathered to some use. I started to blog about tiny houses as they captivated and intrigued me. I literally put the words together and almost immediately purchased the domain TinyHouseBlog.com. I began sharing every few days in blog format the different types of structures I had been admiring online.

To see if there was interest in what I was writing and to see if it was worth my efforts I installed Google Analytics.

The cool thing about Google Analytics is that it not only shows you the number of people visiting your website or blog but also gives you some demographics as well.

Early on I learned that more then half of the Tiny House Blog's audience were women and the majority of them were over the age of 50. I recently competed a survey and found out that most of these women are looking for security and a tiny house that they can potentially own outright and possibly park on their children's property and give them the security they desire.

On the other end of the spectrum was the group in their 20s who I found out were looking for alternative and affordable housing. To many of this generation the tiny house is a first time home and a place to start home ownership.

I also decided to install Google Adsense thinking just maybe I could earn a little money to help cover the cost of hosting the blog and associated expenses. In fact it worked and opened up other doors that I will explain later.

After a while I realized there was, in fact, a real interest in Tiny House Blog as I was receiving over a hundred visitors a day. In 2007 that was really something! I decided to start publishing more often and ramped up to five days a week and then all seven. The blog interest continued to grow and people began to contact me wanting to share their personal story. As traffic grew so did my interest in the blog and I gradually began to shift gears in the direction of the blog. It became a place for tiny housers specifically, to share their story as well as a place to learn about different methods of building.

What started as a hobby and something fun to do turned into a full time career for me. At the end of my second year, I left my day job and during the following year I was able to reach what I considered a full time income. In my sixth year I added the Tiny House Magazine and most recently an iOS App called Tiny House Buzz. Both just offer new opportunities to share the plight of tiny housers.

I am often asked if I live in a tiny house or is this just a business for me? Initially I hemmed and hawed making excuses as to why I did not live in a tiny house. There are real reasons of course. My spouse is not in it all the way and we have a son who is still living at home and still quite dependent on us. But even those are not the heart of the issue.

In nine years I have seen thousands of homes ranging from 90 sq.ft. up to 1,000 sq.ft (and even more!). I've come to the conclusion that there is no set square footage to set as a guideline. One person maybe able to live fine in

100 square feet but if you add a partner or children you have to adjust accordingly.

The "Extreme" tiny house of 100 to 200 square feet has become a dream for many but reality can be totally different.

I have come up with my own philosophy. I want to share it now. I want to encourage those that are living in small spaces and those that just seek to turn their current situation into a tiny-inspired one because this is where I am. This is the life I am living now and here is how I live tiny.

- Downsize your stuff to what you need and to simplify your life.
- Live debt free.
- Work in a job you love.

Easy in theory, I know. Perhaps a bit more detail is needed.

Downsizing Your Stuff

To simplify your life you need to know what you have and what you really need to live and be happy. Most of us have things we have purchased and used only a few times. Otherwise they just take up space and make our lives more complicated. We tend to get caught up in having the latest and greatest in technology; clothes, etc. so we continue to add these things to our lives. Unfortunately though we rarely get rid of the old things or the stuff we don't use. We hang onto it all and let it clutter our lives.

So the first thing we need to do is take inventory of what is important and what is not and start clearing out the things we never use and keep only what is important. At the risk of revealing this on a surface level only I'm going to yield to the real professionals. There are some great e-courses on the Internet instructed by experts in the tiny house movement. I would encourage you to take one of those for more in-depth, hand-to-hand guidance.

If you feel you can do it on your own I suggest start separating your possessions into two distinct sections: things to keep and things to get rid of.

The next step of course is to actually get rid of those things by donating to charities, giving to family and friends, selling on eCommerce sites like Ebay and Craigslist, and discard completely.

Living Debt Free

Similar to decluttering your life of things, when it comes to your finances you also need to run inventory. Sit down and document where your money is going and gain control of it. This is especially important if you are in debt.

When my business got up and running the first thing I did was put all extra funds aside to clear off my credit card payments and car payments. It took dedication and even a certain amount of sacrifice. It was certainly worth it though. There is nothing as enjoyable as living completely debt free though!

The best way to go about finding that financial freedom this is to write it down. Write it all down! You can easily figure out your general monthly expenses, housing, utilities, phone, credit card bills, etc. but they are little more than numbers in your head until you commit them to paper. Take a look at them and think about them. Then break the monthly number into a daily number. Try keeping a notebook with you and each time you purchase something write it down. Commit to owning your expenses so you can work toward owning your financial freedom. This may seem difficult at first but it will really open your eyes to where your money goes and that is essential in order to make living debt free a reality.

The next step though is possibly the most important. With your monthly and daily expenses in mind make a commitment to become debt free. Write it down if you have to. Make a pact with yourself. Deliver an oath. Whatever works for you is what you should do or else this step just won't happen.

Becoming debt free is hard work and requires discipline on a number of levels. It also helps if you have your partner or your spouse working with you. Their involvement is not essential but is certainly an advantage. If you are going to gain control over your spending habits and gaining control of your debt it may even help to literally cut up or altogether get rid of your credit cards. So how is this done? In my experience the snowball method is most effective.

The snowball is not an immediate solution. It takes time and even practice. Because you probably didn't get into debt overnight, it is only fair that it takes time to get out. You need to make a commitment to stick it out till it is done. (Notice a theme yet?)

The key to the snowball method is to stop using your credit cards to pay for things. Some people will literally cut their cards up so as not to use them. Others will put them in a bowl and stick the bowl in a freezer so the ice must first melt in order to gain access to the cards.

The best thing to do though is just get rid of them and only hang onto one to use in an emergency. It must be put away though so it is difficult to use. Whatever you choose you want to have to be forced to think about and even act on the impulse to use a credit card and add to your consumer debt.

So without further ado, the snowball method:

1. Gather all credit card bills together and mark down the payoff amount for each. Also write down your minimum monthly payment.
2. Put your cards in order with the one you owe the least amount to on top followed by the one you owe the second most on and continue until you reach the one you owe least on.
3. After writing down where your monthly income goes designate any extra money you have to create a pool of additional funds. This may mean giving up that daily latte or giving up extra others you simply don't need.
4. Add the additional money to the payment of the first debt on your list. Pay that each month (now including your additional funds) until you have that debt paid off.
5. Once you have paid the first card off put that same money you have been using to pay it off and the additional funds toward the next credit card. Pay that one off and work your way down your list until all cards are paid off. It works, as this is exactly how my family and I got out of debt.

Once your debt has disappeared you can put the money you have been using to pay off debt into a savings account. Before you know it you will be able to purchase that tiny house or small home you have been dreaming of!

Doing the Work You Love

The third step in my philosophy is that you must enjoy your work to really appreciate life on the whole and to open up opportunities that living a simpler life can offer you.

As I mentioned before, starting the Tiny House Blog was a hobby that I was fortunate enough to turn into a career. I had always wanted to be a small business owner but everything I had tried before just didn't work out. This endeavor worked though because I truly enjoyed it and it never quite seemed like work.

Blogging allowed me to use my skills and talents (that have always been a part of me come to find out) in a way I hadn't been able to in previous endeavors. I enjoy photography. I have a degree in graphics, and I enjoy the challenges of running a business. Learning how to market the blog, how to address and deal with people, and how to present things in an easy to read manner as well as provide a place on the Internet people would want to visit often has always been an integral part of Tiny House Blog.

The Tiny House Magazine came from something I discovered several years into the blog. If you work on the Internet you have to keep up with the technology and also learn how to market your niche. I subscribe to a lot of Internet Marketing newsletters and that is how I came upon Ed Dale from Australia who created the software called MagCast. The software was

designed to develop magazines for the Apple NewsStand. When I read about it and found out he was looking for beta testers I just knew I had to check it out. It ended up being a fairly large investment but I felt I had an audience who would appreciate it so I stepped up and purchased it. It added a new outlet and a different style of showing people about tiny houses. Also through the Apple iTunes where the NewsStand was hosted it opened the idea up to new readers who had not heard of the tiny house movement.

The notion of publishing a magazine dedicated to the same content the blog excited me because it combined my graphic experience with my publishing background as well as fulfilling a need I sensed in the Tiny House Community. It started out small and continues to be a modest, grassroots publication. But it fills a need and allows for more in-depth coverage of this very unique lifestyle. During these three years of publication I have been fortunate enough to add some great people that have been instrumental in making the magazine even better as it has grown and flourished. The magazine has also expanded into the Android and PDF versions so that more readers could have access.

I can't honestly say the creation of Tiny House Blog and the success of it as well as the growth of my personal satisfaction has been just because I paid off personal debt or I saved money or I threw some stuff away. In fact, there has been another element not yet even mentioned.

As a person who has gone through the process of downsizing, simplifying, and restructuring my life, I can assure you that as you go through the steps I have outlined you will realize that you don't need quite as much as you once thought in order to be happy. Since starting Tiny House Blog my wife has been able to retire from teaching after a 30-year career primarily because we followed the steps outlined above. Because we chose to live tiny (again, without living in a tiny house, per se) we are now able to travel more and spend more time together. My job can go anywhere with me, and it allows me freedom I never thought possible. Of course even this wouldn't truly be possible without the invention of the Internet. It has opened up this opportunity to more than just myself and, in fact, a new term has even been created to describe the live/work balance: Digital Nomad. That is what I am. Because I can access the Internet with my laptop via phone or WiFi, I can literally work anywhere in the world. The world is my office!

Start with figuring out your passion though. Explore how it may work in a traditional work setting and how it may work via telecommute. There are so many opportunities out there for this circumstance and more are popping up each day. If you are a writer, a video creator, a photographer, or any sort of craftsman, you can probably have a lucrative career without renting an office space or being confined to a cubicle. You may find it helpful to do what I did though. Keep your day job. Let the online or other type of business grow feet of its own to stand on. When you see your income is comparable to your day job income, take the leap. Choose passion over obligation. Remember this if nothing else. Find your passion and learn how to turn that into a revenue stream.

I no longer dread when someone asks me if I live in a tiny house. I don't avoid the topic at all in fact. Instead I briefly explain my philosophy and move forward as if it is the most normal thing in the world because the truth is, the square footage of your home does not have to keep you from living the tiny life.

Where Will The Home Fires Burn?

Can tiny house communities truly put an end to homelessness in our society?

Andrew M. Odom

Having built his first tiny house in 2009, blogger and speaker Andrew M. Odom has become a tiny house advocate on a number of levels in order to advance the idea of a more intentional life for all. He still maintains Tiny r(E)volution and looks forward to adding his voice to *Turning Tiny* by exploring the reasons why tiny houses simply are not an answer to social issues like homelessness and transitional housing.

Jeopardy is perhaps my favorite game show. For those who have been living under a rock since 1964 Jeopardy is a classic game show — with a twist. The answers are given first, and the contestants supply the questions. Let's play a quick round, shall we?

I'll take Tiny House Application for $500, Alex.

"An issue as deep in our society and as complex as human emotion and even dysfunction solved, or not, by placing an already questionable and objectionable roof over someone's head."

[buzzer sounds] *"What is homelessness in America?"*

Even framed by a beloved American game show the subject is still a dicey one. If the same dialogue were brought up in polite conversation the knee-jerk response would more than likely be that in order to truly help someone you must first get them warm, dry, and comfortable. But is that enough framework for a conversation as complex is this one? Is there proof anywhere – statistical proof – that providing basic comforts to humans will put them in a more susceptible mindset to receive help? And should the notion that if you begin to provide basic comforts such as warmth and refuge, that they will

not become complacent and slowly lose drive and ambition? A hypothesis
yes, but one worth examining.

In an Oregon Live article from 2013[11] then CEO of Portland's Dignity
Village, Lisa Larson, admitted that after living in the community for more
than three years, "complacency has set in." When she first arrived she had
given herself a self-imposed deadline of six months in her mind to "get a
job, get safe and get out."

But then throw in the idea of tiny houses to fulfill this gifting of warmth
and food and perhaps medical attention. Do tiny houses in our society today
not bear enough weight in the housing struggle? Is there not *enough* conflict
surrounding the legality of tiny houses? Have we as a society not engaged in
other options to fix or at least ease homelessness? Have we not built shelters?
Have we not funded halfway houses? Have we not instituted voucher systems
and other housing incentives? The conversation doesn't get any more comfortable from here. But without the conversation the game quickly turns into
one resembling Chess wherein opposite sides take turns trying to defeat the
other while hiding behind a line of, well, pawns.

I want to first offer a disclaimer or a point of transparency. I have never
been homeless. I have not volunteered in a dedicated homeless shelter or
housing authority. I have traveled the United States as a Christian missionary and I have worked with the homeless population and with housing solutions alike and I have gathered experiences that are planted firmly in compassion, sympathy, encouragement, pride, and disgrace. But never did I think I
would find myself constantly examining the use of a fledging and harassed
market to put an end to a social injustice. It just seems like adding fuel to an
already burning fire.

One cannot argue with the facts. To date though the only "facts" published – that I am aware of – are those of the recent Family Options Study[12],
which examined more than 2,000 homeless families in a dozen communities
over an 18-month period, and was conducted by the U.S. Office of Housing
and Urban Development in partnership with Vanderbilt University and Abt
Associates.

The researchers analyzed permanent housing subsidy (housing vouchers
such as Section 8), community-based rapid re-housing (temporary rental
assistance), project-based transitional housing (temp housing), and tradition-

al care (shelter). The hard facts? The subsidized housing vouchers, stipends given by the federal government to help families pay for housing costs, overall were found to be the most effective method in stabilizing families, providing domicile for otherwise potentially homeless families, reducing school transitions, and improving overall family well-being.

Before continuing though I want to define Section 8 housing program which is the federal government's major program for assisting very low-income families, the elderly, and the disabled, to afford decent, safe, and sanitary housing in the private market. The Section 8 program allows private landlords to rent apartments and homes at fair market rates to qualified low income tenants, with a rental subsidy administered by Home Forward. "Section 8" is a common name for the Housing Choice Voucher Program, funded by the U.S. Department of Housing and Urban Development.[13] Since housing assistance is provided on behalf of the family or individual, participants are able to find their own housing, including single-family homes, townhouses and apartments. The complaint however is that cities are slowly phasing out affordable, section 8 applicable, living situations. Section 8 neighborhoods are being torn down, closed down, and otherwise allowed to implode.

Further to the point, housing choice vouchers are distributed locally by public housing agencies (PHAs who receive federal funds from the U.S. Department of Housing and Urban Development (HUD) to administer the program). The caveat is that eligibility for a housing voucher is determined by the PHA, based on the total annual gross income and family size and is limited to US citizens and specified categories of non-citizens who have eligible immigration status. The process veils a bureaucratic nightmare: too many people and not enough housing.

Considering tiny houses and tiny houses on wheels average just 186 sq.ft. and are largely illegal by zoning proxy, they are not currently acknowledged by the government on any level.[14] In fact, more municipalities than not jam up tiny houses due to both building codes and zoning codes, which are not at all synonymous. What are the differences between building codes and zoning codes then?

Building codes outline the minimum standards for the construction of any house. The main purpose of building codes (which continue to escape the majority of the tiny house culture) is to protect public health, safety and general welfare as they relate to the construction and occupancy of buildings and structures. Zoning, however, refers to *where* a certain structure can be occupied or where you can locate a house (tiny or not). It is based on health, safe, financial, and environmental considerations.

Zoning can require minimums for emergency vehicle access, neighbor easements, sewer or septic connections, minimums for lot size, rainwater runoff control, square footage of houses, and restrictions on how many residences can occupy a lot or given area (agricultural versus residential, for instance).

To summarize, building codes cover *how* a house is built while zoning covers *where* and how many houses can be placed on a property, and how services and utilities must be accessed. Achieving proper zoning and then building according to building codes is a huge point as to how homeless situations in cities can or cannot adequately be dealt with.

Taking the information known about Section 8 housing and the overall voucher system, mixing it with the building and zoning codes put in place by municipalities, there seems to be just one segment of the homeless population – unmarried, unemployed, individuals – left to receive any worthwhile benefit and even that benefit is less than ideal. The benefit I am referring to comes in the form of homeless shelters, halfway houses, group homes, and other transient waystations. And while there are plenty of arguments suggesting these facilities are in a state of disrepair, a state of emergency, or unsafe to

their own residents, the aforementioned factors still do not set up an ideal situation for the adoption of tiny house communities in which to fight the
social issue of homelessness. In fact, the Family Options Study of voucher
program housing is targeted at family units specifically and ignores the
homeless individual. That much is established, be it as flawed as it is. We are
already stacking problem upon problem and muddying the water for valid
solutions. So the question that must be asked, "can tiny houses be a suitable
housing solution for homeless individuals?" To answer the question free of
presumption and almost stripped of personal opinion one must first look at
the demographic make-up of the homeless individual.

The 2013 Annual Homeless Assessment Report (AHAR) to Congress
outlined the following:

> In January 2013, 610,042 people were homeless on a given night.
> Most (65 percent) were living in emergency shelters or transitional
> housing programs and 35 percent were living in unsheltered loca-
> tions and nearly one-quarter (23 percent or 138,149) of all homeless
> people were children, under the age of 18. Ten percent (or 61,541)
> were between the ages of 18 and 24, and 67 percent (or 410,352)
> were 25 years or older.[15]

The numbers are staggering and show a basic need in our nation. There
is no argument there. There is also no one homeless person stereotype. For
each homeless person there is a backstory. They are someone's son or daughter, brother or sister, and possibly mom or dad. And with 23% being under
the age of 18, they are perhaps runaways or victims of situations beyond their
control who are in need of more than just a roof over their head. The homeless individual is the past, the present, and the future of our United States and
just supplying a shelter in the meteorological "storm" is no substitution for
and should not even be considered as a solution to helping each person claim
a shelter in their personal "storm." Turkish playwright and author Mehmet
Murat ildan illustrates this idea perhaps better than anyone. "Abandoned and
forgotten houses often hide the greatest stories!" As a tiny house community
we may wish to forget the suburban sprawl of the 1960s, or the McMansion
movement of the 1990s, all in substitution for the modern tiny house/small

house movement, but do we really want to forget the inhabitants of all those structures? Do we really want to ignore the stories – the laughs, the smiles, the fears – that are perhaps locked behind doors in houses left unopened by federal stipends and marginal housing life-savers?

From an outsider's perspective it seems that is what the outcropping of tiny house communities for the homeless is doing: masking the real issues that may exist with an aggressive housing arrangement. There is more at stake than just a kumbaya drum circle night.

Historically speaking this is not the first time tiny homes have been used to provide housing for those lacking basic shelter, either. Right at the turn of 19th century the railroad became a vessel for homeless men to both sleep during the night and then find odd jobs across the growing countryside during the day. The problem was that a number of towns along the line were concerned with the hobos and homeless men that would walk the towns and go door-to-door begging. These towns quickly set up "tramp houses" which were little more than 250 sq.ft. buildings designed to serve as temporary shelters as well as keep the homeless in one location. To earn their bed the men would be required to chop wood, procure water, or do other odd jobs. Some tramp houses even went so far as to lock in its residents overnight and then unlock the doors in time for the first train out of town.

The houses themselves were sparsely furnished offering primarily warmth, a bed (or something referred to as a bed), a blanket, and food. The message communicated by these tramp houses was more than clear: stay here, be safe, get some rest, but don't get too comfortable. It is a message that many cities with sponsored homeless villages seem to be projecting but at what cost to the existence of tiny houses and the social acceptance of tiny houses?

Don't tiny houses have a hard enough time breaking down social stigmas? Does using them as homeless shelters of any kind not confuse the issue even further?

Since 2012 there has been a marked increase in tiny house villages aimed at market-ready (houses designed for single-family occupancy that can be bought and sold in an open market system) tiny houses. These villages are intentional communities built on private property held either by an individual, cooperative, or development company. They are zoned as planned urban developments and operated more like an RV park or mobile park than a traditional neighborhood comprised of individually owned homes on individually owned lots. They are even designed to accommodate a co-op board and shared, or communal, spaces. The tiny houses are custom built and offer about as much architectural beauty or neighborhood value as they do daily functionality. They are four walls with a roof and little more. During this same time, though, a few tiny house villages and/or communities have emerged as solutions to urban homelessness. They exist right in the main city rather than on the outer edges or other conveniently removed areas. Dignity Village in Portland, OR is one of these communities and it offers shelter to 60 men and women in various structures. In multiple planned villages these structures rarely exceed 150 sq.ft. and rely on a communal facility for recreation, cooking, and even bathroom considerations.

This is all surface chatter though and serves only as placating language. The issues are much deeper.

- Is the homeless population being served or just being given a place to stay?
- Does a tiny house village for homeless adults do anything for standards of living?
- Are these villages allowing a new breed of Americans to emerge that don't particularly care to work, own, or otherwise be part of the world around them?
- What happens if the private funding runs out? Where will the homeless go then?
- Who governs these communities and if there were a substantial problem how taxing would it be on the cities emergency personnel?
- Do these villages cause a decrease in property values and overall neighborhood attractability?

There is no argument that homeless people are people too (despite the cheekiness of such a saying). But much like there is a reason a family would purchase a 3-bedroom, 2- bathroom home in a gated community, there must be a reason a person is homeless. Do these tiny house villages seek to deal with these issues or are they simply trendy (and more affordable) Band-Aids for a contributing factor to urban blight? At the time of writing there simply are not real statistics to point to either way. While there is plenty of press coverage touting the shelter and safety offered to limited amounts of homeless adults in various cities throughout the United States, there are no real statistics saying whether or not residents are able to assimilate into a more desirable part of society or if they instead get lost in the shuffle and end up where they started. Those are studies that must be made and must be analyzed to intelligently continue the construction and adoption of these villages. In the meantime how long will tiny houses stay en vogue enough for these villages to be seen as anything other than encampments? Similarly, is there any sign that cities are moving to legalize tiny houses throughout so that tiny houses can become housing options for otherwise homeless people outside of the village structure?

At best the tiny house villages designed for the homeless are launching platforms for new ways to use affordable and comfortable tiny houses (not to mention mobile) as part of an aggressive, housing-first, end-to-homelessness strategy. At worst they are little more than social experiments that delicately walk the lines of homelessness evaluation, resident involvement, housing equality, housing quality, public financing, and extreme social structuring. Whatever the case, a data-driven, analytical look at the structure cannot truly be conducted unless a litmus test of some sort is established. Otherwise any evaluation of tiny house villages for the homeless is limited to "he said, she said" reporting. This is also affected by one or more of the following:

- Individuals currently in the tiny house communities are those suffering from chronic homelessness. There is no evidence as to how they ended up homeless or if they have foregone an opportunity to live with friends in some capacity, reside with family, or seek a more formal method of shelter be they faith-based or municipally sponsored. In fact, a recent article published by MYNorthwest.com outlines how Seattle police Sgt. Paul Gracy and his charges try daily to connect with the homeless sleeping under a bridge and along train tracks in his jurisdiction in an effort to connect them with helpful services. As the title of the article states though "Seattle police face constant rejection in efforts to help homeless."[16] I am most drawn to one of the last paragraphs in the article. "I'm winging this," he [Gracy] said. "How do I engage these folks? How do I get them to accept help when they don't want it. What's that magic word?"

- There are rules in place at the villages that add even more exclusivity to the cause. There is no tolerance of drugs or alcohol use and/or abuse. Use and/or abuse can result in a 48-hour expulsion up to permanent expulsion with a stop at mandatory AA meetings along the way. (*see page 10 of the OpportUNITY Village Eugene Village Manual*).[17]
- Before a person can become a resident they must undergo a vetting process of some sort. At Dignity Village in Portland, OR, there is a Village Intake Committee whose "role is to screen potential residents to ensure understanding of Village rules, and to get a sense of who potential Villagers are: their stories, needs, and what they can contribute to the community. The VIC will explain what it takes to live at Dignity Village, and answer any questions about life at Dignity Village, community resources, and necessary steps to obtaining residency."[18] In many cases these interview proceedings are not based on any sort of standard other than inconsistent personality assessment. One is left to assume that if a candidate doesn't meet the criteria of the village he is again put out to the situation he is trying to leave. This does nothing to assist in determining if the cause of homelessness is medical, psychiatric, purely housing-related, or otherwise.
- The structured villages already in existence accept only single individuals or couples, who are able-bodied to contribute to the community. There is no recorded mention of inclusion of disabled persons or families, arguably the most vulnerable members of the homeless population.

At this point the argument becomes even more segmented. Are tiny house villages and communities designed for the homeless truly a solution for homelessness or are they quick fixes for only a certain percentage of homeless people that are able to fit neatly into a statistical demographic? Why tiny houses? Is it because they are small or because they seem affordable or because they are easier to monitor and maintain? A review of several community funding pages and donation links reveals that the tiny houses/cottages/bungalows used in the villages cost on average $2700 each to build. With a community housing even just 10 of these units the startup cost is at least $27,000. That figure doesn't begin to cover any of the soft expenses or operational expenses. What happens if/when the private donations run out? What is the safety net for these villages or will the residents be forced to abandon their houses and turn to homelessness again?

And what about turnaround? There doesn't seem to be any press coverage or village statistics that talk about reentry successes (reentry into a non-homeless situation), cost of turnaround on a tiny house from resident to resident, etc. What is the shelf life of the tiny houses? Are they designed for long-term habitation or are they designed for cost and time effectiveness? Would a tiny house have to be "remodeled" or even replaced every few years? An authentic solution would surely have both short term and long-term designations.

Are these villages being used as a way to raise awareness for tiny houses as tried-and-true housing options for all people or are they a way to bring attention to a larger issue: the imminent failure of our shelter and homeless support systems in American cities?

It is true. At this point there seem to be more questions than answers. But until some of these questions are met head on with statistical data rather than passionate argument with a humanist angle the fact remains that tiny house villages designed and constructed as a way to combat homelessness are at best a stop gap for much larger and deeply rooted issues.

Don't Knock It 'Til You've Tried It

Kate Hopson

For the last year and a half, Kate Hopson, her husband Matt, and their three dogs have been spending life on the road in their renovated 36' fifth wheel. Recently, they've decided to plunge deeper into tiny life and even bigger adventures in an 18' motorhome from the 70s. You can find her occasionally blogging at WheeledandFree.com or sharing the ups and (every so often) downs of full-time RV living on Instagram and Facebook. Her chapter will be an extension of those musings pointing out how living tiny changed her perspective on life and how living with less is actually living with so much more!

I can remember my first thoughts on living tiny: I was in my early tween-hood, having a difficult time keeping my room tidy, and longing for a way to *not* spend my free time cleaning. At the time, our cantankerous Siamese cat had his own "room" that was slightly bigger than a closet, with just enough space for a twin bed and some basic essentials. I'd spend hours longingly staring into his room, scheming how I could organize just a few books and toys and keep my clothes neatly tucked away in a small dresser.

I begged my parents to let us switch rooms. *If only I had less stuff, surely keeping my room clean wouldn't be a problem since there wouldn't be any space to make a mess.* Sadly, my parents didn't give in to my crazy whim. But in their defense, what cat needs his own 12'x13' bedroom?

Though I never got the cat's room, it turns out I was destined to live tiny after all. In the fifteen years following my bright idea, I graduated from high school, left my hometown to attend college, started my career, got married and then moved into a *real* house… the typical American Dream stuff you do transitioning from a kid to an adult.

As a young married couple, Matt and I lived a fairly "normal" life. Both being very dedicated to our jobs, we worked long hours, and because of that, spent little time enjoying much else. We woke up tired, seldom found time for breakfast, commuted through Dallas traffic, spent most of our daylight hours behind a desk, came home to a house and dogs that needed attention, made dinner choices based on convenience rather than nutritional value, tried to relax while worrying about the next day, and then finally shuffled to bed with only a few hours left to recharge. Rinse and repeat, five times a week.

Even though we always managed to squeeze in some fun (we weren't complete robots), life as we knew it was beginning to resemble an exhausting American Rat Race. We were awakening to the fact that time was more important than any commodity; more important than fancy job titles or the things we were able to buy with our hard-earned salaries. We had been living to work instead of working to live... Our souls were craving a change.

Out of the blue one day, Matt threw out the crazy idea of living in an RV. I remember being appalled and thinking, "Only retired people live in RVs!" And of course, there was no way I could ever live in such a small space. My head was spinning. We had three dogs to think about — two of them over 60 pounds. Where would they play? Where would we fit all our stuff? What about our garage full of motorcycles?

Forgetting my old desire to live in a cat room, I tossed Matt's wild suggestion aside, knowing we could never make it work; but despite my solid reasoning against it, the seed was planted. I found myself considering the prospect of a whole new way of living.

At the time, we lived in a house that was fairly large for two people. It was no mansion, but had more than enough room for us and the dogs. As I started assessing our daily habits, I realized the only places we actually spent time in were our kitchen, living room and bedroom; merely a fraction of our whole house. Even the dogs took little advantage of the space, spending the majority of their time lying at our feet.

With my recent reflections about the dogs and unexpected awareness of how much wasted space we were paying to rent, heat and cool, something clicked. The concept of living small became more and more intriguing to me, and in my curiosity, I turned to Google, where I found quite a few people our age working while travelling in RVs. To my surprise, we weren't the only ones with the unconventional thought of ditching a house with a foundation for a home on wheels!

Since I was a graphic designer and Matt a web developer, both our jobs had the capability of being done remotely. After the realization that we could still make a living while taking our careers on the road, the whole idea shifted from preposterous to probable.

I suddenly had so many questions! How much does it really cost to live full-time in an RV? What type of RV is best? What size should you buy? Where do you park it? Can you renovate an RV? The list went on and my brain wouldn't rest until it had all of the answers.

It was a planner's dream. After all of my research, I decided a fifth wheel would be perfect for us, although Matt lobbied for a motorhome since he had spent time traveling in a 40-foot bus before we met. I was very opposed to anything drivable since the visibility of the steering wheel didn't seem homey to me. A fifth wheel also offered more space than a travel trailer, which at the time was the most important factor in my mind, especially since I was still a little concerned about how the dogs would transition to tiny life.

Working with a small budget, the most obvious choice was to find something used and in need of a little love. As an added bonus, I was very eager to tackle a remodel since I had spent years reading DIY blogs without ever having a space of my own to renovate.

Just a few short months after warming up to the idea, I was all in. We searched high and low before finding our new home, a 2002 36-foot fifth wheel, which we affectionately named Lucille.

While all my initial concerns had been eased, we still had the problem of a house FULL of stuff. At a glance it wasn't obvious we had so many things, but what lurked in the nooks, crannies and closets was about to be our enemy. After bringing Lucille home, we began the dreaded task of *DOWNSIZING*. Which may as well be a four-letter-word, because in my opinion, it's the worst thing a person has to do when making the shift to tiny life.

Acquiring "stuff" is a vicious cycle – the more stuff you have, the more space you need to keep it. When starting out on your own as an adult, it's acceptable to have only a few mismatched dishes, one pot for making macaroni and cheese, and if you're lucky, your great-aunt's old couch. But over time, things start to accumulate, whether by your own doing: "I totally needed a fourth set of guest sheets because they were on sale!", hand-me-downs: "Why yes I'll take your old clothes, even though I already have more than I can wear," or gifts: "While I appreciate your thoughtfulness, I now feel obligated to keep this knick-knack forever." Fast-forward the clock, and before you know it, you're living in a three-bedroom house filled with things that haven't been used or even seen in years!

Downsizing can be a daunting, emotional task. Thankfully for us, we didn't have many family heirlooms or things that were difficult to part with; but Matt and I still worried about getting rid of something we might need or miss in the future. Once we made the mental switch of only keeping things, which were useful to us or added joy and value to our lives, we gained some momentum, and it was much easier to let things go. At one point, we were giving things away at a yard sale to any takers, just to be one step closer to our goal.

Our collections, can't-do-withouts, and once-prized possessions were now junk we wanted desperately to be rid of. It took us about 2 months from start to finish to pare down to just the items we'd be taking on our tiny journey. Afterwards, while my memory was still fresh, I wrote a blog post where I shared, *"I won't lie, it was hellacious at times; and toward the end, I wanted to just toss a match in and run away. The funny thing is, it now seems like so long ago, such a fleeting moment in time. I learned a lot about the importance of the things around me, our marriage was stretched but grew stronger, and in the end, the realization of how little we had left was freeing."*

The day we had all of our belongings packed into a 5'x8' trailer was one of the best days of my life. Imagine balancing everything you own on your head. The more things you add, the harder it is to find balance, and the more it weighs you down. Now, imagine removing things from the heavy, wobbly stack one-by-one, until you're able to stand firm and strong on your own two feet. That's the effect downsizing had on us.

Living with less has taught me to be selective with the items that I do bring home. I rarely make impulse buys, and when I decide I need something, I research and then often wait out the purchase to make sure it's a perfect fit. It's easier now to say no to hand-me-downs that aren't something we're truly in need of. When it comes to gifts, our friends and family are considerate of our small space. The things they do give us are often consumables or items we've had on a wish list. I've also learned to invest in fewer, but higher-quality pieces. Not only do they tend to last longer, but I've found I'm more appreciative if we've had to save a while to purchase something. We try to follow the "one thing in – one thing out" rule, which is a lifesaver for keeping clutter at bay. Often, we'll go through cubbies and cabinets just to see if there's anything we haven't used lately that could find a better home with someone else.

When you live with less, wastefulness quickly becomes apparent. Although I had always been somewhat mindful of my effect on the Earth, I wouldn't have considered myself a "green" person. I would usually shut off the water while brushing my teeth, or turn off the lights when leaving a room; but eco-consciousness wasn't at the forefront of my mind until I made the switch to tiny living. In a typical house environment, it's common decency to be mindful of your consumption of resources, but in reality it's easy to use more than needed when the only consequence is a blip on your bill.

Tiny life is drastically different, especially when you don't have the luxury of full-hookups. You learn pretty quickly not to be a water waster when every drop used drains to a tank that ultimately gets full and then requires… *dumping.* By the time your tinymoon is over (and you've become intimately acquainted with the dump valves on the RV underbelly), you might nominate yourself for "Conservationist of the Year" or find yourself playing games to see how little water you can *really* use while making dinner or taking a shower.

It wasn't until we started toying with the idea of spending more time off the grid boondocking, that power consumption became just as critical to us as our water usage. Soon we'll be investing in solar panels, so we've given up most of our power-hungry appliances in favor of manual ones (since our batteries won't offer a never-ending supply of juice). Switching from a traditional electric pot to a pour-over coffee maker and trading our quick and easy electric grinder for a manual one will allow us to have more power for other needs throughout the day. We've also started to utilize reusable items when possible: less paper towels and more cloth napkins, less paper plates and a more earnest approach to dishwashing.

Wasting food food has always made me feel extremely guilty given the fact there are so many people who go without. Since living with a small refrigerator, it's much harder for things to get lost and become science experiments; and consequently, less food makes its way to the trash. While the fridge size may seem like a drawback, it's never hindered our ability to prepare a fresh, tasty meal. In fact, we keep a pretty strict list, applying the "one thing in – one thing out" rule when buying groceries, as well. With such limited space, an extra gallon of milk isn't just an "oops" purchase if there's no room to keep it cool.

It's funny how my priorities evolved from the early days of contemplating tiny life to having actually lived it. Just about 6 months into full-time RV life, I broke my ankle severely. For over three months, friends and family graciously took us in while I was unable to walk. It was then, after living out of a suitcase for so long, we decided that even the minimal belongings we had kept after downsizing were beyond what was genuinely needed.

Not only do I require fewer things to be content, my definition of home has also changed: a functional space to make a meal, a comfy chair to sit and work, a restroom with a shower, a relaxing spot to unwind, and a place to lay my head at night. Add in getting to do all of those things with Matt and the dogs by my side, and I can honestly say I've never enjoyed life more.

Once again, my minimalist wheels started turning, leading to some serious discussion about our beloved Lucille. The spaciousness of our large fifth wheel had been limiting at times. Her size affected where we could stay, and because we work during the week, setup and teardown time often restricted our travel to weekends. While we loved Lucille's extra square footage, hooking and unhooking the truck, putting everything in its place, and pulling her slides in and out took quite a bit of time.

Matt and I really never felt we were living tiny in Lucille. (He sometimes claimed she had too much space!) Though we wouldn't trade our experience with her for anything, the more we thought about decreasing our home size, the more intrigued and excited we became.

At first these thoughts seemed just as outlandish as our original idea of living in an RV. We'd only been in Lucille a short while, plus we'd spent two months renovating to make her our own. Why would we give up a sure thing in favor of the unknown? We tossed around the idea of a smaller travel trailer, or a truck camper, but ultimately a little motorhome was tugging at our heartstrings. Go figure since I was so adamantly against motorhomes just two years ago.

Long story short, at the end of 2015, we purchased Mobi, a 1977 Dodge Travel Mate. We cut our living space by over half, down to a mere 18 feet with no slides. Had we not downsized once already, it's doubtful I would ever have been able to mentally prepare myself for living in a house that can fit in a regular parking space! Our most recent transition was a breeze compared to the brutal move from our house to Lucille. This time, all of our belongings (which once required a 5'x8' trailer) fit into just a few boxes.

When we first set out on this journey, it was with the intent to do something different. Living on the road has brought us a freedom we might otherwise never have experienced. This way of life has given us the most important gift of time — time with each other, time with family, and time for ourselves. And most of all it's made us acutely cognizant of the single fact that you need far less than you think.

The typical American is driven by consumerism. We compare what we don't have to what others do have. We work more to buy more. The more we consume, the less we seem to actually use.

Normal is getting dressed in clothes that you buy for work, driving through traffic in a car that you are still paying for, in order to get to a job that you need so you can pay for the clothes, car and the house that you leave empty all day in order to afford to live in it.
—Ellen Goodman

I am so thankful that tiny living has given us the opportunity to say goodbye to "normal." Taking the uncommon path has improved my life in so many positive ways and will affect me for the rest of my life, no matter the size of my house.

While travelling in an RV or living in a tiny house isn't for everyone (and may not always be for us), my hope is that someone who reads this book will be inspired to give it a chance… Even if it's only by evaluating what surrounds you. Because until you've tried it, you will never know how living with less can truly be so much more.

Part 5

Tiny House Community

It doesn't seem as if the phrase "tiny house" can be said any longer without tacking on the suffix "community." But why? Why do we seek this seemingly fleeting notion of community? Perhaps it is because for so long tiny housers have been victim to all sorts of misunderstanding and community offers that tie that binds, so to speak. In community we find a group of people who have the same interests, religion, race, etc. We are a sort of tribe, working collectively to share similar lifestyles. But just what is community? Is it a commune of sorts? Is it a neighborhood? Is it just a grouping of tiny houses wherein folks create a sort of neighborhood of old? No one truly knows yet, and it has begun to take on many many shapes. The following authors have found their own idea of community though, and there is no shortage of like-minded affection and power in them.

A Lifestyle You Can Live and Believe In

Rod Stambaugh

Rod Stambaugh is the founder and owner of Sprout Tiny Homes, an innovative designer and builder of tiny homes and attainable live-work communities. He not only writes about but believes whole-heartedly that people can be more joyful living the lifestyle created through ditching their "stuff" and enjoying a simpler existence. He hopes to share his message with many more, turning their attention to tiny home communities which, amidst other things, could prove to be a game-changer for rural communities that need a boost to get back on the prosperity track.

Who is Rod Stambaugh? I ask myself that question when I come to a crossroads in my life, and I've seen quite a few crossroads. I tell myself, "Rod Stambaugh is a mover and a shaker. Rod Stambaugh is relentless in pursuit of his dream of building a tiny home empire." That is what motivates me to stay the course. I believe in the tiny home movement. I believe people can be more joyful living the lifestyle created through ditching their "stuff" and enjoying a simpler existence. I believe tiny home communities can be a game-changer for rural communities that need a boost to get back on the prosperity track. I believe tiny home communities are a needed resource for mountain towns where workers are unable to live close to work because of the shortage of housing. I believe . . .

I personally live in two tiny homes. One is in Colorado and is a permanent one-bedroom cottage of about 400 square feet and was probably built in the 1950's. The other is a tiny home on wheels parked at an RV park in California. It is an Aspen model built at the Sprout Tiny Homes facility in Colorado and is 170 square feet in size with a comfy loft where I like to relax on my queen size bed. I have been fortunate in finding a beautiful site to park that is agreeable to hosting a tiny home. The tiny home lifestyle I live allows me to spend valuable time on my growing company, and gives me a tranquil place to relax when I need a break. I know tiny home living first-hand and I love it.

That being said, my mission has become to develop communities in towns where the natives are friendly and tiny homes are welcomed. How do I find these towns? No search necessary – after word got out that Sprout had two tiny home communities on the drawing board, the calls for help came in droves. Those government folks are starting to believe that the tiny house movement is more than a passing fad. It may be the answer to floundering economic development, caused by lack of housing. They are still being cautious – waiting to see how this tiny home community thing plays out. Let me tell you how that's going.

The phones at Sprout ring constantly – calls from people who want to jump on the tiny home bandwagon. For some, HGTV has prepped them and excited them to a point that they truly believe they want to go tiny. Others have done a ton of research and know for a fact they are ready to change their lifestyle. Talk of building your own tiny home for $10,000 or less, parking anywhere you want and moving to new ground when the mood strikes you, happily traveling the country with your cat for company and hooking up at an RV park whenever you feel the need to stop for a rest. I do truly believe that this lifestyle fits for some people, and others need a more stable existence, with a long-term place to live – preferably on their own piece of land.

Reality hits when they find that a completed home costs much more than $10,000, RV parks are not always friendly to tiny homes without RV certification, and local government entities declare your home on wheels to be temporary living quarters or a camp trailer, which you are legally allowed to live in for only a short time, if at all. "Can't park that here!" "Move your trailer off the street!" "No, you cannot live in your friend's back yard and hook into the water, sewer and electric services there." This is not always the case. If you have found the perfect place to exist in your tiny home, I am very happy for you! Many are still searching.

How do I see this playing out in the big scheme of things? City and county codes have to change, and tiny homes need to have a means for certification.

The tiny home industry is in a gray area regarding building codes, certification and best building practices. The early tiny homebuilders built and certified to the RVIA (RV Industry Association) specifications, which are essentially RV standards. The RVIA has taken a recent stance of not accepting tiny home companies to even join the RVIA or certify to the RVIA specification. From a tiny home industry perspective, this is actually a good thing. The RVIA specification is a minimum standard for building RV's. It is stated in RVIA documentation, and by most RV manufacturers, that RV's are not designed or intended for year round living. Tiny homebuilders and owners find themselves in conflict with this stance. Tiny homes should be built to a high standard for use as permanent residences. Standards should include considerations to meet minimum roof snow load, wind design speeds and seismic categories for the area the home will be located. The IRC (international Residential Code) has been adopted and modified by most cities and counties to fit the local land use codes. Building tiny homes to the IRC code is a good goal to aim for from a best practices perspective. IRC code and the square footage of tiny homes may create some conflict with respect to certain room sizes and distances for things like electrical panels, etc.

Sprout Tiny Homes has taken an active role in leading an effort to address the gray area of building codes, certification and best building practices for tiny homes. In May 2015, Colorado Governor John Hickenlooper visited Sprout Tiny Homes in La Junta to understand our business and any challenges we had. During the visit, I was able to spend a good amount of

time with him and was able to convey the need for tiny home building standards and a tiny home friendly zoning template for cities and counties to adopt to address the growing demand for tiny homes to be located within city limits. As a result of that conversation, Governor Hickenlooper suggested that the State of Colorado Office of Economic Development might be of assistance. A grant request was submitted, and Sprout was awarded a small grant to partially fund the creation of the Tiny Home Industry Association aka THIA.

The THIA is a 501(c)6 non-profit national association designed to address tiny home building codes, best building practices, land use zoning code recommendations and general education about tiny homes. Targeted THIA members include tiny home builders, product suppliers to the tiny home industry, insurance companies, planning and zoning administrators, financial institutions and other interested parties with common goals to drive standards and education for the tiny home industry. THIA is a work in progress, and as it evolves, I expect it to be a huge catalyst in helping government entities to make their zoning and building codes more tiny house friendly. THIA will provide recommendations on wording for modified codes for the cities on board with the change, and guidelines for tiny home enthusiasts who are working to convince their city that tiny homes should be allowed.

A few cities have already taken the first step, and many are watching to see how it will work out for those first few. Let's talk about Sprout Tiny Home Communities.

A local resident of Walsenburg was the first to approach me. She and others there sensed the growing popularity of tiny homes and thought inviting them in might be a good way to help turn around their struggling community. She took me on a tour that encompassed every nook and cranny of Walsenburg and portions of Huerfano County outside of town. Walsenburg has had some hard times, with large employers having shut down and laying off hundreds. This caused smaller businesses to fail and there are many empty buildings in the downtown area and there is very little housing that is not old and in need of repair. Walsenburg folks are not willing to just accept the current situation. They love their town and want it to be better for everyone –

a better place to live and work. I am impressed with their efforts to pull themselves up by the bootstraps and get to work to make this happen.

Over the course of a few months, the Walsenburg City Council approved a new ordinance abolishing minimum square footage requirements in their zoning code. Additional requirements were that the homes must be put on some kind of foundation, be connected to the grid / city utilities and be subject to standard property taxes. Sprout purchased a piece of land that was formerly the high school football field, which the city approved for rezoning from Agricultural to Residential, and they have since approved a subdivision plan that will place up to 33 tiny homes on the property. We have completed a survey and an engineering study and are ready to break ground this spring. We hope to have the first tiny homes placed beginning in June. We want to help Walsenburg become the Tiny Home Capital of the World! Economic development is on an upswing and Walsenburg is on its way to becoming a happening place – a destination vacation spot – an artist's haven!

Walsenburg gets it – if people have nowhere to live, companies (who create the jobs) will not locate in their community. The tiny home community will provide homes for employees of the new greenhouse operation that plans to open soon. It will provide homes for teachers, for nurses, for artists, for retirees who are excited to downsize and move to a sustainable community that has all the amenities they need. I believe in Walsenburg and their drive to achieve a better life for the residents of their community! Every day we get emails from people who tell us they want to live in a tiny home community and ask when we will be able to start a tiny home community in their favorite Colorado town.

Salida is the next town to move into my radar. Salida is the opposite of Walsenburg – it is a very desirable destination vacation spot, with skiing in the winter, white water rafting in the summer, award winning biking and hiking trails, numerous restaurants and unique shops. It's a happening place. People want to live and work there. There are tons of jobs, but housing rentals are almost non-existent. There is just no place in town for new people to live. A tiny home community in Salida will provide a ton of answers for them. It will provide lifestyle housing for companies, employees and even vacation rental solutions which is the catalyst for reversing the scary trends we are seeing in these communities. How can you possibly keep employees long-term if there is nowhere close for them to live? Monarch Ski Area, white water rafting companies, the hospital, the school district, local restaurants and shops are all clamoring for housing for their employees.

On the other end of the spectrum are those people who are closing in on retirement age and are deciding how they want to live out their life after "work." They want to ditch the stuff that is weighing them down, sell the large 3000 square foot house that takes up so much of their time, and go tiny. They want to stay active and live in a vibrant community with an abundance of activities. They are attracted to Salida because of the shops, the artistry, the culinary amenities, and the plethora of outdoor activities available in the Chaffee County area, but sadly for them, there is no housing to be had in Salida.

Let's do it! Let's help them fix that problem! Sprout has purchased a 19-acre parcel of land along the Arkansas River that will house 200 tiny homes when fully developed. The city has annexed the land and approved the sub-division plan – another city government that gets it. These homes will be a catalyst to help ease the housing issues and will attract folks who come for the chance to belong to a tight-knit community of people who share their attraction to the simple, healthy lifestyle afforded by tiny home living.

The Salida community will have a range of shared green space areas. There will be a community building to host large gatherings, and a community garden so that farm-fresh vegetables are available to those who are interested. There will be parks for families and some may have storage units for the treasures that you just have to keep, but won't fit in your tiny house. This will be a community where neighbors know each other and are always willing to help. That's the kind of folks who are attracted to tiny home living.

Tiny home living isn't for everyone – it is definitely a lifestyle commitment. The folks who choose to live in tiny home communities will be people who will contribute positively to the local community. Living in the community in which you work, rather than having a long commute, gives people extra time each day to get involved with their neighbors, with their schools, with their government, with life! Placing like-minded people together in a community of homes they have fallen in love with can blossom into a way of living that has the potential to affect the environment. Sustainability is high on the list for tiny home enthusiasts.

What next? Many Colorado mountain towns have the same problem Salida has. Workforce housing is very scarce and employees end up driving long distances to work from rental homes and apartments that are available in out-lying areas. Towns and communities considering tiny home communities as a solution to the housing crisis need to know that the kind of people attracted to them are for lifestyle reasons and not just for a cheap place to live. This is not government-sponsored "affordable" housing. Not to be politically incorrect, but these will not be trailer house communities or temporary RV parking for short-timers. These are tiny home communities that will attract the right kind of demographics to positively contribute to the local community.

Rod Stambaugh and Sprout Tiny Homes will press on in the effort to bring tiny home communities to cities that want to take control of their own destiny and provide a better way for their current and future residents. New, tiny home lifestyle communities are the future of housing. Through the Tiny Home Industry Association, a clear path will be drawn for communities that want to change their outdated codes and include tiny homes in their plans. The future is bright, the future is tiny – I will continue to believe.

Building Community, Changing Lives and Challenging Our Desires

One journey at a time...

Christopher and Malissa Tack

Malissa has been working in the 3D field for the last 10 years and has taken her passion for 3D to the tiny house community. She is currently helping others with their tiny house dreams while creating a small community located in the Pacific Northwest. Husband Christopher works as an Editorial Photographer in the greater Seattle area by day, and tiny house community builder by night. Christopher and Malissa are best known for their Tiny Tack House, that the two of them built themselves, back in 2011. They are perfect for talking about building community, changing lives and challenging our desires, one journey at a time.

I wish I could say turning tiny didn't happen overnight, but it did. If I said it didn't happen overnight it would at very least sound more encouraging to others. But each family has their personal story and this is ours.

For Christopher and I, turning tiny happened really fast, almost so fast that it didn't seem real. It felt like one day we were designing our Tiny Tack House and the next we were four years into living the tiny life. In fact, we didn't need much of a push to get us on the path of downsizing and living a more minimal life. Historically, we had been changing our location every two to three years, whether it be a simple change in apartments or change in states, Christopher and I would find ourselves moving down a different path on a regular basis; a path of less *stuff*. It seemed that with every move we would downsize just a little more because we all know how chaotic it can be to pack and unpack. Less stuff simply meant less to pack!

When we decided to turn tiny, intentionally it wasn't anything new to us. Letting go of things just happened a lot more often and in larger quantities. Since our last days of college, we have repeatedly found ourselves on our own. In other words, since college we have lived without roommates, without family and without friends, sharing our space. For the last ten years, it has been Christopher and I. Since turning tiny though we have been exposed to a whole network of individuals that share the same mindset as us and genuinely want to achieve a happier and healthier life for themselves and the others around them. We immersed ourselves into new friendships, business opportunities and a unique feeling of family. Community was building underneath our feet. We just hadn't noticed it yet.

We moved into our tiny house in the winter of 2011. There was no moving to do; no transfer from build site to homestead. We built and lived in the same spot. We were able to find some acreage out in the countryside, just outside of Seattle, WA. We rented a parking spot, if you will, to build our future tiny on. We continued to hang out on the property once the house was finished, just till we could find some space of our own. Christopher and I were not the only ones on that original property. There was a small house and work garage that the landlord's daughter and son-in-law rented. The garage apartment was then later filled with a young woman who was incidentally taking her first steps towards independence.

During our four years onsite we got to know each other pretty well. During the summer months we would find ourselves sharing gardening tips and planning hikes together. In the winter, when the snow was too deep for our car to get out, they would offer us a ride to the store for supplies. We shared tools and even mowed each others' lawn just as a neighborly gesture. Community was starting to form in just those small gestures, favors, and offerings.

Here is a good case-in-point.

Christopher and I did not design our tiny house to include an oven so naturally we didn't have one. We knew so many people that did, we just figured we could have baking parties; something that would bring us together and allow us all to share in the goods. Collectively we opened ourselves up to the possibility that we were one family on this small chunk of land. Now I'm not one who typically asks for help. It's a hard thing to get over. Saying yes to an offer made by someone else – no matter how close they are in relation – has been a challenge for me. Christopher and I have always had each other to rely on and we had grown comfortable in that.

As time went on though I slowly started opening up and accepting new friendships and subsequently, a sense of community.

All good things must come to an end though. In fact, all good things must come to an end so new adventures can be started. When we look back on most of the life changing moments in our lives there is a blatant recurring theme: movement!

Before even thinking about a tiny house I was working in a dead end job and was feeling stuck. I no longer wanted to be there. I was offered a new job and we moved to New York City. When we wanted to get out of the city – because we realized that big city life just wasn't for us – we packed our things and moved across the U.S., planting ourselves in the Pacific Northwest. Of course, that situation did have one big drawback. We rented a very cheap apartment. It didn't take long before we realized that cheap isn't always the best option.

After those events, living tiny struck us at a vulnerable moment in our lives. We were ready to make the move out of apartment rentals and into something more permanent. We just didn't know exactly how that would look long term. We took the leap anyway. Again, a hurdle. Soon after turning tiny Christopher and I both found us without a steady income. Had our bills been what they were in our rental situation we would have been living in chaos. But because we had turned tiny and not looked back, we were only responsible for 1/3 of what we had been, and was able to make it through! Downsizing could not have happened at a better time in our lives. That being said, the community living onsite that we had originally come to appreciate was no longer working out. Our biggest challenge was that we were five separate individuals living separate lives on the same land. No one moved to the property looking for community. Yes, community did build to a degree because of it. At least we thought it was community. Turns out toes were being stepped on and lines where getting crossed far too often. In my experience community can only be achieved if everyone is onboard with it. People seeking community with others will only find it if they look to those that are also seeking community. Communities that just form carte blanche typically don't last.

Christopher and I knew that our time on that land was up. It was time to move on.

Christopher and I wanted to find individuals who were also seeking community. We wanted the fit to be intentional.

We spent the summer looking at land and properties that would allow us to do just what we wanted but on a slightly smaller scale. We knew what worked and what didn't at our other location so we were able to take those lessons and apply them to our new adventure. Community to us means *we are all in it together* and no one falls without the other. Achievements and advances are made together. We all chip in when times are hard and we all bask in the laughter when times are great. We are allowed privacy to live individually but at the same time stand together in unity. It's not always going to be perfect. We know that. Nothing is perfect. The important thing to remember though is that it needs to work or else it isn't worth the energy. Everyone needs to be fully onboard. Living with others that don't want to be part of a group is a ticking time bomb. Just like any relationship it takes work and an open line of communication and trust. The same goes for building community.

After a summer of searching, during the fall of 2015, Christopher and I purchased a traditional, sticks -n- bricks house with some cleared, open space in the back to park our tiny house. We talked about adding a few other tinies in the backyard and calling it a community. Of course those plans were more long term than anything. We first wanted to prepare the land and make it more inviting before actually inviting others to come stay with us. But, as life does, things changed. Our original goal of starting a small community would have ideally not presented itself for another few years. But that timeline moved up very quickly when we decided to take on a roommate in our new house.

We invited Sean Burke to stay with us in the newly named "common house" while he finished construction on his 'in progress' shipping container tiny house. Not long after Sean joined us on the property we received a phone call from a lovely young family who were, at the time, living in Washington DC. They shared with us their interest in moving to the Pacific Northwest. Looking for a place to call home; not our home, mind you, they were looking for some land in the greater Seattle area so they could search for their own piece of Earth to call home. They needed a place to park in the meantime. Originally they talked about just a short stay but have quickly grown into equal members of our home. It seems that community was forming and has formed very naturally yet also very intentionally.

There are now seven of us living on .28 acres in the greater Seattle area and, at times, that number can get as high as 11. So how is it possible for 11 people to get along in regards to communication, trust and collaboration? It is actually pretty effortless. There is a common house on the land. The house is used as a gathering place for everyone. Anyone that wants to use the facilities such as the laundry room, kitchen, bathroom, etc, are free to do so. As I mentioned before, our tiny house doesn't have an oven. The big house does though. So when it comes time for Christopher to make his amazing chocolate chip cookies, the smell fills the house and clearly drifts out to the back slowly drawing everyone inside for a taste. When one family is heading out to the grocery store it is common for them to ask if anyone else needs anything that can be picked up. We are all very considerate of each other. That alone is essential to the development of a community.

Some of the things that we want to achieve as a community would be creating personal space for everyone, building a community garden, creating a play space for the kids, developing a learning and teaching environment, and effectively becoming a model for using space efficiently. Just because we are located on a small plat within city limits, our ability to live free, healthy and eco friendly, is not and should not be impacted. In addition to the other considerations everyone has the opportunity to create their own private space near their tiny house while still having room to gather for conversations and campfire cookouts. Soon a garden of edible foods, fruit trees and greenery will fill the backyard and become a teaching tool. We will host gatherings on the land and talk about community and positive and progressive change.

It sounds easy. It sounds like our path has been relatively simple. And to some degree it has. But everything is still very new to us. We only just purchased the property in the fall of 2015 so there is still a lot to be done. On the bright side though there are more people onsite now which means more hands on deck for getting projects done like running water and electrical out to the tinies in the back, or building a retaining wall and walking path to and from the common house.

A typical day in our little community looks like this. Christopher and I wake up around 5:20 am every morning and do our standard get ready, eat breakfast and get out the door routine. I take him to the bus stop located just a mile down the road. We only have one car so Chris will usually take the bus and commute into Seattle. This way he doesn't have to worry about traffic or trying to find a parking spot in the city. This means I have the car most days, which comes in handy with running errands and submitting permits for the work that needs to be done on the property. Turns out I'm more of the landlord or caretaker for the property now. I'm in charge of maintaining the common house as well as our tiny in the backyard. I love every second of it though! As it stands, we are currently renting our tiny house out for nightly stays while we work on the land and get it prepped for all the things we have planned. That means I also see to my guests' needs and make sure everyone is happy. Career wise I'm a freelance 3D artist and work from home. It is quite convenient even though it can get challenging to separate the home life and the work life. We are figuring things out though.

Sean also has a full time job located in Seattle. At times I'll give both Chris and Sean a lift to the bus stop where they can hop the same bus to take them right into the downtown area. It's been a nice convenience to be located so close to public transportation. Our newest members to the community, the Carlson's, tend to operate family life from the inside of their tiny house on most days only using the common house for things like laundry, kitchen and bathroom uses throughout.

When not working or commuting or playing city manager we can all typically be found hanging out in the yard, soaking up some springtime sun-

shine, and listening to the birds jumping from treetop to treetop. There isn't any shortage of things to do on the property and the littlest ones onsite always seem to know how to get us adults to take a break. Most times they convince us to create tree branch forts complete with a door opening, windows and even a doorbell of sorts. They are always the tiniest of tinies! The kids love to examine the new flowers popping out of the ground, planting a few of their own even if they are only sticks "pretending" to be flowers.

Sean and Chris return from work later in the evenings and if we're up for it we'll gather together in the common house to talk about things we have planned for the weekend, new friends we have made or we'll just chill out and build a blanket fort, for the kids. There is never a dull moment so far.

Sundays have quickly become our get together and make dinner night. We've been rotating from one family to the next. Each week someone else is in charge of preparing dinner for everyone on the property. We've enjoyed Sean's Pad Thai, the Carlson's stir fry dish and Christopher's Sweet Potato and Chickpea Curry. After dinner is done we like to make homemade ice cream or fruit smoothies before we ultimately call it a night.

It's pretty casual here, but like I mentioned, we are just starting our community experience. We understand that Sean will finish his tiny house at any point and will want to move it to the ocean and drink fancy coffee and watch the sunset over the Puget Sound. We know that the Carlson's might find land on one of the many Islands located in the Pacific Northwest and move their house soon after, ultimately leaving an open space in the backyard. The great thing about community though is that it is not just a geographic location. What we have developed is a community that exists in relationships. Come to find out, I've been part of a community for sometime now. We are building another one now; an extension of the first. Everyone that comes into our lives is family and becomes a small part of our larger community of individuals; one that thrives on seeing positive change in our world. I can only hope to help others on their own path and help make community viable for everyone even though we are still very much in the beginning stages of our little community. In fact, as far as more established communities go there is one located in Portland, OR called Simply Home Tiny House Community.

Simply Home has roughly 3 – 4 tiny houses in the backyard of their common house. Everyone lives in a tiny but uses the main space of the common house for gathering, shared community dinners or spare accommodations for traveling friends and family to overnight. Simply Home also has a community garden that all are welcome to enjoy and they plan different events to help spread the word of community. It is inspiring to say the least.

Community is not at all just a group of individuals living on the same land and doing things with each other. It's also about getting involved in the local community, your own neighborhood and the city around you. It's about connecting with people again and not feeling like you are on this planet alone. It reemphasizes a support system seemingly designed to help you travel your path. Everyone needs a place to sleep for the night. No one should have to curl up on the side of the road. With community you can consider yourself taken care of. If one falls, we all fall. In this world we are all connected even if we've lost the ability to see it. We each get up and go to our jobs, make our dinners and plan our futures. We all have feelings and emotions as well as a deep connection with the world around us. Community is about getting back to that and not just living for us. If I achieve, so should you. The glorious thing is that anyone can start building community right now.

Get out in the world and start volunteering! Join a group of people that make it their mission to do well in the world. Even doing one helpful, unselfish thing a day is a start. Community doesn't have to be tiny houses parked in your backyard. It could be as simple as helping your neighbor brings in their groceries. Point is, community is what you make of it.

From Boneyard To Backyard

How communities are created and how they continue

Lee Pera

Lee Pera is a geographer, educator and community organizer who has lived in 27 different houses in six countries! After all that moving, she was ready for a home, but one that was mobile. She co-founded the nation's first tiny house community in Washington DC while building her tiny house. In *Turning Tiny* Lee will talk about starting a tiny house community with no plan: the plusses and the perils!

The air smelled like summer even though it was already early October and we had a larger than usual crowd because of it. As I scampered about setting up for the final tiny house concert of the season a man on other side of the fence called out to me from across the lawn. "What type of roses are these?" I responded with a glance over my shoulder, "You'd have to ask the owner. It's his garden." By this time in our tiny house community endeavor I was over my frustration that we no longer had a community garden as we had promised the neighbors. Even though I had given up on my original vision I still longed it: a community space where the lines between public and private weren't as rigid as our fence portrayed.

We had started Boneyard Studios on an alley lot in Washington DC to try and create the nation's first tiny house community, something many tiny house enthusiasts had been talking about but no one, at that time, had yet attempted to do. When we began we were a community of four houses and many builders, designers and friends, but over the course of two years it had slowly become a display of one person's projects, which included the garden space. Our original goal was to build our tiny houses together on a cooperatively-governed or owned piece of property, and in that process create a community of supporters through our houses, educational space for the tiny house curious, and space for neighbors to enjoy the property. We succeeded in parts and at times over those two years, but not enough for it to last.[19]

I noticed the man was still standing by the fence staring intently at the roses when I walked out of my house with the cardboard box I had repurposed into a donation bin for the musicians with some duct tape and a sharpie pen. I went over to introduce myself and invite him into the concert. I didn't like chatting with folks from that side of the property because we were separated by a fence that ran the length of the alley that served as a little thoroughfare for the neighborhood, and talking over a fence always felt awkward. As I neared, wishing we had a gate on that side of the property, the man asked if he could bring a rose to his mother. As I said "of course" I noticed the tears in his eyes. I told him to wait and I quickly went back to my house for a scissors. We introduced ourselves while I clipped the rose. Luis explained to me that his brother was buried in the cemetery across the alley and that he liked to go visit him there and meditate. He told me how his mom loved roses and how peaceful the garden made him feel. Even though he declined the invite for the concert, I invited Luis to come in anytime to sit and meditate in the garden, assuring him it was a community garden for all to enjoy. His response made me sad, "I could never do that. It's too beautiful." But not as disappointing as what came next, "Plus, no one has ever invited me in before."

I realized then that what we had tried to create existed only on the surface: a lovely, but superficial display of four tiny houses for the media and for those who wanted to believe we had a tiny utopian community. The reality was that so much effort and control went into making the space a perfect and beautiful showcase that many people, including myself, no longer felt invited or at home in the space. There was an eerie hollowness to its beauty, devoid of the lively, albeit chaotic, energy of the urban area that surrounded us. But this – a perfectly manicured space cut off from the reality around it – is not what I had envisioned when we started Boneyard Studios. And Luis' comment made me realize that anything I did to try and make the space feel more communal and lived in, not just visited; from opening up my house for community work days, to hosting free tiny house concerts, to encouraging friends to drop by and use our common workspace; could not replace the fact that we had a showcase of houses worthy of a museum but not a community of homes and people living together.

A community was why I had wanted to live tiny in the first place. When we started envisioning the Boneyard Studios project over Meetups I organized in fall of 2011 we talked of setting up an LLC to own and govern whatever property we could find. But in the end, one person bought and maintained ownership of the property we found which, at the time, seemed like it might be simpler and faster than setting up a cooperative LLC. I feared it would cause problems in the long run for decision-making and sense of ownership over the project, and eventually it did, but for the majority of that first year our collaborative-decision making process worked out fine. With just a few of us we didn't foresee the need for a governance process. Yet neither did we take the time to clarify our expectations and individual goals in advance, and that led to frustration and miscommunication for all parties. As time went on we learned that we had vastly different views around what we wanted the space to be and whom we wanted it to serve. Unfortunately we didn't discover those differences until we were well into building our houses, now with the eyes of the tiny house world and the media on us, and all of us deeply invested in the project's success.

Before I continue any further into my story, let me stop for a moment to apologize. If you started reading this essay to learn how the first tiny house community in the nation was built and is thriving, I am sorry. I would like to tell you that story, but I can't because it didn't happen. I can, however, tell you a story about taking a risk and building tiny houses in an alley in the nation's capital. I can tell you about cultural values and how those played into differing ideas about what a tiny house community should be. I can tell you about how I created a community through my tiny house build even if it wasn't a physical one. And, while I cannot tell you the story of what it was like for the others involved, I can tell you about the challenges I encountered throughout the process. So, if you care to listen to these stories, please stick with me.

Growing up overseas taught me to be comfortable with change and with things being outside of my control. Moving around every few years I often found myself in situations where I had to think and act quickly without access to all of the information I needed, not necessarily having the time to learn the cultural rules before interacting with people in a new country. Subsequently I have become good at winging it in life. While I'm great at starting endeavors, seeing them through to completion and maintaining projects and relationships are not my strong suit as I've never been in a place long enough to have to do the maintenance work. Knowing this about myself, I knew I didn't want to build my tiny house but preferred to purchase one. I wasn't like many of the tiny house DIY'ers that I know. I got excited about the design of my house, but I wasn't as interested in building tiny as I was in living tiny. Had I been able to buy a tiny house fully built back then I would have. But in 2010, when I first discovered tiny houses, there were no fully built models like there are today.

Given all the moving I had done throughout my life, a tiny house on wheels seemed the perfect solution for me. I figured a little structure would finally allow me to find stability through mobility. While it's easy to romanticize tiny houses when all the images online are of beautiful little houses in stunning landscapes, I knew that wouldn't be my reality in DC, nor did I want to live alone in a little house tucked away in some rural area. What excited me

more than building the house itself was exploring creative ways we can use vacant properties for alternative or temporary housing. I wanted to do this in a community, and I was motivated by the prospect of trying to do it in an urban area like DC, far from the West Coast from where I had relocated.

In late 2010 I made a commitment to myself that I would start my tiny house on the East Coast even if I had to move it to the West Coast to live in it (at the time the only folks I knew living in tiny houses were in the Pacific Northwest). So after a hiatus in Colombia for several months, I returned to the United States and in the summer of 2011 I took a tiny house workshop with Jay Shafer and started hosting regular Meetups with people I met through the workshop. Several months later I met Brian, who also wanted to build a tiny house and do it in a tiny house community. What fortune I had! We started brainstorming and planning our tiny house community project along with a few other folks from the Meetup group. Tumbleweed loaned us a tiny house for an event we hosted to show people what tiny houses were. Along came Jay (*another tiny house Jay!*), a young guy who had just finished graduate work and who also was trying to build a tiny house, and at that moment, Boneyard Studios was on.

We took a risk by building our tiny houses on a non-buildable alley lot in the middle of the city, just two miles from the Capitol. Even though it sounds like everything just fell into place, I had been looking at properties and doing research for well over a year on zoning. Zoning is not an easy thing to understand, even for someone like me who studied geography and urban planning. Wading through the zoning information for two jurisdictions meant going to several websites, downloading documents, cross-referencing numbers and codes and descriptions. It was tedious and confusing. I called and emailed city employees to clarify what was and was not allowed on the different types of property we were looking at. Zoning is black and white, but it doesn't address every scenario so that leaves structures like DIY-built tiny houses on wheels in a grey area. What I learned was that our tiny houses on wheels would be considered travel trailers and it was okay to park a travel trailer on a non-buildable lot in DC as long as that travel trailer did not serve as a permanent, full-time, primary residence. Well, that leaves many scenarios open to interpretation. Can you park your tiny house on your property and use it as your daily, full-time office (as Brian did)? Can you have a sleepover once in a while in your tiny house while you maintain the lease on your apartment where you live (as I did)? Can your tiny house be your primary residence if you only live there half of the year because the other half of the year you are traveling (as Jay did)? Can you allow others to stay in your tiny house while you are living in another state (as Elaine generously did)?

We weren't certain what the answers would be, but we moved forward with what we knew: our tiny houses couldn't be our primary, full-time, permanent residences, but they could be places where we spent a lot of our time. With that knowledge we started our builds, and surprisingly we realized that no one came after us for spending time in our tiny houses. In fact, most people were intrigued and wanted to visit. They wanted to visit a lot! We had so much interest that we started monthly open houses to contain the public visits to pre-determined times so that we had space and time to build. For two years we led thousands of visitors through our houses. In addition to our open house visitors we hosted county and city officials who wanted to talk about tiny houses, zoning, and the opportunities and challenges they presented for cities. But the majority of requests for visits came from journalists...many, many journalists. At first it was exciting, but we quickly learned that most journalists, regardless of what they told us when requesting an interview, reported whatever story they wanted, which usually meant a story about how cute and quaint tiny houses were, rather than substantial treatment of the issues that were important to us: affordable and accessible housing and responsible and sustainable urban development.

My motivation for building a tiny house was not to be cute nor was it to escape from reality or to create a house that would isolate me as I saw tiny houses portrayed by the media. I wanted to live in a house that would force me to live more of my daily life out in the world and create a home that felt a little more like the places I had grown up overseas where a big house in the suburbs was not the end goal in life. I missed the fluidity between public and private spaces that I had experienced in Latin America and the Marshall Islands. I wanted to build a space where my friends would feel like my home was theirs as I had learned to do in Mexico where I was usually told "*mi casa es tu casa*" before I could even learn how to pronounce a new friend's name.

Nor was my motivation for building a tiny house to be totally self-sufficient, but rather to create and be able to rely upon a strong social support system. As a Minnesotan who grew up with the values of independence and self-sufficiency, I knew I *could* build a tiny house by myself, but I knew I would prefer the company and support of others that my colleagues and friends in Ecuador taught me to appreciate. They never understood why I would go on a walk by myself to buy a snack when someone else was so willing to accompany me. Often it was hard to get a private moment for self-reflection during my years in Latin America, but I missed how my friends there prioritized relationships and valued reliance on others. In DC I too often saw grey-suited bureaucrats riding out their years alone on the metro or young professionals trying so hard to show all they've accomplished on their own. This desire for independence and self-sufficiency is very strong in the tiny house movement, but I think we take our self-reliance to the extreme in the United States.

The third cultural value I discovered during our tiny house builds was around the concept of time. Americans are obsessed with efficiencies and time. "Slow down," colleagues in Mexico would tell me, "we must first break bread." It could easily take a day or two – just sitting around the table, eating, drinking chocolate, and getting to know one another – before we ever would attempt to talk business or work. While this might be frustrating for Americans who are obsessed with getting things done on time, I appreciated the lessons I learned in places where time isn't such a priority: just because a process is efficient doesn't mean it is the best process, and there is value in meandering. In Latin America, in the Pacific Islands, and in the Pacific Northwest time didn't matter as much as it does on the East Coast, and things happened without adherence to a strict schedule or project plan. In Latin America, especially, I learned not to bother with devising a plan in the first place because even if I had one it usually would be thrown right out the window as the bus broke down or the highways were shut by a weeklong strike.

You might be wondering, "*What does any of this have to do with tiny houses?*" Well, these cultural values around space, self-sufficiency and time caused significant issues in our community. Originally we had planned to build communal systems like communal water and grey water system. Our friend Robin of Build Tiny designed us a water system for the property, but then my-cofounder decided it would be better if we were all self-sufficient and built our own individual water systems. Both have their advantages and disadvantages, but I believe that the strength in community comes from sharing resources and that we are more resilient when we have others we can support and rely on. I hope that other tiny house communities can see the benefit in developing communal systems and counting on each other, both through physical and social systems.

How we chose to spend our time also caused issues. I often chose to prioritize community building over physically building my house, as I wasn't in a huge rush to finish my house since we couldn't live in them full-time. Both Jay and Brian spent more time prioritizing the physical builds of their houses. I spent a lot of time organizing Meetups and tiny house concerts and workshops rather than putting up walls and painting. I often let deadlines slide when my contractors couldn't show up for weeks to complete a task[20] Since I hadn't devised a design for my house, preferring to "design while doing" as I liked to call my haphazard design process, I spent far too long deliberating decisions that I should have made more quickly. Outside of a shelf in seventh-grade shop class I had never built a single thing, so I figured I would wing this since I do that quite well. Except winging it doesn't work as well in construction as I quickly and painfully learned.

My inability to finish tasks efficiently took a toll on my self-esteem. It was the first time in my life that I really struggled with something and felt like a failure. For too long I let others' critiques fill my head: why was it taking me so long? Why didn't I just hire someone to finish it all for me rather than trying to do it myself? What was wrong with me that I couldn't complete my project as quickly as the guys did? (I was the only woman alongside 5 guys regularly building on the property). If I were to do it over again, I now appreciate the importance of project planning and organization and would spend the majority of my time planning my build. Retrospectively when I think about those questions, though, the answer I keep coming back to centers around the values I learned from living in places outside of the U.S. In DC the type-A, professionally driven crowd, who placed such value on accomplishment, often surrounded me. But my goal was never to build the most innovative and beautiful tiny house in the fastest amount of time. My goal never included my house being featured in design publications. My goal was never even to build a house myself, although I ended up doing just that. Rather my goals centered on building a home, opening up my home to others during the process of building it, and finding a more creative and compassionate community in DC than what I had previously known.

At the end of my life, I doubt I will regret that my tiny house took me twice as long to build as I thought it would. And I know that some of my most cherished memories will be of those community events that I organized and the friends I made through them – the volunteers who came out to help me build, even though they sometimes made mistakes that cost me time later to repair, and the musicians who played tiny house shows, even though the time I spent organizing those might have been time better spent working on my house. I still get down on myself for my house having taken me so long to finish. When that happens and the doubt and self-criticism creep in, I like to reread Dan Webb's piece, "How Long it Took" to remind myself that time doesn't matter all that much in the end, and I'm not the only one who doesn't place such importance on it.

"When people first see my work, a good portion of them ask me one simple question: how long did that take? To which there is a simple answer: I have no idea… Clearly, the time spent is a detail I just don't think about. In fact, I would be hard pressed to think of a detail that matters less. On the other hand, I sure can think of one that matters a whole lot more: total awesomeness. But how long does awesome take? Yeah, I don't know either. What I do know is that the total time spent is moot when all that matters is the end product – I'm sure as hell not getting paid by the hour. If we can all agree that awesome takes awhile, (assuming that it's achieved at all) then a better question might be, why strive for such a lofty goal in the first place?"[21]

So, why should we strive for such a lofty goal as awesome? For me it's because I want to live in a society where people are striving for goals that push the boundaries. When we started the Boneyard Studios project some people called us naïve. They thought we were too idealistic to believe we could form a tiny house community, and when we failed to maintain the physical community they used that as their opportunity to justify why tiny house communities cannot succeed. But tiny house communities are not naïve or unrealistic at all. The challenges we had with Boneyard Studios had very little to do with city policy or zoning. The challenges we had were the cultural values we held and how those influenced our ideas of what a tiny house community would look and act like. Since we started Boneyard Studios back in 2012 there have been tiny house communities popping up across the country. They are succeeding, and showing us that it can be done. We didn't start our tiny house community with a long-term plan, and none of us expected to be living together in the same physical spot forever. Had we planned everything out beforehand and spent years working with the city on zoning, we never would have started and learned the lessons we did to share with others. So, no, it's not naïve to dream and build outside of the status quo. It is naive, however, to think our current model of housing will sustain us in a rapidly changing and increasingly urban society. It is naïve to think we can continue to design and build cities with no thought put into smaller, sustainable, and right-sized housing.

According to Seth Godin, "if you aren't risking, you aren't making." We made a tiny house community. We all took a risk. We all had a role in the formation of the community, and we all had a role in its demise on that original piece of property. All of our individual motivations for building tiny brought us together to form Boneyard Studios in a time when tiny houses weren't yet very popular; however, in the end our values were too different to continue together. One by one my co-founder asked the three of us to leave with our houses so that he could have the property for his business and personal projects. Yet all four of us who had houses there have continued to stay involved in the tiny house world, and none of us let the challenges we encountered deter us from living tiny. Boneyard Studios still exists as a community endeavor in Washington, DC. We host events around tiny houses in partnership with local organizations, and Jay's Matchbox house resides at a local business, which serves as our event space. The former property where we originally started still houses Brian's Minim Home and the Minim Home Company. Elaine's house still resides in a tiny house community in Orlando, Florida.

My house is tucked away in a backyard, but I am far from isolated, as I feared I would be. After a long couple of years I did build a home that is more reflective of the places I grew up, where time isn't managed so tightly and where my relationships matter more than crossing a task off my to-do list. While I built my house so I could move from a city that never felt like home, in the process of opening up my house during the build process I have met a community of creative people in DC who are fiercely passionate about making this city a more affordable and accessible place for all. Surprisingly this is now the longest place I've resided in my entire life, and sometimes I even call it home.

Creating the Agrarian Community

What drew us together was the desire to simplify our lives

Lovare Homestead Collective

Lovare Homestead is a multi-family teaching farm based in Ohio where six families live community style and completely off grid in 6 homes ranging from 150-500 square feet. In *Turning Tiny* those six family stories will unfold to show how communities can form, unite, and build homes that operate complete off-grid, and cultivate organic garden practices as well.

Every community is built out of individuals sharing a goal. At this homestead, we have gathered together to teach each other the things we love and to learn with others what we don't yet understand.

Lovare Homestead is located in the small town of De Graff – just an hour drive from both Columbus and Dayton – in America's Heartland. All 10 of us (5 families total) have come together from different parts of the Midwest to live completely off-grid. We are a collection of oddballs from a variety of backgrounds. What drew us together though was the desire to simplify our lives. There are six tiny houses at Lovare, all of which have differing approaches to Tiny. The differing approaches are important to us. Too often you see those who choose to go tiny labeled as "insane minimalists" or "crazy mountain men." Now, don't get me wrong, we have a few of those and love our insane minimalists and mountain men, but there is more to it than that. Turning Tiny does not mean you have to follow a certain set of rules or live in a space the size of a cardboard box. I think of tiny living as a projection of a state of mind.

Allow me to introduce myself first. I'm Beverly and part of the 4th family to join Lovare Homestead. Tiny living within a community is a lot like what I imagine it was like to live in a suburb in the 1940s or 50s. You can go to your neighbor's house to borrow a cup of sugar, your kids can play at the neighbor's house till dusk without needing to arm them with a cell phone and you can come together with your neighbors to plant a victory garden.

The beautiful part of life at Lovare is that the beauties of the past can be mixed in with the joys of the present day. We have made a lot of advances and have access to information we could have never obtained in the past. I love the ability to create vast online networks of like-minded people to chat and learn about the things that interest us. One of the worse side effects of the online community is that we tend to isolate ourselves from our real-life local community. The residents of Lovare have made it a priority to not only continue chatting and learning, but to share a real life desire to live together. In light of our varied interests and beliefs, one thing we all agree on is the desire to become a presence within our larger community. We will become a space where people from all walks of life can come and learn about such things as tiny and sustainable living. To become this beacon in our community it's also important to open our hearts to new knowledge and be open to learn from the wiser among us.. We have the benefit of being in a beautiful rural area with a lot of farmers who have been working the land since birth. That kind of knowledge and skill cannot be captured in a blog post or a YouTube video.

Everybody that lives at Lovare has had unique experiences that led them to tiny and community living. My own family's journey to Lovare appeared to have happened by accident (at the time), but seems like it was inevitable all along.

My husband, Jason, first mentioned his interest in tiny houses to me when we were dating. I thought he was nuts but decided to marry him anyway. While I found other non-traditional living choices interesting such as intentional communities or even living "off-grid," the notion of living tiny always seemed absurd to me. It became something we would joke about, or something we would bring up when we were feeling frustrated by our hectic lives. Prompted by a stack of bills, a pile of dishes or accidently stepping on one of our son's Legos, one of us would say something along the lines of: "Screw it, let's burn it down and build one of those tiny houses."

Something funny occasionally happens when you repeatedly talk about a topic you view as "out there." It begins to normalize in your mind.

Incrementally you chip away at the strangeness of an idea and begin to see its merits. Thus we found ourselves moving from joking about tiny living, to fantasizing about tiny living, to finally planning our tiny escape.

For those who do want to go tiny, the first roadblock that most of us run into is trying to find land that does not have a minimum square footage requirement. Jason and I were not having much luck in our immediate area so we expanded our search. We happened upon an International Communities posting for a just-forming tiny house community. When Jason first showed it to me I remember thinking: "This can't be real. I thought stuff like this only existed in Portland." We reached out immediately and went to meet Rose and Vincent the following weekend.

Neither tiny nor community living should be jumped into without a lot of soul searching. We already had made the decision to go tiny but it took us a little bit longer to decide if community living would be right for us. Jason and I had talked about it in the past but it still seemed like quite a gamble. However we ultimately decided to take a chance.

Lovare Homestead – our aforementioned "gamble" – was the brainchild of Rose and Vincent. Without their perseverance so many of us would be adrift. Vincent tells his own story about choosing to go tiny:

> Typically tiny house owners are forced to live in trailer parks, back-yards, or on undeveloped acreage far from society whether they want to or not. This doesn't create a sense of community or belonging for them. Too often those of us who live tiny are either seen as a novelty or are isolated from the community by physical distance. We have created Lovare Homestead to rail against those norms. We wanted to create a space for those who wanted to live out their dreams of going tiny.
>
> No one who has joined Lovare has arrived with a completely pre-built tiny house. This causes me to believe that had we not created this community, some of our folks may never have been able to fulfill their dream of going tiny. We want to share with others that may be interested that sustainable and legal tiny house communities are possible.

So what drove me to go tiny? I wanted to simplify my life. When I was 18 I moved into a 2500 sq. ft. house by myself. Not having much while I was growing up, I quickly began accumulating a number of material things to fill in the spaces. While I thought these things would make me happy, they seemed to cause me more stress. Soon after, I decided to downsize. I moved to a smaller house and gave away a lot of what I had amassed. It was if a weight were lifted from my shoulders. Over the next few years I became interested in the tiny house movement and decided to downsize again. Now, other than my tools and my books, all of my other belongings can fit easily in the backseat of my car. That's the beauty of tiny living to me, you get to keep the things that are important to you and your life and leave behind everything else.

Going tiny at Lovare has given me so much. Without a mortgage or utility payments I have gained financial freedom. I am better able to pursue my other passions and it has been remarkably good for my spirits. As I write this I am sitting by the woodstove that is not only keeping me warm during January in Ohio, but is also cooking my dinner. I can look out my window and see the solar panels I installed collecting the last of the day's sun. I honestly do not know what could be more satisfying.

That is something I think all of Lovare can agree on; the satisfaction of living in a life we built for ourselves and sharing it with our local community. Another perspective comes from Cathy, the first person to settle in after Lovare's founding.

When I was a little girl my neighbor Barbie had a playhouse. It had a mailbox and a locked front door. I could only play in it when she wanted to and that, to my displeasure, was not very often. I loved that playhouse. I dreamt of that playhouse. I longed to spend time in that playhouse alone. All through my life, whenever I was in a small space and had time for private thoughts I would ask myself, "Could I live in just this much space?" My answer was always, "Yes!"

As I grew older, I fantasized about getting a piece of land with woods and a stream and building a small cabin in which to live. Fast forward through my doctoral studies, my role as a mother, and a professorship, to a time when tiny houses finally came into vogue. I was thrilled! Not only would I not seem so crazy but resources, networking and ideas were becoming more and more available! I spent hours on Pinterest, Google, Facebook, the Tumbleweed website, and watching tiny house shows, knowing, beyond a doubt, that this is what I was going to do. Eventually, I came upon an Ohio based Meetup and decided to attend a meeting even though it was over two hours away. Rose and her son Nico were there and though I did not get a chance to meet them personally that night. When I saw her Facebook page for Lovare pop up on the Meetup site I quickly contacted her and arranged to meet and chat at the building site of her tiny house.

Between the motivated and welcoming personalities of Rose and Vincent, the possibility of joining their community on land that included a wooded area, and the fact that they had already planned for, and begun, the infrastructure of Lovare, I got very excited. I hoped that I would be chosen to move full-time to the community as they only had room for a certain number of the surging applicants. Being considerably older than they were I wasn't sure I would be seen as a desirable member. Nonetheless they quickly let me know that I was in and this made me very happy!

I decided I did not want my tiny house to be on wheels and that I did not want to start from scratch. I worked with Beachy Barns in Plain City, Ohio to design a 12x18 lofted shed with beautiful dormer windows. I knew I wanted to stay small so I kept a personal goal of staying under 240 sq. ft. so as to not go crazy with designs. In the future, I plan on adding a large 10x10 screened in porch so that I can spend time relaxing outside without the company of mosquitos.

As excited as I am about my tiny house I am even more excited about the Lovare community. Seeing the vision coming to life is inspiring. I look forward to growing food, raising chickens, hosting potlucks, sitting by campfires and sharing dinners in our future community building, canning our crops, enjoying lots of laughter, watching children run about, admiring star filled skies, joining in sing-alongs, helping each other out, and ultimately, sharing lots of love. I am thrilled that we are advocating what we are doing in hopes of inspiring others. To live in a community is so much cheaper than trying to do it all by yourself. It is so much more neighborly, so ecologically efficient, and just a whole lot of fun.

Our newest neighbor is building his THOW (tiny house on wheels) off-site and bringing it to it's more permanent home at Lovare Homestead once complete. Steve arrived at his choice to go tiny at Lovare through another unique happenstance.

My story started about three years ago, just after a divorce. As is the case with most Americans accumulation of assets and other things had become a large a part of my adult life. As the divorce helped me to "pare down" my possessions, I had a strong desire to take it much further. I wanted to get rid of everything but the bare essentials and create a very simple life for myself. My first tiny house was a 30 foot long Morgan Sailboat down in Florida. With less than 200 sq. ft. of interior living space it would definitely be considered tiny living. I enjoyed my time living on the water, but more than that I enjoyed the community of the marina. Within the group there was a vast array of personalities, social and economic situations. There was a sense of community that drew us all together. If you walked up to anyone who had two drinks, one of them would be offered to you. If you were obviously struggling with a boat repair, help would be offered. We were a community of misfits that cared deeply about each other.

Although I found marina life extremely comfortable the need to move back to the Midwest became a priority, as it was impossible to spend enough time with my daughters while living on the water states away. I had been following the tiny house movement online long before the first cable television show aired. With a background in design and construction, the quality and potential uniqueness of each tiny house was very appealing to me.

It was during one of my many tiny house Google sessions that I first ran across Lovare. Upon understanding their plan I immediately knew this was something I wanted. Not only could I duplicate the simple tiny living that I had on the boat but the community aspect could be taken to a whole new level here at the homestead. I had the opportunity to hear Rose speak at the Tiny House Jamboree in Dayton, OH, in 2015. After listening to her session my desire to be involved was only reinforced. I quickly planned a trip to the property to meet with Rose and Vincent and have a look around. On my first day trip here we all sat outside and discussed our lives and our goals for living within the community. I was later accepted as a part of the group that would begin this adventure and I couldn't have been more excited about it.

The immediate need then of course became to build a tiny house. I discussed the project with Eric, a close friend and former partner in a design/build company. He had the space, the tools, and more hands-on construction knowledge than I do and he invited me to come live with him as I built my new home. As I sit here at his kitchen table writing, I am only a few weeks shy of completion. In the past months, I have experienced endless highs and lows as the challenges of building my first tiny house have been revealed and resolved. While design and construction are a passion of mine, I am even more excited to begin the process of becoming a part of the Lovare community; a group of six households who come from very different backgrounds and varied beliefs systems but with enough in common that we have decided to form a community in which we will live, teach, learn, and support each other as we "do life" the best way we know how.

As some of our group has shared our stories here, we have all come to tiny living through different means. Tiny home teaching communities are such a joy and pleasure to all of us here, not only residing at the homestead, but also our greater community in Ohio. They have the ability to enrich people on so many levels. Granted we are still in the infancy of Lovare Homestead. As we grow though we acknowledge and look forward to the work ahead of us, welcoming all that would like to join us on this journey into an agrarian tiny house community.

A Return To Simplicity

The art of slowing down and remembering to live

Elizabeth Singleton

Build us H.O.P.E. is the outreach and development arm for Single Community Services which was founded by author and community visionary Elizabeth Singleton. She along with others works tirelessly around the Phoenix, AZ area to advocate on behalf of the homeless, disabled and mentally ill. H.O.P.E.'s mission is to build an affordable, sustainable tiny house and container model community.

Where the Dream and the Plan Started

As a child I had always dreamed of a community where children who didn't have a place to call home could live. In my mind it was a neighborhood with farming, animals and people who would love them, and all living together in harmony. I spent most of my childhood living on a farm in rural Arizona, so I understood the value and security of a close family. I remember the satisfaction and pride from growing your own foods and sharing with your neighbors. I would often draw pictures of my ideal village. It included homes, activity centers, farming areas, animals, and people, all living together happily. Even now, as I live my life in Phoenix, Arizona I realize those dreams have never left my mind and more and more I find myself returning to them, actually longing for such surroundings to this day.

As a society we have moved away from simple living. We see so many television shows about lifestyles that are based upon accomplishments. We are taught to want more or to adopt a "bigger is better" approach. We are no longer reveling in moments spent sitting on the porch at the front of the house Instead we are pulling into the garage and taking the interior door that leads us directly into our homes. There is no time to see who may be in the neighborhood just outside our aluminum shields. We are removing the opportunities to get to know those around us. So I ask. Are we any happier in our big homes? Do we still have a sense of "belonging" and the security of knowing who lives next door to us? If you didn't see your neighbor for a few days, would you feel the need to stop by just to say hello and check in?

As I got older I had experiences in my life that reinforced my belief in how important being in a shared environment is to our well-being. There was a period of time I was homeless, and yet I was tirelessly supported by others that believed in me, and what I longed to do. It was a time after my divorce, when I was trying to hold onto my house and the mounting debt that I ended up homeless. We slept on friends' couches, in our van and in the back of my office. It took a village to help me get back on my feet. These experiences provided a path for me to move forward and create a life for myself, my family, and others, all based on the idea of being a member of a society that supports and enriches the lives of the people.

In 2005 I began working as a care facility consultant, and I was involved in opening and licensing a variety of care facilities and housing. The need for facilities was primarily driven by the growing number of requests by individuals that were better served with residential treatment and services. I was working with placement agents and I was being asked to provide an alternative for those who could not afford, or did not need the standard residential treatment settings; they needed housing with some supportive services built in. Their income levels created a challenge identifying housing options for them based just on their ability to pay. Many of these individuals ended up living on the street or in unsafe living conditions just to have a roof over their head. My consulting firm started a program to create shared housing. We did this by renting homes and developing shared living spaces. By doing this we were able to rent at a lower, more affordable price. We hired staff to provide support as needed. The request for this setting was overwhelming. We continued to grow and moved to a model of contracting large apartment complexes to provide supportive housing.

When my consulting company developed an affordable housing complex we encouraged the residents to spend time together. Being in the group and also observing the interactions, I saw the positive impact being made on these individuals. They truly became more than just residents, they were each an integral part of the overall, supportive program being created. Once they knew there was someone who cared about their well-being and supported them they became more confident. The residents started the process to reach out and connect with others. This was something that had long been forgotten by many. Their lives had been dominated by just trying to survive.

It became more apparent as I continued to work with, and advocate for, these individuals, that just providing housing was only part of the solution, and there was still something missing. We realized that even though the resident was housed, for many it was hard to make ends meet. They had difficulties paying for their basic needs like food, medication, clothing, and insurance fees. How was this truly affordable?

Housing is the foundation of individual well-being and I firmly believe that housing should be part of the national healthcare discussion. Yet, affordability and lifestyle is just as important. My advocacy opened my eyes to see that we needed more than to just attend meetings and provide statistics on people on the streets. We needed to develop more housing options.

Affordable Housing in the United States
(Let's talk about the problem)

To be called the richest and most developed nation in the Western World, we are sorely lacking in our ability to provide affordable housing for all. Since 2000, rents have risen roughly twice as fast as wages.[22] Furthermore, the number of renters who need low-priced housing has increased.[23]

A 2015 report titled, *Out of Reach* published by the National Low Income Housing Coalition estimates that minimum wage workers in Arizona would have to work 67 hours a week just to afford a one-bedroom apartment at fair market value. The gap in affordable housing units is increasing nationwide faster than the units are becoming available. Currently, conservative estimates indicate the need for 142,000 new affordable housing units in Arizona alone.[24] These trends are not unique to Arizona though.

During the January 2014 *Point In Time* survey (conducted by HUD) of homeless (in shelters, on the streets and those living in unsafe environments) counted 578,424 individuals. Approximately 47% are families and 63% are individuals or couples.[25] This is part of a revolving door of homelessness, or near homelessness, brought on by circumstances such as loss of a job, major medical issues, divorce, and/or domestic violence. Something like a broken down vehicle can cause a person to end up on the street with no identifiable way to get to a job. In fact, one of the biggest challenges for many of the homeless in our society is a path back to what was once a normal life. A lack of affordable housing is one of the significant factors that perpetuate homelessness. I remain driven by the notion that we have to address the need for affordable housing communities and options as a key component to the solution.

The need for more affordable suitable housing options and the lack thereof is what gave birth to Singleton Community Services (SCS), a 501(c)3 grassroots not for profit organization. SCS provides resources, services and housing solutions by offering two distinct housing and service related projects known as Build us H.O.P.E (Housing Opportunities Provided for Everyone) and the Housing Engine.

Why the Tiny House (Finding the Solutions)

I have always been one to think outside the box. I cannot take credit for my personal discovery of the tiny house movement. My daughter Angelica is the one to thank for this. She loves the *Tiny House Big Living* and other remodeling shows. After spending a day feeding the homeless she asked "Mom, why don't we build some tiny homes for the homeless?" I really didn't know much about tiny homes, so I started to research about them. As I read more about the tiny house movement there seemed to be a consistent message throughout each site, each article, and even each new television program. The message centered on slowing down and living a simpler lifestyle. For many it wasn't about completely disconnecting. It was about making choices to live in a way that did not require the "bigger is better" mindset. Instead of watching television shows with the "bigger is better" theme, the movement encouraged people to make conscious choices on keeping the things that mattered to them on a more personal level. The need for the house to drive up to and stay in has been replaced by a sense of getting out into the world and exploring it again. I immediately felt connected to the movement.

Historically speaking, living in a smaller footprint home is nothing new. Since the 1950's the size of American homes has increased dramatically. In 1960, the average home was just at 1,540 sq. ft.[26] and there were 3.3 members in the household.[27] By 2015 the average home had risen to right at 2,600 sq. ft., with 2.5 family members.[28] The average price of a home in 1960 was $12,700. Now $365,000 looks reasonable. It is becoming increasingly more difficult to find and maintain a home, and still have money left to get out and live!

Why are people interested in a tiny home? What are the personal benefits that you gain from making this change? A recent article by Tumbleweed Tiny Homes[29] stated:

> The feedback I receive from the people I speak with daily is that they are no longer interested in exchanging their time working for a large house and filling it up with costly things. Another basic and fundamental economic term is scarcity, and the most precious and limited resource we all have is time. The growing number of converts buying into the tiny house philosophy are regular folks willing to look at their housing choices with a clear and open mind.

According to this article, these are people who are in the mid-30's to their mid-50's and over half of them have college and graduate degrees. Why is this important to look at? I feel it's significant because this population is not looking to escape from living with others, they are looking at creating a lifestyle that is not controlled so much by overall cost of housing. The overall cost to consider needs to include housing (rent or mortgage and interest), utilities, insurance, and property taxes, plus regular maintenance. These "other" costs can, in many cases, add up to more than the rent or the mortgage. The term "house poor" becomes even more significant when you add in those other factors. Many wonder how households earning under $40,000 a year can even afford a home.

So, how do you have the quality of life you want and share a community with others? That's where the Tiny Home Communities have become a positive and supportive alternative. The idea behind these villages is straightforward. Bring together a community of tiny houses and join together in one place to create planned sites that share land, time together, skills, support, and other resources. It can't be emphasized enough that when you are in such an environment, you are able to rely on yourself and others to provide the things needed to have a sustainable and more holistic kind of lifestyle. You connect with the people who live close by. It can start with a wave from your car to another on their way to work. It may continue to sitting on a porch and engaging in a conversation with the others around you. These interactions can lead to relationships that so many of us grew up with. Checking in on your neighbor and seeing how they are doing becomes a very natural part of your life and the way you interact with them. You are able to remove the barriers that create a sense of isolation and loneliness that has become all too representative of our fast-paced, busy lifestyle.

Our Journey to Become Tiny

I think the Build us H.O.P.E. staff and volunteers have watched every tiny home TED talk, YouTube video, and television show out there! We have purchased several books and floor plans on tiny home design. This has been an education, trying to learn all we could about the Tiny Home lifestyle, cost to build, what works and what doesn't work.

I felt we needed to see what "tiny homes living" means to those living the tiny home lifestyle. Over the past two years our team of architects, staff and other housing advocates have traveled to other states and talked with other "tiny home" developments. We wanted to see and hear what was working for them, and what they planned to incorporate as they moved forward. The communities we studied ranged from "tiny home hotels" (booked weeks and weeks in advance) to full communities with shared services. Some of them are designed to offer the resident the ability to become a co-op owner. There were many types recommended for affordable housing. Some I liked and some I didn't agree with. There was also a great deal of advice provided on best practices and also on what not to do.

We spoke with tiny home builders who found their largest customer base included single adults who wanted to have all of the comforts of a permanent home, in a size they could afford and maintain. The homes are designed to maximize the space within the tiny home and to also lead to a more community-oriented lifestyle complete with porches, stoops, and shared services available for all members.

As we were deciding which locations and programs were going to be ones to visit, the one that seemed to be shared on my personal Facebook wall and on the Build us HOPE page the most was for "Community First! Village," in Austin, Texas. This community appeared to be by far the closest in line with our vision. The community was developed by Mobile Loaves and Fishes (MLF) and is a 27-acre master-planned community, providing affordable, sustainable housing and supportive services for the disabled, chronically homeless in Central Texas. I spoke with Alan Graham, the founder of MLF and he set aside the time to provide an extensive tour and background on this community. His willingness to share his experiences was exciting for all of us planning the trip. As we were driving across Texas on our way there, I felt the need to ask multiple times, "are we there yet?" I just couldn't wait to finally meet Alan and see "Community First!" for myself. I was not disappointed at all and Alan continues to be a significant resource and mentor for our program as we move forward.

The major difference between the "Community First! Village" and our designs is the energy sustainability factor. The site is being designed by our architect and a team of sustainability students to maximize renewable components.

What We Learned – Build us H.O.P.E. Tiny Home Community (Our Solution)

Build us H.O.P.E has purchased around 98 acres of land across Arizona with the intent to develop master planned tiny homes pocket communities. This H.O.P.E. model can be utilized to create sustainable communities that will help address the need for affordable housing. The goal is to create affordable communities for populations with income restraints, with the hope of ending the cycle of homelessness.

This is where Build us H.O.P.E. feels the tiny home community will be the model that can be replicated. The sites are being planned by Build us H.O.P.E staff, architectural teams, city government, and tiny home developers for locations that include urban in-fills and rural areas. As we meet with the zoning and planning departments involved, we are finding there is interest and an open mind from the local government agencies. They realize that developing a planned community, based on a sustainable model, is a positive approach to creating the right environment for integrated neighborhoods. Build us H.O.P.E. is utilizing the "micro-home" standard (typically 150 – 480 sq. ft.) in the communities. We are answering questions about the permitting and zoning regulations and are identifying the components we will use for the sustainability of the homes. By working with the local agencies, we can address and resolve any issues regarding the longevity and life of the development. For a number of areas, the IRC 2012 is still the standard, although there is movement toward the IRC 2015 codes. Our collaborators include other tiny home communities, developers, city planners, sustainable urban community developers, architects, funders, and those who live in tiny homes. All of these resources are allowing us to provide information on the changes implemented by other zoning departments throughout the United States. For example, the city of Austin, Texas, has been welcoming in their permitting process for planned tiny home communities. We want to insure the structures are built in a way to last for decades and decades of use and not become blight in the area. This model could reduce the per-unit cost by more than 50%, thereby expanding the resources to house more individuals. Our goal is to create homes that are truly affordable, and will rent for an amount that will not take the majority of a renters' income just to pay for safe shelter alone. By building the tiny homes in a sustainable fashion, and incorporating technologies such as solar and gray water systems (as applicable) we feel we will be able to create the kind of home someone knows they truly can afford to live in. We are building developments that are environmentally sound. We have seen this model work and it has shown that the costs for the community are less overall. With the support of the local community, from corporations to private individuals, we feel we will be able to develop the sites without the overall reliance on public funding and government support.

I want to stress how important it is to learn your city and county zoning requirements for those interested in creating similar projects. We found that statewide each city and county requirement were greatly different. Each of the localities has their own process for moving forward and this is vital information for you to know as soon as possible.

What Will the Tiny Home Community Look Like?

In the beginning I wanted to create a test site of different types of tiny homes, using multiple materials and concepts. I have learned however, the time and affordability of doing so would not allow for such dreams. So our team went with a more practical innovative design.

Our largest master-planned community will include tiny homes, designed in pocket communities. The pocket community design has been shown to create the close-knit groups that learn how to live in a "cohousing" environment. Beyond the housing the rest of the Tiny Home Community will include:

- Main Activity Center, with an auditorium for community and resident events
- Community Gardens with Aquaponics
- Workshops
- Health and well facility, for the Community and the local neighborhoods
- We will create opportunities to be self-sufficient and generate income (for long term sustainability)

It is important to create the connection between the tiny home community and the existing neighborhoods. As with any other permanent neighborhood, key components will be incorporated into the overall plan in order to create a sustainable and long-term environment. A sense of permanence of the components (houses, buildings, shared spaces) needs to be apparent to those who see what is being developed.

By providing the ability to interact, we feel the overall area will benefit by it being there. We want to develop the kind of neighborhood others want to be part of, by living in the community or participating in what the community has to offer. The barriers to affordable housing should not create areas of isolation or detriment. The overall community should be one that others will be drawn to, for all it has to offer to the residents and their neighbors.

From the perspective of the residents, the Communities will allow them to take the smaller steps to re-acclimate to a more modern and busy life. Once the basic need for housing has been taken care of, the focus can be placed on getting back to a place of finding what options are available for them to pursue. The community will support and provide resources that can be utilized to identify the best path for them to take to live the kind of life they want to. For some, the life in this community will become their permanent home, where they can purchase a home and then live, work and lead productive lives within the area.

To be a member of a tiny home community means that you are an important part of the community itself. These members are asked to be part of the community meetings and associations that develop the guidelines for the operation, rules of sustainability and growth. When you, as a resident, know your voice and thoughts will be heard and addressed, you are more willing to listen and contribute.

Build us H.O.P.E. has been looking at the various operations to select best practices in order to incorporate into our model while also fitting the needs of the members, in a permanent community setting. The sites we will build are designed to be there, as permanent residences and common areas, for years and years to come. These are not designed to be transitional communities. These communities are places the residents can choose to live in for as long as they want. The rents or costs of the tiny home itself will be affordable. In many cases that number will be about 50% to 60% of the "average" apartments in the area.

The tiny house movement may also help end the cycle of homelessness by providing affordable housing alternatives and the communities to support them. Remember when you were able to choose your neighborhood based on living around others who wanted to have the same kind of lifestyle? We want to bring that back in a tiny home community. The interest in the communities has been from every social and economic group out there.

Moving Forward

With the proper support, and a viable design, we have found many of the communities have been able to go from a conceptual design to residents living there in a relatively short period of time. We began by hosting a tiny home volunteer meeting, in order to introduce the concept to the local community. This was met with a great turnout and many volunteers who want to be part of the planning and implementation process. The private sector (individuals, local businesses and larger corporations) have become willing partners in a plan that meets the needs for affordable housing and services and can be implemented in a sustainable model. What this means to the community is there is a way to move individuals from homelessness (root of homelessness) to a safe and thriving environment, and they can be a part of the change.

Funding

Build us H.O.P.E will take advantage of many of the mainstream funding types. We will utilize Urban Development Grants, capital campaigns, In Kind Gifts, and other grant resources; web campaigns; in our local area we are planning special events; community sponsorships; campaigns through social media and commercial construction loans.

Conclusion

Every Sunday for the past few years I have been going down to Madison and 12th Avenue in Phoenix, AZ (right outside the "Campus" which is home to the Central Arizona Shelter Services (CASS) to feed the homeless. As an advocate I really can no longer just past out water bottles and food. I am not saying the agencies and outreach programs working with this population are not valuable, they are. However, this s is only a temporary solution to the bigger problem. I truly believe the "tiny homes" movement can be much more than a movement. It can give the residents the opportunity to become our neighbors again.

As for me? I know that eventually I'll live in a tiny home. I feel that simple things in life like being closer to my children and my neighbors, is what I stand to gain. I am looking forward to having the satisfaction of working out in the garden, alongside others who are as excited as I am at seeing what we are creating.

Tiny Homes as Healthcare

Rebecca Sorensen

Rebecca Sorensen has worked with individuals with disabilities and their families for over 18 years. Her work includes program development and evaluation, resource management, individual and family support, and political advocacy. She currently works in Pittsboro, NC for the non-profit XDS, Inc. as a Community Development Consultant organizing and implementing a unique community housing initiative to serve adults living with mental illness. The focus of her work is on healing and recovery through natural interactions and processes. To that end she represents a very special tiny house community that is a group of non-profit organizations and local businesses that have partnered to provide an alternative affordable housing option for individuals with disabilities and who have limited incomes.

My story begins with a set of statistics.

- Over 863,000 adults with developmental disabilities (I/DD) live with caregivers who are over the age of 60.
- Lack of affordable housing stock is a significant contributing factor to continued housing insecurity for adults with disabilities who are living on an average of $721/month. (The maximum Supplemental Security Income provided to adults with I/DD).
- Supplemental Security Income (SSI) recipients who manage to rent a lower cost, non-subsidized unit are likely to be living in significantly substandard housing, in neighborhoods with high crime rates, and using virtually all of their income to pay their rent.
- Over 200,000 non-elderly people with disabilities reside in nursing homes.
- In North Carolina, 146,804 adults with disabilities receive SSI. To rent an average-priced one-bedroom apartment in Durham would cost approximately 102% of the total income for this individual.

- The housing affordability crisis deprives hundreds of thousands of people with disabilities of a basic human need: a place of their own to call home.[30]

For many Americans, these numbers are more than just dismal statistics. They represent our children, our friends, our neighbors, and our loved ones who live, every day, not just with the challenges of their disabilities, but also with few options to increase their opportunity for an independent and meaningful life. Because tiny homes can be far less expensive than traditional homes in terms of taxes, building, heating, maintenance, and repair costs, they offer a unique and innovative solution to the affordable housing crisis experienced by many of our most vulnerable community members.[31]

Living in a tiny home encourages a less cluttered and simpler lifestyle and minimizes ecological impacts.[32] It encourages residents to expand their living space to the world beyond their four walls, and to connect with their neighbors and community members. For adults with disabilities, tiny homes could be the very thing that bridge the affordability gap and offer a living arrangement that is supportive of a person's ability to live as independently as possible. It is this line of thinking, and the collaborative work of many organizations and individuals in our area, that have led to the development of several different initiatives to support adults with disabilities, using tiny homes as healthcare.

A Single System Approach

I learned about tiny homes from my cousin Allie a little over four years ago. She lives near an eco-intentional community in Black Mountain, NC, where many innovative homeowners are pioneering various ways to live sustainably. Tiny homes caught my attention right away, as they offer many implications for potentially serving a population of individuals with disabilities.

Tiny homes can be defined as homes that do not exceed 500 square feet; they are far less expensive than traditional homes in terms of taxes, building, heating, maintenance, and repair costs.[33] Living in a tiny home encourages a less cluttered and simpler lifestyle and minimizes ecological impacts. For adults with developmental disabilities, many of whom are living on

Supplemental Security Incomes of $721 per month, tiny homes are an affordable housing option that do not require a permanent government subsidy or absorb over 100% of the individual's income in rent or mortgage payments.

My son, Raimee, is 19 years old. He is tall, athletic, musically inclined, and described by those who know him as funny, kind, and a little bit devious. Raimee also has a diagnosis of autism and epilepsy. As a child he attended typical Kindergarten, first, and second grade classes. My husband and I took him out of public school at the age of eight when we learned from a classroom aide that Raimee was being bullied by his teacher. Raimee was homeschooled through tenth grade, at which time we discovered a charter high school in Chapel Hill that served at-risk youth and youth with disabilities.

PACE Academy was a perfect match, and our son thrived, both academically and socially. A year and a half into his high school experience, the Department of Public Instruction (DPI) decided to shut PACE down in favor of opening a for-profit virtual charter school owned, not ironically, by DPI's then Director. The decision to close PACE was made ten days prior to the start of the school year, and left many PACE students without a plan or place to go. Many of us parents found ourselves, along with our kids, catapulted into the world of adulthood. Although our family had a general plan for Raimee, we had been living with the assumption that we had a few more years to pull it together. Sometimes, I suppose, it is events such as these that spark the most meaningful solutions.

Like every other 19-year-old boy, Raimee desires autonomy and opportunities to experience independence. Unlike other boys his age, Raimee has a diagnosis whose one predictable trait is its unpredictability. Paired with epilepsy, Raimee's diagnoses make it difficult to identify appropriate ways that he can safely participate in self-determination. And when it comes to housing, there are truly no attractive options.

Here in Chapel Hill, Raimee has the choice of living in an apartment on his own, living in a group home, or living at home with his family. Like many individuals with autism, Raimee has trouble understanding and responding appropriately to potentially dangerous situations. He has yet to master many of the skills required for independent living and moving into an apartment on his own is not an option we could safely pursue. Group homes present another, albeit different, array of challenges. Group home staff, much like those who provide home and community based services funded by Medicaid, are underpaid, under-trained, and tasked with managing a multitude of individuals with different diagnoses. There is a high staff turnover rate, which leads to feelings of instability for residents. Additionally, a third party, often without the family's participation, determines the appropriate fit and quality of care. Group homes require that residents be away from their "home" during the day, and although they are touted as meeting the community integration requirements set forth by Olmstead, research has shown that it is the paid service providers themselves who end up offering the most frequent and enduring forms of social contact for residents.[34] In addition, group home services are expensive. When an individual enters a facility in which Medicaid pays for more than half of the bill, their monthly SSI benefit is reduced to $30. This is the total amount allotted to the resident for "comfort" items not provided by the facility.[35] If a resident is receiving the average maximum amount of SSI, which is $721/month, the cost to live in the group home is more than 95% of their entire income.[36] Lastly, smaller residences were found to have better Quality of Life outcomes for adults with developmental disabilities. In homes of three or fewer residents, the findings were greater instances of personalized support and safety with enhanced social networks.[37]

Our family defines the degree of Raimee's autism as falling somewhere in the middle of the spectrum. Communication is very difficult for him, and he struggles with understanding the perspectives of others. However, Raimee is a really smart guy. When tasks are broken down and explained to him in a way that he can process and understand, he will master those tasks and generalize them to the natural environment. We have learned to never underestimate Raimee's ability to acquire knowledge, to have high expectations, and to be creative and realistic in our teaching procedures. Not surprising is that Raimee learns a skill best when it is not contrived at the table, but when he is learning it en vivo. Which is why the idea of tiny house living makes so much sense for young adults who are living with autism and are in need of an opportunity to safely experience living on their own and managing their own living space.

Our family home is located in western Orange County. Like many counties across the nation, we have strict zoning ordinances that can make living in a tiny home difficult. Residential zoning prohibits community developers from creating very small lots (1,000-2,000 sq. ft.), which is paramount to keeping the housing cost in the affordable range for those living on SSI. Our county, like many others, does not have a residential zone district that would allow lots of that size. However, most counties have provisions that allow existing home-owners to build accessory dwelling units (ADUs) that can be up to 800 square feet. ADUs (also known as granny pods or in-law flats) can be relatively inexpensive to build (averaging $25,000-$50,000), require very little maintenance or upkeep, and can provide a housing option for individuals on the autism spectrum who would greatly benefit from a housing experience that is situated in close proximity to their natural support system. Tiny homes located on family property would not compromise the individual's ability to keep their home and community based waiver services, and according to the cost analysis in Table 1, have the potential to save the State thousands of dollars in group home expenses.

What the cost comparison in Table 1 does not reflect is the additional economic benefit that will occur in ten years when the "mortgage" has been

paid in full. Group home fees will continue for the duration of the resident's stay. Also, while group homes often collect fees from their residents that absorb the majority of their income, the tiny home option would allow residents to keep their SSI and thereby increase their opportunities for independence and participation in community activities and events.[38]

Table 1
Alternative Housing Cost Comparison

Raimee Sorensen: *Single System Case Study*
- 19 year old, diagnosed with autism and epilepsy
- SIS support needs index- 105

Residential Option:
- Res level 3 in <6 bed group home; reimbursed @ $144.19
- Additional Services
- 40 hours week of Community Networking @ $5.35/unit reimbursement
- 1 unit/month of Community Guide @ $150/unit reimbursement
- 1 unit/month of Specialized Consultative Services for BCBA consultation @ $300/ unit reimbursement

Tiny Home Option:
- $40,000 mortgage for build of new tiny home on parent's property in Orange Co. (Est. 10 year mortgage at 3.9%)
- Health and Safety considerations: The individual has a seizure disorder and currently requires 24-hour supervision. If he were to live on his own, it is estimated that he would be safe to be alone at his home for up to 6 hours per occasion, given he has added seizure detection technology. One possible device identified (SmartMonitor) would identify rapid jerking movements and immediately notify designated contacts. After initial purchase of the device, there is a $30 monthly subscription fee.
- Additional services (current service frequencies to continue)
- 46.5 hours/week of In-home Skill Building @ $4.75/unit reimbursement

- 13.5 hours/week of Community Networking @ $5.35/unit reimbursement
- 550 hours/year of Respite (approximately 45 hours/month) @$3.54/unit reimbursement
- 1 unit/month Community Guide @$150/unit reimbursement
- 1 unit/month of SCS services for BCBA consultation @ $300/unit reimbursement

Estimated Monthly Costs

	Residential Group Home	Tiny Home Option
Monthly residential costs	$4,325.00	$403.00
Utilities	-	$20.00
Health and Safety Considerations	-	$30.00
Cost for additional waiver supports	$4,045.20	$6,011.08
Estimated monthly budget	$8,370.20	$6,464.08
Estimated yearly budget	$100,442.40	$77,568.96
Estimated yearly savings		**$22,873.44**
Estimated savings over 5 years		**$114,376.20**

Community

I work as a Community Development Consultant for several collaborates in our area, helping to build communities for special populations in creative and affordable ways. One of the initiatives I work with is the Farm at Penny Lane, whose founder, Thava Mahadevan, is combining farming and tiny homes to build an affordable, therapeutic, and supportive community for adults living with mental illness.

Social care farming is a growing movement that combines agricultural production with health, social, and educational services. Care farms provide opportunities for participants to have social interaction, build skills, and engage in purposeful work. In addition to the more obvious benefits of farming, such as creating access to fresh food and cultivating a connection to nature, farming provides natural opportunities to participate in meaningful and diversified work. It offers multiple task options that can be structured or unstructured, it allows individuals the choice to work alone or with a group, and most often, it produces positive, tangible results.[39] Within this farm environment, Thava and the Tiny Home Community Collaborative are planning to build a village of ten tiny homes.

Similar to adults living with developmental disabilities, many adults living with mental health challenges face extraordinary hurdles with regards to housing security. In fact, over 20 percent of the total homeless population in our country is diagnosed with a mental illness.[40] This number is extraordinarily conservative as it only documents those individuals who are currently receiving services and are located in areas where they are visually able to be included in the count. This statistic does not represent those individuals who are not participating in their treatment program, have not been formally diagnosed, or are living in places or situations where they may not be found or considered to be homeless (such as sleeping in the woods or "couch surfing"). It also does not reflect those individuals who live in fear of losing their housing at any moment, or are taking shelter in residences that are unsafe or substandard, neither of which provides a very solid foundation for the recovery process.

Homelessness not only deprives people of shelter from the elements, it also steals their ability to find respite, to have intimacy, and to have that safe place away from the eyes of the world. Combined with the vulnerability of mental illness, homelessness creates a climate in which recovery in any form is close to impossible. Having a home in a supportive community is a necessary step toward reestablishing that sense of peace that so many of us take for granted. That peace that lets recovery from illness become a priority because you no longer have to wonder where you will lay your head.

The tiny home initiative at the Farm at Penny Lane is building more than just four walls and a roof. We are building a community. Our objective is to provide an affordable housing option that is located within a supportive environment, where participants will have access to fresh food, meaningful and diverse work opportunities, friendship, and therapeutic programs. Providing a home only solves half of the problem; building a circle of support within which an individual with mental illness can have a sense of purpose and feel safe is establishing the foundation for a meaningful and authentic journey to recovery.

Our project is the work of nine different organizations in Chatham county: Cross Disability Services, Inc., Habitat for Humanity, Triangle Community Foundation, Cardinal Innovations Healthcare, Grid-Free NC, Bold Construction, Builders First Supply Company, the Chatham County Fair, and the UNC Center for Excellence in Community Mental Health (CECMH). In a remarkable and whirlwind partnership, we built our first tiny house in five days at the Chatham County Fair. The project drew a large crowd to the fair, and provided our team with a unique opportunity to talk about affordable housing and mental illness to a very broad and diverse population. The house is now located at the Farm at Penny Lane, where it is entering into the first phase of our development plan.

During Phase I, our research team will conduct interviews and focus groups with approximately ten internally selected clients of the UNC CECMH. These clients have agreed to "live" in the tiny home for a short period of time and provide feedback on their experience living within 336 square feet. Data will be collected for one year and will be used to inform the development of Phase II: A tiny house community consisting of five tiny homes. Phase III will follow with the addition of five more homes on the Farm. Our intention is to constantly evaluate and modify our program so that we are meeting the residents' needs, and eventually to replicate the project throughout our state and across the country.

Safe and affordable housing is one of the most urgent public health issues facing our nation. This issue is particularly salient for vulnerable and marginalized populations, such as adults with disabilities, who are frequently relegated to substandard housing in impoverished and unsafe areas where opportunities to develop social connections are limited.[41] It is time to bring innovation, practicality, and humanity into the narrative and forever change the outcomes of this otherwise hopeless trajectory. This is what we are trying to accomplish through the work of the Tiny Home Community Collaborative.

We are surrounded by bureaucratic systems that, in their attempt to solve problems, often overcomplicate the process, and in doing so, forget the most basic elements that are essential to stability and progress for many of our most disenfranchised populations. I would like to propose a simpler perspective: affordable shelter, intentional community, and nutritious food. The undertaking doesn't have to be as monumental as it presents itself. In fact, a big part of the solution is actually quite tiny.

Question Everything

The art of not backing down or out

René Hardee

Wife, Mother, Scientist, and Tiny House enthusiast, Rene' Hardee, turned true change-agent when she petitioned her town of Rockledge, FL to not only accept, but to embrace Tiny Houses into the community. She is aggressively working to bring the City's first Tiny House Neighborhood to fruition! She will no doubt "Question Everything" in *Turning Tiny*.

After one particularly chaotic day in our average, American, 3B/2B, 2000 sq. ft. living, double income life, my husband, in a moment of desperation and frustrated by the demanding needs of a toddler, a newborn, and an exasperated wife, blurted out the phrase that would ultimately take our life down the path we are on today.

"I JUST WANT MY LIFE TO BE AS SIMPLE AS POSSIBLE!"

At the time, I was deeply offended by this declaration. What was that supposed to even mean?

"WELL, WAY TO GET MARRIED AND HAVE KIDS THEN, JERK-FACE!" I shouted towards the sound of his diminishing foot-stomps. I may or may not have thrown a shoe.

Later that night as I was lying in bed, I reflected upon the earlier squabble but this time with a softened heart. Why would he say that? What was he trying to tell me? It seemed like our spats were increasing in number. Why? What were we doing wrong? I felt nervous even asking that question, but desperate to know the answer so we could return to a happy household. In an attempt to shed the negative vibes I was feeling as I drifted off to sleep, I began romanticizing about a time when I felt completely at peace; i.e. "think happy thoughts." My mind floated off to Grad School.

Right around the turn of the century, I was living in a small, 1 bedroom apartment about 20 minutes from Vanderbilt campus in Nashville, TN, and I was making a measly $15,000 per year. But I remember being happy! I had exactly 4 bills and they were always paid on time. I owned one plate, one set of silverware, and one cup. I bought a couch and a table set for $17 at a garage sale. I was wanting for nothing. I always knew where I stood. I felt in control. Life was manageable. Life was easy. Life was just so…SIMPLE!

After a heart-to-heart, my husband and I vowed to simplify our lives. It became our new family motto. But what did that look like? Surveying our surroundings, we lamented over how many rooms in our large house didn't really serve a purpose. For starters, we have two living rooms. Two. I guess one is supposed to be the "formal sitting room" for when you invite solicitors in for tea? The boys each have their own large room. Unnecessary. They even have a separate playroom that they never play in! We have a formal dining room, a large kitchen which we honestly only use about half of, two problematic "rotundas" (for lack of a better word) that serve as feature spaces to transition into different rooms and a 2-car garage that does not hold cars. All of this space eats energy. We pay to heat/cool it. We spend time cleaning it. We buy stuff to fill these rooms so they don't look awkward! We do not enjoy these spaces. What a waste! And to add more insult to injury, this house is considered standard! The American Dream! When we were looking for homes to purchase 7 years ago, this type of house was all that was available. And we didn't question it! We have been programmed since birth to strive for the 3-bedroom, 2-bath, 2000 sq. ft. home. It means success in this country. I get angry just thinking about how much money we have squandered on things that don't really matter to us.

We realized downsizing our possessions would be an easy place to start living more simply. Over the next few months we sold, donated, or trashed approximately 7 carloads full of stuff. Toys, dishes, baby items, clothes, knick-knacks, furniture, books, nothing was sacred. If it was a duplicate or didn't serve an immediate purpose, it went out the door. The effect was instant. We felt lighter; liberated. As if our possessions had been weighing us down. But this positive reaction only whetted our appetite for more.

In 2014, the tiny house movement had started gaining in popularity. As a lover of documentaries, I had recently seen a fascinating one that was speaking to my heart. *TINY* is a documentary about home, and how we find it. The film follows one couple's attempt to build a tiny house on wheels (THOW) from scratch, and profiles other families who have downsized their lives into homes smaller than the average parking space. This could be exactly the answer we were looking for.

Shortly after this viewing I signed up for a local 2-day THOW workshop. I was so excited to finally be interacting with like-minded individuals and experiencing a THOW first-hand. But as much as I enjoyed this weekend of learning, I left the workshop a bit discouraged. It turns out THOWs come with their own set of unique chores and nuisances that didn't really jive with our new family motto of simplicity. And whenever I asked about where to legally put them no one could ever give me a straight answer. It was always "maybe an RV park might take them" or "maybe you could put them out in the middle of nowhere-land where nobody cares," or even "just put them in someone's back yard and pray someone doesn't call the cops on you." Clearly this was a problem.

Skirting the law is not my style. My husband and I both have respectable jobs in town. I have small children who need to go to school. We need to be urban. We need to be in the system.

So off I went to research where tiny houses were allowed. In our home-town the minimum square footage for new construction in a non-HOA area was 1,200 sq. ft. The surrounding county had a lower minimum of 750 sq. ft. but that means you have to be rural. We were not interested in living in an RV park. It just seemed to be too transient of a lifestyle for us. As a whole it seemed like the North West United States had the most tiny house friend-ly cities.

At this point I felt we had 3 options.

- Keep living our "status quo" life and hope that the tiny house move-ment catches on.
- Relocate to a tiny house friendly place. Perhaps Seattle?
- Approach our city about allowing tiny houses.

Now that I knew of this alternative living style I didn't feel I would be content continuing to live in a large house. So A. wasn't an option. We dis-cussed moving, but it just didn't feel right. We love our town. We love our jobs, our church, our friends, family, gym; we love our life! We have planted roots here and just didn't want to start over. So option B. was out. That left option C.

Since I started researching tiny houses I had joined a fair amount of blogs, forums, and Facebook groups, and I began noticing an unsettling trend throughout all of the various sites. The prevailing attitude on these pages seemed to be very negative towards city officials. The sentiment about those people in charge being nothing but "money-hungry" or out to "assert their power over the man" was rampant. Posts of tiny houses being forced out of town or fined for non-compliance dominated the discussions, and served to feed everyone's pre-conceived notions. It probably wasn't true. Right?

I fully admit that I am an optimist: a realistic optimist, but an optimist none-the-less. I give people the benefit of the doubt. I believe people have the best of intentions. I think people genuinely want to say yes and help out. I trust that people are not "out to get me." Experience has taught me that most of the time, I am right. So I was able to set aside any doubts about my city official's intentions and approach the situation with a positive attitude.

Now is the time I would like to make the disclaimer and profess that I have no qualifications what-so-ever in dealing with local government. I had never even been to a council meeting. I didn't even know *who* I should be talking to. Lucky for me my city has a website that lists all the different departments and their responsibilities. Looks like the zoning department was in charge of "land use." Sounded like a good place to start.

I sent the Planning Director a brief e-mail asking for help meeting a family goal. First contact. The date was February 2, 2015. Much to my surprise I received a response fairly quickly agreeing to meet with me. I had scored an entire hour of the City Planning Director's time. Sweet.

I went into the meeting with a goal of gaining understanding. I wanted to fully grasp the concept of zoning, why it was important, and what purpose it served. I think this step is vitally important and helped to make me successful in the end. The Planning Director and City Planner fielded my questions with patience and grace. They took time to explain the different types of zoning categories and what each one meant. They showed me the current land use map highlighting what was currently permissible in each zone. The more I learned, the more questions I had. Their tolerance never wavered.

I confirmed with them what my initial research had turned up; that the minimum square footage of a new construction home in the city was 1,200 square feet. Undeterred, I began testing the boundaries of this regulation. There were some very old homes in the city that had been grandfathered in before the minimum square footage regulation. None were for sale and they were all in desperate need of renovation.

"So, what if I bought an old, small house and renovated it? Could I just knock it down and build another one the same size in its place?" The Planning Director pointed me to another regulation stating that any more than 50% renovation on an existing home was subject to current square footage minimums. One could get around this requirement by renovating little bits of the house over a longer time period, so that eventually you will have updated every square inch, but that just didn't fit the bill of our "simple" prerequisite.

Going back to new construction, the 1,200 sq. ft. minimum requirement was begging for clarification. "What exactly is allowed to be counted towards the 1,200 sq. ft. minimum?," I posed. "Garage? Perhaps a back porch?" The Planning Director raised a little smile and replied with "Any thing under air." At first my mind went racing towards adding air conditioning to a large garage that would eat up the bulk of the square footage minimum, but then I remembered that I was supposed to simplify my life, and heating/cooling/cleaning a large area that served no purpose did not make the grade. So I pressed further. "What about splitting up the square footage? Could I build like two 600 sq. ft. structures and connect them with a covered breezeway or something?" I could tell I had hit upon uncharted territory by the way the City Planner and the Planning Director turned to look at one another. It was as if to say "I dunno. What do you think?" After conferring with themselves for a few moments the City Planner came back with an answer of, "As long as they have the same foundation."

Eureka! I thought to myself. I had found my "in." Well, not quite yet. There was one caveat.

"But only one of the places can have a kitchen," the City Planner counseled. What!? No kitchen? Hrmm! Well maybe we could have like a common kitchen, and have separate living spaces? My mind was wandering off to try and bring resolution to this new challenge. A common kitchen might work, but is that simpler than what I have now? Maybe this wouldn't work after all? I sighed in frustration.

"Well, what exactly constitutes a kitchen?" I asked cautiously, still trying to poke holes in the barriers.

"A kitchen has a stove in it," said the City Planner, quite matter-of-factly.

"Wait, so you're saying it can still have a sink? A microwave? Dishwasher? Toaster? Refrigerator? Even cooktop burners? Just no stove? "

The city officials were nodding their heads almost in unison at my itemized list of typical kitchen appliances.

Maybe I had found my "in" after all?

"So now what if I built four 300 square foot houses and connected them all on the same foundation via a covered breezeway, and only one of the houses had a stove? I could arrange them in a square and put some type of courtyard in the middle. Would that meet the square footage requirement?"

They had caught on to my line of questioning by now and were almost able to predict where I was heading before I even knew where I was going. I hadn't even finished my sentence before the Planning Director responded with, "I think that would meet the square footage requirement."

I sat back in my chair and began reflecting on what just happened. I mean, I fully expected to come out of the meeting with a better understanding of what obstacles I would face in trying to build a tiny house within city limits. I didn't expect to come out with an agreeable solution for legally building a tiny house within the current zoning laws. It happened so fast too. I expected months of back-and-forth discussions. I almost didn't know where to go from here.

And then I suddenly realized what I had just described. In my tiny house research I had stumbled upon architect Ross Chapin and his Pocket Neighborhoods. The images of his intentional communities were everything that I had ever dreamed about. Cute houses, thoughtfully arranged around a common green space, with inward-facing front porches that begged for you to swing the afternoon away and sip iced tea. They comprised a tight-knit neighborhood where people talked to one another and shared dinners together. They were a place where I could feel comfortable letting the kids run in the yard by themselves because I knew they had 10 other households of "extended family" looking out for their well-being. Somewhere neighbors could truly be neighborly.

Four tiny houses arranged in a square with a center courtyard is the classic definition of a Pocket Neighborhood! I frantically dug my phone out of my purse and pulled up photograph after photograph of pocket neighborhoods examples for the planners. I could tell they liked what they saw. I mean, who wouldn't want to live in one?

A Tiny House Pocket Neighborhood ended up being the right solution at the right time for both me and the city. Urban sprawl (also known as "moving to the 'burbs") has left a lot of cities with blighted regions. Once bustling neighborhoods or downtown areas are now old and in need of revitalizing. As the oldest city in Brevard County, Rockledge had experienced its share of blight, and the city was looking to bring it back to life.

Tiny House Pocket Neighborhoods are a perfect solution for urban infill. They allow for many more units per acre than traditional homes, and the housing arrangement fosters strong relationships that compel people to put down roots. Less money is spent on housing yielding more money to be spent within the community. The citizens benefit and the local economy benefits.

From here, I will offer the awesome Rockledge City Planning Team nearly all the credit. They began diligently researching everything about tiny houses, watching the tiny house shows, holding meetings, discussions, researching some more, and ultimately settling upon the creation of a new zoning ordinance specifically tailored for a Tiny House Pocket Community. Nearly this entire ordinance had to be created from scratch, as no other place in the country has blended the two concepts into a specific zoning regulation. But the City of Rockledge was up to the challenge and surpassed all expectations. They exemplified their role in listening and responding to their citizens' needs. I couldn't be more proud of my town.

Over the next several months the draft ordinance would make its way through several Planning Commission hearings and finally up to City Council, all the while taking on feedback and getting tweaked until all parties were satisfied with the result. On September 23rd, 2015, just shy of eight months since first contact, the City Council unanimously voted in favor of adoption of the new zoning ordinance allowing tiny houses in pocket neighborhoods within the city limits of Rockledge Florida. That is record time from concept to approval of such an innovative idea. This speaks volumes about the dedication and teamwork amongst my local government. The City of Rockledge runs like a well-oiled machine.

The night the tiny house ordinance was passed something quite serendipitous happened. A local developer spoke at the hearing and said he already had a piece of property and a concept site plan to utilize the new ordinance. I had been searching for a development partner for several months but always came up empty-handed. Most of them were too busy with million dollar strip mall projects or mega planned unit developments. A one-acre community was not exactly a big money maker. Plus it was new and weird. Real estate development is all about lowering your risk and a project like this was turning risk on its head. What if it didn't sell?

Call it what you will – fate, karma, divine intervention – but the stars just kept aligning to bring this project to where it is today. The chosen property has been rezoned for a tiny house pocket neighborhood, and the developer and I have finally agreed upon a first draft of a site plan. Next, we need to formally submit the site plan to the city and have it approved by all the various departments. After that the building begins.

What started out as a plea to allow one tiny house into the City limits of Rockledge, FL, ended up opening the door for an entirely new kind of community. I often joke to people about how "I just wanted a tiny house for myself but the city is making me build one for everybody!" But, honestly, I couldn't be happier about this community. It's exactly what I've always wanted.

So what's the future for tiny house communities? A wide demographic of people are facing their own unique life challenges and are beginning to question the status quo. They are driven to find alternative living situations. Baby boomers are getting ready to retire and want less household responsibilities. Millennials are up to their eyeballs in student loan debt and the thought of tacking on a 30-year $200K mortgage is even more daunting. Young families who would like to have only one income are seeing tiny houses as viable options. Empty-nesters are realizing a large house is pretty lonely without the kids around. Mature families with two income households desire more quality family time. City officials are looking for ways to encourage urban infill or reduce blight. Tiny house communities can be the single solution to all of these issues.

I view this first Tiny House Pocket Community in Rockledge, FL as a flagship community. Once it is completed I believe it will be a game-changer. People will see that tiny house communities can offer a solution to growing problems across a wide demographic, and municipalities across the country will be eager to replicate them in their cities. They are just looking for someone else to be the first and Rockledge has paved the way.

If you haven't gleaned anything useful from my story, then I'll leave you with this more pointed take-away: question everything! And I mean this in two different senses.

The first? Literally ask questions. If there is something you don't understand, ask for clarification. Don't ever assume you know or suspect the answer. If I would've assumed I knew what my city's definition of a kitchen was, I might not be building a tiny house community today.

In the second sense I encourage you to reflect on you current lifestyle. How's it working for you? What are you lacking? What do you have in excess? Is your time and money supporting your most important priorities? Why not? Do you need your large house? Do you need all your things, or are they keeping you from what you really desire?

I questioned my husband's seemly insulting declaration. I questioned my current living situation. I questioned the heck out of my city zoning officials. I reflected on what things in my life were really important to me and then I questioned what my life would look like if I made those things a priority. I challenge you to do the same.

Making Community Your Business and Your Business Your Community

Matt Ogorzalek and Marnie Khaw

Matt and Marnie co-founded Austin Live|Work, a 10-acre tiny house community and future destination point for land development entrepreneurship. They've found that the 'startup life' has them hobnobbing with many local talents, including skilled tradesmen, designers, engineers, artists and the occasional brush-clearing llamas. If you like tiny homes and business, and especially the business of tiny homes, you may want to check out Austin Live|Work in *Turning Tiny*.

"*We're a middle aged couple, we love our family and we're about to become tiny house community developers. But until we heard the voice, we'd never done a crazy thing in our whole life.*"

Often times, a paraphrased movie quote can help with description. Admittedly, the voice we heard along our "turning tiny" journey wasn't as dramatic as that in *Field of Dreams* (*Field of Dreams.* Dir. Phil Alden Robinson. Perf. Kevin Costner, James Earl Jones, Ray Liotta. Gordon Co., 1989. DVD.) Instead, ours was the kind of voice that emerged and took shape over several years of questioning, philosophizing, theorizing and vision crafting.

Let's start with those questions. Some of the recurring ones were "*Why does my neighborhood feel isolated?*" "*Why am I compartmentalized in my job role?*" Or, "*Why am I in these classrooms learning irrelevant subjects?*" To put simply, the voice was really commenting on the current state of our living, working and learning spaces. This was the drive behind what's now called Austin Live|Work, a tiny house community that fosters startups and entrepreneurship in land development.

Marnie and I had become used to living and working in the city and suburbs and found there was too much inertia with our degrees and office jobs. We were also a little concerned with some of the patterns we've noticed in the economy, so we were looking to hedge by betting on the most reliable investment we knew of: ourselves. We figured that by acquiring some land and living in a tiny house, we could work from home and not do any worse than our previous city slicker lifestyle. Maybe we could have fun creating a meaningful startup company too.

Originally, the attempt was to stay in California to craft this new and improved lifestyle, but it was clear there were more cost-effective choices in 2014. After a few potential locations, the decision was to choose Austin, TX. Austin, which was being called America's fastest growing city, had a big startup and investment network, diverse culture and many excellent food choices, including their well-known food truck scene. By the way, food trucks and tiny homes have got to be cousins, right? In any case, I guess you could say we were smellin' what Austin was cookin', so we packed up and journeyed southeastwards to get some affordable land and tap into this entrepreneurial culture.

We were now eliminating various costs, starting to minimize our belongings and decided to surround ourselves with skilled and passionate locals. We were surprised at how many people we met who wanted to collaborate on a tiny house community project. We'd always had an entrepreneurial streak and had heard of the concept of tiny homes for years. Now it was just a matter of implementation since we thought the idea was solid. Tiny home construction was booming and cities weren't able to keep up with the needs of their clientele. Tiny homeowners and renters needed places and spaces to live, work and learn. The concept of Live|Work communities began to form.

We had made a choice that community was to become an integral part of our life. In our case, we wanted to encourage a culture of entrepreneurship, so it made sense to imbue the 'startup ecosystem'. Fortunately, we've already been approached by hundreds of people who want to 'be the change' in their communities. We don't have any marketing or advertising campaign yet and we can hardly keep up with the responses through the website as well as visitors who ask for a walking tour as they pass by our site. One cool thing we've noticed is that nobody has disliked the idea of a startup ecosystem yet.

Some of the comments we get are "we love what you're doing," or "I want to do something exactly like this," or "I don't know how to describe it but I want to be a part of it." Our car has a license plate that's really noticeable to tiny house enthusiasts, so if we're out shopping at the hardware or grocery store we may have folks standing by the car waiting to chat with us. One of our favorite comments was, "you guys are famous. I just met the tiny house people!" Often times when we're grabbing a bite to eat downtown, we tell the server or owner about our project. We find that occasionally folks will over-hear us from adjacent booths and come to join the conversation because they love tiny houses. All this reinforces the message to us that we need to contin-ue the project and scale it to it's potential.

A day in the life of our community has not always been typical in our first year, however when we do find a routine, it increases our productivity and helps us move on to the next task. Having lots of windows in our tiny house makes it easy to wake up at sunrise. From there, we'll likely take the dog for a walk, talk shop with our builder, see what maintenance or improve-ments need to be made to the 10 acres, the tiny houses or various tools and equipment, take appointments, search for or hire contractors and catch up on emails and phone calls. All this routine can easily be thrown off by the randomness that occurs in a startup ecosystem. We often ask, "Should we stick to the routines or take chances on fleeting opportunities?" Sometimes strange things happen, like when an HBO production team contacted us to film a season of one of their popular series on our land. What would've hap-pened if we signed a contract with them? Who knows, maybe the celebrities would take a look at the tiny houses and add some to their fleet, or perhaps we would take a look at their plush movie trailers and learn about their design tastes. In any case, we've grown to appreciate the randomness and are honing the underappreciated skill of prioritizing and shelving tasks while rec-ognizing and seizing promising opportunities.

Successes are difficult to describe, mainly because when something good happens we immediately start concentrating on the next challenge. However, since we can imagine ourselves sitting outside some 70 degree Sunday after-noon on our newly built tiny house porch with a community-crafted brew in hand, here it goes! The first success was acquiring property outside of a flood zone and with great road access. Our road is new and is engineered well with culverts and bridges. We came to appreciate this after two periods of severe Austin rain when many other neighborhoods were damaged or inconvenienced, but we were not affected. The location is also great because we're situated between several major destination points that will create awareness for us during their events. We've also made connections with those venues that may turn into long-term cross-promotional opportunities. We have access to potable water with great pressure and have also built gray water and compost systems. We were able to release a mysterious oil pipeline easement after diligent research showed our 10-acre property survey was not updated. Not only does this increase our usability and property value, but our neighbors will appreciate this, since it previously split their property in half. It's good to be neighborly, even if it comes through in filing esoteric county documents, right? We installed road base for select travel areas and electricity to 14 tiny house parking spots, created a partially off-grid section for those wanting to power up with renewable energy, partnered with a talented builder who created many amenities, including portable solar-powered systems, vertical food garden structures and a 3,000 square foot workshop for concurrent tiny house builds and community events. Three tiny house builds have been completed on our site so far and we have daily requests for us to build their homes. We have recurring income streams from tiny house rentals and lot rentals. Successes are expected to continue as we meet with passionate and skilled collaborators, our biggest asset and the foundation behind the growing tiny house startup ecosystem.

It's been fun and challenging this last year to experience all the random encounters and opportunities. Challenges can be small and quirky, such as how do you pronounce THOW, the acronym for tiny houses on wheels? Is it |t -hou| or |THou|? Personally, we think it complicates the matter by introducing voiceless fricatives, so we know our choice! Challenges can also be higher level and long-term, like should there be a regional or even global standard for THOW builds and communities and should it be developed through private agile-bodied organizations? The LEED building standard might be a good guide. Before it grew to the current 200,000 or so staff it started out with just 6 volunteers. Tiny houses and the accompanying communities may just end up having their own small and dedicated team to develop standards. That way we can differentiate ourselves from the recreational vehicle and RV park standards we often get lumped in with. Don't get us wrong, we love RV'ers too and are excited about them joining our projects (no pressure RV'ers!). Recognizing some of the unique attributes of tiny houses and tiny house communities will also help banks to structure loans around it's data. We've seen an increase in financing requests from college-aged students and older adults with fixed income and low savings, so hopefully this challenge will be addressed soon. Other challenges include everyday maintenance. There's always a leak to be patched, a house to be leveled, a road to be re-paved or crowned, trash to manage, a battery for the solar unit to be charged or electrical issues to be diagnosed. For contracts, whether they are implicit or explicit, it's a challenge to determine when to barter versus be paid in currency. How detailed should a contract be? We love challenges though, because it means the market is signaling us about the need for growth. 'Growth hacking', if approached right, can create abundance.

Generally, the needs for tiny house communities depend on the demographic. They are also closely related to a person's values. That's why there will always be some sort of 'intentional community'. Experience from the older generations, and Wikipedia for the millennials, will show us that many intentional communities exist, such as kibbutzim, ashrams, communes, eco-villages, survivalist retreats, housing co-ops, fraternity and sorority houses and more. Don't forget our very own co-living startup incubators, right?! Other than the need for affordability, we've noticed a few other like-minded

values and needs from our inquiring enthusiasts. They include community planning that integrates barter, conflict resolution and third-party mediation for disputes, the support of cottage businesses, purposeful collaboration amongst generations, mentorship and apprenticeship programs, workshops that teach both the latest technology and timeless or recession-proof skills and integration of or affiliation with collaborative services like Airbnb, Uber, Taskrabbit, Favor or DogVacay.

Much of our end goal is in choosing the right community model for Austin Live|Work, so that this project can evolve into a lasting and rewarding experience. One of the rewards is if the model grows enough to include consulting opportunities for new and like-minded communities and investment opportunities for those who want to share in the model. Creating an investor atmosphere here will also benefit the community since it will help encourage our early adopters to implement and scale good ideas. Anybody here can become an investor. For example, if our average tiny house renter saves up some funds and decides to collaborate with a neighbor or two on a brilliant idea, they have now started the process of becoming an investor. Entrepreneurship, the world of startups or investing is difficult without structure, so we've given a lot of thought to how this would all function. Thankfully, other investor-minded folks are working with us on this, so we are happy to start planning a structure for incubating, accelerating and seed funding tiny house communities and tiny house technologies. It sounds so 'Silicon Valley'! Well, that's ok with us because they're making some excellent progress there. Have they caught on yet to the value of tiny houses and tiny house communities? Perhaps not, but since we want to see THOWs and communities everywhere, there's never a bad time to share it with the rest of the world.

We foresee the long-term success of tiny house communities depending on a good balance between environmental and economic sustainability. Entrepreneurship, research and development will be a great way to implement this. If you think about where all the research and development is concentrated, it's usually in universities, where students and professors hope to get government or other big-entity funding. That's why another goal of ours is to bring students and academics into the project for more R&D on future land and community design.. 'Tiny House University', if you will. We're experimenting with how R&D can be more effective when broken into smaller manageable community-specific projects across a network or even sub-projects within a single tiny house community. The inclusion of economic research to tiny house communities has also interested us, especially with all the advances in micro tasking, crowd sourcing and peer-to-peer platforms streamlining and 'creatively destructing' stagnant business models. Heck, if game developers can hire experts to study their virtual economies to manage and curb inflation, tiny house communities can learn from this too. There's certainly a potential for all of us to have a niche economy and study all these great topics.

Because we're thinking from a land and community development perspective, we want to learn from previous examples. Sometimes it helps us to ask questions about the far ends of the development perspective, such as "How much could an eco-village scale in network size?" or conversely, "How much environmental consideration could well-funded real estate holding companies or well-optimized agricultural operations give?" There's certainly a lot of debate about topics like this and it can leave one's head spinning. 'Paralysis by analysis' and inertia are enemies to a startup ecosystem, so we're looking for better answers. Thankfully, we keep coming across an approach that fits in well with our philosophy.

Most land or community development acts upon a centralized philosophy. Cities or big corporations have a select few decision makers or people of influence that create their centralized model. For example, cities will incorporate and fund their growth through bond financing. How many people reading this have made direct decisions on these matters? This huge responsibility for having a license to create money is offset by taxpayers who must pay it back. It's safe to say that almost all taxpayers have little direct influence over the decision making process. And that's OK, if people actually want to pay for projects without being directly involved. However, we've noticed that there are many who want to directly contribute to, influence and even be rewarded for their involvement in projects. This means that there is a viable alternative to city development, annexation, zoning and other centralized practices. Perhaps in the near future we will see less suburban sprawl and more holistic design, planning and implementation recognizing universally accepted patterns? Perhaps communities will be interconnected by voluntary agreements and not by force? It's up to all of us. Philosophically, it may come down to how one views the 'metaphorical pie'. Is it finite and will there need to be fighting over the dwindling pieces, or is the pie constantly growing based on the amount of technological innovation or grit and determination of the entrepreneur who drives the economy based on responsible growth? We always think on the bright side here, so we believe in the latter. The 'distributed' community or land development model works well with all our values, in addition to the needs expressed by the emerging tiny house markets.

People are excited about tiny houses for lots of reasons. I'm guessing all the readers have also run into those who don't even get the concept of tiny houses. Sometimes it helps us to think in metaphors or analogies as we prepare for the future. Tiny houses and their communities represent freedom and options. Maybe if we are talking to an engineer, we'd say that tiny houses and their resourceful owners can be looked at like network 'nodes' that have the freedom to travel and find work or investment opportunities by connecting with larger nodes or 'hubs' (i.e. tiny house communities). Pretty far out, huh.

This kind of thinking just resonated with us and honestly, had us kicking ourselves. There's that voice again. "*Why didn't we just start on this years ago?*" I mean, our favorite things are distributed! The cellular network in our body, good soil, the weight load on our tiny house (I'm sure our trailer appreciates this), the Internet, you name it. While nothing is 100% absolute this or that method, we were happy to find that a lot of our favorite networks were clearly leaning towards the distributed or decentralized kind and had their own 'magical' order to it.

These are exciting times. The Internet has brought the information age. We may soon see some huge changes in financial technology with some kind of 'Internet of Value'. Devices may be hooked up in an 'Internet of Things'. Well, we're pretty sold on the idea that these kinds of distributed systems and networks can help the world evolve. Simply put, it's the future and a great way for projects to grow and better recognize their potential so they can split off into other sustainable or regenerative ones. Marnie and I got to thinking, in a very non-hacker-like way, "can we approach land development and communities this way?" Well, a couple of tiny housers can dream about distributed networks, right? Although long overdue, it's about time to start work with all these technologies for another big purpose. Let's call it the 'Internet of Land'. Whatever it's going to be called, land development and community design is going to soon network differently. And fear not, all you baby-boomer tiny house enthusiasts, this is not something that tech-savvy millennials just had an epiphany on. There were some influential authors who have already hinted at this in their circa-1960's books. See, I knew we could all find common ground!

On an inspirational side note, we found that there's nothing that should stop an entrepreneur, including eco-conscious tiny house entrepreneurs, from building as big a business and making as much profit as they want. The ones that succeed in this information age will have to find that thoughtful and ethical balance between environmental and economic sustainability. Heck, since we like growth, let's go one better than sustainability and work on regenerative practices! Simply put, it's ok to think like or become a tiny house magnate. Just do it in a way that would make your family or community proud. There will probably be a few tiny house magnates in our lifetimes. They might even grow out of our startup ecosystem or a tiny house co-living incubator near you.

The future looks bright for Austin Live|Work, tiny houses and the emerging tiny house community network. As we grow older, the need for creating a self-sufficient supportive community is in the back of our minds. Marnie just finished her Master's in Gerontology, so we are also looking to add multi-generational and non-institutional solutions for older adults. We hope to encourage those who read our article, no matter which generation or what background, that they too can start planning their dream lifestyle and implementing on their ideas. Let's build a community!

If I Fail, At Least I Will Fail Big

Finding community in the rubble of pain and loss

Janet Ashworth

Janet is a woman filled by the spirit of an entrepreneur; determined to be a maker, a mover, and a shaker, who has taken her 20 years of sales and marketing experience and combined it with her creative drive to actualize her dream company, "Habitats Tiny Homes" and its accompanying community.

The tiny home movement has swept across the nation like the summer monsoon in India, and most people have seen pictures of them on the Internet or watched one of the numerous shows that have popped up on national television. It seems that almost everyone loves them, even if they would never consider living in one. So what is it about tiny homes that have created this avalanche of interest and why have tiny home owners had to go to battle to legally live in their tiny home on wheels?

My own tiny home journey began with the 2008 economy crash. I had just entered into a new relationship with someone I thought would be my partner long-term. I was also the mother of three incredible teen-aged children, and was making really decent money for the first time in my adult life. Things were pretty darn good. But soon after I moved in with my new love, life took a turn for the worse, and unbeknownst to me, I was about to suffer a string of unfortunate events that would last for years and take almost inhuman strength recuperate from.

From 2008 through 2013, almost every possible life stress imaginable hit me in rapid succession with Muhammad Ali-style vengeance: one blow after another. The initial stressors weren't from negative events. Instead, the initial stresses came from adapting to a new relationship, combining households, and blending families. My partner had a two-year-old son who lived with his mother most of the time, and I quickly found out she was the jealous type who thrived on drama. She began to intentionally cause problems for us. Just minor ones at first, but when I inadvertently discovered that her boyfriend had been physically abusing their son, this small boy came to live with us full-time. All out war ensued. There was a long, expensive custody battle, and the ex-wife drama intensified to the level of a Jerry Springer episode. An intense, emotional battle over a child where one of the parties cares more about the battle than the child, can strain even the best relationship. But that was the just beginning of our problems. Shortly after that, the failing economy caused us both to lose our jobs like thousands of other people across the nation. We began a financial downward spiral, like the last soap bubbles swirling around the bathtub drain, which then developed into a full-fledged sinking like the great ship Titanic in her last moments. First we were late on the credit cards, then the car payments, then the mortgage, and then even covering the basic necessities became difficult.

My partner's way of dealing with the stress was to drink and after a while my stomach would lurch at the sight of him walking in the door with that telltale, wrinkled, brown sack. And who could blame him really? He was a jolly drunk, but substance abuse is difficult on a partner no matter how cheery the perpetrator is when they're indulging. I quickly ascertained that his self worth was wrapped up in how much money he earned, the quality of his belongings, and his golf score. Without these things, his self-esteem seemed to plummet. The more he drank the more I went into fix-it mode. But no matter how valiant my efforts, things continued their downward spiral and the house moved into the initial foreclosure stages. As things got worse and the alcohol ceased to quiet his inner turmoil, he became increasingly unhappy and began to turn toward his religious upbringing for relief. As I ran around like a Marvel super hero with no actual powers trying to solve all our problems, he gave praying a try. As his drinking and praying increased, so did his resentment of me for attempting to manage the constant barrage of problems we faced everyday in a more real-time, earthly fashion. He frequently reminded me that the man is the head of the family. He began to criticize my children and I for not having the same religious beliefs. One day he asked me, "Maybe we're having all these problems because you're not a Christian?" Somehow my spiritual beliefs had caused not only the economic collapse of the entire planet, but also the custody battle with his ex-wife. I knew then that the relationship was doomed.

When the final foreclosure date came and we were given our "be out by" date, I remember trying to uplift his spirits by reminding him that hundreds of thousands of people were having the exact same experience and we should be grateful for the roof over our head and food in our bellies. I also told him it was just a house and as long as our kids were healthy, I felt extremely lucky. So imagine the shock and horror I felt that night when my cell phone rang at 11:00 p.m. As I glanced down at the other-worldly brightness of the screen and saw the name "Chris" in large, glowing letters I knew that things were about to get much, much worse.

Chris was my 23-year old daughter's boyfriend, and boyfriends don't generally call Mom at 11:00 p.m. unless something is wrong, and something was very, very wrong. When I answered the phone, the tone in Chris' voice caused my stomach to plummet like a newly broken elevator down its shaft. He was at the ER with my daughter and she was being prepped for an emergency brain surgery. He wasn't sure exactly what had happened. They were watching a movie and she suddenly complained of a really bad headache and then collapsed upon the floor. It was a 45-minute drive to the hospital that night and her surgery was to last six gut-wrenching hours.

During her surgery the minutes ticked by, each one stretched out like a single rubber band wrapped around a skyscraper high stack of envelopes. My mantra became "just let her live through the surgery." During my unspeakable pain, I was also torn apart for what my two sons and Chris had to endure. All of them were young men in their early twenties and this was a lot to deal with at any age. Writing about this five years later still brings tears stinging back to my eyes, causes my throat to tighten, and my stomach to seize. I remembered telling my partner that we were lucky as long as our kids were healthy and felt as though I gave the secret to my demise to some unknown force that was trying to destroy me.

Miraculously, my daughter did live through the surgery. I then began to focus on just hoping she would wake up from the deep, coma like state she seemed to be in. I spent two miserable weeks sleeping on the floor of her room in the ICU with my boys and Chris, wondering if my daughter would be able to speak, talk, eat, or live her life to the fullest if she did wake up. I felt a glimpse of the wretched, relentless, pounding grief a parent experiences when they lose a child and it scared the shit out of me. The financial hardship, foreclosure, bankruptcy, child custody battle, and relationship problems paled in comparison like a glow stick held up to the mid-day sun. As for my partner, he went completely fetal on me, curled up at home on the bed anesthetizing himself with booze, television, and "The Lord."

My daughter did wake up. She got released from the hospital, married Chris, and spent four years of her young, precious life recuperating. If you met her today, you would never know that she had been so derailed. The relationship with my partner didn't make it however. After four short years of marriage, we went our separate ways. I had endured horrible fights, financial ruin, and religious lectures. It was time I moved out.

So what does this gut-wrenchingly personal account have to do with tiny homes on wheels? When I moved out of our rented home in 2012, I was penniless, in my late 40's, done with relationships, and wondering what the heck I was going to do with my life. I had two very large dogs that I loved dearly and the only place I could afford to rent was a travel trailer parked in a lemon orchard on someone's property. It wasn't very nice either, the trailer, not the lemon orchard. But after I got through with the anger and sadness associated with a recent divorce – when I began to heal from being chewed up by life and spit back out like a bad piece of meat – I was filled with an immense feeling of peace and tranquility. I couldn't believe how fast my housework was after keeping up a four-bedroom household. Any impulse purchases I might be tempted to make were nipped in the bud, as I didn't have room for them. I took frequent hikes with the dogs and started my own garden in the lemon orchard. I read and took naps in a hammock slung in the trees. I took time to go to yoga class and taught myself to paint. And of course spent as much time with my grown kids as possible.

One day I was having a conversation with an acquaintance and was sharing my experience of peace and freedom that living in the trailer had imbibed. I mentioned that I would be happy living in a small space forever, but really didn't like the materials that trailers or RV's were made out of and didn't think they felt like a real home. This person introduced me to tiny homes on wheels. Well, I hadn't ever heard of tiny homes on wheels before, but I immediately did an Internet search and became obsessed with everything tiny. I started to plan and research building my own tiny home. I Googled, Pinned, Tweeted, and Instagrammed everything that had to do with tiny homes and I became determined to build my own in the very near future.

I started to try and save for my tiny home and continued to obsess and talk incessantly about them. I never again wanted to experience a bank-owned home that could be yanked out from under me if I hit a rough patch. I didn't want to continue to rent a home since every year the rents in San Diego continue to climb higher than a Mt. Everest adventure climber trying to beat the latest record. I never again wanted to maintain a large residence and fill it with unnecessary stuff, and knew I would never live with a partner again. A tiny home on wheels was the perfect solution to my long-term housing needs.

As the days swept by filled with tiny home planning, I knew it was also time to focus on my career again. I was living like a college student (sans the fun partying part), and I knew if I was ever going to build my tiny home I would need to start making money again. I began to search for a new job. I had a 20-year sales and marketing background and knew sales was my best career option. But I tried sales job after sales job after sales job. With each new job, I felt like my soul was being denied it's true purpose. Something inside me had changed along with the trauma my daughter experienced and the other hardships. I had experienced difficulties many times before, but it was different this time. The pain had been so intense, and the hardships so relentless, that a place deep inside me had grown as strong as the trunk of a giant redwood in the Sequoia National Forest. This deep place felt powerful and determined. My views on life had been transformed. I now knew that life could change on you fast and the little things that we take for granted most the time became the most precious. A walk on the beach with my dog, the sunset, a kiss, lunch with my daughter or boys, art, listening to live music, and just appreciating life became the most important things. I had never been materialistic, but working just to make money and pay the bills was somehow even less satisfying than before. I wanted to create and be a maker. I wanted to somehow make a difference.

The idea for Habitats Tiny Homes started out like a small annoyance similar to a fresh mosquito bite that hasn't quite yet started to itch. I call it an annoyance because it seemed ridiculous for me to even entertain the thought of starting my own tiny home company. Even though I ate, drank, and breathed everything tiny in my spare time, I had no money or resources, and felt I had no right to start my own business. So just like you would a pesky mosquito, I shooed the idea away. I continued to try different jobs and would last a few months and then quit. The small annoyance became a craving; a full-fledged, Coffee flavored, Haagen Daz-esque style craving that I also ignored. I ignored it as I designed the logo for Habitats Tiny Homes. I ignored it as I – dancing around the room with delight – came up with my tag line "Live Your Big Life in a Tiny Home." I ignored the craving as I ordered my lovely business cards from Vista Print. Then the craving turned into a need that was so powerful it made me angry. "I can't do it!" I would shout at the idea. "Maybe someday I will do it." If I just work hard enough for a little while maybe then I can start a tiny home business. But I knew "maybe someday" was a trap that most of us fall into as we drive our daily commutes in a robot like, road-rage filled stupor every morning and evening. I had seen how fast "maybe someday" can be stolen away. I had seen how, in an instant, my daughter had almost lost her "maybe somedays." It made me want to scream: "follow your dreams" to the world from the top of the highest downtown building.

So I continued to ignore the idea for Habitats Tiny Homes, even as I applied for a small business loan from the only place in town that would loan money to a start-up company with no resources. I thought about all the benefits that tiny homes had to offer the brave souls that were called to live in them. I thought about the local housing crisis in my hometown and in other dense, urban areas. I thought about the hundreds of thousands of people who had been foreclosed upon or evicted in the last few years. I thought about the swelling homeless population; the new homeless that were working in corporate offices only a few years prior. But I also thought about the beautiful, custom designed wood work, adorable floor-plans, sleeping lofts, and creative storage solutions that I was seeing in the tiny homes that were popping up all over the Internet. I thought of the environmental benefits that tiny living could bring to the planet. I thought about all the things that made me, you, and others all over the globe love tiny homes. I decided to leave it up to fate. If I got approved for the start-up loan, I would start Habitats Tiny Homes. And if I went for it, I was going to tap into the new, deep, powerful, determined place inside myself and give it everything I had.

As I waited for an answer from the bank, I continued to research tiny homes and tiny home living. I learned about the difficulties that tiny home owners were experiencing when it came to actually living in these adorable structures. Finding parking was difficult and living in a tiny home full-time was illegal in most places. Neighbors would complain about tiny homes parked in backyards, causing tiny-home owners to have to move from place to place. Even those that owned their own piece of land were finding they couldn't legally park and live full-time in their tiny home. I realized this problem would be even worse in a densely populated, expensive city like San Diego. Even as I hoped and waited for a yes answer from the bank, I realized that starting a successful tiny home company in San Diego meant solving the tiny home parking/living issue here as well.

I continued to research the laws associated with living in a tiny home. I sensed that there needed to be a professional, well organized; master planned, sexy, and somewhat large tiny home community plan. I thought about what I would want if I were to live in a tiny home community and came up with the vision for Habitats Tiny Homes Community. It would be 50 spaces; not huge, but certainly visible. It would be professionally landscaped with edible plants and succulents. San Diego is a desert in a severe draught so planning for ornamental landscaping would be irresponsible. The community would also need to be aesthetically pleasing and as *unlike* a traditional trailer park or mobile home park as possible. It would have a farmer's market style store, a coffee shop, a yoga and meditation hut, a garden, and a community fire-pit. And it would use technologies such as solar power and water reclamation to reduce the carbon footprint of the community.

When I got the yes from the bank I stopped ignoring Habitats Tiny Homes and I ran toward my future. I felt unstoppable, determined, and highly capable. I knew that my sales and marketing background gave me the skills necessary to pitch the idea to the local authorities in a mainstream and corporate way that would feel comfortable to them. I also tapped into my artistic and creative abilities to envision a community concept that would embrace the spirit of the tiny home movement. I also knew that I wasn't scared of failing. I used my small, start-up loan to pay a talented, local landscape architect to put my vision on paper and the concept design is stunning. I also hired a professional Webmaster and am thrilled with my website. These tools would be the face of Habitats Tiny Homes and create the initial impression that my customers would have of my company. It's been three month since Habitats Tiny Homes and Habitats Tiny Homes Community was launched and the response has been far greater and more positive than anything I could have imagined. So far, two local news stations, and the crew of a tiny home documentary in the making have interviewed me. I continue to be contacted by the media regarding future interviews. More than 14 people have reserved their space in the community with $1000.00 deposits reflecting their level of commitment. I've hired a full-time Master Carpenter and have begun my own tiny home build. The framing is finished and this tiny home will also serve as a model for the company. I've also received several orders for tiny homes and I've been asked to write and contribute as an author and voice of the movement.

But, I'm not saying all this in an effort to gain adulation or to brag. What I have to say is this: tiny homes are here to stay and they are a viable and elegant solution to the world's growing housing and environmental challenges. Tiny house communities are popping up across the nation and around the globe and come in all shapes and sizes. Habitats Tiny Homes and Habitats

Tiny Homes Community is an idea that was born from the desires of thousands of people who want to live the tiny home lifestyle and do it legally. This idea chose me to help it come to fruition.

As author Elizabeth Gilbert suggest in her book *Big Magic* that ideas are a living entity that are separate from us yet dependent on us to help them come to fruition. They buzz around the universe trying to find the one person just crazy enough to stop flicking the idea away, or stop ignoring the idea long enough to say "yes."

"Yes" I said to this idea. "I will make this happen. I'm your girl."

Had I kept ignoring the idea, it would have found someone else with enough bravery, determination, and fearlessness to assist it into being and it is my bravery and fearlessness that I will rely on as I help this idea become reality. The thought of creating a home for up to 50 tiny-home owners in San Diego fills my soul with a sense of purpose. I think of the bravery, determination, and fearlessness I now have as the gifts that were given to me for enduring some seemingly insurmountable challenges. When you have stood at the "gates of hell" and suffered great pain, loss and almost lost something that is so precious to you that you would be left a wretched shell of human being, you have no fear of losing any longer. When I embraced this idea and forged ahead I thought, "If I fail, at least I will fail big and I'll fail trying to make a difference"! That, my friends, is living. And it's what "Living Your Big Life in a Tiny Home" is all about.

Chasing Community

On an expedition to find the heart of community

Alexis Stephens

Alexis Stephens and Christian Parsons of Tiny House Expedition, are a filmmaker duo and ordinary couple taking an extraordinary road trip across the US and Canada with their DIY tiny house on wheels in tow. Through their documentary storytelling and direct community engagement, they seek to inspire people to think BIG and build small as means to provide more quality, affordable housing & more connected communities. Creative use of tiny housing is cultivating more connected community experiences and more meaningful relationships, for multi-millionaires to those transitioning out of homelessness; the tiny house itself is just the beginning of *Turning Tiny!*

In the ultimate aligning of the stars and manifestation of many of my personal goals, I somehow found myself in the best relationship of my life, traveling the country in a hand-crafted tiny home on wheels that my boyfriend and I built together. It all began with a few major life changes, much perspiration and a thirst for community.

> *The ache for home lives in all of us, the safe place*
> *where we can go as we are and not be questioned.*
> —Maya Angelou

For most of my life the yearning for home has burdened my spirit. Growing up, I moved at least ten times, across state lines and from one parent's household to the others, living in both rural and suburban settings. Being the new kid was never fun, and feelings of belonging were definitely fleeting. I never felt rooted. It was not until I was adult that I felt like I had a hometown: Winston-Salem, NC. It is the place I've spent the most consecutive years of life, eight to be exact. The ache for acceptance continued to plague me, and any sense of belonging I developed was fragile. I felt isolated and lost, but I was in search of the cure.

A profound perspective shift proved to be the antidote. Fortunately during my divorce, I had few life-changing realizations. First, I realized that I must love myself before I could be adequate partner, friend, or mother. Self-love is crucial to feeling comfortable in your own skin. This comfortability leads to an internal sense of peace; key to finding acceptance and for nurturing healthy relationships. Second, open communication is everything in life. It is the best way to feel heard, have proactive discourse and find solutions to any issue bothering you. Third, I was overwhelmed by my life. My life was running me, not the other way around. Sources of this feeling came from, among other things, too much house to maintain, and to my surprise, too many possessions. My house was a modest 900 square feet, and I was definitely not wealthy. Nevertheless, my house was packed full of junk. It's true. I was a packrat. Over the years, I developed a bad habit of impulse, "feel good" shopping coupled with another bad habit of holding onto everything, from ratty old t-shirts to brochures from places I had visited, and whole host of random odds and ends.

These realizations led me to find a sense purpose and craft a holistic sense of home. I set a handful of complementary goals. I would externalize my feelings and work to improve my relationships, personal and professional, through more open communication. What's more, I would embrace everyday adventure by pushing myself outside of my comfort zone. I would simplify my life in search of inner peace. During this time, I emphasized spending time to nurture my well-being through activities like yoga, learning how to meditate and spending more time outside. I also actively sought out opportunities to connect more with others, including spending more time with friends and in the community— volunteering, attending local community events and starting conversations with folks I didn't know, etc. I discovered my love of building my own community through fostering relationships and direct connection with my neighbors, from all over town. This I found also served to nurture my soul and well-being. I began to feel more comfortable in my skin than ever before, and my sense of home and belonging also grew.

Unfortunately, my feelings of being overwhelmed were not subsiding very much. This is partially to be blamed on my glacially slow start to downsizing. Beginning the process seemed incredibly daunting. My boyfriend and veteran downsizer Christian, proved to be major source of support and coaching. He encouraged me to focus on one room at a time and start with the easy 'pickins' in each room; the true junk items. Item by item and layer by layer, downsizing started to become exhilarating. How good it felt to declutter my space and unburden myself from the noise that was cluttering my mind. It was a healing process, an act of self-love. I was letting go of things that were holding me back, and keeping me from growing. The downsizing process enabled me to see and feel each item for what it was—either something that resonated with me and I loved dearly, something that was crucial to my daily living experience or something that was just taking up space. Truly minimalizing my possessions to uncover myself, learning what was most important to me and what wasn't. This process was taken into overdrive, once the decision was made to go tiny, specifically build our own tiny house on wheels. It all started with a road trip to Michigan and a mutual love of teardrop trailers.

The summer of 2014, Christian and I decided to take a road trip together. We decided a ten hour drive was reasonable, and looked on the map for places we could reach within ten hours of Winston-Salem. Lake Michigan! Neither of us had been, so it was the perfect choice. We had a delightful adventure, stopping at roadside attractions along the way, exploring a beautiful state park and making friends with other campers. It was not without its moments of frustration. Traveling maybe one of the best ways to really get know someone. How you learn or don't learn to communicate with your partner, especially in a small space like in a tent or Honda Element for hours on end, may just make or break your relationship. In our case, we realized how well we worked together and what a special connection we had. We know we wanted to travel more, together. Christian had been researching how to build a teardrop trailer, and we loved the idea of the flexibility and joys of traveling with more creature comforts. One fortuitous day, he mentioned that for a little more money we could build a tiny house on wheels. *What?* I have always loved cozy spaces and cabins but had no idea that you could combine the hominess and durability of a stick-built structure with the mobility of a travel trailer.

(Cue: A research binge.) I plunged myself into reading everything I could find on tiny houses and the tiny house movement. It was absolutely thrilling to learn how TH pioneers were creating their own freedom through tiny living, a do-it-yourself lifestyle. Choosing housing in a way that makes sense for your life— your personality, lifestyle preferences, goals — proves you can create your own freedom. A freedom from the limiting, often unfulfilling status quo of the mainstream American lifestyle was actually attainable. It seemed that small space living was an opportunity to embrace more conscious living, providing more room to develop as an individual. It was also an opportunity to become a more active member of the community. This resonated deeply with me. How perfectly the tiny house lifestyle seemed to fit with this new post-divorce era of my life. I was embracing independence, self-love, simplicity, community and adventure. I was in love, both with tiny houses and with Christian. Time to move forwards to building our own tiny home on wheels!

This newfound love for tiny housing awoke a burning desire to embrace my inner storyteller. In my research, I was struck by the diversity of the movement, so many inspiring advocates and tiny house community projects. These diverse, often grassroots-driven housing projects all have the potential to amplify the individual's tiny living benefits to a broader purpose, making

positive impact in the surrounding community. A growing number of individuals, groups and even cities are embracing tiny housing in variety of forms and community models, for a variety of purposes. A common thread connecting these vibrant projects is an attempt to creatively address modern housing issues and increased need and desire for sustainable living through tiny housing. Beyond that, there appeared to be another heartening common thread. The people behind these projects are what I would call community-makers. My theory is that these community-makers, savvy innovative thinkers and problem solvers, are by nature empathetic towards their neighbors and their surroundings.

Community-makers are central to the heart and soul of the tiny house movement, and their pioneering spirit and projects are on the cutting-edge of the modern housing spectrum. Will all these projects be successes? Probably not, but imagine the stories to be told, lessons to be gleaned and sheer inspiration potential. After hours and hours of research, it became clear to me that the big picture story of the movement, encompassing the grass-roots efforts led by tiny house advocates, along with the TH community experience needed to be told. This joyous light bulb realization meant I could take my love of tiny living on the road to embrace adventure in my own life while sparking meaningful conversations about rethinking housing and the meaning of home. I relished the opportunity to get back to my filmmaking roots. So naturally I pitched Christian, who was already keen on the idea of building a tiny. As a man of adventure who is happiest with a backpack and camera, he quickly agreed.

There's nothing like building a house, an unconventional house at that, to make you reconsider the idea of what makes home, home. We all know a home is more than four walls and roof, whether 130 sq. ft. or 2500 sq. ft. The meaning of home goes far beyond the physical structure; it's also a state of mind. Even though our house was in progress, the sense of home frequently washed over both of us, as we toiled away, often with the help of friends. This warm sense of sanctuary and comfort comes from having a place of our own, especially a place that is being tailored just for you. In life, nothing feels better than having a secure, comfortable place to come back to where you can be yourself.

After nine months of building we completed our tiny home. Christian spent the first night in the house alone, parked in downtown Winston-Salem. The next day we had an epic housewarming party. With the help of friends, sponsors and local community organizations, we temporarily transformed a private green space in downtown into a pop-up park and tiny house community showcase, featuring two tiny houses on wheels and one container house. Approximately 3,000 folks came out to learn about alternative ways of living. How many people from all walks of life showed up, in the oppressive heat, no less, blew us away. The line was long and the conversations were lively. Nothing starts conversations and brings smiles to faces like tiny houses. This event was intended to help further a community wide conversation on the role of tiny housing in Winston-Salem.

After our event, we had a few weeks to settle into our new home and get accustomed to the new rhythms of daily life. And without hesitation, we launched our cross-country journey with a purpose, Tiny House Expedition. We set off with the intention of documenting developing and existing tiny house community projects across the US and Canada. With our adventurous goal in mind, we embarked on our first highway trip with our tiny house on wheels. We had poured our hearts and souls into our house, and now we were sending it off into the great messy, unpredictable world. So, of course, we had to pay our dues to the road. The first stop, Habitat for Humanity ReStore of Cabarrus County, in Kannapolis, NC. We pulled up just in time for the start of the scheduled tiny house open house. There was already a crowd waiting for us. Quickly I opened the front door, only to find the globe of our ceiling fan light shattered on the floor. We had a big day ahead, and I chose not to see this as a bad omen but a learning experience. Later that day, we had the honor of documenting the dedication of the local Habitat's first tiny home (on foundation), part of their pilot program. This all started because of one Habitat employee's passion for tiny housing. Shirley Kennerly kick-started the investigation into adding tiny homes to their housing portfolio. This groundbreaking program, unlike anything the vast majority of affiliates nationwide are doing, seeks to serve a specific population most in need in Kannapolis, and unable to qualify for Habitat's traditional homes. This includes singles or couples on fixed incomes. Their first three planned tiny homes will form a pocket neighborhood within a historic "mill housing" neighborhood. The city of Kannapolis welcomed this development with open arms. Their first tiny home was handicap accessible and the mortgage and utilities came to only $300 per month. The situation was perfectly suited for the new homeowner Barbara. She had longed to be able to set down roots and become an accepted member of society. Barbara had been homeless on and off, and was now unable to work full-time, and is living off of disability. Home ownership is something she thought would always out of her reach. Now thanks to Habitat and her invested sweat equity, her future was now secure. At the dedication ceremony that evening, a big crowd of supporters filled the yard in front of her house. I lost it and was unable to stop crying. I felt so silly to cry in front of the crowd. I was overwhelmed by Barbara's joy and incredibly grateful to be there to document this historic day. It was an unforgettable first stop of many, many more to follow.

A tiny house road trip is an extraordinary experience in an extraordinary mode of transport. Each highway trip feels like an adventure, and a bit like a parade. It's not everyday you see a house traveling 55 miles per hour down the road. There are always delightful reactions from fellow travelers, occasional honks, waves and countless thumbs up and picture taking. Gas stations stops can be quite the social gathering, sometimes overwhelming but always a great educational opportunity. Christian likes to say, tiny houses are like puppies. The biggest, cutest puppy we've ever seen. Everybody wants to touch it and talk about it. Folks come up to us with all kinds of questions. *Why a tiny house? Do you build them? Where did it come from; where's it going? How does it work? What's in it and does it have a bathroom?* The biggest response we get from our random encounters has to be, "I've seen the show!" You might be surprised to learn of how many have commented that they've never seen anything like it and have no knowledge of tiny houses. But what I find remarkable is that I learn this bit of information because these individuals feel compelled to talk to me. At a typical gas station experience, we wouldn't have had reason to connect. The eye catching nature and adorability of the tiny house is an effective ice-breaker and way to get folks thinking more deeply about alternatives to traditional housing, sustainability and what is really needed to be happy. It's heartwarming to realize we are spreading smiles and sparking discussion wherever we go.

The spontaneous conversations and sometimes friendships that form from brief encounters with those we meet at stops along the way, especially at events, is perhaps the highlight of our trip.

Many such conversations have occurred at RV parks where we often park. Our first RV park experience was especially memorable.

It was a lovely park in rural Virginia with a saltwater pool, situated in the backyard of a local racetrack. Within moments of arriving a dozen RV'ers swarmed our tiny house. They were curious and excited. Most of these folks were full-timers. Two guys offered us help with a propane issue we were having. One couple invited us to dinner, which we happily took them up on. To their delight, we couldn't resist offering an impromptu open house. This was the first tiny house on wheels they had ever seen in-person or at all, and they wanted to learn all about it.

Later at dinner we learned that this couple had fallen on hard times and been living in their RV for three years. They found that small space living was quite liberating but the wife, who was a tiny house enthusiast, longed for a homier space built from more quality materials. For now, this was not in the cards but when there was a little more money saved up, they could have their own THOW. In the morning, as we prepared to leave, a sweet little girl stopped by with a gift. It was a mini replica of our tiny home. My heart melted. To this day her picture still hangs on our fridge.

Months later, we found ourselves in the sunshine state exploring a different kind of RV park: Orlando Lakefront, a Tiny Home and RV Community. It's a growing community in a revitalized 1950's RV park, featuring a beautiful lake and bird sanctuary. It's one of the first RV parks in the nation to transition to a "Tiny House Park." The heartbeat of this lush tiny home community is James Taylor, the tiny house host with the most. He's a charismatic tiny house community advocate always looking for opportunities to help others pursue their tiny house dreams. As the part-time community manager, he is the point person for all interested in living tiny at the community. Adam Money, the owner of Orlando Lakefront, seeks to create both an aesthetically pleasing and warm, friendly community environment for all residents. He's in no rush to show traditional RV'ers the door as many have been long time residents in good standing. Adam sees a long-term opportunity to transform his park, and he wants to do it gradually.

During our short whirlwind stay we were immediately embraced by the tiny house residents we met. We shared stories of tiny living and our hobbies, laughing until our cheeks hurt. The sense of home we felt was unmistakable. Yes, this was our tribe. The tiny housers were a diverse group, ranging in age from early twenties to late sixties. They socialize together often, and offer each other help with daily activities and emotional support, when called for. Sometimes overzealous tiny house enthusiasts will venture into the community and look in their windows. As a result, the tiny house neighbors developed a texting system instead of knocking, to ensure boundaries are being respected.

This tiny house tribe is a tribe in the purest sense, a collection of individuals sharing a common interest. Tiny house community means connecting over the common ground of tiny houses, but it's so much more. The house is the launch pad for a more connected, meaningful lifestyle. Tiny house living encourages closer connection to your surroundings and naturally, more social interaction with your neighbors.

Several thousand miles down the road, we pulled into another tiny house community, lovingly referred to as the "Airstream Park" by its residents.

Llamalopolis – as some people also refer to it as – is a tiny house and Airstream village in the Fremont East District in the heart of downtown Las Vegas. In the fall of 2014 the park was just another empty lot. Long ago it had been an RV park and still retained some of its infrastructure like hookups, though now in disrepair. Along came a visionary by the name of Tony Hsieh, the CEO of Zappos. He was looking for a new place to call home, and just so happened he owned a combined total of 33 Tumbleweeds and Airstreams. An idea came along to park all these at the old RV park to conduct a community experiment. Tony invited 30 friends to stay at the lot for one week to explore ideas for how to create a functioning, sustainable community. A simple setup on what was just an empty, paved lot, now brought to life by group of dreamers and friends. During their stay, they would all gather around the fire to cook, talk and listen to music. After a couple of nights, Tony and several others already knew they wanted to stay for good. For Tony, an extraordinarily successful man, this would become his full-time residence. A simple and definitely unique urban tiny house community model has organically evolved, to best meet the needs of its residents; while the structure of the community has deliberating been molded to foster daily spontaneous social encounters. The park is continually evolving and now has the goal of achieving net zero energy.

We entered Llamalopolis through a llama decorated gate, and immediately found ourselves in an enchanting semi-covered tunnel filled with twinkling lights and lined with trees. Later we learned this recycled element came from a local Christmas display. You can just make out the tiny homes in the background, and you can clearly smell the nearby alpaca pin. It opens up to the "living room"; an outdoor, shared space centered around two fire pits and a stage. Christian and I certainly didn't know what to expect when we came for a visit. We were completely taken back by how to down-to-earth the residents are. They come from varied professional and socioeconomic backgrounds. They were all a delight to have as neighbors. They proved to be fun, kind, and fascinating neighbors, including both full-time and part-time residents. The community itself felt like a big, warm family including a wide assortment of animals (chickens, alpacas, dogs and cats). We ended up staying for two weeks and couldn't have felt more welcomed or more at home.

Regarding the structure of the community, the shared common areas act as an extension of living space for each resident and their respective sleek Airstream or cozy Tumbleweed tiny house, which all face toward these spaces. The entire community is enclosed by 5 ft. high fence. This helps maintain a sense of safety, and we found, also fosters a connected community feel. The style and vibe of the community is reminiscent of Burning Man. The air is filled with music and smoke from the fire pits, that are always burning once the sun goes down. Spontaneous conversations and impromptu potlucks are common. We learned that there's an emphasis on each resident contributing to the community. These contributions are based around an individual's natural gifts and abilities. For instance, resident Daniel Park is a professional musician, and he often contributes music for the enjoyment of his neighbors. One evening I contributed a home-cooked meal. As we got to know our temporary neighbors, we were intrigued to learn that many of them are introverts. Resident Krissee remarked that she loved people, but left to her our own introverted tendencies, she wouldn't regularly interact with others, even though this was an important part of maintaining a healthy sense of wellbeing. Living at the park was a perfect opportunity for her to enjoy her neighbors' company, and always have the option of retreating to her private cozy haven. For Tony, living here isn't about living small at all. In fact, he said this was the biggest home he has ever lived in. His life was outside his tiny home, or his "bedroom." The community life, he found, is essential to feeling part of something more meaningful, a more alive way of life.

Through our travels thus far, Christian and I are left with a more poignant meaning of home. For us, home is a sense of community; a feeling of belonging and security. It is a place of our own and connection with others, that enables us to our best selves. It's also more literally our cozy tiny home, and simply being together.

As we continue to travel, we hope to find more communities around the country embracing a greater diversity of homes and residents. When surrounded by a supportive environment we can all find a sense of belonging. We all tend to care more about our neighbors when we know them, when it's personal. Nothing can be more destructive than being isolated from society, feeling like you don't belong. When people really care about a community and embrace its diversity, they can make it better. They can create a sense home for themselves and all of their neighbors. Christian and I take this to heart. We are both chasing community and crafting our own. Now, time to continue our adventure!

Simply Home Community
Sharing our lives in tiny cohousing

Lina Menard

Lina Menard is a small house designer, dweller, builder, consultant, and advocate who keeps a blog calledThis Is The Little Life, featuring vignettes about simple living in small spaces. Through her sustainable design consulting company, Niche Consulting LLC, Lina helps people design and build their own tiny dream homes and communities. In *Turning Tiny*, Lina shares her experience as one of the first residents at Simply Home Community, a tiny cohousing community in Portland, OR, where she lives in her gypsy wagon, The Lucky Penny.

The Proposal

We were at a Portland Alternative Dwellings' Tiny House Mixer one evening when Tony popped the question.

"So… do you want to move in with me?" he asked.

It was the most exciting proposal I'd ever received.

"Yes!" I replied enthusiastically. "Yes! Yes! Yes!"

Then I caught myself as the 'what ifs' began.

"I mean, probably." I hedged. "With the contingency that I have to see the place and feel like it's a good fit. But yes, of course! Yes, please!"

It was the spring of 2014 and I had been working four 10-hour days on my Vardo each week while also working three 10-hour days as the sustainability coordinator for a green building project. My days were exhilarating and utterly exhausting. I didn't have time to think about where to park my tiny house on wheels once it was done; however, by this point I'd lived in a travel trailer, a yurt, and two tiny houses on wheels. I had developed a robust faith that the universe had some crazy new plan up her sleeve for me.

So when happy-go-lucky, geek extraordinaire, cowboy carpenter Tony told me that he, his wife Aline, and our fellow tiny house enthusiasts Karin and Ben were saving a spot for me in the first tiny cohousing community in the country, it felt like a veritable miracle. All I had to do was visit the community, agree to the Community Living Agreements, and claim my spot. I'd been fantasizing about tiny house community for the better part of a decade. Now I was being invited to join a tiny house community that four other people had worked their tails off to manifest. We scheduled a day for me to come and visit the property so I could make a final decision.

Rewind: My Turning Tiny Journey

For as long as I can remember, I've intended to someday design and build myself a house. I was that kid who spent long afternoons designing houses with Legos and building forts under the back deck. When I learned about the social and environmental benefits of cohousing in my ninth grade Human Ecology class I had a eureka moment that sustainable design is more impactful on the community level than the household level. I especially loved the cohousing model where everyone has a little space of their own and shares extensive common spaces, giving them access to things they wouldn't otherwise have.

Because of this early encounter with community planning, I decided my life goal was to live in and help design thriving communities. My fascination with community development and sustainability – and intentional communities in particular – continued throughout high school and college. When I dedicated my undergraduate thesis to intentional communities, I marveled at how the benefits of community living are exponential rather than linear. I discovered there are practical reasons to share resources from an environmental and financial standpoint; people can lower housing costs and ecological footprints as they own less and share more. However, the deal-sealers for me have always been the social and emotional benefits. I especially loved hearing about coming home to a home-cooked meal several nights a week (while only cooking a couple times a month), having lots of hands (and brains and backs) for work parties, and creating traditions together through celebrations and holidays.

I knew that someday I wanted this sort of collective lifestyle for myself. In 2007 some friends and I attempted to create a cohousing community with "normal size" homes in Walla Walla, Washington, but we weren't able to rally critical mass. Many meetings, bylaws, conference calls, and articles of incorporation later, our group dissolved and the members made other housing plans. Around the same time, I learned about tiny houses when a colleague left a Yes! Magazine story on my desk about Dee Williams, who was soon to become my tiny house hero. I sent an email to one of the members of our cohousing group, floating the idea of creating a cohousing community of tiny houses. She was as fascinated as I was, but we weren't sure there would be other people interested in tiny house community.

Fast Forward: Envisioning Tiny House Community

Now let's fast forward five years, from that moment in 2007 when I decided tiny houses and cohousing should really get acquainted, to the summer of 2012. I was living in a backyard cottage (also known in Portland as an accessory dwelling unit or ADU) and studying construction project management for my masters degree in urban planning at Portland State University. I had my summer dream job finishing out Tandem, a tiny house that's now located at Caravan – The Tiny House Hotel for nightly rental. By this point I had lived in a travel trailer as well as Bayside Bungalow – a tiny house on wheels that I rented from my pal Brittany Yunker. I was also doing My 200 Things Challenge so I could move into a 12' diameter yurt. I had been trying out different small spaces to inform design decisions for the tiny house on wheels I was going to build myself.

That summer I wrote a blog post about my vision for tiny cohousing. You can jump on over to my blog to read it in its entirety if you like, but I'll sum it up here. My big idea was to create a tiny cohousing community in the city by purchasing a big lot with a small existing home (which would become a common house) and parking a handful of tiny houses in the backyard as detached bedrooms. I imagined that the common house would include a big living room for gatherings, a dining room for shared meals, laundry facilities, and a bathroom with toilet, bathtub, shower, and sink so that the tiny houses wouldn't necessarily need to have these things. And, of course, most importantly, there would be a common kitchen in which to cook tasty things with full-sized cookie sheets and a freezer that actually keeps the ice cream cold. (After living in tiny houses with tiny freezers for two years I'd learned that even ice-cream-loving-lil-ol-me can't eat a pint of it at once, no matter how melty it is!)

I could see this tiny cohousing community in my mind's eye and I was hoping that my urban planning experience would help me make it happen. Two years later, this fantasy was a reality, and even better, I was one of the lucky first residents!

The Ingredients for Tiny House Community

If there was a recipe for creating tiny cohousing, it might read something like this:

At least 4 people with "can do" attitudes
Several dozen potluck dinners
Countless brainstorming sessions
2 winks and 1 nod
1 set of Community Living Agreements
Several dozen handwritten letters
1 afternoon on a bicycle
At least 1 person (preferably two) with excellent credit and a well-paying job
1 30-year mortgage
4 tiny houses on wheels

But, of course, the instructions are a little complicated and the prep time is horribly underestimated. So here's how it worked out for us at Simply Home Community.

In the summer of 2012, while I was envisioning a tiny cohousing community, my friends Karin and Tony were each building their own tiny houses on wheels. I'd met Tony and Karin through Portland Alternative Dwellings workshops and they were as interested in tiny house community as I was. Ben Campbell, whom I met when I coordinated a Pedalpalooza Tiny House

Bike Tour was also planning to build himself a tiny house and he was interested in community living, too.

All things considered, these were still the early days of this most recent wave of the tiny house movement. Tiny houses weren't yet A Thing here in Portland (nor anywhere else). So people wouldn't go looking for "tiny house" on a Meet Up or Facebook group. Our means were subtler. We found each other through word of mouth or sometimes we'd just spot a tiny house while biking through a neighborhood and tape a note on the door. One way or another, we were finding our people.

We began convening monthly potlucks for tiny house enthusiasts to discuss the possibilities. Our group started out with four. Then we were six. Then ten. And before long a group sixteen of us were meeting regularly. Of course, none of us had spaces big enough to host said potlucks since most of us lived in tiny houses at this point. So we gathered up at parks in the summertime. During the rainy season (which is the other nine months of the year here in Portland) we met up at brewpubs and eventually at Good Life Medicine Center, which was founded by Karin.

Originally the primary goal of our group was to make tiny houses legal so that we could put a bunch of them together. We created all sorts of plans for how to legalize tiny houses. We broke into subcommittees so that we could look for land, discuss petitions, draft proposals, and hold meetings with city officials. We were trying to figure out if it made sense to convert an existing RV park, place tiny houses on a sliver of leftover land from a transportation project as a "holding use" until a project of "higher and better use" came along, or develop a planned unit development. We were exploring funding options and zoning variances for these ventures. We quickly discovered that we were both out of our league financially and ahead of our time. City officials we spoke to typically explained that they had bigger fish to fry. They were addressing issues of violence, inequity, and access. The reminded us of those useful old adages "ask forgiveness, not permission" and "code enforcement is on a by-complaint basis." We got the sense that there were plenty of blind eyes turned towards us and our little houses – and we realized that might not be such a bad thing after all.

Learning the Lingo

One of the pivot points for our tiny house community group was when I went down to the bureau of planning and development with a woman who owned a property with an existing home and wanted to put tiny houses in the yard to rent. We met with someone from the building department and explained what we were trying to do.

He knitted his eyebrows and said "Hold up. So this 2000 square foot house, is it permitted?" We explained that it was.

"And these other ones," he continued. "They're on wheels?"

"Yes, they're basically custom built travel trailers," we explained.

"Well then, they're not our jurisdiction. They exist in the air space, but not on the ground. They're not buildings. They're vehicles. You'll need to talk to zoning."

So we went over to talk to zoning and explained our vision for tiny cohousing again.

"Let me get this straight…" the zoning guru said. "You have six people – which is the maximum number of unrelated individuals who can make up a household – who share an existing house and some of them want to park their recreational vehicles on the property?"

"Well…" I hesitated, ready to explain it all over again.

"Right…?!" she said, this time nodding slowly and giving us two exaggerated winks.

"Oh, yes," I replied. "That's exactly what we are trying to do."

"Well as long as you're complying with all setbacks and all use requirements, I don't think there would be a zoning issue," she said.

And *that* is how we were spoon-fed the way to create a tiny house community in Portland at that time.

I reported back to the group about the conversation we'd had with the zoning official and suggested we create a tiny cohousing community like I'd been fantasizing about. Maybe we could move forward with a community like this in a single-family residential zone because as long as we really *did* all use the common house and treat our tiny houses like detached bedrooms, we were basically operating as a single household in a shared house.

Some folks dropped out of the group at that point because they didn't want to move forward if tiny houses weren't legal yet. And I could certainly relate. I'd been nervous a few times myself. But I'd also lived in small "pre-legal" structures all across the city for the past few years. By this time Portland was already the epicenter of the tiny house universe, so we figured it was the best place to create the first tiny cohousing community. Portland is exploratory, experimental, and entrepreneurial. We're not afraid to give it a go and laugh at ourselves, and our mistakes if we make a royal mess of it. The city wasn't actively rallying around tiny houses but they certainly weren't doing anything to stop our endeavors.

So the Land Scouting Committee moved forward full-steam ahead and I hunkered down to work on my tiny house. And then we reconvened in that magic moment I first described where Tony made me an offer I couldn't refuse.

Creating Simply Home Community

Meanwhile, here's what they were up to. In the spring of 2014 Tony, Aline, Karin, and Ben met weekly (and sometimes more often) to arrange the logistics of creating Simply Home Community. They worked hard to create a set of Community Living Agreements, which everyone could agree to live by. The Community Living Agreements is a dynamic document that provides guidelines on everything from dogs and drugs to dinners and dishes.

Karin, Tony, Ben, and Aline also formed an LLC and created a set of bylaws to arrange for financial and legal systems. However, when they began looking at how the LLC could purchase property, they discovered banks tend to offer more favorable rates to individuals (and especially to married couples) than to companies. So they determined that the best course of action was to have Tony and Aline purchase a property and transfer ownership of the land over to the LLC. They scouted for property all across the city, with a focus on large lots and relatively affordable land values.

After several months of working with a realtor, Tony decided to get serious. He's the what-are-we-waiting-for sort of person and standard operating procedure for real estate transactions was frustrating him. So he spent a morning handwriting letters explaining what we were trying to do and then spent an afternoon riding around the NE Portland on his bicycle, putting letters on people's doors. He got three responses from homeowners interested in selling their property for a tiny house community. The property he and Aline selected was a third of an acre with a 1400 square foot 1930s farmhouse, a garage, majestic trees, flowers, established fruit trees, and several spots in the yard that were simply begging for tiny houses to be parked there.

Settling In

Tony and Aline moved into the top floor of The Big House in July of 2014 and began making it home. I moved into the basement of The Big House a few weeks later. (My tiny house was still under construction at Green Anchors and I wanted to get it a further along before I brought it to Simply Home.) The three of us in The Big House started trying out the Community Living Agreements right away and began revising them as we learned the quirks of our house.

Karin moved to Simply Home in late August with her beloved house, Serenity (named, of course, after the home, sweet home of our favorite space pirates). She had built her tiny house a couple years prior and lived in a few other spots already by the time she founded Simply Home Community. She wanted to be fully engaged as a community member and she was excited to dig in the dirt and grow a garden in a place that would be hers for the foreseeable future. Her little house seemed to put down roots as soon as Karin nestled her into her spot behind the plum tree.

Tony's little house arrived in September. He had been building his tiny house, The Rustic, when he and Aline met and he lived in it for about a year while they were dating. However, Aline explained that, as much as she loved him and the tiny house, she didn't want to raise their children in a tiny house, thank you very much! Now that they had plans to start a family, Tony brought his tiny house to Simply Home Community to rent it out and give someone a chance to try on tiny for themselves.

Ben moved his little house to Simply Home Community in September after a mighty push to finish it up, which included a great many of his friends and his tiny house heroes. His vardo was parked right under the oak tree at the end of our path and he built himself a little porch so that he could sit there to enjoy the comings and goings.

My not-quite-finished-yet tiny house, The Lucky Penny, joined the others at Simply Home Community in mid-October and we tucked her into the spot between The Big House and The Rustic. In this location, the skylight provided an awesome view of the birch tree overhead and The Big House was conveniently right next door.

Shortly after I moved in we had a renter join us in The Rustic, bringing our count up to six. We hosted a housewarming party in November. It happened to fall on the coldest day of the year, so it was nice to have our friends come visit to celebrate and warm our houses. The party was complete with little treats in the little houses, lots of fabulous food and drink, music and dancing, movies on the projection screen, and a fire in the fire pit. It was so nice to be home!

Our Visible and Invisible Structures

Once our houses were settled onto the land, we began to make improvements to the property. One of our first community projects was constructing a bike shelter. (It's Portland, after all, and we've got to uphold the 2 bikes per person ratio!) Shortly after, we built a garden shed and a wood shed. We've dug into the garden, too, planting veggies and fruits. We've done our best to

keep up with the bounty of this land and we've gotten even more ambitious for this next year.

We also began settling into routines and rhythms. We have a meeting every week, alternating between logistics meetings and heart meetings. Logistics meetings are the time to take care of business while heart meetings have included everything from visioning sessions and personality tests to baking cookies and enjoying the soaking pool at McMenamin's. We have work parties (also known as "play parties") for two hours every Sunday morning to work in the garden or do home improvement projects. (Anyone who can't make it to work party makes up for their time at some other point during the week.) We also rotate through our "bashi chores" – taking turns putting the compost out, sweeping the floors, and tidying the communal bathroom in The Big House. We save money by sharing resources including a bulk buy for food, a shared Netflix account, and a family phone plan. We also help pay the mortgage with our lower than market rent, so it's seven people paying it, instead of two!

Knowing we can get a hug one way or the other when we come home is definitely a perk, but for most of us, our very favorite thing about living here is community dinners. Since there are seven of us, we each have a night of the week that we cook. This means we all cook dinner only once a week but we get to come home to a home-cooked meal the other six nights of the week. (And if we can't make it to supper our meal is packed away in the fridge for our lunch the next day.) Additionally, as Tony puts it, "them that cooks, don't do dishes." Dinners are a chance for us to catch up on what's happening in each other's lives and since everyone has a different cooking style, we have plenty of variety.

Once a month we host a Simply Home Tiny House Community Tour to show our property to other people who want to see inside a tiny house or create a tiny house community of their own. We're always excited to share our challenges and lessons learned to help others avoid the mistakes we've made and learn from our triumphs. We explain that our biggest challenges were finding a group of people that were committed to living this way. We've learned that community is not for everyone, nor is every community or every time right for those people who are community-oriented. We've all had opportunities to grow and we've learned a great deal about how to live well together. Fortunately, this piece of land and this group of people are all in the right place at the right time.

Making "Community" Simply "Home"

Technically our one-year mark at Simply Home Community was in July if you count from the date we closed on the property, but we celebrate in the fall because that's when we all moved in and made it a community. By the time we celebrated our one-year anniversary, we'd already had quite a few transitions. Two of our community members had left and we'd added three new members: Lindsey lives in the bedroom on the main floor of The Big House, Jake moved into our basement bedroom, and Isha is renting The Rustic. (We also have another community member on the way since Aline and Tony are expecting a baby this summer!)

Ben and his little house have moved to a friend's house in the neighborhood and my little house, The Lucky Penny, was relocated to the spot under the oak tree. I love looking up at the branches, the stars, and the rain through my skylight. From this perspective, Raffi – my Devon Rex cat – and I enjoy seeing people come and go and watching the garden grow. However, my lil' house won't be in this spot long-term because I fell in love with the guy next door (really and truly!) and now we're planning a new tiny for two which will occupy this spot. Jake is also considering building himself a tiny house next summer and Karin has started scheming her Vardo, too.

Today was a fairly typical day here at Simply Home Community. I enjoyed breakfast with my sweetie before he headed to work. While I was doing my bashi chore for this month – taking out the garbage – I wished Jake a good day while he headed to work via bike. Then I began working on project management for design clients of mine. Tony and I took a break to chat for a bit and he showed me a project he's been working on. This afternoon I had lunch on my porch in spot of sunshine and watched the cats play tag in the garden. I greeted Karin on her way to teach a class as she passed my little house and greeted her again when she returned. Now, as I sit here on my window seat, writing while listening to light spring rain on my roof, Isha and Jake are finishing up building raised beds for this year's garden. Before long the dinner bell will ring, signaling time to come enjoy the food that Lindsey has cooked up for us. Afterwards we'll have a logistics meeting to work through the details of our upcoming Simply Home retreat and Isha and I will share the timeline for our new tiny house build.

It's a good little life! I'm excited to see tiny houses pop up across the country and exceedingly grateful for this place and these people who have made "community" simply "home"!

Photos courtesy of Guillaume Dutilh and Billy Ulmer.

Part 6

Tiny House Business

As with any emerging trend and industry advancement or major change there comes about a series of cottage businesses that tailor products and services specifically to that industry. It certainly is no different for the tiny house movement. It was only a matter of time before multitudes of tiny house builders would pop up nationwide, festivals, associations, and tiny house appliances would be profiled as well as any number of businesses in between. Anything for a buck, some would say. But there still exist those businesses and those business-minded people who see not just a land of opportunity but a way to fulfill a valid need with quality solutions. The businesses now catering to the tiny home community are inevitably validating the movement in so much as giving them an exclusive product line and exposure. Tiny house business also gives consumers a chance to customize their homes and be on top of the latest fads. These businesses may be new or young but they are all shooting for the same goal: create quality solutions for an emerging market while still building revenue. Here are just some of their stories.

From Cradle to Grave
Salvage mining and salvage building

Brad Kittel

Brad Kittel – creator, designer, builder, spokesperson, and now, author – has developed an entire philosophy around the concept of "sustainability through salvage." Together with his crew of like-minded salvagers he builds Tiny Texas Houses that are as much as 99% "pure salvage" and offer all the amenities of a new construction house. He is more than happy to share his ideas around salvage mining and his believe that we all have the power to create solutions to our global problems by even the simplest of choices we make on a daily basis.

In 1981, I built a tiny house on wheels inside a 66-passenger school bus. I lived in that bus for 3-1/2 years. In it, I traveled the country and lived for extended periods after graduating college in the state of Florida. From Florida I headed up to Alabama and then across to the Seattle, Washington area before dropping back down to Las Vegas, eventually spending six months rebuilding and repairing the bus motor. Once fixed, my home ushered me over to Oklahoma, and finally to our resting location deep in the heart of Texas!

I pulled my coach to a halt on July 4th, 1984, with expired tags, no insurance, an expired inspection, and towing a Dodge pickup truck with a motorcycle in the back of it. In my pocket was about $640 but at the time I had no friends or promise of a job. I had my health though and a whole lot of sunshine.

Not long after my son Adam was born (and now a family man), I sold both the bus and the motorcycle. My housing scale had changed. I moved up the American Dream ladder to a 650 sq.ft. house in East Austin (which at the time was a less than admirable part of the city). Soon after though, we bought a 1,000 sq.ft. house and my inner city real estate business began growing exponentially. I was a broker and what we now call a "house flipper." I bought and fixed up the worst of the houses in the area, cleaning them up and providing desirable housing options at first time homebuyer prices. Business was good, I was doing well, and we upgraded again, this time to a 2,500 sq.ft. house.

Over the years I won a number of revitalization awards for creative rehabs and neighborhood cleanup and restoration projects (primarily in an area now known as French Place in Austin, TX). At one point in my business career, just before the dot com boom, I even opened the largest cybercafé in Texas. Soon after I semi retired to Gonzales, TX to spend more time with my son. I felt we still needed more space though so we upgraded yet again into a 2,800 sq.ft. house. Later on we added an addition raising our square footage to just at 4,500 sq.ft. During that decade I also founded Discovery Architectural Antiques which was the largest architectural warehouse and/or storefront in the Southern USA at 137,000 sq.ft. During its prime, we had a sawmill, a wood shop, and a cabinet/door shop.

I had developed a new passion though and one that led everyone to think I was crazy. I wanted to build tiny Texas houses out of 95% pure salvage to show we could use all the massive inventories I had collected to create solutions for sustainable living. We would not just reduce or eliminate construction energy costs but actually bank enough saved energy to literally power the house for 100 years or more! I introduced Tiny Texas Houses and life began to change. Little did I know how long it would take to get where we are today and down which roads I would travel to create a house using minimal new energy to get the materials and to build the house too.

The tiny house industry has a number of definitions at this point and many include wheels. I chose a path though with one focus: homes transportable with a big trailer that leaves once the house gets to the homestead. If one wants to move it again one day they can. To assist in the process I like a crane to ease the setting in and backing out of the house from the actual ground spot. That said, my houses have been as big as 12' x 32', constructed completely of wood, including a fold down porch roof, sometimes both in front and back. This embodies a process of salvaging materials, building with them, making the houses transportable, developing out of the box designs I call Space Magic, and building houses to last for a century. This is the ethos upon which Tiny Texas Houses is based.

Salvage mining and salvage building create healthy environment houses that will last for much longer than the owners who build them, if cared for properly. We can unleash billions of dollars in hidden resources that cannot be duplicated or matched anywhere else in the world to use in the next generation of houses. Houses that are small but that will benefit both the people and the planet. The healthy, toxin free, sustainable resources we can bring back to life are far greater than what we have left on the planet to strip off. My personal objective is to prove this to people before the incredible wealth is all gone, thrown into landfills. We are literally throwing away materials that can create homes for the homeless and our veterans, women and children, all who silently wonder and lament over how they will survive through a winter, or even life for that matter, without proper domiciles. From a business standpoint I have created a way for this to turn from hypothesis into action that rewards participants. I have shown how it works and how it can help foster creativity, imagination, hope, and sustainable lifestyles. I call it the Pure Salvage Living Renaissance.

I live in a tiny house again and actually love it more than any I have owned before. The notion of a small space and a simplified life is one I share with countless others, followers of the downsizing movement. There is a desire to be free of debt and assets that once fueled a fire in generations following WWII. As an aging generation retires, most have no choice but to accept the challenge of downsizing. For some it will be painful. Others though consider it being freed of our anchors that could easily leave us drowning in possessions we can no longer afford or maintain. 72,000,000 "Baby Boomers" are rapidly learning they will not be living in the style they are accustomed to once they retire, if they even can retire. I should know. Having been through the full cycle of tiny house to big house and back, I gained a valuable foundation for realizing the benefits of living simple. So many years later I have gravitated back such that my current house has essentially the same floor space as my first house in the shell of a bus.

Ten years ago, when I started Tiny Texas Houses, I foresaw tiny houses becoming an industry that could create a path out of the matrix of taxes, insurance, homeowner's fees, property maintenance and the expenses that will otherwise enslave homeowners for the duration of their lives. It has been good to see others agree – not just older folks either – but young people 25-35 years old who seem to be getting past the 'American Dream' candy that post-WWII Americans ate 60+ years ago and have now exchanged for anti-depressants. Many are escaping the trappings of a media-centric world and choosing a new style of living focused on relationships and experiences. Distractions are being left behind in favor of living life instead of watching it. The key to this tiny house movement is understanding that the focus is not just on a house but rather the lifestyles in America and their ability to change in years to come.

A reckoning has come about where the big house of the 'American Dream' is no longer a desire of the people or deemed a wise investment. People are looking for smaller places now and there is a social upheaval. Organic living is becoming a focal point with key points being simplifying one's life and reducing stress when possible. Now is the time when creative thought is going to provide solutions to existing and burgeoning problems such as how to build new houses without taking more resources from the planet and creating more toxins in the world. I believe it is time to focus on how much energy we can save before we finish building the house that will in turn save natural resources (as well as energy in order to make glass, hardware, sinks, and more) rather than just how much money can be saved in the actual construction process. This is the true test of sustainability. How little energy can you take from the planet to build a home, live a life, and be truly happy? It is not a dream so much as a shift in the paradigm. A true-to-form Pure Salvage Living Renaissance can take hold and begin to create solutions that millions can benefit from, as well as our planet, if given the chance.

One of the cottage industries I see rising from the ashes of house consumption are the creation of Art Houses. As a society we have a rich history that is full of hidden treasure. I have chosen this as my personal medium for creating Art Houses. I build with 95% pure salvage. These are one of a kind houses created solely to inspire others to build millions of organic cottages and tiny houses, each unique and personal. This business can easily go national and provide a unique path for home ownership that empowers people who otherwise can not buy a home. Potential homeowners are encouraged and in some cases required to barter their time and talents to build their house as well as others. It is an exchange of human energy for homestead.

The Pure Salvage Outposts are co-ops in that they will create homesites, work spaces, shared tools, and ample materials for people to get together and build themselves houses to live in for the rest of their lives.

The notion of using salvage to do this is what I affectionately call the 'Grave to Cradle' cycle. It is a philosophy in action and is designed to create sustainable housing that will last for centuries, be portable, and toxin free. If taught and implemented the ideology shows how to get most of the required materials for nothing more than human energy. The only modern materials are domestically manufactured. New products are barely needed to make the organic cottages energy efficient and sustainable, just some insulation, screws, nails, plumbing, wiring, and house wraps.

I have created houses as small as 63 sq.ft. and as big as 350 sq.ft. on the main floor, and up to 550 sq.ft. of livable space if you count the lofts in a portable Tiny Texas House. They have not been light weight nor intended to be pulled with a common truck but instead a semi and special trailer. My houses are a way of showing what extremes we can take sustainable living through salvaging. The largest standing virgin forest in the world is sitting in America, slowly being thrown away into landfills, burned, or left to rot. This incredible virgin forest is disguised in the form of giant barns, buildings, and houses across much of our nation's landscape. We can harvest this to cre-

ate sustainable houses, businesses, and much more with just a bit of sweat equity.

I have spent the last decade proving what is possible for men and women, experienced and inexperienced, from all walks of life, to salvage houses in as little as 5 days, in order to get what they need to build a home. My houses are intended to inspire people to build their own and then continue paying forward by teaching others. Some people will prefer to work salvaging the houses while others build or hunt down the next resource structures.

This method of building minimizes the contaminants, toxins, and use of most plastics, vinyls, and manufactured parts, or imports for the entire house building process. By the numbers 20 gallons of gas used during the salvaging of a house is often enough to not only power the compressor for the nail kicker, but also fuel the truck to haul the materials to the work space where the new houses will be built. Likewise, the building process for the two houses to be created from the salvaged one will amount to less than 20 gallons of diesel fuel for saws and a compressor for nail guns. Upon further analysis it is easy to see that on a modern house construct it takes more than 20 gallons of fuel to create the glass for the windows alone.

I created Tiny Texas Houses to prove the merit in salvage construction as well as to educate others about salvage construction. Getting others to understand and invest in this theology has proven to be the hardest task.

I began this adventure with the commitment to create 100 different styles of sustainable Tiny Texas Houses. My long-term hope was then to create a metric for salvage materials to rate construction by inspiring others to shoot for at least 50% or better and thus show they are truly sincere about making a difference in sustainable building. This standard and ethos in construction could save enormous valuable resources spent on housing each year and make longevity and salvage materials a higher priority in housing construction. So far, I have created over 75 examples of what we can do if we set our minds to this ethos and new standard of sustainable organic housing that utilizes the incredible reserves of salvage we have stashed across this country awaiting a new life.

My business is fueled by my belief that we have an obligation to create housing that is clean and healthy giving our children a better world than we were given. Tiny houses grouped together as villages of like-minded people are a path I see us moving toward voluntarily, and I see it as a good thing to view communes as a path to community instead of fearing or making fun of them. We have the potential to build millions of tiny houses for young adults who want to live an alternative lifestyle that breaks free from the McMansion mold. It also frees others – especially senior citizens – who are beginning to see the folly of owning giant houses that go largely unused, thereby depleting savings at an alarming rate.

My idea of business is not solely based in profit margins though. I have spent ten years freely giving away the pictures, training, and means for others to embark on a journey of salvage construction too. Tiny Texas Houses has sought to educate others through Salvage Bootcamp seminars and construction workshops. Thankfully salvage building seems to be catching on now. Hopefully the growing fascination with this perspective will continue and more builders will participate. I predict that more millionaires will be made from the salvage industry than any other small business venture in the next decade.

It's important to note that I refer to salvage mining and salvage building as an industry. Because of it millions will be employed, billions will be unleashed in assets, and many families will create cottage industries of their own from what was once considered trash. The myriad of occupations that will dovetail into this are perfect for the retraining of so many whose occupational specialties have become obsolete or outdated. This puts the work back into Americans hands and bolsters economies on all levels.

The Pure Salvage Living Renaissance opens the path to healing. Everyone wins! The work and investment made by generations that came before us can be saved and restored and become a palpable investment in our very own future.

My "Grave to Cradle" philosophy, Tiny Texas Houses, and the experiences I have gathered in my own quest for happiness fuels a Space Magic transformation I find myself sharing daily with our society. Using human energy – literally our hands and minds – is the most responsible and perhaps the most honorable way to preserve history, honor our forefathers hard work by transforming trashed places into treasure spaces, one home at a time.

So Much In So Little

Building a business in a growing, tiny marketplace

Mike Bedsole

Mike Bedsole is the owner of Tiny House Chattanooga and Tiny House Trailers USA. He and the business are based in Chattanooga, TN, with their construction warehouse located in Cleveland, TN. Mike's construction background is mainly home remodel and repair, and he turned Tiny in 2014. Mike is committed to putting "So MUCH in SO little" for the Tiny House of your dreams and to help you Turn Tiny!

Buy it at auction. Buy it when it's in foreclosure. Buy it because the neighborhood is right. It doesn't matter. The outcome is the same. Go in and assess the damage and prescribe the repair. Call in the sub-contractors. Fix the drywall, add a bathroom, and put down some floating hardwood flooring. Add a granite countertop to the kitchen and slap on a fresh coat of paint in the bedrooms. Call the agent. List it. Sell it. Set aside the revenue from the sale and start looking for the next investment. It is called the 'Art of Flipping' and like so many others during the late 90s and early part of the millennium I was heavily involved. Perhaps not as involved as I was in my previous career which was centered on a restaurant franchise location in the Chattanooga, TN area, but involved nonetheless. But like it was with the eateries, I became a bit bored and disenchanted with the return on investment. It seemed fruitless and I was hungry for something with a greater return in both profit AND job satisfaction. That opportunity presented itself rather precariously as I was recovering from neck surgery and had little else to do but read, draw, and watch TV. It seemed as if every time I tuned in to the DIY and home shows I was presented with these tiny house structures, ever growing in popularity. They were cool. They were a challenge. And they were going to be my foray back into a business that would allow me to be creative, hands-on, and excited, all at once!

In December of 2014 I had to have a cervical spinal fusion for a bulging disk. It was even less fun than it sounds. Recovery time was estimated to be 3-4 months. That is a long time to do nothing when for years I had been used to a fast-paced and busy lifestyle. During that period of rehabilitation though I was introduced to a new style of living and a new style of building. I saw on television people who were giving up larger 3-bedroom/2-bathroom stick-built tract houses for something smaller, *much* smaller. What was most interesting to me though is that the houses didn't seem to have any less structural integrity or be any less eye-catching. These tiny houses weren't simply wooden "single wides" but rather actual homes that had subsequently been built on wheels. They weren't a Winnebago with shingles, but rather a custom house on a trailer foundation. Almost instantly my mind began to focus in on how I could be part of all this.

I had long been someone who prided myself on not needing much to survive. I am a pretty simple guy and the idea of packing so much creativity into a living situation that was attractive, well-built, mobile, and sustainable was where I knew I wanted to give my attention. I had to first figure out where to begin. I took a leap of faith and on Jan. 1, 2015 and launched Tiny House Chattanooga. Chattanooga is a town that has come to identify itself with its enthusiasm for sustainable living, green building and outdoor adventure and I wanted to have my business name tied to this awesome place I call home. I decided I needed to do some homework beyond just having a business name and logo and way beyond just watching early episodes of Tiny House Nation. In February of that same year I attended a Tumbleweed workshop led by Guillaume Dutilh who himself had built a 20 ft. tiny house inspired by Jay Shafer's Fencl design. It was on display that day and I was able to actually see one of these homes and see how it was built; the nuances, structural details, joints, etc. It was an exceptionally cool house but seemed a little cramped for me. At the time I didn't really know that Guillaume was traveling the country in it with another person (and a dog) and therefore wanted a smaller, more efficiently towable house, and had subsequently filled it with enough for two people. The tight feeling of the space got me thinking a tiny house would better serve if it used all the available width of the trailer. I also walked away with some very good ideas for tiny house interior features. I left knowing that a tiny house on wheels of any size would hardly be livable if – like a more traditional sticks 'n bricks build – it wasn't started on the right foundation. I started researching and understanding more about trailers.

It's important for a tiny house builder to understand that one size does not fit all when building a home on a mobile frame. I have history with trailers. In past business experiences, with friends, and even with family, I have done a lot of towing. I personally own a dump trailer, two box trailers, a 23' boat (with trailer), and rent a 30' travel trailer on a yearly basis. I know about tongue weight and gross weight and cargo weight and how it all plays into the chassis design and effects that actual towing capabilities. Because of that history and knowledge I quickly connected with trailer manufacturers around the country to find out what was readily available but also to be sure I would be building on the correct trailer design for the structure. After talking with over 30 trailer manufacturers across the country, we narrowed it down to the few superior choices that we use today. From there I formed Tiny House Trailers USA. The trailer is the tiny home's foundation; the planning and the build must start from there.

I may be getting ahead of myself though.

Before building my first tiny house (even though at this point I had a trailer to build on and was committed to producing something outstanding) I needed to work out if this direction was one I wanted to go in because of the design and build challenge or if there was something more behind it all within me. I was and am still motivated in large part to the values behind the tiny house movement as well as the commitment and passion of tiny house people. In our consumer nation it is a big leap of faith and resolve to give up the big house filled with stuff, the garage full of cars, the 4-wheelers and boats, and whatever else spells out success, and instead live towards a smaller footprint, a command over personal finances, and a reduction in possessions. The decision to live tiny is an individual one and for each person who decides to go tiny there is a personal motivation. Whether it be strictly downsizing, getting out of rental situations and owning your own home, or even just because they are unique little structures, the tiny house at large allows a person to live a comfortable, customizable, and responsible life without over-extending oneself or living beyond their needs. I had just sold myself on the idea and I was now truly ready to build.

When I was at the Tumbleweed workshop one of my initial thoughts was that the house on display came across as quite heavy. Granted it used a generous portion of traditional framing and interior wood, I still felt like it could be lighter and more economic for the towing. In addition I wanted to make sure that all the space available in regards to width was used. Tiny House Chattanooga homes needed to be stylish and well appointed, use all available space, and be the lightest and strongest homes on the market!

I had remembered seeing a video on YouTube from a guy in New Zealand that built his entire house of steel studs. I thought the idea had a lot of merit and so I reached out to FrameCAD, the New Zealand company that made the light-gauge steel framing, through email and asked if there was a fabricator in the United States. It took nearly four months to track down a solid answer but I was finally put in touch with Mark McQuain , owner of Volstrukt. Volstrukt, LLC provides steel framing solutions using the FrameCAD cold formed steel systems.

That meeting gave birth to the very first galvanized steel framed tiny house in the United States built via the FrameCAD system. That very tiny house – the Nooga Blue Sky – found its way to the first Tiny House Jamboree and brought a lot of attention to Tiny House Chattanooga.

Clad in tongue and groove pine siding the Nooga Blue Sky holds on to the traditional tiny house aesthetic while keeping its weight down. The entrance to the home is a set of double doors, which goes back to my philosophy on using all available space. The double doors bring light in and make the space seem larger than it is while also being highly functional for bringing things in and out. Stylistically the house also has two different roof pitches offering depth and dimension creating more of a traditional home look than just a singular pitch roofline. This design element allows the loft to be as large as possible and as comfortable as any. We think the most obvious choice for our tiny houses is the generous inclusion of windows. We use large windows in strategic places. Inside the houses I try very hard to stick with my desire for smart space appropriation. There are steps leading up to the loft that double as storage drawers. The kitchen has a drop down bar for bar seating that even has a leaf for adding more guests. I tried to build a first house that would be one I would both be proud to live in and feel like I didn't have to sacrifice anything I might have in a larger home. We offer soaking tubs in our homes, washer/dryers, full-size sinks, sleeping arrangements for multiple people, off-grid solutions, and dress it all up with beautiful wood framing and finishing. Because we are a customer-oriented business though we take special pride and have truly built our business model around custom tiny homes for real people.

I understand that interested parties have varying budgets. Some clients may come to us and not want to spend over $30,000 while others may come to the design desk prepared to spend $80,000. Neither end of the spectrum should alter how a business treats a client though. The tiny house community is such an inviting one, filled with authentic people who are looking to make a difference in their lives as well as the world around them, we work that much harder to do business with the same attitude. And why shouldn't we? We are just over a year old and we have been fortunate enough to thrive in this growing tiny house marketplace. We want people to mention Tiny House Chattanooga and the tiny house movement all in the same breath. When a client comes in the very first thing we do is thank them for trusting us with their dream. From there the process is one that makes the build easier, the client happier, and the product as perfect as possible.

We begin a custom build by going over the needs of the individual. That is paramount. If a tiny house business doesn't make an attempt to understand their client from the outset the build will never be accurate. We go to great lengths to detail how the tiny house will function now and in the future. From that point we sketch out a working budget based on the financial standpoint of the client.

One of the misconceptions of tiny houses is that they are smaller and therefore should be infinitely less expensive. This is common sense on paper but not always in practice. A number of elements have to be custom made in a tiny house, all of which take a lot of man hours. Weight has to be thought about and then rethought at every step. All of these elements translate into dollars and cents and because THC is a business like any other, and offering the most value to our customers while maintaining a profitable business is always a balance. We try to do so while keeping our clients needs at the front of our minds. Budget is so important for all involved. We try very hard to guide our clients in all of their choices in order to make sure their tiny house will function and feel the way they expect it to. That includes warning them of improper building techniques we have seen in the marketplace and showing them in depth how we build. This part of the process is helped out by the fact that not only am I the primary builder and the contractor on the build but also the Sales Rep. for Tiny House Chattanooga. Right now I feel like being with a client from the start of the process is highly important. What is good for the goose is good for the gander, so to speak. I like to remain the point of contact for all clients, be it as their designer, their builder, or even just their advisor. And with our company growing as it is I am spending more time working with clients in a desk capacity and hiring highly qualified, local builders to take a spot on the line. I feel like that is a large part of keeping our business successful as well. You have to know your limits.

One of the primary goals of the tiny house community is to become a nationally recognized, legal form of housing. Part of achieving that will be showing the enhancement to our communities through tiny houses. Right now one way of doing that is showing the quality and safety of tiny houses as well as showing how they contribute to local economies and standards of living. If multiple tiny house companies come to the forefront but deliver less than stellar product and never tap into local craftsmen to fill needed positions the stigma will remain that tiny houses are a fad and are not interested in doing anything other than flying under the radar. That simply will not advance the business or the acceptability of the movement. That is primarily why we are expanding as fast as we can in the local market. There are incredibly talented builders and designers in my local area. As our business continues to grow and we see more clients it only makes sense to bring those folks on board our team to increase the basic tenants of our business.

Beyond even the local market I have plans for a national expansion. Region by region a client will be able to have a Tiny House Chattanooga design built for them without leaving their hometown. Our facilities already allow us to build multiple houses at once. But I want to make it possible and financially feasible for a home like the Nooga Blue Sky to be built on the West Coast, East Coast, and all points in between. From a business standpoint I want to maintain a business model with a strong turnaround time so a client does not have to wait 6 months for their build to be finished. I don't want to be limited by a narrow mindset or a narrow operating margin. Tiny House Chattanooga has the capability and the desire to be larger than that and to rewrite the standard operating procedure of tiny house building. I want to offer a 'best of both worlds' type scenario.

Tiny House Chattanooga is available to build a highly custom work of mobile art and lifestyle but can also produce a more basic spec build to customers who are looking for just a shell or a strong foundation for their personal build. It starts even more basic than that though. A successful tiny house builder and company must be able to see the client for who they are, understand what they want, and commit to their build, be it small or large. To put "SO MUCH in So Little" you must be able to see the customer's big picture.

Tiny House Insurance 101

Protecting your tiny home investment

Martin Burlingame

Martin Burlingame is the foremost insurance expert on tiny homes and the tiny home movement. His agency has built custom programs to handle the complex insurance needs of a variety of different industries. The Tiny Home program is available in over 40 states and is unique to the industry.

Thinking about investing in a tiny home and joining the tiny house movement? Don't be fooled. Tiny homes are a significant investment, and protecting this investment may keep you up at night. To handle the complex needs of the tiny world for the sake of insurance is a challenge on its own. With my expertise on new movements and ability to build programs for complex insurance products, I'm able to help out tiny home buyers to find a way through the maze of insuring their property. My passion from tiny homes started with the Tiny House Jamboree in 2015 where the energy of the event helped me grasp the passion of the tiny movement. I love the outdoors and enjoys hiking and backpacking with my children and the Boy Scouts. What better way to combine family, passions and enjoyments than in a tiny! Now onto insurance and protecting your investment!

Buying insurance for your home is almost second nature, but insuring tiny homes incurs a special set of problems. Is a tiny house on wheels a house, or is it a trailer? Is it a stationary primary dwelling, or is it a mobile vacation home? Are you living in it, or are you planning to rent it out for short stays? What happens if your tiny house burns or, in the worst case, is stolen? Insurance companies have difficulty grasping these different scenarios and providing you with the protection you need at a reasonable price. These are questions that need to be explored and need to begin much more broad conversations regarding the insuring of a tiny house on wheels from start to finish.

Builder's Risk: Building or Finishing Your Own Tiny

First and foremost in the world of tiny, the issue of Builder's Risk needs to be addressed. Sometimes called Course of Construction, this type of insurance covers the tiny house during construction and until the home owner occupies the tiny home. Builder's Risk is a relatively common insurance policy in the world of stick-built conventional homes where banks demand a policy to protect their interest while the builder builds the home. In the tiny world, as the value of these homes increases with customization and new options, customers and tiny home builders need a Builder's Risk policy that can handle tiny homes.

This type of policy covers the Tiny Home structure at a predetermined value – the end value once all work is complete – and usually is bought in 3-, 6-, 9-, or 12-month increments, depending on the length of time you plan on working on your tiny. Builder's Risk policies do not cover liability, rather, this policy covers the physical structure in case of fire, theft, or other major perils. Insurance companies pay on an actual cash value, so if you are 50% finished on a $50,000 tiny home, the insurance company would cover $25,000 – or half – of the value. If you buy a shell and then customize it, the shell value is included in the insurance valuation. Issues may arise if you build your own tiny, but you are not a licensed contractor. Insurance companies may have reservations with the construction of key components unless licensed professionals – such as electricians, plumbers, heating and gas installers – do the work. Once the tiny home is finished, it's time to buy insurance in order to live in it and become part of the movement.

Basic Types of Homeowners Insurance

Typically, two types of homeowners insurance cover a home – Property Insurance and Liability Insurance. Property protection is broken down further into four sub-components: the dwelling itself, separate structures, contents, and loss of use. These are often referred to as Coverage A – D and may appear that way on your policy. Liability insurance is subdivided into Personal Liability and Medical Expenses. Let's define these types of property insurance without sinking into the dreaded world of insurance lingo.

Property

Dwelling (Coverage A). "Dwelling" coverage is insurance language for the actual value of the structure you live in – your dwelling. A dwelling may be an everyday home, a small cabin in a remote area, or a mobile home. In the tiny home world, "dwelling" typically means the tiny home value, along with any upgrades or custom features you may have added. Coverage for the dwelling does not cover clothes, plates, bedding, or the solar powered coffee maker you may have bought to make the tiny home experience unique and wonderful.

Separate Structures (Coverage B). Separate structures are akin to a detached garage or large barn on your property. In the tiny home world, insurance for a separate structure is not needed unless you have managed to pack a horse stable and greenhouse into your reduce area!

Contents (Coverage C). Contents is the stuff you own that is contained inside your tiny home. Despite the huge amount of downsizing you have done to fit into a tiny home, most likely you have accumulated many items that you need and want for your new way of life. Clothes, furniture, bedding, kitchenware (including the solar coffee pot), the TV, and that hammock you want to take naps in, all count as contents. We recommend you do an inventory, pricing everything before deciding on how much contents you want to cover on the policy. You will be surprised at how much stuff you actually have!

Loss of Use (Coverage D). Loss of use is the coverage everyone seems to forget about until they are displaced by a fire and need money for hotel rooms and food for an extended period of time. Hence, loss of use coverage insurance pays you when you are displaced from your home due to events beyond your control. This coverage is optional for tiny homes but is recommended if you are using the tiny as your primary house.

Liability

Personal Liability. Personal liability coverage pays damages to people who are injured by you or your property. This would cover the tree falling on your neighbor's car, your dog biting someone, or slip-and-falls. This portion of the policy covers you for negligence, not intentional acts, and will extend to family members living with you. Since tiny homes are often used as secondary or vacation homes, owners should discuss this coverage with an insurance agent. Liability coverage can be extended from a primary residence, purchased separately, or may require an endorsement if you rent or lease your tiny home. Also, problems may arise due to geographic location of a tiny home. Some insurance companies do not cover homes in every area of country and may not be able to offer secondary dwelling type endorsements.

Medical Expense. Medical coverage pays the medical expenses, up to a certain amount, incurred by an accident on your property or away from your property if caused by you or a family member. For example, your friend's child trips on the stairs of your tiny, breaks an arm, and goes to the hospital. Medical expenses may include reasonable charges for medical, surgical, x-ray, ambulance, or dental.

Trip Insurance

While many in the tiny home movement plan on a stationary life (i.e. Fresno, CA), others plan on traveling the country and moving their tiny home at least once or twice a year. Traveling requires trip insurance and is completely different than your homeowner policy that expects you to remain in one location with a physical address. Trip insurance is written on an inland marine policy form similar to construction equipment. The insurance handles claims during the movement of the tiny home but is typically written in one-year increments with a penalty if cancelled early.

Special Issues with Insuring Tiny Homes

Tiny Home Classification

Why are tiny homes different when it comes to insurance coverage? Tiny homes impose a special set of issues in regard to insurance coverage because tiny homes can be classified in three ways:

1. As a primary or secondary dwelling fixed at one location
2. As a primary or secondary dwelling that is mobile, and finally,
3. As a trailer

Usage and Insurance Rating

A tiny home's insurance rating depends on the owner's plans for the use of the home as well as what an insurance agent is able to procure. While tiny home classification and insurance rating do not seem like difficult concepts to grasp, matters become complicated when it comes to how insurance companies handle the business of insuring property. Company A may want to write a home's insurance coverage in the city, but when you move your tiny to the mountains, Company A will no longer cover you because of your new location. Company B may be fine with remote locations but cannot handle the movement of the tiny, so when you call to tell Company B that you are going from Maine to California, they have a meltdown. So you decide to go with Company C because the company specializes in insuring trailers. You go on your merry way only to find out that Company C cannot provide coverage once you become stationary and need liability protection.

Geographical Location

Now that your head is spinning and you are muttering your hatred of insurance companies and insurance agents, add into the mix the geographi-

cal location of a tiny home. Maybe Company A is a West Coast company and can't write in Florida where you now have parked your tiny for the winter. You come back from a walk on the beach and call your agent only to find out that a) s/he is not licensed in Florida, and/or b) your insurance company cannot write insurance coverage in Florida. The company cancels your insurance, and you are back to square one.

The nature of tiny homes makes them mobile in two ways. They can move constantly from place to place, acting as a trailer, or they can move to a location for an extended period, and then move to another location for another extended period, acting as a permanent dwelling. Insurance policies must adapt to this new way of life. Tiny home owners need an insurance policy that will cover a permanent dwelling, yet gives the Tiny Home owner the flexibility of moving the tiny home from point A to point B

A Tiny Home Insurance Solution

Fortunately, there is a viable solution to these daunting insurance issues for tiny homes. Commercial Insurance Group, LLC (CIG), based in Colorado Springs, Colorado and licensed in 40+ states, has developed a custom insurance program especially for the Tiny Home movement. The program issues an insurance policy to cover a tiny home as a permanent dwelling and adds a trip endorsement to cover a tiny home while in transit.

With this custom program, tiny home owners use a web application or cell phone app to log on to an Internet website and notify their insurance agent when they decide to move their tiny home. A temporary insurance endorsement for five to ten days is added to the tiny home owner's insurance policy (an endorsement, for those who love to speak insurance) that covers the tiny home while in transit. Once the tiny home reaches its destination, the home owner again logs on or accesses the phone app to notify the insurance agent of the new location. On a side note, for those tiny home owners going off the grid, latitude and longitude coordinates can be sent via cell phone GPS. When the insurance agent receives the permanent location, the policy is endorsed with the new location so that the tiny home is covered under a dwelling policy rather than the trip endorsement. With the flexibility of moving from dwelling to mobile and back to dwelling with a single application, home owners avoid the hassle of having separate policies issued and cancelled each time they want to move their tiny home to a different location, since many insurance companies do not cover from state to state. With this custom program, the complications of state-to-state moves are greatly reduced.

Tiny Insurance for a Big Movement

The tiny house movement has grown tremendously over the past decade, and insurance companies had to grow and adapt along with this movement. Navigating homeowners insurance is complicated enough without the added dimension of tiny home mobility. Fortunately, tiny home owners now have options ensuring that not only are their tiny home investment and its contents covered when stationary, but also when in transit anywhere in the United States. With this peace of mind, tiny home owners can enjoy their new home as the unique property experience that it is both now and in the future.

Building a Business

Steve Weissman

After downsizing his life in 2004, Steve Weissmann discovered Tumbleweed Tiny Houses. He instantly developed a love affair with tiny houses, and in 2007 bought the company and opened shop in California. Over the past 9 years he's grown Tumbleweed to become the largest tiny house business in the US and has continually pioneered this growing industry.

It is not the critic who counts, not the man who points out how the strong man stumbles, or where the doer of deeds could have done them better. The credit belongs to the man who is actually in the arena, whose face is marred by dust and sweat and blood; who strives valiantly; who errs, who comes short again and again, because there is no effort without error and shortcoming; but who does actually strive to do the deeds; who knows great enthusiasms, the great devotions; who spends himself in a worthy cause; who at the best knows in the end the triumph of high achievement, and who at the worst, if he fails, at least fails while daring greatly, so that his place shall never be with those cold and timid souls who neither know victory nor defeat.

About one year ago my wife shared that quote from Theodore Roosevelt. She said it summed me up pretty good and so promptly hung the quote in my office directly behind my chair. Now everyone that sits in my office can look up and figure me out in the time it takes to read that paragraph.

My fingerprints are literally all over this company. It took me nearly a decade to realize that, but now that we have nearly 100 people working at Tumbleweed Tiny House Company it's becoming pretty obvious. By nature I'm a rather private person. The idea of writing about both business and myself is truly uncomfortable. I'm an agent of change and I have a story that perhaps no one has ever really heard before.

Today Tumbleweed is the largest player in the tiny house industry. Most people assume it is because we were first but I firmly believe that it is instead my three rules for success:

Rule 1: Set goals

Rule 2: Communicate clearly

Rule 3: Persist, persist, persist

These rules are akin to a 3-legged stool. It will topple if you remove even one leg.

When I falter personally it is usually because of Rule #2. That is most definitely my Achilles Heel. It goes back to my desire to be private and guarded which started in early childhood. I was so dang shy. I remember hiding under my mom's dress when she would drop me off to kindergarten. I was *that* kid.

In 5th grade we had to write a report on what we wanted to be when we grew up, and I took that assignment very seriously. I did a lot of research on all the professions out there and decided that I wanted to be the CEO of my own company. My report was very well organized and earned me an A+. And from that day on my vision for my future never wavered once. The three rules took hold and guided me to where I am today. The road was not always smooth though.

As a young man I wasn't a gifted communicator. Other people didn't really make sense to me and as such I wanted to learn how to use a computer before they were cool (the year was 1983). My dad said the only way to do that was to find a teacher. So I started asking people if they had a computer and would teach me how to use one. Luckily my neighbor had a computer and wasn't about to turn down a ten-year-old boy full of curiosity. In short order I became a spreadsheet loving, computer nerd, long before that was cool. By the time I was in 7th grade I was building amortization tables and profit and loss statements in Visicalc II, the first spreadsheet computer program for personal computers. It turns out I was a bit of a quant. Some people can read sheet music and hear music right off the page. I can read a P&L (Profit & Loss Statement) and read the company's story. I found my dual love in business numbers and computers.

I enrolled in college as a computer science major and quickly realized that this degree wouldn't get me to the CEO chair so I changed my major to Quantitative Economics and Decision Science and graduated in 1995.

On my 8-hour drive home from college – ready to start my new life – I had an epiphany that was critical to my development. On I-5 near Bakersfield, California I realized that all my decisions were based on a scale where I measured desire versus fear. And in almost every instance fear was the victor, a very sobering and depressing realization. I lived with the fear of rejection, fear of failure, and fear of inadequacy, and on and on. About three months later I finally found the solution to overcome my fears was to constantly put myself in uncomfortable situations and expand my comfort zone little by little. I knew that in order to succeed I had to fail, and fail often. So I did!

By the age of 26, I think my social skills were now passable. But I toiled in mediocrity for a couple more years uncertain as to why. On my 28th birthday I randomly wandered into a Borders Book Store and saw a book titled "Developing the Lead Within You" by John Maxwell. I picked it up and started reading right in the store. Now mind you, I took pride in the fact that I had so much knowledge I would never need to read another book after graduating college because I already knew it all. But this book shook me right from the start, and so I bought it – the first book of my adult life that wasn't required reading.

I ate it up. And then I read every book that the author recommended and I read more books and more books. I couldn't stop. I devoured titles ranging from human behavior to marketing, to accounting to investing, to negotiating and on and on. I've literally read hundreds of books to continue to grow my knowledge. It was the link I was missing and I even began to call the authors of the books that really impacted me and meet them and absorb more knowledge. I grew and developed and was now ready to be a CEO.

About this same time – In my 30's – I started downsizing into smaller and smaller homes. I never heard about tiny houses, and didn't know anyone else who was doing what I was doing. Living in a small space just wasn't a thing. Yet I found that the extra space was a burden for me. I hated to shop. I didn't really care about possessions, and I absolutely despised household cleaning chores. I eventually moved into the smallest house in town that I could find. It was a cute little granny unit that was smaller than a 2-car garage. It boasted one open room with a kitchen, a bathroom, a closet and a sleeping loft. Sound familiar?

One day a friend of mine told me about someone in town who lived in a smaller house than me – like way smaller. About a week later I saw my first Tumbleweed and instantly fell in love with it. I knew that I wanted to be involved. I started volunteering my time in 2006 and a year later I bought half of the "company." I put the words company in quotes because at the time Tumbleweed was more idea than business. It had no business license or business plan; just a website that sold a few house plans and some "books" that were really just brochures printed at Kinkos and stapled together. Sales hovered around $4,500 per month.

But we were off and running. It was a labor of love that I toiled at on weekends and evenings after my regular job. I never anticipated that it would become what it is today. I just really loved the designs and the fact that I could nerd out on something really cool and maybe even make some money doing it.

By 2010 Tumbleweed was making enough money for me to leave my restaurant business behind and focus on tiny houses. "This is actually how you make a living?" a customer asked me with a strange look on her face. I remember agreeing how strange that was. At the time, there were only a handful of people in the world in the tiny house industry. I myself was worried that tiny houses were a fad and this leap into full time 'Tumbleweeding' was a big risk – especially since I had a newborn baby at home.

Lo and behold, tiny houses started to grow in popularity and based on my online marketing skills, Tumbleweed built a very strong foundation. We now had more web traffic and Facebook fans than any other RV manufacturer in the nation and more than all but one homebuilder.

In 2012 I acquired the remaining 50% of Tumbleweed, got a loan, and moved the company out of my garage and into a real office. My goal was to make it easy for anyone to own a tiny home. At the time I believed it was very hard to do that and there was a huge opportunity if we could figure it out. Tiny houses were mostly illegal, nearly impossible to finance and insure, plus incredibly hard to place. So in 3-step rule fashion we set out to become the first company to join RVIA, offer financing, get insurance for our units, and get green certified. I pushed hard to make the pricing transparent and easy to understand – both from an overall cost and a monthly cost for those who got a loan. We reached out to hundreds of lenders – never deterred by the onslaught of "no" responses. The same pattern repeated with insurance companies, warranty companies, etc. I also created ten specific and measurable goals to make it easy for a customer to own a tiny home – all with deadlines for us to achieve. We were off and running.

But for the establishment, tiny houses were too risky and the opportunity too small to put resources into. We had no historical data and the closest comparison were park model RVs, which had been struggling in sales for the past twenty years.

Today the scene is starting to change and the TV shows have played a very large role in that. Tiny houses are hot commodities. I'm 100% certain that we are at the beginning of a long and very exciting trend that will continue to grow hundred-fold over the next twenty years.

So why have I changed from thinking this is a fad to believing this is a landmark industry? I started studying other social trends and saw so many similarities. The industry is not without issues though. Zoning and coding plague us all and it only helps to understand what roadblocks there are and why.

First off, there are five types of tiny houses. In fact

some of these have been around for a very long time and haven't gained traction. I don't think all five are going to grow, only some.

Here's the list:

- Tiny House RVs up to 8'6" wide
- Park Model RVs over 8'6" wide
- HUD homes
- Mobile homes
- Homes on foundations that meet International Building Code

Each of those listed above require a license to build and a license to sell it. Depending on what you are doing, you may need a vehicle manufacturer's license, or a vehicle dealers' license, a contractor license, a real estate license and so on. The first two are technically vehicles and the last three are considered homes.

The die-hard tiny house fan will notice that I've left off "Tiny Houses on Wheels." It's a long discussion best summed up in this way: not only does it require new zoning, it requires a whole new category of codes to both build and sell those units. The path for the others on the list will occur much faster and one could eventually morph into the dream of what a "Tiny House on Wheels" might become. From a zoning perspective it can gain traction in a reasonable amount of time, but from a sales license perspective it is a much harder climb. At some point, it needs to be a house or RV so a proper license can be obtained to sell it. The notion that a business will be able to sell fifty "Tiny Houses on Wheels" in a year without an existing sales license is unrealistic.

Considering that the "houses" on that list have been around for a very long time and never gained traction leads me to believe they won't. Rather I see the tiny house RVs as the trend of the future, which is why we ditched our homes on foundations a couple years ago.

The big drawback to tiny house RVs is that it is a vehicle and not a house – and therefore not intended for full time living. And that actually makes sense to me from a public safety perspective. The code to manufacture an RV really isn't up to par for full time living requirements. A manufacturer can make a roof with a 5lb. snow load and meet code. Now that's a problem.

At the same time, there is a huge interest from people around the country to allow for tiny houses in the zoning code. Over the past year hundreds of zoning officials, mayors and town planners have contacted us because so many advocates across the nation are telling them to legalize tiny houses. The planners want them too and they are asking questions to learn more about tiny houses in general. There are over 17,000 municipalities in this country and they all have their own zoning rules. This is the big challenge. No matter how big though, we are starting to see some zoning departments make changes. Typically, they will remove the minimum size requirements for houses, or allow for more uses for RVs on residential properties. I predict the growth will occur for both the Tiny House RVs 8'6" or less and the really tiny homes on foundations.

So what is going to happen to tiny houses in terms of housing trend?

The law of customer diffusion explains the theory about adaptation of a new product. You see it transform industries from computers to cell phones. But more analogous to tiny houses, you see it in social change reforms from housing codes, to health care reform, to the legalization of gay marriage and marijuana. I studied those examples to better understand how the laws around tiny houses will change.

Social changes meet financial resistance or personal value resistance. For instance, gay marriage doesn't have any financial implications to those who oppose it, but those who do oppose it do because of their personal values. Marijuana is similar but oddly has financial benefits to nearly everyone from its legalization. On the flip side, there isn't a moral objection to healthcare for everyone, only a financial objection that giving healthcare to everyone will raise the costs for people who already have it. Housing codes for the most part didn't have resistance, but still took time.

So how much time does social change take? I've spent years researching these trends and here is what I learned (for those of you who want to cite sources, my apologies, since I honestly don't remember where I picked up this knowledge). If you have resistance, it usually takes 35-40 years to reach the 50% saturation. Without resistance it takes 20-25 years. We are talking about generational shifts. My best guess is that tiny houses are in the 20-25 year range for 50% of the zoning departments to alter their current codes. However, if opposition takes hold, tack on another fifteen years to my estimate.

In the beginning it will go very slowly and the changes will be almost unnoticeable. We may see a 1% success rate within the next five years. But because there are no case studies to compare recent results to it is hard to confirm that number. Cities like Fresno will be the example in as little as five years that everyone else is looking at. That's when the real conversation starts to flow. And little by little, the zoning departments will start to alter their rules. More people in other towns will see the change happening there and want it in their hometown. From town to town, and ultimately state to state, we will start to see big changes in about ten years.

Our industry will continue to grow within the parameters of this trend, and the flavors of business will change as well. Today all tiny house businesses seem to fall into one of three categories: hand, brand or land.

Hand – These are the craftsmen and the builders, who currently make larger homes and decide to start building tiny homes as well. If they succeed, they will eventually stop making larger homes and focus on tiny homes. Most are contractors and only a few actually want to grow the business to a point where they are no longer selling or building themselves but rather managing a large team of people. Almost all tiny house businesses fall into this category.

Brand – These are the non-builders who venture into the tiny house world and want to build a company and have unique models. They'd rather work on sales and marketing than swing a hammer. I fall into this category and there are only a few others.

Land – Developers who have land and decide to build/sell tiny houses on their land. For these businesses, the profit is in the land. They'd rather negotiate land deals than swing a hammer. So far there are only a few players on this side, but expect a lot more.

As the system progresses we'll see more land guys "and" some new entrants that will come in on the volume side. I call them the "and" because there will be quite a few of them and they will be fairly indistinguishable. I'm certain that as tiny house sales pick up, some of the park model RV manufacturers will use their economies of scale to come up with affordable "and" tiny houses for the land guys to sell lots of.

Right now, something interesting is happening. People are entering the tiny house business for one of two reasons. They either love it, or they have a contractor business that isn't successful enough so they are jumping into this hot trend to get more business. I've been doing this for almost a decade and those reasons haven't changed. When the big boys enter, most of the smaller companies will go out of this business and back to building conventional homes. Those of us who do survive that major shift will have done so because we followed solid business rules – not because we built the "best" tiny house around. If you believe that building the absolute best tiny house in the world is going to insure success and you also believe that anyone building a mediocre house will go out of business then you could use that logic to argue that the Big Mac is hands down the #1 best burger in the world.

Today my job revolves around employees, finances, planning, goal setting, and accountability. In all of this and as my business grows I unfortunately become more removed from the thing I love, the tiny house. It is a small loss for being able to grow a business such as Tumbleweed and pursue those passions.

I live a charmed life because I get to live my dream building a business with the greatest product I've ever seen. It's what I have wanted to do since I was just ten-years-old.

Tiny House Hotel – Getting Bigger
How a 1,000 year flood built WeeCasa

Kenyon Waugh

Kenyon, a serial entrepreneur, has always had a different way of looking at the world. Untroubled by worry, he works to show people that they, alone, determine what is possible.

"That way is even worse"

It had been raining for several days, not the norm for Colorado, yet not completely out of the ordinary. Neighbors and friends would say things like: "This [rain] is why I moved from Seattle" or "We need the moisture." People went about their lives slightly inconvenienced not anticipating anything out of the ordinary.

I woke up very early on September 12, 2013 to get to the office for an important presentation with a potential customer and investor at my company. It was still raining as I slipped out of the house quietly around 5:30 am. The town was quiet and not many people were moving around. I was blindly going about my drive to the office, when I saw a sheriff's car in the middle of road with lights flashing and an officer waving her arms at me. The officer came over to my car. She said, as if annoyed by my cluelessness, "You're not going this way. The river is over the road and there is about three feet of water flowing over it." Still focused on the task at hand, I said, "Oh, that's ok, I'll head up the canyon and around to Boulder." She looked at me, now visibly annoyed by my cluelessness, "That way is even worse. Go home and get prepared to be in town for a couple of days."

I turned back still trying to figure out how I was going to get to the office – clueless as to the magnitude of the situation. When I arrived home, the local news was reporting on flooding near Lyons. I logged on Facebook and saw a number of local people had already posted about their middle of night knocks on the door with evacuation instructions. It seemed like the river was raging.

As the town woke up, more information was flowing through Facebook. The phone was ringing earlier than normal. My family started to paint a picture that we were surrounded by water on all sides. The entire town had been broken into seven separate islands with a raging river flowing between us. We were instructed to "prepare" for a couple of days. The school district called stating that school was cancelled for the day.

After the schools call the rain slowed down and even stopped for a bit for the first time in several days. It felt like a normal day. We had electricity, water, Internet, and cable TV. Everything around our house was wet from days of rain, but nothing too far out of the ordinary.

My family and I walked into town to see what was going on. It quickly became obvious that this was not a normal day. It was a day that would change our lives and the lives of many residents in our small mountain town forever.

Two to three feet of water flowed down Main Street, through the Lyons Fork Restaurant, through the St. Vrain Market, through the library moving swiftly and causing damage – a *lot* of damage. We walked to the river pedestrian bridge on Fourth Avenue where the water is typically 6-18 inches deep but now was 10 feet or more deep, with all sorts of debris flowing in it. The calming trickle had become a torrent of violent water and carnage. We could see homes in the North and South Saint Vrain confluence area that were now underwater, damaged, and even uprooted. Cars had shifted from their parking spots by the raging river.

Everyone we came upon had the same stunned look on his or her face; we all stared at the water not saying anything. The only noise was water rushing by and causing damage, objects being swept into other objects, trees and branches breaking and adding to the current. Later that night the electricity went out. The water shut off as well as the gas service. We were trapped on an island.

It would be four days before my family was able to leave. During that time our neighbors and friends banded together and looked out for each other. We had a town barbeque to share meat and other perishables. The elementary school became a temporary shelter. At a morning meeting in the town, park residents demanded supplies and support from the sheriff as he shouted out the news starting with the words that still ring in my ears, "A bullhorn is just one of the things we do not have!" Helicopters flew overhead. Military vehicles took the elderly and sick out of town. Our situation was very real but not yet digestible.

My family was lucky. Our house was not damaged. Unfortunately almost 100 families were not so lucky. Lyons lost both of its mobile home parks and many houses owned by 2nd, 3rd and 4th generation town residents. We were not able to return to our home for nearly eight weeks, a short time compared to those who are still not settled nearly two and a half years later.

Rebuilding and Recovery

Over the next several months our town leadership sprang into action. There were town hall meetings. There were FEMA (Federal Emergency Management Agency) meetings and appointments, insurance calls to make, and a tremendous outpouring of support as we all tried to return home and resume some semblance of normalcy.

One of the mobile home parks in Lyons – Riverbend – was destroyed; literally wiped out. These mobile homes were not simply flooded but rolled and damaged beyond repair. FEMA notified us that this mobile home park would not be rebuilt because it was located in a floodplain. The owners aided homeowners with clearing the debris and restoring the property. The newly imposed floodplain restrictions limited the uses of the property and what could be developed on the six acres of now cleared land. The solution was a special event venue.

That's when the idea hit me. If Lyons is going to have a new event venue with the closest chain hotel 16 miles away we should develop short term lodging.

WeeCasa is Born

I had long been fascinated with tiny houses and loved the idea of limiting the amount of stuff we possess. My wife and I have been backpackers for most of our lives and on our Appalachian Trail "thru-hike" had become obsessive about what we carried on our backs for the 2,000+ miles. We went so far as sharing one spork to eat our one daily hot meal. So living "light" is in my DNA.

Looking through FEMA floodplain regulations something that clicked for me read, "Recreational vehicle parks and campgrounds are often good uses for floodplains, particularly when flooding usually occurs during seasons when these facilities are not in use or where there is plenty of warning time prior to a flood." A lightbulb went off! We could build a private RV park that had tiny houses on wheels: RV's!

Being classified as an RV park we can host guests up to 30 days, but we can't allow people to live in tiny houses on the property.

My wife and I invested in the Riverbend property when the current owners were looking to get some new partners involved with changing the use of the property. We saw this beautiful piece of property right on the river that had caused so much damage as a place to rebuild. We recruited investors to start the WeeCasa business.

We wanted to have enough tiny houses to accommodate the wedding parties and decent sized groups. We would have ten tiny houses for rent as a hotel for people coming to Lyons for weddings and festivals. Craigslist provided the first two houses on the property: one new construction and one that had been saved from the flood north of Lyons. We spent a couple of weeks setting up the business plan and necessary permits.

We met Rod Stambaugh from Sprout Tiny Homes at a post-flood town meeting and discussed some creative ways to get tiny houses on site. We placed an order for eight tiny houses for Sprout to build in a jointly developed floor plan. Things were underway.

Over the summer, I left my corporate job to focus exclusively on WeeCasa. Brent, one of our partners, developed an incredible website and we registered with reservation software and credit card processing companies. We emailed promotional pricing to all of the people hosting events at Riverbend and reservations started to trickle in.

We hired Karen as our Operations Director who went about setting up the homes for hotel guests. Her attention to detail and ability to focus on many different tasks helped us create a great stay experience. Together with Brent and his wife, Karen decorated the tiny houses and outfitted them with French Press coffee makers, high quality linens, local artwork and great personal touches making the rooms both beautiful and functional.

What Is a Tiny House?
(We don't have regulations for that)

As many familiar with the tiny house movement know, not everyone is excited about tiny houses. Those in local government are tasked with implementing and enforcing the zoning and building regulations that take weeks, months and years to finalize. Tiny houses rarely fit into those rules and regulations.

With the event season approaching we started in earnest to build the infrastructure to support the tiny houses. The town utilities had been damaged in the flood but we expected them to be back in place before our first guests arrived in May. We were making good progress until we hit some roadblocks.

The new FEMA rules and the scale of the damage had taxed our town staff. We struggled to keep up with new requirements and new interpretations of regulations. The foundation on which we had built our business plan was shifting under us.

As for booking our first guests, unfortunately, we decided to build WeeCasa nearly nine months after most of our wedding events were scheduled, so many attendees had already planned other accommodations. We started weekly tours to grow interest in WeeCasa. Our tours were very popular as many people had never been inside a tiny home. Some weekends we had over 50 people schedule or stop by our tours. They marveled at the new units and many booked reservations to come and live tiny! Many people talked with us about building their own tiny house or buying a tiny house. It was exciting to see the response.

As our opening day approached we had to get creative. We had guest reservations and we needed to be open. We installed a water system: 4,000 gallons of tanks and a pump. We rented a construction generator to power the units. One of our partners, Steve, led the effort to get all of this in place. Without his herculean efforts, ingenuity and tenacity, we would have been sunk before we started.

We made it through 2015 and closed for the winter in November 2015 with almost 500 stay nights on the books. We were already getting inquiries for the 2016 season as the snow and cold weather started.

We have recently finalized the entire infrastructure but it took us a full season to do so. In 2016 we will re-open for the season and plan to remain open all year around.

I've Seen Tiny Houses on TV but I've Never Actually Stood in One!

WeeCasa was opened as a hotel, a dealership and a place to expose and educate people about tiny living and tiny houses. We wanted to allow people the opportunity to come and see, stay, talk about, fantasize about and plan their own tiny adventures.

We started giving tours three times a week. The first tour had three participants who were planning to buy a tiny house and move out of their apartment. We talked for hours while they walked through our five different floor plans. When they left, we were all excited. Over the summer the tours grew larger and larger in size. We started having 150 or more people attend the tours. Many came back to stay with us for a night or a weekend. We were gaining momentum.

I was fascinated by people's stories about how they discovered the tiny home movement. They talked about the benefits of tiny homes in general and the key benefits they were personally seeking. We spent hours pouring over floor plans and critiquing how we would design a 20-foot, and even a 24-foot home. We talked composting toilets, solar panels, electricity, and propane. We talked, we listened and the sheer volume of people that showed up for our tours was amazing. We were on to something!

We started working with other builders to place homes on the property and to participate in tours. We were slowing becoming part of the Colorado tiny house community. We met with SimBlissity Tiny Homes, Tiny Diamond Homes, Rocky Mountain Tiny Houses, and several smaller builders. We met Angie and Bobby from Tiny House America when they rolled through Lyons on their Tiny House Road Trip.

At some point we heard about the Tiny House Jamboree in Colorado Springs and decided to drive down to see what the "scene" was like. We were bleeding money from the sheer cost of the generator so the prospect of WeeCasa participating in the Jamboree with a booth or making a bigger investment wasn't even an option. We thought we would be there about two hours to walk around and see the sights, talk to some builders and other folks. When we arrived, it was insane with 10,000 people on just the first day. People stood in lines for up to 45 minutes just to see the inside of a tiny house. The positive energy and enthusiasm was amazing. We might be crazy in our endeavor but we weren't the only ones!

Gaining Momentum

As the season went on we hosted more guests who were also tiny home enthusiasts. One of our first guests called later in the summer saying he felt confident and ready to buy a tiny house after staying with us. Those guests later brought the film crew from one of the tiny house reality shows to our property for filming. Several of our homes were featured on these same television programs throughout the summer. The local newspaper wrote several articles highlighting WeeCasa. There were blog posts, an increase in our Facebook "friends," and just a general online buzz. We marketed with pro-

motions and our occupancy increased. We joined AirBnB and our occupancy increased even further.

We ended our season in November just shy of our original occupancy target. We closed as we were still waiting on all the necessary connections to utilities.

In December 2015 we held our first Wee Winter Festival on the property. Skye, one of our partners, created a great two-day event with tiny home tours, food, and live music. It was held on the same weekend as several Town of Lyons events and our sponsors helped get the word out. More than 700 people came for the tours, to learn more about tiny houses and to enjoy our winter fireworks. We even pulled three tiny houses in the Town's Parade of Lights. It might just be the world record for the "Most Tiny Houses in a Parade."

It was the perfect way to end our first season.

The Future of WeeCasa is Getting Bigger

When we designed the infrastructure we built 22 tiny house "slips" hoping that we could grow over time.

Since the Wee Winter Festival we have been approached by numerous builders and private individuals interested in parking their tiny houses on our property. This exciting opportunity is allowing us to provide more diversity in the houses we have on site and allows others to become part of our Tiny House Hotel.

We plan to have the entire park filled with tiny homes by the end of 2016 and will be open year-round starting in the Spring of 2016. We are also starting to work with others from around the country interested in building a WeeCasa-type hotel based in their area on our experiences. The Town of Lyons has embraced WeeCasa and we are excited about the things to come.

When people ask me, "How's it going at WeeCasa?" I always respond, "Getting Bigger!"

Tents, Ships, and Rivets
Wally Byam's Airstream

Dale "Pee Wee" Schwamborn

Dale "Pee Wee" Schwamborn is part of the Wally Byam and Airstream heritage. He has traveled on Airstream Caravans to Mexico, Central America, Canada, Africa (advance scout), and the Middle East. Pee Wee worked at the California factory. Today he gives lectures about Wally Byam, Helen Byam Schwamborn, and the African Caravan.

There is a cliché telling us that when a child is born the child receives parents and family as accorded by birth. My heritage is steeped in the Byam and Schwamborn families.

Helen Byam Schwamborn, my mother, and Wally Byam her first cousin were siblings whose fathers were brothers. Wally and Helen bonded in the 1930's and became good friends. The Byams and Schwamborns went camping together and other social activities.

In 1951 Wally Byam decided to expand the Airstream image by forming his first Caravan to Mexico and Central America. Wally asked my parents if I could going camping in the California High Sierras for a week. Wally gave me a nickname on the hike, Pee Wee; it has been part of my Airstream life now for 65 years. Our time camping gave Wally the opportunity to evaluate Dale now Pee Wee for traveling as his guest on his 1st Caravan.

In 1955 Wally needed someone to organize, and plan Caravans for him. He hired my mother, Helen. The Airstream owners formed a Club, which Helen was in charge of managing the Headquarters, the Wally Byam Caravan Club International. There were several additional Caravans I went on the two most memorable were the 1956 European Caravan, traveling with my mother. The other was working for Wally as the Advance Scout on the 1959 African Caravan from Cape Town to Cairo. The African Caravan lasted ten months including the Middle East, Balkans and joining a European Caravan in Trieste, Italy.

Wally and Helen were a team, and the most important aspect in their relationship was Helen was Wally's sounding board, I can only imagine about what was said between. All discussions were held in confidence. I'm asked about what they talked about. I have no idea.

In 1960 Wally wrote a very telling letter to Helen that's shows the years they shared together. "Your thinking and analysis has helped me a great deal. Again I give thanks for your excellent judgment—which I have never known to be anything but perfect. I am really proud of my little cousin. Thanks again, Wally."

Wallace Merle Byam passed away in 1962. What was a loss to the Airstream and the recreational vehicle world was even a greater family loss. Wally was my cousin, friend, mentor and employer and I dearly miss this wonderful man.

Helen Byam Schwamborn went on to work with Airstream as a board member. She was also on the board for the Wally Byam Foundation and other notable duties. She helped in the planning for the Around-the-World Caravan trans-continental travel from Singapore to Portugal. Visiting a geographical feast by going to India, Nepal, Thailand, Afghanistan, Iran, Syria, Turkey, Europe and most notably traveling to the Soviet Union and parking in Red Square.

After serving two years in U.S. Army I went to work for Airstream in their California factory for five years.

Helen retired at the age 75, in 1979.

In 1983 Gerard Letourneau, Airstream president, acknowledges Helen's contribution to Airstream in a letter.

He said, "…without the WBCCI and its support to the company, the future would have been doubtful for the company. Your earlier efforts to make the Club what it is today is recognized and sincerely appreciated. Indirectly, your help "saved" Airstream more than anyone could realize."

My mother passed away in 2004.

Since her passing I have worked with several writers for articles and books. The most notable is Russ Banham and his marvelous Airstream history as penned in Wanderlust, Airstream at 75.

Today I give talks about Wally Byam, Helen Byam Schwamborn, and the 1959 Airstream Wally Byam African Caravan. For *Turning Tiny*, this is Wally Byam's story.

> *It didn't matter how big our house was;*
> *it mattered that there was love in it."*
> —Peter Buffett, *Life Is What You Make It: Find Your Own*
> *Path to Fulfillment*

Wally Byam is universally recognized as the father of the travel trailer industry in America. He knew travel trailers as no one else ever did. But just manufacturing wasn't enough for Wally Byam. Wally not only built them, he used them; he not only used them himself but through the Wally Byam Caravans he opened unlimited vistas of trailer travel to thousands who searched for adventure and new experiences.[42]

Wallace Merle Byam came from pioneer stock and was born in Baker City, Oregon.

His life experiences including that of a sheephearder began to accumulate and guide him towards a self-contained trailer and a following of loyal owners traveling the compass in the United States and overseas. As a youth he tended his grandfather's sheep in the rolling hills of eastern Oregon, living in a shepherd's cart. This largely outdoor lifestyle certainly played a part in his later love of camping, especially in the California High Sierras.

Wallace learned to live in close quarters with just a bed, food storage and survival essentials with sparse space for anything else.

In 1921 he graduated from Stanford University in History. His degree isn't his only achievement though. He was a seaman many times over as a cabin boy on the Alaska fishing routes, and a sailor landing in Tahiti. His time at sea also contributed to his understanding of small spaces as he learned to live with a bunk and a locker in pocket-sized berthing quarters.

Wally stayed the avid camper enjoying the healthy hikes, open range and clean air.

Marion James and Wally Byam were married on June 21, 1924, and quickly became a tent camping couple enjoying the lifestyle of life outdoors. Marion was not however, fond of sleeping on or even near the ground launching a desire within Wally to find a more suitable camping situation for he and his bride. Though the exact details are not known it is widely believed that Byam bought a Ford chassis in the late-1920s from an auto junk dealer. This early trailer was more of a tent contraption on the Model T chassis. It was a start and launched Byam into a new, yet fledgling business, in which he was intent on designing a tear-drop shaped camping trailer and even manufacturing them.

> Throughout the late twenties I—and hundreds of others like me—continued to experiment with our back yard models. We discarded a thousand screwball ideas for every one that worked. I built boxes, tents, and trailer bodies on Model T chassis in effort to solve the whole problems of mobile living…[43]

Byam sold complete trailer kits, and finished trailers he built in his Los Angeles backyard. By 1930 he had abandoned advertising and publishing (his trade at the time) to become a full-time builder of Masonite travel trailers. The Airstream Company was incorporated in 1931. The Torpedo was the first factory-produced Airstream model, and by early 1932.

This home-crafted trailer was the 17' Torpedo, slept four adults with one double bed in the rear and two single bunks capable of being mounted along the sides, cold running water, a sink, a two-burner gas stove, a shower, and provisions for a commode. It is important to note that Byam's plans were for the basic shell alone and that the inside still had to be outfitted with any mechanics the owner may want. The Torpedo was made of Masonite rather than the aluminum Airstream known today. The monoque construction in that there is no frame. The body is the frame. The tongue is bolted to wooden stringers under the front floorboards. It was quite a creation for Depression-ridden America!

Wally Byam was an inventor and a cultivator. He kept up with the times and the availability of materials and designed the Airstream Airlite offering new floor plans and lengths to compete in the burgeoning manufacturing field and the advancement in customer requirements.

The modern Airstream gained its look from a much earlier advancement. In 1917 Anthony Fokker and Hugo Junkers applied duraluminum to Luftwaffe planes to make them lighter. This also required them to engineer pneumatic tools and a wide range of rivets to attach the metal. This allowed Hawley Bowlus, an engineer working with pilot Charles Lindbergh, to apply riveting to gliders and ultimately, travel trailers. He is best known for his Bowlus Road Chief travel trailer, the first technical application of duraluminum and rivets to manufacture a trailer.

From all of this rich manufacturing heritage Wally Byam saw the potential to engineer his own aluminum and rivet travel trailer. He began from the ground up and engineered and designed the Airstream Clipper in 1936. This addition, and its rivet design ultimately gave birth to the 1947 postwar Airstreams, which have continued into the 21st Century. The innovation doesn't stop there.

In 1941 Airstream received a contract from the Farm Security Administration to build emergency housing for defense workers in San Diego, California. Wally would take his understanding of small spaces and essential living to the mobile real estate world building simple, 8' x 20' hous-

es that would contain a bedroom, a kitchen, and a dinette. Other provisions would be made for showering and laundry. The relocatable housing trailers were designed to be used by families and dormitories to house single men.[44]

On December 7, 1941, The Day of Infamy, the United States declares war on Japan and the Axis and almost instantly switches American manufacturing from consumer goods to war materials. Airstream was forced to take a hiatus for nearly six years due to material shortages.

Wally Byam went to work at Lockheed's Burbank plant supervising some 300 employees as well as teaching at University of California at Los Angeles. During this period he fined tuned his knowledge in using sheet metal, riveting, constructing jigs and fixtures, and other essential skills in aircraft manufacturing.

In a series of notebooks from this period it became apparent that Wally was preparing to break into the camping world with a catalog, a how-to book and designs for camping gear. Camping had always been second nature to him. The notebooks outlined everything it would take to open an outdoor camping store and catalog center including how to finance the endeavor, how to begin operations, and even how to craft a book that would help the novice camper.

Wally never brought this dream to fruition though and towards the end of the war Curtis Wright contacted Wally Byam about designing and managing a new trailer venture. Wright had the financial backing and experience in manufacturing trailers to open said company and in 1946 the Curtis Wright trailer came to fruition. Their relationship was short lived and ended towards the end of 1946 or early 1947.

Byam reopened Airstream in 1947 and by 1948 demand was booming.

Even with his rediscovered success Wally Byam expressed a concern about the travel trailer industry. Through the Great Depression, war years, and post-war housing there was a stigma attached to "trailers." Too many trailers became derelicts in trailer parks or vagrant housing dotting the landscape. The more gentile home owners came up with a derogative connotation for trailer dwellers, "Trailer Trash." The phrase didn't distinguish between stationary travel trailers and mobile homes from those used by families on vacation or weekend jaunts. Wally gave a gift to the industry by his unwavering determination to change the attitudes towards travel trailers. From a small note he wrote:

WHAT IS A TRAVEL TRAILER?
A travel trailer is one whose un-laden weight is not more than the normal passenger car that tows it – used mainly for travel and not as a residence exclusively and legally towable without permits in any state in which it is used.

In 1948 Wally Byam and his close and life-long friend Cornelius Vanderbilt, Jr. took an Airstream to Europe. Neil was a journalist, writer, and lecturer, and wanted to capture Europe on film three years after the war's end. This was Byam's first European experience and had a profound influence on his life.

After the trip Wally authored a book entitled *Fifth Avenue on Wheels*. In it he dispensed insights and tips as well as ideas and wisdom on both travel and life. In its pages he continued to advocate a change in opinions about recreational vehicles.

Byam noted that the wealthy families built their mansions on Fifth Avenue in Manhattan. He then drew upon his relationship with Neil Vanderbilt and the Vanderbilt Mansion on Fifth Avenue to analyze prestige, travel, and trailers, in general. Byam enlisted his advertising background to increase his company's sales as well as make a major breakthrough in the travel trailer industry. Both were needed for the continuance of Airstream.

In 1951 he planned his first Wally Byam Caravan to Mexico and Central America. It lasted four months and successfully laid the groundwork for future trips. The media picked up immediately the unique way that groups might travel together. Hometown newspapers covered the trip, and national media followed the Caravan. It opened the doors for the recreational vehicle owners to hitch up and travel. The sleeping industry received an injection to enjoy the wonders in traveling with their homes towed behind their family's automobiles. On a more personal note Wally and Marion James divorced in 1952. Wally soon remarried to Estelle "Stella" North Hall.

In 1955, those hearty Caravanners that traveled on six Caravans wanted to be able to reunite in a Club. In Kentville, Nova Scotia Airstream owners wrote a constitution and bylaws voted on it, paid their dues and the Wally Byam Caravan Club became a reality. Airstream financially supported the Club, but Club matters were carried out in accordance with their by-laws. The Wally Byam Caravan Club incorporated in 1957. We must recognize that the Tin Can Tourist Club is the oldest ongoing recreational vehicle organization. The WBCCI is a single travel trailer Club that grew to over a 30,000-trailer membership.

Over the next decade Airstream organized additional Caravans to Mexico, Central America and Canada.

The Wally Byam Caravans expanded to include Cuba, 1956 Europe, 1959 African Caravan, and 1963 Around-the-World Caravan. The 1956 European Caravan spent six months touring western Europe, and had a write up in the June 1957 National Geographic magazine. The African Caravan traveled overland from Cape Town, Union of South Africa to Cairo, Egypt United Arab Republic, then to the Middle East and Europe. The Around-the-World Caravan traveled over 31,000 miles from Singapore to Portugal and lands' end. It took them 403 days with stops on the way in India, Nepal, Afghanistan, Iran, Turkey to name only a few of the countries traveled through, and they even parked the group in Red Square in Moscow, Soviet Union.

The 1959 Wally Byam African Caravan established a new role for Caravanners: a Caravan Scout. It is a tale worthy to be told by David Livingstone, the missionary and African explorer. At 20 years old I was extremely fortunate to hold this title on the African Caravan.

The job description was a simple one: check road conditions, find campsites, find local conveniences and talk with officials. Officials applied to town clerks, mayors, tourist guides, and government officers, for travel considerations and permissions. The scout truck itself was even a testament to reduced living space. With an interior space of approximately 7-1/2' x 13', it was everything Byam built upon in his career.

Having a back door created an aisle to the front of the unit. The sitting area's back was the upper bunk that was held in place by two chains when in the up position. The galley consisted of a small single sink, a two-burner gas range, a small 3 cubic foot gas refrigerator. For hot water, over the kitchen, was a Junkers instant water heater. The shower had a marine toilet and mounted shower head. There was a black or septic tank, but no grey or dirty water tank. The thirty-gallon water tank had an exterior filler pipe and cap. Water was obtained by carrying and filling the water tank with a jerry can and rarely at a service station with a hose. There were no water hookups available in Africa.

In another feat of engineering U.C.L.A provided a water purification system that filtered out the smallest parasite that would be encountered on the trip. The entire trip was completed without boiling water or adding chemicals. There were several doctors on the caravan who were always adamant about boiling water but the new technology of filtered water proved too much to resist!

The scout truck was a ton and a half Chevrolet rail, with the Airstream compartment attached to the frame. It was equipped with a four-wheel drive, a front mounted winch, a standard 30-gallon gas tank and two 50-gallon auxiliary gas tanks. The tanks were always topped of when gasoline was available. It was assumed that 10 mpg would give the caravan 1300 miles of driving.

There is one question frequently asked, "What did you eat during the trip?" "Who did the cooking?" I cooked and the assistant did the dishes, an equitable division of labor.

This is a quotation in a letter written to my parents.

We took the spare time and allotted it to servicing the truck, filling up the propane, washing the van, doing our laundry, etc. At this point the question arises – "do you boys do your own cooking? I do the cooking and Nick does the dishes. Our meals in the African Scout Car are varied. For breakfast some pancakes, or hot oats, maybe bacon, sausage and eggs, possibly with potatoes. Milk or tea is the morning beverage. For lunch we generally eat light, soup. Dinner is varied – steak, spaghetti, potatoes, peas, string beans, carrots, and plenty of fresh fruit. Also on our menu is macaroni, pot roast, lamb chops, smothered steak, etc. Desert is generally fruit, but we do have cake, Jell-O and ice cream. I do the shopping and all of food I bought in the market, so far we haven't had to live out of cans, and all of our food is fresh.

Living in approximately 80 sq. ft. for over ten months was wonderful, amazing and unbelievable.

Wally Byam's mind was always in motion. He was constantly considering trailer enhancements, designs, materials and marketing moves. It is no wonder then that when he returned from the 1959 African Caravan, he put his team to work on a project; for the sake of mystery, "Project Bambi."

He and Stella spent four months in a scaled down custom Airstream. Wally understood that a couple could travel in comfort in a small trailer that didn't require a top of the line tow vehicle. He wanted a trailer that was capable of being towed by a smaller vehicle altogether. The Bambi had a 13-foot exterior body length and an exterior width of 81 inches. The interior floor space approximately 81.3 sq. ft. and became a very popular model.

Wally had another idea in the late 1950s. He created a two-mold small fiberglass trailer. It looked similar to a Casita trailer. The prototype, the only one produced, was ready to test in 1962. The mold designer and fiberglass department manager took it all the way to Managua, Nicaragua that year. Airstream quietly shelved the project for reasons still undetermined. Today the prototype is in Colorado being restored.

Sadly Wallace Merle Byam passed away on July 22, 1962.

In our eyes, Wally Byam was the prime vehicle on which the travel trailer road to its present-day popularity and usefulness in an age of recreational prosperity.

It will never be argued that Wally Byam will remain an exciting and important chapter in the annual of travel trailering.

—Art Griffin, Editor and Publisher, *Trail-R-News*

Wally was delightfully human... he decided that Airstream and Wally Byam should be synonymous. No one who knew him, however distantly, ca regret not knowing him better, for at heart he was sentimentalist who was determined that he would sell people an object that would make their lives happier, and then show them how to use it.

—Jack Kneass, Managing Editor, *Trail-R-News*

His handpicked team continued on though turning Airstream into the industry leader it is today.

Stella Byam eventually sold the company to several members of the Airstream Board in the early 1960s. The company remained private until 1966 when it went public. In less than a year Beatrice Foods, a conglomerate, purchased the company.

In 1973 the RV industry underwent its first near miss when the oil crisis crippled the United States and gasoline prices skyrocketed. Changes had to be made. Automobile requirements in the United States changed and large sedans with super plus horsepower engines gave way to small mid-size and compact cars with reduced engine capacities. What would the RV industry do?

The recreational world switched to light weight trucks with traction, transmissions and horsepower to tow trailers. This led to van conversions, motorhomes, and fifth wheels joining the existing travel trailer industry. As a company Airstream changed as well. It was purchased by Thor Industries and its product line expanded.

The RV industry likewise changed introducing light weight feather trailers, traditional trailers, class "B" conversions, hefty fifth wheelers, and behemoth motorhomes; with varieties and modifications too numerous to categorize.

In recent years vintage recreational vehicles have grown in popularity. The Tin Can Tourists, Vintage Airstream Club and other organizations anchor enthusiasts. There is a thriving industry remodeling, and refurbishing the old RV's. Vintage trailers fit very nicely with the do-it-yourself families.

There is a phenomenon today with all recreational vehicles, the "full-timers." Most full-timers are retired and want the fresh air, the horizon and adventure more than a stationary dwelling and physical assets. Let's call them "road warriors" for they go everywhere and their numbers of kindred spirits is growing. As with the tiny house movement, living space in the recreational vehicle world is determined by the individual, financial means, environmental beliefs, life styles, locality, and fluidity, tenants Wally Byam understood all too well.

From Tiny Shops to Tiny Houses

Marc McQuain

After starting a career in residential design and construction, Marc McQuain got involved with retail development. While living in Dubai during the last recession, he used an engineered, lightweight, steel framing system to develop a relocatable, small format, modular retail shop. Upon returning to the United States in 2015, he discovered the exploding tiny house movement and was able to employ his engineering designs to help right-size the industry.

In the spring of 2007 I was debating the pros and cons of relocating my family to Dubai to take advantage of the business opportunities arising out of the region's rapid retail development. Our young company, Vindico Retail, specialized in large scale Retail and Mixed-Use development and had done well, but the size and maturity of the US retail market meant that I was on the road a lot more than I was home.

We had been approached a few times about opportunities in the Middle East and usually declined, however, that spring I was averaging about one weekend a month at home in San Jose with my wife and children and the rest of the time spread across various projects on the East coast. We had another opportunity in Dubai that was on the verge of being too good to pass up, but what clinched the deal was the fact that they were building more large-scale retail projects in that one city, than were under development in the entire USA. No matter how busy we got I was nearly assured that I would get to spend every evening at home with my family.

Arriving in Dubai, we did what most people did when they got there. We set a budget, hired a relocation specialist to help us navigate the white-hot residential market, and started looking at property after property that either didn't suit or we were out bid, or too slow to commit. Our "bargain" rent was nearly $7,000 per month but Vindico had just signed a large contract and the villa was a good size for entertaining and in the "right" neighborhood for the Managing Director of an up-and-coming company.

After securing a place to live we went home to San Jose and began the big purge. We had a dumpster dropped in front of the house and over the next couple of weeks and weekends we started my second favorite part of the international relocation – getting rid of all the "extra" stuff! This was going to be my sixth international relocation. My wife was working for Apple at the time and had committed to staying stateside through the launch of the first iPhone. This meant I would have to run the garage sales, which I wasn't thrilled about. It did, however, represent an unprecedented opportunity to get rid of stuff.

In the days before we left the US we further organized our material selves into the things we "need" for the next two months and everything else. We locked the "needed" pile in a closet with lots of caution tape and "do not pack" signs (we learned the hard way how poorly post-it notes or the "this, but not that" systems worked in our previous moves).

The movers came, packed everything into a shipping container and after one more stop at our new storage unit, we headed off to the airport.

About 30 hours later we arrived on the doorstep of our villa in Dubai. This was the beginning of my favorite part of an international relocation – the six to eight weeks that you have until the container that is packed with all your other gear finally tracks you down and explodes in your new home. For me this has always been when I am at my most efficient. I know where everything is. I tend to put things back where they are supposed to go. I don't have to plan my weekends around wrangling stuff, and the kids play with the things they have instead of walking past a mountain of toys and games to say they are bored.

The challenge with the new house was that it was twice as big as the one we had moved from. In addition to replacing all the stuff that I had managed to sell or get rid of we now had to furnish almost an entire house from scratch. Eventually our container arrived. The mini-Christmas feeling that happens when people are reunited with 67 cubic meters of stuff (a lot that they had forgotten about and most that they hadn't needed) settles into the more mundane days of unpacking boxes every evening to fill the shelves, closets and garage until eventually all the boxes are stacked at the curb to be recycled.

We worked very hard for about a year and things were going well. We had signed several new contracts, moved to a bigger office, and hired new staff. My original plan of staying two to three years to get the company up and running started to look a lot more like three years as the news from the States and the UK became more and more depressing. The Global Financial Crisis was wreaking havoc in our industry. We heard stories and received emails every week from colleagues in the architectural, construction, development and retail sectors that were losing their jobs, their homes and their companies. It was a difficult time and we felt thankful that, whether through business acumen or dumb luck we found ourselves working in a part of the world that would avoid slowing down at any cost. There seemed to be plenty of money and cancelling a project, or laying people off was viewed as being weak in a market that was built largely on bravado: selling huge dreams based on pretty renderings, speculation, and blind trust that the double digit growth would continue.

Eventually, Dubai went the way of the rest of the world. People were laid off and eventually projects were cancelled. We realized pretty quickly that we had been naïve in being thankful that we were in Dubai. In 2008 and 2009 the United Arab Emirates (UAE) was still a frontier market (they reached emerging market status in 2014) so where the recession in the U.S. and other mature markets was playing out based on the same rules of previous recessions this was a first for the UAE and there was no structure for bankruptcy, or liquidation as things started to unravel.

For individuals who had moved to the UAE this meant that the home and car loans that they easily secured by signing a security check for 100% of the loan value became due and payable within days of being laid off. As the central bank began freezing personal bank accounts, thousands of expatriates found themselves in a position where missing their next mortgage or car payment left them choosing between packing a suitcase and leaving or the risk of going to jail. While not everyone was living beyond their means even those who had been in the country for years and had built a responsible future for their families, were forced to abandon much of what they had worked for due to no fault of their own. The urban myth of rows of cars lined up at Dubai international airport was a reality.

I suppose in some ways, without the recession we wouldn't be part of the tiny house movement today.

For our business, the next few years would be very difficult. We went from twelve contracts to a single project. We had to lay off dozens of people, many of whom we knew would have no choice but to return to their home countries and probably never return. We were owed large sums of money that were never repaid. My family moved out of the villa, my wife and kids returned to the states, our stuff got piled into a storage unit, and I spent a year staying with friends, or funds permitting, in monthly or weekly hotel rooms.

I spent a lot of time at our office during those days. There wasn't a lot to do but not being there seemed too much like giving up, so every day and most evenings were spent trying to find new work or think of a way to help get the business back on track.

The lone project we still had was not easy. It was a very high profile retail scheme being developed by one of the region's biggest government developers and had been designed by one of the UK's world renowned architects. It was a beautiful building, but, unfortunately, it wasn't a very good retail space, which made it challenging for our client's tenants. One of the issues we grappled with was an inability to install mezzanines within the tenants shops. We had lots of space but the building's structural design didn't allow for the installation of additional areas. After countless failed attempts we finally came across a building system that could provide a mezzanine structure that was both strong enough and light enough to solve our mezzanine dilemma.

We received a submission from a small company who proposed using a lightweight steel system instead of the much heavier steel being proposed by other builders. We had used metal framing for years and I assumed that this was the same so I visited their workshop to understand how their calculations could be so different and to see how the mezzanines were being constructed. Instead of seeing a shop full of experienced metal workers cutting and fabricating the mezzanines, what I saw instead was what I would learn was a state of the art roll-forming machine. The machine reminded me of the 3D printers that were always being talked about but instead of a roll of plastic filament this machine had a 1-ton coil of galvanized steel being fed into it. I watched as one of the mezzanines was designed on the computer and then loaded onto a USB stick that was plugged into the roll-forming machine where it was extruded into what looked like a child's erector set with all the parts pre-punched and labeled so that the small team of workers could assemble the entire structure in just a short time. After years in the design and construction sector this new system was a revelation. By using the computer designed and manufactured cold rolled steel structure we were able to deliver the mezzanines faster and cheaper than any other method.

A feature of a place like Dubai is that it draws people from all over the world. In addition to the mixing of cultures and ways of doing things, such diversity brings a myriad of ways to solve an issue. The roll- forming system that was brand new to me was commonplace in New Zealand and has been used in residential construction for over 20 years. There were quite a few roll-forming machines in the region due to its rapid growth. Most were being used to build large-scale residential projects throughout the Middle East.

During the late nights in the empty office a couple of recurring themes kept surfacing. The first was sustainability. The retail sector had been paying lip service to sustainability for a few years but it was finally starting to be taken seriously. The other was activating vacant shops. The malls in Dubai are much larger than most of the malls in the USA and Dubai Mall, one of the world's largest, has over 1200 shops and restaurants. Unfortunately, many of the malls open with long runs of vacant units, a catch-22 that makes the difficulties in getting shops open adversely affect the shops that did open. Given that our company built its reputation on some of the most successful mall openings in history, this conundrum became a big focal point.

When I saw the roll-forming machine I knew it had the potential to solve one of the biggest stumbling blocks for an idea that had been kicking around for some time. We had built small "bump back" shops to activate vacant spaces on past shopping center projects, but the problem with these was that they were very expensive one-offs and as soon as a permanent tenant was found they were thrown in the dumpster. The roll-forming machine allowed us to design a modular shop unit that could be installed very quickly and then removed and relocated to another vacant space when a permanent tenant was found. We convinced our one remaining client to let us install a prototype and over the next two nights, with the help of a couple of laborers I designed and installed what we later developed into the first ever PocketShop.

In addition to creating a new form factor for a temporary shop that could be installed in one night and removed or relocated in just four hours, we also inadvertently created a way for new tenants that either couldn't afford, or didn't have a track record, to operate in high profile retail environments. In a market that typically says 'no' to things that aren't proven, both landlords and tenants were very positive about this innovative new concept. We launched a new business, POP Retail, with new partners and restructured Vindico to allow me to spend more time on the new business.

My family was able to rejoin me in Dubai as the market started to bounce back through 2011 and 2012. My oldest son Jayson would spend the next couple of years working around the clock to install PocketShops at night and spend the days helping with other aspects of the business. Vindico was recovering and POP Retail was growing quickly. As things continued to improve I had to focus more of my time on Vindico and on the bigger retail projects that were now starting back up again. Although we had tried to keep a low profile on what we were doing in Dubai with the PocketShops, word was gradually starting to get out and we were receiving calls from other regions wanting to start PocketShop programs of their own. This recession had been different for many retailers as well. While a lot of stores closed for good, due to the length and severity of the downturn there were not the normal crop of new retailers waiting to fill the void. This, coupled with the accelerated changes in online retail, meant Landlords were struggling to fill space. We knew we needed to make a few changes so that we could push the sustainability agenda and create more flexible retail environments.

In 2014 with both businesses doing well it was time to return to the US. We had deployed over 150 PocketShops with more than half of the brands in them being either new to the region or new to retailing. In order to focus on PocketShops we purchased our own roll-forming machine and set up a small manufacturing company in Austin, Texas. We went through another international move. Our 2-3 year trip to Dubai ended up being closer to eight years. Time flies. When I finally made it back to San Jose to see what we had left in our storage unit, there was nothing that was worth relocating to Texas with us. We could have paid for the contents of the unit many times over with the monthly rental fees but we had simply lost track of what we had and where things were. Time for another purge. It was great to be back stateside and we were really looking forward to the challenge of a product-based business.

We ordered the roll- forming machine at the start of 2015 but before it had even arrived our sales rep from Framecad (the New Zealand based manufacturer of the system) asked if we would be interested in building small houses. Our first response was "thanks for the referral, but we are committed to focusing on the PocketShops and sticking to the industry we know best." We didn't want to be a residential builder. After the fourth or fifth call and a few more from a very persistent builder named Mike Bedsole from Chattanooga who, after a year of research, was adamant that Lightweight Steel Framing was the best way to frame a tiny house, I figured I should at least do a little research. I needed to better defend my reasoning if I was going to continue to get calls about these little houses. While the tiny house movement was off and running in the US, we were pretty isolated and had never come across the term.

I started with the video that was creating the interest. A gentleman in New Zealand named Bryce Langston had made a series of videos (Living Big in a Tiny House) showing how he had used the Framecad lightweight steel framing system to build a small house on a trailer. The videos were well produced and informative and definitely showed the benefits of the steel framing for this application. Of course I was already a convert, I had just spent a year convincing my business partner that we should invest the first profits we had seen in a very long time into our own machine. But, as I watched more videos I would alternate between excitement and concern.

On the one hand, it was very exciting to see the similarities between what we had been doing in the retail sector as a small company with a single voice and how a similar message regarding downsizing and a more sustainable approach to residential could capture the imagination of thousands of people. On the other hand, some of the videos that showed people building their own tiny houses were cause for concern. You didn't need a lot of architecture or building experience to see that many of the homes were being built on trailers that were never meant to carry a house and that the framing and other construction methods that were being used could become serious safety issues.

Many of the people who had taken the time to blog or upload video of their projects were young and eager to challenge the conventional wisdom as to where how they should live. However, it was easy to see how a shift to a simpler life could benefit people from all walks, and at many different stages of life.

As I spoke with more friends and family members it was interesting how many people were aware of the movement. While there were a couple of naysayers, most people that I talked to watched the shows and talked about the idea of a simpler life as though they were talking about an around the world trip, like it was something that they could only dream about. It struck me as odd that something this aspirational could be so easily within the reach of so many. Most aspirations require more of something; more time, more money, more exercise. The tiny house movement required less of almost everything.

My wife reminded me of all the people we were able to help realize their retail aspirations with PocketShops and how similar this was to Tiny houses, so, I made a couple of phone calls. The first was to my business partner, Peter Row, who lived in Australia, and like me had never heard of a tiny house. I explained what the houses were, why they were on trailers, how it was similar to what we were about to do with retail (except much further along the curve) and why I thought it was important for the movement to grow. He asked the usual questions, is it a trend or a fad? Who is doing it? What's the difference between tiny houses, RVs and mobile homes? It was a long call. My chief recollection was that we kept coming back to there being so many positives that it would be a terrible tragedy if it never came to fruition not least because the houses we were seeing had these inherent safety concerns.

Because the tiny houses were not covered under any formal codes they didn't have to go through a building plan review or building inspection process. That doesn't mean that people weren't building their tiny houses to their local codes.

In fact, as more professional builders entered the THOW arena the houses certainly benefitted even without formal signoffs. However, the most glaring omission that still remained was the fact that many building codes don't require a structural review for one and two story houses. So, individuals and even builders didn't think they were skipping an important step in ensuring their tiny house was built safely. There are states, like California, that require an engineer's review on all homes. But even states without a blanket requirement still recommend that complex or non-standard designs be reviewed by an engineer. A house being driven down the road definitely qualifies as both non-standard and complex.

My second call that day was to tell Mike that we would build the frame for his house. Jayson had returned to the states and was now our lead designer so the two of them designed our first Tiny House and we rolled it later that week. He arrived that weekend and we erected the house frame on his trailer. It took just a few hours and by Sunday evening he was heading back to Chattanooga.

On Monday we rolled our second tiny house. Peter and I had agreed that if we were going to take a slight detour on our retail journey it would be worth getting a little first-hand information. The second annual Tiny House Convention was being held in Portland, Oregon the following weekend so we erected the house frame on a trailer and packed a bag for the 2000-mile trip from Austin to Portland.

A quick call to the engineer to see if it was possible to drive the frame across country without any sheathing on it was met with what sounded like a shoulder shrug followed by a "why would you do that?" but ended with a few concerns about the amount of wind load on each individual stud. We ran around town to pick up signage and our freshly embroidered shirts and hit the road Wednesday evening.

The engineer was right about the wind load; even though the house was a very light 1,200 lbs., it towed like it weighed ten times that. We made many more fuel stops than expected as a result of the wind drag and hit a snowstorm in Colorado that required a 4-hour detour through Wyoming but after 37 hours on the road we arrived on Friday evening. The steel frame looked the same as when we had left Austin!

The show started the next morning and it was an interesting mix of reactions. There were a few people who seemed genuinely hostile to the fact that we had a steel house (not to mention matching embroidered polo shirts.) One person said that steel "just didn't feel right" for a tiny house, but for the most part what we were struck by was the enthusiasm and passion that the participants had for tiny houses. The last retail convention I had been to had tens of thousands of people but most of the passion was reserved for the golf course. The 350 people who had come to this show couldn't have been more excited and were eager to learn whatever they could from the speakers as well as from the handful of tiny houses that were on display. It was a great event for us because we got to stand inside our first group of tiny houses and see the enthusiasm of the people behind the movement.

My sense when we left the conference was that the tiny house movement was in transition. It made sense that the people who had been involved in the early days would be resistant to builders and businesses crashing their party, but what they had created was too important to not grow.

I spent a lot of that spring and early summer back in Dubai but when I returned to Austin at the end of July we decided that if we were going to build more tiny houses we should go to the first Tiny House Jamboree in Colorado Springs which was less than two weeks away. We were excited that it was only half the distance to drive as the last show! We designed a new tiny house that included a roof deck, a large patio, outdoor kitchen, as well as adding a garage with a deck that was accessed by an alternating tread staircase.

The Jamboree was nothing short of amazing. We arrived on Thursday and erected the whole stage. We were expecting to spend Friday catching up on emails and doing other work but when the gates opened there were people literally running from the entrance to get into the tiny houses. We made a lot of new friends and met a few kindred spirits, like Damon and Natalie at Trailer Made Trailers, who shared our vision for specializing and making the best product we can to support the movement. The rest of the weekend was just as crazy and we left Colorado Springs as excited about the people that we continued to meet as we were about our future role in the movement. Whether they were builders or future do-it-yourselfers, everyone we met was very keen to be involved.

Many people ask me if the tiny house movement reached its tipping point at the Jamboree. I usually say that it has but it has not been able to "tip" yet because we still have a major hurdle to overcome with regard to how tiny houses and small houses can be incorporated into communities and how they can be a meaningful part of our future town planning. Once we figure out where to put tiny houses, the pent up demand will be truly disruptive to the existing residential market.

We think an important step to allowing tiny homes to be legally placed means ensuring that lawmakers have confidence that they are built to acceptable standards. By using an engineered steel frame we are using a state of the art construction method that far exceeds the residential status quo and is designed for its intended purpose.

The biggest driver for most people is the amount of weight that can be saved when building with a steel frame versus wood. Many of the other benefits; sustainability, superior strength, more flexibility in design, lower maintenance and longer life, resistance to mold, termites and fire, become more important as the projects move into the later stages of construction.

Our tiny house building partners like the time that can be saved when using our frames but one of the things we most enjoy hearing from our do-it-yourselfers is how quickly their house got underway once they received their framing. An unfortunate statistic within the tiny house community is how many houses get started but never get finished. It is great to help people create momentum at the start of their projects and ensure that the design that they have chosen is safe and engineered to take them down whatever path lies ahead.

In the months following the Jamboree we developed several other engineered designs and we have continued to work with both tiny house builders and do-it-yourselfers. What we thought was going to be a quick detour to help a few do-it-yourselfers get off on the right foot has turned into an exciting and very rewarding experience for both my family and my business. Tiny houses are currently the dominant part of our steel framing business.

The tiny house movement embodies so many aspirational qualities that there seems to truly be something for everyone. Whether it is being more organized, having financial freedom, or the ability to travel, living a more sustainable life, or investing extra time and resources into more rewarding experiences versus having more stuff.

For us, the Turning Tiny process has happened over many years. It started with a combination of the freedom we experienced at the beginning of each overseas relocation, along with seeing how well the rest of the world does at living within much smaller footprints and much simpler lives. We are looking forward to being a part of the tiny house movement for years to come.

When Business Dreams Become Business Realities

Andrew Stewart

Andrew Stewart's path to the tiny house movement is paved with experience in outdoor adventure, travel abroad, and even foreign language studies. Together with his father Andrew began Mill Creek Ranch Resort in Austin, TX to showcase how affordable cottages could be used to create resort communities. His view of *Turning Tiny* exceeds just the standard one-off, factory model, and instead focuses on the business of developing tiny home resorts and community around the country, allowing residents to live big while living small.

I was honored and a bit surprised when I was asked to contribute my family's experience with tiny houses to the *Turning Tiny* book. As owners and operators of Mill Creek Ranch Resort, we occupy a distinct niche in the tiny house universe. Our resort features 399 sq.ft. park models (or cottages, if you will) that are classified as recreational vehicles by the RVIA. We also offer 100 spaces for traditional recreational vehicles making us a diverse and inviting community in the east Texas town of Canton. To date our focus has been offering tiny houses as vacation homes rather than primary residences. So far it has been a true recipe for success offering the best to us in regards to business and our guests and residents in regards to lifestyle!

In 2004 my parents' small town suffered a huge loss in that one of its major employers – Champion Factory – closed shop. While others saw an obvious setback my father saw opportunity. He knew that if he applied his authentic brand of capitalist philanthropy to the situation he could bring the factory back and create employment opportunities for those who had recently lost theirs. My dad was not interested in traditional manufactured housing. It was not his area of expertise. He was an entrepreneur and an educated chemical engineer. In fact, in 1990 he and a partner founded Murex, a company that provided gasoline blendstocks to refiners. It was there that he developed and adopted a principle of adapting to all the changing conditions within a marketplace. As a result Murex still is a nimble company that has changed focus numerous times over the years yet still remained relevant and successful. Suffice to say, my father has never really been afraid to jump into unfamiliar waters and since he was not an expert in the mobile home business he sought help. Turns out one of his neighbors had made a career in the mobile home industry and served as a great consult.

My dad asked the gentleman what the recently closed, 140,000 sq.ft. plant could be used for other than the traditional mobile homes that it had been making. The answer was park models.

Not a mobile home, yet not an RV either, park models appealed to a number of target markets and proved to be my family's entry into the world of tiny houses. My father again made a shrude business move, and brought in a retired CFO from the mobile home sector, the owner of a transport company, and the former manager of the factory itself. My father was assembling the best of the best so that he could create a company that would serve a need as well as offer jobs to a recently paralyzed community.

Soon after, my father came to me to see if I had any ideas about what kind of park models we should build. In our twenties my wife and I we spent time traveling and camping in a VW Westphalia and loved the efficiency of the tiny space. We understood perhaps more than anyone that every corner and nook of the van was designed to be both functional and beautiful. Later, while thinking of building a house on some land we own outside of Austin, Texas, we became fans of the work of Sarah Susanka and her *Not So Big House* collection. We were drawn to the idea of quality over quantity and designs that emphasize comfort, beauty and a high level of detail. In park models, we saw an opportunity to apply some of Ms. Susanka's principles as well as the efficient design of the VW Westphalia. 399 sq.ft. does not allow for wasted space. We all agreed we wanted to build small, expertly constructed, second homes that featured beautiful finishes, and efficient use of every square foot. The existing equipment and set up of the factory made it fairly easy to shift from building standard single and double wide mobile homes to higher end park models. Pretty quickly after we started building park models, we realized that helping people find a place to park them was going to be an essential next step. We had seen park models used in a few RV resorts, so my father started looking for some land nearby where we could build a resort that was capable of accommodating the very park models we were building in the factory. We found a small cattle ranch not too far away in Canton, Texas. It was across the street from the First Monday Trade Days which features home furnishings, imports, and every imaginable collectible. This shopping event alone attracts hundreds of thousands of shoppers a year, so we decided that this would be a high profile location for a resort featuring park models. The land was also home to an existing RV park that we could absorb into our resort. We went to work with a few RV park designers to come up with a reasonable plan.

Every plan we saw was crowded, packing in as many rental spaces as possible. We wanted to remain faithful to the concept of quality over quantity. To do so we decided on a design that took advantage of the natural beauty of the land as well as giving people more shared common space. As the plan developed I began to see a little village of park models surrounded by creeks, ponds, and trees. I wanted this to be a tranquil, beautiful, and safe place for people to enjoy and interact with nature, so we decided that we would use golf carts instead of cars to access the park models. To this end we now have a concierge system to help you unload your car upon arrival and carry your personal belongings and supplied to your house. Once settled, you can walk anywhere you want or you can rent a golf cart for your stay.

As Mill Creek continued to grow, we realized we were going to need a rental model for our resort. We wanted our focus to be on ownership rather than just rental units. We researched other resorts with park models, studied their business models, and formed our own plan. We wanted to feature the park models as an affordable way to have a vacation home. My family knew from our own personal experience of owning a vacation home, that there are a number of additional costs in having a second home: property taxes, utilities, home owners association fees, and maintenance costs, all of which can make a vacation home a very expensive proposition. The model we were putting together at Mill Creek Ranch Resort would allow people to have a vacation home that could, in turn, generate enough rental income to cover or at least off set the expenses of a second home ownership. We set up a rental-sharing program that allows for the resort to be profitable and the cottage owners to have a second home cum second income.

Another perk is that since park models are considered RV's for property tax purposes and the cottage owners don't have to buy the land, we are able to provide a second home without adding the burden of property taxes to the owner. We started out by offering a variety of options for rental sharing, but have now settled on a 70/30 split with 70% funneling to the resort and 30% to the owner. The resort takes care of the maintenance of the park model itself as well as the pools, landscaping, marketing, advertising, and booking.

Mill Creek Ranch Resort has been in successful operation now for nearly eight years and in that time we have come to the conclusion that in order to keep up with the demands of the market we need to expand the resort into a nationwide network. We want our park model owners to have sister parks around the country that they can visit where they will be confident that they will enjoy the same level of amenities they enjoy at Mill Creek Ranch Resort. It may prove a challenge since Mill Creek proudly offers water features near every cottage, nature trails, sporting courts, Frisbee golf, a well-appointed lodge, event spaces, outdoor pavilions, playgrounds, and swimming pools, but it is one we are certainly up for. In fact, we have recently entered into a conversation with EcoVentures, LLC to find similar resorts that will help create a remarkable network, as well as to develop new properties, or partner with parks to help them develop their properties. There is no doubt that a

nationwide network of resorts, will give people the opportunity to have tiny homes in beautiful locations across the county at a reasonable price.

As the tiny house movement has grown, we have had a growing number of requests for a permanent living option at Mill Creek Ranch Resort. When had no real idea that people would want to live full time in 399 sq.ft. Because of the increased interest in tiny houses though, we have begun to explore creating a permanent tiny house community. We have more than 200 acres of land that we have not begun to develop and it seems perfect for the next phase of our ideas. A number of the inquiries we have received have come from local artists and artisans who represent at the First Monday Trade Days. Largely because of them we envision a community with studio space, community gardens, and chicken coops even. We are constantly encouraged by the endless opportunities in our future. For a lot rental fee people could settle their tiny house and join a vibrant community.

What my father originally envisioned was little more than way to provide a future for my family and a future for his community. What we have developed is a future for the nation though and we couldn't be more proud of where the tiny house world is taking us!

Tiny Obsession – Big Results

How a one-man micro-cabin crusade has done so well

Derek "Deek" Diedricksen

Derek "Deek" Diedricksen is an designer, builder, and blogger, and author of "Microshelters," and "Humble Homes, Simple Shacks." This Boston-area tiny house addict built his first "non-fort"/cabin in 1987 after reading Lester Walker's "Tiny Houses," and hasn't looked back. Since then, he and his brother Dustin have taught building workshops "From Fargo To Sydney," have been featured in the NY Times, Boston Globe, and yahoo.com's homepage, hosted and designed for the HGTV series "Tiny House Builders," and have been chosen to speak at events ranging from SxSW in Austin, TX, to institutions such as M.I.T, Vanderbilt, and Walden Woods. Derek's blogs at RelaxShacks.com.

Ya' know, I've often been asked one question (well, aside from "Deek, did you play with mercury as a kid?"), time and time again when it comes to what I do for a living, and that's just it, "How the heck did you arrive at doing what you're now doing?" The funny thing is, with three past books I've written (including the damn-hard-to-find "Quick Camps, and Leg Cramps" tiny shelter book I once sold out of my basement) and over three hundred YouTube videos, I've never really touched upon it. Sure, I've had the conversation quite a few times with select "lifers" and "vets" in the scene like Steven Harrell of TinyHouseListings, Tiny r(E)volution's Andrew Odom, and Kent Griswold of TinyHouseBlog, but I've never really yacked about it, or blurted forth my "story," if you want to call it that, on paper. And lets face it, in this burgeoning scene, most people are just concerned with pretty pictures, a quick viral-worthy, or bait-able, internet tag line, or some hot babe hosting an online video – it sells, it works, always has, and will continue to, and doesn't usually require depth or good content. But when I was asked to write about this facet of, and the lineage of what I'm now doing, it surprised me, yet didn't (and made me wonder "how can I work babes, some killer lead title, and something viral-destined into all of it?").

But back to reality.

"Darin, this is going to bore the pants off people," I said, when talking with this book's helmsman, "They want my usual juvenile jokes, self-depre-cation, and hope on how they can build a house for $45.87 in under a week (newsflash: you can't). My forte is salvaging, and recycling junk that I work into whimsical tiny houses, tree houses, and backyard offices!? This is just a big curve ball of seriousness for anyone who half knows about my work! You sure about this?" Perhaps Darin too, had played with mercury as a kid?

Well, Darin Z. was sure, and the more I thought about it, it did make a bit of sense. For starters, here's the thing: at one point I was only the sixth blog out there – on friggin' planet Earth – that was dedicated to tiny houses. For this reason, it was pointed out, I just might have some insight into what makes a tiny house-based business last. I mean, I've seen so many of them come and go, and with the new television and media attention that "tiny" keeps receiving (hell, HGTV was even foolish enough to let me host, design, and build for them for a short series!), it seems that many traditional builders out there are misleading themselves into thinking that this whole conversion-to-tiny game will result in them rolling up at their next high school reunion like monacle-donning Monopoly-guy lookalikes, or Ivanka Trump, in no time flat. Well, rude awakening time, people, the "game," as I see it, takes a hair more than knowing how to throw a T-111 shed onto a rusty Craigslist-gleaned Jayco pop-up trailer frame. I WISH it were that easy. But then again, in a way, it HAS been easy, and here's why, AND what differentiates some of the builders from others.

Ok, and I'm going to sound like a total jerk by saying this, but I'm a total tiny house, tiny shelter, and small space addict, and have been since 1987, when I got ahold of Lester Walker's book "Tiny Houses," and set upon build-ing my first serious cabin. What I'm getting at is that this is no passing fad for me, and that's the case with many others I consider not only friends, but suc-cessful and innovative builders in the scene. Guys like Joe Everson from Tennessee Tiny Homes, Dan Louche from Tiny Home Builders, and old-school stalwarts David and Jeanie Stiles – we're all total nerds who truly love and believe in the concept of living smaller or more reasonable lives by taste, necessity, or environmental approach. We each have our reasons, but not one of us, got into this to be TMZ-reportable, or rolling in riches... and none of us are. I make a decent living by working my skinny white butt off, and these other guys/gals do the same. Now, I could attempt eloquence in prose and flow from one idea to another, but instead, I'm going to cut to the chase of what I think makes a tiny house business work, whether it be by design, intent, or approach. I'll leave you my "word of wisdom" and then I'm off to the next project, which I will barely have time for, but will say "yes" to, simply because I love doing this. And that segues right into one of my main points.

Love It To Death (Well, not literally)

LOVE, I mean friggin' LOVE what you're doing. Goal one should NOT be the Rolex with a tiny house outlined in emeralds on it, nor the Kardashians by your side. Its just like rock bands. All the best, coolest, and most talented musicians didn't do it for fame or girls/guys, they did it because they just loved playing, and by absolutely loving what they were doing, it was no longer "work," and they thrived, were innovative, and fully immersed themselves in their work. If you've got that going for you, you're on the right track, and your insane hours won't feel as laborious as they would, say, mopping floors, at a slaughter house. Yes, this tip is completely un-profound, but I can't tell you how many people I see who just don't seem to exude a true love for what they're doing with tiny houses – and it shows. I once saw someone speak who came out and said "My goal is to be on top of the tiny house world and be famous" – those very words, in one sentence, showed me that this person was into the scene for the wrong reasons. Don't be this person.

All Wimps Need Not Apply

Be prepared to put in some serious hours, sweat, and occasional tears, doing what you aim to do. This is especially true as we've reached a point where there's a new tiny house building company every 35.8 seconds. I'm not knocking new builders, in fact I think its great, encourages healthy competition and (sometimes) better design. Again, this isn't any paradigm shift in "tips towards a better business," but you really need to bust ass to stand out in what's becoming a pretty saturated movement. Some noteworthy builders that don't sleep, and bleed for their art: Abel Zimmerman from Zyl Vardos, Mike Bedsole and his crew from Tiny House Chattanooga, and Brad Kittel from Texas, BA Norrgard from A Bed Above My Head, Macy Miller of MiniMotives, Andrew and Gabriella Morrison, and well, so many more you and I don't have time to write or read about. Each one of them kills it by killing themselves, and trying to offer up something by way of individuality, and to offer something missing from the scene. Go check out their work, and other likeminded builders and businesses and ask yourself "What are these guys doing right," from their online presence, to their techniques, to their personalities, work ethic, and public involvement. Its a whole lot more complicated than sitting pretty with a tiny house you just completed, and waiting for the photographers to roll in. These people work HARD.

Stand Out

Individuality. This one is pretty damn important. If you're going to build a boring, standard, or substandard, shed with gun-slit-tiny windows, with little sense and taste in size and placement, and then try to pass it off as a real deal "high end" tiny house, slap a price tag of $45k on it, and think to yourself "Easy Street, here I come!", well, you've just built yourself the worlds largest, rolling, paper weight because that beast isn't going anywhere fast. LOOK at what makes certain designs work, and what makes them appealing, while conversely deciphering what doesn't fly, what others missed, and what you might change. Change things up and evolve when need be. Don't get to comfortable doing the same thing over and over – your work will end up predictable and boring, and never stand out from the pack.

Spend It Like a "Fool"

There's the old saying "You have to spend money to make money," and man is that ever true. I LOVE building with salvaged materials, but you have to know where you can save money (while not sacrificing strength or good aesthetics), and where you need to spend, or invest, it. Heck, even with my hands-on workshops, I have to front THOUSANDS of dollars before a single person signs up. Its painful and stressful, but I do this because it ensures I'm doing things the right way, as best as I can, and for the maximum benefit of the students who have invested THEIR hard earned money to be part of what I'm doing. Its worked for me though, and I've set up and hosted almost twenty workshops and every single one of them has sold out. So know that individuality sometimes can come with the towed-aspects of having to invest and spend in order to create a better product. Its a fine line to ride, and one that can hurt the wallet. I'd personally rather make a little less money for my insane output of time and work, than have someone walk away unhappy. We have one of the longest running fully hands-on workshops out there, so I feel we must be doing something right with this approach.

You ARE NOT The Best

Realize/be aware that there are a ton of people out there who can out-build and out-design you, and don't let that discourage you – let it inspire you. Don't copy the work of others, but don't be afraid to let it inspire you, or allow you to try out new angles in design, decor, or spatial layouts. Furthermore, CITE and give credit to you mentors and influences. I see SO many builders who clearly cop someone's design, almost fully, and

then don't give them a single nod. I frequently slip in stories of my inspirational upbringings when interviewed, as these people that helped me on my path to who I am, deserve credit. To walk the walk, here I go again. My biggest influences, or those who greatly inspired me with their word: David and Jeanie Stiles, Lloyd Kahn, Dan Price, and Harlan Hubbard. If you don't know them, look those names up – they're all GREAT.

The Not-So-Profound Art of Reciprocation

Don't look at others as a competition; reciprocate. There are quite a few bloggers out there who ask for help, and then never return the favor. This is common etiquette, and a few of them have quickly earned the reputation as "one-way streets." Its not one huge gladiatorial competition. Help others out, and they'll (hopefully) help you in a time of need. I won't mention any names, but there are a handful of people and builders out there who are fully immersed in the "Three M's" mindset, as I like to call it – "Me. Me. Me!"

Make Coffee Your Friend

Seriously. You don't like coffee? Tough. Learn to love it. You'll need it. There's no room for decaf sissies in such a business. I'm kidding, but I do drink about 5-6 cups a day, sucked through the straws of recently downed pixie sticks, and even then, I'm exhausted, but still lovin' it (cue: cheesy McDonald's jingle). Oh, but don't drink McDonald's coffee – its terrible and doesn't have enough "oompfh" to help you along. But seriously, on to number eight....

Donate, Help Out, Pitch In

Most businesses, never mind those just in the tiny house realm, miss this one, especially as they're starting up and counting every penny along the way. Launching a business isn't easy, so I also recommend easing into the process from one career to another and not just blindly jumping full throttle into the game. However, as I do wholeheartedly understand that with a tough, struggling, long-hours, fledgling business, that giving up goods, money, or more time, is the last thing you might want to, or be able to do, I feel its something that should be done – and not just politically. Do this, and help others out, because its the right thing to do. Someone needs help with a build for the homeless? A young couple needs a prize or two from you for their crowd-funding campaign? Well, if you can, DO help. Aside from the fact that its often FUN to help out others, help them succeed, and that it makes you feel good (your "good turn daily"), I guarantee that the action is contagious and leads other to do the same, whereupon it might ultimately come back to you. Don't do it for that reason though, and simply always try to be nice, helpful, and friendly. its important, believe me, especially in customer service. And be nice all the while, and not some smarmy, over-critical, holier-than-thou, know it all in the game – no one likes that, especially on message boards. You'll soon earn a really bad reputation for yourself. Help people, be friend-ly, and have some tact.

Yes, Even the "Stupid" Emails

Answer those emails – even the "stupid" ones. Why, because everyone is coming from a different background and different level of knowledge. Even the "incessant dumb question" person could become a potential supporter, or client. They think enough of you to make YOU the person to ask, so do give them the time of day – within reason, of course. William Rockhill of Bear Creek Carpentry, a friend of mine, and talented builder is a good example of this- ultra friendly, patient, and knowledgeable, and its for those reasons I asked him to be a moderator for one of my tiny house boards. Be THAT guy.

Do Almost Any Interview That Comes Your Way

I've seen two of three builders/bloggers more or less publicly claim that, "I won't do an interview unless its to a blog/audience as big as mine, if not bigger." This is what they called time-management blogging (or business) by the book. I don't like it – at all. While this makes perfect business sense, there is more to a business than just crunching numbers and making profit (a whole other chapter in an of itself). Don't be an ass – DO those interviews if you do have the time.

"But Deek, time is money!" Again, you might be missing the point if you think that. Here's how I approach or see this. When I'm asked to do an interview, from a big paper, to the dinkiest of podcasts, OR radio stations, I try to go ahead and do them – all of them. Yes, some of the interviews can end up being "somewhat of a waste of time," BUT, I've had so many of these once dinky-blog ones, go on to reach huge amounts of people, or just the RIGHT person – which can then lead to another interview, another gig, another book sale, another invite to talk at a home show, or another new acquaintance and friend in the scene – you get the point. Have FUN doing these interviews, don't look at them through "Charts, graphs, and marketing-research-eyes," stop thinking you're so overly important, and help these people out. I personally try to do almost any interview that comes my way, and I if don't end up doing one, its never intentional, but simply because I'm swamped, and/or forgot (so DO ask the interviewee to check back with you down the road if you're especially busy). To save time, a "Frequently asked questions" section on your website isn't a bad idea, although I sort of feel that it comes off as arrogant (while it should not). I've done so many interviews for college papers when I know I'll never ever even see a copy of the final result, but still, I have fun doing these, and am surprised, flattered, and thankful that people even care to ask. Basically, don't blow interested parties off.

Give Back

Not for the simple sake of PR (which of course is a great side effect of it), but giving back, event-wise, is a great idea. Want to get your name or product out there, well, consider setting up some fun event that all are welcome to. As I mentioned, I host hands-on tiny house building workshops and have for almost six years now, and I feel lucky that people are so interested in these classes. While I can't host those workshops for free (they cost me a small fortune to get off the ground), I do set aside some money from each, and remind myself every once in awhile to host, or help with a free event for those who don't have the funds to make my workshops. Additionally, I often buy a lot of art (that I don't need and don't have wall space for) from independent artists as my way of helping and giving back. Its my way of thanking the scene, it brings people together, and I've met so many great builders, dwellers, artists, and musicians by doing so – many of which have helped to further inspire me, or give me new tangents of idea for projects, builds, or collaborations.

You're Gonna Lose Here and There

Its inevitable, and the key is to LEARN from your business and design mistakes. This one's older than Aesop's Fables, but still, and will continue to hold true. Every day is a lesson, and don't let a mistake or failure go by without learning from it. Learn to not beat yourself up when you make a mistake too – we all do, and all will.

Photograph All!

Get GOOD photos, on a GOOD camera (or by a professional) or everything you do. Video too. You can't convey the quality, eccentricity, or appeal of your work to prospective buyers, press, or your own blog readers if you're taking your photos on a disposable camera from the dollar store. You worked hard on these builds, so at least give them the properly chronicled respect of a good photo session. Staging a cabin with decor and art goes A LONG way too. It's an extra step and cost, and more energy expended, but well worth it. A cabin staged in photos looks cozier and gives off a more lived-in vibe for people who aren't so visual or as imaginative. A cabin photographed as such is much more likely to sell, or attract attention. Have fun with this!

Devour Continual Inspiration

"Deek, I know all there is about style, design, and function," says the self-absorbed fool. This is the thought process of someone whose business will eventually suffer. I won't say that it's as extreme a tip as "Evolve or Die," but I think its EXTREMELY important to continually DEVOUR whatever inspiration you can. Keep current and on top of things. Yes, there are now 45,986 new-jack tiny house blogs (some of them amazing!), and you'll never have time to keep up with the all, but DO spend some time to check up on blogs, other builders, message boards and discussion groups, to read design magazines, watch YouTube tutorials and tours, and to generally inform: "keep up with the Joneses." This is fun for me, and never feels like work –

and it all wraps into my very first recommendation a few pages back. Speaking of which, I love writing much less so than building and designing, so I'm wrapping this up, and heading outside to continue work on a prefabricated tree house office/guest space for the Make-A-Wish Foundation. If you read all my previous tips, THAT one covers about FIVE of my points! See how I did that and it all comes full circle?

What's Your Tiny?

A question for business, life, work, and play

David Papen

David Papen, President of Ecologic Modulars, has a passion for building houses with efficient size and design. He knows and shows, from over 30 years of experience in the housing production facility industry that anyone can have their own dwelling, big or tiny. David has literally built thousands of houses of all sizes and styles, and is most excited about the simple and efficient craftsman quality and designs that come with the tiny house movement.

What's your tiny? That's the question everyone should be asking themselves. Tiny Living is a life choice that isn't just about our homes. It's a path to a bigger life that will leave a smaller footprint behind, that we as a people should adopt in all aspects of our lives. Don't think of it as a minimalist lifestyle at all. When you think about a lifestyle choice, the first thing you should consider is the first half of the word: LIFE. And you shouldn't expect your life to be more than just existing, but actually living. What is living but a collection of experiences all stitched together to create the life-print of you? So think of what you want your life-print to look like. What do you want to see on your canvas? Fun? Children? Travel? Comfort? Financial Freedom? Those are the top five answers it seems when you ask people of things that they want and they feel are a necessity to get to the number one answer: LOVE MY LIFE!

In my opinion, tiny is a way to create that life. In more ways possible than you can imagine. Not just in living but if you go to the essence of what tiny living is, more efficient and probably more natural, you can take the blueprint of this philosophy and take it to work, work places, business, play, and yes, also homes.

So, what is YOUR version of tiny?

My name is David Papen and I have been building tiny homes since 1996. It all started when I wanted to have a place so I could stay and visit my children as I worked in Tennessee. My children lived in Missouri. I built it out of necessity, not to minimalize my lifestyle or for earth hugging values I was trying to pass on to my fellow man. No, necessity, and necessity alone were the driving factors behind my first build. I wanted to get that out in the open so no one states that I am seeking some kind of accolade for being a pioneer or the first of a movement. In fact, I find it interesting if anyone could make such a claim! Tiny has always been here and almost always been a build of necessity. Not of value or lifestyle. Many notable writers, artists, poets, and musicians, including Mark Twain and many others, have built tiny out of necessity, to find solitude and space for inspiration.

I think at a root we all have joined this movement for the same reasons. Tiny has become an art that is practical and admirable on so many levels. An expression. Even an extension of ourselves that says who we are, what we find beautiful and express what we stand for.

I have been a builder for more than 30 years and what attracted me most to this industry was that I could make it my art, that I could express myself in a way that I could not have been doing while building the countless hotels and suburbia homes that I have constructed. I could use my imagination, I could do the things I always wanted to and use materials and fashion them in such a way that would have been to cost prohibitive in a larger home or dwelling. If you look around you, in your neighborhood, you probably see redundancy in every build, a theme of practical and basic. No grand expression or originality. No awe factor! I love that I can get more awe factor from 170 sq.ft. that most can get in 3,000. That's awesome! That's why a designer wants to design, why a writer wants to write, and a musician wants to play music.

People ask me why do you think there is such a buzz for tiny? In my opinion it's not living smaller. It's not because we are just trying to minimalize or pass on a lifestyle. It's that we are doing both of those things with style. It's the art of it all! Each and every build has some form of beauty. Some nook. Some cranny that's all its own and sets it apart from all the others. Whether it's use of space or color, its design, its art. That is why people stand in a two-hour line to see these units. That's why we the designers and the do-it-yourselfers pick up the pencils and hammers. It's the art of it all and the self-expression. Who would have ever thought that necessity would become an art form! But here it is and I am so proud to be a tiny part of it.

I have been so blessed to have been invited into many people's lives and homes, tiny or not, and to be allowed to build or view that piece of art that they have or want and created. If you look at both the person and the tiny, side by side, it's so amazing to see the little details. You can see bits of both in each of them. That should be all of our goals: to create architecture that expresses something, or more importantly, someone.

Now, I am in no way going to tell you that if you live a tiny lifestyle that fairy dust will fall from the sky and dust your days with little magic sprinkles of goodness and you are going to love your life and all your troubles will be over! It's not going to happen! You are still going to have the same set of troubles you have now. They are just going to happen in a smaller area.

So what's my tiny? Well, my tiny started out of necessity as I said but has evolved to a much larger scope if you will, in business. When I met Darin

Zaruba with EcoCabins I was already a tiny believer. I have been building tiny for a long time and he proposed a merger of resources and talents. I was in! We shared a like-minded business plan that was built around the tiny house movement, but more importantly its philosophy. Small businesses in a big business platform, meaning all of the small businesses feed the larger business by serving a common product and thus helping the mother company grow to big business by sheltering the smaller ones.

Each of the smaller company's mission would be to serve itself but also serve the needs of the larger by self-providing its resources and profits to feed the needs of the other, all for the benefit of this new philosophy of living small.

The Eco System – Nature's Formula for life put into business! Our company EcoCabins is the brand and the sales platform. Ecologic Modulars, a craftsman-quality, high-efficiency production-facility model as the builder. Ecologic Supplies is the materials supplier. Ecologic Villages represents the developments and its people. Wordup is the marketing arm. Tiny Toters, is the transportation company, and so on. And Tiny House Jamboree serves as the event that pulls the community and the industry together. All are under the same umbrella with a mission to work with all the tiny world of builders to bring them together, to learn from one another and all, and to grow our world of tiny.

My turning tiny is at the same time therefore not so tiny at all. It's huge! It started with a small house to see my kids but has evolved to a way of life that includes business, family, and friends I have met along the way.

Tiny doesn't have to stop simply at the dwellings and it shouldn't. We should, can, and are, in our case, taking it to the workplace. Most manufacturing plants have a floor space of 100,000 sq.ft. or greater. We have been able to engineer a production facility that produces the same amount of floors as most of our large competitors twice the size. Using a station build assembly process instead of a line build, means less people, less space, and more volume.

My tiny has become the factory and the factories we are developing, and which we are adding to our ecosystem of production facilities and supply lines and still allowing that freedom of expression and art that people want in the design of their tiny. It's NOT EASY to re-tool a system that's been stuck in a trailer house modular cookie cutter world since its inception, but we are doing it! We are turning the industry into tiny too, and it's working! We have made new innovations both in build and art that could not have been achieved without a team of like-minded professionals, sharing the same passions.

That's why I feel the tiny business in the big business platform is so important too. It's become a family, a tiny world banding together that we all can bounce ideas off of and collaborate with and create. I feel this is so important that we also find a way to tiny the workplace. Even more important than our homes, in an ever-expanding world of industry and commerce, finding a way to accomplish the same thing in a smaller footprint is paramount. Look around your workplace. Think of ways to make it smaller and challenge our industry leaders to follow suit. We have their ears right now. Let's use our imagination and lead them to a smaller footprint of industry, guide our fellow humans to find their tiny, their art form, and their expression of themselves in all that they do and seek the reward that comes with less.

Finding Freedom

Josh Barry

Josh Barry, a passionate rugby player, enlisted in the US Marine Corps at 17. Upon completion of his enlistment, Josh moved back to Denver, CO and founded Freedom Pergola LLC. Josh was given an opportunity to take over the sales program for Freedom Yurt Cabins, a company founded in 2014 by his father, Richard Barry. In April of 2016, EcoCabins and Freedom Yurt Cabins formed a partnership and established Freedom Outdoor Structures where Josh was promoted to President.

It's 5:30 am. You wake up, wipe the sleep from your eyes, and sigh because you feel as if you need a crane to pull your morbid existence from its eight-hour slumber. On any normal day you'd at least have the energy to make it to the bathroom and flick on the light before warming up the shower. Today seems especially dreary though and the thought of exiting your cotton cocoon seems unbearable. You roll over and face your nightstand, catch a glimpse of something you see every day, and contemplate in a way you haven't for a long time. It's a picture – a figment of the past. It's a reminder of a life you used to live but for some reason, stopped living.

As you lay in silent mediocrity, you start to wonder why this picture looks so different than the man who will inevitably greet you in the mirror as soon as you rise for your morning wash. Sure, 15 years of monotony has deepened the lines on your forehead and your hair isn't the same shade of sandy blonde that it used to be. But there's something haunting staring back at you from that photo. Your gaze is trapped on a pair of hazel eyes that shine with a youthful brilliance you haven't experienced for years. Those eyes belong to a man who stands on the edge of a waterfall in the Rocky

Mountains of Colorado, and he's spreading his arms wide as if to show the world behind him that he is the master of his own destiny. He doesn't carry the overwhelming burden of a life unlived that seems to be crushing you this morning and keeping your from even standing on your own two feet. It is at this moment that you start to ponder on how you've misplaced the sparkle in that boy's eyes. You admit to yourself that you might do anything to get it back. Where did it all go wrong? How could such an energetic teen become a shell of depression and disappointment after such a short time? What steps led you to this low point in life that seems to be marked by a morning where you contemplate all of your life's decisions? Was it the job you took straight out of college that has slowly sucked the life out of you these past few years? Could it be the mountain of debt you've piled up through student loans, a car payment, mortgage, and credit cards? What about the realization that you might never own the ground under your own two feet or the roof over your head? What is it that makes a man truly free, and why don't you have it? Better yet, what can you do to find it?

The image I just painted is what I like to call "my nightmare" and I use it as a constant reminder of the life I wish to avoid; I must avoid. Sure I've experienced that defeated feeling of rising early on a Monday morning to do a job I'm not particularly passionate about. I joined the Marine Corps at the ripe old age of 17 and earned a degree in obedience from the 'School of Hard Knocks' as I like to call it. Actually, I'm quite proud of my military service and I treasure not only what it taught me, but also the fantastic men and women I was able to serve next to day in and day out. In fact, I worked in an Airframe shop where we repaired and fabricated metal components for F-18 fighter jets. Eventually I rose to a position of moderate authority where I was in charge of supervising maintenance and coordinating our shop's functions from start to finish. And while it was certainly entertaining and fulfilling to fix $40 million aircraft in support of my nation's defense, I was never quite satisfied with the lifestyle. It would be a bold faced lie if I were to describe myself as the type of person who falls in line easily. On more than one occasion, I've been accused of marching to the beat of my own drum while those around me kept cadence with each other. I suppose that my inner identity could be likened to a stubborn mule: compliant when he needs to be, but always looking for an opportunity to shake the reins and blaze his own trail.

After coming to grips with my stubborn nature, I felt it wise to part ways with the Marine Corps and attempt to blaze a little trail of my own. I separated from the Corps under honorable conditions in November of 2014 and quickly put rubber to the road on as I headed back to my home state of Colorado. Upon my return I spent some time with my father, Richard Barry.

Dad has always been a trailblazer in his own regard and classifies himself as a perpetual "tinkerer" and "jack of all trades, master of none." He'd spent the last decade developing a structure that was meant to provide sustainable housing for the masses. It was based on the traditional Mongolian concept of a Yurt, which nomadic people have used for centuries as portable shelter. However, in my dad's innovative style, he'd managed to put his own spin on the concept and create a round, modular, hard walled house that he dubbed the *Freedom Yurt Cabin*. His company was in the process of taking the Yurt Cabin from concept to production and he needed help spreading the word about his new creation. Since I had no specific job prospects and was in the process of transitioning from military service to civilian life, I decided to come on board and make myself useful in any way possible.

As I began to research the budding tiny house movement, my first stop was the tiny house blog owned and operated by Kent Griswold. Kent is one of the most kind and generous human beings who I have ever had the privilege of meeting, and his insights into the tiny house movement have been invaluable to me, and my career in the industry.

One of the first things Kent and I discussed was the average tiny house enthusiast and what they were like. I felt a sense of freedom and adventure as I pictured myself in the shoes of a tiny house frontiersman, traveling across the nation in a 200 sq.ft. house on wheels or starting a homestead on a few acres surrounding a small cabin in the woods. I was fascinated to learn that the tiny house movement is something that does not appeal to a specific race, gender, political leaning, or socio-economic background. In fact, it seemed as if the followers of this movement were a fairly even cross section of America as a whole! This was infinitely intriguing to me, and as I began spending more time around tiny house enthusiasts at events like the Tiny House Jamboree, I was careful to observe the cornucopia of people who seemed so interested in our Freedom Yurt Cabin, other small and tiny structures, and sustainable living within one's means. This observation would lead me down a road where I would experience a paradigm shift in how I planned to live my life, and would cause me to commit to inspire others to shift their thinking in a similar direction.

A few months after my initial work with Freedom Yurt Cabins had begun and I was first exposed to the tiny house community, the concept of "downsizing" would come into play within my own family. I spent most of my childhood in a comfortable, 3500 sq.ft. home in Centennial, Colorado where the suburban lifestyle reigned supreme. Food was never further away than the local supermarket and free time was spent going to movies, hanging out in mega-malls, or playing team sports. It wasn't until the autumn of 2015 that my family felt the calling to simplify our lives and reconnect with God's creation. While our lives in Centennial were certainly safe and comfortable, we had becoming disenchanted with the lack of appreciation that was shown in our community for our ability to live such cozy lives. My parents feared that their children were becoming jaded by a society in which kids often value their video game consoles over inter-personal relationships with their friends and neighbors. On top of that, the price of housing was at an all time high in the Denver area and our little piece of that suburban sprawl had grown significantly in value. With three of my younger siblings still living at home, my parents saw a perfect chance to turn their attention towards moving away from the city and putting down roots somewhere further from the complications of our modern American way of life.

After months of searching we found a perfect little house on a few acres of land bordering the Pike National Forest in Sedalia, Colorado. Though it was less than half the square footage of the house we had grown up in, my family settled in comfortably and began hiking, fishing, hunting, and living off the land. We sifted through the tons of unwanted items we had hoarded in our prior residence and were amazed at how easily we gave most of them away. Slowly but surely, we became aware of the excessive importance we had placed on material possessions when living in suburbia, and we transitioned our thoughts to sustainability and clean living. My mother purchased chickens and goats to provide our family with organic sustenance and we all observed as her priorities changed from day to day. She looked back on her life in Centennial and was awed by how quickly she became accustomed to milking goats, hiking through the picturesque forests that surrounded our home, chopping and storing wood, and keeping a fire lit during the winter. My brothers who used to collect golf balls to sell to neighborhood dads now found themselves working with their own two hands and learning carpentry, farming techniques, and daily survival skills. Life was certainly not easier, but the reward of a hard day's work could be relished in the evening with a home-cooked meal shared amongst kin next to a warm fire.

After witnessing such a dramatic shift in my own family's mind-set, priorities, and daily life, I came to understand the tiny house movement, homesteading, downsizing, and simplifying trends in a much deeper way. Over the months in which my family's lifestyle had changed so drastically, I had met people like Melissa Fletcher from Yurts of Hawaii and Kenny Grigar, owner of Off Grid Hardware in Taos, New Mexico. I began to see that among Millennials and Baby Boomers alike, there is a significant portion of the American population that is growing tired of the status quo. The cliché life plan of a college degree, tens of thousands of dollars in student loans, a car payment, marriage, two kids, and a thirty year mortgage is now being challenged by a lifestyle that offers greater satisfaction and flexibility. Day after day, I was introduced to people who had purchased tiny houses on wheels and spent years traveling the beautiful landscapes of the United States, working remotely from Wi-Fi hotspots, and reconnecting with nature and humanity. I began to understand that these pioneers of alternative living would not only need affordable homes to call their own, but that this movement would need legitimate representation and a prominent platform from which its followers can voice their opinions and allow their lives to be examples for others to emulate.

While tiny houses on wheels may appeal to the general public as structures that incite plenty of romantic fantasies, my experiences showed me that these homes may not actually serve as a realistic way to solve the housing crisis facing our nation. For landowners and those folks less driven by wanderlust, wheels on a home may be less than desirable. And while millions of people have marvelled over the ingenuity of fitting all of life's necessities into a sub-200 sq.ft. floor plan, most would be more comfortable with a bit more space. Don't get me wrong. I'm as enamoured as anyone when I step foot in a well-designed tiny house! The craftsmanship and creativity on display rarely cease to amaze anyone who spends even a few minutes inside a well built home on wheels. However, it is important to understand that, for better or for worse, we live in a nation where housing is strictly regulated. In isolated instances, members of the tiny house community have fought diligently with individual municipalities so that zoning regulations can be changed and communities of tiny homes can be established legally. While it is certainly not my intention to downplay the actions of these sojourners for sustainable housing, I think true "sustainability" must be considered. I do not believe it is realistic nor sustainable to assume that we, as a community which is passionate about alternative housing, will be able to change the minds of tens of thousands of municipal building departments around the country so that our homes of choice will be permitted. Rather, I feel it is best in this situation to conform ever so slightly to existing regulations and take advantage of those provisions, which are already in place. The International Residential Code (IRC for short) is the regulatory document to which most single and dual family residences in the United States are built, and it is widely recognized as a veritable Bible of modern residential building. When a building inspector is handed a set of plans that show adherence to the IRC, he is exponentially more likely to issue a permit. Of course, when dealing with tiny houses, there may still be regulations in place in many municipalities, which require structures to adhere to minimum square footage requirements. For structures like our Freedom Yurt Cabin, this is less of a problem. In fact, our company has already commissioned IRC compliant Yurt Cabins to be designed, most of which will be between 350 and 600 sq.ft. We hope that the world will begin to see this as a sign of legitimacy from our company as customers will have the luxury of being able to live in IRC compliant structures while still paying a fraction of what they would for a modern, site-built home.

Since early on in the journey, which I have previously described, my goal has been to enact the concept of freedom in my own life and to allow others to live life more abundantly as well. It pains me to see such large portions of American society who live constantly within the status quo and seem chained to its standards, and I only wish to inspire those individuals to break free from the confines of their limited reality. Nothing could be more critical to achieving true freedom than to own the ground under your own feet and the roof under which you lay your head at night. Just as I watched my own family change from complacent suburbanites to trailblazing pioneers in a matter of weeks with a only a slight relocation outside of city limits, it is my most fervent hope that many more Americans will take up the challenge to be financially and personally independent from the normal confines of city and suburban living. I truly believe that structures like the Freedom Yurt Cabin will play a key role in promoting a paradigm shift in the way the average American thinks about housing.

It All Starts with a Good Foundation

Damon C. DesChamp

Trailer Made Custom Trailers is the largest supplier of tiny house foundations on wheels in the nation. Damon DesChamp and his wife Natalie Doolittle have warmly welcomed the tiny house industry to the Trailer Made family, and have shipped hundreds of tiny house specific trailers all over the country over their year in business together.

The old adage, "A house is only as good as the foundation on which it is built," rings true in so many things in, and out, of the construction world. Everything begins with a foundation; from education, to love and relationships, to family, careers, and so on, until you realize that the first step is always the most important one.

I, Damon C. DesChamp, and my partner in life and in business, Natalie J. Doolittle, founded Trailer Made Custom Trailers in June 2013, out of a necessity for a foundation on which to build a new career, a new life, and to seek out one thing to do to change a small part of the world. With it we wanted to be the best at that one thing. So, with a new relationship, a new business, and a new path, we decided to do something that neither of us had ever done before: build a new enterprise from square one. Little did we know what adventures, stresses, victories and defeats awaited us when I said one day, "Honey, I think I am going to build a trailer today and see what I can come up with?" Famous last words, indeed.

I worked for almost twenty years in the financial sector of the auto industry, working long and thankless hours for car dealership groups around the country before returning to school for a fresh start on a new career.

Natalie came from a childhood development background as a teacher, and then for nearly fifteen years as a Pampered Chef consultant and director. While this may be a real head scratcher when someone tries to connect the dots on how a couple made the decision to start a trailer manufacturing operation, in retrospect, we wouldn't have made the company what it is today without each other's individuality, imagination, vision, compassion, skills, and work ethic. Even the two of us still often scratch our own heads and ask each other "How did this happen?" The answer is simple. You don't choose your path in life; you just discover it! As it turned out, we were destined to change the tiny house world, and we haven't looked back!

Like any new business there was a blank slate in front of the two of us, and we were free to write our own destiny (good or bad). More than anything, that what drove each of us to be the very best we could be at our respective duties operating a business. Keep in mind that neither of us had worked in a related industry in the past.

I had grown up in a small town in Missouri where every boy grows up working or hanging out in all kinds of "shop" environments. Relatives and parents of friends were small business owners. Life was like a giant shop class. This town in Missouri at one time was known as the "utility trailer capital of the nation," and a lot of the kids worked for various trailer companies during the summers, or evenings and weekends, gathering some pretty valuable skills along the way. Natalie was a preschool teacher until the birth of her daughter in 2003, when she then decided to leave teaching and begin a career as a consultant for The Pampered Chef. This afforded Natalie the opportunity to be a full time mom to her child and still be a full time business operator for herself and her family. The two of us have a very strong, yet eclectic set of skills that blend wonderfully together to have created truly a business that is "the best of both worlds."

From a very humble beginning in a small shop in Northglenn, Colorado, and from the first trailer my first real employee (and close friend) built and advertised on Craigslist 'for sale by owner', the Trailer Made Custom Trailers network of dealers and builders has reached more than 35 states in the U.S., and now supplies the foundations to over 200 professional tiny home builders nationwide, and thousands of their beloved DIY tiny housers. That first day with trailer #1 kick started an idea that has largely been forgotten in today's economy: do right by the customer, do it for the customer, and run your business with integrity. What a concept, right? With just some guerrilla style advertising and offering "custom trailers" built to order per each client, the reputation of Trailer Made has spread quickly throughout Colorado, fueled largely by markets like the off-road enthusiasts, oil and energy clients, and the construction trades. We have found ourselves overwhelmed with requests for designs that nobody else in the trailer industry either had the courage to tackle, or just didn't have the time to be bothered to build. There is a fine line between bravery and stupidity, but either way these "one-off" projects serve as a repeated trial-by-fire that have honed the skills of Team Trailer Made in very short order. This cast a huge neon light on a niche market that was being ignored by the "big box" manufacturers. Their "here's what we offer, take it or leave it" attitude filled the sails of Trailer Made's ship as it set sail forward into uncharted waters.

A few months into the custom trailer-building venture, a gentleman walked in with a folder containing some graph paper sketches in it, and asked if we had ever heard of a tiny house. At the time, Natalie and I were occasional fans of the television shows about tiny houses and their owners, but that was about the extent of our knowledge. This prospective client had given us some raw details about the tiny home design, its intended purpose, who the client would be, and what task we would be charged with if we accepted his design to build for him. So Trailer Made set out on the rather daunting task of building a foundation for a home that can be hooked up and pulled down a road at 65 miles per hour. Tiny house trailer number one really showed the flaws in design and building practices at that time around the industry. Most tiny homes up to that point were still being built on car hauler or utility trailers, and for some applications, that was, and still can be sufficient. I had a lot of back and forth conversations with the tiny home builder (who was also a start-up enterprise at the time), and together we all learned what was great about the first iteration of a tiny house trailer, and more importantly, what can be improved on going forward.

Fast-forward to Trailer Made tiny house foundation version 2.0 and now even 3.0. People were hearing and seeing on the Internet that there was a company in Colorado custom building "tiny house trailers." The floodgates opened to Trailer Made. Singles, couples, millennials and baby boomers alike were dropping by, emailing, and calling for tiny house trailers every single day. I had been continuing my education in welding, fabrication, and structural engineering, and this new opportunity in the tiny house community was perfect to create something that would really change the world and also serve as a "laboratory" of sorts for my reincarnation as a fabricator and engineer. Natalie (the real brains behind the operation) was able to operate the business on a day-to-day basis, keep everyone paid and employed, and make sure the lights were on each day.

The two of us thoroughly enjoyed the different walks of life that we encountered in the new tiny house clientele that sought out our foundation trailers. As it turns out both Natalie and I had stumbled onto something that fed each of our souls. Natalie had the personal interaction now with tiny housers that she had loved while teaching and doing home shows for Pampered Chef, and I got to be the "mad scientist" in the shop, armed with a little imagination and a welding machine. In essence I was getting to relive my youth growing up in Missouri in dirty, yet fascinating shops and garages. Who knew that guy that walked in with graph paper in hand would impact both of our futures so significantly? By the way, that "guy" was a gentleman named Byron Fears, and is the co-proprietor, with his wife Dot, of the Simblissity Tiny Home Company. Who knew?

After completion of the first tiny house foundation, Natalie and I both thought we would likely never be asked to build a tiny house trailer again. Yet just three years later, Trailer Made Custom Trailers is the nation's leading

supplier of tiny home foundations on wheels, delivering between 50-60 tiny home foundations per month, to thirty-five states outside of Colorado, and we account for more than 80% of the company's volume in sales! It appears the owners have "discovered" their path in life after all.

I mentioned before that Natalie and I wanted to 'change the world' somehow before we departed from it. When someone talks about changing the world, most people just roll their eyes. But, for a moment, just consider the many different reasons that someone may consider going tiny. Maybe you are a student just out of college, and you have a crippling amount of student debt that you have to pay back before your life can ever really "begin." You could be the parents of the aforementioned student, and that student has siblings that also want to attend college, and the average cost of student housing is around $12,000 per year, per student. Maybe you are a local musician/single father who has lived in a mobile home until it is unfit for occupancy for you and your little girl, and you desperately want to provide a new home for your family, and your only option is to do it with your own two hands. Maybe, you are an entrepreneur trapped inside a construction worker's life, and you want to "build a tiny house just to see how it goes." You could be someone drawn to the outdoors, not the indoors, and living tiny is just another reason to get out and enjoy the world for what it is. Perhaps, just maybe, you were in real estate investment in your past life as a finance professional and you barely survived the housing bubble burst of 2007, and you have a new perspective on "wants versus needs?" The list goes on and on as to why someone is drawn to the tiny house movement. No one at Trailer Made ever tires from hearing every single story shared by a new tiny house client.

Just as the tiny house movement is a constantly evolving and changing community, so too are we. We don't say "here it is, take it or leave it." We consult, educate, learn from the client, and often give guidance on what works and what may be challenging for a build project. We have developed working and personal relationships with hundreds of builders all over the country who, by and large, have far more experience in home building than we do as a steel fabrication company. This has been the single most important factor in our growth and success. We listen to feedback, both good and bad, from the novice first time DIY'er, all the way to the other end of the spectrum. This has helped us with our R&D and product development to the point that we never want to rest on our laurels and say that we are done improving our products. Anyone who tells you they are an "expert" in something is missing one key skill: how to learn. I don't feel that anyone in the tiny house industry is an expert. Natalie and I are not. We are instead, and should always remain, students of the movement. We get to pass on knowledge that we have learned from other industry members. To this day we ask of others as many questions as they ask of us. This skill was taught to us by the thousands of DIY'ers that we want to thank for the life lesson.

A few years in the tiny house industry has given us confidence and credibility in our advice to homebuilders of all skill levels. We have an immense network of building professionals all over the country to seek counsel from if we get stumped on a building related topic. It is a really powerful thing to be the first, visit, call or email when someone begins their tiny house journey, and we don't take that lightly at all. We are beholden to our tiny house family members, and we constantly want to evolve the industry, the movement, and the technology and information available to the industry as a whole. With Natalie and myself being parents of three children, it is the paternal instinct in both of us to be fiercely protective of our tiny housers, and we have no issue helping a client separate fact from fiction when it comes to building their forever tiny home. If we ruffle a few feathers along the way, so be it. At least we hold true to our standard of operating our company with integrity and with the customer's best interests in mind.

The bottom line is we are one big, giant, world wide "tiny" family, complete with in-fighting, dysfunction, and the occasional drunk obnoxious uncle, but also with comradery, love, compassion, knowledge, wisdom and gratitude.

It is truly a remarkable experience to pick up the phone on any given day, and hear from a "friend" in the tiny house world. Most of these friends we have never had the opportunity to ever meet in person, shake hands with, or exchange a hug. Does this mean they aren't friends? Absolutely not! At the first Tiny House Jamboree in 2015, Natalie and I were both on an emotional roller coaster for the entire weekend. We had hundreds of people that we had spoken to over the phone, or emailed back and forth, but never met face to face, come to our tent and introduce themselves, just for the sake of it! We had clients and new friends from Texas, Ohio, Arizona, Michigan, Wisconsin, Arkansas, Virginia, Tennessee, Pennsylvania, Connecticut, California, Utah, Idaho, and more, (and maybe one or two from Colorado and Wyoming?) drop by to show off their progress pictures, photos of their completed homes, and most importantly, to share their own personal stories of their journey. Of course some parts of the Jamboree was all business, where people wanted to talk nuts and bolts about design, pricing, deliveries, and future joint business partnerships between them and Trailer Made. The really humbling and overwhelming part of the whole experience for both of us was the good ol' fashioned "chit chat" that we got to enjoy with our past, present and future tiny house clients all weekend long.

A young couple from Colorado Springs, and one of our first tiny house clients, surprised us with an invitation to their completed home just down the road from where the Jamboree was held that year. When I saw what they had accomplished between just the two of them, I was so blown away that I became visibly emotional. Natalie and I were so proud of that couple that day, and we had to eat a little bit of humble pie at the end of their journey, because we quietly had doubts that the two of them could make it to the finish line on their project. I think that moment was an epiphany for me, and I knew from then on I would be a champion of the DIY tiny house movement, no matter what!

Today, Trailer Made is proud to employ as many tiny house enthusiasts as we can find. If you don't speak tiny house language fluently, chances are you don't have much of a future with our company. Our guys and gals thoroughly enjoy the opportunity to have their work seen on television, on a website, a blog, or on a social media feed. It is a sort of badge of honor to be so tied to an industry that is still so young, and know that you have helped play a small part in its evolution. We are even involved in educational programs all over the country at the high school and college level that have implemented tiny house construction into their students' curriculum, so we are already educating and creating the tiny house movement of the next generation! If the next few years have anything in store for us like the last few years have had, we are running headlong into a very exciting future indeed! As the industry steers toward standardization, and legitimization, we see more and more walks of life hopping the tiny fence over to our wonderfully unique and quirky world.

Having the opportunity to speak with hundreds of new (and seasoned) members of the tiny house community on a monthly basis has really put into perspective how many different things this industry means to so many people. You could be that broke college student, you could be broke parents of a college student, you could be the broke real estate investor turned welder. No matter what made you decide to pick up this book and read it, the common thread is as thick as an oak tree; you love the tiny house movement in some way, and the tiny house movement has the love to welcome you to the family.

Redefining Housing – Simple I Smart I Sustainable
A philosophy for living life, doing business, and finding home

Darin Zaruba

As a visionary entrepreneur, builder, developer, and manufacturer in the housing industry, Darin Zaruba recently shifted his business focus – turning tiny in both philosophy and design. He jumped into the tiny house movement with both feet in all arenas, with a wish to professionalize the movement at the same time. He is building business and industry around it and with that is making sure there are attainable and realistic housing options for all needs on any human scale.

It is no accident that I find myself drawn to tiny houses, and small, sustainable houses. Thinking back to my childhood I was practically raised in one without even knowing it.

I grew up in my grandparents' house, in Loveland Colorado. As modest as it was my grandparents also owned two small cabins in the mountains less than thirty minutes away. At 10' by just 20' and without indoor plumbing and running water, the cabins were Thoreau-esque. Growing up there virtually every weekend helped me to understand the concept of what we would now call sustainability, and helped me to understand life, as complex or as simple as it can be, in general. Even today I am taken with the little box concept Thoreau outlined so well.

> I used to see a large box by the railroad, six feet long by three wide, in which the laborers locked up their tools at night, and it suggested to me that every man who was hard pushed might get such a one for a dollar, and, having bored a few auger holes in it, to admit the air at least, get into it when it rained and at night, and hook down the lid..., and in his soul be free.

My grandparents never subscribed to the larger sense of the American Dream and if they did they never projected it or acted on it. In fact, we lived very modestly in a simple 3-bed/2-bath home. I don't remember a lot of excess. But at the same time I don't remember going without or having to sacrifice much. Modesty was probably the central theme and while I certainly had the understanding that one doesn't need excess to be happy I also understood inside that material possessions weren't, in themselves, evil. But I did want more, and started early down that spiral of acquiring more and more to find happiness

After my grandfather passed and my family had to put my grandmother into assisted living we started going into their books and more closely taking a look at their financial state. They had a net worth that I do not think any of us were prepared for! In their meager living they were able to achieve a balance of happiness and wealth. I quickly realized I wanted to find that too, but the American dream has a way of pushing you to excess. I'll admit it's a very hard cycle to break, much like an addiction.

As a middle school student I was fascinated with role-playing games. I didn't walk around wearing a cloak or having people call me Lygar the Destroyer in the hallways. I was particularly fascinated with the worlds my fellow players created on paper: castles and dungeons to endlessly create and explore. That sense of exploring space and creation translated into a high school passion for architectural drawing and drafting. I realized with a pencil and a few plastic guide tools I could create homes and office buildings and public spaces and really develop locations that would allow a community to thrive. It was an escape for me. I did not know it then but no matter how much I enjoyed drawing, computers would be introduced into my life, and everything would change.

I took my first computer drafting class and was hooked! Until this time drafting and architectural design was actually all that kept me going to school each day. I was either disinterested or bored with everything else being taught. Just as soon as I was introduced to computer drafting I began to design my first house. As I think back I can hear myself almost saying, "Oh crap! This is awesome." It was a huge change in my life and one that would set the stage for everything to follow.

I also quickly realized that what was happening was the playing field was being leveled unfairly. Computers were turning applied arts and sciences like architecture and drafting into commodities. Joe Blow next to me – without a shred of artistic ability or foresight – was now able to create the same things I had once thought was a special skill of mine. I decided at that point that I did not want to go through life being a commodity. I wanted to be artistic and a visionary. I needed to find something new. Even though I took some architectural courses and basic drafting courses while at University of Nebraska at Kearney, I shifted my mindset more to business.

My first startup after four years working for an outdoor retail chain in the business development department – was an outdoor guide service, survival training, teambuilding company, and rental shop, all in one. Our excursions put us in tents and snow caves and other tiny spaces for countless nights. I learned how to be extremely efficient and space conscious in this style of living. However, I wasn't as passionate about it long term as I thought, especially in relation to the revenue it provided.

During this entire time I was also dabbling in branding, marketing, teambuilding, and investing. Those interests and that work led into a couple partnerships and new business developments. It was at this point that everything started to pay off and my ideas started to take off. By age 27 I had started and was operating my first successful consulting business and working with some incredible leaders of business and industry, including in the hous-

ing and development industries where my passion always lied – albeit somewhat dormant.

A mentor in this housing and building industry approached me and wanted my expertise to help him start a fund for mobile homes and affordable housing. I've always believed in seizing opportunity and not letting a chance to learn something new pass by so I jumped. We joined up and in about a year we raised several million dollars and put it into mobile home notes. We were, in essence, buying mortgages. When I saw the demand for affordable housing and the relatively untapped nature of the market I recognized a larger opportunity. I started a sales group in Arizona and Colorado that originated the loans. We would essentially buy mobile homes for affordable housing options, fix them, flip them, and carry the mortgage for deserving people.

I use that term so loosely now but it is probably worth a definition from my standpoint. In America, "mobile home" has such a negative connotation. It is used synonymously with trailer; single wide, doublewide, house trailer, and other words. It is unfortunately too often used to, more or less, describe a sub-culture of America that has no pride in their house, doesn't care what their yard looks like, and is typically undereducated and a burden on society. This could not be further from the truth however! The most complete definition of a mobile home is a prefabricated structure, built in a factory to the HUD code on a permanently attached chassis before being transported to a site and lived in as a permanent home. That's it. In more ways than not that is what tiny house trailers today are: mobile homes. Yes, not a lot of them are factory built, but they are still fastened to trailers and carried to a site where they are set up as a permanent or semi-permanent home.

It was through this flipping of mobile homes that I started to make real money and is really where a good portion of my business is even now. I am proud to say I've been involved in land development, student housing projects, fix and flips, modular construction, and even custom homes. From each one I've gathered information and ideas that have led me to my thoughts today, and I am even more of a manufactured housing advocate now. When I was tip-toing through the door of the tiny house community I was bringing all of this knowledge and experience with me. The past decade has indeed prepared me for my current role as a tiny house and alternative housing advocate.

I was given a copy of Sarah Susanka's *The Not So Big House* right about the time of the subprime mortgage crisis in 2007 and 2008. Watching house after house fall into foreclosure and people literally put out into the street I recognized a dire need for a change in this nation. People needed affordable places to live. Manufactured housing was starting to shake its stigma and be seen as a socially acceptable way to live. The mentality of America and our definition of home had to change and I could see the groundwork for that change being laid. It just so happens that around these years I also became aware of the tiny house movement. The houses themselves reminded me of my grandparents' cabin so many years ago yet their mobility was so similar to what I had most recently been working with. America was starting to talk about downsizing and minimalism and using all sorts of buzzwords associated with a tiny house movement. I could feel a bubble being blow up around this burgeoning market and thought process. As a businessman I realize that is the key to successful business. You not only have to keep your ear to the ground but you have to recognize a market even before it recognizes itself. Between 2010 and 2012 a tiny house market was emerging with a focus on eco-conscious, sustainable, and responsible living.

I followed the tiny house movement and loved it, the craftsmanship, the ingenuity, the unique designs and pride in ownership the owners had. I looked at the overall movement and saw it was mostly a band of like-minded gypsies building individual houses based on their construction skillset. But that model lacked vision and direction to me. I saw that the tiny house movement at that time lacked structure. It lacked a future. It did have a couple established and well-known building companies, and others emerging, but the movement even just two years ago, needed somewhere to go and someway for it to become a more obvious home choice for the masses. To get to that point several obstacles had to be addressed:

- To what standards do tiny houses on wheels need to be built?
- What is the build cost of a tiny house on wheels?
- Can they be mass-produced in any way?
- How can Joe American transition his life into a tiny house?

For the movement to continue growing and begin to make a real impact on our world it needed to rise above the pied pipers that were forming well-meaning associations and alliances and organizations of tiny house enthusiasts, armed with little to no actual knowledge of the building industry, or complex building, coding and zoning issues. In many cases, the things I was reading were doing more harm than good and walking people down the wrong road. The movement needed just that: to move. Move forward. Move back. Move somewhere. It couldn't just stand still anymore.

So around late 2013 I rebranded my housing company into a more eco-responsible one putting an emphasis on sustainable living as a whole with a focus on smaller spaces and factory-built technology. Under our new name, EcoCabins, I felt like we were moving in the direction of what I wanted to do from here on out. I had come to a place where all that I had learned to date and all those lessons about simple living and fiscal responsibility my grandparents illustrated, were being embodied under one roof. It's not about tiny houses. It has never just been about tiny houses. It never will be. It is about simple, smart, and sustainable living. I took my entire factory history and experience and decided to focus on the development of a new paradigm. People are undergoing a monumental change of heart and mind regarding housing and home and what the "American Dream" experience looks like in this millennium. With my company I am trying to be ahead of that paradigm shift and it requires understanding and experience in philosophy, finance, and motivation.

If you create or reposition a company that can successfully take all of those components, mix them together, and turn out beautiful, craftsman quality houses at an affordable price, you have a leg up on where the [tiny house] movement needs to go and where the nation needs to go. And what's more, we need to know how to celebrate that paradigm shift.

I am reminded everyday by clients and colleagues that factory built housing – modular housing, if you will – needs its moment in the spotlight because the stigma of "trailers" that once existed is quickly disappearing. I have always come back to factory built being the most efficient, responsible and frankly, the best construction out there. And factory built housing isn't limited to a 3/2 configuration that has 4 feet of fake river rock up the bottom and vinyl siding the rest of the way to the eaves. Factory built houses can range from tiny house trailers at 150 sq.ft. to mansions with a half dozen bathrooms and twelve bedrooms. Factory built just means that the home is built indoors, in a controlled production facility, with a set of uniform standards and practices, and guided by regulated government codes and actual certifications. It is built on a concrete budget with materials and elements pre-selected by the purchasing party.

In my opinion factory production construction is the best process of building, period. It's more efficient. It's more reliable. When done right it is even more sustainable. You know exactly what your house will look like when finished. You know exactly how long it will take for the house to be built. You know exactly when the house will be ready to move in to. There are no real surprises. The factory follows stringent building codes, using an inventoried amount of materials, makes precise cuts and fits, and works even when it's sleeting outside. Because in factory construction we build to highly regulated codes, we can't hide mistakes or bury McDonald's lunch bags in the wall cavity and sheetrock over it. We are held to the highest standards and there is no time or tolerance for anything less. As you can tell, I am a huge advocate for it in many ways.

We also live in a "twitter world" where we are used to going on Amazon and shopping. We want things now, without wait. By in large, consumers don't require the level of intimacy that has existed before. We don't want to wait until the sheetrock is on the walls to decide which of thirty shades of green we want on the dining room walls. We want to order, get our shipping confirmation, and then go on about living until delivery. Not only do we live in this twitter world but now we live in this world of need versus want where people are taking very hard and long looks at their own relationships with consumption and space. They're asking, "Do I really need all of this? Do I want to pay to heat and cool four bedrooms that no one even sleeps in?" And what we're seeing – what the tiny house movement has brought to the forefront – is this turning tiny paradigm. More and more people are turning to smaller spaces because of a several factors. They learned invaluable lessons from the mortgage bubble, the American salary is not keeping up with the cost of living so their monthly budgets are lower and have less flexibility, they want to own their own home, and they want to invest in relationships rather than just things.

And so just a couple of years ago when I realized that tiny houses and tiny houses on wheels were becoming more and more popular each day. I knew that the paradigm I was noticing around 2013 was coming to fruition and as a business I was poised to cater to this segment of buyers and enthusiasts. I also heard that a lot of people were finding it hard to find a qualified builder for their tiny house plans. They were losing money or ending up with a horrible product. I didn't see any recognizable building standards and I don't think a single person was building to code. It seemed like a version of the wild, wild, west with construction mercenaries. In a way I understood that because what I was noticing is the number of sites and tiny house dwellers that were selling plans to build their house but were offering no support or even recommendations as to building them. There were few actual houses for sale. That is when I knew it was time for my company to jump into the tiny house market and build a model. I was prepared to deliver homes that are simple, smart, and sustainable. The only thing left was to build a tiny house model, from a production facility, and introduce her to the world.

Two tiny house designs always really stood out to me: that of Macy Miller and that of Andrew and Gabriella Morrison. They both were attractive, clever, spacious, and perfect canvases for higher end interior products and finishes.

I had been following Andrew and Gabriella Morrison for a couple of years through their Tiny House Build website and blog. Ironically Andrew Morrison was giving a TEDx talk on the tiny house movement in Colorado Springs just minutes from my office. I reached out to him to talk about their hOMe and the possibility of an affiliation of some kind. We got together and talked for a couple of hours about the realm of possibilities within the tiny house movement as both a passion and a business. I definitely pitched to them and admitted that I felt their hOMe was a perfect fit for my newly retooled production concept. I wanted to be a builder of their tiny house plans. I wanted to provide a version of their hOMe to end-users or, in this case, homebuyers. I was prepared to connect A to C. It seemed almost like a no-brainer to the three of us as they were being asked regularly to recommend a builder for their hOMe plans. From that initial conversation, a simple collaboration and now a friendship were born and we had found our niche.

Around this same time – 2014 – EcoCabins entered a park model (a 399 sq.ft. factory built home) in the Colorado Springs Parade of Homes. It was the first time nationally that anyone had entered a small, ANSI-coded house (read: park model RV) in a national, parade event. A television interview with ABC NewsChannel 13 allowed me to quickly share why our entry was so special. In a real estate market where the average new construct cost upwards of $230,000, our $59,000 base model was rewriting the playbook. We were offering a supreme quality, affordable housing option. We took home the coveted People's Choice Award that year in the under $300,000 category. It was said that the parade attendance increased by as much as 20% with people clamoring to see our "out-of-the-box" model. During those parade weeks it became commonplace to hear visitors, including retirees and small families, saying things like "I could do this" or "I really want one of these." I initially thought our model would resonate with those looking for vacation homes or second homes but it turns out the attraction was for a single residence or a viable, downsized way of living full-time. The exposure we received and the exposure small houses and tiny houses received were simply overwhelming.

That sort of victory naturally brought opposition and within weeks I found myself sitting in the office with three other homebuilders almost having to defend the unit and our involvement. I knew the parade needed to start thinking outside of the box and we were in a position to do just that. I continued to push the envelope reminding my competitors that I, too, was a homebuilder. My style was to construct in a facility and deliver to the site rather than to construct directly on site. It wasn't comparing apples to oranges. It was comparing Fuji to Granny Smith! What eventually came to light during that meeting was resentment to our process and our growing popularity. One homebuilder even said, and I basically quote, "I just don't want you playing in the same sandbox as us because we don't want to compete against that." That statement became a light bulb moment for me.

I quickly realized that I was making the establishment very nervous. I was appealing to a market segment that was evading those companies. I also distinctly remember being asked in that meeting, "What's next? A tree house?" Without even having to think I responded with: "Why not? There are people living in tree houses right now and some of those are million dollar tree houses!" I added to the conversation the idea that next parade I would go even smaller and introduce the hOMe tiny house we're presently constructing. It was obvious the time was right to move forward in my belief that simple, smart, and sustainable was where the market was going. That moment was the genesis of the Tiny House Jamboree.

As I rolled that idea of a big event around in my head for a bit and talked to some trusted friends and colleagues about it I came to the realization that what was needed was a showcase for small and tiny homes. Instead of being mentioned in someone else's bulletin, they needed their own spotlight. I decided to invite other local and regional homebuilders. I invited national tiny house builders. I invited direct competitors. I wanted anyone who was willing to show up and showcase their rolling masterpieces. The idea continued to blossom, a team was assembled and with little more than a grassroots social media campaign, a lot of word-of-mouth exposure, a few large-audience mentions such as a feature article in Tiny House Magazine, and a healthy dose of curiosity, my team and I were able to put together and execute the Tiny House Jamboree in about six months! It was incredible for all involved. Three things truly motivated me during those months and ultimately made me decide to take the idea of the Jamboree from pencil to pen.

1. The establishment needed to be rocked
2. The small house and tiny house movement needed large, national exposure and validation
3. And it needed leadership.

Until this point the tiny house movement had no real leadership. There was no real organization or singular motivation. There was no real equal representation and far too many misguided, misinformed voices trying to speak over one another. I have always believed that a rising tide doesn't isolate vessels. When the tide rises, all boats do as well. I knew the Jamboree was going to be a huge financial risk and probably even a failure in regards to turnout. But I am now incredibly proud that I was able to basically throw the world's first $100,000 tiny house party for thousands of people! The Jamboree was not a profitable venture at all but it was something that exceeded all expectations and really gave the movement the boost it desperately needed.

Make no mistake. Even though the venture wasn't profitable I am a businessman at heart. I am also a believer in sustainability and purposeful living.

Since that parade of homes in 2014 I wanted nothing more than to keep driving home the message that small living is a solution to a number of problems for a growing market and that there is no reason – no excuse, even – small homes can't be equally as beautiful and well-built as their more traditional counterparts. Being able to drive that bus and offer that sort of leadership is important to me. I want to be an industry leader in all things that I do and I wanted to take the focus off of the people and small minds that I saw as being detrimental to the movement. The movement deserved professionalism, and I was in a position to provide that.

After all was said and done and summer came to an end I needed quite a bit of time to wind down. The Jamboree was a huge endeavor and attracted an estimated 40,000 people from all over the world over that three-day weekend. I needed to debrief with the team and think about what was next for us. I honestly didn't know if I could do a second event the following year or even if I wanted to. The initial plan was not to create an annual event but by September 2015 – hardly a month after the first Jamboree ended – I was all but being threatened to announce the second Jam. I took some time to think about it but soon realized that the momentum created by the Tiny House Jamboree was one that could absolutely change the state of the real estate market in America both in the foreseeable future and the long-term. It has to be done and so it is.

So what's next? That's the fun part… this is literally the genesis of something that is bigger than me, bigger than a business, and yes… even bigger than a movement. Who knows where it will go, but one thing is for sure: it is going. The movement, its people, the homes, and the stories have inspired me and humbled me and definitely changed my viewpoint on how to live. I am honored to be a small part of it.

With this compilation book, packed with amazing life changing stories, I tried to capture the moment and hope to encourage you to jump in and turn tiny too: whatever tiny means to you. With you are many others and the movement continues to grow. It's a flow and a paradigm shift that is now strong enough to really make a change. The story will continue. More stories will arise. Maybe some time from now we are able to fill another book with more amazing stories. So maybe until then, good luck turning tiny!

Notes

1. http://www.census.gov/prod/2013pubs/p60-245.pdf

2. Quote from Anne Lamott's *Traveling Mercies*: "I think I already understand about life: pretty good, some problems." – Sam Lamott, at (age seven)

3. One successful session of meditation was during my week of framing and sheathing. The structure was framed, and exterior sheathing was being affixed. It was incredibly loud inside the shell, with 8-10 people hammering on the outside. I put earplugs in, laid down, and was transported to a space to which I've never been able to return. It was literally as though my house was cradling me.

4. MAGIC Camp – Mentor a Girl in Construction – holy smokes. It was a partnership with NAWIC (National Association of Women in Construction) and in 5 days we and 16 area high school girls with construction professionals as their mentors built the subfloor, and framed, house-wrapped and sheathed my house.

5. I chose the title "luminary" for myself in 2014 when I was designing my new business card for my position with Jay Shafer and we were all about being offbeat. One of the definitions of luminary, according to Merriam-Webster, is a person of prominence or brilliant achievement; a body that gives light. What I liked most about that definition is the part about giving light. It's a recurring theme for me – in my intentions that I wrote for MAGIC Camp, I wrote that I hoped my house was a "glowing orb of light." I like light. I like sharing my light, and shining light on others.

6. David Friedlander, "Talking to Jay Shafer About Making The Universal House," 30 May 2014, TreeHugger, 30 May 2014 < http://www.treehugger.com/tiny-houses/jay-shafer-makes-the-universal-house.html>

7. That is, in the increasingly likely event our wages and cost of living don't balance out.

8. Hey, I was a good worker but not *that* good.

9. Local NIMBYs like Mark Rayavec of the Venice Stakeholders Association and nationwide critics like talk show host Steve Harvey come to mind as those who most vociferously oppose our lifestyle in the media.

10. Not her real name.

11. www.oregonlive.com/portland/index.ssf/2013/10/dignity_village_residents_figh .html

12. www.huduser.org/portal/portal/sites/default/files/pdf/FamilyOptions Study_final .pdf

13. http://www.homeforward.org/landlords/what-is-section-8

14. http://thetinylife.com/tag/infographic/

15. https://www.hudexchange.info/resources/documents/ahar-2013-part1.pdf

16. http://mynorthwest.com/11/2914928/Seattle-police-face-constant-rejection-in-efforts-to-help-homeless?google_editors_picks=true)

17. http://media.wix.com/ugd/bd125b_ 286951ebcfad4362954cdccd20dea940.pdf

18. http://dignityvillage.org/services/village-intake-committee/

19. The Boneyard Studios concept was conceived of in late 2011 by Lee Pera and Brian Levy who were shortly thereafter joined by Jay Austin and Elaine Walker. Boneyard Studios was incorporated as an LLC in late 2012. By Fall 2014 the houses owned by Jay, Lee, and Elaine had all left the property where Boneyard Studios began. Boneyard Studios still exists as an entity in DC hosting events and education around tiny houses. Minim Homes owns the property where the tiny house community once resided and now operates a showcase space for small designs there.

20. It's really hard to find contractors who will do a small task here or there on a tiny house. Ironically building an efficient space like a tiny house is not an efficient process because you don't have the economy of scale

21. "How Long it Took" http://danwebb.squarespace.com/writing/2015/5/1/how-long-it-took.html

22. The Rent is Still Too Damn High – And Getting Higher (Zillow.com/research/jan-2015-market-report-8951)

23. The Housing Affordability Gap for Extremely Low-Income Renters In 2013 (The Urban Institute)

24. "Metro Phoenix needs more affordable housing" (The Arizona Republic, Catherine Reagor, March 27, 2015)

25. The 2014 Annual Homeless Assessment Report (AHAR), Part 1 (The United States Department of Housing and Urban Development)

26. Statista.com – 183657

27. Forbes.com – #67719e334295

28. Forbes.com – #67719e334295

29. Tiny Houses are no longer exclusive to the alternative crowd (tumbleweedhouses.com – #6051604)

30. Cooper, E., Knott, L., Schaak, G., Sloane, L., and Zovitoski, A. (2015). Priced out in 2014: the housing crisis for people with disabilities. *The Technical Assistance Collaborative, Inc. Consortium for Citizens with Disabilities.* Retrieved from http://www.tacinc.org/media/52012/Priced%20Out%20in%202014.pdf

31. Ferraro, C. (February 21, 2009). "Small but perfectly formed." *Financial Times.*

32. Ferraro, C. (February 21, 2009). "Small but perfectly formed." *Financial Times.*

33. Ferraro, C. (February 21, 2009). "Small but perfectly formed." *Financial Times.*

34. Cummin, R., and Lau, A. (2003). Community integration or community exposure? A review and discussion in relation to people with intellectual disabilities. *Journal of Applied Research in Intellectual Disabilities.* 16:145-15.

35. Social Security Administration (2011). "Supplemental Security Income Program." 2011 Annual Report of the SSI Program. Retrieved from https://www.socialsecurity.gov/OACT/ssir/SSI11/ProgramDescription.html

36. Cooper, E., Knott, L., Schaak, G., Sloane, L., and Zovitoski, A. (2015). Priced out in 2014: the housing crisis for people with disabilities. *The Technical Assistance Collaborative, Inc. Consortium for Citizens with Disabilities.* Retrieved from http://www.tacinc.org/media/52012/Priced%20Out%20in%202014.pdf

37. Francis, G., Blue-Banning, M., and Turnbull, R. (2014). Variables within a household that influence quality-of-life outcomes for individuals with intellectual and developmental disabilities living in the community: discovering the gaps. *Sage Journals,* 39(1): 3-10.

38. Social Security Administration (2011). "Supplemental Security Income Program."

39. Hassink, J., Elings, M., Zweekhorst, M., van den Nieuwenhuizen, N., & Smit, A. (2010). Care farms in the Netherlands: Attractive employment-oriented and strengths-based practices in the community. *Health & Place,* 16: 423-430.

40. National Alliance to End Homelessness (2016). "Poor health and homelessness." Retrieved from www.endhomelessness.org/pages/mental_physical_health

41. Wilson, A. (2015). C. Felix Harvey Project Narrative. Unpublished manuscript.

42. From the 1963 Wally Byam Store Catalog

43. Trailer Travel Here and Abroad by Wally Byam page 17

44. Los Angeles Times April 24, 1941